TWO INDUSTRY LEADERS. ONE SUPERIOR TEACHING TOOL.
INFINITE LEARNING POSSIBILITIES.

...want to ...classroom ...able online content or deliver your class totally at a distance, Harcourt accommodates all your distance learning needs. Harcourt, a leader in providing lifelong learning solutions, in partnership with WebCT, a leading platform in electronic learning, brings you and your students the industry's most robust online courses.

WebCT facilitates the creation of sophisticated Web-based educational environments. It provides a set of course design tools to help you manage course content, a set of communication tools to facilitate online classroom collaboration, and a set of administrative tools for tracking and managing your students' progress.

Via the WebCT platform, Harcourt offers the following program choices:

1 **WebCT Testing Service.** If testing is all you want, we will upload the computerized test bank into a course with no publisher content. If you like, we will even host it for you on our server.

2 **Free access to a blank WebCT template.** With a qualified adoption, Harcourt will host a course (without any Harcourt content) for you to input your original materials and use in your classroom.

3 **Customized course creation.** Harcourt will create an online course from your original content, your school's content, Harcourt's content, or any combination of these. Contact your local Harcourt representative for more details.

Harcourt WebCT Manuals
If you adopt a Harcourt Online Course, your students will receive Harcourt's Guide to the World Wide Web and WebCT packaged with the textbook.

(ISBN 0-03-045503-0)

To view a demo of any of our online courses, go to **webct.harcourtcollege.com.**

MANAGERIAL ACCOUNTING

A FOCUS ON DECISION MAKING

MANAGERIAL ACCOUNTING

A FOCUS ON DECISION MAKING

STEVE JACKSON
University of Southern Maine

ROBY SAWYERS
North Carolina State University

HARCOURT COLLEGE PUBLISHERS

Fort Worth Philadelphia San Diego New York Austin Orlando San Antonio
Toronto Montreal London Sydney Tokyo

Publisher	Mike Roche
Acquisitions Editor	Bill Schoof
Market Strategist	Charles Watson
Developmental Editor	Jennifer Sheetz Langer
Project Editor	Jim Patterson
Art Director	Brian Salisbury
Production Manager	Lois West

Cover Illustration: Photos supplied by © Don Couch Photography and Photo Disc © 2001. Montage by Bill Brammer Design.

ISBN: 0-03-021092-5
Library of Congress Catalog Card Number: 00-100121

Copyright © 2001 by Harcourt, Inc.

Address for Domestic Orders
Harcourt, Inc., 6277 Sea Harbor Drive, Orlando, FL 32887-6777
800-782-4479

Address for International Orders
International Customer Service
Harcourt, Inc., 6277 Sea Harbor Drive, Orlando, FL 32887-6777
407-345-3800
(fax)407-345-4060
(e-mail)hbintl@harcourt.com

Address for Editorial Correspondence
Harcourt College Publishers, 301 Commerce Street, Suite 3700, Fort Worth, TX 76102

Web Site Address
http://www.harcourtcollege.com

Printed in the United States of America

0 1 2 3 4 5 6 7 8 9   048   9 8 7 6 5 4 3 2 1

Harcourt College Publishers

To those who influence our decisions:
Cheryl, Christina, Kent and Ben
Amber and Robyn

THE HARCOURT SERIES IN ACCOUNTING

PRINCIPLES OF ACCOUNTING INTEGRATED FINANCIAL/MANAGERIAL

Cunningham, Nikolai, and Bazley
ACCOUNTING: Information for Business Decisions

TECHNOLOGY COMPONENTS

Guided Exploration, LLC
Interactive Decision Cases for Financial Accounting

Bell, Kirby, and Gantt
Guide to Understanding and Using Annual Reports
Second Edition

Davis
OMAR (Online Multimedia Accounting Review): The Accounting Cycle

COMMUNICATION

McKay and Rosa
The Accountant's Guide to professional Communication: Writing and Speaking the language of Business

FINANCIAL

Hanson and Hamre
Financial Accounting
Eighth Edition

Porter and Norton
Financial Accounting: The Impact on Decision Makers
Third Edition

Porter and Norton
Financial Accounting: The Impact on Decision Makers
Alternate Second Edition

Stickney and Weil
Financial Accounting: An Introduction to Concepts, Methods, and Uses
Ninth Edition

Knechel
The Monopoly Game Practice Set

MANAGERIAL

Jackson and Sawyers
Managerial Accounting: A Focus on Decision Making

Maher, Stickney, and Weil
Managerial Accounting: An Introduction to Concepts, Methods, and Uses
Seventh Edition

INTERMEDIATE

Williams, Stanga, and Holder
Intermediate Accounting
Fifth Edition
1998 Update

ADVANCED

Pahler and Mori
Advanced Accounting: Concepts and Practice
Seventh Edition

FINANCIAL STATEMENT ANALYSIS

Stickney and Brown
Financial Reporting and Statement Analysis: A Strategic Perspective
Fourth Edition

AUDITING

Guy, Alderman, and Winters
Auditing
Fifth Edition

Rittenberg and Schwieger
Auditing: Concepts for a Changing Environment
Third Edition

THEORY

Bloom and Elgers
Foundations of Accounting Theory and Policy: A Reader

Bloom and Elgers
Issues in Accounting Policy: A Reader

GOVERNMENTAL AND NOT-FOR-PROFIT

Douglas
Governmental and Nonprofit Accounting: Theory and Practice
Second Edition

REFERENCE

Bailey
Miller GAAS Guide
College Edition

Williams
Miller GAAP Guide
College Edition

PREFACE

AN INTRODUCTION TO THIS TEXT

"If by education we mean the cramming of a pupil's mind with facts or rules, without any real conception of their meaning or of the relations in which they stand to each other, it is perfectly safe to say that it is a waste of time. This kind of education fits a man for a certain groove, in which he moves in a routine way, a mere piece of mechanical machinery, incapable of independent thought or action. *If confronted with a new condition, to which his rules do not apply, he is helpless, and is liable to make mistakes that are disastrous, because his action is based on insufficient knowledge of the foundation principles . . .*"

Walton, 1917, Journal of Accountancy

In the above statement lies the primary motivation for our writing a new textbook for the study of Managerial Accounting: a *desire to encourage a transition away from a purely third-person delivery by classroom instructors toward a first-person discovery by students both within and outside of the classroom.*

To encourage *discovery learning*, this textbook links **discussion** and **assignments** to needed student skills in managerial decision making. It further illustrates the discussion through use of realistic and interesting companies in every chapter. While educators should expose students to structured uses of tools and information (which aid in good management decisions), accounting education at the turn of *this* century also demands preparation for a world of unstructured problem solving.

The ever-expanding body of knowledge needed in this information age requires that students take responsibility for **life-long** discovery learning. Our approach encourages students to exploit the material presented by allowing its contents to awaken in them a curiosity about how managers solve some of the complex problems and what judgment processes are inherent in today's highly competitive global environment.

Accounting itself has always been referred to as the *language of business.* Business does not exist because of accounting, but accounting exists because businesses need a way to communicate. Accounting information is used for decision-making, planning and controlling activities. Today's competitive global environment requires that accounting information systems have a customer focus so as to provide quantitative and qualitative information useful for decision-making. This requires accounting information to be relevant and reliable in order to be useful to that end. Therefore, managers must learn to be active participants in the design of the information systems used and the reports that are generated from those systems. They must not be passive users of accounting information.

This textbook does provide the background accounting information and tools for using that information that are vital for success in the management environment. However, here the emphasis is on the analysis and interpretation of information rather than on its preparation. This enables us to teach students to think not only "how" but also "why" and to make informed decisions.

We present an approach that we eagerly invite you to explore—an approach which allows both instructor and student to discover an understanding of decision-making in business and will prepare the student for success in all areas.

INTENDED AUDIENCE

In the past, management accountants were traditionally thought of as the recorders and preparers of accounting information. They were typically separated from the rest of the management team and were rarely involved in the major decision-making process. In

"This is truly a managerial accounting approach."

SHEILA AMMONS, AUSTIN COMMUNITY COLLEGE

today's very competitive, global economy, management accountants *have* become part of the management team, actively participating in formulating and implementing the businesses' strategy.

Our textbook and supporting package is intended for all business majors: accounting, management, marketing, finance, human resources, and general business, indeed it is intended for all who will *use* accounting information to make business decisions. Non-business majors will also find this text useful, as the real-world focus and use of accounting information in decision-making are important skills in all areas of life and work. We teach without the use of journal entries or other accounting procedures since our focus is on using accounting information by managers in an organization.

We anticipate that all students in your managerial courses have had at least one term of financial accounting. This text is designed to stand alone and work well in succession to any of the popular financial accounting texts currently on the market.

KEY FEATURES

While the contents of the book are similar to other managerial accounting textbooks, it is truly focused on decision-making and using accounting information for analysis of business problems. We introduce a basic, four-step decision-making model in Chapter 1.

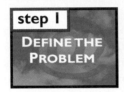
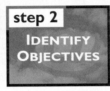

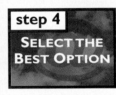

The most important element in the decision-making emphasis of this text is providing students with the structure of the decision-making model. The decision-making model is incorporated throughout the text to reinforce learning. The book integrates material on current issues such as technological advances, global competition, ethics, total quality management, cross-functional teams, activity based costing and the value chain throughout the text. Finally, it would be practically impossible to properly address current issues in managerial accounting without addressing changes in knowledge management and accounting information systems. Chapter 13 focuses on developments in knowledge management and accounting information systems for improved managerial decision-making.

The end of chapter assignment material differs from other texts in that a significant proportion of the longer problems and cases will, through the use of the decision model, require the student to analyze, predict, and extend the solution to make business decisions. These problems/cases require the student to work with unstructured situations, which have more than one defensible decision. The text *and* assignment materials both include extensive use of qualitative information. End-of-chapter assignment material also includes a few problems/cases that focus on group learning or outside research requiring short written solutions. Each chapter also includes a continuing case designed around a computerized business simulation.

PEDAGOGY

This textbook is designed to capture and maintain student focus and interest. The textbook is designed in full-color, with a very visual format to stimulate student interest in the text material.

The text has several types of critical thinking questions in the text designed to alert students to any lack of understanding of material covered before moving on to subsequent areas.

Concept Questions are answered in the text immediately following the question.

Pause and Reflect questions are inserted where needed to alert the student to stop and reflect on what they have learned so far, applying ideas to various situations. Due to the nature of the questions, Pause and Reflect questions do not have answers in the text. Our intent is to teach students to think critically, and to evaluate more than one possible solution to business problems.

PAUSE & Reflect

 Key Concepts and definitions are also highlighted in the text and reference is made, where appropriate, to the decision model.

Key Formulas are highlighted where presented in the text.

In The News features, are real world stories, to help students grasp and apply the real-world significance of many of the topics discussed.

Management Actions and Decisions are interviews with managers and users of accounting information in today's business environment. These enhance the learning of concepts by allowing the student to see how decisions are made in the "real world."

Cross Functional Applications highlight the use of accounting information by managers in all areas of business. Our hope is to spark the interest of business students, to emphasize the reasons accounting information is important to understand.

TECHNOLOGY FOCUS

Finally, due to the rapid development of technology available to organizations to conduct their businesses, we have incorporated **Technology Focus** features, which correlate to chapter topics on such issues as Electronic Commerce and Electronic Data Interchange (EDI).

Liberal use of photos further illustrates topics and enhances the understanding of the text material. End-of-chapter assignment material as well as the text material has been classroom tested to minimize errors and misstatements.

Each chapter features a variety of fictional, yet interesting and realistic companies as an example(s) of chapter concepts. We also feature a **Continuing Case** on "Big Al's Pizza Inc." This case builds on lessons and solutions from preceding chapters. It provides a dynamic setting for students to grasp the impact their decisions make upon a business, and promises to be fun as well. The Continuing Case dovetails with **Templates** in MS Excel providing students the dynamic tools to explore possible outcomes by working with numbers on interactive spreadsheets. Three to five Excel templates for end-of-chapter problems are also available to provide students with the opportunity for more analysis and experience with modern applications in business.

BIG AL'S

SPECIFIC CHAPTER COVERAGE

We have written a 16-chapter text designed for a one-semester course. The book is divided into five sections:

- The Costing of Products and Services.
- The Nature of Costs in Decision-Making.
- Planning, Performance Evaluation and Control.
- Contemporary Topics in Management Decision-Making.
- Other Topics of Interest.

CHAPTER 1

ACCOUNTING INFORMATION AND MANAGERIAL DECISIONS

This chapter defines accounting information and its uses by both external and internal users. The chapter then describes the decision-making role of management in planning, operating and controlling and provides a framework for assessing decisions that commonly face managers of organizations.

"This chapter presents a good overview of management accounting and its users. New acronyms, such as ERP are also used—good! The role of managers is good, and adequately explained....The human resource aspect is a role frequently overlooked or minimized. The decision model is a good addition. I have not seen it before in a management accounting text."

JAMES MAKOFSKE, FRESNO CITY COLLEGE

CHAPTER 2

THE PRODUCTION PROCESS AND PRODUCT (SERVICE) COSTING

Chapter 2 begins with a description of the production process for both traditional manufacturing companies with inventory and manufacturing companies with little or no inventory. The chapter also provides an introduction into basic cost terminology applicable to manufacturing companies, merchandising companies and service providers and concludes with a description of cost flows in each type of company.

CHAPTER 3

PRODUCT COSTING MEASUREMENT DECISIONS

Chapter 3 begins with a discussion of the basic systems that companies use to accumulate, track and assign costs to products and services and contrasts and compares job costing, process costing and operations costing. Chapter 3 introduces the concept of cost pools and cost drivers and how they are used to allocate overhead using plant-wide and departmental overhead rates. The chapter includes a discussion of the use of overhead estimates (predetermined overhead rates) in product costing and the treatment of over or under- applied overhead. The appendix of the chapter introduces backflush costing (a costing system that is appropriate for companies employing just-in-time (JIT) manufacturing techniques) and discusses process costing in more detail.

"...The TopSail [Construction Co. in Chapter 4] example was a very clear, concise and comprehensive illustration of the application of ABC. Sometimes explaining the concepts of ABC is very difficult, as students often have a difficult time relating to the types of activities in many manufacturing environments..."

DANIEL R. BRICKNER, UNIVERSITY OF AKRON

CHAPTER 4

PRODUCT COSTING FOR MANAGEMENT DECISIONS: ACTIVITY BASED COSTING AND ACTIVITY BASED MANAGEMENT

In this chapter, we revisit the problems of overhead application and discuss the use of an alternative product costing system called activity based costing (ABC). The benefits and limitations of ABC are discussed, as is the application of ABC to selling and administrative activities and in a JIT environment. The last part of the chapter discusses the use of activity information in controlling and managing costs (activity-based management).

CHAPTER 5

THE NATURE OF COSTS

This chapter introduces concepts and tools that will be used in Chapters 6 through 8. Chapter 5 begins with a definition of cost behavior and illustrates the concepts of fixed costs, variable costs and mixed costs. Next, the chapter revisits the concept of relevant costs as they apply to variable and fixed costs. The chapter also describes the impact of income taxes on costs and introduces the concept of the time value of money and its impact on costs incurred in different time periods.

CHAPTER 6
COST BEHAVIOR AND DECISION MAKING: COST, VOLUME, PROFIT ANALYSIS

In this chapter, we focus on one aspect of the nature of costs (cost behavior) and develop a set of tools that focus on the distinction between fixed and variable costs. These tools include measures of a company's contribution margin, contribution margin ratio and operating leverage - the cornerstones of cost-volume-profit (CVP) analysis. The effect of income taxes on CVP analysis is also discussed.

"The authors did a thorough job [in Ch. 6] of explaining CVP analysis and related topics—contribution margin, breakeven, target profit, operating leverage, income tax effects, and variable costing. Break-even analysis utilizing ABC is also discussed. The reinforcement of the decision model was a good inclusion."

JEANNE YANAMURA, UNIVERSITY OF NEVADA-RENO

CHAPTER 7
ACCOUNTING INFORMATION, RELEVANT COSTS, AND DECISION MAKING

In Chapter 5, we emphasized that only relevant costs and factors should be considered by managers when making decisions. Following the decision-making framework developed in Chapter 1 and building on what we know about the nature of costs from Chapter 5, we analyze a variety of decisions affecting managers in Chapter 7. These decisions include an examination of general pricing issues and the pricing of special orders. The chapter also examines decisions to outsource labor, whether to make or buy a component used to manufacture a product, whether to add or drop a product or service, and how to utilize limited resources to maximize profit. We also consider the impact of ABC on these decisions.

CHAPTER 8
LONG-TERM (CAPITAL INVESTMENT) DECISION ANALYSIS

In this chapter, we develop tools that aid managers in making long-term decisions to purchase new property, plant and equipment (capital investment decisions). The use of net present value and internal rate of return methods in both screening decisions and preference decisions is discussed, as is the impact of income taxes on the analysis. The impact of new manufacturing techniques on capital investment decisions and the importance of qualitative factors in the analysis are also discussed. An approach to long term purchasing decisions that does not take into consideration the time value of money, the payback method, is also mentioned.

CHAPTER 9
THE USE OF BUDGETS IN PLANNING AND DECISION MAKING

In this chapter we introduce the concept of budgeting and discuss how budgets assist managers in planning and decision making. We discuss and demonstrate the preparation of operational budgets for a traditional manufacturing company with inventory as well as for a company operating in a JIT environment. The chapter also covers the use of operational budgets in merchandising and service companies. We pay special attention to the preparation and use of the

"This is the best coverage [in Ch. 9] of the use of Budgeting that I have seen in a Principles of Management Accounting textbook. It is thorough, straightforward, and has good examples."

LYNETTE CHAPMAN, SOUTHWEST TEXAS STATE UNIVERSITY

cash budget for managerial decision making and tie it into the preparation of the statement of cash flows used extensively by external users. Finally, we discuss static and flexible budgets with particular emphasis on the impact of ABC on flexible budgets, and the preparation and use of non-financial budgets.

CHAPTER 10

THE USE OF BUDGETS FOR COST CONTROL AND PERFORMANCE EVALUATION

Corinne's Country Rockers

In this chapter, we expand the discussion of flexible budgeting, and introduce the concept of standard costs and variance analysis as tools to help managers "manage by exception" and evaluate performance in their control function. The chapter ends with a discussion of budgeting culture and the various behavioral issues involved in the budgeting process.

CHAPTER 11

OTHER TOOLS FOR COST CONTROL AND PERFORMANCE EVALUATION

G&B
GARCIA&BUFFET CPAS

In this chapter we discuss decentralized organizations with an emphasis on the different decisions that must be addressed in a decentralized environment. We also discuss the impact of responsibility accounting and segment reporting on decision making in decentralized organizations. We discuss performance evaluation in cost, revenue, profit and investment centers and introduce measures of performance such as return on investment (ROI), residual income and economic value added (EVA) commonly used in investment centers. We conclude the chapter with a discussion of segment performance and transfer pricing issues between segments.

CAMELBACK MOUNTAIN COMMUNITY BANK

Birdie Maker

> "[Chapter 11 is a] good combination of objectives: responsibility accounting, decentralized operations, cost, profit and investment centers, segment margins and departmental income statements ... right place for performance evaluations and transfer pricing."
> **JACQUELINE SANDERS, MERCER COUNTY COMMUNITY COLLEGE**

CHAPTER 12

NON-FINANCIAL MEASURES OF PERFORMANCE

In this chapter we introduce the concept of the balanced scorecard and discuss how the balanced scorecard integrates financial and non-financial measures of performance. We discuss the four perspectives of the balanced scorecard approach: the financial perspective, the customer perspective, the internal business perspective and the learning and growth perspective. We relate measures of quality, timeliness, marketing effectiveness and productivity to each perspective of the balanced scorecard. We conclude the chapter by referring to previous examples in the text to highlight the variety of non-financial measures of performance used by companies.

TINA'S Fine Juices

TopSail Construction

Happy Daze Game Co.

> "I think this [Ch. 13] is a great topic. Accounting has always been an information system, but now its role is being broadened into information for financial and non-financial data. It's not the debits and credits anymore, but efficiency factors, module relationships and sharing information. It's decision-making based on customer orientation along with the bottom line results. It is a merging of technology, marketing, human resources, accounting, finance and management."
> **JIM MEIR, CLEVELAND STATE COMMUNITY COLLEGE**

CHAPTER 13

THE MANAGEMENT OF INFORMATION AND KNOWLEDGE FOR BETTER DECISIONS

In this chapter we introduce the reader to the concept of knowledge management—the process of formally managing information and knowledge resources in order to facilitate access and reuse of that information and knowledge. Information and knowledge resources may vary for each company, but include traditional sources of data provided by the accounting information system as well as such things as internal memos, training manuals, customer information, and of course the biggest knowledge resource of them all—a company's employees. Just as information and knowledge resources vary among companies, knowledge management systems may vary as well. Typical knowledge management tools include knowledge warehouses and enterprise resource planning (ERP) systems. Knowledge management tools facilitate supply-chain management, customer relationship management, and internal decision making.

CHAPTER 14

MANAGEMENT FRAUD AND INTERNAL CONTROL

 In this chapter we discuss the importance of good internal control and its affect on the reliability of accounting information used in decision making. We discuss the internal control function from a management perspective and from the perspective of the external auditor or CPA. We discuss the most common types of fraud (including inventory theft, price fixing, phantom vendors, kickbacks and financial statement fraud) and show how internal control systems can prevent or uncover these abuses. Finally the chapter looks at the role of the accounting managers and external auditors in providing assurance that the reported financial information is fairly presented and reliable.

CHAPTER 15

THE STATEMENT OF CASH FLOWS

In the previous fourteen chapters of this textbook we have concentrated on using internally generated accounting information for managerial decision making. In this chapter we present an in-depth discussion of the preparation and use of the cash flow statement. While this statement is primarily used by parties external to the organization, we discuss its importance to managerial decision making and its links to the cash budget produced for internal purposes.

CHAPTER 16

FINANCIAL STATEMENT ANALYSIS

In this chapter we concentrate on another typical financial accounting topic with emphasis on preparing ratios used by stockholders, creditors and other user groups. We also relate some of the ratios to internal uses in decision making. The ratios covered are related to the decision making process of internal management as well as the outside users mentioned above.

"The chapters [15 and 16] compare quite favorably [to other books available]. These are extremely difficult chapters to write and for students to comprehend, due to the nature of the material. I am quite pleased with the approach taken and the examples given.
GEORGE VIOLETTE, UNIVERSITY OF SOUTHERN MAINE

SUPPLEMENTAL RESOURCES

Harcourt College Publishers offers a wide variety of supplemental materials and packages to complement the main text and course for both instructors and students. A descriptive list follows. Instructors should contact their local Harcourt College Publishers sales representative or e-mail us at *accounting@harcourt.com* to learn more about the value-added packages and discounts available for their students.

FOR INSTRUCTORS

Solutions Manual *with checklist of Key Figures* *Written by Steve Jackson and Roby Sawyers* A comprehensive manual, written by the authors, containing all the solutions to the end-of-chapter items. Open ended discussion questions have several possible answers listed, with none being the absolute correct answer.

Instructor's Manual *Written by Steve Jackson and Roby Sawyers* A comprehensive resource for instructors, this manual was written by the authors to provide additional teaching tips, outlines, tips for finding guest speakers, instructional outlines for using the videos with classes. This manual has been created closely with the PowerPoint lecture slides to provide a cohesive and seamless teaching package.

Test Bank *Written by Suzanne H. Lowensohn, Barry University* Sue Lowensohn was a colleague of Steve Jackson's at the University of Southern Maine and has been closely involved with this project since its inception. The test bank is fully compatible with the approach of the authors. The test bank contains over 1,500 questions to evaluate students' progress through the course material. Continuing with the text's vision of teaching decision-making and critical thinking skills, it contains questions which require students to evaluate accounting information. A selection of various formats is available including multiple choice, short answer, problems and short cases.

Computerized Test Bank Available in Windows format, the computerized version of the printed test bank enables instructors to preview and edit test questions, as well as add their own. The tests and answer keys can also be printed in "scrambled" formats.

Request Test Service Harcourt College Publishers makes test planning quicker and easier than ever with this program. Instructors can order test masters by question number and criteria over a toll-free telephone number. Test masters will be mailed or faxed within 48 hours.

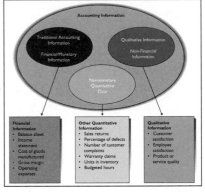

Overhead Transparencies A selection of textbook illustrations and examples are available in transparency acetate form. Also included are solution acetates for all numerical end-of-chapter concept application exercises, problems and cases.

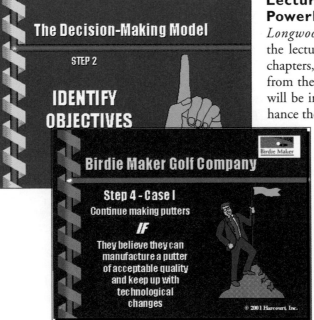

Lecture Software in Microsoft PowerPoint *Created by Kristine Palmer, Longwood College* An asset to any instructor, the lectures in PowerPoint provide outlines of chapters, graphics of illustrations and examples from the text. Selected end-of-chapter exercises will be included in a clear, crisp fashion to enhance the presentation.

Custom Videos In partnership with successful, well-known companies such as IBM, Lycos, Stride Rite and Pizzeria Uno's, this exciting and innovative video package was developed to find out how managers use accounting information to make decisions. Topics illustrated include break-even analysis, pricing decisions, process controls, and the use of accounting information systems in organizations.

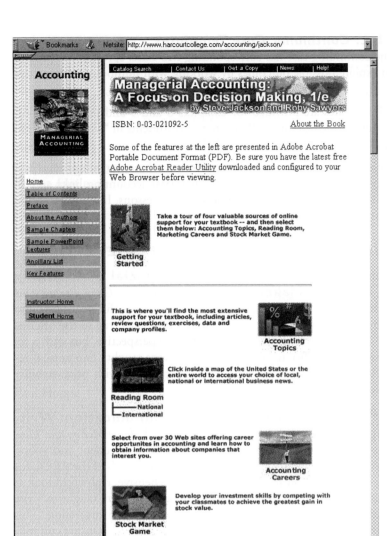

Managerial Accounting has a **Companion Web site** www.harcourtcollege.com providing additional instructor and student resources including managerial accounting links and an accounting resource library of articles with applications to text lessons, student Internet activities, and tutorials to enhance the classroom experience. Harcourt College Publishers has also collaborated with Eric Sandburg and Crystal Barkley Corporation to develop a Web Site especially for accounting. This site contains a wealth of accounting resources and student exercises to aid instructors and students in obtaining company information, annual reports, current news, links to SEC filings, and stock quotes. These resources can be located at www.harcourtcollege.com/accounting/.

Distance Learning

For professors interested in supplementing classroom presentations with online content or who are interested in setting up a distance learning course, Harcourt College Publishers, along with WebCT and Blackboard, can provide you with the industry's leading online courses.

WebCT and Blackboard facilitate the creation of sophisticated Web-based educational environments by providing tools to help you manage course content, facilitate online classroom collaboration, and tracking your students' progress. If you are using WebCT in your class but not a Harcourt Online Course or textbook, you may adopt the *Student's Guide to the World Wide Web and WebCT* (ISBN 0-03-045503-0). This manual gives step-by-step instructions on using WebCT tools and features.

In conjunction with WebCT, Harcourt College Publishers also offers information on adopting a Harcourt online course, WebCT testing service, free access to a blank WebCT template, and customized course creation. For more information, please contact your local sales representative. To view a demo of any of our online courses, go to webct.harcourtcollege.com.

FOR STUDENTS

Study Guide *Written by Steve Jackson, Roby Sawyers, and James Makofske of Fresno City College* A true study aid, this manual lists learning objectives with key concepts to aid students with the fundamentals of the course. In addition, it provides students with self-test questions, exercises and problems that actively engage students in applying what they have learned as well as preparing them for exams.

Student PowerPoint Notes We have provided a complete set of student notes in a manual so that all topics within the chapters are covered and less pressure is placed upon instructors to cover all topics in class. Students can spend more time focusing their attention on class discussions rather than rushing to write down all the information being provided. Therefore, students can simply add to the lecture information in the space provided next to every corresponding slide.

Dick Bundons	Johnson County Community College
Gregory Burbage	Sacramento City College
Joseph Catalina	Hudson Valley Community College
Curtis Clements	Baylor University
Alan Cohen	Ithaca College
Mark Comstock	Missouri Southern State College
Michael Cornick	University of North Carolina
Randolph Coyner	Florida Atlantic University
Charles Croxford	Mercer College
Dan Daly	Boston College
James Damitio	Central Michigan University
Elizabeth Davis	Baylor University
Wayne J. Davis	Indiana University of Pennsylvania
Patricia Doherty	Boston University
Robert Edney	Rider University
Rafik Elias	Cameron University
Peter Ben Ezra	George Washington University
Neil Fargher	University of Oregon
Linda Ferrell	Evergreen College
Robert D. Fesler	Tennessee Technical University
Don Foster	Tacoma Community College
Ken Fowler	Mankato State University
Harland Fuller	Illinois State University
George Gardner	Bemidji State University
Jackson F. Gillespie	University of Delaware
Arnold Glickman	Queens College
John Gobo	Hudson Valley Community College
John Godfrey	Springfield Technical Community College
Ellsworth C. Granger	Mankato State University
Gary Grudnitski	San Diego State University
Susan Gustin	West Virginia University
Chandra Gyan	Miami University
Joseph Hagan	East Carolina University
Jan Heier	Auburn University
John Hill	Delgado Community College
Nancy Hill	DePaul University
Bernice Hill	Spokane Falls Community College
Rofert Holtfreter	Central Washington University
M.A. Houston	Wright State University
Richard Hulme	California State Polytech University
Raj Iyengar	Catholic University of America
Philip Jones	University of Richmond
N. Leroy Kauffman	Western Carolina University
Annemarie Keinath	Indiana University–Northwest
Marsha Kertz	San Jose State University
Zafar Khan	Eastern Michigan University
Ronald Kilgore	University of Tennessee
Judy Kimm	Monterrey Peninsula College
Stacy Kline	Drexel University
Mehmet Kocakulah	University of Southern Indiana
Greg Kordecki	Clayton College and State University
Thomas Kozloski	Drexel University
Robert Kravet	Fairfield University
L. Kuhn	Louisiana State University
Chor T. Lau	California State University–Los Angeles
Charles Liclair	Cochise College

Managerial Accounting has a **Web site** www.harcourtcollege. ing additional instructor and student including managerial accounting links a accounting resource library of articles with a plications to text lessons, student Internet activities, and tutorials to enhance the classroom experience. Harcourt College Publishers has also collaborated with Eric Sandburg and Crystal Barkley Corporation to develop a Web Site especially for accounting. This site contains a wealth of accounting resources and student exercises to aid instructors and students in obtaining company information, annual reports, current news, links to SEC filings, and stock quotes. These resources can be located at www.harcourtcollege.com/accounting/.

Distance Learning

For professors interested in supplementing classroom presentations with online content or who are interested in setting up a distance learning course, Harcourt College Publishers, along with WebCT and Blackboard, can provide you with the industry's leading online courses.

WebCT and Blackboard facilitate the creation of sophisticated Web-based educational environments by providing tools to help you manage course content, facilitate online classroom collaboration, and tracking your students' progress. If you are using WebCT in your class but not a Harcourt Online Course or textbook, you may adopt the *Student's Guide to the World Wide Web and WebCT* (ISBN 0-03-045503-0). This manual gives step-by-step instructions on using WebCT tools and features.

In conjunction with WebCT, Harcourt College Publishers also offers information on adopting a Harcourt online course, WebCT testing service, free access to a blank WebCT template, and customized course creation. For more information, please contact your local sales representative. To view a demo of any of our online courses, go to webct.harcourtcollege.com.

FOR STUDENTS

Study Guide *Written by Steve Jackson, Roby Sawyers, and James Makofske of Fresno City College* A true study aid, this manual lists learning objectives with key concepts to aid students with the fundamentals of the course. In addition, it provides students with self-test questions, exercises and problems that actively engage students in applying what they have learned as well as preparing them for exams.

Student PowerPoint Notes We have provided a complete set of student notes in a manual so that all topics within the chapters are covered and less pressure is placed upon instructors to cover all topics in class. Students can spend more time focusing their attention on class discussions rather than rushing to write down all the information being provided. Therefore, students can simply add to the lecture information in the space provided next to every corresponding slide.

Big Al's Pizza Inc. *Continuing Case Templates* *Created by Steve Jackson and Roby Sawyers* The continuing case has corresponding MS Excel spreadsheets providing dynamic tools to explore possible outcomes by working with numbers on interactive spreadsheets.

Interactive MS Excel templates are provided for Chapters 8 and 9 and selected end-of-chapter exercises throughout the text on our Web site to aid students in "what-if" analysis using time value of money tools and interactive budgets.

Managerial Accounting has a **Companion Web site** www.harcourtcollege.com providing additional activities and resources including managerial accounting links and an accounting resource library of articles with applications to text lessons, Internet activities, and tutorials to enhance the classroom experience.

NEW FROM HARCOURT COLLEGE PUBLISHERS

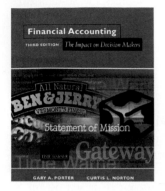

A Great Companion to Managerial Accounting is **Financial Accounting: The Impact on Decision Makers, Third Edition** *by Gary Porter and Curt Norton* The first edition of Porter/Norton was the most successful new entry into the financial accounting market in 20 years. This third edition holds true to the original vision of teaching the subject from both the preparer and user perspective, but with a revision focused on greater accessibility to the variety of students taught. Two annual reports (Gateway and Ben & Jerry's) and an annual update program with price stability guarantee highlight the third edition package.

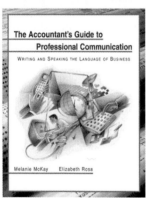

The Accountant's Guide to Professional Communication: Writing and Speaking the Language of Business *by Melanie McKay and Elizabeth Rosa* This stand-alone text handbook is a great addition to a student and young professional's accounting reference library, fitting perfectly with the goals of the AECC for enhancing accounting communication skills. It gives a comprehensive, real-world look at all forms of communication used by accounting professionals. Users are taught to write and speak more effectively as preparation for entering the accounting profession. This text, which virtually "teaches itself", can be used independently in an accounting communication course or as a supplement to enhance any course covering financial reporting, managerial accounting, auditing, or tax accounting topics. Both accounting and non-accounting business majors alike will find this book to be an indispensable reference tool they will want to keep on their office shelves upon entering the "real world".

REVIEWER FEEDBACK

We would love to list all the great feedback we have received from students and faculty who have aided us with writing *Managerial Accounting,* yet it would be impossible to thank everybody. We hope our thanks is manifested and evidenced through the incorporation of their suggestions in the final product. However, we do list a few comments that assure us—and hopefully you—that we are on-target:

"Overall, I am impressed by the clarity and pedagogy of this [text]. It seems to provide good foundation materials for a Managerial Accounting course. It is fairly aggressive in including complex problems, but compensates by providing a clear understandable description of the problem solving process. Using this text should help students to become better users of accounting information and better decision makers." Douglas Johnson, Arizona State University.

"I especially like the "In the News" features... the authors have used examples that relate well to the students. [Also] I love having the Contribution Model covered along with Break/Even and Taxes. Currently this is the only text I have seen where Break/Even and ABC are explained together." Lynette Chapman, Southwest Texas State University.

"The examples and illustrations were outstanding... the illustration of flows of manufacturing costs is one of the clearest I've seen." Mark Comstock, Missouri Southern State College.

ACKNOWLEDGEMENTS

No book can ever be developed without the help of others who teach the course. We want to give our thanks to the individuals involved in the development of *Managerial Accounting: A Focus on Decision Making*.

Reviewers

Sheila Ammons	Austin Community College–Northridge
Walter Austin	Mercer University
Cindi Bearden	Birmingham Southern College
Dan Brickner	University of Akron
Richard Brody	University of Nevada–Las Vegas
Lynette Chapman	Southwest Texas State University
Mark Coffey	Western New England College
Mark Comstock	Missouri Southern State College
Joe Donelan	University of West Florida
Hubert Gill	University of North Flordia
Brenda Hartman	Tomball College
Gene Hartley	North Central Missouri College
Michael Haselkorn	Bentley College
John Haverty	St. Joseph's University
Paul Hoppe	Golden Gate University
Richard Hulme	California State Polytechnic University–Pomona
Douglas Johnson	Arizona State University
Becky Jones	Baylor University
Celina L. Jozsi	University of South Florida
Il-Woon Kim	University of Akron
Kathy Lancaster	California Polytechnic State University
Gina Lord	Santa Rosa Junior College
Sue Lowensohn	Barry University
Dianna Matthew	Ball State University
Marina Nathan	Houston Community College
Charlotte Pryor	University of Southern Maine
Priscilla Reis	Idaho State University
Jacqueline Sanders	Mercer County Community College
Vic Stanton	California State University–Hayward
Arden Trine	University of Wisconsin–Oshkosh
George Violette	University of Southern Maine
Stephen Wheeler	University of the Pacific
Steven Wong	College of Alameda
Jeanne Yanamura	University of Nevada–Reno

Survey Respondents

Steven Adams	California State University–Chico
Noel Addy	Mississippi State University
Richard Aldridge	Western Kentucky University
Felix Amenkhienan	Radford University
Vidya Awasthi	Seattle University
William Bentz	Ohio State University
Arthur Berman	Chemeketa Community College
Delano Berry	Florida International University
Phillip Blanchard	University of Arizona
Loraine Boland	Western Washington University
Ken Boyce	Seattle Central Community College
Bruce Bradford	Fairfield University
Rodney R. Brooker	Glendale Community College
Carol Brown	Oregon State University

Dick Bundons	Johnson County Community College
Gregory Burbage	Sacramento City College
Joseph Catalina	Hudson Valley Community College
Curtis Clements	Baylor University
Alan Cohen	Ithaca College
Mark Comstock	Missouri Southern State College
Michael Cornick	University of North Carolina
Randolph Coyner	Florida Atlantic University
Charles Croxford	Mercer College
Dan Daly	Boston College
James Damitio	Central Michigan University
Elizabeth Davis	Baylor University
Wayne J. Davis	Indiana University of Pennsylvania
Patricia Doherty	Boston University
Robert Edney	Rider University
Rafik Elias	Cameron University
Peter Ben Ezra	George Washington University
Neil Fargher	University of Oregon
Linda Ferrell	Evergreen College
Robert D. Fesler	Tennessee Technical University
Don Foster	Tacoma Community College
Ken Fowler	Mankato State University
Harland Fuller	Illinois State University
George Gardner	Bemidji State University
Jackson F. Gillespie	University of Delaware
Arnold Glickman	Queens College
John Gobo	Hudson Valley Community College
John Godfrey	Springfield Technical Community College
Ellsworth C. Granger	Mankato State University
Gary Grudnitski	San Diego State University
Susan Gustin	West Virginia University
Chandra Gyan	Miami University
Joseph Hagan	East Carolina University
Jan Heier	Auburn University
John Hill	Delgado Community College
Nancy Hill	DePaul University
Bernice Hill	Spokane Falls Community College
Rofert Holtfreter	Central Washington University
M.A. Houston	Wright State University
Richard Hulme	California State Polytech University
Raj Iyengar	Catholic University of America
Philip Jones	University of Richmond
N. Leroy Kauffman	Western Carolina University
Annemarie Keinath	Indiana University–Northwest
Marsha Kertz	San Jose State University
Zafar Khan	Eastern Michigan University
Ronald Kilgore	University of Tennessee
Judy Kimm	Monterrey Peninsula College
Stacy Kline	Drexel University
Mehmet Kocakulah	University of Southern Indiana
Greg Kordecki	Clayton College and State University
Thomas Kozloski	Drexel University
Robert Kravet	Fairfield University
L. Kuhn	Louisiana State University
Chor T. Lau	California State University–Los Angeles
Charles Liclair	Cochise College

William Link	University of Missouri
Jan Mardon	Green River Community College
S.A. Marion	Westchester Community College
Mercedes Martinez	Rio Hondo College
Mike Merz	Boise State University
Ronald Milne	University of Nevada–Las Vegas
Robert Minnear	Emory University
Kanalis Ockree	Washburn University
Peter Oehlers	Widener University
Roger Rasmussen	Sierra College
Vafant Raval	Creighton University
Roy Regel	University of Montana
Michael J. Rose	Butler County Community College
Marilyn Salter	University of Central Florida
Franklin Schuman	Utah State University
Mike Shapeero	Bloomsburg University
Kimberly Shaughnessy	James Madison University
Debbie Shinnea	Purdue University–Calumet
Kenneth Sinclair	Lehigh University
Gordon R. Smith	Florida State University
Earl Smith	Rose State College
William F. Smith	Xavier University
Earl Spiller	University of South Carolina
Michael Stemkoski	Utah Valley State College
Michael Tyler	Barry University
Bernadette Vehec	Valencia Community College–East
James Wallace	University of California
Linda Whitten	College of San Mateo
Jane Wiese	Valencia Community College–East
Ray Williams	Mankato State University
Pete Woodlock	Youngstown State University
Martha Woodman	University of Vermont
Robert Wrenn	Los Angeles Harbor College
Myung-Ho Yoon	Northeastern Illinois University
Jeffrey Yost	Arizona State University–West

We appreciate the assistance of those who have worked on the text and ancillary package to ensure accurate information. A special thanks to Alice Cash and Lee Dworksy for their dedication to this project, and thanks to James Meir at Cleveland State Community College who technically reviewed the test bank for both accuracy and content.

We owe a special thanks to the members of our respective departments at the University of Southern Maine and North Carolina State University for their helpful input, thoughtful comments and for allowing us the time to complete this textbook. In particular, we thank Dorothy Rosene for her encouragement in starting the book and Al Chen and George Violette for their advice and support throughout this project and indeed for many years before.

We would also like to thank Doug Johnson at Arizona State for his encouragement when we were doctoral students at ASU and for his efforts during the review of this book. Also, a special thanks to Mike Martel for his help with Chapter 13.

We are grateful to the editorial, marketing, and production team at Harcourt College Publishers for their invaluable efforts: Mike Roche, Bill Schoof, Craig Avery, Charlie Watson, Jim Patterson, Brian Salisbury, Lois West, Linda Blundell, Lili Weiner, and especially Jennifer Langer who guided us through the project so well.

We dedicate this book to our wives, children, and families for their loving support and encouragement, and in memory of Professor David Hoffman and Wilbur R. Jackson.

Steve Jackson
Roby Sawyers

Steve Jackson, C.P.A., is Assistant Professor of Accounting at the University of Southern Maine. He earned a Ph.D. from Arizona State University and a B.S. from the University of Montana. He has published articles in such refereed journals as *The Journal of Accounting and Finance Research*, *The Journal of Economic and Social Measurement*, *The Accounting Educators Journal* and *The Journal of Accountancy*. His major research interest is in the accounting education area.

Dr. Jackson's professional activities include membership in the American Institute of Certified Public Accountants and the American Accounting Association. He is a former staff accountant with Touche Ross & Co. in Seattle and has over 12 years of public accounting experience. He has been a faculty member at Northern Arizona University, Western New England College, the University of Southern Mississippi as well as the University of Southern Maine. He has over 15 years of teaching experience and has taught courses in managerial and cost accounting, auditing, and financial accounting.

He was awarded three excellence in teaching awards while a doctoral student at Arizona State University and also received three teaching awards while at the University of Southern Mississippi one of which was the outstanding faculty award given by the USM Gulf Coast Accounting Society. He has previously published two managerial accounting study guides and an Instructors Manual/Test Bank for a major managerial accounting textbook. He also is the recipient of the University of Southern Maine Faculty Senate Intellectual Contributions award for the School of Business.

He lives in Portland, Maine with his wife where he enjoys fly-fishing, golf, the Portland Sea Dogs, and watching football. He has three children and a dog named Boots.

Roby Sawyers, C.M.A., C.P.A. is Associate Professor of Accounting at North Carolina State University. He earned a Ph.D. from Arizona State University, a Masters in Accounting from the University of South Florida and a B.S.B.A. from the University of North Carolina at Chapel Hill. He has published articles in a variety of journals including the *Journal of Accountancy*, the *Journal of Business Ethics*, *the Journal of the American Taxation Association*, *Advances in Taxation*, *The Tax Adviser*, and *Auditing: A Journal of Practice and Theory*. His research interests include individual behavior and decision making in a variety of contexts as well as corporate ethics. He has over 10 years of teaching experience and has taught courses in managerial and cost accounting, individual and business taxation, and the taxation of estates, gifts and trusts. He has also taught a variety of continuing education and review courses for the American Institute of CPAs, the Institute of Management Accountants and McGladrey and Pullen, LLP.

Dr. Sawyers' professional activities include membership in the American Accounting Association, the Institute of Management Accountants, and the American Taxation Association. He has served as an appointed member of the American Institute of CPAs tax division and is a member of the North Carolina Association of CPAs. He has worked in public accounting and currently provides tax and consulting services to a variety of individual and business clients.

He lives in Raleigh, North Carolina with his wife, daughter and cat. He volunteers his time serving the homeless population in the area and enjoys hiking, camping, singing in the church choir, managing his farm, and attending college basketball games.

BRIEF CONTENTS

CONTENTS

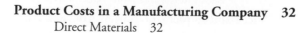

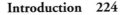

Sunset Airlines

Clayton Herring Tire Co.

Birdie Maker

Bud and Rose's Flower Shop

Amber Valley

Harbourside Hospital

Chapter 1

ACCOUNTING INFORMATION AND MANAGERIAL DECISIONS

Study Tools

A Preview of This Chapter

In Chapter 1, we begin the study of managerial accounting by discussing what is meant by accounting information and how accounting information is used by both internal and external users to make decisions. The chapter also describes the decision-making role of managers in organizations, provides a decision framework for assessing those decisions, and discusses the role of relevant factors, risk, and ethics in decision making.

Key concepts include:
- Accounting information includes both financial (quantitative) and non-financial (qualitative) information used by decision makers.
- Managerial accountants facilitate management decision making.
- Accounting information systems are constantly evolving to meet the changing demands of its users.
- Never make decisions with just the numbers! Always consider non-numerical (qualitative) information.
- Sunk costs are not relevant.
- Future costs that do not differ between alternatives are not relevant.
- Opportunity costs are relevant.

A Preview of Upcoming Chapters

Chapters 2 through 4 provide an introduction into the basics of production processes used by manufacturing companies, cost flows in manufacturing, merchandising and service companies, and basic product and service costing methods used in different types of organizations.

LEARNING OBJECTIVES

After studying the material in this chapter, you should be able to:

LO1 Understand the uses and users of accounting information

LO2 Understand the decision-making role of managers

LO3 Apply a basic four-step decision-making model

LO4 Evaluate the role of relevant factors and decision making

LO5 Understand and evaluate the role of risk in decision making

LO6 Understand and evaluate the role of ethics in decision making

The main focus of accounting is decision making. In fact, the American Accounting Association defines accounting as "the process of identifying, measuring and communicating economic information to permit informed judgments and decisions by users of information" (A Statement of Basic Accounting Theory, 1966, 1). All organizations—large and small; manufacturing, merchandising, or service; profit or nonprofit—have a need for accounting information. The primary role of accounting is to provide useful information for the decision-making needs of investors, lenders, owners, managers, and others both inside and outside the company. However, the needs of internal users and external users often differ. This chapter defines accounting information and its application by both external and internal users. The chapter then describes the decision-making role of management in planning, operating, and controlling and provides a framework for assessing decisions that commonly face managers of organizations. The chapter also provides a discussion of the role of relevant factors, risk, and ethics as they pertain to decision making. ■

┌───┐
│ **INTRODUCTION**   │
└───┘

All types of organizations, from large multinational manufacturing companies like Ford Motor Company to small custom furniture manufacturers, have a need for accounting information. Retailers such as Wal-Mart and locally owned hardware stores, large service companies such as FedEx and local CPA and law firms, and even nonprofit organizations such as the American Red Cross and small local museums and homeless shelters need accounting information. This information is used by internal managers in their day-to-day decision making and also by external users like investors, creditors, donors, and even the Internal Revenue Service.

┌───┐
│ **ACCOUNTING INFORMATION**   │
└───┘

LO1
Understand the uses and users of accounting information

Accounting information is provided by a company's **accounting information system (AIS).** Traditionally, the AIS was simply a transaction processing system that captured financial data resulting from accounting transactions. For example, the AIS would document a transaction to purchase materials by recording a journal entry showing the date of purchase, a debit to raw materials inventory, and a credit to accounts payable or cash.

Under this view of AIS, accounting information was simply financial information (sales, net income, total assets, costs of products, etc.) expressed in terms of dollars or other monetary units (e.g., yen, francs, pesos). Other nonmonetary information—such as (1) the number of units of materials or inventory on hand, (2) the number of budgeted labor hours to produce a product, (3) the number of units necessary to break even, and (4) the time it takes to manufacture a product—were likely collected and processed outside the traditional accounting information system. The use of multiple information systems within a company causes a number of problems. It is costly to support multiple systems. Perhaps more important, it is difficult to integrate information coming from different systems and to make decisions for a company with multiple sources of information. In addition, other useful information concerning transactions—such as the quality of the material purchased, the timeliness of its delivery, or customer satisfaction with an order—might not be captured at all and therefore not evaluated by management.

Over the past few years, **enterprise resource planning (ERP) systems** have been developed in an attempt to address these shortcomings. ERP systems integrate the traditional AIS with other information systems to capture both quantitative and qualitative data, to collect and organize that data into useful information, and to transform that information into knowledge that can be communicated throughout an organization (see Exhibit 1-1). These systems can be customized to provide specific and relevant information to different types of users. For example, information for tax reporting purposes must conform to the requirements of federal, state, and local taxing authorities, whereas information used in preparing financial statements and annual reports for shareholders and creditors must meet the requirements of generally accepted accounting principles (GAAP) and the Securities Exchange Commission (SEC). On the other hand, information provided to internal users (managers) is thoroughly integrated across the organization and yet is customized to the needs and desires of the particular user.

www.sec.gov

With an ERP system, the sale of a product not only generates financial information by updating the cost of goods sold and profits, but the system also updates inventory records, adjusts production schedules if necessary, and orders raw materials. In addition, delivery time, warranty claims, and service calls can be tracked and are available to managers across the organization. Therefore, production managers would know when to expect shipments of materials. Sales representatives could access information about expected delivery times to their customers, and customer service representatives could see records of previous service calls. All of this information contributes to the cost-effective management of a company and to better decision making.

Throughout our study of managerial accounting information and its use in decision making, the importance of considering both quantitative and qualitative information is

EXHIBIT I-I   A Contemporary View of Accounting Information

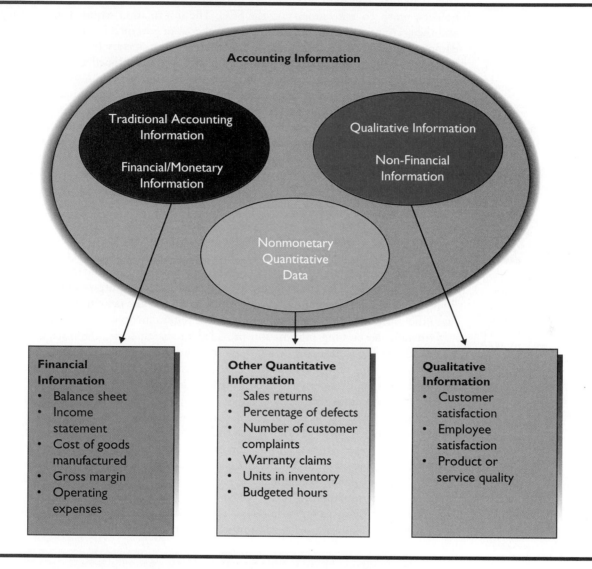

emphasized. The uses of ERP systems as decision-making tools are discussed more fully in Chapter 13. At this point, it is simply important to understand that in order to provide managers with the information they need to effectively plan, operate, and control their businesses, financial data must be linked to nonfinancial (qualitative) data, transformed into useful information and knowledge, and communicated throughout an organization.

 Key Concept: *Accounting information includes both financial (quantitative) and non-financial (qualitative) information used by decision makers.*

THE USERS OF ACCOUNTING INFORMATION

EXTERNAL USERS

There are many different users of accounting information both external and internal to the organization. Stockholders, potential investors, creditors, government taxing agencies and regulators, suppliers, and customers are all external users. What type of information do external users need? Stockholders and potential investors want information to help them analyze the current and future profitability of an organization. Companies that have issued stock to the public (or those that plan to) provide this information in the form of annual reports, registration statements, prospectuses, and other reports issued to shareholders, prospective investors, and the SEC. The information required in these reports and the accounting methods used to prepare them are governed by the SEC and GAAP. Although this information is primarily quantitative and monetary (sales and net income), it also may include nonmonetary information such as units shipped and market share. It also may include qualitative information, such as "Management's discussion and analysis of financial condition and results of operations," which is found in annual reports.

What about smaller companies that are owned by just a few members of a family (closely held) or nonprofit organizations like the Red Cross? External users of financial information such as banks or potential donors to nonprofit organizations still need accounting information to make the proper decision about lending or donating money. However, their needs may differ from those of stockholders and potential investors. Creditors generally want to assess a company's overall financial health and may be particularly interested in a company's cash flow or ability to repay their loans. Potential contributors to nonprofit organizations may have a need for both monetary information, such as how much of the Red Cross's budget is spent for charitable purposes, and nonmonetary information, such as how many women with children are served by the local homeless shelter.

Government agencies (federal, state, and local) have very specific information needs, including the measurement of income, payroll, and assets for purposes of assessing taxes. This accounting information is typically provided on income tax returns, payroll reports, and other forms designed specifically to meet the requirements of each agency.[1]

Generally, accounting information provided to shareholders, creditors, and government agencies is characterized by a lack of flexibility (its content is often dictated by the user), the reporting of past events using historical costs (financial statements for the previous three years), and an emphasis on the organization as a whole.

Suppliers and customers are also external users. However, their accounting information needs are likely to be very different than those of other external users and may be more clearly aligned with the needs of internal users. For example, suppliers of car parts to General Motors need detailed information on inventory levels of specific parts in order to know when to manufacture and ship parts. Bank customers may want to check on their account or loan balances before making a major purchase. Someone buying a new computer may want to check on the expected delivery date or whether a product is backordered before placing an order. This type of information needs to be much more detailed and timely than that provided to most other external users.

www.redcross.org

TECHNOLOGY FOCUS

Wal-Mart Stores Inc., which pioneered the idea of retailer and supplier sharing sales data, recently expanded the amount of data available to suppliers from five quarters to two years. Wal-Mart shares data on sales, profit margin, and inventory levels with over 7,000 suppliers who access Wal-Mart's database 120,000 times per week ("Wal-Mart Expands Access to Product Sales History," *Wall Street Journal*, August 18, 1999, B8).

Automobile manufacturers must provide suppliers with detailed inventory records so that parts like these engine blocks can be provided on a timely basis.

---

[1]It should be noted that many nonprofit organizations that do not pay income taxes are still required to provide information to the Internal Revenue Service that is available for use by donors and other interested parties.

INTERNAL USERS

Internal users of accounting information include individual employees as well as teams, departments, regions, and top management of an organization. For convenience, these internal users are often just referred to as managers. Managers are involved in a variety of activities including planning, operating, and controlling. These activities all involve making decisions both on an individual basis and in teams (see Exhibit 1-2).

THE DECISION-MAKING ROLE OF MANAGERS

PLANNING

Planning involves the development of both the short-term (operational) and the long-term (strategic) objectives and goals of an organization and an identification of the resources needed to achieve them. Operational planning involves the development of short-term objectives and goals (typically, those to be achieved in less than one year). Examples of operational planning for Ben & Jerry's include planning the raw material and production needs for each type of ice cream for the next four quarters or determining the company's short-term cash needs. Operational planning for a hospital would include budgeting for the number of physicians, nurses, and other staff that are needed for the upcoming month or determining the appropriate level of medical supplies to have in inventory. Operational planning also involves the determination of short-term performance goals and objectives including meeting customer service expectations, sales quotas, time budgets, and so on.

Strategic planning addresses long-term questions of how an organization positions and distinguishes itself from competitors. For example, Ben & Jerry's strategy for producing high-quality ice cream is very different from that used for producing a store brand of lower-priced ice cream. Long-term decisions about where to locate plants and other facilities, whether to invest in new state-of-the-art production equipment, and whether to introduce new products or services and enter new markets are strategic planning decisions. Strategic planning also involves the determination of long-term performance and profitability measures such as market share, sales growth, and stock price.

LO2
Understand the decision-making role of managers

www.benjerry.com

Identify some potential strategic planning decisions that would be made by a nonprofit organization whose mission is to provide medical services to the poor.

EXHIBIT 1-2 Percentage of IMA Survey Respondents Who Work on Cross-Functional Teams

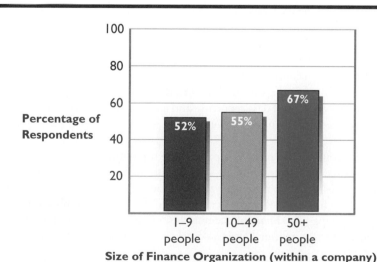

SOURCE: "Counting More, Counting Less: The 1999 Practice Analysis of Management Accounting," Institute of Management Accountants, 10.

OPERATING

Operating activities encompass what managers must do to run the business on a day-to-day basis. Operating decisions for manufacturing companies include whether to accept special orders, how many parts or other raw materials to buy (or whether to make the parts internally), whether to sell a product or process it further, whether to schedule overtime, which products to produce, and what price to charge. Other operating decisions affecting all organizations include assigning tasks to individual employees, whether or not to advertise (and the corresponding impact of advertising on sales and profits), and whether to hire full-time employees or to outsource.

CONTROLLING

Controlling activities involve the motivation and monitoring of employees and the evaluation of people and other resources used in the organization's operations. The purpose of control is to make sure the goals of the organization are being attained. It includes using incentives and other rewards to motivate employees to accomplish an organization's goals and mechanisms and to detect and correct deviations from those goals. Control often involves the comparison of actual outcomes (cost of products, sales, etc.) with desired outcomes as stated in the organization's operating and strategic plans. Control decisions include questions of how to evaluate performance, what measures to use, and what types of incentives to implement. For example, a company that emphasizes high-quality products and excellent customer service may evaluate and reward production workers who have exceeded goals based on these virtues (such goals, for example, may involve specifying the percentage of allowable defective units or scrap, monitoring customer complaints, or a myriad of other factors).

THE ROLE OF THE MANAGERIAL ACCOUNTANT

**www.rutgers.edu/
Accounting/raw/ima**

In 1996 the Institute of Management Accountants (IMA) commissioned a "Practice Analysis of Management Accounting." Through surveys of 4,000 accountants working in organizations and detailed interviews of accountants at nine corporations, the IMA practice analysis provides a detailed view of what managerial accountants do and are expected to do in the future. This study was updated in 1999.

So what do they do? Managerial accountants have traditionally been thought of as the bean counters or number crunchers in an organization. However, the practice analysis found that advances in accounting information systems and other changes in the past five or ten years have resulted in the automation of traditional accounting functions involving data collection, data entry, and data reporting and a corresponding shifting of those functions from management accounting to clerical staff. The study found that

> management accountants in many companies have been liberated from the mechanical tasks of their work. Instead of collecting information, management accountants are expected to use that freed-up time to analyze it. Instead of preparing financial statements, they interpret the financial information and explain the business implications to managers. They are doing more financial planning and more financial modeling. They work with managers to make informed business decisions. (Siegel and Kulesza, 1996, 21)

Management accountants have become decision-support specialists who "see their role as distilling diverse information, putting it into a useful format, and facilitating management decision making" (Siegel and Kulesza, 1996, 22) (see Exhibit 1-3).

 Key Concept: *Managerial accountants facilitate management decision making.*

EXHIBIT 1-3 Change in Nature of Work of Management Accountants over the Past Five Years

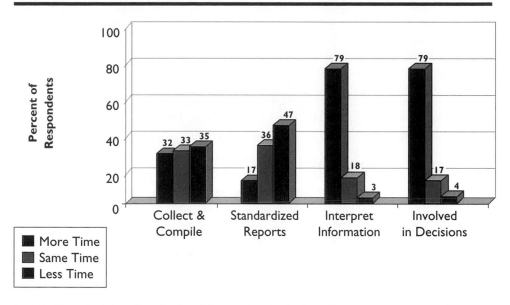

Percent of Respondents

	More Time	Same Time	Less Time
Collect & Compile	32	33	35
Standardized Reports	17	36	47
Interpret Information	79	18	3
Involved in Decisions	79	17	4

■ More Time
■ Same Time
■ Less Time

SOURCE: "Counting More, Counting Less: The 1999 Practice Analysis of Management Accounting," Institute of Management Accountants, 7.

MANAGEMENT ACTIONS AND DECISIONS

www.medco.com

GARY LUBIN
Merck-Medco Managed Care, LLC

Effective decision making is critical in today's business environment. According to Gary Lubin, vice president of sales, planning, and operations, for Merck-Medco Managed Care, LLC, "business is about making decisions; the better the decision, the better the result."

Merck-Medco Managed Care, LLC, is the leading prescription-drug benefit management (PBM) company in the United States, managing more than 350 million prescriptions each year for more than 50 million Americans. Its clients include *Fortune* 500 corporations, unions, health maintenance organizations, Blue Cross/Blue Shield plans, insurance carriers, and similar organizations providing health benefit coverage. The company manages retail networks of 55,000 pharmacies and dispenses through its own mail-order pharmacies.

In his position at Merck, Lubin (a licensed CPA with an accounting degree from Washington University and an M.B.A. from Harvard) is responsible for establishing procedures on the selling cycle (proposal requests, product pricing, resource allocation) and market sizing (identifying the market potential, identifying opportunities for products, etc.). He is also responsible for evaluating market opportunities and their impact on resource allocation, forecasting, and other general administrative activities (succession planning, budgeting, etc.).

At Merck-Medco, "decisions are viewed broadly as an action to also include reports or analyses. While seemingly obvious, decisions must add value to the organization—or it is not worth allocating resources to do the work. The days of doing work 'just-in-case' are long gone. Good decisions are driven by good analysis, supported by information, and, ultimately, based on high-quality data. For example, when Merck has to decide which prospective customers to target, we use managerial accounting techniques to frame our alternatives, understand the tradeoffs, and identify risks. Accounting information becomes the common denominator and an important way to evaluate different options."

THE ROLE OF OTHER MANAGERS

Managers are found in all functional areas of an organization including marketing, operations/production, human resources, and finance. What kind of accounting information does this diverse group of managers need and what is the role of the managerial accountant in providing it? Although managers rely on the same information provided to external users, they have other needs as well. In addition, information flow is a two-way street. Whereas managers in other functional areas rely on accounting information to make decisions, managerial accountants also rely on information provided by marketing, operations/production, human resources, and finance.

MARKETING MANAGERS

Marketing is the "process of planning and executing the conception, pricing, promotion, and distribution of ideas, goods, services, organizations, and events to create and maintain relationships that satisfy individual and organizational objectives" (Boone and Kurtz, 1998, 9). Marketing managers need to know how much a product costs in order to help establish a reasonable selling price. They need to know how a given advertising campaign and its resulting impact on the number of units sold is expected to affect income. They need to know how enhancing a product's features or changing its packaging will influence its cost. Commissions paid to sales representatives may be based on a company's profits. All of these marketing decisions require accounting information. Note that information also flows from marketing to accounting. For example, marketing will provide sales forecasts and estimates to managerial accountants for purposes of budgeting.

OPERATIONS/PRODUCTION MANAGERS

The operations and production function produces the products or services that an organization provides to its customers. Production and operations managers are concerned with providing quality products and services that can compete in a global marketplace. They need accounting information to make planning decisions affecting how and when products and services are produced. They need to know the costs of producing and storing products in order to decide how much inventory should be kept on hand. They need to know the costs of labor when making decisions to schedule overtime to complete a production run or when deciding how many physicians are needed in the emergency room. These decisions are also influenced by information provided by the marketing managers including the expected customer reaction if products are not available when orders are placed or if doctors are not available when patients need them.

Operations and production managers have been forced by a global economy and increasing customer demands to change the methods used to produce products and services. As a consequence, they have placed demands on accounting information systems to provide even more timely and accurate information for decision making as well. The information provided by accounting information systems is constantly evolving to meet the demands of its users.

 Key Concept: *Accounting information systems are constantly evolving to meet the changing demands of its users.*

FINANCE MANAGERS

The finance function is responsible for managing the financial resources of the organization. Finance managers make decisions about how to raise capital as well as where and how it is invested. Finance managers need accounting information to answer questions such as whether money should be raised through borrowing (issuing bonds) or selling stock. Finance managers make decisions concerning whether a new piece of manufacturing equipment should be purchased or leased and whether a plant expansion should be paid for in cash or by borrowing money from the bank.

HUMAN RESOURCE MANAGERS

Although all managers who supervise, motivate, and evaluate other employees are human resource managers, the human resource function is concerned with the utilization of human resources to help an organization reach its goals. More specifically, human resource managers support other functions and managers by recruiting and staffing, designing compensation and benefit packages, ensuring the safety and overall health of personnel, and providing training and development opportunities for employees. These decisions require input from all other functional areas. What kind of accounting information do human resource managers need? Human resource decisions such as hiring new employees are often made under budget constraints. Ensuring safe workplaces for employees may involve the redesign of manufacturing processes. Accountants can provide information regarding the cost of the redesign. The decision to train employees to use new equipment may require an analysis of the costs and benefits of the new program.

A SUMMARY OF ACCOUNTING INFORMATION USED BY INTERNAL AND EXTERNAL USERS

In general, accounting information needed by internal users differs from that needed by external users in the following ways:

- It is more flexible.
- It is geared to the specific company and user and does not have to meet the requirements of the SEC, GAAP, or government taxing agencies.
- It is more forward-looking, often emphasizing the future rather than the past.
- It is more timely, sometimes sacrificing accuracy in the process.
- It emphasizes segments of an organization more than the company as a whole.

Exhibit 1-4 summarizes the external and internal users of accounting information, the type of information typically needed by these users, and the source of the information.

AN INTRODUCTION TO DECISION MAKING

Although the problems and questions facing marketing, production, finance, and human resource managers of organizations are all different, the decision-making process that they follow is remarkably uniform. In fact, it is the same decision-making model that you are likely to use when making nonbusiness decisions. Do you remember the decision-making process you went through the last time you made a major decision? It could have been a decision to purchase or sell a car, a computer, or a stereo system. It could have been a decision to attend a particular college, accept a summer job, or perhaps even to get married.

Decisions such as these have many variables or factors that must be considered. If you were making a decision to purchase a car, you would consider variables such as its cost, features, color, and financing options. If you were making a decision about what college to attend, factors might include the cost, proximity to your home, and academic reputation. Different decision makers might even consider different factors for the same decision situation. For example, the color of a car may not be important to one buyer but critical to another. The number and type of variables considered might be different for each individual and for each decision the individual makes.

Decisions may have to be made under time, budget, or other constraints. Your choice of a car may be limited to those that cost under $10,000. Your decision to accept a summer job may be limited to those that are within 30 miles of your home. Your decision to

EXHIBIT I-4 External and Internal Users of Accounting Information

Users	Type of Accounting Information Needed	Provided in
Shareholders and creditors	Sales, gross profit, net income, cash flow, assets and liabilities, earnings per share, etc. While this information is primarily monetary, it may also include nonmonetary information (units in inventory). This information is often provided in summary form (for the company as a whole) and typically is historic in nature.	Annual reports, financial statements, and other available documents
Government agencies	Varies by agency but includes taxable income, sales, assets, comparisons of actual expenditures to budgets, etc. This information is usually provided for the company as a whole and is historic in nature. It can include both monetary and nonmonetary information.	Tax returns and other reports
Customers and suppliers	Order status, shipping dates, inventory levels, etc. This information must be very detailed and timely to be useful.	Limited-access databases available to specific customers and suppliers
Marketing, operations and production, finance, and human resource managers	Timely and detailed information on sales and expenses, product costs, budget information, and measures of performance. Often includes nonmonetary data (direct labor hours, units to break-even, etc.). Accounting information is often needed for segments of an organization and is more likely future oriented than historical.	Cost reports, budgets, and other internal documents

attend a college may have to be made by a certain date. In addition, many decisions are made with missing information or at least with imperfect information. In deciding which car to buy, you would probably want to consider the cost of future repairs for different models. Although you might estimate these costs by using sources such as *Consumer Reports,* you will not know with certainty. Decisions may not be perfect, but they should be the best you can make given the information that is available to you at the time. The process you go through is to gather all the information you can to reduce the risk of an incorrect or less than optimal decision.

Decisions often lead to other decisions. Once you have decided to buy a car or a stereo, you need to make other decisions such as whether to pay cash or to finance the purchase, or whether to buy an extended warranty. It does seem like life is a never-ending string of decisions.

In this chapter we discuss decision problems in general and how to gather as much relevant information as possible to reduce the risk of incorrect decisions. The decision-making model presented here will allow you to approach complex decisions in an orderly fashion.

Decision making is the process of identifying different courses of action and selecting one appropriate to a given situation. All decisions require using judgment. The quality of the decision often depends on how good that judgment is. Judgment refers to the cognitive aspects of the decision-making process. By cognitive, we mean taking a logical, thinking approach to making decisions rather than just making decisions on the spur of the moment. In this section of the chapter, we learn how to structure a decision problem so that we will use better judgment when making decisions.

Using a basic decision-making model does not guarantee that all our decisions will be correct, but it will allow us to increase the odds of making a good decision. A lot of decisions have more than one acceptable solution, as do a lot of the problems and cases in this textbook. The trick is to pick the *best* solution for each particular decision-making situation.

Outline as best you can the process you went through in selecting the last major item you purchased.

A DECISION-MAKING MODEL

STEP 1: DEFINE THE PROBLEM

When faced with a problem, the first step is to define it accurately. Managers (and students) often act without a clear understanding of the real problem. In fact, many bad decisions are made simply because the decision maker is trying to solve the wrong problem. For example, a company experiencing a reduction in sales might erroneously define the problem as low sales volume (and attempt to solve the problem by providing increased sales incentives) when the real problem is poor quality of the product sold. Problem definition requires the cooperation of managers in all functional areas of an organization. Whereas a single manager might focus on the reduction in sales, input by accounting, operations, marketing, and sales managers will most likely result in a clearer picture of the underlying problem causing the reduction in sales (poor quality). This may lead to even further refinements such as identifying the specific type of material that is causing the quality problem. Accurately defining a problem requires a willingness to listen to others, good judgment, and lots of practice.

LO3
Apply a basic four-step decision-making model

| Step 1 | **DEFINE THE PROBLEM** |

In retrospect, should you have considered other options and variables when making your most recent big purchase?

STEP 2: IDENTIFY OBJECTIVES

The second step in the decision-making process is to identify the objectives in finding a solution to the problem. Objectives may be **quantitative** (to buy at the best price or to increase net income), **qualitative** (to buy the highest-quality component or to increase customer satisfaction), or a combination of the two.

| Step 2 | **IDENTIFY OBJECTIVES** |

STEP 3: IDENTIFY AND ANALYZE AVAILABLE OPTIONS

The third step in the decision-making process is to identify the options available to achieve your objectives and analyze those options. This step requires the consideration of relevant variables affecting the problem and of alternative courses of action. Most decisions require the decision maker to consider more than one option and multiple variables.

| Step 3 | **IDENTIFY AND ANALYZE AVAILABLE OPTIONS** |

DILBERT BY SCOTT ADAMS

DILBERT reprinted by permission of United Features Syndicate, Inc.

These variables should include both quantitative and qualitative factors. The key here is to identify only the variables that are relevant to a particular decision. The concept of relevant factors is discussed in more detail on page 15.

IN THE NEWS   **www.consumerreports.com**

Every year Consumer Reports publishes an issue called a "Buyers Guide." This guide provides a variety of qualitative information to aid your decision in purchasing products evaluated by this organization.

STEP 4: SELECT THE BEST OPTION

 Step 4   SELECT THE BEST OPTION

The fourth and last step is to select the best option. We need to answer the question of how well each of our options will achieve our objective or objectives. This is sometimes the most difficult step in the process. Just as our options and variables included both quantitative and qualitative factors, our solution should consider both as well. As a general rule you should never make decisions based only on quantitative information. Often, qualitative information is at least as important as or more important than quantitative information.

▶ **Key Concept:** *Never make decisions with just the numbers! Always consider nonnumerical (qualitative) information.*

MANAGEMENT ACTIONS AND DECISIONS   **www.medco.com**

To be successful in a business like Merck-Medco, "employees need to possess a broad array of skills and must be able to think through and look beyond the numbers." When hiring entry-level positions, Gary Lubin looks for students who have an appreciation for the breadth of tools and techniques that can be applied to understand a business situation as opposed to the depth of any one technical tool.

GARY LUBIN
Merck-Medco Managed Care, LLC

What were the risks in your decision to purchase a particular product?

At this stage, the decision maker must also recognize that decisions are often made in the face of uncertainty. This step in the decision process will involve our preference for risk and our estimate of what chance the future events have of happening. The impact of risk on decision making is discussed more completely on page 16.

To summarize, we follow these four steps in the process of making decisions (see Exhibit 1-5):

1. Define the problem.
2. Identify objectives.
3. Identify and analyze available options.
4. Select the best option.

Evaluate your decision to purchase a product. Was your decision a good one?

Once we have completed the preceding process and chosen the best option, we must then implement our decision and evaluate the results. We may have to go back to step one and repeat the process if the decision turns out to be less than optimal.

EXHIBIT 1-5 The Decision-Making Model

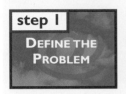
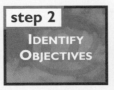

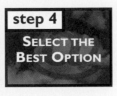

| step 1 | step 2 | step 3 | step 4 |
| DEFINE THE PROBLEM | IDENTIFY OBJECTIVES | IDENTIFY AND ANALYZE AVAILABLE OPTIONS | SELECT THE BEST OPTION |

RELEVANT FACTORS AND DECISION MAKING

Step 3 in our decision-making model is to identify and analyze relevant factors affecting the decision. How do decision makers determine if a factor is relevant? Relevant factors are those that affect a particular decision. Therefore, they must be factors that differ between alternatives. In deciding between automobiles, if they all have the same options at the same cost (air conditioning, AM/FM stereo, etc.), then those options are not relevant to the decision. Very often, costs are key factors that must be considered in decisions. As with other factors, **relevant costs** are those that differ between alternatives. Another way to view relevant costs is to identify those that are avoidable or can be eliminated by choosing one alternative over another. In choosing between automobiles, if one car has air conditioning and another does not, the cost of air conditioning is relevant because choosing one of the alternatives could eliminate that cost.

Sunk costs are costs that have already been incurred. Because sunk costs cannot be avoided, they are not relevant in decisions. In your decision to trade in your old vehicle, the amount that you paid for it may appear to be important. However, because that cost is sunk, it cannot be avoided, is not relevant, and should not be considered in your decision.

 Key Concept: *Sunk costs are not relevant.*

Concept Question: *As a production manager of a manufacturing company, you have become aware of a new machine that can reduce the cost of making a product by 30 percent. However, when you approach your boss about buying the new equipment, he says that you can't buy it until the old equipment is fully depreciated in two more years. Is the depreciation on the old machine a relevant cost? What factors are relevant?*

Concept Answer: Depreciation on the old machine is sunk and therefore is not relevant. ■

If sunk costs are not relevant, what about other costs that will be incurred in the future? Are all costs that are not sunk relevant? Again, the key is that relevant costs are avoidable costs. If future costs do not differ between alternatives, they are not avoidable (they will be incurred regardless of the alternative chosen) and therefore are not relevant. In your choice of an automobile, if the cost of an option is the same, then that cost is not relevant in your decision.

 Key Concept: *Future costs that do not differ between alternatives are not relevant.*

Opportunity costs are the benefits forgone by choosing one alternative over another and are relevant costs for decision-making purposes as well. For example, in choosing to go to college, you are forgoing the salary you could receive by working full time. Almost all alternatives have opportunity costs. In choosing to work instead of going to school, the

Step 3 | IDENTIFY AND ANALYZE AVAILABLE OPTIONS

LO4
Evaluate the role of relevant factors and decision making

Making a decision to stop producing a product is a difficult one that depends on an analysis of both quantitative costs and qualitative factors. For example, assume you are the manager of a consumer electronics manufacturing company that makes televisions and videocassette recorders (VCRs). What quantitative costs would be relevant in making the decision to stop making VCRs? Remember, relevant costs are those that can be avoided by choosing one alternative over another. What qualitative factors should be considered?

In making the decision to stop producing VCRs, what opportunity costs might be involved? Consider, for example, alternative uses of the facilities and other products that might be manufactured instead of VCRs.

opportunity cost is the higher salary that you might earn if you choose to go to school. Opportunity costs are sometimes difficult to quantify but nevertheless should be considered in making decisions.

 Key Concept: *Opportunity costs are relevant.*

RISK AND DECISION MAKING

LO5
Understand and evaluate the role of risk in decision making

As mentioned earlier, most decisions involve **risk.** A decision maker's goal is to consider (and possibly to minimize) the risk of decisions. One of the factors that come into play when selecting the best option (Step 4) is the attitude toward risk. If the decision makers are risk seekers, then they will rate the alternatives one way. If they are risk averse, they will probably rate the alternatives differently. For example, risk-averse decision makers may rate an automobile that has been in production a couple of years and has a history of being reliable more highly than a brand new model with no track record.

A quantitative method of considering the risk of decision factors is by adjusting the discount rate used in time value of money calculations (see Chapter 8 for a more detailed discussion of this important concept). Cash flows occurring further in the future might be discounted at a higher interest rate than cash flows occurring in the next year or two. Increasing the interest rate in present value calculations has the impact of decreasing the present value of those cash flows.

A second way of adjusting for risk is by considering the probability that certain events will occur. For example, in the choice of an automobile the interest rate on the loan may be an important factor. However, a particular dealer may not guarantee the interest rate before the loan is approved. Knowing that the probability of the rate changing is 50 percent, the rating can be adjusted accordingly to take this risk into account.

A third method of considering risk is through **sensitivity analysis.** Sensitivity analysis is the process of changing the values of key variables considered in the analysis to determine how sensitive decisions are to those changes. For example, if the purchaser of an automobile is not 100 percent sure of qualifying for the best possible loan package at all the dealers, he or she may want to consider the cost of that automobile, taking into account all possible finance packages. If this adjustment changes the decision, then the decision is sensitive to changes in that variable. If it does not change the decision, the decision is not sensitive to that variable.

ETHICS AND DECISION MAKING

LO6
Understand and evaluate the role of ethics in decision making

Ethical issues frequently arise in the course of personal decision making. Sometimes the ethical issues are clear (should you keep the money in the wallet you found or return it to its owner) but at other times may be a little cloudy. For example, what ethical responsibilities does the owner of a used car have in telling a prospective buyer about potential problems?

Likewise, ethical issues in business decisions may be fuzzy. Although most of us would agree that it would be unethical for businesses to sell products that are known to be unsafe to customers, cigarette manufacturers do just that every day. Is the use of inexpensive foreign labor by shoe and apparel manufacturers an acceptable business practice or a serious lapse of ethical responsibility? Is the release of chemicals into the environment as a by-product of an electric utility or a paper mill an acceptable cost of providing products to a demanding customer or an unacceptable and unethical practice?

Regardless of how you feel about these and other ethical issues, companies must consider the implications of such decisions. As special interest groups grow more vocal about environmental issues and working conditions, consumers boycott products and switch brands, and investors consider ethical and social criterion in making investments, ethical

MANAGEMENT ACTIONS AND DECISIONS

www.medco.com

The importance of high ethical standards in business cannot be overstated. At Merck-Medco, Gary Lubin notes that new employees "must understand the importance of quality and completeness; appreciate the process as well as the result; exhibit self-confidence; work well both independently and in teams; and above all, demonstrate high ethical behavior."

GARY LUBIN
Merck-Medco Managed Care, LLC

Pricing decisions are an important consideration for companies attempting to maximize their profitability. However, pricing decisions are likely to influence other factors (such as the volume of products sold) and cannot be made in isolation. The impact of changing prices on the number of units sold is usually not known with certainty. How might you as a manager take this risk into account in determining the selling price of your products?

decisions become crucial business decisions. In fact, research finds a strong link between companies that express a clear commitment to ethics and a company's financial performance. In a study of the 500 largest publicly held companies in the United States, those with a strong commitment to ethics were ranked among the top 100 financial performers twice as often as those without a strong commitment (Verschoor, 1997).

Ethical problems arise in organizations for a number of reasons. Sometimes, pressure to reach unrealistic short-run goals may lead to unethical behavior like padding budgets or using poor-quality materials in production to save money. Strictly adhering to an organizational hierarchy can be problematic when subordinates blindly follow orders. In the past, managers often viewed their goals in strictly monetary terms—to earn a profit and to increase shareholder wealth. More recently, there has been a call for a return to the view of business as a moral practice in which managers are concerned about the ethical consequences of what they do. In this view, decisions must be made in an environment that encourages the evaluation of a multitude of values, not only dollars and cents.

Do companies have responsibilities to other stakeholders?

Concept Question: **What ethical responsibilities does a company have to its shareholders, employees, customers, and the communities in which it is located?**

Concept Answer: While companies take various approaches to ethical responsibility, they often provide guidance to their employees concerning what is acceptable ethical behavior through the use of a formal code of ethics.[2] Codes may be very specific and mention acceptable and unacceptable behavior or just provide a general framework and value system that can be used by employees in their day-to-day decision making. For example, Ben & Jerry's mission statement consists of three interrelated parts:

1. Product—to make, distribute and sell the finest quality all-natural ice cream and related products in a wide variety of innovative flavors made from Vermont dairy products.
2. Economic—to operate the company on a sound financial basis of profitable growth, increasing value for our shareholders, and creating career opportunities and financial rewards for our employees.
3. Social—to operate the company in a way that actively recognizes the central role that business plays in the structure of society by initiating innovative ways to improve the quality of life of a broad community—local, national, and international. ■

PAUSE & Reflect

Is adhering to laws and regulations sufficient to ensure ethical behavior in organizations?

A variety of professional organizations also have ethical codes of conduct that apply to their members. In 1997 the Institute of Management Accountants issued a revised code

---

[2]Berenebeim (1992) reports that 84 percent of U.S. companies surveyed had an ethics code, and 45 percent have enacted them since 1987.

PAUSE
& *Reflect*

A supplier offers to sell you aluminum used in the manufacture of aluminum baseball bats at a sizable discount. After inspecting the aluminum, you find that while it meets your technical qualifications, in some cases it shatters under extreme use. What objectives might you consider to explicitly take into account your company's ethical responsibilities in this situation? What relevant factors should be considered?

of ethics for management accountants stating that "practitioners of management accounting and financial management have an obligation to the public, their profession, the organizations they serve, and themselves, to maintain the highest standards of ethical conduct." The full text of the code is provided in the appendix to this chapter.

With a little elaboration, our four-step decision model is sufficient to handle the consideration of ethical issues. In Step 2, objectives should include the consideration of a company's ethical responsibilities. This might include statements like "the decision should result in a higher-quality product or a safer product for customers." It might require explicit acknowledgment that the well-being of employees will be considered in the decision or that the decision must not harm the environment. Ethical decision making requires managers to consider who will be affected by the decision and how.

If a company's objectives include the consideration of ethical responsibilities, then it is important to identify the major principles, laws, and values that have a bearing on the decision in Step 3. Principles include qualities like integrity, honesty, and respect for others. Laws affecting business decisions include the Internal Revenue Code and the Foreign Corrupt Practices Act of 1977, which makes it illegal for U.S. corporations to make improper payments or bribes to help in the acquisition of sales. Values include such things as the importance of the quality and safety of products but also include the desire to earn a profit or protect one's job. If a company's ethical responsibilities are adequately and explicitly acknowledged in Step 2 and Step 3 of the decision model, selecting the best option in Step 4 will consider ethical objectives as well as the monetary impact of a particular decision.

IN THE NEWS   **www.anheuser-busch.com**

In 1996 Anheuser-Busch launched a campaign to discourage beer distributors from carrying microbrews. They offered discounts and subsidized advertising and limited distributors' ability to bring rival brews to bars and retailers. When the distributors began to abandon the microbrews, the microbrews brought suit against Anheuser-Busch. Anheuser-Busch maintains the actions are legitimate and legal.

APPENDIX

STANDARDS OF ETHICAL CONDUCT FOR PRACTITIONERS OF MANAGEMENT ACCOUNTING AND FINANCIAL MANAGEMENT

Practitioners of management accounting and financial management have an obligation to the public, their profession, the organizations they serve, and themselves, to maintain the highest standards of ethical conduct. In recognition of this obligation, the Institute of Management Accountants has promulgated the following standards of ethical conduct for practitioners of management accounting and financial management. Adherence to these standards, both domestically and internationally, is integral to achieving the Objectives of Management Accounting. Practitioners of management accounting and financial management shall not commit acts contrary to these standards nor shall they condone the commission of such acts by others within their organizations.

COMPETENCE

Practitioners of management accounting and financial management have a responsibility to:

- Maintain an appropriate level of professional competence by ongoing development of their knowledge and skills.
- Perform their professional duties in accordance with relevant laws, regulations, and technical standards.
- Prepare complete and clear reports and recommendations after appropriate analyses of relevant and reliable information.

CONFIDENTIALITY

Practitioners of management accounting and financial management have a responsibility to:

- Refrain from disclosing confidential information acquired in the course of their work except when authorized, unless legally obligated to do so.
- Inform subordinates as appropriate regarding the confidentiality of information acquired in the course of their work and monitor their activities to assure the maintenance of that confidentiality.
- Refrain from using or appearing to use confidential information acquired in the course of their work for unethical or illegal advantage either personally or through third parties.

INTEGRITY

Practitioners of management accounting and financial management have a responsibility to:

- Avoid actual or apparent conflicts of interest and advise all appropriate parties of any potential conflict.
- Refrain from engaging in any activity that would prejudice their ability to carry out their duties ethically.
- Refuse any gift, favor, or hospitality that would influence or would appear to influence their actions.
- Refrain from either actively or passively subverting the attainment of the organization's legitimate and ethical objectives.
- Recognize and communicate professional limitations or other constraints that would preclude responsible judgment or successful performance of an activity.

- Communicate unfavorable as well as favorable information and professional judgments or opinions.
- Refrain from engaging in or supporting any activity that would discredit the profession.

OBJECTIVITY

Practitioners of management accounting and financial management have a responsibility to:

- Communicate information fairly and objectively.
- Disclose fully all relevant information that could reasonably be expected to influence an intended user's understanding of the reports, comments, and recommendations presented.

RESOLUTION OF ETHICAL CONFLICT

In applying the standards of ethical conduct, practitioners of management accounting and financial management may encounter problems in identifying unethical behavior or in resolving an ethical conflict. When faced with significant ethical issues, practitioners of management accounting and financial management should follow the established policies of the organization bearing on the resolution of such conflict. If these policies do not resolve the ethical conflict, such practitioners should consider the following courses of action:

- Discuss such problems with the immediate superior except when it appears that the superior is involved, in which case the problem should be presented initially to the next higher managerial level. If satisfactory resolution cannot be achieved when the problem is initially presented, submit the issues to the next higher managerial level. If the immediate superior is the chief executive officer, or equivalent, the acceptable reviewing authority may be a group such as the audit committee, executive committee, board of directors, board of trustees, or owners. Contact with levels above the immediate superior should be initiated only with the superior's knowledge, assuming the superior is not involved. Except where legally prescribed, communication of such problems to authorities or individuals not employed or engaged by the organization is not considered appropriate.
- Clarify relevant ethical issues by confidential discussion with an objective advisor (e.g., IMA Ethics Counseling Service) to obtain a better understanding of possible courses of action.
- Consult your own attorney as to legal obligations and rights concerning the ethical conflict.
- If the ethical conflict still exists after exhausting all levels of internal review, there may be no other recourse on significant matters than to resign from the organization and to submit an informative memorandum to an appropriate representative of the organization. After resignation, depending on the nature of the ethical conflict, it may also be appropriate to notify other parties.

SUMMARY OF KEY CONCEPTS

- Accounting information includes both financial (quantitative) and nonfinancial (qualitative) information used by decision makers. (p. 5)
- Managerial accountants facilitate management decision making. (p. 8)
- Accounting information systems are constantly evolving to meet the changing demands of its users. (p. 10)

- Never make decisions with just the numbers! Always consider nonnumerical (qualitative) information. (p. 14)
- Sunk costs are not relevant. (p. 15)
- Future costs that do not differ between alternatives are not relevant. (p. 15)
- Opportunity costs are relevant. (p. 16)

KEY DEFINITIONS

Accounting information system (AIS) A transaction processing system that captures financial data resulting from accounting transactions within a company (p. 4)

Enterprise resource planning (ERP) systems Systems used to collect, organize, report, and distribute organizational data and transform that data into critical information and knowledge (p. 4)

Planning The development of both the short-term (operational) and the long-term (strategic) objectives and goals of an organization and an identification of the resources needed to achieve them (p. 7)

Operating activities The day-to-day operations of a business (p. 8)

Controlling activities The motivation and monitoring of employees and the evaluation of people and other resources used in the operations of the organization (p. 8)

Decision making The process of identifying alternative courses of action and selecting an appropriate alternative in a given decision-making situation (p. 12)

Quantitative Can be expressed in terms of dollars or other quantities (units, pounds, etc.) (p. 13)

Qualitative Deals with nonnumerical attributes or characteristics (p. 13)

Relevant costs Those costs that differ between alternatives (p. 15)

Sunk costs Costs that have already been incurred (p. 15)

Opportunity costs The benefits forgone by choosing one alternative over another (p. 15)

Risk The likelihood that an option chosen in a decision situation will yield unsatisfactory results (p. 16)

Sensitivity analysis The process of changing the values of key variables to determine how sensitive decisions are to those changes (p. 16)

CONCEPT REVIEW

1. Accounting information systems generate both monetary and nonmonetary accounting information. List two examples of each.

2. Is information produced by an accounting information system all quantitative? Why or why not? Give examples.

3. Define quantitative and qualitative information. Include in your definition some examples.

4. When purchasing a new car, give examples of quantitative and qualitative information. Would a car purchase decision include both types of information?

5. List the most common external users of accounting information and what type of information they might need.

6. List the most common internal users of accounting information and what type of information they might need.

7. Discuss how a financial report for an internal user might differ from a financial report prepared for an external user.

8. Define strategic and operational planning.

9. Define control from a management perspective.

10. Assume that you have a 16-year-old son who has just received his drivers' license. Your son does not do all of the assigned work in his high school classes. What could you do to "control" his behavior regarding doing the assigned work in school? In other words, what sort of rewards or incentives would be appropriate to motivate him?

11. How has the role of the managerial accountant changed over time? What do managerial accountants do?

12. What type of accounting information do marketing managers need to make better decisions?

13. What type of accounting information do operations/production managers need to make better decisions?

14. What type of accounting information do finance managers need to make better decisions?

15. What type of accounting information do human resource managers need to make better decisions?

16. List and describe the four steps of the decision-making model.

17. How can risk be addressed in the decision-making model?

18. Define sunk costs and opportunity costs, and discuss their importance in decision making.

APPLICATION OF CONCEPTS

19. You are faced with the decision of choosing a new car. You have narrowed your options to four different types of automobiles that fit your needs.

	Automobile 1	**Automobile 2**	**Automobile 3**	**Automobile 4**
Price	$12,000	$13,000	$14,000	$15,000
Options	Radio, $250	Cassette, $350	CD player, $500	CD/Cassette player, $750
Air	None	$1,200	$1,250	$1,200
Automatic Transmission	$1,000	$1,200	$1,250	$1,500
Power Package	None	$850	$1,250	$500

Required

A. Define as best you can the decision problem that you face in choosing the best automobile for you.

B. What would be your objectives in choosing an automobile? Separate the objectives into qualitative and quantitative areas. In your specific situation what would be your most important objective and why?

C. As you will recall, Step 3 of the decision-making model requires you to identify all available options. Discuss what you consider to be the available options, in your decision to choose a new automobile. Discuss all relevant quantitative and qualitative variables affecting these options.

D. Which of the four automobiles is the best quantitative choice? Why?

E. List and discuss qualitative factors that may cause you or any other decision maker to choose an automobile that is not the best quantitative choice.

20. Kent Jackson, an English major, has to decide which course to enroll in during the summer session. A science course he wants to take is being offered at a cost of $800 plus laboratory fees of $10 per class (25 classes total). His other choice is a writing workshop with tuition of $950. In addition to selecting a course, Kent needs a place to stay during the summer. Although he already paid $500 for a dormitory room, Kent has decided he can no longer live on campus. There are two rooms available: a private residence that would cost him $900 and a semiprivate room that would cost $600. Kent could sublet his dormitory but feels he should keep it empty in case he changes his mind and returns to campus in the fall.

Required

A. What other costs should Kent consider in making his decision?

B. What are some qualitative factors Kent might want to consider before he makes his decision? Why?

C. Discuss all relevant variables pertaining to this decision.

D. If Kent has a fixed amount of $2,000 to live on during the summer, how would this fact affect his decision?

21. A friend has informed you of an opportunity for a part-time job that you are considering accepting during your last semester before graduation. It would start at the beginning of your last semester and require working 20 hours per week at a rate of $15 per hour. It would also provide some good experience that could lead to a full-time job after you graduate. However, it would require a 2-hour round-trip commute, 4 days a week. In addition, you currently receive a scholarship of $1,000 per month, which stipulates that you cannot work off campus. Consequently, if you accept the job, you will have to give up the scholarship. You expect to register for 15 credit hours (5 classes) during your last semester and have been told that each of the courses is very demanding. In addition to class time, you expect to study about 30 hours each week.

Required

Using the decision-making model introduced in the chapter:

A. Define the problem you face in deciding whether to accept the job.

B. Using your own personal situation, define your objectives related to the problem identified in part A.

C. What are your options, and what factors are likely to be relevant in making your decision?

D. What opportunity costs are associated with the decision?

E. Is the decision risky? How would you take risk into account when making your decision?

22. Many airlines offer special low rates to certain destinations, but these rates are available only to customers that can fly on short notice. Sometimes low hotel rates are also available at the last minute. How can this behavior be explained in terms of relevant costs?

23. Bob would like to impress Jessica on their first date and is wondering whether he should make dinner or whether they should go to a nice restaurant. What factors are relevant in the decision?

24. It's final exam time for Janet and she is panicking because she doesn't have enough time to study for her last two exams. She currently has the same average in both calculus and history. With sufficient study time, she estimates that she could increase her grade in calculus by 15 points and her grade in history by 10 points. However, she has only six hours of study time available. Janet estimates that she can increase her final grade in calculus by 2 points for each one hour studied and increase her final grade in history by 3 points for every hour of study. To maximize her additional points, how much time should Janet study for each exam?

25. Is it ethical for a U.S. company operating in a foreign country to offer bribes to suppliers or government officials if it is an acceptable business practice in the foreign country?

26. Recently, a story on *60 Minutes* highlighted the widespread practice of automotive service businesses attempting to sell customers unneeded parts and services. What are the ethical issues involved? Who are the stakeholders?

27. As an engineer with a multinational aerospace firm, you become aware of a potential defect in an airplane engine part. Your tests indicate that at low temperatures, a seal may leak, allowing hot gases from the engine to ignite. Although the risks of such a leak are very low, the consequences are potentially disastrous. What ethical issues are involved? Who are the stakeholders? What should the manager do?

CONTINUING CASE | BIG AL'S PIZZA EMPORIUM

Big Al's Pizza Emporium is a pizza restaurant in Tempe, Arizona. Big Al's is very successful because it is located close to a major university and most of the restaurant's business is from college-age customers. Big Al's would like to expand the business and sell pizzas to grocery stores, convenience stores, and school cafeterias. The restaurant staff would prepare and freeze the pizza for wholesale distribution. In order to expand, the business must acquire new kitchen space and equipment. The pizza restaurant is not capable of handling any additional volume. Big Al's has hired you to evaluate the proposed expansion and to lead the company through the first year of operations.

Required

1. What information do you think Big Al's should gather in order to analyze the feasibility of the expansion?

2. What do you think it costs to produce a 16-inch pizza? Make sure you include all ingredients and some labor time, but for this estimate don't worry about the equipment needed.

3. What equipment do you think the restaurant needs to acquire?

4. Using the decision model presented in this chapter, determine the problem definition.

5. What variables should be considered?

6. What qualitative factors should be considered in the decision?

Chapter 2

THE PRODUCTION PROCESS AND PRODUCT (SERVICE) COSTING

Study Tools

A Review of the Previous Chapter

Chapter 1 provided an overview of accounting information, its users, and the types of decisions that are made by both external and internal users of accounting information.

A Preview of This Chapter

In this chapter we learn about basic production processes used by manufacturing companies, cost terminology, the flow of costs in manufacturing, merchandising and service companies, and the impact of product costs and period costs on a company's income statement and balance sheet.

Key concepts include:
- Costs flow in the same way that products flow through a production facility.
- Product costs attach to the product and are only expensed when the product is sold whereas period costs are expensed in the period in which they are incurred.

A Preview of Upcoming Chapters

Chapter 3 provides an introduction into the cost systems used to accumulate, track, and assign costs to products and services, and the particular difficulties and problems caused by the allocation of overhead. Chapter 4 discusses the allocation of overhead to products using activity-based costing (ABC), and how activity information is used to help managers control and manage costs.

LEARNING OBJECTIVES

After studying the material in this chapter, you should be able to:

LO1 Understand basic production processes used by traditional manufacturing companies with and without inventory

LO2 Apply the concepts of product costs for manufacturing, merchandising, and service-oriented companies

LO3 Understand basic cost flows applicable to manufacturing, merchandising, and service companies

LO4 Evaluate the impact of product costs and period costs on a company's income statement and balance sheet

Product (and service) costing is important for both external users and managerial decision making. Externally, the cost of products and services must be known to value inventory (for products) and to determine the gross profit on sales. Internally, managers must know the costs of products and services for a variety of reasons including making pricing decisions and budgeting for expected cash disbursements. The costing of products and services is described in Chapters 2, 3, and 4. Chapter 2 begins with a description of the production process for both traditional manufacturing companies with inventory and manufacturing companies with little or no inventory. The chapter also provides an introduction into basic cost terminology applicable to manufacturing companies, merchandising companies, and service providers and concludes with a description of cost flows in each type of company. In Chapter 3, we discuss systems that companies use to accumulate, track, and assign costs to specific products and services and some of the issues related to measuring and allocating overhead and other product costs. In Chapter 4, we discuss some of the problems inherent in traditional methods of overhead allocation and describe a contemporary costing system called activity-based costing that may be more appropriate for internal decision making. ■

INTRODUCTION

Regardless of the type of company involved, costs are associated with the products and services produced and sold. Although it might appear simple to determine the cost of a product or service, as you will see in the next few chapters, the process can be quite complicated. How should companies determine the costs of producing products and providing services? What costs should be included? Before we can answer these questions, we should also ask why companies want to determine their product costs. For example, a company might be preparing financial statements to be used by a bank in determining whether to make a loan to the company, or it may be filing its income tax return for the year. Generally accepted accounting principals (GAAP) and tax laws govern costing for financial statement purposes and for tax purposes, respectively. On the other hand, a company might want to determine the cost of a particular product in order to determine its sales price or to estimate a product's profitability. Cost information is also helpful for budgeting and evaluation purposes. Costing for internal decision making is the focus of Chapters 2, 3, and 4.[1]

MANUFACTURING, MERCHANDISING, AND SERVICE ORGANIZATIONS

LO1
Understand basic production processes used by traditional manufacturing companies with and without inventory

Every company provides a product or service to customers and clients. **Manufacturing companies** (such as Intel, Toyota, mom-and-pop bakeries, or custom furniture makers) take raw materials and produce new products from them. Retail and wholesale merchandising companies sell products that someone else has manufactured. Examples include large department stores like Sears and Target as well as the independent record shop or clothing store on the corner. In contrast to manufacturing and merchandising companies, service companies do not sell a tangible product as their primary business. Service providers are the fastest growing segment of the U.S. economy employing roughly 75 percent of the workforce. Service providers include such diverse companies and industries as airlines, hospitals, automobile repair shops, brokerage firms, law firms, and CPA firms.

THE PRODUCTION PROCESS

PAUSE & Reflect

Grocery stores sell products that other companies have manufactured but they may also have their own bakeries in which they transform raw materials into new products. Should they be classified as manufacturing or merchandising companies? Brokerage firms sell information to clients. Is information a product or a service?

Manufacturing companies purchase raw materials from other companies and transform them into a finished product. This transformation typically requires labor and the incurring of other costs such as utilities, the depreciation of factory equipment, or supplies. Manufacturing companies may produce a single product or many products. Likewise, companies may have only a few customers or many thousands. The process used to manufacture these products depends on the specific product or products made, the customers that buy the product(s), and the company itself. Some companies are very labor intensive whereas others rely heavily on automation. Some companies choose to make very high-quality products whereas other companies emphasize low cost. Some companies choose to carry large amounts of inventory whereas others manufacture their products in small batches and make their products just in time to meet customer demand.

MANUFACTURING IN A TRADITIONAL ENVIRONMENT

Traditionally, the factory of a manufacturing company is organized so that similar machines are grouped together. For example, a furniture manufacturer might have areas de-

---

[1] It should be noted that companies might want to cost other objects in addition to products. For example, a company might want to know the costs of a particular department or division or even the costs of servicing a particular customer.

Traditional furniture manufacturers such as this one retain varying levels of products in their work-in-process inventories so that workers at each step along the process will never experience idle time on the job.

voted to cutting and rough sanding, shaping the cut lumber into furniture pieces (like chair legs), using lathes and routers, drilling holes and dovetailing joints, assembly of the furniture pieces, and finishing. As raw material (in this case lumber) is processed in each area, it is "pushed" to the next area for further processing. Lumber is brought into the factory from the warehouse and is cut and rough sanded according to specifications for specific products. It is then moved to another area in the factory where chair legs, bed posts, and tabletops are shaped from the rough lumber. Next, it might move to an area containing drill presses and machines to make dovetail joints. After drilling and jointing, it would be moved to still another area for assembly. In this area, workers would glue or screw the various parts together and attach necessary hardware and glass. After assembly, the furniture is moved to an area where it is sanded again and varnish or paint finishes are applied. It would not be unusual for one or more of these areas to be in different buildings or sometimes in entirely different plants. After leaving the finishing department, the furniture is ready for packing and selling to customers.

In this traditional system, it was normal (and perhaps even desirable) to accumulate **raw materials inventory** and finished products inventory (called **finished goods inventory**) to serve as buffers in case of unexpected demand for products or unexpected problems in production. It was also normal to accumulate inventories of partially completed products (called **work-in-process inventory** or WIP). WIP might result for example when furniture pieces that have been drilled and jointed are pushed to the assembly area before the workers in that area are ready for them.

PAUSE & Reflect

Can you think of other reasons that it may be desirable to have buffers of inventory on hand?

MANUFACTURING IN A JIT ENVIRONMENT

One of the big changes affecting manufacturing companies in the past 20 years or so has been the adoption of **JIT (just-in-time) production systems.** In an effort to reduce costs and become more efficient producers, companies began to focus on the costs and problems associated with the traditional manufacturing facility and the practice of carrying large amounts of inventory.

Concept Question: In addition to costs of storage and insurance, what are some of the other costs of holding large amounts of inventory?

Concept Answer: In addition to the obvious costs of storage and insuring inventory, traditional manufacturing systems may result in other not-so-obvious costs including the production of lower-quality products with more defects. The buffers that seem so desirable may in fact lead workers to pay less attention to detail and work less efficiently. In addition, the organization of factories in which similar machines are grouped together greatly increases the time necessary to manufacture products and makes it more difficult to meet special orders or unexpected increases in demand without having large amounts of inventory on hand. ■

In a just-in-time system, materials are purchased and products are made "just in time" to meet customer demand. Unlike traditional production, the process begins with a customer order and products are "pulled" through the manufacturing process. Under ideal conditions, companies operating in a JIT environment would reduce inventories of raw materials, work-in-process, and finished goods to very low levels or even zero.

Without a buffer of extra finished goods and raw materials, it is imperative that companies employing JIT be able to manufacture products very quickly. This typically entails restructuring the factory itself. In the traditional factory, similar machines were often grouped together resulting in raw materials and unfinished products being handled and moved a great deal from area to area. In the traditional factory, it also was difficult and time consuming to switch production from one product to another (from tables to chairs for example) because the same machines were used for both. In contrast, factories in a JIT environment are typically organized so that all the machinery and equipment needed to make a product is available in one area. These groupings of machines are called manufacturing cells. The use of cells minimizes handling and moving of products. It also reduces or eliminates setup time (the time needed to switch production from tables to chairs) because we now have one cell devoted just to the manufacture of tables and one cell devoted just to the manufacture of chairs. Sometimes, workers are trained to operate all of the machinery in a manufacturing cell, increasing speed and efficiency even more. Dell Computer Corp uses just-in-time manufacturing techniques to assemble build-to-order personal computers. As you can see in Exhibit 2-1, Dell can ship a computer to a customer within 12 hours of receiving an order. The actual assembly takes under two hours.

www.dell.com

IN THE NEWS

In mid-1999, Toyota and General Motors announced plans to manufacture and deliver custom automobiles to customers within 10 to 12 days of receiving an online order. ("General Motors Looks to the Future with Internet Unit," *Wall Street Journal*, August 11, 1999, B4.)

Concept Question: *Using the decision-making model introduced in Chapter 1, discuss the problem, objectives, and options facing a company like GM in deciding to employ JIT techniques in their manufacturing operations. What factors and variables are relevant in their decision?*

Step 1 DEFINE THE PROBLEM

Concept Answer: The problem facing GM and other automobile manufacturers is that traditional manufacturing practices in which cars are manufactured and delivered to dealers before the car is sold are costly and can be inefficient. When consumer demand changes (i.e., consumers demand more sport utility vehicles than estimated), manufacturers and their dealers are sometimes left with large amounts of unsold cars. In addition, when consumers can't get the cars they desire, they may get angry and decide to purchase from another manufacturer resulting in lost sales and customer ill-will.

Step 2 IDENTIFY OBJECTIVES

GM likely has multiple objectives including reducing the costs associated with holding large amounts of inventory, decreasing the time it takes to deliver a vehicle to a customer, increasing the flexibility of the manufacturing facilities, and increasing the quality of automobiles produced.

EXHIBIT 2-1 JIT Business in Action at Dell Computer Corp.

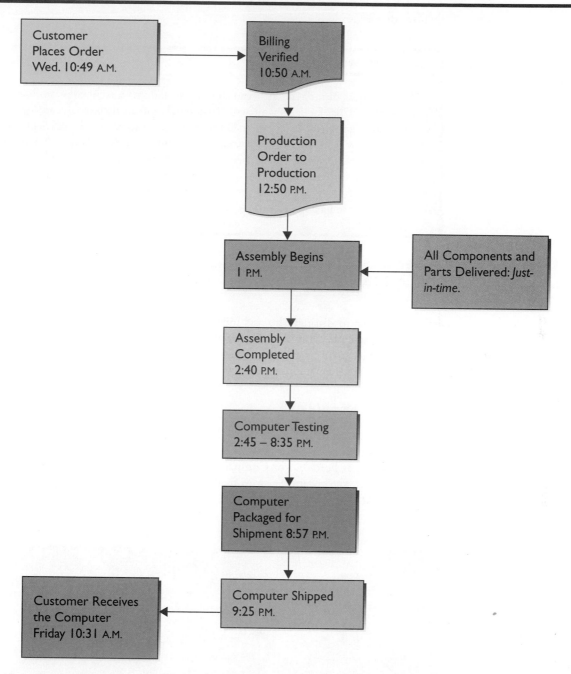

SOURCE: Adapted from Stephanie Losee, "Mr. Cozzette Buys a Computer," *Fortune* (1997).

GM's objectives might be met in a number of ways. Among the options it may consider are more (or less) automation of manufacturing facilities (without adopting JIT practices), doing away with the dealer network by requiring customers to order cars directly from GM, reducing the number and variety of car and truck models offered to customers, and adopting JIT techniques in its manufacturing processes. GM should consider the impact of each of these options on its objectives of reducing the costs of holding inventory, decreasing delivery time, increasing flexibility, and increasing quality. GM should also consider the impact on the existing work force, suppliers, dealers, customers, shareholders, and other stakeholders. ■

Step 3   IDENTIFY AND
         ANALYZE AVAILABLE
         OPTIONS

Regardless of the size of the company involved, the number or products made, or the type of manufacturing system used, manufacturing companies must know how much their products cost.

IN THE NEWS

When U.S. car manufacturers began to make small cars to compete with foreign imports in the 1970s, foreign manufacturers routinely priced their small cars lower than did U.S companies. While foreign manufacturers were probably more efficient and had lower costs than their U.S. counterparts, U.S. manufacturers found that they really did not have a good idea how much their different lines of automobiles really cost! They routinely overcost the high-volume small cars they manufactured and undercost the lower volume large cars. This bias in costing high-volume and low-volume products is discussed more in Chapter 4.

PRODUCT COSTS IN A MANUFACTURING COMPANY

LO2
Apply the concepts of product costs for manufacturing, merchandising, and service-oriented companies

It is convenient to distinguish costs incurred directly in the manufacture of a product (manufacturing costs) from those incurred elsewhere in the company (nonmanufacturing costs). **Manufacturing costs** are costs incurred in the factory or plant and typically consist of three components: *direct materials, direct labor,* and *manufacturing overhead.*

DIRECT MATERIALS

Direct materials are defined as materials that can be directly and conveniently traced to a particular product or other cost object *and* that become an integral part of the finished product. At Ford Motor Company, sheet metal and tires are direct materials. At Dell Computer, the computer chips made by Intel and used in Dell computers are direct materials.

Companies often will not make the effort to count every screw, rivet, or nail in a product and would rather elect to classify these items as Indirect Materials.

Direct materials typically cause few problems in the costing of products. The amount of direct material used in making products can usually be accurately measured using engineering studies and the accounting system of most companies is capable of tracing the materials used and the costs of those materials to specific products. However, questions do arise and judgment is often needed to correctly classify materials as direct or indirect.

Materials that we know are used in the manufacture of products but cannot be measured with reasonable accuracy and easily and conveniently traced to a particular product are indirect costs **(indirect material).** For example, the rivets and welding materials used by Ford Motor Company and the screws and solder used by Dell Computer would probably be classified as indirect materials.

DIRECT LABOR

Direct labor is the labor cost (including fringe benefits) of all production employees who work directly on the product being made or service being provided. Sometimes direct labor is called touch labor to reflect the hands-on relationship between the employee and the product or service. Assembly-line workers are the clearest example of direct labor. Like direct material, identifying direct labor cost is usually straightforward and accurate. Time sheets may be used to keep track of the work employees perform on different products and the wages they are paid. Other labor cost incurred in the manufacture of a product (such as the cost of work performed by janitors, maintenance workers, and even supervisors who do not work on the products directly) is classified as an indirect cost **(indirect labor).**

MANUFACTURING OVERHEAD

All costs incurred in the factory that are not properly classified as direct material or direct labor are called **manufacturing overhead.** These costs may include utilities, depreciation of factory equipment and buildings, rent, repairs and maintenance, insurance, and so on. Manufacturing overhead also includes indirect materials and indirect labor and may include overtime and idle time costs for direct labor workers. In a traditional manufacturing environment, the costs included in manufacturing overhead are most often indirect in nature and cannot be conveniently and accurately traced and assigned to a specific product. Remember our machinery and equipment was typically used to make multiple products making it difficult to trace the cost of a machine to a specific product. Although many overhead costs in a JIT environment will also be indirect in nature (rent and utilities for example), more of the costs are likely to be direct in nature. For example, in a JIT environment the cost of machinery in a manufacturing cell can be traced to a specific product (tables) if it is only used to make tables.

Because of the indirect nature of most overhead costs and the inability of companies to directly measure the amount of overhead included in products or to trace manufacturing overhead to products, accountants have come up with various methods of allocating manufacturing overhead to products. Traditional methods of allocating overhead using job and process costing are discussed in Chapter 3. A contemporary method called activity-based costing is discussed in Chapter 4.

NONMANUFACTURING COSTS

Nonmanufacturing costs consist of those costs that are incurred outside the plant or factory and typically are categorized as selling and administrative costs. While nonmanufacturing costs are necessarily incurred in running a business, they are not directly incurred in the production of products. A general rule of thumb is to imagine the product not being produced. If a particular cost would still occur, then it is generally a nonmanufacturing cost. Common examples of nonmanufacturing costs include advertising costs, commissions paid to salespersons, administrative and accounting salaries, and office supplies. Nonmanufacturing costs also include rent, insurance taxes, utilities, and depreciation of equipment when used in selling and administrative activities.

Concept Question: *Classify the following costs as manufacturing or nonmanufacturing costs:*
  1. Depreciation of factory machinery
  2. Depreciation of vehicles used by salespersons
  3. Lease expense on factory equipment
  4. Lubricants used for maintenance on factory machinery
  5. Factory supervisors' salaries
  6. Heat, water, and power used in the factory building
  7. Material used to construct the product
  8. Materials used in packaging the finished product for shipment
  9. Fringe benefits paid to assembly line workers
  10. Depreciation of furniture used in the employee cafeteria
  11. Overtime paid to assembly line workers

A manufacturing firm buys computers that are used to control the production process and to process accounting information for management. Are the costs of the computers (depreciation) classified as manufacturing or nonmanufacturing costs?

Concept Answer: The key to identifying costs as manufacturing or nonmanufacturing is to think about where in the process the cost occurs. If the cost occurs in the factory while the product is being produced, it is a manufacturing cost. If the cost occurs after the product is produced or outside the manufacturing area, then it is a nonmanufacturing cost. In the Concept Question above, numbers 1, 3, 4, 5, 6, 7, 9, and 11 are manufacturing costs while the remainder are not. ■

Concept Question: *Which of the items in the previous Concept Question would be considered manufacturing overhead?*

Concept Answer: Numbers 1, 3, 4, and 6 would be considered manufacturing overhead. In addition, overtime paid to assembly line workers (number 11) may be considered overhead. This is discussed more fully in Chapter 3. ■

LIFE-CYCLE COSTS AND THE VALUE CHAIN

This simple classification of costs as manufacturing or nonmanufacturing leaves a lot to be desired. How should costs associated with research and development be classified? What about costs that are incurred in the engineering and design of products or costs that are incurred after the sale due to warranty work or other customer service? **Life-cycle costing** takes into account all the activities in an organization's **value chain.** The value chain of an organization is simply the set of activities that increase the value of an organization's products and services. A typical value chain includes research and development, design, production, marketing, distribution, and customer service activities (see Exhibit 2-2). Life-cycle costing therefore includes all of the costs incurred throughout a product's life, not just in the manufacturing and selling of the product.

COST FLOWS IN A MANUFACTURING COMPANY—TRADITIONAL ENVIRONMENT WITH INVENTORY

If companies simply used all the materials they purchased to make one product, finished making all the units of that product that they started, and sold everything they finished,

EXHIBIT 2-2 Life-Cycle Costs

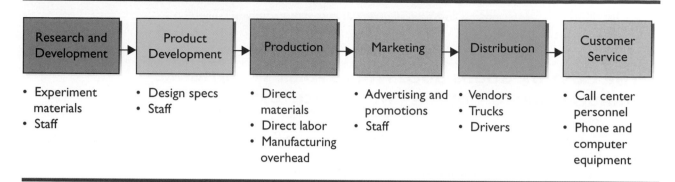

Research and Development	Product Development	Production	Marketing	Distribution	Customer Service
• Experiment materials • Staff	• Design specs • Staff	• Direct materials • Direct labor • Manufacturing overhead	• Advertising and promotions • Staff	• Vendors • Trucks • Drivers	• Call center personnel • Phone and computer equipment

calculating the income or loss from selling the product would be relatively easy. However, when multiple products are made or when materials are not all used, or goods are not all finished, or products are not all sold, the process becomes more difficult.

To accurately cost products of manufacturing companies, manufacturing costs must somehow be traced or allocated to each individual product as it is being produced and then move through various inventory accounts as the product(s) progress toward eventual completion and sale. At the point of sale, the cost of producing the product (the cost of goods sold) must be matched with the sales price to compute a profit or loss on the sale (called gross margin or gross profit). Subtracting nonmanufacturing costs from the gross margin provides a measure of profitability for the company as a whole. When materials are not all used in production, goods are not finished, or finished goods are not all sold, costs must be accounted for in the appropriate raw material, work-in-process, or finished goods inventory accounts.

Manufacturing costs include direct material, direct labor, and manufacturing overhead. These costs are also called product costs because they attach to the product as it goes through the production process. Picture a product moving down an assembly line. As labor, material, and overhead costs are incurred, they attach to the product being produced and remain with that product until it is sold. Costs flow in the same way that products flow through a production facility.

 Key Concept: Costs flow in the same way that products flow through a production facility.

LO3
Understand basic cost flows applicable to manufacturing, merchandising, and service companies

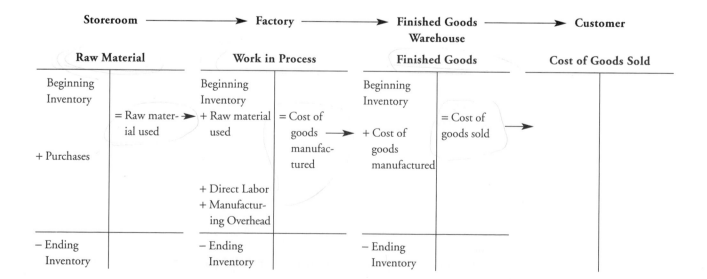

Storeroom	→	Factory	→	Finished Goods Warehouse	→	Customer
Raw Material		**Work in Process**		**Finished Goods**		**Cost of Goods Sold**
Beginning Inventory		Beginning Inventory		Beginning Inventory		
	= Raw material used →	+ Raw material used	= Cost of goods manufactured →	+ Cost of goods manufactured	= Cost of goods sold	→
+ Purchases						
		+ Direct Labor + Manufacturing Overhead				
− Ending Inventory		− Ending Inventory		− Ending Inventory		

This basic cost flow model is appropriate (with slight variations) for companies using either job costing or process costing systems. The differences between job costing and process costing systems are discussed more fully in Chapter 3.

THE COST OF GOODS SOLD MODEL FOR A TRADITIONAL MANUFACTURING COMPANY WITH INVENTORY

To illustrate the production process and some of the associated problems with costing products, we will use a fictional company called Northern Lights Custom Cabinets. Northern Lights Custom Cabinets manufactures and sells custom ordered kitchen and bathroom cabinets. The company primarily sells to building contractors but occasionally deals directly with homeowners. Northern Lights is located in Anchorage, Alaska, and has been in business only a few years, so management is still learning the business and how to properly determine the cost of each cabinet.

Northern Lights has an engineering and design division, which is involved in all custom cabinet jobs. Quality control dictates that the engineering and design division must design all cabinets. Northern Lights strives to minimize the costs of production without sacrificing quality. Once the design phase of each cabinet job is complete, the material must be ordered. The material is stored in the raw materials warehouse until needed for each job and is then moved to the production area.

The production factory is separated into three distinct areas: (1) cutting, (2) assembly, and (3) finishing. In the cutting area, all wood is cut into the required pieces based on the plans from the engineering and design division. The pieces are all numbered and bundled for each particular section of the cabinet job. After cutting is completed, the bundles are moved to the assembly area where the cabinets are constructed using glue and wood dowels. The assembled cabinets are moved to the finish area where they are finished and stored for delivery to the home. This process can take up to one month to complete and is very labor intensive. After the cabinets have been completed they are delivered to the home. Because each job is custom, Northern Lights also provides installation services for an extra charge.

Northern Lights purchases raw materials and stores the materials in a warehouse that is separate from the production facility or factory. While these materials are in the warehouse the costs of the raw materials are included in a raw material inventory account. Northern Lights began 1999 with raw materials costing $10,000 on hand and purchased an additional $40,000 of raw materials during the year. Therefore, the company had $50,000 of raw materials available for use during the year.

Description	Item	Amount
Raw materials on hand to start the period	Beginning inventory of raw materials	$10,000
Acquisitions of raw materials during the period	+ Cost of raw materials purchased	+ 40,000
The pool of raw materials available for use during the period	= Raw materials available for use	= $50,000

When the raw material is moved to the factory, the raw material costs move with the material to a work-in-process inventory account. Any raw materials not used during the year remain in the raw materials inventory account. Northern Lights moves $45,000 of raw materials to the factory for use in manufacturing cabinets; $5,000 of raw materials remains in raw materials inventory.

Description	Item	Amount
The pool of raw materials available for use during the period	Raw materials available for use	$50,000
The amount of raw materials used in production (and moved to a WIP account)	− Raw materials used in production	− 45,000
Raw materials on hand at the end of the period	= Ending inventory of raw materials	=$ 5,000

Raw Materials		**Work in Process**	
$10,000	$45,000		
+40,000			
$ 5,000			

As direct labor costs of $65,000 are incurred (factory workers work on the cabinets), the cost of the workers is added to the raw material cost in the work-in-process inventory account. Likewise, as manufacturing overhead costs ($85,000 of machine costs, rent, depreciation, utilities, indirect material, etc.) are incurred they are added to the work-in-process account. As long as each set of cabinets remains in the factory, the costs associated with them are recorded in the work-in-process account.

If there is no beginning inventory of work in process and everything that is started in 1999 is finished (there is no ending inventory of WIP), then the cost of goods manufactured is simply the sum of raw materials used, direct labor, and manufacturing overhead. When beginning or ending inventories exist, the cost of goods manufactured must be adjusted accordingly. At the beginning of 1999, Northern Lights had $15,000 of unfinished cabinets (started in 1998) in the factory. These cabinets were completed in early 1999. However, the company got even further behind in 1999 resulting in $20,000 of cabinets being partially finished at the end of 1999. Therefore, the cost of goods (cabinets) manufactured in 1999 and transferred to finished goods was $190,000.

Description	Item	Amount
Work-in-process on hand at the beginning of the period	Beginning inventory of WIP	$ 15,000
The amount of raw materials used in production	+ Raw materials used	+ 45,000
The amount of direct labor cost incurred	+ Direct labor	+ 65,000
The amount of manufacturing overhead incurred	+ Manufacturing overhead	+ 85,000
Work-in-process at the end of the period	− Ending inventory of WIP	− 20,000
The cost of goods manufactured during the period	= Cost of goods manufactured	=$190,000

Work in Process		**Finished Goods**	
$15,000	$190,000		
+45,000			
+65,000			
+85,000			
$20,000			

Northern Lights
custom cabinets

When a cabinet is sold, the accumulated costs in the finished goods inventory account are moved to the cost of goods sold account. If there is no beginning inventory of finished goods and all of the goods finished in the current year are sold (there is no ending inventory), the cost of goods sold is equal to the cost of goods manufactured. However, when beginning and ending inventories exist, the cost of goods sold must be adjusted accordingly. Northern Lights had one order (costing $30,000) that was not delivered to customers by the end of 1998. Likewise, at the end of 1999, the company had $5,000 of cabinets that were finished but not sold. Therefore, the cost of goods (cabinets) sold during 1999 was $215,000.

Description	Item	Amount
Finished goods on hand at the beginning of the period	Beginning inventory of finished goods	$ 30,000
The cost of goods manufactured during the period	+ Cost of goods manufactured	+ 190,000
Finished goods on hand at the end of the period	– Ending inventory of finished goods	– 5,000
The cost of goods sold during the period	= Cost of goods sold	=$215,000

Finished Goods		Cost of Goods Sold	
$ 30,000	$215,000		
+190,000			
$ 5,000			

COST FLOWS IN A MANUFACTURING COMPANY—JIT ENVIRONMENT

How do cost flows differ in a manufacturing company utilizing JIT? Remember, in a JIT environment, the physical flow of goods is streamlined by the use of manufacturing cells that largely eliminate inventories of raw materials, WIP, and finished goods. Cost flows are streamlined as well. While the mechanics of an accounting system for companies utilizing JIT are covered more fully in the appendix to Chapter 3, direct material, direct labor, and overhead costs can essentially be accumulated directly in a cost of goods sold account. Since raw materials are immediately placed into production when purchased there is no need to record their purchase in a separate raw materials inventory account. Likewise, since all goods are typically finished and shipped out immediately to customers, there is no reason to keep track of WIP or finished goods inventories.

Description	Item	Amount
The amount of raw materials purchased and used in production	Raw materials purchased and used	$ 50,000
The amount of direct labor costs incurred	+ Direct Labor	+ 65,000
The amount of overhead cost incurred	+ Manufacturing overhead	+ 85,000
The cost of goods sold during the period	= Cost of goods sold	=$200,000

MERCHANDISING COMPANIES AND THE COST OF PRODUCTS

Wholesalers and retailers purchase merchandise from other companies in finished form. With the exception of packaging and other minor changes, they simply offer the products for resale to other companies (wholesalers) or to the ultimate consumer (retailers). Therefore, the product cost of a wholesaler or retailer is simply the purchase price of the merchandise the wholesaler or retailer sells.

Because merchandising companies simply purchase goods for resale, the flow of costs in a retail or wholesale establishment is fairly simple. On the balance sheet, merchandising companies use a single account for inventory, called merchandise inventory. The costs incurred in inventory are simply the costs to purchase the inventory.

How are the costs incurred in purchasing inventory for resale expensed? You may recall from financial accounting that the principle of matching revenue from sales with the costs associated with that revenue means that the cost of purchasing merchandise is expensed as cost of goods sold as the merchandise is sold. However, the cost of goods sold is not necessarily equal to the cost of merchandise purchased during the period. If merchandise is purchased and not sold or if merchandise that was purchased in another period is sold in the current period, cost of goods sold must be adjusted accordingly.

The Cost of Goods Sold Model for a Merchandising Company

Description	Item	Amount
Merchandise on hand to start the period	Beginning inventory	$15,000
Acquisitions of merchandise during the period	+ Cost of goods purchased	+ 63,000
The pool of merchandise available for sale during the period	= Cost of goods available for sale	= $78,000
Merchandise on hand at the end of the period	− Ending inventory	− (18,000)
The expense recognized on the income statement	= Cost of goods sold	= $60,000

COST FLOWS IN A SERVICE COMPANY

Many similarities exist between the costing of products in a manufacturing company and the costing of services. Like product costs, the cost of services includes three components: direct material, direct labor, and overhead. However, the proportions of each may vary dramatically. Service companies typically have few direct materials (or indirect materials for that matter) and large amounts of direct labor and overhead.

In a movie studio, costumes and props are direct material and the salaries of actors and directors would be direct labor. Overhead would include the costs of the studio itself and all of the recording and production equipment. Camera operators and other support people would more than likely be classified as indirect labor because they would likely work on more than one film at a time. In a CPA firm or law firm, direct material costs would likely be very small whereas direct labor costs for CPAs and attorneys would be very large.

Concept Question: In a CPA firm, paper is used in the preparation of tax returns. Is the paper likely to be considered direct or indirect material? Secretarial staff may be used to enter *data into a computer for tax return preparation or for making copies of returns. Is the secretarial labor properly classified as direct labor or indirect labor?*

Concept Answer: The paper would likely be considered indirect material because it is probably immaterial in amount and accounting for the paper used in each return would be difficult and inconvenient. On the other hand, if a significant amount of secretarial time is spent inputting data, it is likely that the CPA firm would keep track of those hours and trace them directly to a tax return as direct labor. Secretarial time spent on copying would most likely be considered indirect labor. Note that indirect material and indirect labor are still treated as costs of providing services by the CPA firm.

Although service companies have both direct and indirect costs, in general they have larger proportions of indirect overhead costs. For example, in a hospital, although the costs of specific drugs and special tests or X-rays can be traced to a specific patient, the costs of operating rooms and equipment and the salaries of administrators, discharge personnel, orderlies, and maintenance workers would all be indirect. ■

Concept Question: *Would a service company ever have the need for a WIP account?*

Concept Answer: Work-in-process (WIP) accounts could be used on projects that were incomplete at month end, such as audits by CPA firms, lengthy legal cases by law firms, and consulting engagements that are long term. In fact this is a very common way to account for the accumulation of costs on these types of engagements. ■

PRODUCT COSTS AND PERIOD COSTS

LO4
Evaluate the impact of product costs and period costs on a company's income statement and balance sheet

Manufacturing costs are called **product costs** or inventoriable costs because they attach to products as they go through the manufacturing process. Direct material, direct labor, and overhead costs remain with the product until the product is sold. It is only when sold that product costs are expensed as cost of goods sold on the income statement. Until the sale of the product, the costs of manufacturing are included in one of three inventory accounts: raw material, work-in-process, and finished goods. These inventory accounts appear on the balance sheet along with other assets and liabilities. On the other hand, nonmanufacturing costs are called **period costs** because they are expensed in the period incurred. Selling and administrative costs are expensed immediately on the income statement in the period in which they are incurred (see Exhibit 2-3).

EXHIBIT 2-3 The Path to the Income Statement—Product and Period Costs

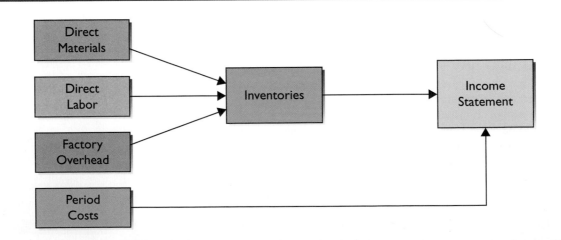

Key Concept: *Product costs attach to the product and are only expensed when the product is sold whereas period costs are expensed in the period in which they are incurred.*

Balance sheets of a traditional manufacturing company (Ben & Jerry's Homemade Inc.) and a merchandising company (Circuit City) are shown in Exhibit 2-4. Note that merchandise inventory makes up about half of Circuit City's total assets but a much smaller portion of Ben & Jerry's total assets.

www.benjerry.com
www.circuitcity.com

Income statements (called a statement of operations by Ben & Jerry's and a statement of earnings by Circuit City) are shown in Exhibit 2-5. Income statements show the expensing of product costs as goods are sold (called cost of sales and buying and warehousing by Ben & Jerry's and Circuit City, respectively) and period costs (selling, general, and administrative expenses).

Note that the information provided in the balance sheets and income statements of Ben & Jerry's and Circuit City is historical in nature, is in summary form, and is provided for the company as a whole. This is typical of financial information provided to external users (stockholders, investors, and creditors).

EXHIBIT 2-4   Consolidated Balance Sheets (Partial) (In thousands)

Consolidated Financial Statements
Consolidated Balance Sheets
(In thousands except share amounts)

ASSETS	December 26, 1998	December 27, 1997
Current assets:		
Cash and cash equivalents	$ 25,111	$ 47,318
Short term investments	22,118	481
Trade accounts receivable: (less allowance of $979 in 1998 and $1,066 in 1997 for doubtful accounts)	11,338	12,710
Inventories	13,090	11,122
Deferred income taxes	7,547	6,071
Prepaid expenses and other current assets	3,105	2,378
Total current assets	82,309	80,080
Property, plant and equipment, net	63,451	62,724
Investments	303	1,061
Other assets	3,438	2,606
	$ 149,501	$ 146,471

continued on next page

EXHIBIT 2-4   Consolidated Balance Sheets (Partial) (In thousands)

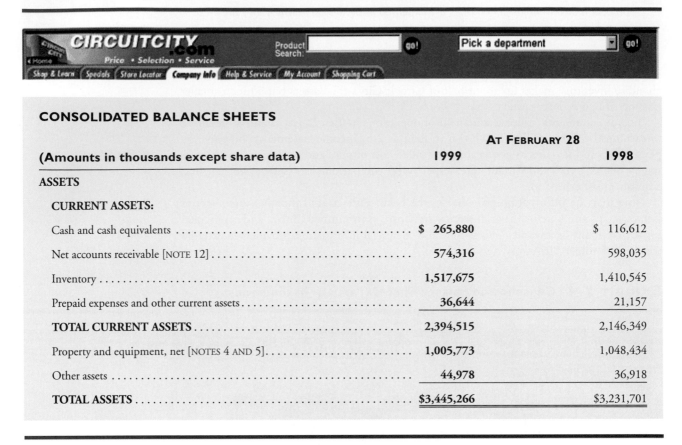

CONSOLIDATED BALANCE SHEETS

(Amounts in thousands except share data)	AT FEBRUARY 28	
	1999	1998
ASSETS		
CURRENT ASSETS:		
Cash and cash equivalents	$ 265,880	$ 116,612
Net accounts receivable [NOTE 12]	574,316	598,035
Inventory	1,517,675	1,410,545
Prepaid expenses and other current assets	36,644	21,157
TOTAL CURRENT ASSETS	2,394,515	2,146,349
Property and equipment, net [NOTES 4 AND 5]	1,005,773	1,048,434
Other assets	44,978	36,918
TOTAL ASSETS	$3,445,266	$3,231,701

EXHIBIT 2-5   Income Statements (Partial) (In thousands)

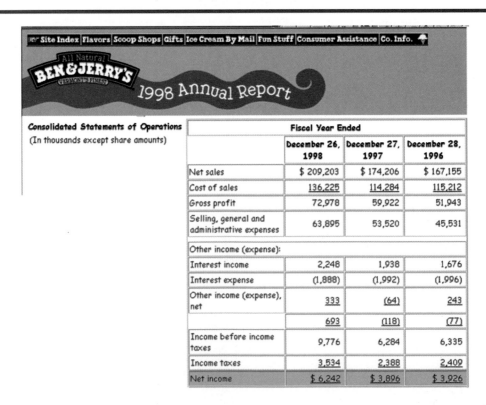

Site Index | Flavors | Scoop Shops | Gifts | Ice Cream By Mail | Fun Stuff | Consumer Assistance | Co. Info.

BEN&JERRY'S — 1998 Annual Report

Consolidated Statements of Operations (In thousands except share amounts)	Fiscal Year Ended		
	December 26, 1998	December 27, 1997	December 28, 1996
Net sales	$ 209,203	$ 174,206	$ 167,155
Cost of sales	136,225	114,284	115,212
Gross profit	72,978	59,922	51,943
Selling, general and administrative expenses	63,895	53,520	45,531
Other income (expense):			
Interest income	2,248	1,938	1,676
Interest expense	(1,888)	(1,992)	(1,996)
Other income (expense), net	333	(64)	243
	693	(118)	(77)
Income before income taxes	9,776	6,284	6,335
Income taxes	3,534	2,388	2,409
Net income	$ 6,242	$ 3,896	$ 3,926

continued on next page

CONSOLIDATED STATEMENTS OF EARNINGS

(Amounts in thousands except share data)	1999	%	1998	%	1997	%
		YEARS ENDED FEBRUARY 28				
NET SALES AND OPERATING REVENUES	$10,804,447	100.0	$8,870,797	100.0	$7,663,811	100.0
Cost of sales, buying and warehousing	8,359,428	77.4	6,827,133	77.0	5,902,711	77.0
GROSS PROFIT	2,445,019	22.6	2,043,664	23.0	1,761,100	23.0
Selling, general and administrative expenses [NOTE 11]	2,186,177	20.2	1,848,559	20.8	1,511,294	19.7
Interest expense [NOTE 5]	28,319	0.3	26,861	0.3	29,782	0.4
TOTAL EXPENSES	2,214,496	20.5	1,875,420	21.1	1,541,076	20.1

In contrast, companies provide very detailed financial statements for use by internal managers. A manager of a Circuit City store would want to know detailed information on sales of specific merchandise (televisions, VCRs, stereo components) and accessories. A divisional manager would want sales information for each store in his or her region. Marketing and production managers at Ben & Jerry's need to know the gross margin for each product, not just the overall gross margin. Managers also need detailed information on the balance sheet. For example, managers at Circuit City would want to know exactly how many of various products are in inventory and how long they have been there.

IN THE NEWS   www.paramount.com

Actors, writers, and directors sometimes contract with movie studios to receive a percentage of a movie's profits in lieu of a set salary. However, misunderstandings concerning how profits are defined have led to problems. As an example, although *Forrest Gump* is the fifth highest grossing movie ever produced with domestic ticket sales of $330 million, a year after its release, Paramount Studios reported a $63 million loss. At that time, ticket sales amounted to $191 million but expenses were reported to be $254 million. Among the expenses were $50 million in production costs, $74 million in marketing costs, $62 million in distribution costs, $62 million in payments to actors and producers, and $6 million in interest. Apparently, Paramount expensed all of the product costs associated with the movie as soon as it was released rather than matching costs with revenues earned over time.

SUMMARY OF KEY CONCEPTS

- Costs flow in the same way that products flow through a production facility. (p. 35)
- Product costs attach to the product and are only expensed when the product is sold whereas period costs are expensed in the period in which they are incurred. (p. 41)

KEY DEFINITIONS

Manufacturing companies Companies that purchase raw materials from other companies and transform those raw materials into a finished product (p. 28)

Raw material inventory Inventory of materials needed in the production process but not yet moved to the production area (p. 29)

Finished goods inventory Inventory of finished product waiting for sale and shipment to customers (p. 29)

Work-in-process inventory Inventory of unfinished product (in other words, what is left in the factory at the end of the period) (p. 29)

JIT (just-in-time) production systems The philosophy of having raw materials arrive just in time to be used in production and for finished goods inventory to be completed just in time to be shipped to customers (p. 29)

Manufacturing costs Costs incurred in the factory or plant to produce a product. Typically consists of three different elements: direct materials, direct labor, and manufacturing overhead (p. 32)

Direct materials Materials that can easily and conveniently be traced to the final product (p. 33)

Indirect material Material used in the production of products but not directly traceable to the specific product (p. 33)

Direct labor Labor that can easily and conveniently be traced to particular products (p. 33)

Indirect labor Labor used in the production of products but not directly traceable to the specific product (p. 33)

Manufacturing overhead Indirect material and labor and any other expenses related to the production of product but not directly traceable to the specific product (p. 33)

Nonmanufacturing costs Costs that include selling and administrative costs (p. 33)

Life-cycle costing Includes all of the costs incurred throughout a product's life, not just in the manufacturing and selling of the product (p. 34)

Value chain The set of activities that increase the value of an organization's products and services. The value chain typically includes research and development, design, production, marketing, distribution, and customer service activities (p. 34)

Product cost Also called inventoriable costs because they attach to the products as they go through the manufacturing process (p. 40)

Period cost Costs that are expensed in the period incurred. Attached to the period as opposed to the product. (p. 40)

CONCEPT REVIEW

1. Are the terms *cost* and *expense* synonymous? Why or why not?

2. Compare the terms *direct* and *indirect* cost.

3. In 1990, a study found that overhead of U.S. manufacturers was 50 percent greater than that of Japanese manufacturers and 20 percent greater than that of European manufacturers. What impact will this have on the U.S. companies? Why might U.S. companies have higher overhead?

4. What are some of the reasons that companies want or need to determine accurate product costs?

5. Discuss the differences between costing a product (such as building an airliner) and costing a service (such as flying passengers on an airline).

6. What has changed in the manufacturing environment in the past 20 years or so that has caused some companies to reevaluate their product costs?

7. Describe what a JIT environment means. What are some of the pluses and minuses of making a product or producing a service just in time to be sold?

8. Define the three components of manufacturing costs.

9. Define nonmanufacturing costs.

10. Define life-cycle costs.

11. Compare product and period costs. Why is the designation important?

12. Why is manufacturing overhead considered an indirect cost of a product?

APPLICATION OF CONCEPTS

13. Tom's Thimbles, a manufacturing company, began the month with raw materials costing $7,000 on hand; purchases during the month totaled $15,000. If $6,000 of raw materials were remaining at the end of the month, what was the amount used for production during the current month?

14. Danielle's Dresses manufactures women's clothing. In 2001 wage and salary expenses included the following:

Machine operators	$100,000
Quality control supervisors	50,000
Fabric cutters	25,000
Factory janitor	8,000
Company president	100,000 — period cost

Required

A. What was the amount of direct labor incurred in 2001?

B. What was the amount of indirect labor incurred in 2001?

15. Coed Novelties manufactures key chains for college bookstores. During 2002, the company had the following costs:

Direct materials used	$41,000
Direct labor	28,000
Factory rent	12,000
Equipment depreciation—factory	4,000
Equipment depreciation—office	750
Marketing expense	3,500
Administrative expenses	50,000

45,000 units were produced in 2002.

Required

A. What are the total product costs for 2002?

B. What is the product cost per unit?

C. What are the total nonmanufacturing costs for 2002?

D. What is the net income for 2002 if 40,000 units are sold for $4 each?

16. Deskmakers is a new company, which manufactures desks. In their first month of operation, they began and completed 500 desks. The following production information has been provided:

Direct material cost per unit	$ 18
Estimated indirect material costs	220
Direct labor hours per unit	4
Cost per direct labor hour	15
Estimated indirect labor cost	400
Factory rent	2,000
Marketing expense	750
Administrative expenses	1,600

Required

A. What is the cost of direct labor per desk?

B. What were the total overhead costs for the first month's production?

C. What were the total product costs for the first month's production?

D. What are the total period (nonmanufacturing) costs for the first month's production?

E. What would the net income for the first month be if 500 of the desks were sold at a price of $85 each?

17. Christopher's Creations had the following information available for the month of January:

	Beginning	**Ending**
Raw materials inventory	$110,000	$115,000
Work-in-process inventory	55,000	58,000
Finished goods inventory	41,000	37,000
Raw materials purchased		121,000
Direct labor (2,500 hrs@$12)		30,000
Overhead		53,000

Required

A. How much raw material was used in January?

B. What is the cost of goods manufactured in January?

C. What is the cost of goods sold in January?

18. Pottery Works, which produces pottery bowls, had the following summary cost information:

Direct materials used	$24,000
Direct labor	22,000
Factory rent	6,000
Equipment depreciation	7,500
Units produced	25,000
Marketing expense	15,000
Administrative expense	13,000
Shipping charges	5,000

Required

A. Based on the above information, what is the manufacturing cost per unit?

B. If 24,000 of the 25,000 units are sold, what is the cost of goods sold?

C. If 24,000 of the 25,000 units are sold, what is the value of ending inventory?

19. The following payroll records for Signmakers reflect amounts paid in March.

Assembly line workers	$15,000
Janitorial staff	2,000
Maintenance workers	5,000
Production supervisors	22,000

Required

A. What is the amount of indirect labor costs for March?

B. What is the amount of direct labor costs for March?

20. The following direct labor information pertains to the manufacture of Stone hinges:

Direct labor hours to make one hinge	6
Number of hours per week, per worker	40
Weekly wages per worker	$700

Required

A. What is the direct labor cost per unit?

21. Fred's Furniture manufactures modern furniture. In 2001 wage and salary expenses included the following:

Machine operators	$250,000
Quality control supervisors	150,000
Fabric cutters	125,000
Factory janitor	28,000
Company president	150,000

Required

A. What was the amount of direct labor incurred in 2001?

B. What was the amount of indirect labor incurred in 2001?

22. Campus Coolers manufactures portable coolers with college logos. During 2002, the company had the following costs (in thousands):

Direct materials used	$41,000
Direct labor	28,000
Factory rent	22,000
Equipment depreciation—factory	12,000
Equipment depreciation—office	750
Marketing expense	5,500
Administrative expenses	30,000

4,500,000 units were produced in 2002.

Required

A. What are the total product costs for 2002?

B. What is the product cost per unit?

C. What are the total period costs for 2002?

D. What is the net income for 2002 if 3,000,000 units are sold for $25 each?

23. Doormakers is a new company, which manufactures doors. In their first month of operation, they began and completed 1,500 doors. The following production information has been provided:

Direct materials cost per unit	$ 35
Estimated indirect material costs	1,100
Direct labor hours per unit	4
Cost per direct labor hour	12
Estimated indirect labor cost	4,000
Factory rent	5,000
Marketing expense	750
Administrative expenses	1,500

Required

A. What is the cost of direct labor per door?

B. What were the total overhead costs for the first month's production?

C. What were the total product costs for the first month's production?

D. What is the unit product cost?

E. What are the total period (nonmanufacturing) costs for the first month's production?

F. What would the net income for the first month be if 1,250 of the doors were sold at a price of $95 each?

24. Purple Pants, Inc. had the following information available for the month of January:

	Beginning	**Ending**
Raw materials inventory	$315,000	$310,000
Work-in-process inventory	65,000	58,000
Finished goods inventory	32,000	25,000
Raw materials purchased		227,000
Direct labor (2,500 hrs@$12)		30,000
Overhead		155,000

Required

A. Determine the raw materials used in January.

B. Determine Purple's cost of goods manufactured in January.

C. Determine Purple's cost of goods sold for January.

25. You are the President of Box Creations. Your new accountant, who had recently graduated from Not-so-good University, presented you with the following income statement for the month of January:

Sales Revenues	$660,000
Total January Expenses	595,000
Net Income	$ 65,000

By talking to the production departments, you learn that 60,000 units were produced in January at a cost of $420,000 (total product costs). The sales department notes that 55,000 units were sold for $11 each. Monthly administrative and marketing costs total $75,000.

Required

A. Based upon this information, prepare a corrected income statement for January.

B. Explain what was wrong with the new accountant's income statement.

26. Urns Unlimited, which produces decorative urns, had the following summary cost information:

Direct materials used	$22,000
Direct labor	10,000
Factory rent	5,000
Marketing expense	3,000
Administrative expense	11,000
Shipping charges	5,000
Equipment depreciation	3,500
Units produced	15,000

Required

A. Based on the above information, what is the manufacturing cost per unit?

B. If 14,500 of the 15,000 units are sold, what is the cost of goods sold?

C. If 14,500 of the 15,000 units are sold, what is the value of ending inventory?

27. Leacy's Department Store features women's fashions. In 2002, the store had $514,000 in merchandise at the beginning of the year. Annual purchases totaled $463,000.

Required

A. If the year-end inventory revealed $488,000 on hand, determine the cost of goods sold for 2002.

B. What was the pool of merchandise available for sale during the period?

C. If sales were $675,000 and other costs were $115,000, what was net income for the year?

28. Jack's Slacks is a local men's clothing store. Jack buys clothing and accessories from manufacturers and marks them up by 55 percent. Jack began the year with $155,000 ($240,250 retail value) and bought $350,000 (retail value $542,500) more items during the year. Ending inventory is $95,000 (retail value $147,250).

Required

A. What were Jack's sales for the year?

B. What was Jack's cost of goods sold for the year?

C. What was Jack's gross margin for the year?

29. Below are some costs incurred in 2003.

Material costs

Aluminum	$271,000
Oil and grease for production machinery	3,000
Screws and nails	5,000

Labor costs

Equipment operators	$ 80,000
Equipment mechanics	54,000
Factory supervisors	90,000

Required

A. What is the total direct material cost for 2003?

B. What is the total direct labor cost for 2003?

C. What are the total indirect costs for 2003?

D. Explain why you considered some costs indirect.

30. Dunn Computer Company began manufacturing personal computers for small businesses at the beginning of 1999. During the year, Dunn purchased 30,000 mouse pads with the company's name and logo at a cost of $2.50 each. The marketing manager used 2,500 of the pads as an advertising gimmick at a local trade show, and 25,000 of the pads were packaged with computers that were manufactured during 1999. Eighty percent of the computers were finished during the year and of that amount, 90 percent were sold.

Determine the cost of the mouse pads that would be included in the following accounts as of December 31, 1999, and specify whether the account would appear on the balance sheet or income statement:

a. Raw materials

b. Work in process

c. Finished goods

d. Cost of goods sold

e. Advertising expense

31. Ehmke Technologies manufactures storage devices for personal computers. Although most of the company's sales are to computer manufacturers, about 30 percent of sales are made directly to individuals via mail order. Ehmke Technologies recently hired you as a sales manager. Your duties include dealing directly with the computer manufacturers that buy your company's products and supervising the employees who take phone orders from individual customers. Because most of your time is spent dealing with the manufacturing companies, the company's vice president for marketing says your $45,000 salary should be classified as a manufacturing cost. The company's controller says it should be classified as a selling expense.

Required

A. Which viewpoint is correct? Why?

B. The company's president doesn't understand what all the fuss is about and says the company's income will be the same regardless so who cares! Is she right? Explain your answer.

32. Eldred Inc., a manufacturing company, prepays its insurance coverage for a three-year period. The premium for the three years is $19,000 and is paid at the beginning of the first year. Three-fourths of the premium applies to factory operations and one-fourth applies to selling and administration activities.

Required

Answer the following questions for the first year of coverage:

A. What amount of the cost should be considered product costs?

B. What amount of the cost should be considered period costs?

33. Erdmann Inc. manufactures area rugs. Among Erdmann's 1999 manufacturing costs were the following salaries and wages:

Rug weaving machine operators	$155,000
Factory foreman	65,000
Machine mechanics	50,000
Factory maintenance workers	45,000

Required

A. What was the amount of direct labor incurred in 1999?

B. What was the amount of indirect labor incurred in 1999?

34. Ertz Inc. recently changed to a just-in-time philosophy from a traditional costing philosophy. How will this new philosophy affect the work-in-process inventory balance in the future? Can management expect to see a change in the finished goods inventory balance? Explain your answer.

35. The following direct labor cost information pertains to the manufacture of televisions at Estes TV:

Time required to manufacture one television	6 direct labor hours
Number of workers	45
Number of hours per week each employee worked on manufacturing televisions	38
Weekly wages per worker	$ 1,200
Workers' benefits as a percentage of wages	35%

Required

  A. What is the cost of direct labor per television?

  B. What is the cost of indirect labor per television?

  C. Explain the difference between direct and indirect labor.

36. Favre Co. produces complete sets of football pads and has prepared the following summary of cost information:

Direct materials used	$4,000
Direct labor	2,000
Factory rent	4,000
Factory equipment depreciation	3,500
Units produced	7,000
Marketing expense	5,000
Administrative expense	3,000

Required

  A. Based on the preceding data, calculate the manufacturing cost per set of pads.

  B. Explain why you included or did not include each cost item.

37. The following cost and inventory data are taken from the books of Evans Co. for the year 1999.

Costs Incurred

Raw material purchased	$125,000
Direct labor	75,000
Indirect labor	40,000
Equipment maintenance	10,000
Insurance on factory	12,000
Rent on factory	30,000
Depreciation on factory	20,000
Factory supplies	11,000
Advertising expense	15,000
Selling and administration expense	21,000

Inventory Balances	1/1/99	12/31/99
Raw materials	$10,000	$17,000
Work in process	20,000	31,000
Finished goods	30,000	25,000

Required

  A. Calculate the cost of goods manufactured.

  B. Calculate the cost of goods sold.

  C. List the costs not included in the above requirements and discuss why you elected to exclude them.

  D. If raw material and work-in-process inventories had decreased during the year, would the financial statements be different? How?

38. Fausel Company manufactures wooden rocking chairs. Fausel purchased the following materials in June:

1,500 springs (part of the rocking mechanism) at a cost of $15,000, each chair uses two springs

Glue at a cost of $1,500 (enough to manufacture 500 chairs)

Stain at a cost of $500 (enough to manufacture 500 chairs)

Wood at a cost of $5,000 (enough to build 1,000 chair frames)

Fausel produces 500 chairs during June and has no beginning balances of raw materials, WIP, or finished goods inventory

Required

    A. Which of these material costs should be classified as direct? Which as indirect?

    B. If Fausel finishes only 400 of the 500 chairs on which production was started, what is the balance in the finished goods inventory account?

    C. If 380 of the finished chairs are sold, what is the cost of goods sold?

    D. What is the June 30 balance in the work-in-process inventory account?

39. Cape Fear Inc. is a clothing store located in a major shopping mall. The company buys clothing and accessories from a number of manufacturers and generally marks them up 60 percent over cost. At the end of 1999, Cape Fear Inc. had clothing and accessories in the store with a cost of $60,000 (retail value of $96,000). During 2000, the company bought an additional $220,000 of clothing. Cape Fear Inc. had sales during 2000 of $420,000.

Required

    A. What was the cost of goods sold for 2000?

    B. What was the ending inventory of merchandise at December 31, 2000?

40. Fletcher & Fuller LLP is a local CPA firm that prepares approximately 1,000 tax returns each year for its clients. The managing partner of the firm has asked for information concerning the costs of preparing tax returns from the accounting department. He has been provided with the following report:

Average wage per hour of tax preparation staff	$35
Average wage per hour of clerical staff	$12
Average number of hours per return (preparation)	10
Average number of hours per return (clerical)	2

Required

    A. What is the average direct labor cost of preparing a tax return at Fletcher & Fuller?

    B. What are the options available for reducing the cost of preparing tax returns? What are the implications of these options?

    C. Fletcher & Fuller has the option of purchasing tax preparation software for $5,000 per year. If the software is used, the hours needed to prepare the return would decrease to three hours per return and the clerical time would increase to four hours because of additional computer operator time. How would the purchase affect the cost of labor per tax return?

    D. Does it appear to be a good business decision to purchase the software? What other costs must be considered?

    E. What are the qualitative aspects of the preceding decision?

41. Gagstetter Manufacturing was organized on January 1 of the current year. Independent investors financed the business totally. These investors have stipulated that the company must show a profit by the sixth month or the financing would be stopped. Gagstetter has shown losses for the first four months but was expecting to show a profit in the fifth and current month. After reviewing the income statement for the fifth month (May) the president, Craig, was disappointed with the performance and called an employee meeting. At the meeting Craig informed the employees that based on the performance for the first five months and in particular the month of May, he saw very little hope of a profit by the sixth month. He also informed the employees that they should prepare to close the business. Promptly after the employee meeting the controller quit, leaving you in charge of the accounting function. The latest financial information is given below:

Gagstetter Manufacturing
Income Statement
For the Month Ended May 31, 1999

Sales		$325,000
Less:		
Raw material purchased	$140,000	
Direct labor	75,000	
Indirect labor	10,000	
Utilities	25,000	
Depreciation	30,000	
Insurance	15,000	
Rent	12,000	
SG&A expense	30,000	
Advertising	25,000	
		362,000
Net loss		$(37,000)

Other Information:

Inventory Balances	4/30/99	5/31/99
Raw material	$10,000	$30,000
Work in process	15,000	22,000
Finished goods	50,000	70,000

Seventy-five percent of utilities, depreciation, insurance, and rent are related to the factory while 25 percent of those costs are related to selling and administrative activities.

Required

A. Redo the income statement for May. (Include a statement of cost of goods manufactured and a statement of cost of goods sold.)

B. Do you agree with the president's assessment of the situation? Why or why not?

C. How will you explain to the investors why your income statement is different from the one the controller presented earlier?

42. Barcourt Inc. manufactures baseball bats and has recently had a fire that destroyed most of the inventory and almost all of the accounting records. The controller at Barcourt Inc., Dana Genzel-Diaz, has approached you to reconstruct the records. She gives you a box of charred accounting records with which you are to reconstruct the income statement for the month of the fire. The following is the reconstruction of the accounting records:

Direct materials used	$ 9,000
Direct labor	4,000
Manufacturing overhead	11,000
Total manufacturing costs	?
Beginning work-in-process	?
Ending work-in-process	6,000
Cost of goods manufactured	21,000
Sales	35,000
Beginning finished goods inventory	7,000
Cost of goods manufactured	?
Goods available for sale	?

Ending finished goods inventory	10,000
Cost of goods sold	?
Gross margin	?
Selling and administrative expense	7,000
Net income	?

Required

A. Supply the missing data.

B. Prepare a new complete income statement.

43. Hemphill Inc. manufactures soccer balls and has recently had an earthquake that destroyed most of the inventory and almost all of the accounting records. The controller at Hemphill Inc., Chip Gillikin, has approached you to reconstruct the records. He gives you a box of partially destroyed accounting records with which you are to reconstruct the income statement for the month of the earthquake. The following is the reconstruction of the accounting records:

Direct materials used	$19,000
Direct labor	14,000
Manufacturing overhead	?
Total manufacturing costs	35,000
Beginning work-in-process	11,000
Ending work-in-process	13,500
Cost of goods manufactured	?
Sales	50,000
Beginning finished goods inventory	?
Cost of goods manufactured	?
Goods available for sale	?
Ending finished goods inventory	14,000
Cost of goods sold	25,500
Gross margin	?
Selling and administrative expense	?
Net income	15,500

Required

A. Supply the missing data.

B. Prepare a new complete income statement.

44. Hardball Inc. manufactures baseballs and has recently had a flood that destroyed most of the inventory and almost all of the accounting records. The controller at Hardball Inc., Mary Goodwin, has approached you to reconstruct the records. She gives you a box of partially destroyed, wet accounting records with which you are to reconstruct the income statement for the month of the flood. The following is the reconstruction of the accounting records:

Direct materials used	$16,000
Direct labor	?
Manufacturing overhead	17,000
Total manufacturing costs	48,000
Beginning work-in-process	12,000
Ending work-in-process	?
Cost of goods manufactured	46,000
Sales	50,000
Beginning finished goods inventory	7,000
Cost of goods manufactured	?
Goods available for sale	?
Ending finished goods inventory	?
Cost of goods sold	8,000
Gross margin	?
Selling and administrative expense	?
Net income	13,000

Required

A. Supply the missing data.

B. Prepare a new complete income statement.

45. Slots R Us owns a gambling boat on the Gulf Coast and has recently experienced Hurricane Jennifer, which severely damaged the boat and almost all of the accounting records. The controller at Slots R Us, Tim Guglielmo, has approached you to reconstruct the records. He gives you a box of partially destroyed, wet, windblown accounting records with which you are to reconstruct the income statement for the month of the hurricane. The following is the reconstruction of the accounting records:

Direct materials used	$18,000
Direct labor	13,000
Manufacturing overhead	31,000
Total manufacturing costs	?
Beginning work-in-process	?
Ending work-in-process	12,000
Cost of goods manufactured	?
Sales	90,000
Beginning finished goods inventory	19,000
Cost of goods manufactured	60,000
Goods available for sale	?
Ending finished goods inventory	17,000
Cost of goods sold	?
Gross margin	?
Selling and administrative expense	20,000
Net income	?

Required

A. Supply the missing data.

B. Prepare a new complete income statement.

46. Northern Lights Custom Cabinets manufactures and sells custom-ordered kitchen and bathroom cabinets. The company primarily sells to building contractors but occasionally deals directly with homeowners. Following is a summary of inventory and cost information for 1999:

	Balance 1/1/99	Balance 12/31/99
Raw material inventory	$10,000	$15,000
Work-in-process inventory	15,000	12,000
Finished goods inventory	30,000	32,000

During the year raw material used in the production of cabinets was purchased for $350,000. Northern Lights also incurred $200,000 for labor cost in the factory and had $175,000 in manufacturing overhead for the year.

Required

A. Determine the amount of direct material transferred to work-in process in 1999.

B. Calculate total manufacturing costs for 1999.

C. Calculate total cost of goods manufactured for 1999.

D. Calculate cost of goods sold for 1999.

Ethics

47. As controller, you have been asked to prepare and submit financial statements to your company's bank as part of a loan application. From previous conversations with bank loan personnel, you know your company's cost of goods sold as a percent of sales is unusually high. Your supervisor has asked you to reclassify some product costs as period costs thereby decreasing the cost of goods sold to an acceptable amount. Because your total costs would be the same (just classified differently), your supervisor says there is nothing wrong with making the reclassification. Discuss the ethical issues involved in this decision.

48. Business Games Inc. (BGI) has designed the ultimate business board game. The game has been on the market for 10 years and the company has sold more than 20 million games. The games sell for $9 to stores and the suggested retail price is $15. BGI has computed the cost of producing the games to be $5.40. The cost includes direct material, direct labor, and overhead. Management of BGI has decided the time is right to produce a special edition of the game in a mahogany collector's box. They will also design a special game board and new game pieces. Your job is to set a new sales price and decide if the special game should be produced. You receive the following report from the accounting department to help you with your decision:

	Present Game	**Special Game (estimated)**
Direct material	$1.25	$30.50
Direct labor	2.00	3.50
Overhead	2.15	2.15
	$5.40	$36.15

Required

    A. Is the cost information provided above sufficient to determine a sales price for each game? Why or why not?

    B. What qualitative factors should be considered in deciding whether to produce and sell the special game?

49. Finding ways to decrease product costs is an area of increasing concern for many manufacturers. Conduct an Internet search of the *Wall Street Journal* and other business publications to find recent articles dealing with product costing. Summarize the cost-cutting efforts of three manufacturers discussed in the articles.

50. Arrange a visit to a locally owned restaurant or coffeehouse and ask the manager how the establishment determines the cost of its products. What is included in the cost of a cup of coffee or a meal?

www.intel.com
www.circuitcity.com

51. Examine the financial statements of a manufacturing company (like Intel) and a merchandising company (like Circuit City). Compare their balance sheets and the percentage of total assets in inventory. What similarities and differences do you see?

CONTINUING CASE | BIG AL'S PIZZA INC.

Big Al's Pizza Inc. (a new subsidiary of Big Al's Pizza Emporium) has been established to produce fresh, packaged 16-inch pizzas for wholesale to grocery stores, convenience stores, and school cafeterias. The Marketing Department has finished its market research and they have determined that the current total market demand for fresh, packaged 16-inch pizzas is 150,000 units per month. As a new entrant to the market, the goal set by the company is to sell 25,000 pizzas in the first month and 325,000 pizzas for the year. Following the first quarter, their goal is to increase sales by about 10 percent each year.

Big Al's deals exclusively with Pizza Products Inc. to purchase all material and equipment. Pizza Products Inc. is a supplier of a full range of pizza supplies from raw materials to semi-finished products. They offer three levels of products, the Gold Brand, their best quality and most expensive brand, to their Bronze Brand, the most basic and cost-effective choice. Their Silver Brand is their mainstream and mid-priced product.

Big Al's will have 10 production lines with five workers on each line. Each worker is responsible for one of the five stages of production—dough, sauce, cheese, toppings, or packaging. Following is a flowchart of the production lines showing the time needed at each workstation. These time estimates include normal downtime, breaks, and so on.

Dough Maker 2 Minutes → Sauce Maker 2 Minutes → Cheese Maker 2½ Minutes → Toppings 3 Minutes → Packaging 2 Minutes

Moving products between stations takes approximately 30 seconds. So the total time to produce one pizza is the total of all the time needed at each step plus two minutes for product movement (4 at ½ minute) or 13½ minutes per pizza. The slowest step in the process is applying the toppings at three minutes so the production process is limited to 20 pizzas per hour (60 minutes divided by 3 minutes). All production-line workers work eight hours per day. Because Big Al's has 10 production lines they can produce 200 pizzas per hour or 1,600 pizzas per eight-hour shift.

Assuming 20 workdays per month, Big Al's has the capacity to produce 32,000 pizzas per month or 384,000 pizzas per year. However, during the first year, their estimated production is 325,000 pizzas.

Pizzas are produced in batches of up to 1,600 pizzas based on the specific orders received from grocery stores, cafeterias, and convenience stores. All pizzas are shipped daily.

Following are the projected costs for Big Al's Inc.:

Material Costs

Complete Dough Shells	$.35 per unit: Gold Level
	$.25 per unit: Silver Level
	$.20 per unit: Bronze Level
Complete Sauce Package	$.55 per unit: Gold Level
	$.45 per unit: Silver Level
	$.40 per unit: Bronze Level
Complete Cheese Package	$.40 per unit: Gold Level
	$.35 per unit: Silver Level
	$.25 per unit: Bronze Level
Complete Meat Package	$1.10 per unit: Gold Level
	$.90 per unit: Silver Level
	$.80 per unit: Bronze Level

Complete Assembly Package	$.25 per unit: Gold Level
	$.20 per unit: Silver Level
	$.15 per unit: Bronze Level

Labor Costs

Direct labor employees are paid on an hourly basis based on hours actually worked. Once production line workers finish a day's scheduled production, they are sent home. The maximum they can work each day without incurring overtime costs is 8 hours. The overtime premium is an additional 50 percent of the basic hourly rate of $5.00. Assume 20 workdays per month. Supervisors and other indirect labor employees are salaried.

Rate for direct labor	$5.00 per hour (plus 30% fringe benefits)
Indirect Labor:	
Supervisor	$3,500 per month (including fringe benefits)
Other indirect labor	$2,000 per month (including fringe benefits)

Overhead Costs

Rent on Production Facility	$1,000/month
Utilities	$1,500/month
Other overhead:	
Indirect material	$2,500/month
Maintenance costs	$1,500/month
Quality Inspection costs	$2,000/month
Equipment (lease cost)	$2,500/month

The lease is for a term of 5 years. However, it can be terminated at any time with a penalty of $10,000.

Selling and Administrative Costs

Administrative salaries	$4,000/month (including fringe benefits)
Salaries of sales staff	$5,000/month (including fringe benefits)
Product promotion and advertising	$2,000/month
Rental of office space for administrative and sales staff	$2,000/month
Utilities, insurance, etc.	$500/month
Lease of office furniture and equipment	$800/month

Required

Using the cost information given:

A. What are the estimated direct material costs per pizza at each cost level?

B. What are the estimated direct labor costs per pizza?

C. What are the estimated manufacturing overhead costs per pizza?

D. What is the estimated total manufacturing cost per pizza at each cost level?

E. Big Al's production facility is organized in a very traditional fashion. Dough preparation, sauce preparation, topping preparation, cheese preparation, and packaging are all done in separate areas of the factory. In addition, employees on the production lines are responsible for only one task. Can you think of other ways to organize the production facility that might be more efficient?

F. If you had to set a sales price for each type of pizza, what would it be? In addition to product costs, what other costs must the sales price cover?

G. Identify all period costs for Big Al's Pizza Inc. How much are they per month?

PRODUCT COSTING MEASUREMENT DECISIONS

Study Tools

A Review of the Previous Chapter

Chapter 2 gave us an overview of the production process and the costing of products and services in an organization.

A Preview of This Chapter

In this chapter we learn about the specifics of costing products and services using job costing, process costing, and operations costing, and the particular problems caused by the allocation of overhead to products. The chapter introduces the concept of applying overhead to products using cost drivers and the issues that must be considered by managers in choosing a suitable cost driver.

Key concepts include:
- Overhead cannot be directly tracked to products and services but must instead be allocated using cost drivers.
- Understanding what causes overhead costs to be incurred (what drives them) is the key to allocating overhead.
- Accuracy in overhead application has become much more important as overhead costs have increased and make up a larger portion of the total costs of products.
- In order to provide relevant information for decision making, overhead must often be estimated.

A Preview of Upcoming Chapters

Chapter 4 extends the discussion of overhead application and provides an introduction into the use of activity-based costing and activity-based management.

LEARNING OBJECTIVES

After studying the material in this chapter, you should be able to:

LO1 Understand the differences between job, process, and operations costing; and how they are used to accumulate, track, and assign product costs

LO2 Understand the basics of job costing

LO3 Analyze issues related to the measurement of direct materials, direct labor, and overhead costs in job costing

LO4 Analyze problems related to the application of overhead costs to products

LO5 Analyze the role of cost pools and cost drivers in overhead application

LO6 Evaluate topics related to the choice of cost driver and the use of estimates in overhead application

LO7 Evaluate the advantages and disadvantages of using plantwide versus departmental overhead rates

LO8 Understand the basics of backflush and process costing (appendix)

In Chapter 2, we defined product costs and discussed the flow of costs in manufacturing, merchandising, and service companies. Chapter 3 begins with a discussion of the basic systems that companies use to accumulate, track, and assign costs to products and services. These systems are called job costing, process costing, and operations costing. Job, process, and operations costing have the same goals—to accumulate, track, and assign direct material, direct labor, and overhead costs to the products and services produced by a company. While direct material and direct labor can usually be traced directly to products and services, due to their indirect nature overhead costs must be allocated to the products or services provided by a company. Chapter 3 introduces the concept of cost pools and cost drivers and explains how they are used to allocate overhead using plantwide and departmental overhead rates. The chapter includes a discussion of the use of overhead estimates (predetermined overhead rates) in product costing and the treatment of over- or underapplied overhead. The appendix of the chapter introduces backflush costing (a costing system that is appropriate for companies employing just-in-time manufacturing techniques) and discusses process costing in more detail. ■

INTRODUCTION

LO1
Understand the differences between job, process, and operations costing; and how they are used to accumulate, track, and assign product costs

As a reaction to decreasing sales in its restaurants, McDonald's Corp. proposed a radical price reduction on its Big Mac in early 1997. The sandwich (usually priced around $1.90) would be offered for 55 cents with the purchase of fries and a drink. The proposal required the approval of a majority of franchisees. As an owner of a local McDonald's, you estimate that the cost of making a Big Mac is 63 cents. Would you vote for the proposal?

www.mcdonalds.com

One of the most important roles of managerial accountants is to help determine the cost of the products or services being produced and sold by a company. Cost information is equally important for manufacturing and service businesses and is used by managers across the organization. Pricing decisions made by marketing managers, manufacturing decisions made by production managers, and finance decisions made by finance managers are all influenced by the cost of products.

In today's competitive environment, managers must be aware of the impact of financial decisions on the overall success of their business. For example, marketing managers need to set a competitive price that will capture the needed market share and provide a fair profit. If the price of the product is set too low, a larger market share may be captured but the business may not earn a satisfactory profit. On the other hand, if the price of the product is too high, the business may not capture sufficient market share to remain competitive. These pricing decisions require product cost information in order to set an optimal price. Pricing decisions are discussed more fully in Chapter 7.

APPLICATION IN BUSINESS
www.gm.com

After the labor strike in 1998, General Motors instituted an aggressive marketing campaign including large price rebates in order to gain back market share.

Production managers make decisions concerning whether to buy components used in manufacturing a product or to make them internally. For example, an automobile manufacturer could choose to make batteries used in their cars or to buy them from an outside supplier. The cost to make the battery compared to the cost of buying it would be important in this decision. The company would also consider qualitative factors such as the reliability of the supplier and quality of the battery. This and other production decisions are also discussed in Chapter 7.

Hospitals are a great example of process costing. Each service, test, or treatment, such as an X-ray or blood test results in a process by a hospital worker that incurs a cost. These can be tracked to an overall unit, or for the entire care facility.

PRODUCT COSTING SYSTEMS

Just as different companies use different techniques to manufacture products or provide services, companies use different product costing systems to accumulate, track, and assign the costs of production to the goods and services produced. Companies that manufacture customized products or provide customized services to clients use a costing system called **job costing,** which accumulates, tracks, and assigns costs for each job. Jobs are simply the individual units of a product. For a custom homebuilder, each house is a job. For a CPA firm, a job might be an individual tax return, an audit engagement, or a consulting engagement for a particular client. For a print shop, each order for wedding invitations, graduation announcements, or custom letterhead is a job. For a hospital, each patient is a job.

On the other hand, companies that produce a homogeneous product on a continuous basis (oil refineries, breweries, paint and paper manufacturers, for example) use **process costing** to accumulate, track, and assign costs to products. Rather than accumulating the costs for each unit produced and directly tracking and assigning costs to each unique unit, process costing accumulates and tracks costs for each process as products pass through the process and then assigns costs equally to the units that come out of each process. A process is simply the work that is performed on a product. For a paint manufacturer, blending and pouring are processes. For a bread baker, mixing, baking, and slicing are processes. The details of process costing are demonstrated in the appendix to this chapter.

Operations costing is a hybrid of job and process costing and is used by companies like clothing or automobile manufacturers who make products in batches—large numbers of products that are standardized within a batch. For example, a clothing manufacturer might make 5,000 identical shirts in one batch. Each batch is costed like a job in job costing but each shirt in the batch is costed like a homogeneous product in process costing. The table summarizes the types of products that would most likely be costed using job, operations, and process costing.

LO2
Understand the basics of job costing

Clothing manufacturers are an example of operations costing as they specialize in mass production.

System	Job Costing	Operations Costing	Process Costing
Type of Product	Custom	Standardized within batches	Homogeneous
Examples	Construction, movie studios, hospitals, print shops, CPA, and law firms	Automobile and clothing manufacturers	Beverages, oil refineries, paint, paper, rolled steel

COSTING SYSTEM

BASIC JOB-ORDER COSTING FOR MANUFACTURING AND SERVICE COMPANIES

LO3

Analyze issues related to the measurement of direct materials, direct labor, and overhead costs in job costing

Northern Lights Custom Cabinets uses job costing to accumulate, track, and assign costs to the cabinets it produces. The direct material, direct labor, and overhead costs for a specific job are accumulated on a job cost report. This report may be kept manually or be totally automated. Regardless, its role is to keep track of the material, labor, and overhead costs that are incurred for a particular job. A job cost report for Northern Lights is shown in Exhibit 3-1.

MEASURING AND TRACKING DIRECT MATERIAL

Measuring direct material cost should be a relatively easy task for Northern Lights. The company only has to identify the amount of material actually used in each job and attach the proper cost to it. Northern Lights uses a variety of material including wood, Formica,

EXHIBIT 3-1 Cost Sheet for Job 101

Northern Lights Custom Cabinets

Job Number: 101　　　　　　　　　　　**Customer: Robyn Gray**
Date Started: March 6　　　　　　　　**Date Finished: March 9**
Description: Smith house

Direct Materials		Direct Labor			Manufacturing Overhead		
Type	**Cost**	**Employee**	**Hours**	**Amount**	**Hours**	**Rate**	**Amount**
Oak	$875	Staley	12.6	$255.15	22.4	$16.67	$373.41
Marble	600	Chen	4.5	91.13			
Particle Board	78	Kent	5.3	107.33			
Brass Pulls	330						
Cost Summary		Direct Materials			$1,883.00		
		Direct Labor			453.61		
		Manufacturing Overhead			373.41		
		Total			$2,710.02		

and marble for countertops, and stained glass, glue, screws, dowels, and stain in constructing a finished set of custom cabinets. Although some of the more common materials are stored in inventory, exotic, and more expensive woods and marbles and hardware items such as handles and pulls are typically purchased just in time for their use in a particular job. As raw material is needed for a particular cabinet job, it is recorded on the job cost record. In Exhibit 3-1, you can see that Northern Lights used oak and marble in the manufacture of Job 101 (for the Smith house) as well as particleboard. These materials can all be traced directly to Job 101 and are treated as direct materials. Also included as direct material are various pieces of hardware such as handles and drawer pulls. The amount and type of direct materials used in a job depend on the specific set of cabinets built. Because they will differ with each job, they must be accumulated, tracked, and assigned by job.

Some of the materials are stocked in inventory whereas others are purchased just in time for use in a job. It would not make good business sense for Northern Lights to stock a large amount of expensive hardware items for cabinets when some of the special hardware items may only be used once a year. On the other hand, because oak is used in over 50 percent of cabinets, Northern Lights chooses to keep enough on hand to meet two to three months of expected demand.

In the Smith house (Job 101), the customer has requested that the countertop be made of a synthetic marble, a material that is very durable but has a tendency to crack while being cut. Sure enough, as the material is being cut, it cracks and has to be discarded. How should the cost of the cracked material (spoilage) be treated? If the spoilage is considered normal, the cost is included in the determination of product costs. **Normal spoilage** results from the regular operation of the production process and includes the discarded ends of a sheet of wood or marble. If the broken marble is considered normal spoilage, its cost is treated as part of the direct material cost for the job being produced. On the other hand, other reasons, perhaps improper handling, poorly trained craftspeople, or equipment that is in poor condition cause **abnormal spoilage.** If the marble was broken because a saw blade has not been properly sharpened, it would probably be considered abnormal spoilage.

Concept Question: *How would you treat the cost of abnormal spoilage? Would it be fair to treat it as part of the direct material cost for the job being produced? Should the cost of abnormal waste be passed on to the customer as an increase in the sales price?*

| Step 1 | DEFINE THE PROBLEM |

Concept Answer: Abnormal spoilage should probably be included in manufacturing overhead where the cost is spread across all jobs completed during the period. Abnormal spoilage should probably not be treated as direct material where it would be considered in the cost of a specific job. ■

Concept Question: *Northern Lights also uses a variety of wooden dowels, screws, glues, and finishing nails in the construction of cabinets. However, you should note that these are not listed as direct materials on the job cost report in Exhibit 3-1. Why? How is Northern Lights accounting for the cost of these materials?*

| Step 2 | IDENTIFY OBJECTIVES |

Concept Answer: Although it may be physically possible to track the specific screws, glue, and nails to a particular cabinet, the cost of doing so is great and the benefits are few. Northern Lights has chosen to treat these materials as indirect material that will be allocated to the Smith job as part of overhead. ■

Companies that primarily provide services to clients or have minimal material costs may not treat any materials as direct. For example, a law firm that primarily prepares wills and other paper documents may choose to treat the costs of paper as an indirect material (part of overhead). Likewise, although CPA firms may use a lot of paper and other materials processing tax returns for clients, they may not track the paper to specific jobs on a job cost report. On the other hand, a hospital might choose to itemize every pill (even aspirin) and other medication given to a patient and every bandage used in an operation on a patient's job cost report (the patient's case file).

Concept Question: Why might a hospital keep track of every aspirin given to a patient?

Concept Answer: Tracking the use of pills and other medications to a patient provides other valuable benefits to doctors and the hospital. Doctors need to know exactly what medications have been given and when. Although it may also provide a way to charge patients for the cost of medications they consume during a hospital stay, the costing of the medications is probably not as important as the tracking itself. ■

MEASURING AND TRACKING DIRECT LABOR

LO4
Analyze problems related to the application of overhead costs to products

The measurement of direct labor cost also should be a relatively easy task. Direct labor cost refers to labor that is directly related to the manufacture of a product or the provision of a service. Assembly-line workers in a manufacturing setting and CPAs working on tax returns are examples of direct labor. On the other hand, personnel such as manufacturing supervisors, janitorial staff, and maintenance personnel in a manufacturing company and secretarial staff in a CPA firm are considered indirect labor and are included in overhead. The costs of direct labor for a specific job are accumulated on a job cost report, but most companies keep track of each employee's time by requiring the completion of time sheets. Time sheets may be prepared by hand or totally automated and integrated with the job cost system. Regardless of the form used, employees must keep track of how much time they spend on specific jobs. For assembly-line workers, management needs to know how much time is spent manufacturing a specific product. For CPAs and attorneys, the managing partner needs to know how many hours are spent servicing a particular client.

The cost of direct labor is simply calculated by multiplying a wage rate for each employee by the number of hours that each employee works on each product. However, in addition to the hourly cost of labor, wage rates must also include the cost of **fringe benefits** as well. These fringe benefits include the employer's cost for health, dental, and other insurance, retirement plans, and so on. The employer portion of social security tax and state and federal unemployment taxes would also be included. Studies have shown that fringe benefits typically cost a company 30 to 35 percent of the base wage of each full-time employee. The job cost report in Exhibit 3-1 shows that three employees of Northern Lights Custom Cabinets worked 22.4 hours on Job 101 at a cost of $20.25 per hour. This cost includes a $15 hourly wage rate plus benefits of $5.25 per hour.

Concept Question: Due to a power outage, Northern Lights incurred idle time while working on Job 101. Would Northern Lights most likely treat this idle time as overhead or an additional cost of direct labor assigned directly to Job 101?

Concept Answer: Not all the time that direct labor workers are paid for is spent productively. For example, if machinery and equipment break down or if materials are not available when needed, **idle time** results. How should idle time of direct labor workers be treated? Although idle time could be traced to a specific job (the job that is being worked on when the idle time occurs), most companies choose to treat idle time as an overhead cost rather than a cost of a specific job. ■

Overtime premiums paid to direct labor workers cause similar classification problems. Overtime is typically paid at 150 percent of the normal wage rate (sometimes called "time and a half") for hours worked in excess of 40 per week. For example, lets assume that the hourly pay for an assembly-line worker is $15. An overtime premium for this worker would be $7.50 per hour, increasing the total hourly wage to $22.50. With fringe benefits at 35 percent, the cost of labor rises to $33.75 per hour. Overtime may be incurred for a number of reasons. Sometimes, production problems cause a company to get behind on a job. When this happens, the company may choose to incur overtime costs (work over the weekend) to finish up a job on time. In other situations, a company might accept an order knowing that it will require the scheduling of overtime.

Concept Question: On Friday morning, the building contractor who had ordered Job 101 called Northern Lights and said he needed the cabinets next Monday instead of next Wednes-

day. The Northern Lights staff worked eight hours on Saturday, and the company incurred overtime premiums in order to finish the job by the new due date. How should Northern Lights treat the overtime premium—as part of direct labor or overhead? Should this overtime increase the selling price to the customer?

Concept Answer: In practice, the treatment of overtime costs depends on the reason the overhead is incurred. If overtime is incurred as a result of production problems, most companies treat the cost as overhead. On the other hand, if the overtime results from the acceptance of a rush order, most companies would treat the overhead as a direct labor cost that would be assigned directly to the specific job (and would most likely be included in determining its price). ■

In highly automated manufacturing environments, the cost of direct labor has been reduced significantly as automated machinery and robotics have replaced direct labor workers. This shift in product costs from labor to overhead has had important implications for product costing. Whereas the cost of direct labor is relatively easy to accumulate, track, and assign to products, overhead costs are a different matter.

MANUFACTURING OVERHEAD

Overhead is the most difficult product cost to accumulate, track, and assign to products. Unlike direct materials and direct labor, overhead is made up of lots of seemingly unrelated costs—rent, depreciation, insurance, repairs and maintenance, utilities, indirect labor, indirect material, and so on. In addition, in traditional manufacturing environments most overhead is indirect in nature. As a result, it cannot be directly tracked to products and services but must instead be allocated. Although many overhead costs in a just-in-time (JIT) environment will also be indirect in nature (rent and utilities, for example), more of the costs are likely to be direct in nature. For example, in a JIT environment the cost of machinery in a manufacturing cell can be traced to a specific product (tables) if it is only used to make tables.

LO5
Analyze the role of cost pools and cost drivers in overhead application

▶ **Key Concept:** *Overhead cannot be directly tracked to products and services but must instead be allocated using cost drivers.*

Allocation involves finding a logical method of assigning overhead costs to the products or services produced by a company. If a company only produces one product, the allocation would be simple. We could just divide the total overhead cost by the total number of units produced. If our total overhead costs incurred during the year were $100,000 and we produced 20,000 identical tables during the year, it would be logical to assign $5 of overhead to each table ($100,000/20,000 tables). However, what if we make 10,000 tables and 10,000 chairs? Does it still make sense to allocate overhead based on the number of units produced? Probably not. A more logical approach might be to allocate the overhead to the tables and chairs based on the number of direct labor hours or machine hours consumed in the manufacture of each. If chairs take twice as long to manufacture as tables, twice as much overhead would be allocated to them. The choice of allocation base requires a thorough understanding of what causes overhead costs to be incurred.

THE ROLE OF COST POOLS AND COST DRIVERS

Understanding what causes overhead costs to be incurred is the key to allocating overhead. The choice of a logical base on which to allocate overhead depends on finding a cause-and-effect relationship between the base and the overhead. A good allocation base is one that drives the incurrence of the overhead cost. Therefore allocation bases are often referred to as **cost drivers.** A cost driver causes a cost to be incurred.

LO6
Evaluate topics related to the choice of cost driver and the use of estimates in overhead application

Key Concept: *Understanding what causes overhead costs to be incurred (what drives them) is the key to allocating overhead.*

One way to think about cost drivers is to imagine something causing something else to happen. A cost driver for overhead is an activity that causes overhead to be incurred. If we wanted to allocate the cost of utilities incurred to run machines in the factory to products, we would want to find a cost driver that causes the utility costs to be incurred. In this case, the time the machines were in use (machine hours) might be an appropriate allocation base. In our previous example, if it takes twice as many machine hours to make chairs than it does to make tables, chairs would correspondingly be allocated twice as much utility cost.

Other overhead costs associated with machines, such as depreciation and repairs and maintenance, could be allocated using the same cost driver. In companies that are more labor intensive, the cost of utilities might be allocated using direct labor hours as the cost driver. In that case, if it takes three labor hours to make a table and only one labor hour to make a chair, a table would be allocated three times as much overhead as a chair. The choice of cost driver depends on the specific company and the production processes it utilizes in providing products and services to customers but as you can see, it definitely has an impact on the cost of products and services.

Concept Question: *Northern Lights incurs utility costs of $1,000 during the month and starts and finishes 12 cabinet jobs. Each job requires machine time but the time varies greatly depending on the materials used and the difficulty of the job. Job 101 required 22.4 labor hours whereas Job 104 required 60 hours. The total labor hours during the month totaled 500. If Northern Lights allocates utility cost using labor hours as the cost driver, how much of the utility cost should be allocated to Job 101? How much to Job 104?*

Concept Answer: Utility costs are $2 per direct labor hour ($1,000/500 direct labor hours). Therefore, $44.80 of utility costs (22.4 × $2 per hour) should be allocated to Job 101 while $120 of utility costs (60 hours × $2 per hour) should be allocated to Job 104. ■

PAUSE & *Reflect*

In a law firm, overhead costs consist of the cost of office space for attorneys, the salaries of secretaries, the cost of research material, and so on. What allocation base might be used as a cost driver for overhead in a law firm?

Overhead consists of a variety of different costs with potentially different drivers for each. For example, the salaries of janitors and supervisors in the factory are overhead costs. The costs of rent and insurance for the factory building are overhead costs. The costs of indirect materials are overhead costs. Instead of identifying cost drivers for each component of overhead, companies have traditionally lumped overhead into similar **cost pools** to simplify the task. In the most extreme case, companies lump all overhead into one cost pool for the entire factory. Other companies have separate pools of overhead for each department. Still others use cost pools for each activity performed in making a product. Regardless of the number of cost pools and method of overhead allocation used, overhead rates are calculated using the same basic formula:

Manufacturing Overhead/Cost Driver

DEPARTMENTAL OVERHEAD RATES

LO7
Evaluate the advantages and disadvantages of using plantwide versus departmental overhead rates

In traditional manufacturing companies and service industries, direct labor hours or direct labor cost have often served as cost drivers. As recently as 1991, a survey of U.S. manufacturing companies found that 62 percent used direct labor hours or dollars as their overhead cost driver (Cohen and Paquette, *Journal of Cost Management,* fall 1991). Another 13 percent used machine hours as the cost driver. Allocating overhead based on direct labor or machine time worked well (and still does) when companies make only a few products, when they incur relatively small overhead costs compared to labor and material costs, and when that overhead is related to the volume of products produced.

For example, as demonstrated in Exhibit 3-2, a takeout pizza restaurant with a single location and no delivery might apply overhead using a single plantwide (storewide) prede-

EXHIBIT 3-2 Applying Overhead Using a Plantwide Rate

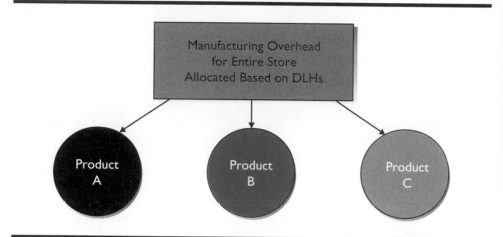

termined overhead rate. The costs of pizza ovens, rent, utilities, and other overhead costs would be lumped into one storewide cost pool and allocated to products (pizzas) based on the amount of labor time (direct labor hours, or DLHs) it takes to make each pizza. In this case, the cost of overhead is relatively small and is likely to be related to the number of pizzas made. In other words, it is volume based.

However, as companies make more diverse products and become more heavily automated, the use of plantwide cost pools and single cost drivers may provide less than accurate cost information. Companies using departmental overhead rates form separate cost pools for each department. The overhead in each cost pool can then be applied to products based on different cost drivers. Consider the pizza restaurant again. To expand its market to wholesale customers (grocery stores), the restaurant buys a new automated pizza oven, new mixers, and new packaging machinery, and it expands its facility. The new oven, mixers, and packaging machinery are used entirely to make pizzas for the wholesale market while the takeout market is served with the existing oven and mixer. In this scenario, it would probably make sense for the restaurant to accumulate overhead costs into two cost pools—one for the takeout department and one for the wholesale department. Although the overhead costs associated with the takeout activities might still be allocated based on direct labor hours incurred, a better driver of the costs associated with the wholesale activities (which is more heavily automated) might be machine hours, or MHs (see Exhibit 3-3). Although the use of departmental rates in this example is probably not significantly more difficult or time consuming than the use of a plantwide rate, that is not always the case.

Concept Question: Using the decision-making model introduced in Chapter 1, the management team of RGS Inc. has identified a problem (Step 1) caused by their current method of allocating overhead to products using a plantwide rate based on direct labor hours. Although their new product requires substantial machine time to manufacture, it requires very little direct labor resulting in an allocation of only a small amount of overhead. As a result, the company's management accountant feels the new product is being undercosted and underpriced. Management's objective (Step 2) is to develop a method of allocating overhead to products that will provide accurate costs for both their traditional labor-intensive product and their new product. The team is considering using multiple overhead rates as one option (Step 3). What factors are likely to be relevant in their decision?

Step 1	DEFINE THE PROBLEM
Step 2	IDENTIFY OBJECTIVES
Step 3	IDENTIFY AND ANALYZE AVAILABLE OPTIONS

Concept Answer: The choice of a single plantwide overhead rate or multiple overhead rates depends on a variety of factors and an analysis of the costs and benefits of each approach. The use of a single plantwide rate is easier, less time consuming, and cheaper than the use of multiple departmental overhead rates. But departmental rates can provide more accurate cost information.

EXHIBIT 3-3 Applying Overhead Using Departmental Rates

Manufacturing Overhead
for Entire Store

Department A
(Take-out Department)
Allocated Based on DLHs

Department B
(Wholesale Department)
Allocated Based on MHs

Product
A

Product
B

Product
C

This is particularly true when multiple products are produced, the products consume resources differently, and departments perform very different activities. Regardless of whether a single rate or multiple rates are used, choosing an appropriate cost driver is an important factor. ■

In heavily automated manufacturing environments, direct labor costs have shrunk to as little as 5 percent of total production costs whereas overhead costs have soared to 60 percent or more of total product costs. It's not hard to see why. Consider a modern automobile manufacturing plant. High-tech computers control robots that weld, paint, and perform other jobs that were previously done by humans. These machines are very expensive and are treated as part of overhead cost. As overhead costs have increased and make up a much larger portion of the total costs of products, accuracy in overhead application has become much more important as well. Overhead allocation using multiple cost pools and overhead rates based on the activities performed in a company is discussed in Chapter 4.

 Key Concept: *Accuracy in overhead application has become much more important as overhead costs have increased and make up a larger portion of the total costs of products.*

THE USE OF ESTIMATES

It is not unusual for managers to want to estimate the cost of a product before it is actually produced. Having timely cost information is useful for pricing decisions as well as production decisions. However, because the actual amount of many overhead items will not be known until the end of a period (perhaps when an invoice is received), companies often estimate the amount of overhead that will be incurred in the coming period. For example, a manufacturer of computers that are custom made to meet customer requirements needs to know the cost of producing each computer so it can establish a sales price. Customers place orders 24 hours per day and the company's policy is to ship computers to customers within 48 hours of the order. Although the company has records of each component and other material used in the assembly of the computer and knows the exact amount of time workers spend putting the computer together (remember the job cost report discussed earlier), calculating the actual amount of overhead cost incurred is virtually impossible to do in a timely manner. Why? Because the amount of most overhead items such as utilities expense, maintenance expense, supplies, and so forth will not be known until after the computer is assembled and shipped. The only alternative, short of requiring the customer to wait until the end of the period to know the actual price of the computer, is to estimate the amount of overhead on each computer and set the sales price accordingly. Using estimates has another advantage as well. It is not unusual for overhead to fluctuate during the year. For example, the utilities costs incurred by Ben & Jerry's (whose factory is located in Vermont) during the winter are likely to be higher than those incurred in the summer. If Ben & Jerry's used actual overhead costs to cost products, the ice cream the company makes in February would cost more than the ice cream it makes in May. Using estimates smooths out or normalizes seasonal and random fluctuations in overhead costs. Thus, this method of costing is often called normal costing.

www.benjerry.com

 Key Concept: *In order to provide relevant information for decision making, overhead must often be estimated.*

PREDETERMINED OVERHEAD RATES

Companies that estimate the amount of overhead cost incurred in costing products allocate overhead using predetermined overhead rates. **Predetermined overhead rates** are calculated using a slight modification of the basic overhead rate formula:

 Key Formula: *Predetermined overhead rate (for a cost pool) = Estimated overhead for the cost pool/Estimated units of the cost driver*

Companies utilizing robotics in their manufacturing facilities often have predetermined overhead rates due to factual information available on the cost of the machinery and the amount of work that a particular machine can handle in a set amount of time.

Predetermined overhead rates are typically calculated using annual estimates of overhead and cost drivers although some companies do more frequent calculations. The allocation of overhead using predetermined overhead rates is called an application of overhead. The amount of overhead applied to a product is calculated by multiplying the predetermined overhead rate by the actual units of the cost driver incurred in producing the product or service. The cost of a product or service for a company utilizing normal costing therefore includes an actual amount of direct material, an actual amount of direct labor, and an applied amount of manufacturing overhead based on estimates.

Calculating predetermined overhead rates is a three-step process. Step 1 involves the identification and estimation of the indirect overhead costs included in the plantwide or departmental cost pool. Step 2 involves the identification and estimation of the appropriate allocation base (the cost driver). Step 3 is the actual computation of the predetermined overhead rate.

As an example, let's assume that Northern Lights has chosen to lump all overhead into one cost pool for the entire factory (a plantwide cost pool). The company identifies overhead costs as including the cost of utilities, insurance, and rent for the factory building; depreciation and repairs and maintenance of manufacturing equipment; supplies used in the factory; and the salaries of a production supervisor and janitor in the factory. The company further estimates that these costs should total about $100,000 in the next year. Since Northern Lights is very labor intensive, it has chosen labor hours as the cost driver and estimates using 6,000 labor hours during the next year. Dividing the estimated overhead of $100,000 by the estimated allocation base of 6,000 labor hours results in a predetermined overhead rate of $16.67 per labor hour.

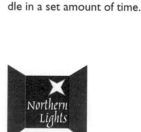

$$\frac{\$100,000}{6,000} = \$16.67 \text{ per labor hour}$$

In other words, for every labor hour worked on a product the company should apply $16.67 in overhead cost. As you can see in Exhibit 3-1, since Job 101 required 22.4 labor hours, it was allocated $373.41 of overhead.

THE PROBLEM OF OVER- AND UNDERAPPLIED OVERHEAD

Because overhead is applied to products using predetermined overhead rates based on estimates, it is likely that actual overhead costs (when they become known) will differ from that applied. If applied overhead is greater than actual overhead, the company **overapplied overhead.** If the applied overhead is less than actual overhead, the company **underapplied overhead** for the period. Over- and underapplied overhead can occur for a couple of reasons—estimating the overhead incorrectly or estimating the cost driver incorrectly. For example, Northern Lights had a predetermined overhead rate of $16.67 per direct labor hour ($100,000 estimated overhead/6,000 estimated direct labor hours). If during the year, 6,000 direct labor hours are actually incurred in making cabinets, our total applied overhead will total $100,000. But what if our actual overhead costs total $101,000? Northern Lights will have underapplied overhead by $1,000. What impact does the underapplication have on the cost of cabinets produced by Northern Lights?

Because applied overhead is accumulated in work in process (WIP) and then transferred to finished goods as units are completed and then to cost of goods sold as units are sold, if everything is sold, adjusting for over- or underapplied overhead simply involves adjusting the balance of the cost of goods sold account. If Northern Lights sells all the cabinets it produces, its cost of goods sold would be understated by $1,000. But what if some of the cabinets were not sold, or perhaps not even finished? Then the $1,000 should be allocated in some fashion to work in process, finished goods, and cost of goods sold to recognize that all three accounts are too low. This allocation is usually based on the balance in each account. As an alternative, if the amount of the adjustment is small, companies may choose to adjust only the cost of goods sold account.

APPENDIX

ADDITIONAL TOPICS IN PRODUCT COSTING

BASIC PROCESS COSTING

LO8
Understand the basics of backflush and process costing (appendix)

Companies that produce beverages and other products (paint, paper, and oil) in a continuous flow production process typically use process costing. As mentioned previously, instead of accumulating, tracking, and assigning direct material and direct labor costs directly to each job, process costing systems accumulate and track direct material and direct labor costs by department and then assign the costs evenly to the products that pass through each department. Likewise, instead of applying overhead to each specific job, overhead is applied to each department and then assigned evenly to each product that passes through. Although the application to job or department differs, the amount of overhead applied is calculated in exactly the same way. After predetermined overhead rates are developed, overhead is applied by multiplying the predetermined overhead rate by the actual units of cost driver incurred in each department. A comparison of the cost flows in job costing and process costing is shown in Exhibit 3-4.

In companies with no beginning or ending inventories (all units are finished), the mechanics of process costing are very simple. Because all the units produced are identical, costs accumulated and tracked in each department can simply be averaged across all the units that are produced. If $30,000 of direct material costs and $70,000 of direct labor and overhead costs are incurred in the blending department, and 10,000 gallons of product are produced, the cost of blending each gallon is obviously $10 per gallon and the 10,000 finished units cost $100,000 to produce.

EXHIBIT 3-4 A Comparison of Cost Flows

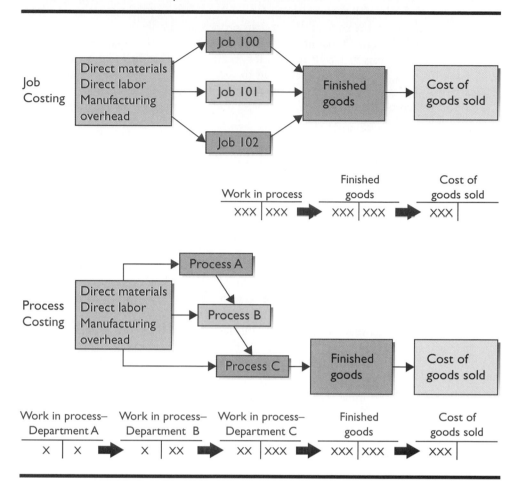

However, problems quickly arise when companies have inventories. Let's assume that the blending department finishes blending only 8,000 gallons while 2,000 gallons are left in ending work in process at the end of the year. These 2,000 gallons are 50 percent complete and will require additional materials, labor, and overhead during the next period before they are finished. Should each gallon (finished or unfinished) still cost $10 in this case? That would mean that our 8,000 finished units cost $80,000 whereas our 2,000 unfinished units cost $20,000. Of course, that would not make sense because we would expect our finished units to cost more per gallon than those that are only half finished!

To get around this problem, we need to calculate the number of **equivalent units** completed during the period. If two units are uniformly 50 percent finished at the end of a period, we have finished the equivalent of one complete unit. In the previous example, we partially finished 2,000 units with each unit uniformly 50 percent complete. How many finished units could we have completed using the same amount of direct materials, labor, and overhead? The 2,000 units that are 50 percent finished are the equivalent of 1,000 finished units. Therefore, our total equivalent units finished during the period are equal to 9,000—the 8,000 units we actually finished plus another 1,000 equivalent finished units in ending inventory.

Our cost per equivalent unit is therefore $11.11 ($100,000/9,000 equivalent units) and the 8,000 finished units cost $88,880 whereas the 2,000 units in ending inventory (1,000 equivalent units) cost $11,120 ($100,000 − $88,880). Process costing and the calculation of equivalent units are substantially more complicated when companies have both beginning and ending inventories of work in process. The details of process costing with beginning inventories are beyond the scope of this book.

Another difference between job costing and process costing is that process cost systems often require multiple WIP accounts—one for every process. As products are moved from one process to another, the costs of the previous process are simply transferred to the next process. For example, a paint manufacturer accumulates and tracks direct material, direct labor, and overhead costs to a WIP account for each process (blending and pouring). The total costs for each process are then assigned to the paint by dividing by the number of gallons of paint that comes out of each process. The total cost of each gallon is therefore the sum of the costs assigned from each process and an average of the costs incurred in each process.

BACKFLUSH COSTING

Companies utilizing just-in-time manufacturing techniques generally have little or no inventory of raw material, WIP, or finished goods. Remember that products are typically produced only after an order has been placed so theoretically all units produced will be sold. Although managers still need to know the cost of goods produced using JIT techniques, the costing process used is greatly simplified by recording all manufacturing costs directly into cost of goods sold. As can be seen in Exhibit 3-5, instead of sequentially tracking manufacturing costs through raw materials inventory, WIP, finished goods, and cost of goods sold, manufacturing costs are flushed directly into cost of goods sold. At

EXHIBIT 3-5   A Comparison of Cost Flows

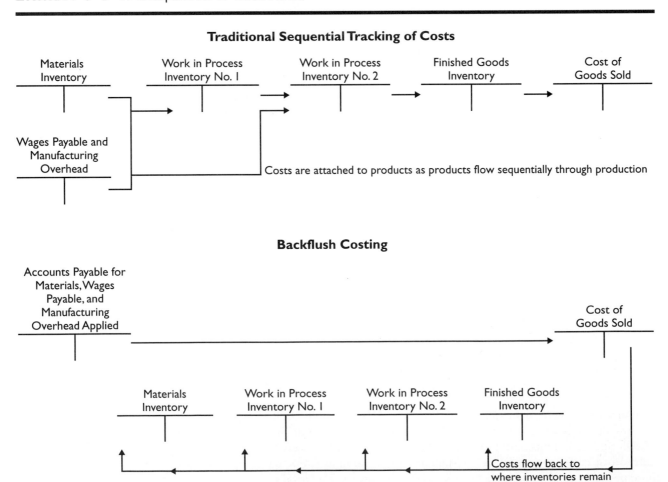

the end of the period, if the company has small amounts of inventory on hand, manufacturing costs are backflushed into the appropriate inventory account. This is the exception rather than the rule. In most cases, we would expect all costs to remain in cost of goods sold.

A chief attraction of **backflush costing** is its simplicity. Simple systems, however, generally do not yield as much information as do more complex systems. Criticisms of backflush costing focus mainly on the inability of the accounting system to pinpoint the uses of resources at each step of the production process. Managers, however, keep track of operations by personal observations, computer monitoring, and nonfinancial measures. In a backflush costing system, control shifts away from accounting numbers toward critical physical measures observable by management in the factory.

SUMMARY OF KEY CONCEPTS

- Overhead cannot be directly tracked to products and services but must instead be allocated using cost drivers. (p. 67)
- Understanding what causes overhead costs to be incurred (what drives them) is the key to allocating overhead. (p. 68)
- Accuracy in overhead application has become much more important as overhead costs have increased and make up a larger portion of the total costs of products. (p. 70)
- In order to provide relevant information for decision making, overhead must often be estimated. (p. 71)

KEY DEFINITIONS

Job costing A costing system that accumulates, tracks, and assigns costs for each job produced by a company (p. 62)

Process costing A costing system that accumulates and tracks costs for each process performed and then assigns those costs equally to each unit produced (p. 62)

Operations costing A hybrid of job and process costing; used by companies that make products in batches (p. 63)

Normal spoilage Spoilage resulting from the regular operations of the production process (p. 65)

Abnormal spoilage Spoilage resulting from unusual circumstances including improper handling, poorly trained employees, faulty equipment, and so on (p. 65)

Fringe benefits Payroll costs in addition to the basic hourly wage (p. 66)

Idle time Worker time that is not used in the production of the finished product (p. 66)

Overtime premium The additional amount added to the basic hourly wage due to overtime worked by the workers (p. 66)

Allocation The process of finding a logical method of assigning overhead costs to the products or services produced by a company (p. 67)

Cost drivers Factors that cause or drive the incurrence of costs (p. 67)

Cost pools Groups of overhead costs that are similar; used to simplify the task of assigning costs to products using ABC costing (p. 68)

Predetermined overhead rates Used to apply overhead to products; calculated by dividing the estimated overhead for a cost pool by the estimated units of the cost driver (p. 71)

Overapplied Overhead The amount of applied overhead in excess of actual overhead (p. 72)

Underapplied Overhead The amount of actual overhead in excess of applied overhead (p. 72)

Equivalent units The number of finished units that can be made from the materials, labor, and overhead included in partially completed units (p. 73)

Backflush costing A costing system in which manufacturing costs are directly flushed into cost of goods sold instead of flowing through inventory (p. 75)

CONCEPT REVIEW

1. Give an example of an organization that might use a job-order costing system and explain why.

2. Job costing is most appropriate for what type of product?

3. Describe a situation when backflush costing would be appropriate.

4. What type of costing system would a service organization, such as public accounting firms, be most likely to use?

5. The concept of equivalent whole or completed units is necessary in what type of costing system?

6. If Clinton Company uses normal costing, when would an adjustment to the applied overhead account increase product costs?

7. When should a normalized overhead rate be used?

8. What is a predetermined overhead rate? Why is it needed? How is it computed?

9. Why would a company decide to use a predetermined overhead rate instead of the actual overhead cost incurred?

10. What are some of the variables that must be considered in selecting a base to be used in computing the predetermined overhead rate?

11. What is overapplied overhead? What is underapplied overhead?

12. List two reasons why overhead might be overapplied.

13. List two reasons why overhead might be underapplied.

14. Explain the importance of product cost information in the context of management decision making.

15. Distinguish between job-order and process costing.

16. Why is it easier to accumulate costs using a process costing system?

17. How are work-in-process accounts maintained in a company using process costing?

18. Define the term *equivalent units of production.*

APPLICATION OF CONCEPTS

19. George is a typical employee who works 40 hours per week. Last week George spent 4 hours talking football with his supervisor and only had 36 productive hours, although he was paid for all 40 hours that he was at work. He is paid $6 per hour. In a job costing system, how should his labor costs be classified?

20. BN Rabbit Enterprises calculates predetermined overhead rates for each department. In the feeding department, total overhead costs were $3,400 in 1999, and are expected to total $4,000 in 2000. There were 325 pens in 1999 and plans for 400 pens in 2000.

Required

   A. If the number of pens is used as the cost driver, calculate the 2000 predetermined overhead rate (rounded to the nearest cent).

   B. If the number of pens is used as the cost driver, calculate the amount of overhead applied in 2000 if there were actually 390 pens in operation.

   C. Based on the rate computed in B, if actual overhead was $5,000, what was the amount of under- or overapplied overhead in 2000?

21. At Lamply and Associates LLP, overhead is assigned to clients based upon direct labor hours. At the beginning of 2002, estimated overhead costs were $106,000 and estimated direct labor hours were 10,800. Actual overhead costs amounted to $116,400, and 10,904 direct labor hours were worked.

Required

   A. Compute the predetermined overhead rate used to apply overhead to clients. (Round to the nearest cent.)

B. How much overhead should be applied to a client whose file notes 120 direct labor hours in 2002? (Round to the nearest cent.)

22. Carl's Pottery Barn had no beginning or ending WIP inventory balance. Costs transferred to WIP during the month included $400 for direct labor and $375 for indirect costs. If the month's cost of goods manufactured totaled $1,050, how much direct material was used during the month?

23. Carl's Pottery Barn uses number of minutes in the firing oven to allocate overhead costs to items. In a typical month, 5,000 firing minutes are expected, and average monthly overhead expenses are $350. During January, 5,000 firing minutes were used, and total overhead costs were $275. Compute Carl's predetermined overhead rate, applied overhead for January, and the amount of over- or underapplied overhead for the month.

24. During the month of March, TAL Productions purchased $30,000 of direct materials. Total manufacturing costs were $115,000. Indirect labor costs were $20,000 and direct labor costs were $25,000. There was no beginning direct materials inventory, but ending direct materials inventory was $10,000. Total manufacturing overhead costs must have been how much?

25. Lowen Enterprises applies overhead using direct labor hours. The following information is available for the year:

Expected direct labor hours	600,000
Actual direct labor hours	540,000
Overhead applied	$2,950,000
Actual overhead	$2,800,000

Required

What was the overhead application rate?

26. Grandma R knits made-to-order rugs. The following is an incomplete job cost report for job 314.

DIRECT MATERIALS			DIRECT LABOR		OVERHEAD
Type of yarn	Cost	Date	Knitting hours	Total cost	Total applied
Blue - 4 skeins	$14	1/23	5	$40	$4.50
Brown - 2 skeins	11	1/24	7	?	?
Green - 2 skeins	13	1/25	3	24	$2.70

Required

A. What is the direct labor cost per hour?

B. What is the direct labor cost for January 24?

C. Based upon this job cost report, how is overhead being assigned to each rug?

D. How much overhead should be applied for the January 24 knitting?

E. What is the total manufacturing cost for this rug?

F. Which yarn is the most expensive?

27. Jenny's Jingles manufactures holiday decorations. Overhead is applied to products based upon direct labor hours. Last year, total overhead costs were expected to be $85,000 based upon an estimated 8,500 direct labor hours. Actual expenses totaled $88,750 for 8,400 actual hours.

Required

A. Compute the predetermined overhead rate.

B. How much overhead should be applied to a job that was completed in three direct labor hours?

C. What is the amount of over- or underapplied overhead at the end of the year?

28. The following events took place during the year for the Billy Joelle Company:

Purchased $100,000 of raw materials

Incurred 4,500 direct labor hours

Paid indirect labor costs of $25,000

Incurred utilities, rent, and depreciation totaling $45,000

Direct materials used in production amounted to $70,000

Applied overhead at 125 percent of direct labor costs

Direct labor averages $11 per hour

$200,000 of products were transferred to finished goods

Products valued at $188,000 were sold

All beginning inventory balances were zero.

Required

A. Calculate the direct materials ending inventory.

B. Calculate the work in process ending inventory.

C. Calculate the finished goods ending inventory.

D. Calculate the over- or underapplied overhead for the period.

29. Martha's Magnets creates special order magnets for its customers. The company's estimated overhead cost for the year is $11,000 and the number of direct labor hours is typically 2,100. In the first month, the following jobs were completed:

	Job 101	Job 102
Direct materials used	$1,100	$1,450
Direct labor cost	1,500	1,250
Direct labor hours	150	125

Required

A. What was the company's predetermined overhead rate using direct labor hours as a base?

B. How much overhead was applied to each job?

C. What were the total manufacturing costs for each job?

30. Tripp Sound Works Inc. estimated its overhead costs for 19X0 to be $1,750,000. Tripp expected to produce 350,000 units during the year. During 19X0, the company incurred overhead costs of $1,600,000 and produced 400,000 units. What rate would be used to apply manufacturing overhead costs to products? Calculate the amount of manufacturing overhead costs applied to units produced. Calculate the amount of under- or overapplied manufacturing overhead for the year.

31. The following events took place during the current year for Moody Blues Company.

1. Purchased direct materials	$100,000
2. Incurred direct labor costs	$ 60,000
3. Incurred indirect labor costs	$ 30,000
4. Incurred utilities, rent, and depreciation	$ 50,000
5. Direct materials issued to production	$ 85,000
6. Overhead is applied at $9 per machine hour	
7. Machine hours used	10,000
8. Transferred to finished goods	$210,000
9. Cost of goods sold during period	$190,000

Required

   A. Calculate the direct materials ending inventory.

   B. Calculate the work-in-process ending inventory.

   C. Calculate the finished goods ending inventory.

   D. Calculate the over- or underapplied overhead for the period.

32. Clapton Company applies overhead costs to products at a rate of $2.50 per direct labor hour. The company uses a separate overhead account. The following data relate to the manufacturing activities of Clapton Company during October:

	October 1	October 30
Direct materials inventory	$ 60,250	$61,750
Work-in-process inventory	44,000	43,500
Finished goods inventory	24,150	23,000

Factory Costs Incurred during the Month

Direct materials purchased	$155,000
Direct labor costs incurred	$270,000 (27,000 direct labor hours)
Factory utilities	35,000
Factory rent	52,000
Factory supervisor	43,000
Depreciation on factory equipment	25,000

Required

   A. Calculate the cost of direct materials used during October.

   B. Using normal costing, calculate the cost of units completed during October and sent to the finished goods storeroom.

   C. Using normal costing, calculate the cost of goods sold during October. Assume the company waits until the end of the year to adjust cost of goods sold for the over- or underapplied overhead.

33. For the month of May, Guess Who CPAs worked 300 hours for Albert Flasher and 400 hours for Glamor Boy. Guess Who bills clients at the rate of $150 per hour. The accounting staff is paid $55 per hour. The accounting staff is estimated to work a total of 800 hours during the month, but 100 of these hours are not expected to be billed to clients. The estimated amount of service overhead costs to be paid during the month is $9,600. Service overhead is assigned to clients based proportionally on direct labor hours. The company also spent $5,000 in marketing and administrative costs.

Required

   A. Calculate the predetermined overhead rate and the amounts applied to Albert Flasher and Glamor Boy.

   B. If actual overhead costs incurred were $10,000, would overhead be over- or underapplied?

   C. In a CPA firm, would this appear to be the best way to apply overhead? Why?

34. The Beatle Products Company uses a job costing system. The company estimated its annual overhead to be $100,000 and the number of direct labor hours for the year to be 20,000 hours. In the first month, the following jobs were completed:

	Honey Pie	Savoy Truffle
Direct materials used	$11,000	$14,500
Direct labor cost	$23,000	$12,500
Direct labor hours	1,500 hours	1,250 hours

Required

A. What is the company's predetermined overhead rate using direct labor hours as the base?

B. What is the overhead assigned to Honey Pie?

C. What is the overhead assigned to Savoy Truffle?

D. What is the total manufacturing cost of Honey Pie?

E. What is the total manufacturing cost of Savoy Truffle?

35. KENCOR Brewery uses the latest in modern brewing technology to produce a prize-winning beer. In both 1999 and 2000, KENCOR produced and sold 100,000 cases of beer and had no raw material, work-in-process, or finished goods inventory at the beginning or end of either year. At the end of 1999, the company installed machines to perform some of the repetitive tasks previously performed with direct labor. At the beginning of 2000, KENCOR's bookkeeper estimated that net income would increase from $530,000 in 1999 to $706,000 in 2000.

	1999 (Actual)	2000 (Estimated)
Beer Sales (100,000 cases)	$1,000,000	$1,000,000
Less: Cost of goods sold		
Direct material	150,000	150,000
Direct labor	125,000	25,000
Applied overhead*	$ 95,000	$ 19,000
Gross profit	$ 630,000	$ 806,000
Less: Selling and administrative costs	100,000	100,000
Net income	$ 530,000	$ 706,000

*For 2000, overhead was applied at the 1999 rate of $9.50 per direct labor hour for an estimated 2,000 hours of direct labor. A total of 10,000 direct labor hours were worked in 1999. KENCOR's bookkeeper estimates that 5,000 machine hours will be worked in 2000.

However, when actual overhead is used to calculate net income at the end of the year, net income decreased from $530,000 in 1999 to $435,000 in 2000.

	1999 (Actual)	2000 (Actual)
Beer Sales (100,000 cases)	$1,000,000	$1,000,000
Less: Cost of goods sold		
Direct Material	150,000	150,000
Direct Labor	125,000	25,000
Actual Overhead:		
Lease Expense	25,000	25,000
Utilities Expense	15,000	30,000
Depreciation (equipment)	50,000	200,000
Equipment Maintenance	$ 5,000	$ 35,000
Gross Profit	$ 630,000	$ 535,000
Less: Selling and administrative costs	100,000	100,000
Net Income	$ 530,000	$ 435,000

Required

Step 1 DEFINE THE PROBLEM

A. What potential problems do you see in the bookkeeper's estimate of income for 2000?

Step 2 IDENTIFY OBJECTIVES

B. Based on the information given, would you change the cost driver or predetermined overhead rate for 2000? What cost driver would you suggest?

Step 3 IDENTIFY AND ANALYZE AVAILABLE OPTIONS

C. Using the cost driver and predetermined overhead rate you suggested in B, recalculate KENCOR's estimated net income for 2000.

D. KENCOR has set a goal of increasing net income in 2001 to $550,000. However, sales are expected to be flat. Using the decision model from Chapter 1, identify some options for KENCOR. How might they reach their goal of increasing income to $550,000? What qualitative factors should be considered in their decision?

Step 4   SELECT THE BEST OPTION

36. Boots R Us manufactures hunting boots. The company is currently trying to choose the best method of allocating manufacturing overhead to boots produced. Following is information from the accounting department of Boots R Us:

Estimated Income Statement

Sales	$1,000,000 (10,000 pairs of boots)
Direct materials	300,000
Direct labor	150,000 (10,000 hrs)
Estimated overhead	100,000
Net profit on boots	$ 450,000
Estimated machine hours	15,000

Required

A. Compute the predetermined overhead rate for Boots R Us using (1) direct labor hours, (2) direct labor dollars, and (3) machine hours.

B. If actual labor cost was $170,000 for 10,500 direct labor hours and actual machine hours used were 18,500, what would be the applied overhead using the three predetermined overhead rates computed in Part A?

C. If actual overhead is $115,000, compute over/underapplied overhead for all three allocation bases used in Parts A and B.

D. Compare the over- and underapplied overhead calculated with the three different drivers in C. Why do different drivers result in different amounts of applied overhead? Which cost driver appears to be best?

Step 3   IDENTIFY AND ANALYZE AVAILABLE OPTIONS

E. What other factors must Boots R Us consider in choosing a cost driver?

37. Scott Herring Hammocks has two departments: assembly and packaging. The company uses a job order cost system and computes a predetermined overhead rate in each department. The assembly department bases its rate on machine hours, and the packaging department bases its rate on direct labor hours. At the beginning of the year, the company made the following estimates:

DEPARTMENT

	Assembly	Packaging
Direct labor hours	10,000	50,000
Machine hours	40,000	2,000
Manufacturing overhead	$600,000	$250,000
Direct labor cost	$100,000	$500,000

Required

A. Compute the predetermined overhead rate for each department.

B. The job cost sheet for job 8260 (50 hammocks), which was started and completed during the year, showed the following:

DEPARTMENT

	Assembly	Packaging
Direct labor hours	5	20
Machine hours	50	20
Materials	$725	$225
Direct Labor cost	$ 50	$200

Compute the total applied overhead for job 8260.

C. If the company uses a plantwide rate (based on direct labor hours) to apply overhead, what is the total applied overhead for job 8260?

D. What problems could using a plantwide rate cause for managerial decision making?

38. Northern Lights Custom Cabinets is a very labor-intensive operation so it has elected to apply overhead costs to products using direct labor hours as the cost driver. The following data relate to the manufacturing activities of Northern Lights Custom Cabinets during January 2000:

custom cabinets

	January 1	January 31
Direct materials inventory	$ 50,250	$51,750
Work-in-process inventory	34,000	33,500
Finished goods inventory	14,000	13,000

Factory Costs Incurred during the Month

Direct materials purchased	$ 75,000
Direct labor costs incurred	170,000 (17,000 direct labor hours)
Factory utilities	35,000
Factory rent	50,000
Factory supervisor	50,000
Depreciation on factory equipment	25,000

Required

A. Calculate the cost of direct materials used during January.

B. Using normal costing, calculate the cost of units completed during January and transferred to the finished goods showroom.

C. Using normal costing, calculate the cost of goods sold during January. Assume the company waits until the end of the year to adjust cost of goods sold for the over- or underapplied overhead.

CONTINUING CASE | BIG AL'S PIZZA INC.

As discussed in Chapter 2, Big Al's Pizza Inc. produces fresh, packaged 16-inch meat pizzas for wholesale to grocery stores, convenience stores, and school cafeterias. Big Al's deals exclusively with Pizza Products Inc. to purchase ingredients and equipment. The cost of material, labor, overhead, and selling and administrative costs is provided in Chapter 2.

During the first year of operations, Big Al's determined the cost of overhead to be allocated to each of its pizzas by dividing the total amount of overhead expected to be incurred for the year by the expected annual production. The predetermined overhead rate for its first year of operation was therefore:

> Predetermined overhead rate =
> $198,000/325,000 pizzas = $.609 per pizza.

During the first month of operation (January), Big Al's produced 25,784 pizzas. Actual direct material costs were $56,250 (materials were purchased at the silver quality level) and actual direct labor costs were $38,740 for 5,960 hours worked. Actual overhead during January was equal to $17,200.

In its second year of operations, Big Al's has decided to expand the product line by producing a new veggie pizza. The pizza will require the purchase of a veggie package from Pizza Products Inc. at a cost of $.60, $.50, or $.40 respectively for gold, silver, and bronze quality levels. Of course, the meat package will not be required. All other ingredients remain the same and prices remain the same.

The veggie toppings require additional processing time (cutting and dicing) of approximately 1 minute per pizza. Therefore, the total time to apply toppings for a veggie pizza is 4 minutes compared to 3 minutes for a meat pizza. The remaining processing time for dough, sauce, cheese, and packaging is the same for the new veggie pizza and the meat pizza. Total processing time for the veggie pizza is therefore 14 1/2 minutes compared to 13 1/2 minutes for the meat pizza.

The new veggie pizza is not expected to affect sales of the meat pizza. In the second year of operations, Big Al's expects to produce and sell about 350,000 meat pizzas and 25,000 veggie pizzas.

Increasing production is expected to increase overhead costs by 5% in year 2. Direct labor costs are not expected to change. The costs of product promotion and advertising are expected to increase to $3,000 per month. All other selling and administrative costs are expected to remain the same as in year 1.

Actual production during January of Year 2 was 28,761 meat pizzas and 2,118 veggie pizzas. Actual direct material costs were $62,550 for the meat pizzas and $3,400 for the veggie pizzas. Actual direct labor costs were $43,605 for the meat pizzas and $3,037.50 for the veggie pizzas representing 6,460 and 450 direct labor hours respectively. Actual overhead costs during January were $19,825.

Required

Using the information given:

Year 1

A. Comment on Big Al's allocation of overhead based on the estimated number of pizzas to be produced. Was it appropriate when Big Al's only produced one type of pizza?

B. Using normal costing, what was the cost of the 25,784 meat pizzas produced in January?

C. Was overhead over- or underapplied in January?

Year 2

D. Can Big Al's still allocate overhead based on the number of pizzas produced in Year 2?

E. What appears to be the most logical cost driver for allocating overhead in Year 2?

F. Compute a predetermined overhead rate for big Al's using the cost driver you identified in E.

G. Using normal costing (and the predetermined overhead rate calculated in F) compute the total manufacturing cost for the 28,761 meat pizzas and the 2,118 veggie pizzas made in January of Year 2.

H. Assuming Big Al's applies overhead in Year 2 based on the number of units expected to be produced, compute the total manufacturing costs for the meat pizzas and the veggie pizzas made in January.

I. The marketing manager of Big Al's estimates Year 3 sales of 385,000 meat pizzas and 30,000 veggie pizzas. The production manager is concerned about being able to produce that number of pizzas without incurring significant overtime or making changes in the production process. In terms of the 4-step decision-making model, outline the problem, potential objectives, and options that the management team of Big Al's should consider.

PRODUCT COSTING FOR MANAGEMENT DECISIONS: ACTIVITY-BASED COSTING AND ACTIVITY-BASED MANAGEMENT

Study Tools

A Look at the Previous Chapter

Chapter 3 provided an introduction into product costing in different types of production environments and different types of companies and the difficulties of allocating overhead to products.

A Preview of This Chapter

In this chapter we learn about the benefits of applying overhead to products using activity-based costing (ABC) and the use of activity-based management (ABM) to aid in controlling costs and making better decisions.

Key concepts include:

- Unit-level costs are performed each time a unit is produced. Batch-level costs are performed each time a batch of goods is produced. Product-level costs are performed as needed to support the production of each different type of product. Facility-level costs simply sustain a facility's general manufacturing process.
- The key feature of an ABC system is allocating overhead costs based on activities that drive costs rather than the volume of number of units produced.
- Traditional volume-based costing systems often result in over-costing high-volume products and undercosting low-volume products.
- Activity-based management focuses on managing activities to reduce costs and make better decisions.
- The successful implementation of ABC and ABM requires a long-term commitment by top management and the cooperation of all functional areas of a business organization.

LEARNING OBJECTIVES

After studying the material in this chapter, you should be able to:

LO1 Discuss activity-based costing (ABC) systems

LO2 Apply ABC systems to cost products and services

LO3 Analyze the use of cost drivers in ABC systems

LO4 Apply ABC systems to selling and administrative activities

LO5 Understand the application of ABC in a JIT environment

LO6 Evaluate the benefits and limitations of ABC systems

LO7 Understand activity-based management (ABM) and the value chain

A Preview of Upcoming Chapters

Chapters 5 through 8 build on the concepts of product costing introduced in Chapters 2 through 4. In Chapter 5, the nature of costs is discussed and students are introduced to concepts of cost behavior, relevant costs, the impact of income taxes, and the time value of money on costs and decision making.

In this chapter, we revisit the problems of overhead application and discuss the use of an alternative product costing system called activity-based costing (ABC). Assigning overhead to products and services using traditional allocation methods and volume-based cost drivers may not provide adequate information to managers to make good decisions. Activity-based costing (ABC) provides more accurate cost information by focusing on the activities or work that is performed in the manufacturing of a product or provision of a service and the cost drivers associated with those activities. The benefits and limitations of ABC are discussed, as is the application of ABC to selling and administrative activities and in a just-in-time (JIT) environment. The last part of the chapter discusses the use of activity information in controlling and managing costs (activity-based management). ∎

INTRODUCTION

The previous chapter examined a number of problems associated with the application of overhead to products and services. Due to the indirect nature of overhead and the fact that overhead consists of a variety of seemingly unrelated costs, it is often difficult to determine how much overhead should be included when costing specific products and services. To complicate matters further, in order to provide timely cost information to managers, overhead costs must often be estimated.

In the past, overhead typically made up a smaller portion of the total cost of a product or service. The environment was one of "labor intensive" manufacturing. With labor as the dominant activity and therefore the cost driver, direct labor hours worked was a logical activity base with which to allocate overhead to products. As the manufacturing environment matured and the use of machines or robotics in production has increased, overhead cost became a larger percentage of the total manufacturing cost. In heavily automated manufacturing environments, direct labor costs have shrunk to as little as 5 percent of total production costs, whereas overhead costs have soared to 60 percent or more of total product costs (see Exhibit 4-1). It's not hard to see why. Consider a modern automobile manufacturing plant. High-tech computers control robots that weld, paint, and perform other jobs that used to done by human labor. High-tech computer operated equipment like robots are very expensive and are treated as part of overhead cost. As overhead costs increase and make up a larger portion of the total costs of products, accuracy in overhead application has become much more important. At the same time, advances in information technology have allowed even the smallest businesses to take advantage of computers. These advances have provided more and more timely information to managers than ever before.

ACTIVITY-BASED COSTING

LOI

Discuss activity-based costing (ABC) systems

Traditional overhead allocation methods, which use one or two volume-based cost drivers to assign overhead costs to products, can provide misleading product cost information in heavily automated manufacturing environments in which companies make a variety of diverse products. Volume-based allocation methods work best if the manufacturing environment includes mostly unit-level costs (costs that vary with every unit produced or the volume of production).

However, costs incurred in setting up machinery to make different products, costs incurred in designing a new model, and costs incurred in providing manufacturing facilities

EXHIBIT 4-1 Percentage Change in Manufacturing Costs

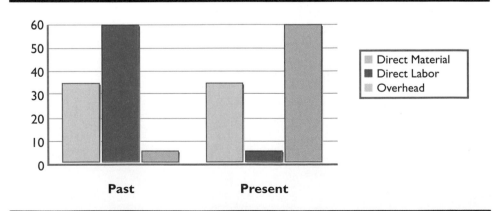

are not incurred every time an individual unit (a table) is produced. Rather, batch-level costs like machine setups are only incurred when a batch of products (100 tables) is produced. Likewise, product-level costs (designing a new model) are only incurred when a new product is introduced. Finally, facility-level costs like the rent on the factory building are incurred to sustain the overall manufacturing processes and don't vary with the number or type of products produced.[1]

Examples of unit, batch, product and facility level overhead costs are provided in the table below.

Overhead Costs and Cooper's Hierarchy

Unit-Level Costs	**Product-Level Costs**
Supplies for factory	Salaries of engineers
Depreciation on factory machinery	Depreciation of engineering equipment
Energy costs for factory machinery	Product development costs (testing)
Repairs and maintenance of factory machinery	Quality control costs
Batch-Level Costs	**Facility-Level Costs**
Salaries related to purchasing and receiving	Depreciation of factory building or rent
Salaries related to moving material	Salary of plant manager
Quality control costs	Insurance, taxes, etc.
Depreciation of setup equipment	Training

 Key Concept: *Unit-level costs are incurred each time a unit is produced. Batch-level costs are incurred each time a batch of goods is produced. Product-level costs are incurred as needed to support the production of each different type of product. Facility-level costs simply sustain a facility's general manufacturing process.*

When concentrated at the unit level, it makes sense that the number of units produced should be correlated with the amount of overhead costs allocated to each unit. However, as companies incur more and more batch, product, and facility-level costs, the correlation between the volume of product produced and the allocation of overhead becomes very fuzzy. **Activity-based costing (ABC),** which is based on the concept of assigning costs based on activities that drive costs rather than the volume or number of units produced, provides more accurate costing in these situations. **Activities** are procedures or processes that cause work to be accomplished. Activities consume resources and products consume activities.

LO2
Apply ABC systems to cost products and services

 Key Concept: *Overhead costs are assigned to products in an ABC system in two stages. In Stage 1, activities are identified and overhead costs are traced to each activity. In Stage 2, cost drivers are determined for each activity and costs are assigned to products.*

Examples of typical activities of a company are shown in the first column of the following table. It should be noted that overhead costs can be traced to more than one activity. For example, utilities may be related to purchasing, engineering, and machining activities. An employee who provides maintenance services and runs machines in the factory might have his salary split between machining and maintenance activities. Likewise, while depreciation of factory equipment is related to machining, depreciation of other equipment might be related to maintenance or quality control activities.

---

[1]This classification of costs as unit-level, batch-level, product-level, and facility-level is commonly referred to as Cooper's hierarchy.

Activities and Cost Drivers

Activity (level)	Potential Cost Drivers
Purchasing (batch)	Number of purchase orders or number of parts
Receiving (batch)	Amount of material or number of receipts
Product testing (product)	Number of change orders, number of tests, hours of testing time
Machine setups (batch)	Number of setups
Machining (unit)	Machine hours, labor hours, or number of units
Customer orders (batch)	Number of orders, number of customers
Maintenance of machines (unit)	Machine hours
Quality control inspections (unit, batch, or product)	Number of inspections, number of parts
Supervision (batch or product)	Number of supervision hours
Plant occupancy (facility)	Square footage, number of employees, labor hours, machine hours
Product movements (batch)	Pounds of material handled

COST DRIVERS

LO3
Analyze the use of cost drivers in ABC systems

In Stage 2, cost drivers for activities are chosen. As discussed in Chapter 2, cost drivers should cause or drive the incurrence of costs. For example, costs of purchasing might be driven by the number of purchase orders processed, whereas engineering costs might be driven by the number of parts in a product. Typical cost drivers for the activities identified in the table above are provided in the second column of the table.

Unit, batch, and product level activities are assigned to products using cost drivers that capture the underlying behavior of the costs that are being assigned. Facility-level costs, however, are usually not allocated to products or allocated to products in some arbitrary manner. For example, in the previous table, plant occupancy is a facility-level activity that would include costs like plant managers' salaries, depreciation of the factory building, rent, taxes, and insurance. Allocation of these costs would require the use of arbitrary cost drivers like square footage, number of employees, labor hours, or machine hours.

CHOOSING COST DRIVERS TO MOTIVATE BEHAVIOR

Cost drivers should generally be chosen based on a cause-and-effect relationship between the driver and the specific cost being considered. However, cost drivers may have motivational effects that must be considered as well. As an example, consider an activity like taking customer orders by telephone. Although there might be a causal relationship between the time spent on each call and the various costs of the customer order activity, if objectives of the customer order department include increasing sales per customer and improving customer service, using the time spent on each call as a cost driver might give employees a mixed message. If time on the phone relates to the assignment of cost, employees will be encouraged to spend as little time on the phone as possible to minimize the cost and also possibly answer more calls. As an alternative, if the number of sales is used as a cost driver, employees will be less likely to cut a call short, risking a lost sale or a dissatisfied customer.

Concept Question: Overhead costs incurred in purchasing materials and supplies used in production are often related to the number of purchase orders processed by a company (the more purchase orders processed, the higher the purchasing costs). Using the decision making model introduced in Chapter 1, what objectives might a company have in choosing a cost driver for these overhead costs (Step 2)? What other cost drivers might be considered as options in Step 3? What factors should be considered in deciding whether to use the number of purchase orders as the cost driver for purchasing costs?

Concept Answer: Step 2: Objectives might include reducing overhead costs related to purchasing, ensuring high quality supplies and materials, ensuring timely delivery of materials and supplies, etc. The particular objectives of a company determine the options to be considered in Step 3.

Step 2	IDENTIFY OBJECTIVES
Step 3	IDENTIFY AND ANALYZE AVAILABLE OPTIONS

Step 3: Other possible cost drivers include the number of different parts needed in production, the number of suppliers or even the proximity of suppliers to your business. Factors to be considered in making a decision concerning a cost driver include the out-of-pocket costs of purchasing materials and supplies, the costs of storing materials and supplies, the reliability of suppliers, the quality of materials and supplies purchased, etc. ■

It should be recognized that every business (because of different types of production processes and products) would have a different set of activities and costs drivers. In addition, the more complex the business or the production process, the more complex the ABC system is likely to be. Management must work together to design an appropriate cost system for the business.

TRADITIONAL OVERHEAD ALLOCATION AND **ABC**—AN EXAMPLE

As an example, let's consider TopSail Construction, a fictional beach housing contractor. TopSail Construction usually builds about 30 houses per year. On average, it takes about 5 months (20 weeks) to build each house. As in all manufactured products, the cost of a house consists of three main components: direct material, direct labor, and overhead.

TopSail Construction

Many different types of materials are used in the construction of a house. Raw materials needed in home construction range from lumber and roofing to insulation, sheet rock, brick, siding, and more. These types of raw materials can usually be accumulated, tracked, and assigned to specific homes with relative ease and thus are classified as direct materials. Indirect materials would include such things as nails, screws, and glue that are not worth the effort to try and measure with complete accuracy.

Direct labor is also fairly straightforward in the construction business. Like many building contractors, TopSail does not employ brick masons, electricians, plumbers, sheet rock installers, and painters but rather uses subcontractors to perform this work. Because subcontractor labor can be traced directly to each house built, these costs are classified as direct. TopSail only has six full-time employees. Two are carpenters that work directly on houses; they are also classified as direct labor costs. Two are construction supervisors whose primary job is to supervise the subcontractors and inspect the work done on each house. The construction supervisors typically spend their days going from house to house. TopSail consequently classifies their salaries as indirect labor. TopSail also employs a full-time administrative assistant and a secretary in the office to handle the ordering of materials and processing of change orders for each house as well as payroll, billing, accounts payable, and other accounting and administrative tasks related to the business. Because about one half of the time of the office staff is spent directly on manufacturing duties, one half of the cost of their salaries (indirect labor) and other office expenses such as rent, insurance, utilities, and supplies (overhead) is treated as a product cost. The other half is related to administrative duties and is treated as a period cost. In addition, TopSail has two part-time employees who deliver materials every morning and clear construction debris after work is complete each day. The salary of these workers is classified as indirect labor.

TopSail Construction incurs other overhead costs including the cost of tools (saws, drills, etc.) used on the job, trucks used for material delivery and cleanup, trucks used by the construction supervisors, rent of construction trailers used as temporary offices at large construction sites, and so on. TopSail estimates that its overhead costs will total $485,000 in 2000. The following table provides a breakdown of this estimate.

Estimated Overhead Costs for 2000

Overhead Item	Estimated Cost
Indirect materials	$180,000
Indirect labor:	
Construction supervisors	130,000
Office staff	30,000
Part-time workers	30,000
Other overhead:	
Office expenses	48,000
Tools	15,000
Trucks and other equipment	40,000
Rent on construction trailers	$ 12,000
Total	$485,000

If TopSail produced only one type of house, the overhead allocation process would be very simple. As discussed in Chapter 3, all the company would have to do is divide the total overhead of $485,000 by the number of houses constructed. If TopSail constructed 30 houses in 2000, each house would be allocated $16,167 of overhead costs. However, to meet the specific needs of customers, TopSail builds both standard homes in large subdivisions and custom homes (on the beach) of different design, size, and features. The construction of custom homes requires TopSail to give more attention to the proper allocation of overhead costs to each house.

TopSail Construction

Using a traditional volume-based overhead allocation method would result in Top-Sail Construction using only one predetermined overhead rate such as direct labor hours to allocate overhead to houses. If TopSail estimates that the total direct labor hours used in 2000 in building homes will be 88,000, then it would have a predetermined overhead rate of $5.51 per hour of direct labor used to construct each house ($485,000/88,000 direct labor hours). If a standard house takes 2,400 hours of labor to build, it would be allocated $13,224 of overhead costs. Likewise, a custom home requiring 4,000 direct labor hours would be allocated $22,040 of overhead costs. The following table illustrates the total cost of a standard house and a custom house using traditional volume-based costing.

Traditional Volume-Based Allocation Method Using Direct Labor Hours

Cost	Standard House	Custom House
Direct material	$ 75,000	$112,500
Direct labor	60,000	100,000
	(2,400 hours at $25 per hour)	(4,000 hours at $25 per hour)
Overhead	13,224	22,040
	(2,400 hour at $5.51 per hour)	(4,000 hours at $5.51 per hour)
Total costs	$148,224	$234,540
Sales price	$178,000	$281,500

TopSail typically establishes a sales price equal to about 120 percent of total manufacturing costs. Remember, this is not all profit, as TopSail must still cover all selling and administrative costs (half of its office expenses, advertising, commissions on sales made by real estate agents, etc.). If all of the overhead costs were related to the amount of labor hours needed to build the house, then a volume-based overhead allocation system would provide management with the information needed to make good decisions.

However, because TopSail builds two types of houses, a standard beach house with very few options and a custom home designed for beach property that will have many different options, the traditional volume-based overhead allocation method may not provide the best information to management. The custom house requires much more inspection activity and typically has many more change orders than the standard house. In addition, the materials used in a custom house are more varied resulting in more frequent purchases and deliveries. The use of an activity-based costing system might be more appropriate. In the next section, we explore TopSail's use of ABC.

STAGE 1: IDENTIFICATION OF ACTIVITIES

The first step in the implementation of an ABC system is the identification of production activities and the tracing of overhead costs to each activity. Remember that activities are processes or procedures that cause work to be accomplished. TopSail Construction identifies five primary activities that consume the resources of the company:

1. Inspections
2. Purchasing

3. Supervision
4. Material delivery and handling
5. Processing of change orders

The following table provides the overhead costs associated with each activity. Note that the total overhead is $485,000 regardless of whether it is allocated using volume-based drivers or using ABC.

Estimated Overhead Costs for 2000

Activity	Estimated Cost
Inspections	$ 50,000
Purchasing	30,000
Supervision	100,000
Material delivery and handling	225,000
Processing change orders	$ 80,000
Total	$485,000

An example of "Standard" beach houses.

An example of a "Custom" beach house.

STAGE 2: IDENTIFICATION OF COST DRIVERS AND ALLOCATION OF COSTS

Once the activities have been identified and overhead costs traced to each activity, cost drivers must be identified for each activity. The cost drivers chosen are as follows:

TopSail Construction

I. Inspections: Cost driver = Number of inspections

2. Purchasing: Cost driver = Number of purchase orders

3. Supervision: Cost driver = Hours of supervisor time

4. Material delivery and handling: Cost driver = Number of deliveries

5. Change orders: Cost driver = Number of change orders

As you can see from the cost drivers chosen, they are more closely related to the activity than direct labor hours. It simply makes more sense to allocate the cost of processing change orders based on the number of change orders processed rather than the number of labor hours to build each house.

TopSail estimates that it will make 20 standard houses and 10 custom houses during the next year. TopSail further estimates that each standard house will require weekly inspections over the estimated 20 week construction period (20 per house), whereas the custom homes will require daily inspections (100 per house). Custom homes built on the beach must meet specific state and local building codes to withstand hurricane force winds and tidal surges. They require more detailed inspections at more frequent time intervals than TopSail's standard homes.

Standard houses also require less supervision time (125 hours) than a custom house (150 hours). Custom homes require different and more varied materials than the standard house. Thus, TopSail expects that material will be ordered and delivered about 30 times over the five-month construction period for a standard house (1.5 times per week on average), whereas the custom house will require about three orders and deliveries per week. Finally, TopSail expects to process considerably more change orders with the custom house (30 per house) compared to only 10 for the standard house. The following table summarizes the total number of inspections, purchase orders, supervision hours, deliveries, and change orders TopSail expects next year.

Estimated Cost Driver Activity

Cost Driver	Standard Houses (each)	Standard Houses (total for 20 houses)	Custom Houses (each)	Custom Houses (total for 10 houses)	Total
Number of inspections	20	400	100	1,000	1,400
Number of purchase orders	30	600	60	600	1,200
Supervision hours	125	2,500	150	1,500	4,000
Number of deliveries	30	600	60	600	1,200
Number of change orders	10	200	30	300	500

In the following table, predetermined overhead rates are calculated for each activity and cost driver, just like we did using a plantwide or departmental overhead rate with volume-based cost drivers.

TopSail Construction: Activity-Based Costing

Activity	Total Estimated Cost	Cost Driver and Estimated Amount	Predetermined Overhead Rate
Inspections	$ 50,000	Number of inspections (1,400)	$35.71 per hour of inspection time
Purchasing	30,000	Number of purchase orders (1,200)	$25 per purchase order
Supervision	100,000	Hours of supervisor time (4,000)	$25 per supervisor hour
Material delivery and handling	225,000	Number of deliveries (1,200)	$187.50 per delivery
Processing change orders	$ 80,000	Number of change orders (500)	$160 per change order
Total overhead	$485,000		

The following table illustrates the total cost of a standard house and a custom house using an activity-based costing system.

Activity-Based Costing System

Cost	Standard House	Custom House
Direct materials	$ 75,000	$112,500
Direct labor	60,000	100,000
Inspections	714	3,571
Purchasing	750	1,500
Supervision	3,125	3,750
Material handling and delivery	5,625	11,250
Processing change orders	$ 1,600	$ 4,800
Total costs	$146,814	$237,371

TopSail Construction

If we compare the two methods of allocating overhead costs to standard and custom houses, we can see why volume-based allocation and activity-based costing resulted in different amounts of overhead being applied to each house and we can see the impact these differences could have on sales price decisions for management. Allocating overhead costs using an activity-based costing system results in greater allocations of overhead to the custom house because it consumes more of the purchasing, inspection, supervision, material handling, and processing change order activities than the standard house. Although the custom house was also allocated more overhead under the volume-based costing system, the amount is different (as is our rationale for the allocation). Under a traditional volume-based costing system, the custom house was allocated more overhead than the standard house simply because it consumed more direct labor hours. Remember that the custom house required 4,000 direct labor hours, whereas the standard house required only 2,400 direct labor hours. Notice that using volume-based costing resulted in overcosting the standard house and undercosting the custom house compared to costing under ABC.

One important aspect of ABC systems is the elimination of cross subsidies between products. Cross subsidies occur when high-volume products like the standard house are assigned more than their fair share of overhead costs. At the same time, more complicated low-volume products like the custom house are allocated too little overhead. This cross subsidy may make high-volume products appear unprofitable when they may not be, or it may make them appear to show less profit than they actually do. Activity-based costing systems eliminate the cross subsidy between high- and low-volume products.

 Key Concept: *Volume-based costing systems often result in overcosting high-volume products and undercosting low-volume products. This cross subsidy is eliminated by the use of ABC.*

Concept Question: *Under what circumstances would volume-based costing and activity-based costing result in exactly the same overhead allocation?*

Concept Answer: Volume-based costing and activity-based costing result in different allocations of overhead when products consume activities in different proportions. On the other hand, volume-based costing and activity-based costing result in the same allocations of overhead when products consume resources in the same proportions. For example, producing a standard house consumed 2,400 direct labor hours while producing a custom house consumed 4,000 direct labor hours (see the table on page 91). Based on this consumption of resources, the standard house was allocated 37.5 percent or $13,224 of overhead while the custom house was allocated 62.5 percent or $22,040 of overhead. If the standard house and custom house had consumed all resources related to inspections, purchase orders, supervision, deliveries, and processing change orders in the same proportion as they consumed direct labor (37.5 percent for the standard house and 62.5 percent for the custom house), the total overhead allocated to each house using volume-based costing and ABC would be exactly the same. ■

Although the differences may seem slight, consider the impact of the cost differences on TopSail's pricing policy. Under ABC, TopSail would price the standard house at $176,000 instead of $178,000 and the custom house at $285,000 instead of $281,500. In the very price conscious standard housing market, overpricing the standard house by $2,000 could result in a loss of sales, which could impact TopSail Construction's profit margin. Likewise, in the more flexible custom home market, TopSail could have likely priced its custom house at a higher price than that indicated by traditional costing methods.

As this example illustrates, the allocation of costs using activity-based costing is more accurate and reflects the consumption of costs based on the activities that drive them rather than on one volume-based cost driver. In addition to providing management with more accurate cost information for pricing decisions, it also affects a variety of other decisions discussed in Part II of this book.

ABC SYSTEMS IN SERVICE INDUSTRIES

Service providers currently make up the fastest growing segment of the U.S. economy employing almost 75 percent of the workforce. As service companies expand the scope and quality of services offered, the need for fast, accurate costing information becomes more important. Can ABC be used to cost services as well as products? Do the same principles that we learned for manufacturing companies apply to service businesses? The answer is yes! In fact, ABC is every bit as important for service providers as it is for manufacturing companies. Although ABC was developed for use primarily by manufacturing companies, it has gained widespread acceptance in the service sector.

LO4
Apply ABC systems to selling and administrative activities

IN THE NEWS

In a recent survey, 61 percent of nonmanufacturing companies (financial, nonprofit, utilities, and service organizations) reported adopting ABC compared to 45 percent of manufacturing companies.

Source: Krumwiede, "ABC: Why It's Tried and How It Succeeds," *Management Accounting,* April 1998.

However, implementing ABC in service companies is not without its problems. One common problem is that the type of work done in service companies tends to be non-repetitive. Unlike highly automated manufacturing companies, analyzing the activities of a service provider can be difficult when the activities differ greatly for each customer or service. In addition, service-oriented companies are likely to have proportionately more facility-level costs than do manufacturing companies. Remember from our earlier discussion that facility-level costs are allocated arbitrarily to goods and services (if at all).

ABC AND SELLING AND ADMINISTRATIVE ACTIVITIES

The principles of ABC can be applied to selling and administrative activities as well. Instead of computing the cost of a product or service, the goal is to determine the cost of providing a selling or administrative service. For example, a company might use ABC to determine the cost of providing payroll services. This information can be used to help management determine whether to continue processing payroll in-house or whether to outsource.

IN THE NEWS   www.usps.gov

The U.S. Post Office recently used activity-based costing to help determine the costs and benefits of allowing customers to pay using debit and credit cards. In this case, the Post Office focused on the impact of using debit and credit cards on customer satisfaction even though cost savings were also likely to be seen.

Source: Carter, Sedaghat, and Williams, "How ABC Changed the Post Office," *Management Accounting,* February 1998.

ABC AND JUST IN TIME (JIT)

LO5
Understand the application of ABC in a JIT environment

ABC can be used by companies employing traditional manufacturing techniques with inventory and by those utilizing just-in-time (JIT) production systems. JIT systems were described in Chapter 2 as production systems in which materials are purchased and products are produced just in time to be used in production or sold to customers. Because factories are typically redesigned in a JIT environment so that all machinery and equipment needed to make a product is available in one area (a manufacturing cell), overhead costs are more likely to be traced to products as unit-, batch-, or product-level costs in a JIT environment. Fewer overhead costs are likely to be considered facility-level costs requiring arbitrary allocation. Although utilizing JIT production techniques does not eliminate all facility-level costs, combining ABC and JIT should result in even more accurate product costing.

COST FLOWS AND ABC

The flow of costs from raw materials to work-in-process to finished goods and cost of goods sold is not affected by the implementation of activity-based costing. Although the existence of multiple overhead rates (rather than plantwide or departmental rates) may make the application of overhead more complex, the cost flows remain the same as that described in Chapter 2 for manufacturing companies with inventory, manufacturing companies operating in a JIT environment, service companies, and merchandising companies.

BENEFITS AND LIMITATIONS OF ABC

Because of the increase in global competition, companies must strive to achieve and sustain a competitive advantage. This requires organizations to continually improve performance in all aspects of their business operations. By focusing on continuous improvement, organizations can minimize scrap in the manufacturing process, reduce lead times for customer deliveries or vendor shipments, increase the quality of products and services produced, and control manufacturing and nonmanufacturing costs.

LO6
Evaluate the benefits and limitations of ABC systems

Activity-based costing systems provide more and more accurate cost information that focuses managers on opportunities for continuous improvement. Throughout their planning, operating, and control activities, managers use the information provided by ABC systems. In Chapter 1, planning was defined as the development of short- and long-term objectives and goals of an organization and an identification of the resources needed to achieve them. Using ABC in the budgeting process provides more accurate estimates of these resources.

One of the biggest advantages of ABC is the increased accuracy of cost information it provides for day-to-day decision making by managers (operating decisions). Managers use ABC information to make better decisions related to adding or dropping products, making or buying components used in the manufacturing process, marketing and pricing strategies, and so forth.

ABC also provides benefits related to the control function of managers. Costs that appear to be indirect using volume-based costing systems now are traced to specific activities using cost drivers. This allows managers to better see what causes costs to be incurred leading to better control.

However, ABC is not for everyone and the benefits of increased accuracy don't come without costs. Accumulating, tracking, and assigning costs to products and services using ABC requires the use of multiple activity pools and cost drivers. High measurement costs associated with ABC systems are a significant limitation. Companies may decide that the measurement costs associated with implementing ABC systems are greater than the expected benefit from having more accurate cost information. For example, if the market dictates prices, such as with commodity products, and companies have little control over pricing their products, highly reliable product costs may not be necessary for pricing. However, ABC may still prove valuable for planning and cost-reduction efforts.

IN THE NEWS

It has been reported that 54 percent of companies using ABC are using it for decision making outside the accounting function and 89 percent of companies using ABC say it was worth the implementation costs.
Source: Krumwiede, "ABC: Why It's Tried and How It Succeeds, *Management Accounting,* April 1998.

In general, companies that have a high potential for cost distortions are more likely to benefit from ABC. Cost distortions are likely when companies make **diverse products** that consume resources differently. Products that vary a great deal in complexity are typically diverse, but differences in color or other seemingly minor differences in products can lead to product diversity when these differences materially change the products and affect the resources they consume.

Are the standard houses and custom houses built by TopSail Construction diverse products?

Concept Question: *A furniture manufacturer makes hand-made custom dining room tables and chairs. Both products are very labor intensive and are made using the same saws, drills, lathes, sanders, and other equipment. Are the tables and chairs diverse products?*

Concept Answer: Although the products are certainly different, they are probably not diverse. They probably consume overhead resources in similar proportions. However, if they were made using different equipment and manufacturing processes, they probably would be considered diverse. ■

Companies that have a large proportion of non-unit-level costs are also likely to benefit from ABC. Remember, unit-level costs vary with the number of units produced and can be allocated with reasonable accuracy using volume-based cost systems and drivers. On the other hand, volume-based costing systems can result in distortions when allocating batch-, product-, and facility-level costs.

Companies that have relatively high proportions of overhead compared to direct materials and direct labor are likely to benefit from ABC as well. This is often the case with highly automated manufacturing companies or companies that have adopted JIT techniques. Note that service companies, such as law or CPA firms, may also have high overhead costs compared to direct material and direct labor and likewise may benefit from the implementation of ABC.

Activity-Based Management and ABC

Although activity-based costing focuses on allocating overhead costs to products based on activities, **activity-based management (ABM)** focuses on managing activities to reduce costs and make better decisions. As mentioned in the previous section, one of the benefits of ABC is that it makes managers more aware of exactly what causes costs to be incurred. For example, the number of different parts and supplies used might drive costs incurred in ordering parts and supplies. This knowledge allows managers to take steps to reduce those costs by redesigning products to use similar or fewer parts.

 Key Concept: *Activity-based management focuses on managing activities to reduce costs and make better decisions.*

In the News	**www.daimlerchrysler.com**

Since implementing ABC in 1991, Chrysler estimates that it has saved hundreds of millions of dollars by simplifying product designs.
Source: Ness and Cucuzza, "Tapping the Full Potential of ABC," *Harvard Business Review,* July 1995.

ABM and the Value Chain

LO7
Understand activity-based management (ABM) and the value chain

One of the goals of ABM is to identify and eliminate activities and costs that don't add value to goods and services. In today's competitive business environment, customers demand high-quality products and services, and organizations that supply these products and services must strive to make sure that each step in the production process adds value to the product or service. The value chain (see Chapter 2) is the term used to describe this linked set of value-creating activities. These activities include everything from research and development to customer service after the sale (see Exhibit 4-2) and include the following:

1. *Research and development.* The creation and development of ideas that lead to new products and services.
2. *Product development.* The detailed development of the research and development ideas that results in new products and services.

Without a soul, there's just a shell. Without passion, these would just be cars.

Passion is such a strong emotion. It causes us to live, breathe and sweat our hearts out for the things we care most about. For Chrysler, it is about creating extraordinary cars. Cars born from breakthrough design and brought to life through innovative engineering. It's the passion in our cars that stirs you and your soul to respond. For more information, call us at 1.800.CHRYSLER or visit our Web site at www.chrysler.com.

ENGINEERED TO BE GREAT CARS **CHRYSLER**

3. *Production.* The use of resources to produce a product or provide a service.

4. *Marketing.* Providing potential customers with information about the attributes of products or services available that results in customers purchasing the products or services.

5. *Distribution.* The actual delivery of products or services to customers.

6. *Customer service.* Providing customers with needed support or service during and after the sale.

VALUE-ADDED AND NON-VALUE-ADDED ACTIVITIES

However, not all activities create value. **Non-value-added activities** don't add value to the finished product or service. Non-value-added activities are those that can be eliminated without affecting the quality or performance of a product. Examples of non-value-added activities include storage of materials, work-in-process and finished goods, moving of materials and parts from storage to the factory in a manufacturing company, idle time of employees while waiting for work, and so on. Likewise, packaging products (unless done for health/safety reasons or to make a product more appealing to a consumer) might be considered a non-value-added activity. Companies that have successfully implemented quality improvement programs resulting in extremely low numbers of defective products may

EXHIBIT 4-2 The Value Chain

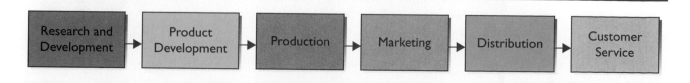

consider quality inspections as a non-value-added activity. These companies would argue that if products are designed correctly and production processes are monitored and controlled effectively, quality of products will be assured throughout the process. Consequently, inspections of finished products are redundant and don't add value to the product.

Can you think of a situation in which you would consider quality inspections to increase the value of a product or service?

To be competitive, companies must strive to eliminate or minimize non-value-added activities. Remember that activities cause costs. So reducing or eliminating non-value-added activities would correspondingly reduce costs. The use of JIT production techniques can eliminate (or at least minimize) non-value-added costs associated with inventory storage, product movements, and other activities involved with ordering, receiving, and handling inventory. Likewise, the implementation of total quality management (TQM) programs can significantly reduce non-value-added costs associated with quality inspections, resolving customer complaints due to defective or poor quality products and services, recalls, warranties, and so on. TQM is discussed more fully in Chapter 12.

SUCCESSFUL IMPLEMENTATION OF ABC AND ABM

Utilizing activity-based costing information to reduce costs, eliminate non-value-added activities, and manage more effectively requires the cooperation of all functional areas of a business organization and top management.

CROSS FUNCTIONAL APPLICATIONS
Perhaps nowhere else is cooperation among accountants, marketing managers, production managers, human resource managers, and finance managers more critical than in the implementation of activity-based costing and management systems.

Without active involvement in the process, marketing managers may balk when price changes are thrust upon them, production managers may be hesitant to change a production process used successfully for many years, and human resource managers may criticize the motivational and behavioral implications of suggested changes. Successful implementation also requires a strong commitment from upper management in terms of vocal support, resources provided, and prioritization among the company's other initiatives such as TQM and JIT.

The full benefits of ABC and ABM require a long-term commitment by management. The benefits of ABC and ABM are simply not realized overnight, and management must be willing to focus on the long-term benefits that are possible through their implementation.

 Key Concept: *The successful implementation of ABC and ABM requires a long-term commitment by top management and the cooperation of all functional areas of a business organization.*

MANAGEMENT ACTIONS AND DECISIONS
www.andersen.com

According to Mike Riggins, an associate partner with Andersen Consulting in its Utilities Practice Division, companies believe that ABC and ABM give them a competitive advantage in their market space. Companies in the service sector have been embracing ABC/ABM in record numbers over the past decade. This trend is especially true of companies whose industry groups have encountered great changes due to deregulation (i.e., airlines, telecommunications, utilities, etc.).

In working with various large electric utilities across the United States, Riggins has seen many different levels of ABC/ABM imple-

MIKE RIGGINS
Andersen Consulting

(continued)

mentations and utilization. Companies that have been the most effective at maximizing their investment in ABC/ABM have usually followed a life cycle that involves three distinct focus areas, as shown in Exhibit 4-3.

ABM is not a "flavor of the month" approach to cost management, and as such it requires lasting lifestyle changes for the organization. Implemented properly, significant benefits (cost reductions as well as revenue enhancements) can be recognized in each phase of the ABM life cycle. Put simply, ABM becomes a way of life for an organization, is ingrained as a part of the organization's day-to-day operations, and becomes a catalyst helping move companies toward continuous improvement and market leadership.

EXHIBIT 4-3 The ABM Life Cycle

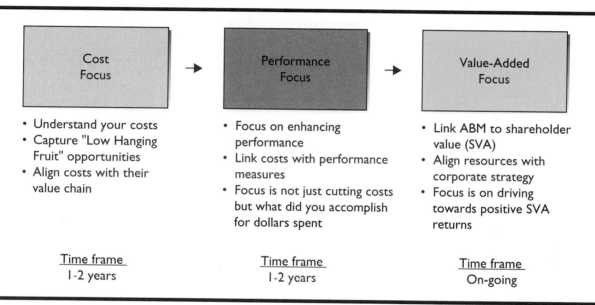

Cost Focus	Performance Focus	Value-Added Focus
• Understand your costs • Capture "Low Hanging Fruit" opportunities • Align costs with their value chain	• Focus on enhancing performance • Link costs with performance measures • Focus is not just cutting costs but what did you accomplish for dollars spent	• Link ABM to shareholder value (SVA) • Align resources with corporate strategy • Focus is on driving towards positive SVA returns
<u>Time frame</u> 1-2 years	<u>Time frame</u> 1-2 years	<u>Time frame</u> On-going

SUMMARY OF KEY CONCEPTS

- Unit-level costs are incurred each time a unit is produced. Batch-level costs are incurred each time a batch of goods is produced. Product-level costs are incurred as needed to support the production of each different type of product. Facility-level costs simply sustain a facility's general manufacturing process. (p. 87)

- Overhead costs are assigned to products in an ABC system in two stages. In Stage 1, activities are identified and overhead costs are traced to each activity. In Stage 2, cost drivers are determined for each activity and costs are assigned to products. (p. 87)

- Volume-based costing systems often result in overcosting high-volume products and undercosting low-volume products. This cross subsidy is eliminated by the use of ABC. (p. 95)

- Activity-based management focuses on managing activities to reduce costs and make better decisions. (p. 98)

- The successful implementation of ABC and ABM requires a long-term commitment by top management and the cooperation of all functional areas of a business organization. (p. 100)

KEY DEFINITIONS

Activity-based costing (ABC) A system of allocating overhead costs that assumes that activities, not volume of production, cause overhead costs to be incurred (p. 87)

Activities Procedures or processes that cause work to be accomplished (p. 87)

Diverse Products Products that consume resources in different proportions (p. 97)

Activity-based management (ABM) A system that focuses on managing activities to reduce costs and make better decisions (p. 98)

Non-value-added activities Activities that can be eliminated without affecting the quality or performance of a product (p. 99)

CONCEPT REVIEW

1. Discuss the impact of robotics on today's manufacturing environment.

2. Is product cost information absolutely accurate? Why or why not?

3. Discuss the impact of information technology on accounting systems.

4. Discuss the importance of choosing the right cost driver and the potential impact of choosing the wrong cost driver.

5. What are the four categories of overhead costs in Cooper's hierarchy? Briefly define each.

6. Define activity-based costing.

7. Will activity-based costing benefit every business? Why or why not?

8. What are the two stages of cost allocation in an activity-based costing system? Briefly define each.

9. Define the term *activities* as used in activity-based costing systems.

10. What exactly are cross subsidies between products? How can they be controlled?

11. How do activity-based costing systems provide better information for continuous improvement in manufacturing?

12. Discuss the differences in activity-based costing systems for selling and administration activities.

13. Discuss activity-based costing systems in service businesses. How are they different from those used in manufacturing businesses?

14. Why is it important for management to distinguish between value-added and non-value-added activities?

15. Give examples of some common non-value-added activities.

16. The decision process to choose a cost driver can be very important. Use the decision model introduced in Chapter 1 to discuss the process one might go through to choose a cost driver.

APPLICATION OF CONCEPTS

17. The Fancy Drapery Company sells draperies suited for large or small windows. The company has decided to adopt an activity-based costing system. Last year the company incurred $650,000 in overhead costs related to the following activities:

Activity	Allocation Base	Overhead Cost
Purchasing	number of purchase orders	$250,000
Receiving	number of shipments received	150,000
Sales	number of sales orders	250,000

The activities for large and small window draperies were as follows:

	Large	Small
Purchase orders	5,000	10,000
Shipments received	7,500	12,500
Sales orders	6,500	8,500

Required

A. What is the overhead rate for purchasing?

B. What is the overhead rate for receiving?

C. What is the overhead rate for sales?

D. How much of the purchasing overhead should be assigned to the large draperies?

E. How much of the purchasing overhead should be assigned to the small draperies?

F. How much of the receiving overhead should be assigned to the large draperies?

G. How much of the receiving overhead should be assigned to the small draperies?

H. How much of the sales overhead should be assigned to the large draperies?

I. How much of the sales overhead should be assigned to the small draperies?

J. If a customer requested a bid on a specially designed drapery that would probably require five purchase orders, how much purchasing overhead would you include in the bid?

18. The Bouncy Baby Crib Mattress Company sells large and small mattresses and is considering the adoption of an activity-based costing system. Last year the company incurred $800,000 in overhead costs related to the following activities:

Activity	Allocation Base	Overhead Cost
Purchasing	number of purchase orders	$400,000
Receiving	number of shipments received	300,000
Sales	number of sales orders	100,000

During the year, 15,000 purchase orders were issued (7,500 each for large and small mattresses), 20,000 shipments were received (12,500 for large and 7,500 for small), and 25,000 sales orders (15,000 for large and 10,000 for small) were processed.

Required

Determine the amount of overhead that should be assigned to each product using activity-based costing.

19. The following overhead cost information is available for the Christopher Corporation for the year ended June 30, 2002:

Activity	Allocation Base	Overhead Cost
Purchasing	number of purchase orders	$400,000
Receiving	number of shipments received	100,000
Machine setups	number of setups	400,000
Quality control	number of inspections	150,000

During the year, 30,000 purchase orders were issued, 25,000 shipments were received, machine setups numbered 2,700, and 22,000 inspections were conducted. A total of 11,000 direct labor hours were charged to various products. The corporate managers are trying to decide whether they should stick with a traditional allocation method, where overhead is allocated based upon direct labor hours, or switch to an activity-based costing system.

Required

A. Determine the overhead rate based upon direct labor hours.

B. Determine the overhead rate for each of the activities.

C. A job card for one particular batch of products had the following specifications:

Direct labor hours	7
Purchase orders	7
Shipments received	10
Setups	3
Inspections	3

Compute the estimated overhead allocated to this batch under traditional allocation and activity-based costing.

D. Are there any differences in your two answers from Part C? If so, why? Which method do you think is better? Why?

20. The following cost information is available for the Brenda and Steve Corporation for the year ended June 30, 2004:

Activity	Allocation Base	Overhead Cost
Purchasing	number of purchase orders	$125,000
Receiving	number of shipments received	60,000
Machine setups	number of setups	200,000
Quality control	number of inspections	105,000
Direct material	$15 per unit for deluxe items; $11 per unit for regular items	
Direct labor	$18 per hour (including benefits)	

During the year, 30,000 purchase orders were issued, 20,000 shipments were received, machine setups numbered 2,500 and 25,000 inspections were conducted. 11,500 direct labor hours were charged to various products.

Required

A. The corporate managers are trying to decide whether they should stick with a traditional allocation method, where overhead is allocated based upon direct labor hours, or switch to an activity based costing system. Determine the overhead rate based upon direct labor hours and the overhead rate for each of the activities.

B. A job card for one particular batch of 100 deluxe units had the following specifications:

Direct labor hours	7
Purchase orders	7
Shipments received	10
Setups	3
Inspections	3

Compute the estimated overhead allocated to this batch under traditional allocation and activity-based costing.

C. Which costing method do you think is better? Why?

21. The following cost information is available for the Brenda and Steve Corporation for the year ended June 30, 2004:

Activity	Allocation Base	Overhead Cost
Purchasing	number of purchase orders	$150,000
Receiving	number of shipments received	50,000
Machine setups	number of setups	250,000
Quality control	number of inspections	125,000
Direct material	$14 per unit for deluxe items; $10 per unit for regular items	
Direct labor	$20 per hour (including benefits)	

During the year, 30,000 purchase orders were issued, 20,000 shipments were received, machine setups numbered 2,500, and 25,000 inspections were conducted.

Required

A customer has contacted Brenda and Steve Corporation requesting comparative bids for an order of 100 deluxe units and 100 regular units. Brenda and Steve estimate the following activities related to the bids:

	Regular	Deluxe
Direct labor hours	7	10
Purchase orders	7	7
Shipments received	10	10
Setups	3	4
Inspections	3	4

Compute the bids for deluxe and regular units.

22. Surfs Up manufactures surfboards. The company produces two different models of boards, the small kahuna and the big kahuna. Data regarding the two products follow:

Product	Direct Labor Hours per Unit	Annual Production	Total Direct Labor Hours
Big	1.875	8,000 Boards	15,000
Small	.875	40,000 Boards	35,000

Additional information about Surfs Up:

The big board requires $75 in direct materials per unit while the small board requires $40. The direct labor rate for the company is $13 per hour. The company has always used direct labor hours as the activity base for applying overhead to product. Manufacturing overhead is estimated to be $1,575,000 per year. The big board is more complex to manufacture than the small board because it requires more machine time.

Because of the big board's requirement for the additional machine work, the company controller, Tim Guglielmo, is considering the use of activity-based costing to apply overhead to product. Tim has identified three separate activity centers in the manufacture of the boards.

Activity Center	Cost Driver	Traceable Costs	Annual Total	TRANSACTIONS Big	Small
Machine setups	Number of setups	$100,000	225	100	125
Special design	Design hours	$225,000	1,000	900	100
Production	Direct labor hours	$900,000	50,000	15,000	35,000
Machining	Machine hours	$350,000	11,000	10,000	1,000

Required

Assume that Surfs Up continues to use direct labor hours as the base for applying overhead cost to product.

A. Compute the predetermined overhead rate.

B. Determine the cost to produce one unit of each product.

Assume that the company decides to use activity-based costing to apply overhead cost to product.

C. Classify the activity centers into the four levels defined by Cooper: unit, batch, products, and facility.

D. Compute the overhead rate for each activity center. Also compute the amount of overhead cost that would be applied to each product.

E. Determine the cost to produce one unit of each product.

F. Explain why overhead cost shifted from the high-volume product to the low-volume product under activity-based costing.

G. Discuss the concept of cross subsidies between products as it applies in this case.

23. David Hall Inc. manufactures plastic and ceramic outdoor eating dishes. The company's western plant has changed from a labor-intensive operation to a robotics environment. As a result, management is considering changing from a direct-labor-based overhead rate to an activity-based costing system. The controller has chosen the following activity cost pools and cost drivers for factory overhead:

Overhead Cost		Cost Driver	Number
Purchase orders	$200,000	Number of orders	25,000 orders
Setup costs	$300,000	Number of setups	15,000 setups
Testing costs	$420,000	Number of tests	18,000 tests
Machine maintenance	$800,000	Machine hours	50,000 hours

Required

A. Compute the overhead rate for each cost driver.

B. An order for 50 ceramic dish sets had the following requirements:

Number of purchase orders	3
Number of setups	20
Number of product tests	7
Machine hours	150

How much overhead would be assigned to this order?

C. Would you expect the new ABC system to allocate a different amount of overhead per set?

D. Discuss why using an ABC system could provide better information to decision makers regarding the setting of a sales price. What other advantages might David Hall Inc. realize from the new ABC system?

24. Tom Hall Inc. manufactures sailboats and has two major categories of overhead: material handling and quality inspection. The costs expected for these categories for the coming year are as follows:

Material handling	$100,000
Quality inspection	$300,000
Total number of material moves	500
Total number of inspections	200

The plant currently applies overhead using direct labor hours as an activity base. The estimated amount of direct labor hours is 50,000.

Chris Hamilton, the plant manager, has been asked to submit a bid and has assembled the following data on the proposed job:

Direct materials	$3,700
Direct labor (1,000 hours)	$7,000
Overhead	?
Number of material moves	10
Number of inspections	5

Chris has been told that many similar companies use an activity-based approach to assign overhead to jobs. Before submitting his bid, he wants to assess the effects of this alternative approach.

Required

A. Compute the total cost of the potential job using traditional overhead application (i.e., direct labor hours to assign overhead).

B. Compute the total cost of the job using activity-based costing with the new cost drivers to allocate overhead (i.e., the number of material moves to allocate material handling costs and the number of inspections to allocate the quality inspection costs).

C. Discuss the difference and what impact the change might have on the decision regarding the bid price.

D. Using the decision model presented in Chapter 1, complete the following tasks:

(1) Define the decision problem Chris faces.

(2) Identify the key objectives in the decision problem.

(3) Identify the different options that Chris has in solving this decision problem.

Step 1	DEFINE THE PROBLEM
Step 2	IDENTIFY OBJECTIVES
Step 3	IDENTIFY AND ANALYZE AVAILABLE OPTIONS

25. Jon Haufe Inc. manufactures TVs that are specifically designed for use in sports bars. The company has budgeted manufacturing overhead costs for the year as follows:

Type of Cost	Cost Pools
Electric power	$2,500,000
Inspection	1,500,000
Budgeted overhead costs	4,000,000

Under a traditional cost system, the company estimated the budgeted capacity for machine hours to be 40,000 hours. Jon Haufe Inc. is considering changing to an activity-based cost system. Thus, the following estimates were provided:

Type of Cost	Activity-Based Cost Drivers
Electric power	50,000 kilowatt hours
Inspection	10,000 inspections

The following information was provided concerning the production of 2,000 units of model #1003:

Direct materials cost	$50,000
Direct labor costs	$75,000
Machine hours	10,000
Direct labor hours	5,000
Electric power—kilowatt hours	20,000
Number of inspections	1,000

The accounting department has provided management with the following report:

Traditional Costing System

Overhead rate per machine hour	$ 100
Manufacturing costs for 2,000 units of #1003:	
Direct materials	$ 50,000
Direct labor	75,000
Applied overhead	$1,000,000
Total	$1,125,000
Cost per unit	$ 562.50

Activity-Based Costing System

Electric power overhead rate	$50/kilowatt hour
Inspection cost overhead rate	$150/per inspection
Manufacturing costs for 2,000 units of #1003:	
Direct materials	$ 50,000
Direct labor	75,000
Applied overhead	$1,150,000
Total	$1,275,000
Cost per unit	$ 637.50

Required

A. Explain the difference between activity-based costing and conventional costing methods and how ABC might enhance the financial reporting of Jon Haufe Inc.

B. If Jon Haufe Inc. were setting a sales price based on a 20 percent markup, how would profit be affected if the company *did not* change to an ABC system?

26. Grandma's Rocking Chair Company produces 1,000 units of Rocking Chair A and 1,000 units of Rocking Chair B. Currently, the company uses a traditional cost system, but it is considering an activity-based cost system. It wants to know what the cost of inspection would be for both products assuming the following:

	Product A	Product B	Total
Number of inspections	2	10	12
Cost per inspection	$1,000	$1,000	$12,000
Direct labor hours per unit	3,000	2,000	5,000

Required

A. Under traditional costing, how much of the $12,000 inspection cost would be allocated to Product A and Product B, respectively?

B. Using activity-based costing, how much of the $12,000 inspection cost would be allocated to Product A and Product B, respectively?

C. Discuss what caused the difference. Would this difference affect management decisions? How? What method is more accurate? Why?

27. Worth Hawes Manufacturing has just completed a major change in its quality control (QC) process. Previously, QC inspectors at the end of each major process had reviewed products, and the company's 10 QC inspectors were charged as direct labor to the operation or job. In an effort to improve efficiency and quality, Worth Hawes Manufacturing purchased a computer video QC system for $250,000. The system consists of a minicomputer, 15 video cameras, other peripheral hardware, and software.

The new system uses cameras stationed by QC engineers at key points in the production process. Each time an operation changes or there is a new operation, the cameras are moved, and a QC engineer loads a new master picture into the computer. The camera takes pictures of the unit in process, and the computer compares them to the picture of a "good" unit. Any differences are sent to a QC engineer who removes the bad units and discusses the flaws with the production supervisors. The new system has replaced the 10 QC inspectors with 2 QC engineers.

The operating costs of the new QC system, including the salaries of the QC engineers, have been included as overhead in calculating the company's plantwide factory overhead rate, which is based on direct labor dollars.

The company's president is confused. His vice president of production has told him how efficient the new system is, yet there is a large increase in the factory overhead rate. The computation of the rate before and after is as follows:

	Before	**After**
Budgeted overhead	$1,900,000	$2,100,000
Budgeted direct labor	1,000,000	700,000
Budgeted overhead rate	190%	300%

"Three hundred percent," lamented the president. "How can we compete with such a high factory overhead rate?"

Required

A. Discuss the development of factory overhead rates. Why do we need factory overhead rates and how are they computed? Discuss the accuracy of the computation of a factory overhead rate.

B. Explain why the increase in the overhead rate should not have a negative impact on Worth Hawes Manufacturing.

C. Explain, in the greatest detail possible, how Worth Hawes Manufacturing could change its overhead accounting system to eliminate confusion over product costs.

D. Discuss how an activity-based costing system might benefit Worth Hawes Manufacturing.

E. Use the decision model presented in Chapter 1 to answer the following questions.

> **Step 1** DEFINE THE PROBLEM

(1) Present a description of the decision problem facing the company in choosing a new costing system.

> **Step 2** IDENTIFY OBJECTIVES

(2) What are the key objectives involved in the decision problem as defined here?

(3) What option does the company have in this decision problem?

> **Step 3** IDENTIFY AND ANALYZE AVAILABLE OPTIONS

28. The Teresa Heine Company manufactures multimedia equipment designed to be sold to universities. The company's southeastern plant has changed from a labor-intensive operation to a robotics environment. As a result, management is considering changing from a direct-labor-based overhead rate to an activity-based cost method. The controller has chosen the following activity cost pools and cost drivers for the factory overhead:

	Overhead Cost	**Cost Driver**	**Annual Cost Driver**
Purchase orders	$200,000	number of orders	10,000 orders
Setup costs	$ 25,000	number of setups	5,000 setups
Testing costs	$ 48,000	number of tests	6,000 tests
Machine maintenance	$350,000	machine hours	10,000 hours

Required

A. Compute the overhead rate for each cost driver.

B. An order for 1,000 video projectors had the following requirements:

Number of purchase orders	3
Number of setups	5
Number of product tests	20
Machine hours	1500

How much overhead would be assigned to this order?

C. What could management do to reduce the overhead costs assigned to these video projectors? What would be the impact on company net income of reducing overhead assigned to the video projectors?

D. Use the decision model presented in Chapter 1 to answer the following questions:

> **Step 1** DEFINE THE PROBLEM

(1) Define the decision problem faced by Teresa Heine Company in Part C.

> **Step 2** IDENTIFY OBJECTIVES

(2) What are the company's key objectives in solving this decision problem?

Step 3 — IDENTIFY AND ANALYZE AVAILABLE OPTIONS

Step 4 — SELECT THE BEST OPTION

(3) What options are available to the company in solving this decision problem?

(4) What options do you think are best and why?

29. The Law firm of Duffy and Rowe provides legal services for clients. During the year, corporate clients required 5,000 hours of legal services, whereas individuals required 3,000 hours. The firm has traditionally used direct labor hours to assign overhead. However, Duffy believes services to businesses cost more than services to individuals and wishes to adopt activity-based costing. The firm's revenues and costs for the year are as follows:

	Corporate	Individual	Total
Revenue	$150,000	$150,000	$300,000
Expenses			
Lawyers' salaries	$100,000	$ 50,000	$150,000
Overhead			
Filing	$ 10,000		
Quality control	5,000		
Data entry	25,000		
Total overhead	$ 40,000		

Rowe has kept records of the following data for use in the new activity-based costing system:

		ACTIVITY LEVEL	
Overhead Cost	Cost Driver	Corporate	Individual
Filing	Number of clients	5	5
Quality control	Number of hours spent	75	25
Data entry	Number of pages entered	1,000	1,500

Accounting has prepared the following pro forma income statements:

Traditional Costing Income Statement

	Corporate	Individual	Total
Revenue	$150,000	$150,000	$300,000
Expenses			
Salaries	100,000	50,000	150,000
Overhead	$ 25,000	$ 15,000	$ 40,000
Total costs	$125,000	$ 65,000	$190,000
Operating profit	$ 25,000	$ 85,000	$110,000

Income Statement Using Activity-Based Costing

	Corporate	Individual	Total
Revenue	$150,000	$150,000	$300,000
Expenses			
Salaries	100,000	50,000	150,000
Overhead			
Filing			
($1,000 × 5)	$ 5,000	$ 5,000	$ 10,000
Quality costs			
$50 × 75	3,750		
$50 × 25		1,250	

Data entry

($10 × 1,000)	10,000		
($10 × 1,500)		15,000	
Total overhead	$ 18,750	$ 21,250	$ 40,000
Total costs	$118,750	$ 71,250	$190,000
Profit	$ 31,250	$ 78,750	$110,000

Required

Recalculate the computation of overhead in the two income statements. Include the calculation of the individual overhead rates. Discuss the best way to allocate costs in this example and include the approximate difference in profits between corporate and individual clients. Why would activity-based costing be preferred as a cost allocation method?

BIG AL'S

| CONTINUING CASE | BIG AL'S PIZZA INC. |

As you will recall from Chapter 2, Big Al's expects to incur the following overhead costs in Year 1. Costs are expected to increase by 5 percent in Year 2.

Year 1 Overhead Costs (Estimated)

Rent on Production Facility	$1,000/month
Utilities	$1,500/month
Indirect Labor:	
Supervisors	$3,500 per month (including fringe benefits)
Other indirect labor	$2,000 per month (including fringe benefits)
Other overhead:	
Indirect material	$2,500/month
Maintenance costs	$1,500/month
Miscellaneous factory costs	$2,000/month
Equipment (lease cost)	$2,500/month

Lee Dworsky, the accounting manager at Big Al's has just returned from a conference on activity-based costing and thinks that Big Al's should consider implementing an activity-based costing (ABC) system at the beginning of Year 2. Lee has identified five primary activities taking place in the production facility at Big Al's, has traced overhead costs to each activity, and has identified a cost driver for each activity as follows:

Year 2 Overhead Costs (Estimated)

Activity	Monthly Overhead Cost	Cost Driver
Material delivery and handling	$4,410	Number of shipments
Assembly of pizzas	$5,670	Direct labor hours
Packaging	$1,260	Number of pizzas
Storage of materials	$3,150	Refrigerator space
Quality inspections	$2,835	Number of inspections

The estimated activity for each cost driver is:

Cost Driver	Meat Pizza (350,000 pizzas)	Veggie Pizza (25,000 pizzas)	Total
Number of material shipments	52	104	156
Direct labor hours	?	?	?
Number of pizzas	350,000	25,000	415,000
Refrigerator space (cubic feet)	2,500	700	3,200
Number of inspections	75,000	3,000	78,000

Required

A. Using the overhead categories identified above (for Year 1), classify Big Al's overhead costs as unit level, batch level, product level, or facility level.

B. Based on information provided in Chapters 2 and 3, calculate the number of direct labor hours expected to be incurred in manufacturing 385,000 meat pizzas and 30,000 veggie pizzas.

C. Using the activities and drivers above, calculate a predetermined overhead rate for each activity.

D. How much estimated overhead would be allocated to a meat and veggie pizza using ABC?

E. Compare the estimated overhead allocation using ABC to the estimated overhead allocation using direct labor hours or number of pizzas.

F. What are some of the advantages and disadvantages of using ABC in this case?

G. Would you suggest that Big Al's adopt an ABC system?

Part II

THE NATURE OF COSTS IN DECISION MAKING

Chapter 5

THE NATURE OF COSTS

Study Tools

A Review of the Previous Chapter

Chapter 4 completed the first part of the book dealing with the costing of products and services. Up to this point we have focused our attention on methods used to cost products and services, the difficulties that arise in product costing, and the decisions faced by managers in reacting to those difficulties.

A Preview of This Chapter

In this chapter we examine the nature of costs. Students are introduced to concepts of cost behavior, relevant costs, and the impact of income taxes and the time value of money on costs and decision making.

Key concepts include:
- Costs behave in predictable ways.
- Within the relevant range, fixed costs are constant in total and vary per unit, variable costs vary in total and are constant per unit, and mixed costs vary in total and vary per unit.
- It can be misleading to always view variable costs as relevant and fixed costs as not relevant.
- Managers must consider the impact of taxes on decisions.
- Managers must consider the time value of money when making long-term decisions.

A Preview of Upcoming Chapters

In Chapter 6, the concept of cost behavior is developed further and students are introduced to a variety of tools (contribution margin ratio, operating leverage, break-even) used in CVP analysis. Chapter 7 extends the discussion of relevant costs and examines a number of decisions made by managers in their day-to-day activities. Chapter 8 examines the use of time value of money tools in long-term (capital budgeting) decisions.

LEARNING OBJECTIVES

After studying the material in this chapter, you should be able to:

LO1 Understand the nature and behavior of fixed, variable, and mixed costs

LO2 Analyze mixed costs using regression analysis and the high-low method

LO3 Understand the concept of relevant costs and apply the concept to decision making

LO4 Understand the impact of income taxes on costs and decision making

LO5 Understand the time value of money and its impact on costs and decision making

Understanding the nature of costs is of vital importance to managers. Understanding how costs behave, whether costs are relevant to specific decisions, how costs are affected by income taxes, and how to adjust costs incurred in different periods for the time value of money allows managers to determine the impact of changing costs and other factors on a variety of decisions. This chapter introduces concepts and tools that will be used in Chapters 6 through 8. Chapter 5 begins with a definition of cost behavior and illustrates the concepts of fixed costs, variable costs, and mixed costs. Next, the chapter revisits the concept of relevant costs (introduced in Chapter 1) as they apply to variable and fixed costs. The chapter also describes the impact of income taxes on costs and examines the effect of the time value of money on costs incurred in different time periods. ■

INTRODUCTION

In Part I we defined and determined the cost of a product or service. We now focus our attention on the nature of those costs and how they are used in decision making. While some costs may increase or decrease as production volume changes, whereas other costs remain stable, specific costs behave in predictable ways as volume changes. This concept of predictable **cost behavior** based on volume is very important to the effective use of accounting information for managerial decision making.

 Key Concept: *Costs behave in predictable ways.*

THE BEHAVIOR OF FIXED AND VARIABLE COSTS

LO1
Understand the nature and behavior of fixed, variable, and mixed costs

Fixed costs are costs that remain the same in total but vary per unit when production volume changes. Facility-level costs like rent, depreciation of a factory building, the salary of a plant manager, insurance, and property taxes are likely to be fixed costs. Summarizing this cost behavior, fixed costs stay the same in total but vary when expressed on a per-unit basis.

Rent is a good example. If the cost to rent a factory building is $10,000 per year and 5,000 units of product are produced, then the rent per unit is $2.00 ($10,000/5,000). If production volume decreases to 2,500 units per year, the cost per unit will increase to $4.00 ($10,000/2,500). If production volume increases to 7,500 units, the cost per unit decreases to $1.33 ($10,000/7,500) per unit. However, the total rent remains $10,000 per year.

On the other hand, **variable costs** vary in direct proportion to changes in production volume but are fixed when expressed as per-unit amounts. As production increases, variable costs increase in direct proportion to the change in volume, and as production decreases, variable costs decrease in direct proportion to the change in volume. Examples

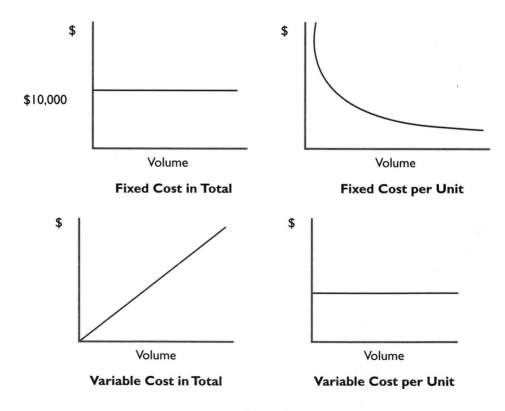

Fixed Cost in Total

Fixed Cost per Unit

Variable Cost in Total

Variable Cost per Unit

include direct material, direct labor (if paid per unit of output), and other unit-level costs like factory supplies, energy costs to run factory machinery, and so on.

Strictly speaking, a cost that varies in direct proportion to changes in volume requires a linear (straight-line) relationship between the cost and volume. However, in reality costs may behave in a curvilinear fashion. Average costs or cost per unit may increase or decrease as production increases. For example, utility costs per kilowatt-hour may decrease at higher levels of electricity use (and production). Managerial accountants typically get around this problem by assuming that the relationship between the cost and volume is linear within the relevant range of production. In other words, the cost per unit is assumed to remain constant over the relevant range. The **relevant range** is the normal range of production that can be expected for a particular product and company. The relevant range can also be viewed as the volume of production where the fixed and variable cost relationship holds true. As you can see in Exhibit 5-1, within this narrower range of production, a curvilinear cost can be approximated by a linear relationship between the cost and volume.

APPLICATION IN BUSINESS

Although direct labor is often treated as a variable cost, in reality it may behave more like a fixed cost in many companies due to the negotiation of employment contracts with unions. For example, airlines may agree to employment contracts for pilots and flight attendants that guarantee a minimum number of hours each week. This means that even if they are not working (flying), the costs are still there. If they were only paid for actual hours worked and not guaranteed a minimum salary, the cost would be considered a variable cost.

Consider the behavior of direct material costs as production increases and decreases. If the manufacture of a standard classroom desk requires $20 of direct material (wood, hardware, etc.), the total direct material costs incurred will increase or decrease proportionately with increases and decreases in production volume. If 5,000 desks are produced, the total direct material cost will be $100,000 (5,000 × $20). If production volume is increased to 7,500 units (a 50 percent increase), direct material costs will also increase 50

EXHIBIT 5-1   Curvilinear Costs and the Relevant Range

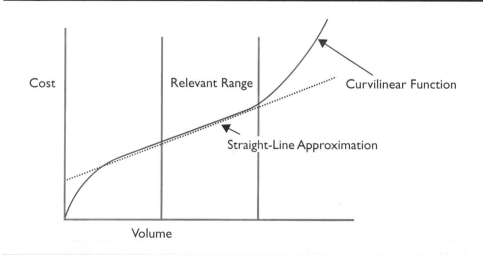

percent to $150,000 (7,500 × $20). However the cost per unit is still $20. Likewise if production volume is decreased to 2,500 desks, direct material costs will decrease by 50 percent to $50,000. But once again, the cost per unit remains $20.

A graphical representation of fixed and variable costs is presented in Exhibit 5-2. Note that rent remains $10,000 per year regardless of the level of production and that variable costs vary in total as production increases. Also note that variable costs can be represented by a straight line starting at the origin and continuing through each data point, and that total variable costs are zero when production is equal to zero.

THE COST EQUATION

Expressing the link between costs and production volume as an algebraic equation is useful. The equation for a straight line is:

$$Y = a + bx$$

The *a* in the equation is the point where the line intersects the vertical (*y*) axis and *b* is the slope of the line. In Exhibit 5-2, if *y* = total direct material costs and *x* = units produced, *y* = $0 + $20*x*. The y intercept is zero and the slope of the line is $20. For every one unit increase (decrease) in production (*x*), direct material costs increase (decrease) by $20. You can see that direct material costs are variable because they stay the same on a per-unit basis but increase in total as production increases. Likewise, we can express the fixed cost line as an equation. If *y* = rent cost and *x* = units produced, *y* = $10,000 + $0*x*. In this case, the *y* intercept is $10,000 and the slope is zero. In other words, fixed costs are $10,000 at any level of production within the relevant range.

EXHIBIT 5-2 Fixed and Variable Costs

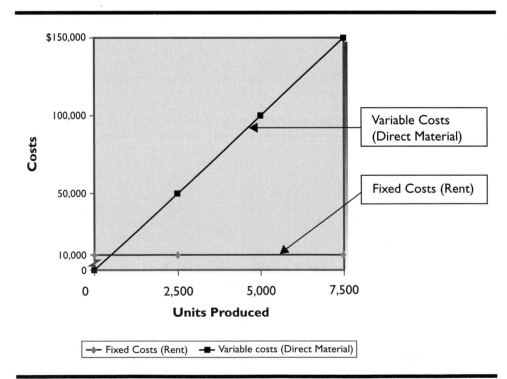

COST BEHAVIOR AND DECISION MAKING

Understanding how costs behave is vitally important when making production decisions, preparing budgets, and so on. To further explore this, let's consider Big Al's Pizza. After operating for one month, the owner of Big Al's Pizza Emporium asked his accountant how much it cost to make 2,100 pizzas last month. Big Al's incurred $4,200 for direct materials (pizza dough, cheese, and other ingredients), $3,150 for direct labor, and $8,400 for overhead (rent, utilities, insurance, depreciation of pizza ovens, supervisor salary, etc.). As shown in the following table, Al calculated the cost of a pizza (the cost of goods sold) as $7.50 ($15,750 total costs/2,100 pizzas).

Cost	Amount	Per Unit
Direct materials	$ 4,200	$2.00
Direct labor	3,150	1.50
Overhead	8,400	4.00
Total	$15,750	$7.50

He then estimated that since production was expected to increase to 2,600 pizzas next month, his total cost of goods sold should be $19,500 (2,600 pizzas × $7.50 each).

Concept Question: *Do you agree with Al's calculation of cost of goods sold? Why or why not?*

Concept Answer: It depends! Although Al did calculate the cost of 2,100 pizzas to be $7.50, this per-unit amount is going to change as the volume of pizzas changes if any of the costs of making pizzas are fixed. Remember fixed costs stay constant in total but vary on a per-unit basis. ■

Concept Question: *Assume that direct materials and direct labor are variable costs and that $6,300 of overhead is fixed. The remainder of the overhead cost is a variable utility cost of $1.00 per pizza. With this new information, how much total costs should Al expect to incur next month if 2,600 pizzas are produced?*

Concept Answer: As you can see in the following table, the total cost of making 2,600 pizzas is expected to be $18,000 or $6.92 per pizza. The cost per pizza has decreased from $7.50 to $6.92 as production volume increased from 2,100 to 2,600 pizzas. ■

Costs	Amount		Per Unit
Direct materials	$ 5,200	($2 × 2,600)	$2.00
Direct labor	3,900	($1.50 × 2,600)	$1.50
Variable overhead	2,600	($1 × 2,600)	$1.00
Fixed overhead	$ 6,300	($8,400 − $2,100)	$2.42
Total	$18,000		$6.92

Although the traditional income statement introduced in Chapter 2 is good at separating product and period costs, it commingles fixed and variable costs. Therefore, cost of goods sold consists of both fixed and variable costs and will differ at different levels of production. Even though the traditional income statement's focus on cost of goods sold and gross margin is useful for external reporting purposes, an income statement focusing on

cost behavior is more useful for internal decision making. A contribution margin-based income statement focusing on cost behavior is discussed more fully in Chapter 6.

Although there are many advantages to automation and a stable workforce, the impact of increasing fixed costs on the day-to-day decisions made by managers must not be ignored. The impact of cost structure on decision making is discussed in more detail in Chapter 6.

STEP COSTS

Classification of costs is not always a simple process. Some costs vary but only with relatively large changes in production. Batch-level costs related to moving materials may vary with the number of batches of product produced but not with every unit of product. Product-level costs associated with quality control inspections may vary when new products are introduced. Costs like these are sometimes referred to as **step costs.** In practice, step costs may look like and be treated as either variable costs or fixed costs. Although step costs are technically not fixed costs, they may be treated as such if they remain constant within a relevant range of production. Consider the costs of janitorial services within a company. As long as production is below 7,500 desks, the company will hire one janitor with salary and fringe benefits totaling $25,000. The cost is fixed as long as production remains below 7,500 units. However, if desk production exceeds 7,500, which increases the amount of waste and cleanup needed, it may be necessary to hire a second janitor at a cost of another $25,000. However, within a relevant range of production between 7,501 and 15,000 units, the cost is essentially fixed ($50,000). A graphical representation of a step (fixed) cost is shown in Exhibit 5-3.

Step costs may look like variable costs in other cases in which the steps are relatively small. Consider the cost of electricity used in baking pizzas at Big Al's Pizza Emporium. Al generally bakes five pizzas at a time in one of two pizza ovens. The electricity costs of the oven are the same whether one pizza or five pizzas are being cooked. Technically, the costs vary with batches of five pizzas. However, within a relevant range of production, the costs per pizza are likely to be stable (a variable cost).

MIXED COSTS

LO2
Analyze mixed costs using regression analysis and the high-low method

Mixed costs present a unique challenge because they include both a fixed and a variable component. Consequently, it is difficult to predict the behavior of a mixed cost as production changes unless the cost is first separated into its fixed and variable components. A good example of a mixed cost is the cost of a delivery vehicle for a Big Al's Pizza Emporium. Let's assume that Al enters into a lease agreement for a new delivery van that calls for a lease payment of $400 per month. Every month Al is required to

EXHIBIT 5-3 Step Costs

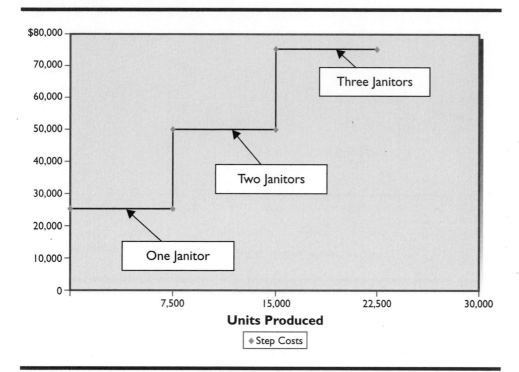

make the $400 payment regardless of whether any deliveries are made, hence $400 of the cost is fixed. However, Big Al's also incurs costs related to driving the vehicle (gasoline, oil, maintenance costs, etc.) that vary with the number of deliveries made (and miles driven). If these costs average $1.50 per delivery and 200 deliveries are made during the month, Al will incur an additional $300 of variable costs for a total cost of $700. If 100 deliveries are made, the additional cost will be $150. While the variable portion of the cost of the delivery van varies in total as the number of deliveries increases or decreases, it remains fixed when expressed per unit ($1.50 per delivery). On the other hand, the fixed portion of the cost remains constant in total ($400) but varies when expressed per unit.

Although the fixed and variable components of the delivery van cost are obvious, in many cases they may be difficult to identify. As shown in the table below, Big Al's has incurred the followed overhead costs over the last seven weeks.

PAUSE
& Reflect

Can you think of other common examples of mixed costs?

Week	Pizzas	Total Overhead Costs	Cost per Unit
1 (Start-up)	0	$ 679	N/A
2	423	1,842	$4.35
3	601	2,350	3.91
4	347	1,546	4.46
5	559	2,250	4.03
6	398	1,769	4.44
7	251	1,288	5.13

Is the overhead cost a fixed, variable, or mixed cost? Clearly, the cost is not fixed, because it changes each week. However, is it a variable cost? Although the cost changes each week, it does not vary in direct proportion to changes in production. In addition, remember

EXHIBIT 5-4 Mixed Costs

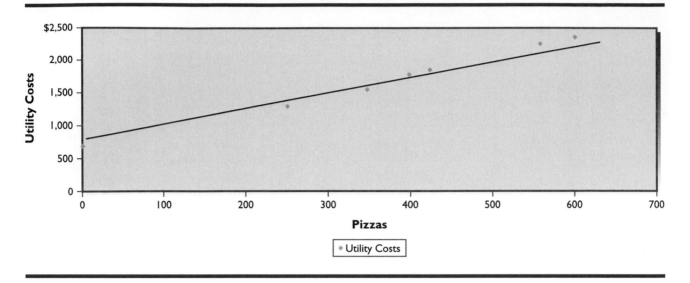

Utility Costs

that variable costs remain constant when expressed per unit. In this case, the amount of overhead cost per pizza changes from week to week. A cost that changes in total and also changes per unit is a mixed cost. As you can see in Exhibit 5-4, a mixed cost looks somewhat like a variable cost. However, the cost does not vary in direct proportion to changes in the level of production (you can't draw a straight line through all the data points) and if a line were drawn through the data points back to the y-axis, we would still incur utility cost at a production volume of zero. Like a fixed cost, a mixed cost has a component that is constant regardless of production volume.

Once we know that a cost is mixed, we are left with the task of separating the mixed cost into its fixed and variable components. However, unlike the lease example, it is not clear how much of the utility cost is fixed and how much is variable. In the next section, we demonstrate the use of a statistical tool called regression analysis to estimate the fixed and variable components of a mixed cost.

SEPARATING MIXED COSTS INTO THEIR FIXED AND VARIABLE COMPONENTS

A variety of tools can be used to estimate the fixed and variable components of a mixed cost. When we separate a mixed cost into its variable and fixed components, what we are really doing is generating the equation for a straight line with the *y* intercept estimating the fixed cost and the slope estimating the variable cost per unit.

 Key Concept: *Within the relevant range, fixed costs are constant in total and vary per unit, variable costs vary in total and are constant per unit, and mixed costs vary in total and vary per unit.*

Continuing our example of Big Al's Pizza Emporium, after the initial seven-week startup period, Al compiles data regarding the total overhead cost and the number of pizzas produced in the next 12 months. As you can see in the following table, because the overhead cost varies in total and on a per-unit basis, it must be a mixed cost. A graph of the data is shown in Exhibit 5-5.

Month	Pizzas	Overhead	Per Pizza
1	2,100	$ 8,400	$4.00
2	2,600	10,100	3.88
3	2,300	8,800	3.83
4	2,450	9,250	3.78
5	2,100	8,050	3.83
6	2,175	8,200	3.77
7	1,450	6,950	4.79
8	1,200	6,750	5.63
9	1,350	7,250	5.37
10	1,750	7,300	4.17
11	1,550	7,250	4.68
12	2,050	7,950	3.88

REGRESSION ANALYSIS

A statistical technique used to estimate the fixed and variable components of a mixed cost is called least squares regression. **Regression analysis** uses statistical methods to fit a cost line (called a regression line) through a number of data points. Note that although the data points in our example do not lie along a straight line, regression analysis statistically finds the line that minimizes the sum of the squared distance from each data point to the line (hence the name least squares regression).

EXHIBIT 5-5 Overhead Costs

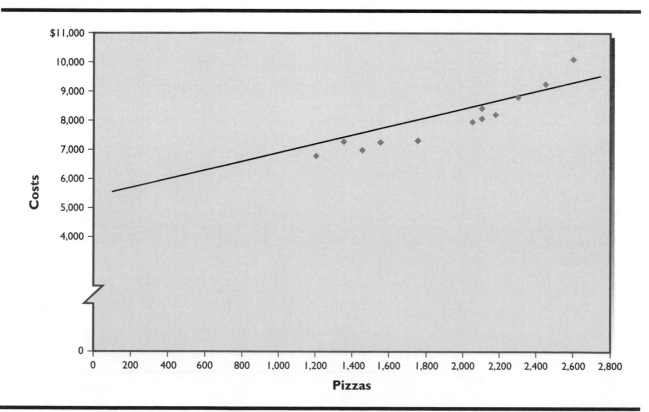

USING A SPREADSHEET PROGRAM TO PERFORM REGRESSION ANALYSIS

Using a spreadsheet program to estimate regression models is a relatively simple process. We are going to use Excel in this example, but all spreadsheet programs are very similar. The first step is to enter the actual values for our mixed cost (called the **dependent variable** in regression analysis since the amount of cost is dependent on production) and the related volume of production (called the **independent variable** since it drives the cost of the dependent variable) into a spreadsheet using one column for each variable. Using data from Big Al's Pizza Emporium for overhead costs incurred and pizzas produced for the first 12 months of operations, the results are shown in the Excel spreadsheet (see Exhibit 5-6).

The next step in Excel (see Exhibit 5-7) is to click on the tools option from the toolbar and choose data analysis from the pull-down menu. From the data analysis screen, scroll down, highlight regression, and either double-click or choose OK.

The regression screen will prompt you to choose a number of options. The first is to input the y range. The y range will be used to identify the dependent variable (overhead costs) found in column c of your spreadsheet. You can either type in the range of cells or simply highlight the cells in the spreadsheet (be sure not to include the column heading), and click on the icon in the y-range box. The next step is to select the x range for the independent variable (volume of pizzas). Once again, you can enter the cells directly or highlight the cells in the second column of your spreadsheet.

After inputting the appropriate y and x ranges, your Excel spreadsheet should look like the example shown in Exhibit 5-8. Click on OK, and the regression model summary output appears as shown in Exhibit 5-9.

EXHIBIT 5-6

Month	Pizzas	Overhead
1	2,100	$ 8,400.00
2	2,600	$10,100.00
3	2,300	$ 8,800.00
4	2,450	$ 9,250.00
5	2,100	$ 8,050.00
6	2,175	$ 8,200.00
7	1,450	$ 6,950.00
8	1,200	$ 6,750.00
9	1,350	$ 7,250.00
10	1,750	$ 7,300.00
11	1,550	$ 7,250.00
12	2,050	$ 7,950.00

EXHIBIT 5-7

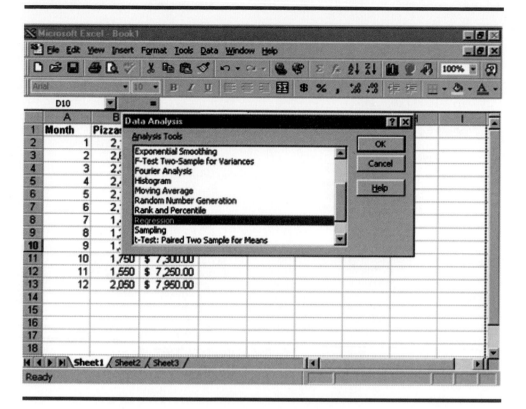

EXHIBIT 5-8

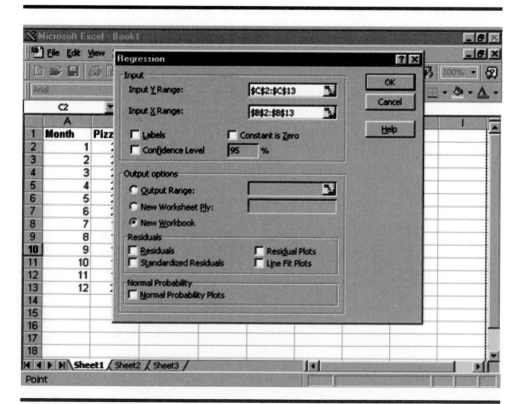

EXHIBIT 5-9

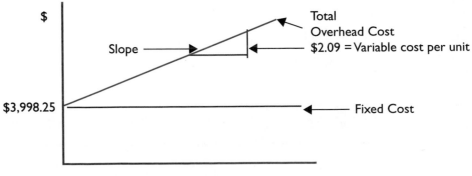

How is the summary output interpreted? First note toward the bottom of Exhibit 5-9 that the estimated coefficient (value) of the intercept (the y intercept) is 3,998.25 and the estimated coefficient (value) of the x variable (the slope) is 2.09. So, the fixed cost component of our mixed overhead cost is estimated to be $3,998.25 and the variable cost component is estimated to be $2.09 per pizza.

Using the least squares regression results, we can compute the regression line for overhead costs at Big Al's Pizza Emporium:

Total overhead cost = Fixed cost + Variable cost per unit × Volume
Total overhead cost = $3,998.25 + 2.09 × Volume

Graphically, the line for the total overhead costs can be expressed as seen in the illustration below.

Total Overhead Costs for Big Al's Pizza Emporium

$ [vertical axis]

Slope ⟶

Total Overhead Cost
$2.09 = Variable cost per unit

$3,998.25 ⟵ Fixed Cost

Volume of Pizzas

We can use this equation to help predict the amount of overhead costs that will be incurred for any number of pizzas within the relevant range. The relevant range is that range of activity within which management expects to operate or the range in which this equation is useful or meaningful. Our predictions should be limited to those activity levels within the relevant range. Based on last year's data, Big Al's expects to produce between 1,200 and 2,600 pizzas each month. Next month, Big Al expects to produce 1,750 pizzas. Based on the regression equation, Big Al estimates total overhead costs to be $7,655.75 ($3,998.25 + ($2.09 × 1,750 pizzas)).

REGRESSION STATISTICS

The regression statistics section at the top of Exhibit 5-9 provides useful diagnostic tools. The multiple R (called the correlation coefficient) is a measure of the proximity of the data points to the regression line. In addition, the sign of the statistic (+ or −) tells us the direction of the correlation between the independent and dependent variables. In this case, there is a positive correlation between the number of pizzas produced and total overhead costs. The **R square** (often represented as R^2 and called the coefficient of determination) is a measure of goodness of fit (how well the regression line "fits" the data). An R^2 of 1.0 indicates a perfect correlation between the independent and dependent variables in the regression equation; in other words, 100 percent of the data points are on the regression line. R^2 can be interpreted as the proportion of variation in the dependent variable that is explained by changes in the independent variable. In this case, the R^2 of .8933 indicates that over 89 percent of the variation in overhead costs are explained by increasing or decreasing pizza production.

Concept Question: Based on the regression results, we previously estimated that overhead costs should be $7,655.75 when 1,750 pizzas are produced. However, looking back at month 10, you will note that actual overhead costs were $7,300 when 1,750 pizzas were produced. Why aren't we able to compute the actual overhead costs in previous months using the regression results?

Concept Answer: Because the R^2 is less than 1.0. There is not a perfect correlation between the number of pizzas produced and overhead costs incurred. Another way to look at it is that all the data points used to compute the regression equation are not on the computed regression line. ■

An R^2 of less than 1.0 implies that other independent variables might have an impact on the dependent variable. For example, outside temperature and other environmental factors might impact overhead costs incurred by Big Al's. Multiple regression is a technique in which additional independent variables are used to help predict changes in a dependent variable. If we added additional variables to our regression model, we would probably get a better predictive model. However, it is unlikely that we will ever identify all the relevant variables that cause the total cost to change. Nor is it necessary. The goal of separating a mixed cost into its fixed and variable components is to help managers predict costs in the future, not to compute an exact breakdown.

Can you think of other variables that might have an impact on total overhead costs?

OTHER USES OF REGRESSION ANALYSIS

Regression analysis can be used in a variety of ways in managerial decision making. For example, marketing managers may be interested in predicting changes in sales based on changes in advertising expenditures and other variables. Production managers interested in quality control might collect data on overtime worked in a factory and compare that to the number of defective items produced to see if increases in overtime affect the amount of defective goods produced. This could lead management to hire additional workers rather than working existing workers excessive amounts of overtime.

However, regression analysis must be used with caution. The precision of a computerized statistical technique like regression analysis can be misleading. Regression results after all are only estimates. First and foremost, high correlations between independent variables and dependent variables and "good" models do not necessarily indicate a cause and effect relationship. It is important that managers use common sense and their intimate knowledge of what activities really drive costs before attempting to model cost equations.

ESTIMATING REGRESSION RESULTS USING THE HIGH-LOW METHOD

If we didn't have access to a computer regression program or for some reason didn't want to use this tool, we could estimate the regression equation using a simpler technique called the high-low method. The high-low method uses only two data points (related to the high and low levels of activity) and mathematically derives an equation for a straight line intersecting those two data points. Though technically inferior to regression analysis (which uses all the data points), from a practical perspective, the high-low method can often provide a reasonable estimate of the regression equation.

In the table on page 123, the high level of activity occurred in Month 2 when 2,600 pizzas were produced and $10,100 of overhead cost was incurred. The low level of activity occurred in Month 8 when only 1,200 pizzas were produced and overhead costs totaled $6,750. The slope of the line connecting those two points can be calculated by dividing the difference between the costs incurred at the high and low levels of activity by the difference in volume (number of pizzas at those levels). Remember, the slope of a line is calculated as the change in cost over the change in volume, in this case the difference in cost to produce pizzas over the difference in volume of pizzas made. As with the regression equation, the slope of the line is interpreted as the variable cost component of the mixed cost:

$$\frac{\text{Change in cost}}{\text{Change in volume}} = \text{Variable cost per unit}$$

Inserting the data for Big Al's Pizza Emporium, the variable cost is $2.39 per unit ($10,100 − $6,750)/(2,600 − 1,200). This compares with our regression estimate of $2.09. We then solve for the fixed cost component by calculating the total variable cost incurred at either the high or the low levels of activity and subtracting the variable costs from the total overhead cost incurred at that level. Mathematically, if

$$\text{Total overhead costs} = \text{Fixed Costs} + \text{Variable cost per unit (number of pizzas)}$$

then

$$\text{Total overhead costs} - \text{Variable costs} = \text{Fixed Costs}$$

At the high level of activity, total overhead costs are $10,100 and variable costs equal $6,214 (2,600 pizzas × $2.39 per pizza). Therefore, the fixed cost component of overhead costs is estimated to be $3,886 (total overhead costs of $10,100 less variable costs of $6,214) and the total overhead cost is estimated to be $3,886 + $2.39 (number of pizzas produced).

Why is this equation different from the least squares regression equation? Regression is a statistical tool that fits the "best" line through all 12 data points, whereas the high-low method mathematically derives a straight line between just 2 of the data points. By using the 2 points at the highest and lowest levels of activity, we are forcing a line between those points without regard to the remaining data points. If one or both of these points is unusual (an outlier), the result will be a cost line that is skewed and therefore may not be a good measure of the fixed and variable components of the mixed cost.[1] Therefore less than optimal decisions could be made due to the skewed data.

In the case of Big Al's Pizza Emporium, let's see how the high-low estimate would impact our prediction of total overhead costs next month when 1,750 pizzas are produced. Using the high-low estimate of the cost equation, we would predict total overhead costs of $8,068.50 ($3,886 + $2.39 × 1,750 pizzas). This compares with our estimate of $7,655.75 using the cost equation generated from the regression analysis.

Given the simplicity of generating regression equations using spreadsheet packages and hand-held calculators, the need for computing cost equations in practice using the high-low method is questionable. However, it remains an easy-to-use tool for estimating cost behavior.

COST BEHAVIOR, ACTIVITY-BASED COSTING, AND ACTIVITY-BASED MANAGEMENT

Whereas we have examined the behavior of unit-level costs related to changes in production volume (number of pizzas and number of deliveries), costs are affected by changes in other cost drivers as well. In Chapters 3 and 4, we introduced the concept of activities as procedures or processes that cause work to be accomplished (purchasing, receiving, production, plant occupancy, etc.) and cost drivers as allocation bases that cause or drive the incurrence of costs. Some of these drivers are related to volume (machine hours and labor hours), but drivers of batch and product level costs are more likely related to the complexity of a product (number of parts, number of inspections) or product diversity (number of setups, number of purchase orders). Although these costs may not vary in direct proportion to volume, they may vary in direct proportion to other cost drivers.

Regression analysis can be used to help managers identify the "best" cost drivers of activities for use in activity-based costing (ABC) and activity-based management (ABM). For example, an activity like processing customer orders might vary with the number of orders or the number of customers. Regression analysis can be used to identify which of the two possible independent variables best explains the variation in the dependent variable (costs of placing customer orders).

COST BEHAVIOR IN MERCHANDISING AND SERVICE COMPANIES

In merchandising firms, sales revenue is a common cost driver. The cost of merchandise purchased is a variable cost (it varies in direct proportion to changes in sales revenue). The cost of labor is often fixed (although seasonal hires may behave more like variable costs) and many other costs of facilities are fixed. Service-oriented companies have a variety of cost drivers depending on the industry. For example, a mortgage loan department might classify costs according to how they behave with respect to the number of loan applications processed, whereas an airline might look at number of passengers, passenger miles, and so on.

RELEVANT COSTS AND COST BEHAVIOR

As mentioned in Chapter 1, relevant costs are those that are avoidable or can be eliminated by choosing one alternative over another. Relevant costs are also known as differential or incremental costs. In general, variable costs are relevant in production decisions because they vary with the level of production. Likewise, fixed costs are generally not relevant because

LO3
Understand the concept of relevant costs and apply the concept to decision making

---

[1]It should be noted that the presence of outliers is a problem in regression analysis as well.

they typically don't change as production changes. However, variable costs can remain the same between two alternatives and fixed costs can vary between alternatives. For example, if the direct material cost of a product is the same for two competing designs, the material cost is not a relevant factor in choosing a design. However, other qualitative factors relating to the material (like durability) may still be relevant. Likewise, fixed costs can be relevant if they vary between alternatives. Consider rent paid for a facility to store inventory. Although the rent is a fixed cost, it is relevant to a decision to reduce inventory storage costs through just-in-time (JIT) production techniques if the cost of the rent can be avoided (by subleasing the space, for example) by choosing one alternative over another.

 Key Concept: *It can be misleading to always view variable costs as relevant and fixed costs as not relevant.*

THE IMPACT OF INCOME TAXES ON COSTS AND DECISION MAKING

LO4
Understand the impact of income taxes on costs and decision making

TAXES AND DECISION MAKING

We always need to consider tax laws and the impact income and other taxes have on costs, revenues, and decision making. Just as an individual should consider the impact of income taxes on a decision to hold or sell a stock, managers must consider the impact of taxes in a variety of decisions. The first key to understanding the impact of taxes on costs and revenues is the recognition that many costs of operating businesses are deductible for income tax purposes and that most business revenues are taxable. Second, the form of a transaction may impact the amount of tax that is paid or whether a cost is tax deductible. For example, structuring a purchase of a building as a lease with a corresponding payment of rent has different tax implications than a purchase of the same building. Third, the payment of taxes requires cash outflow and reduces the amount of cash available for other purposes in a business organization. Therefore, the impact of taxes must be considered in a variety of managerial decisions including production decisions, cost-volume-profit analysis, the purchase of property and equipment, and budgeting.

 Key Concept: *Managers must consider the impact of taxes on decisions.*

AFTER-TAX COSTS AND REVENUES

The computation of after-tax costs and after-tax revenues is really very simple. Consider an example in which your current taxable cash revenue is $100 and tax deductible cash expenses equal $60. Taxable income is therefore equal to $40. If the tax rate is 40 percent, $16 of income taxes will be paid, leaving you with $24 cash after tax. Now consider the impact of spending an additional $20 on tax deductible expenditures. This reduces your taxable income to $20. With a 40 percent tax rate, $8 of income taxes will be paid instead of $16 (you saved $8 of income tax) and you will be left with $12 after tax. Even though you spent an additional $20, your cash flow decreased by only $12 ($24 less $12).

Revenue	$100	$100
Expense	60	80
Taxable Income	$ 40	$ 20
Tax (rate = 40%)	16	8
After-tax cash flow	$ 24	$ 12

Mathematically, the after-tax cost of a tax deductible cash expenditure can be found by subtracting the tax savings from the before-tax cost or by simply multiplying the before-tax amount by (1 − tax rate):

$$\text{After-tax cost} = \text{Pretax cost} \times (1 - \text{Tax rate})$$

So if the before-tax cost is $20 and the tax rate is 40 percent, the after-tax cost is $12. ($12 = $20 × (1 − .40)). In this case, the impact of income taxes is to reduce the "real" cost of a tax-deductible expense to the business and to increase cash flow.

Income taxes also have an impact on cash revenues received by a business. Continuing our original example, if taxable cash revenue increases by $20, taxable income will increase to $60 ($120 minus $60). After payment of $24 of income taxes, you will be left with $36 of cash. An increase in revenue of $20 increases your cash flow by only $12 ($36 minus $24). Why? Because the $20 is taxable and results in the payment of an additional $8 of income tax ($20 × .40). Mathematically, the formula to find the after-tax benefit associated with a taxable cash revenue is analogous to the formula for after-tax cost. The after-tax benefit of a taxable cash receipt can be found by subtracting the additional tax to be paid from the before-tax receipt or by simply multiplying the pre-tax receipt by (1 − tax rate):

$$\text{After-tax benefit} = \text{Pretax receipts} \times (1 - \text{Tax rate})$$

So if the before-tax receipt is $20 and the tax rate is 40 percent, the after-tax benefit is $12 ($12 = $20 × (1 − .40)). In this case, the impact of income taxes is to increase the "real" cost to the business and to decrease cash flow.

BEFORE- AND AFTER-TAX NET INCOME

In a similar fashion, managers can calculate the impact of taxes on net income. If we have a tax rate of 40 percent and net income of $1,000,000, we will have a tax liability of $400,000 (40 percent of the $1,000,000) and be left with $600,000 after tax. This is exactly the same thing that happens to our paychecks as individuals. If an individual earns $1,000 per week and faces a 30 percent income tax rate, the individual's take-home pay (after considering income tax withholding) is only $700. Mathematically,

$$\text{After-tax income} = \text{Pretax income} \times (1 - \text{Tax rate})$$

Although tax laws are very complex and computing tax due is rarely as simple as applying one rate to net income, estimating the income tax impact on cash receipts and disbursements is important in managerial decision making.

APPLICATION IN BUSINESS   www.irs.gov

In the past twelve years there have been 9,500 changes to the Internal Revenue Code making tax planning a nightmare for many small businesses. Major tax bills during that time include The Tax Reform Act of 1986, The Omnibus Budget Reconciliation Acts of 1987, 1989, 1990, and 1993, and The Taxpayer Relief Act of 1997. Particularly problematic is Congress's habit of making temporary tax changes that expire every few years. Although the changes are made on a temporary basis due to budget considerations, they are almost always extended at the last minute. Making decisions in an environment characterized by constantly changing tax rules is challenging to say the least.

THE TIME VALUE OF MONEY AND DECISION MAKING

LO5
Understand the time value of money and its impact on costs and decision making

When decisions are affected by cash flows that are paid or received in different time periods, it is also necessary to adjust those cash flows for the time value of money (TVM). Because of our ability to earn interest on money invested, we would prefer to receive $1 today rather than a year from now. Likewise, we would rather pay $1 a year from now than today. A common technique used to adjust cash flows received or paid in different time periods is to discount those cash flows by finding their present value.

> **Key Concept:** *Managers must consider the time value of money when making long-term decisions.*

To fully understand the calculations involved in finding the present value of future cash flows, it is necessary to step back and examine the nature of interest and the calculation of interest received and paid. The concepts of time value of money are developed more completely in Chapter 8.

SUMMARY OF KEY CONCEPTS

- Costs behave in predictable ways. (p. 116)
- Within the relevant range, fixed costs are constant in total and vary per unit, variable costs vary in total and are constant per unit, and mixed costs vary in total and vary per unit. (p. 122)
- It can be misleading to always view variable costs as relevant and fixed costs as not relevant. (p. 130)

- Managers must consider the impact of taxes on decisions. (p. 130)
- Managers must consider the time value of money when making long-term decisions. (p. 133)

KEY DEFINITIONS

Cost behavior How costs react to changes in production volume or other levels of activity (p. 116)

Fixed costs Costs that remain the same in total when production volume increases or decreases but vary per unit (p. 116)

Variable costs Costs that stay the same per unit but change in total as production volume increases or decreases (p. 116)

Relevant range The normal range of production that can be expected for a particular product and company (p. 117)

Step costs Costs that vary with activity in steps. They may look like and be treated as either variable costs or fixed costs. While step costs are technically not fixed costs, they may be treated as such if they remain constant within a relevant range of production (p. 120)

Mixed costs These costs include both a fixed and a variable component. Consequently, it is difficult to predict the behavior of a mixed cost as production changes unless the cost is first separated into its fixed and variable components (p. 120)

Regression analysis The procedure that uses statistical methods (least squares regression) to fit a cost line (called a regression line) through a number of data points (p. 123)

Dependent variable The variable in regression analysis that is dependent on changes in the independent variable (p. 124)

Independent variable The variable in regression analysis that drives changes in the dependent variable (p. 124)

R square (R^2) A measure of goodness of fit (how well the regression line "fits" the data) (p. 127)

CONCEPT REVIEW

1. Discuss the importance of understanding cost behavior in decision making.

2. Define fixed costs.

3. Define variable costs.

4. Describe the behavior of direct material cost in total and per unit as production volume changes.

5. Describe the relevant range and how it relates to cost behavior.

6. How will fixed costs expressed on a per-unit basis react to a change in the level of activity?

7. When production increases how do fixed manufacturing costs react on a per-unit basis and in total?

8. Give the equation that best describes the fundamental relationship among total costs (TC), fixed costs (FC), and variable costs per unit (V).

9. Describe the behavior of mixed costs when production volume changes.

10. Discuss the meaning of dependent and independent variables in regression analysis.

11. Discuss the trend toward more fixed costs in a manufacturing environment and how that trend affects the cost per unit when production volume changes.

12. Describe step costs and give an example.

13. Describe a situation where the normal expected behavior of direct labor cost may change.

14. Discuss the impact of taxes on costs and how that affects decision making.

15. Discuss the meaning of R square in regression analysis. What does an R square of 1 mean?

16. Discuss situations in which the high-low method may provide inaccurate estimates of fixed and variable costs.

APPLICATION OF CONCEPTS

17. You run a regression analysis and receive the following results:

Multiple R	.71196
R Square	.50688

Adjusted R Square	.50438
Standard Error	1.43764

Analysis of Variance

	DF	Sum of Squares	Mean Square
Regression	1	418.52992	418.52992
Residual	197	407.16375	2.06682

F = 202.49935   Signif F = .0000

VARIABLES IN THE EQUATION

Variable	Coefficients	Standard error	t Stat	P-value
X variable 1	7.93958	.055794	14.230	.0000
Intercept	204.070	.261513	−.780	.4361

Required

A. What is the fixed cost?

B. What is the variable cost per unit?

C. What is the cost equation?

D. How much variance in the y-variable (cost) is explained by the x variable?

E. If the above regression was for production costs and 250 units of x are produced, what are total fixed costs?

F. If the above regression was for production costs and 300 units of x are produced, what are total variable costs?

G. If the above regression was for production costs and 350 units of x are produced, what are total production costs?

18. Fancy Shoe Manufacturers documented their production levels and overhead costs for the past five months.

	Production	Overhead Cost
January	10,600 pairs	$40,250
February	10,575	41,000
March	11,500	44,250
April	12,500	45,250
May	11,000	43,750

Required

A. Using the high-low method, what is the variable cost per unit?

B. Using the high-low method, what is the fixed cost?

C. Using the high-low method, what is the overhead cost equation?

D. Using the high-low method, what would you expect the total cost of producing 12,000 pairs of shoes to be?

19. You run a regression analysis and receive the following results:

Multiple R	.39429
R Square	.15547
Adjusted R Square	.14964
Standard Error	.44416

Analysis of Variance

	DF	Sum of Squares	Mean Square
Regression	1	5.26588	5.26588
Residual	145	28.60536	.19728

F = 26.69262   Signif F = .0000

VARIABLES IN THE EQUATION

Variable	Coefficients	Standard error	t Stat	P-value
X Variable 1	11.0323	.021353	5.166	.0000
Intercept	8833.07	.090586	9.751	.0000

Required

A. What is the fixed cost in this regression analysis?

B. What is the variable cost per unit?

C. Prepare the cost equation based upon these results.

D. Does this regression equation "fit" the data well? What information did you examine to answer this question?

20. Minor Corporation anticipates net income of $1,200,000 this year. They are considering an equipment lease that would result in a $175,000 deductible expense this year. The tax rate is 35 percent.

Required

A. What would be the tax expense and net income after taxes for the anticipated net income (without the lease of the equipment)?

B. What would be the tax expense and net income after taxes if the equipment is leased?

C. What would be the after-tax effect of the lease expense?

21. Christopher Corporation documented their production levels and utility costs for the past six months.

	Production	Utility Cost
January	113,000 units	$1,712
February	114,000	1,716
March	90,000	1,469
April	115,000	1,619
May	112,000	1,698
June	101,000	1,691

Required

A. Using the high-low method, what is their utility cost equation?

B. What would be the expected utility cost of producing 120,000 units?

C. Using the above data and a spreadsheet program run a regression analysis. Discuss any differences in the results and the potential impact on decision making.

22. Collins Company has the following current year costs:

Variable costs	$6 per unit
Fixed costs	$7,000

The Company plans to enter into an arrangement with a supplier that will result in a 50-cent decrease per unit in variable costs next year. They will also reduce their rental space, which will decrease fixed costs by 10 percent.

Required

A. If current year production is 12,000 units, what are total fixed costs?

B. If the company makes the changes discussed above, what will be the new cost equation?

C. Given the new cost equation, determine estimated total costs if production remains at 12,000 units.

23. Hester Company incurred a total cost of $10,000 to produce 500 units of output. A total of 550 hours was incurred for this effort. If the variable cost was $10 per direct labor hour, then how much was the fixed cost?

24. Hickman Company produces two products, Bert and Ernie; Hickman has provided you with the following data. Production and cost data for the two products are as follows:

Number of Units (Bert)	Total Cost
1	$ 10
10	100
100	1,000

Number of Units (Ernie)	Unit Cost
1	$5,000
10	500
100	50

How would you describe the behavior of costs for Bert and Ernie?

25. Simon Company operates in a relevant range from 1,000 to 1,500 units and incurs the following overhead costs:

Units Produced	Utilities	Lease costs	Indirect labor costs
1,000	$10,000	$15,000	$13,000
1,500	$12,500	$15,000	$15,600

Required

A. Classify the above costs as fixed, variable, or mixed.

B. At a production volume of 1,300 units, what are Simon Company's total estimated overhead costs?

26. Garfunkel Company incurs the following overhead costs at production volume of 2,000 and 8,000 units:

Units Produced	Maintenance Expense	Rent	Indirect labor
2,000	$24,250	$21,000	$22,000
8,000	$67,000	$21,000	$88,000

Required

A. Describe the cost behavior of each element of overhead cost listed above.

B. At a production volume of 9,000 units, what are Garfunkel's expected overhead costs?

27. The controller of Sawyer College has determined that a janitor can clean an average of 20 dorm rooms each day. Bay View Dorm has 100 rooms and is projected to be 80 percent full for the spring semester (January to May). In the summer (June to Au-

gust) the dorm is used only for summer camps so is projected to be only 50 percent full. In the fall semester (September to December) the dorm is projected to be 100 percent full. Sawyer College outsources their maintenance and housekeeping services from another company that charges Sawyer College $2,000 per month for each janitor hired.

Required

A. Compute the cost for janitorial service for Bay View Dorm for each of the three periods of time.

B. What cost behavior pattern best describes janitorial costs for Bay View Dorm?

C. How would you predict the costs of janitorial services for the dorm in the future?

28. Chris Gaines has leased a new automobile using a special lease plan. If the auto is driven 1,000 miles or less during a one-month period the lease payment is $250. When the mileage ranges between 1,001 and 1,500 miles, the lease payment becomes $300. For 1,501 to 2,000 miles, the lease payment rises to $350.

Required

A. How would you describe the lease cost described above?

B. If Chris always drives between 1,200 and 1,400 miles per month, how would you classify the lease cost for planning purposes?

C. If Chris's monthly mileage ranges from 0 miles to 1,800 miles, how would you classify the lease cost for planning purposes?

29. Data from the duplicating department of Hope Services for the previous six months are as follows:

	Number of Copies Made	Duplicating Department's Costs
January	20,000	$17,000
February	25,000	19,500
March	27,000	21,000
April	22,000	18,000
May	24,000	19,000
June	30,000	24,000

Regression output from the previous data is as follows:

Coefficient of Intercept	2807.895
R square	.967696
Number of observations	6
X coefficient (IV)	.686842

Required

A. What is the variable rate per copy for Hope Services?

B. What is the fixed cost for Hope Services?

C. Based on the regression output for Hope Services, what equation should be used to compute an estimate of future total costs?

D. If 26,000 copies are made next month, what total cost should be incurred?

E. Based on the information given, how good will the equation described in Part C be at predicting the total cost each month for Hope Services?

30. Regression results for Robyn's Flower Shop Inc. are as follows:

Dependent variable—overhead costs	
Independent variable—direct labor costs	
Coefficient of intercept	$4,000
Coefficient of independent variable	3.00
Correlation coefficient	.67
R square	.45

The company is planning on operating at a level that would call for direct labor costs of $10,000 per month for the coming year.

Required

A. Using the regression output for Robyn's Flower Shop Inc., give the equation that best represents the overhead cost equation.

B. What percentage of variation in overhead costs is explained by the independent variable in the regression output for Robyn's Flower Shop Inc.? How good will the equation be at predicting total cost?

C. Discuss how the prediction ability could be improved.

31. Calculate the after-tax impact of the following situations.

Before-Tax Cost	Tax Rate	After-Tax Cost
(1) $25,000	40%	?
(2) 50,000	20	?
(3) 35,000	35	?
(4) 75,000	25	?
(5) 85,000	45	?

32. Calculate the after-tax impact of the following situations.

Before-Tax Revenue	Tax Rate	After-Tax Revenue
(1) $100,000	40%	?
(2) 200,000	20	?
(3) 135,000	35	?
(4) 175,000	25	?
(5) 185,000	45	?

33. Mandy Lifeboats Cruise Co. is in need of better information for planning new cruises. You have been retained as a consultant to provide a planning model. You are provided with the following information regarding last year's average costs for 12 cruises on the MS Robyn, a cruise ship that has a maximum capacity of 525 passengers and has a crew of 250. All cruises on the MS Robyn are either seven or ten days in length.

Cruise	Days	Passengers	Total Cost
1	7	455	$3,150,100
2	7	420	2,975,250
3	7	473	3,175,950
4	7	510	3,266,150
5	7	447	3,145,100
6	7	435	3,100,150
7	10	445	3,650,150
8	10	495	3,700,150
9	10	480	3,670,350
10	10	505	3,750,000
11	10	471	3,675,000
12	10	439	3,650,900

The total cost of a cruise includes all costs of running the ship (fuel, maintenance, depreciation etc.) and meals, entertainment and crew costs.

Required

    A. Using the number of passengers as the independent variable, run a regression analysis (or use the high-low method) to arrive at the total cost formula for a cruise.

    B. How accurate is the planning model calculated in A?

    C. What are the total fixed costs per cruise?

    D. What are the variable costs per passenger?

    E. What other independent variables might be used by Mandy to predict total cruise costs? Using regression analysis or the high-low method, calculate the cost equation using this new independent variable.

    F. Using the decision-making model described in Chapter 1, define the problem facing Mandy (Step 1), their likely objectives in choosing a planning model (Step 2), and options and factors they would likely consider (Step 3).

    G. Using the best planning model you can develop using the data presented above, what is the estimated cost of a 10-day cruise at full capacity of 525 passengers?

Step 1	DEFINE THE PROBLEM
Step 2	IDENTIFY OBJECTIVES
Step 3	IDENTIFY AND ANALYZE AVAILABLE OPTIONS

34. B.B. Lean, a major retailing and mail-order operation, has been in business for the past 10 years. During that time, the mail-order operations have grown from a sideline to represent over 80 percent of the company's annual sales. Of course, the company has suffered growing pains. There were times when overloaded or faulty computer programs resulted in lost sales, and the scheduling of temporary workers to augment the permanent staff during peak periods has always been a problem.

    Tom Humes, manager of mail-order operations, has developed procedures for handling most problems. However, he is still trying to improve the scheduling of temporary workers to take telephone orders from customers. Under the current system, Humes keeps a permanent staff of 60 employees who handle the basic workload. Based on his estimate of the upcoming telephone volume each week he determines the number of temporary workers needed for the next week. The permanent workers are paid an average of $10 per hour plus 30 percent fringe benefits. The temporary workers are paid $7 per hour with no fringe benefits. The full time workers are very seldom sent home when volume is light but are not paid for hours missed. Temporary workers are paid only for the hours worked. Tom normally keeps three supervisors at $1,000 per month but adds one additional supervisor when the temporary workers are used.

    Humes has decided to try regression analysis as a way to improve the prediction of total costs of processing telephone orders. By summarizing the daily labor hours into monthly totals for the past year, he was able to determine the number of labor hours incurred each month. In addition, he summarized the number of orders that had been processed each month. After entering the data into a spreadsheet, Hall ran two regressions. Regression 1 related the total hours worked (permanent staff plus temporary workers) to the total cost to run the phone center, and Regression 2 related the number of orders taken to the total cost. The output of these regressions is as follows:

Month	Total Cost	Total Hours	Number of Orders
January	$134,000	9,600	10,560
February	133,350	9,550	10,450
March	132,700	9,500	10,200
April	134,000	9,600	10,700
May	133,675	9,575	10,400
June	139,900	10,100	10,700
July	143,820	10,500	11,100
August	140,880	10,200	10,450
September	137,940	9,900	10,200

October	153,620	11,500	12,200
November	163,420	12,500	12,900
December	150,680	11,200	11,490

Regression Equation: TC = FC + VC (orders) or TC = FC + VC (hours). Where: TC = Total Cost; FC = Fixed Cost, and VC = Variable Cost per hour or order.

	Regression 1	Regression 2
Intercept (FC)	36,180.42	21,595.15
X Variable (VC)	10.21475	10.95427
R-Square	.997958	.890802

Required:

A. What are the equations (planning models) for each of the two regressions?

B. Tom Humes estimates that they will receive 12,470 orders and 12,000 hours worked during the month of January. Predict the total cost of running the phone center using both cost equations. Round your answer to the nearest whole number.

C. Tom needs to choose one of the models to use to predict total costs for next year's monthly budget. Using the decision model presented in chapter one:

Step 1 — DEFINE THE PROBLEM

Step 2 — IDENTIFY OBJECTIVES

Step 3 — IDENTIFY AND ANALYZE AVAILABLE OPTIONS

1. Define the problem faced by Tom (Step 1).

2. What are the objectives of the decision problem (Step 2)?

3. What are Tom's options (Step 3)? Can you think of other independent variables that might be used to predict the costs of the phone center?

4. What other factors should Tom consider?

35. Hunziker Rapid Delivery Service wants to determine the cost behavior pattern of maintenance costs to their delivery vehicles. The company has decided to use linear regression by employing the equation y = a + bx for maintenance costs. The prior year's data regarding maintenance hours and costs and the results of the regression analysis are given in the following table:

	Hours of Activity	Maintenance Costs
January	480	$4,200
February	320	3,000
March	400	3,600
April	300	2,820
May	500	4,350
June	310	2,960
July	320	3,030
August	520	4,470
September	490	4,260
October	470	4,050
November	350	3,300
December	340	3,160

Regression Output

Coefficient of Intercept	684.65
X Coefficient	7.2884
R square	.99448

Required

A. Based on the data derived from the regression analysis, what maintenance costs should be budgeted for a month in which 420 maintenance hours will be worked?

B. What is the percentage of the total variance that can be explained by the regression equation?

36. Data from the duplicating department of Kool Kopy Company for the previous nine months are as follows:

	Number of Copies Made	Duplicating Department's Costs
January	20,000	$17,000
February	25,000	11,000
March	27,000	27,000
April	22,000	18,000
May	24,000	30,000
June	30,000	24,000
July	22,000	18,000
August	23,000	18,500
September	34,000	26,000

Regression Output

Coefficient of intercept	729.9013
R square	0.447444
X coefficient	0.757405

Required

Review the preceding actual data and the regression output.

A. Do you think the data could be improved by removing any outliers? If so, identify likely outliers from the data given and state reasons why you would remove them.

B. Would removing these data points change the regression output? How?

C. Give reasons for the change and direction the values may move. Give reasons why you might want to leave the data as is.

37. Data from the duplicating department of Hope Services for the previous six months are as follows:

	Number of Copies Made	Duplicating Department's Costs
January	20,000	$17,000
February	25,000	19,500
March	27,000	21,000
April	22,000	18,000
May	24,000	19,000
June	30,000	24,000

Required

A. Using the high-low method, separate the fixed and variable expenses and give the resulting equation.

B. Compare the equation generated in Part A to the equation generated by the regression output in Problem 29, Part C. Explain the difference. Discuss why one method may be better than the other for identifying fixed and variable cost components.

C. If Hope Services estimates that it will make 23,000 copies in July, what will be the total duplicating costs? What will be the total fixed and variable costs for July?

D. If Hope wanted to predict total duplicating costs for 50,000 copies, would either the model in Problem 29 or the model calculated here do a good job of estimating total cost at the level of production? Include a discussion of the relevant range.

38. Hunziker Rapid Delivery Service wants to determine the cost behavior pattern of maintenance costs to their delivery vehicles. The prior year's data regarding maintenance hours and costs are given in the following table:

	Hours of Activity	Maintenance Costs
January	480	$ 4,200
February	320	3,000
March	400	3,600
April	300	2,820
May	500	4,350
June	310	2,960
July	320	3,030
August	520	4,470
September	490	4,260
October	470	4,050
November	350	3,300
December	340	3,160
Total	4,800	$43,200

Required

A. Using the high-low method, compute the fixed costs and the variable rate and give the resulting equation.

B. Compare the equation in Part A to the regression results in Problem 35. Compare the equations and comment on the difference.

C. Explain what is the best method for management to use in cost analysis at Hunziker Rapid Delivery Service?

39. Data from the duplicating department of Kool Kopy Company for the previous nine months are as follows:

	Number of Copies Made	Duplicating Deptartment's Costs
January	20,000	$17,000
February	25,000	11,000
March	27,000	27,000
April	22,000	18,000
May	24,000	30,000
June	30,000	24,000
July	22,000	18,000
August	23,000	18,500
September	34,000	26,000

Required

A. Using the high-low method, identify the fixed costs and the variable cost per unit and show the resulting equation.

B. Compare the equation generated in Problem 36 using regression analysis to the equation in Part A. Comment on the differences. Why do you think this model using the high-low method is different? What, if anything, could be done to improve the accuracy of the high-low model in this problem?

CONTINUING CASE BIG AL'S PIZZA INC.

During the first two years of operations, Big Al's overhead costs have fluctuated from month to month. Although overhead appears to go up and down according to the number of pizzas produced each month, the accounting manager has noticed that that is not always the case. For example, in the 14th month of operations, the manufacturing facility was closed for almost 10 days due to severe weather and production for the month was very low. However, overhead costs were only about 25 percent lower than those incurred in the previous month. In an effort to estimate overhead costs in Year 3, the manager has collected the following information from his records over the last 24 months of operation and has asked for your assistance in analyzing the data.

Month	Pizzas produced	Total overhead costs
1	25,784	$17,200
2	25,897	17,300
3	25,750	17,450
4	26,352	17,600
5	27,567	17,950
6	28,492	18,125
7	27,398	17,900
8	28,112	17,955
9	29,499	18,507
10	28,879	18,295
11	29,344	18,325
12	29,399	18,550
13	30,879	19,825
14	15,167	14,800
15	28,379	18,732
16	29,765	19,832
17	30,334	19,965
18	30,761	19,786
19	31,300	20,359
20	31,804	20,149
21	31,795	20,508
22	32,016	20,489
23	32,379	21,166
24	32,675	20,852

Required

A. Does the data present any special problems that might impact the accuracy of using either the high-low method or regression analysis to predict overhead costs? What suggestions would you make to company accountant Lee Dworski before analyzing the data?

B. Use the high-low method to estimate the fixed and variable components of total overhead costs.

C. Use regression analysis to estimate the fixed and variable components of total overhead costs.

D. Should the accounting manager consider using another independent variable (instead of pizzas produced) to predict overhead costs?

E. During Year 3, Big Al's estimates January production of 33,000 pizzas. Based on this estimate of production, how much overhead would you estimate for Big Al's?

F. How else might Lee Dworski estimate overhead costs in Year 3?

Chapter 6

COST BEHAVIOR AND DECISION MAKING—COST-VOLUME-PROFIT ANALYSIS

Study Tools

A Review of the Previous Chapter
In Chapter 5, we examined the nature of costs. Students were introduced to concepts of cost behavior, relevant costs, and the impact of income taxes and the time value of money on costs and decision making.

A Preview of This Chapter
In this chapter, the concept of cost behavior is developed further and students are introduced to a variety of tools (contribution margin ratio, operating leverage, break-even) used in cost-volume-profit (CVP) analysis.

Key concepts include:
- The contribution margin income statement is structured to emphasize cost behavior as opposed to cost function.
- For every unit change in sales, contribution margin will increase or decrease by the contribution margin per unit multiplied by the increase or decrease in sales volume.
- The contribution margin per unit and the contribution margin ratio will remain constant as long as sales vary in direct proportion to volume.
- The payment of income taxes is an important variable in target profit and other CVP decisions.
- Variable costing is consistent with CVP's focus on differentiating fixed from variable costs and provides useful information for decision making that is often not apparent when using absorption costing.

A Preview of Upcoming Chapters
Chapter 7 extends the discussion of relevant costs and examines a variety of decisions made by managers in their day-to-day activities.

LEARNING OBJECTIVES

After studying the material in this chapter, you should be able to:

LO 1 Discuss the basic concepts underlying CVP analysis

LO 2 Determine the format and use of the contribution margin income statement

LO 3 Use the decision-making model in CVP analysis

LO 4 Analyze what-if decisions using contribution margin per unit, contribution margin ratio, and operating leverage

LO 5 Compute a company's break-even point in a single and multiproduct environment

LO 6 Use break-even analysis in an activity-based costing environment

LO 7 Analyze target profit before and after the impact of income tax

LO 8 Identify the assumptions inherent in CVP analysis

LO 9 Identify the differences between variable costing and absorption costing and the use of variable costing for decision making

In Chapter 5, we emphasized the importance of understanding the nature of costs. In this chapter, we focus on one aspect of the nature of costs (cost behavior) and develop a set of tools that focus on the distinction between fixed and variable costs. These tools include measures of a company's contribution margin, contribution margin ratio, and operating leverage—the cornerstones of cost-volume-profit (CVP) analysis. CVP analysis provides marketing and operations managers with useful information concerning sales necessary in order to break even or to earn a target profit and how profit is affected when the costs, volume, or prices of products or services are changed. The effect of income taxes on CVP analysis is also discussed. ■

INTRODUCTION

LO1
Discuss the basic concepts underlying CVP analysis

Some of the more important decisions managers make involve the analysis of the relationship between the cost, volume, and profitability of products produced and services provided by a company. **Cost-volume-profit analysis (CVP)** focuses on the relationship between the following five factors and the overall profitability of a company:

1. The prices of products or services
2. The volume of products or services produced and sold
3. The per-unit variable costs
4. The total fixed costs
5. The mix of products or services produced

THE CONTRIBUTION MARGIN INCOME STATEMENT

LO2
Determine the format and use of the contribution margin income statement

As mentioned in Chapter 5, the traditional income statement required for external financial reporting focuses on function (product costs versus period costs) in calculating the cost of goods sold and a company's gross profit. **Gross profit** is the difference between sales and cost of goods sold. However, since cost of goods sold includes both fixed costs (facility-level costs) as well as variable costs (unit-level costs like direct material), the behavior of cost of goods sold and gross profit is difficult to predict when production increases or decreases.

APPLICATION IN BUSINESS

Gross profit (usually as a percentage of sales) is used by investment analysts as a measure of cost control and efficiency in the manufacturing process and thus is useful in assessing the value of a company

In contrast, the contribution margin income statement is structured by behavior rather than by function. In the figure below, a traditional income statement and a contribution margin income statement are shown side by side so you can see the difference.

Comparison of Income Statements

Traditional			Contribution Margin		
Sales		$1,000	Sales		$1,000
Less: Cost of goods sold			Less: Variable costs		
Variable costs	$350		Manuf. costs	$350	
Fixed costs	150		S & A costs	50	
Total cost of goods sold		$ 500	Total variable costs		$ 400
Gross profit		$ 500	Contribution margin		$ 600
Less: S & A costs			Less: Fixed costs		
Variable costs	$ 50		Manuf. costs	$150	
Fixed costs	250		S & A costs	250	
Total S & A costs		$ 300	Total fixed costs		$ 400
Net income		$ 200	Net income		$ 200

As you can see, although the net income is the same for both statements, the traditional statement focuses on the function of the costs, whereas the contribution margin income statement focuses on the behavior of the costs. In the traditional income statement, cost of goods sold and selling and administrative costs include both variable and fixed costs. In the contribution margin income statement, costs are separated by behavior (variable versus fixed) rather than by function. Note, however, that the contribution margin income statement combines product and period costs. Variable costs include both variable product costs (direct materials) and variable selling and administrative costs (commissions on sales), whereas fixed costs likewise include both product and period costs.

 Key Concept: *The contribution margin income statement is structured to emphasize cost behavior as opposed to cost function.*

Because of the focus on cost behavior, the information in the contribution margin income statement is very useful for managerial decision making. For example, a contribution margin income statement for HD Inc. (a manufacturer of floppy disk drives for computers) is shown below. Note that per-unit cost information is also shown in the statement. This information is helpful in understanding the usefulness of the contribution margin income statement.

	Total	Per Unit
Sales (100,000 units)	$200,000	$2.00
Less: Variable costs	80,000	.80
Contribution margin	$120,000	$1.20
Less: Fixed costs	40,000	
Net Income	$ 80,000	

CONTRIBUTION MARGIN PER UNIT

As you can see in the income statement above, the contribution margin is $1.20 per unit. What exactly does that tell us? It tells us that every floppy disk sold by HD Inc. contributes $1.20 toward the payment of fixed costs. Once fixed costs are covered, each unit sold will contribute $1.20 toward net income. Remember that variable costs vary in total with production and remain constant when expressed as a per-unit amount. As long as total sales vary in direct proportion to the number of units sold, **contribution margin per unit** will also remain constant.

Note what happens to HD's contribution margin if one additional unit is produced and sold. Increasing sales by one unit increases contribution margin by $1.20. Assuming that fixed costs don't change, net income increases by the same $1.20.

	Total	Per Unit
Sales (100,001 units)	$200,002.00	$2.00
Less: Variable costs	80,000.80	.80
Contribution margin	$120,001.20	$1.20
Less: Fixed costs	40,000.00	
Net income	$ 80,001.20	

What happens if HD Inc. increases sales by 100 units? As you can see, contribution margin and net income increase by $120 (100 units × $1.20 per unit) to $120,120 and $80,120, respectively.

	Total	Per Unit
Sales (100,100 units)	$200,200.00	$2.00
Less: Variable costs	80,080.00	.80
Contribution margin	$120,120.00	$1.20
Less: Fixed costs	40,000.00	
Net income	$ 80,120.00	

What happens if sales decrease by 1,000 units? Contribution margin and net income will decrease by $1,200 (1,000 units × $1.20 per unit).

	Total	Per Unit
Sales (99,000 units)	$198,000.00	$2.00
Less: Variable costs	79,200.00	.80
Contribution margin	$118,800.00	$1.20
Less: Fixed costs	40,000.00	
Net income	$ 78,800.00	

As you can see, the use of contribution margin per unit makes it very easy to predict how both increases and decreases in sales volume impact contribution margin and net income.

 Key Concept: *For every unit change in sales, contribution margin will increase or decrease by the contribution margin per unit multiplied by the increase or decrease in sales volume.*

Concept Question: *How much net income will HD Inc. earn if sales decrease to 90,000 units?*

Concept Answer: Note that you can calculate the change in net income from any starting point. From 99,000 units, net income will decrease by $10,800 (9,000 units × $1.20 per unit) to $68,000. You can get the same answer starting at 100,000 units. A 10,000 unit reduction in sales will reduce income by $12,000 (10,000 × $1.20 per unit) to $68,000. ■

In the figure below, note what happens when sales volume decreases to 33,334 units. At this point, HD Inc.'s net income is zero. The company is at the break-even point when the contribution margin just covers fixed expenses and net income is zero. The calculation of a firm's break-even point is discussed in more detail later in the chapter.

	Total	Per Unit
Sales (33,334 units)	$66,668	$2.00
Less: Variable costs	26,668	.80
Contribution margin	$40,000	$1.20
Less: Fixed costs	40,000	
Net income	$ 0	

CONTRIBUTION MARGIN RATIO

The contribution margin income statement can also be presented using percentages as shown in the following income statement. The **contribution margin ratio** is calculated by dividing the contribution margin in dollars by sales dollars:

$$\text{Contribution Margin Ratio} = \frac{\text{Contribution Margin (in \$)}}{\text{Sales (in \$)}}$$

The contribution margin ratio can be viewed as the amount of each sales dollar contributing to the payment of fixed costs and increasing net profit—that is, 60 cents of each sales dollar contributes to the payment of fixed costs or increases net income. Like the contribution margin per unit, the contribution margin ratio will remain constant as long as sales vary in direct proportion to volume.

	Total	Percentage
Sales (100,000 units)	$200,000	100%
Less: Variable costs	80,000	40
Contribution margin	$120,000	60% (120,000/200,000)
Less: Fixed costs	40,000	
Net income	$ 80,000	

 Key Concept: *The contribution margin per unit and the contribution margin ratio will remain constant as long as sales vary in direct proportion to volume.*

Like contribution margin per unit, the contribution margin ratio allows us to very quickly see the impact of a change in sales on contribution margin and net income. As you saw in the income statement on page 148, a $200 increase in sales (100 units) will increase contribution margin by $120 ($200 × 60%). Assuming fixed costs don't change, this $120 increase in contribution margin increases net income by the same amount. On page 148, we decreased sales by 1,000 units ($2,000) resulting in a decrease in contribution margin and net income of $1,200 ($2,000 × 60%).

 Key Concept: *For every dollar change in sales, contribution margin will increase or decrease by the contribution margin ratio multiplied by the increase or decrease in sales dollars.*

Concept Question: *Using either contribution margin per unit or contribution margin ratio, calculate HD Inc.'s net income (loss) when sales are as follows:*

1. *25,000 units or $50,000*
2. *50,000 units or $100,000*

Concept Answer: Using the contribution margin per unit of $1.20, if sales are 25,000 units, the contribution margin will be $30,000 (25,000 × $1.20 per unit). Subtracting fixed costs of $40,000 leaves a net loss of $10,000. The contribution margin can also be calculated by multiplying sales of $50,000 by the contribution margin ratio of 60%. In a similar fashion, when sales are equal to 50,000 units ($100,000) contribution margin is equal to $60,000 and net income is equal to $20,000. ∎

Go back and calculate the contribution margin ratio in the HD Inc. income statements presented on the last few pages. Make sure you understand the calculations. You will see that it is always 60 percent.

THE CONTRIBUTION MARGIN AND ITS USES

To illustrate the many uses of the contribution margin income statement in managerial decision making, let's look at the income statement of Happy Daze Game Company. Happy Daze produces just one game but plans to increase its product line to include more

new games in the near future. The latest income statement for Happy Daze is presented below.

Happy Daze Game Company

	Total	Per Unit	Percentage
Sales (8,000 units)	$100,000	$12.50	100%
Less: Variable costs	72,000	9.00	72%
Contribution margin	$ 28,000	$ 3.50	28%
Less: Fixed costs	35,000		
Net income (loss)	$ (7,000)		

In this case, Happy Daze is losing $7,000 on sales of $100,000. What would happen if sales were to increase by 3,000 units? Using what we know about the contribution margin income statement, we can see that every unit sold contributes $3.50 or 28 percent of every sales dollar toward fixed costs. If Happy Daze sells 3,000 more units, contribution margin and net income will increase by $10,500 (3,000 × $3.50). We can use the contribution margin ratio to arrive at the same solution. Increasing sales by 3,000 units at $12.50 per unit will increase sales dollars by $37,500. With a contribution margin ratio of 28 percent and no changes in fixed costs, a $37,500 increase in sales will increase net income by $10,500 ($37,500 × 28%). What does this mean for Happy Daze? If the company can increase sales volume by 3,000 units (without changing anything else), it will show a profit of $3,500 instead of a loss of $7,000.

However, increases in sales may not happen in isolation. In order for Happy Daze to increase sales by 3,000 units, management might choose to lower the sales price, increase incentives to the sales staff, improve the quality of the product, or perhaps increase the advertising budget. As you will see in the next section, CVP analysis helps managers determine the impact on net income when these and other "what-if" decisions are made.

WHAT-IF DECISIONS USING CVP

LO3
Use the decision-making model in CVP analysis

In Chapter 1 we introduced a decision making model. This model is summarized in Exhibit 6-1. The first step in the decision-making model is to accurately define the problem. While it might be convenient to identify Happy Daze's problem as its net loss, the real problem is that contribution margin is not sufficient to cover fixed costs. Defining the problem in this way allows a more complete identification of objectives and options in Steps 2 and 3.

EXHIBIT 6-1 The Decision Model

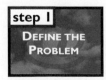
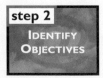

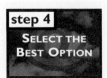

Step 2 in our decision process is to identify objectives. In this case, Happy Daze has two primary objectives—to increase net income and to maintain high-quality products.

Step 2 IDENTIFY OBJECTIVES

Step 3 is to identify Happy Daze's options. Our identification of the problem as one of contribution margin not being sufficient to cover fixed costs is helpful in fully exploring options in this step. For example, contribution margin can be increased in one of two ways: by increasing sales without a corresponding increase in variable costs (or by a greater percentage than variable costs) or by decreasing variable costs without a corresponding decrease in sales (or by a greater percentage than sales). As an alternative, Happy Daze could focus on decreasing fixed costs while holding contribution margin steady or some combination of the two. Within each of these general options, Happy Daze has a multitude of specific alternatives available that require an analysis of relevant variables.

Step 3 IDENTIFY AND ANALYZE AVAILABLE OPTIONS

After consultation with marketing, operations, and accounting managers, the CEO of Happy Daze identifies three options that she would like to consider in more depth:

1. Reducing the variable costs of manufacturing the product
2. Increasing sales through a change in the sales incentive structure or commissions (which would also increase variable costs)
3. Increasing sales through increasing advertising (a fixed cost)

OPTION 1

When variable costs are reduced, contribution margin will increase. So the question becomes: what can be done to reduce the variable costs of manufacturing? Happy Daze could find a less expensive supplier of raw material. The company could also investigate the possibility of reducing the amount of labor used in the production process or of using lower-wage employees in the production process.

LO4
Analyze what-if decisions using contribution margin per unit, contribution margin ratio, and operating leverage

In either case, qualitative factors must be considered. If Happy Daze finds a less expensive supplier of raw materials, the reliability (shipments may be late, causing down time) of the supplier and the quality (paper products are not as good, adhesive is not bonding) of the material must be considered. Reducing labor costs also has both quantitative and qualitative implications. If less labor is involved in the production process, more machine time may be needed. Although this option certainly lowers variable costs, it also raises

fixed costs. Using lower-skilled workers to save money could result in more defective products due to mistakes made by lack of experience on the part of the workers. Another possible result of using fewer workers is that it can adversely affect employee morale. Being short staffed can cause stress on workers due to the likelihood that they will be overworked.

A key point in Step 3 is that a decision maker should consider only those costs and other factors that are relevant to the decision. In other words, only those costs and other factors that vary between each of the options should be considered.

Happy Daze decides to decrease variable costs by reducing the costs of direct labor. This reduces variable costs by 10 percent and, as shown in the following analysis, results in an overall increase in net income of $7,200.

Happy Daze Game Company Impact of Reducing Variable Costs by 10%

	Current	Option 1
Sales	$100,000	$100,000
Less: Variable costs	72,000	64,800
Contribution margin	$ 28,000	$ 35,200
Less: Fixed costs	35,000	35,000
Net income (loss)	$ (7,000)	$ 200

OPTION 2

The CEO of Happy Daze would also like to consider providing additional sales incentives in an effort to increase sales volume. For example, the marketing manager estimates that if Happy Daze raises the sales commission on all sales above the present level by 10 percent, sales will increase by $30,000 or 2,400 games. (The additional sales commission will be $3,000.) The results of Option 2 are shown below.

Happy Daze Game Company Impact of Increasing Sales Incentives (sales increase to $130,000)

	Current	Option 2
Sales	$100,000	$130,000
Less: Variable costs	72,000	96,600
Contribution margin	$ 28,000	$ 33,400
Less: Fixed costs	35,000	35,000
Net income (loss)	$ (7,000)	$ (1,600)

Happy Daze can increase net income by $5,400 by increasing the sales commission by 10 percent on all sales of more than $100,000. The new variable costs are calculated by using a variable cost percentage of 72 percent on sales up to $100,000 and 82 percent on all sales of more than $100,000. However, note that Happy Daze still has a net loss under this option. In addition, it is important to remember that the increase in sales is an estimate, and actual sales may be higher or lower than $130,000. As you can see in the following income statement, if sales increase by $40,000 instead of $30,000, income will increase by $7,200 and Happy Daze will report net income of $200.

Happy Daze Game Company Impact of Increasing Sales Incentives (sales increase to $140,000)

	Current	Option 2A
Sales	$100,000	$140,000
Less: Variable costs	72,000	104,800
Contribution margin	$ 28,000	$ 35,200
Less: Fixed costs	35,000	35,000
Net income (loss)	$ (7,000)	$ 200

In Option 1 and Option 2, the ultimate change in net income can be determined by focusing solely on the change in contribution margin. Fixed costs are not relevant in either analysis because they do not vary. However, as you will see in Option 3, that is not always the case.

OPTION 3

The marketing manager estimates that spending an additional $10,000 on advertising will increase sales by $40,000 or 3,200 games. Contribution margin is again relevant because it differs between options. In addition, fixed costs are relevant in analyzing Option 3, because the increase in sales will only occur with an increase in advertising (a fixed cost).

What is the impact of Option 3 on the contribution margin and net income of Happy Daze? As shown below, increasing sales by $40,000 (3,200 games) will increase contribution margin by $11,200 [(12.50 − 9) × 3,200] or [40,000 × .28]. However, because fixed costs will also increase by $10,000, net income will increase (the net loss will decrease) by only $1,200.

Happy Daze Game Company Impact of Increasing Advertising

	Current (8,000 units)	Option 3 (11,200 units)
Sales	$100,000	$140,000
Less: Variable cost	72,000	100,800
Contribution margin	$ 28,000	$ 39,200
Less: Fixed cost	35,000	45,000
Net income (loss)	$ (7,000)	$ (5,800)

Step 4 requires the CEO of Happy Daze to select the best of the three options. How well does each option meet the stated objectives of increasing net income while maintaining a high-quality product? The CEO of Happy Daze should analyze each alternative solution in the same manner and choose the best course of action based on both quantitative and qualitative factors.

Step 4 | SELECT THE BEST OPTION

From a quantitative perspective, Option 1 results in an increase in net income of $7,200, Option 2 increases net income by $5,400, and Option 3 increases net income by $1,200. However, remember that if sales increase to $140,000 in Option 2A, net income will increase by $7,200. The increase in sales predicted in Option 3 is also not known with certainty. Step 4 requires an assessment of the risk inherent in each option, and the sensitivity of a decision to changes in key assumptions. For example, in Option 3 the marketing

www.dell.com

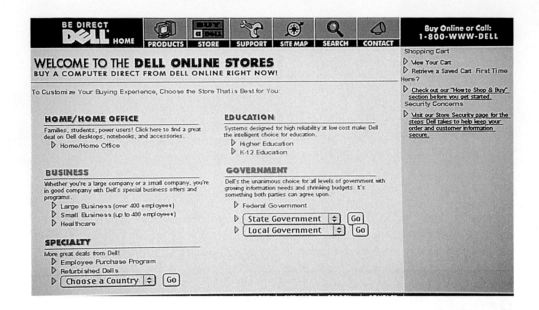

manager thinks that increased advertising could increase sales by as much as $60,000. This would result in an increase in income of $6,800. Option 1 has little quantitative risk because the decrease in costs is known with certainty, no increase in sales is projected, and it is always easier to lower costs than it is to raise sales. Based only on a quantitative analysis, Option 1 appears to be Happy Daze's best choice. However, Happy Daze must also consider the impact of the three options on the quality of their product. Of particular concern, Happy Daze should consider whether reducing labor costs in Option 1 will have a negative impact on the quality of their product. If the reduction in labor costs results from using lower paid but inadequately skilled workers, quality may be adversely affected.

CHANGES IN PRICE AND VOLUME

Managers in almost all companies frequently make decisions using CVP analysis. One decision concerns how a price change (and the resulting change in sales volume) will impact net income. Changes in sales price can have a significant impact on sales volume. Raising the sales price may result in a decrease in sales volume. However, the impact on total sales revenue may be offset by the increase in sales price. Likewise, a decrease in sales price may result in an increase in sales volume without a corresponding increase in total sales revenue.

The change in volume is a projection based on the best information available at the time. Changes in sales price can be difficult to reverse. After a sales price is lowered, customers may react unfavorably to a later unexpected increase. Consequently, risk analysis is very important in these decisions.

CROSS FUNCTIONAL APPLICATIONS	*These business strategy decisions involve individuals in many areas of an organization, such as marketing, sales, production management, and even human resources personnel for hiring decisions. The implications of a bad decision in this area can affect the firm's bottom line.*

CHANGES IN COST, PRICE, AND VOLUME

Changes can be made to cost, price, and volume at the same time. In fact, changes in cost, price, and volume are never made in a vacuum and almost always impact one or both of the other variables. As an example let's look at ZIA Motors, a manufacturer of automobiles. ZIA sells only one type of automobile (the Zoomer) at the low end of the price range. The car provides good, basic transportation but has experienced a significant drop in demand (and therefore profitability) in the past year. As a result, ZIA has decided to improve the quality of the Zoomer and market the car as a higher-quality but still economical alternative to its better-known American-made competitors. The cost of direct material and other variable costs in the redesigned model will increase by 20 percent (from $6,000 to $7,200) due to higher labor costs and the use of higher-quality engine materials and insulation to provide a quieter ride. Fixed costs will also increase due to the additional machinery needed. ZIA will need to invest $100 million in new equipment and robotics resulting in annual depreciation of $20 million. They also plan a $10 million advertising and public relations campaign to let the buying public know about the enhancements to the car. ZIA also plans to increase the sales price of the redesigned Zoomer from $8,000 to $10,000. The marketing department estimates that these changes will increase demand by somewhere between 2,000 and 10,000 cars per year. (Current demand is 30,000 cars.) When pressed for its best forecast, the marketing department estimates new sales at 35,000 automobiles. Current and projected income statements for ZIA are shown below.

Current and Projected Income Statements for ZIA Motors

	Current	**After Proposed Changes**
Sales	$240,000,000	$350,000,000
Less: Variable costs	180,000,000	252,000,000
Contribution margin	$ 60,000,000	$ 98,000,000
Less: Fixed costs	75,000,000	105,000,000
Net income	$ (15,000,000)	$ (7,000,000)

As you can see, although net income increases with the proposed changes, ZIA is still losing money on the Zoomer. Even though contribution margin increases by $38 million, fixed costs increase by $30 million resulting in an overall increase in net income of $8 million.

IN THE NEWS	**www.hyundai.com**

Hyundai has been dealing with the public perception of the quality of their automobiles for years. In the past, Hyundai had a reputation for building inexpensive, lower-quality cars and has struggled to raise the selling prices of its newer cars to reflect their higher quality.

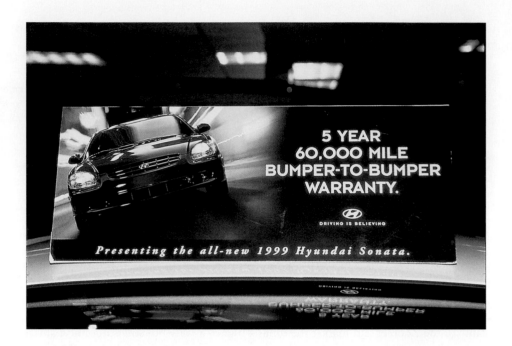

Concept Question: *If sales only increase by 2,000 cars, how much will income increase (decrease)? What if sales increase by 10,000 cars?*

Concept Answer: These types of what-if questions can be answered most easily using concepts of CVP analysis already at your disposal. In the previous example, if the proposed changes are made, the sale of each car will contribute $2,800 toward fixed costs and ultimately net income. In other words, the contribution margin of each car sold is $2,800 ($10,000 sales price less $7,200 variable costs). If 32,000 cars are sold, total contribution margin will be $89,600,000 (32,000 × $2,800). Although this is an increase of $29,600,000, the change in fixed costs must also be considered. Because fixed costs increase by $30,000,000, income will actually decrease by $400,000 if only 32,000 cars are sold. On the other hand, if 40,000 cars are sold, contribution margin will be $112 million, an increase of $52 million (40,000 × $2,800). This more than offsets the $30 million increase in fixed costs and income will increase by $22 million. ■

Step 4 | SELECT THE BEST OPTION

Step 4 of the decision model explicitly recognizes the uncertainty inherent in many decisions. In this case, our decision is sensitive to assumptions made concerning the demand for the remodeled car. If demand for redesigned Zoomers is only 32,000 cars, net income will actually decrease and ZIA will choose not to make the changes. If sales increase to 35,000 or 40,000 cars, income will increase under the proposed changes.

Concept Question: *At what level of sales will ZIA be indifferent to making the proposed change? In other words, at what level of sales will ZIA Motors' current loss of $15 million remain the same?*

Concept Answer: Because fixed costs increase by $30 million under the new proposal, contribution margin must also increase by $30 million for ZIA Motors to be equally well off under the proposed changes. A $30 million increase in contribution margin requires a new contribution margin of $90 million and sales of 32,143 cars. (32,143 cars × $2,800 contribution margin per car = $90 million (rounded).) ■

BREAK-EVEN ANALYSIS

In addition to what-if analysis, it is useful for a company to know how many units or the dollar amount of sales that are necessary for it to break even. The **break-even point** is the level of sales where contribution margin just covers fixed costs and consequently net income is equal to zero. Break-even analysis is really just a variation of CVP analysis in which volume is increased or decreased in an effort to find the point at which net income is equal to zero.

Break-even analysis is facilitated through the use of a mathematical equation derived directly from the contribution margin income statement. Another way to look at these relationships is to put the income statement into equation form:

$$\text{Sales} - \text{Variable costs} - \text{Fixed costs} = \text{Net income}$$

or

$$\text{Net Income} = (\text{Sales price per unit} \times \text{Volume}) - (\text{Variable cost per unit} \times \text{Volume}) - \text{Fixed cost}$$

Substituting symbols we have the following:

$$NI = SP\,(x) - VC(x) - FC$$

where x = sales volume. Because SP − VC = contribution margin, the formula is simplified to

$$NI = CM(x) - FC$$

Because NI = 0 at the break-even point, total CM must equal FC,

$$CM(x) = FC$$

and the volume of sales in order to break even (x) can be calculated by dividing FC by CM:

$$\text{Break-even (units)} = \frac{\text{Fixed cost}}{\text{Contribution margin per unit}}$$

By dividing the contribution margin of each product into the fixed cost, we are calculating the number of units that must be sold to cover the fixed costs. At that point, the total contribution margin will be equal to fixed costs and net income will be zero. For example if Happy Daze has fixed costs of $35,000 and the contribution margin per unit is $3.50 as shown earlier, the break-even point is computed as follows:

$$
\begin{aligned}
\text{Break-even (units)} &= \frac{\text{Fixed costs}}{\text{Contribution margin per unit}} \\
&= \frac{\$35,000}{\$3.50} \\
&= 10,000 \text{ units}
\end{aligned}
$$

We can use a similar formula to compute the amount of sales dollars needed to break even:

$$\text{Break-even (\$)} = \frac{\text{Fixed costs}}{\text{Contribution margin ratio}}$$

Using the amounts from the previous example,

$$\text{Break-even (\$)} = \frac{\$35,000}{28\% \text{ (see page 150)}}$$
$$= \$125,000$$

Concept Question: *Refer to the income statement on page 155 for ZIA Motors. How many Zoomers does ZIA have to sell under the proposed changes in order to break even?*

Concept Answer:

$$\text{Break-even (units)} = \frac{\text{Fixed costs}}{\text{Contribution margin per unit}}$$

$$= \frac{\$105,000,000}{\$2,800}$$

$$= 37,500 \text{ units} \ \blacksquare$$

Graphically, the break-even point can be found by comparing a company's total revenue with its total costs (both fixed and variable). As seen in Exhibit 6-2, the break-even point is the volume at which total revenue is equal to total cost.

EXHIBIT 6-2 Break-Even Graph

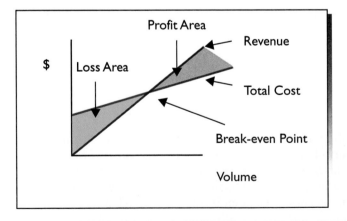

BREAK-EVEN CALCULATIONS WITH MULTIPLE PRODUCTS

Break-even calculations become more difficult when more than one product is produced and sold. In a multiproduct environment, a manager calculating the break-even point is concerned not so much with the unit sales or the dollar sales of a single product but with the amount of total sales necessary to break even. This requires the calculation of an "average" contribution margin for all the products produced and sold. This in turn requires an estimate of the sales mix—the relative percentage of total units or total sales dollars expected from each product.[1] However, customers (and sales volume) will not always behave in the manner that we predict. For example, although the expected sales product mix may be 600 units of Product A and 400 units of Product B, we can only estimate our customers' buying habits from past experience. If the sales product mix ends up being 700 units of A and 300 units of B, the break-even analysis will change accordingly.

Assume that Happy Daze adds another game to its product line. The company estimates that the new game will achieve sales of approximately 50 percent of the old game. So if 8,000 units of the old game were sold, Happy Daze would expect to sell about 4,000 units of the new game. The expected sales product mix (in units) is therefore two-thirds $\left(\frac{8,000}{12,000}\right)$ old game and one-third $\left(\frac{4,000}{12,000}\right)$ new game. The new game will be priced at $15 per unit and requires $11 of variable production, selling, and administrative costs so the contribution margin per unit is $4. The game will also require an investment of $15,000 in additional fixed costs. A summary of the price and cost of the old and new games is provided below.

LO5
Compute a company's break-even point in a single and multiproduct environment

Happy Daze Game Company

	Old Game (8,000 units)	Per Unit	New Game (4,000 units)	Per Unit
Sales	$100,000	$12.50	$60,000	$15.00
Less: Variable cost	72,000	9.00	44,000	11.00
Contribution margin	$ 28,000	$ 3.50	$16,000	$ 4.00
Less: Fixed cost	35,000		15,000	
Net income (loss)	$ (7,000)		$ 1,000	

The calculation of "average" contribution margin is *really* a weighted average. Although the simple-average contribution margin of the old game ($3.50) and the new game ($4.00) is $3.75, the weighted average is $3.67 (rounded). This can be seen most easily by examining the total column of the income statement.

Happy Daze Game Company

	Old Game (8,000)	Per Unit	New Game (4,000)	Per Unit	Total (12,000)	Per Unit
Sales	$100,000	$12.50	$60,000	$15.00	$160,000	$13.33
Less: Variable cost	72,000	9.00	44,000	11.00	116,000	9.67
Contribution margin	$ 28,000	$ 3.50	$16,000	$ 4.00	$ 44,000	$ 3.67
Less: Fixed cost	35,000		15,000		50,000	
Net income (loss)	$ (7,000)		$ 1,000		$ (6,000)	

---

[1]Calculating the optimum mix of products to produce given limited resources and demand constraints is addressed in Chapter 7. The optimum mix will result in the highest overall contribution margin and also the highest overall profit for a company.

Happy Daze Game Co.

Dividing the total contribution margin of $44,000 by 12,000 units sold gives us a total contribution margin of $3.67 (rounded) per unit. The weighted average contribution margin can be calculated more directly by multiplying the unit contribution margin for each game by the proportion of each game in the sales mix and adding the resulting numbers. This effectively weights each product's contribution margin by the relative sales mix for that product.

$$\text{Old game} = \frac{2}{3} \times \$3.50 = \$2.33 \text{ (rounded)}$$

$$\text{New game} = \frac{1}{3} \times \$4.00 = \$1.33 \text{ (rounded)}$$

$$\text{Weighted average contribution margin} = \$3.66$$

The weighted average contribution margin for Happy Daze Game Company is therefore $3.66 per game (rounded).

Concept Question: *Assuming a sales mix of 50 percent old games and 50 percent new games, calculate the new weighted average contribution margin for Happy Daze. Does it increase or decrease? What if the sales mix changes to 40 percent old games and 60 percent new games? Why does the weighted average contribution margin continue to increase as Happy Daze sells more new games and fewer old games?*

Concept Answer: With the sales mix at 50 percent old and 50 percent new, the weighted average contribution margin becomes $3.75 [(.50 × 3.50)+(.50 × 4.00)]. When the mix changes to 40 percent old and 60 percent new, the weighted average contribution margin changes to $3.80 [(.40 × 3.50) + (.60 × 4.00)]. Notice that when the volume shifts toward selling more of the product with the highest contribution margin, the weighted average contribution margin increases. ■

The break-even formula for a company with multiple products is therefore as follows:

$$\text{Break-even (units)} = \frac{\text{Fixed costs}}{\text{Weighted average contribution margin per unit}}$$

Happy Daze's break-even point is therefore: $\left(\frac{\$50,000}{3.67}\right)$ or 13,624 units (rounded). How is this number interpreted? Remember that the weighted average contribution margin is dependent on the sales mix. Likewise, the break-even point is dependent on the sales mix (two-thirds old games and one-third new games). Assuming a sales mix of two-thirds to one-third, Happy Daze must sell 9,128 old games and 4,496 new games (rounded) to break even.

$$\text{Old game: } 13,624 \times \frac{2}{3} = 9,083$$

$$\text{New game: } 13,624 \times \frac{1}{3} = 4,541$$

Concept Question: *Refer to the previous concept question. If the sales mix changes to 50 percent old games and 50 percent new games, what will be the impact on the break-even point? What if the sales mix changes to 40 percent old games and 60 percent new games?*

PAUSE & *Reflect*

Imagine how difficult it is for large retail stores such as Wal-Mart or REI to compute a break-even point for the entire store or company.

Concept Answer: As the sales mix changes and Happy Daze sells more new games with a higher contribution margin, the break-even point will decrease. ■

www.walmart.com
www.rei.com

The break-even point calculated using a weighted average contribution margin for multiple products is only valid at the sales mix used in the calculation. If the sales mix changes, the break-even point will also change. Obviously, the more products involved in the sales mix, the more sensitive the calculation becomes to changes in sales mix.

BREAK-EVEN CALCULATIONS USING ACTIVITY-BASED COSTING

Computing break-even when using activity-based costing (ABC) requires some slight modifications to the general formulas presented thus far. Conventional CVP analysis assumes that all costs are either variable or fixed. In ABC, costs are classified as unit, batch, product, or facility level and CVP analysis must be modified accordingly. Whereas unit-level costs behave like true variable costs and vary directly with volume, and facility-level costs behave like fixed costs, batch- and product-level costs are likely to vary with drivers related to the complexity of a product or product diversity. Along with fixed costs, batch- and product-level costs are included in the numerator of the break-even formula. However, unlike traditional break-even analysis, they are allowed to vary with changes in their appropriate cost drivers. Although it may appear that the value of CVP would diminish when using ABC, in fact CVP analysis may be even more useful in decision making because the cost behavior information in an ABC system is more accurate.

The break-even equation when using ABC is modified as follows:

LO6
Use break-even analysis in an activity-based costing environment

$$\text{Break-even (units)} = \frac{\text{(Fixed costs + Batch-level costs + Product-level costs)}}{\text{Contribution margin per unit}}$$

In the formula, batch-level costs are equal to the cost per unit multiplied by the appropriate batch-level driver(s) and product-level costs are equal to the cost per unit multiplied by the appropriate product-level driver(s). The contribution margin per unit is calculated

by subtracting unit-level variable costs from the sales price. The main differences between the two calculations are as follows:

1. The fixed costs differ. Some costs that were previously identified as being fixed may actually vary with nonunit cost drivers (batch- and product-level costs).
2. These nonunit-level variable costs are included in the numerator along with fixed costs.

An ABC analysis of Happy Daze's product costs is shown below.

Sales price:	$12.50 per unit
Variable cost:	
Direct material	$ 3.00 per unit
Direct labor	$ 2.00 per unit
Variable overhead	$ 4.00 per unit
Total variable cost	$ 9.00 per unit
Setup cost (batch)	$10,000 (10 setups @ $1,000 per setup)
Testing cost (product)	$ 5,000 (200 testing hours @ $25 per testing hour)
Facility-level fixed costs	$20,000

Putting these numbers into the ABC break-even formula results in the following:

$$\text{Break-even (units)} = \frac{(\$20,000 + \$10,000 + \$5,000)}{\$3.50}$$
$$= 10,000 \text{ units}$$

Concept Question: *Why is the break-even point using the ABC break-even formula the same as that computed using the conventional break-even formula?*

Concept Answer: Using the conventional break-even formula, fixed costs are $35,000 and consist of true fixed costs and nonunit-level variable costs associated with setups and testing. As long as the number of setups and inspection hours remain constant, the break-even will be the same under conventional break-even analysis and ABC. ■

However, if setups or the number of inspection or testing hours change, break-even will be different. Conventional break-even calculations ignore the changes in batch- and product-level costs. (Remember that they are treated as fixed under a conventional break-even analysis.) But these activity levels can change. For example, if Happy Daze discovers that it can reduce the direct labor involved with production of games from $2.00 to $1.85 per unit, its contribution margin will increase to $3.65 and the break-even point will decrease to 9,589 units (rounded). Using the conventional break-even formula would lead one to believe that the reduction in direct labor does in fact reduce the break-even point. However, what if Happy Daze has to increase the amount of time spent inspecting or testing the product as a result of the reduction in direct labor? Because the ABC system treats inspection or testing time as a nonunit-level variable cost, the additional hours of inspection time will impact the break-even point. If the reduction in direct labor adds an additional

70 inspection hours, total costs will increase to $6,750 (270 hours × $25 per hour) and the break-even point will be as follows:

$$\text{Break-even (units)} = \frac{\$20,000 + \$10,000 + \$6,750}{\$3.65}$$
$$= 10,069 \text{ units (rounded)}$$

As can be seen from this computation of the break-even point using the ABC formula, the break-even point actually is higher than before the reduction in direct labor. Why is that? At a sales volume of 10,000 units (the old break-even point) the reduction in direct labor is $1,500 (10,000 × .15) but the increased inspection expense is $1,750 (70 hours × $25). So what appears to be a cost reduction really isn't. Break-even analysis using ABC allows managers to more clearly see these tradeoffs, often leading to better decisions.

TARGET PROFIT ANALYSIS (BEFORE AND AFTER TAX)

The goal of most businesses is not to break even but to earn a profit. Luckily, we can easily modify the break-even formula to compute the amount of sales (units or dollars) needed to earn a target profit (before tax). Instead of solving for the sales necessary to earn a net income of zero, we simply solve for the sales necessary to reach a target profit.

LO7
Analyze target profit before and after the impact of income tax

$$\text{Sales} - \text{Variable costs} - \text{Fixed costs} = \text{Target profit (before tax)}$$

or

$$\text{Target profit} = (\text{Sales price per unit} \times \text{Volume}) - (\text{Variable cost per unit} \times \text{Volume})$$
$$- \text{Fixed cost}$$

Substituting symbols we have

$$\text{TP (before tax)} = \text{SP}(x) - \text{VC}(x) - \text{FC}$$

where x = sales volume. Because SP − VC = contribution margin, the formula is simplified to

$$\text{TP (before tax)} = \text{CM}(x) - \text{FC}$$

or

$$\text{CM}(x) = \text{FC} + \text{TP (before tax)}$$

To solve for x, divide each side by CM:

$$\text{Sales volume (to reach a target profit before tax)} = \frac{[\text{FC} + \text{TP (before tax)}]}{\text{CM}}$$

**Happy
Daze**
Game Co.

Happy Daze has decided that it must earn a target profit of $100,000 or the owners/stockholders will not want to continue their investment in the business. The question is how many games does the company have to sell to earn that amount of profit? Using the target profit formula presented earlier and the data for the old game from page 150, consider the following equation:

$$\text{Sales volume (to reach a target profit before tax)} = \frac{(\$35{,}000 + \$100{,}000)}{\$3.50}$$
$$= 38{,}572 \text{ units (rounded)}$$

Although Happy Daze must only sell 10,000 games to break even, the company must sell 38,572 games to reach a before-tax target profit of $100,000. In fact, once we know that Happy Daze's break-even point is 10,000 units, we can directly calculate the sales necessary to reach a target profit of $100,000 using the CM per unit. Because each additional unit sold (above the break-even point) will contribute $3.50 towards net income, Happy Daze must sell an additional 28,572 units $\left(\frac{\$100{,}000}{3.50}\right)$ to earn a profit of $100,000.

Concept Question: *Using your knowledge of CVP analysis, how many units must Happy Daze sell in order to earn a target profit of $50,000?*

Concept Answer: To reach a before-tax target profit of $50,000, Happy Daze must sell 24,286 units calculated as follows:

$$\text{Sales volume (to reach a target profit before tax)} = (\$35{,}000 + \$50{,}000)/\$3.50$$
$$= 24{,}286 \text{ units (rounded).} \blacksquare$$

The multiple product break-even and ABC break-even formulas can be modified in a similar fashion to solve for the sales necessary to reach a target profit. In a multiple product environment:

$$\text{Sales volume (to reach target profit)} = \frac{\text{(Fixed costs + Target profit)}}{\text{Weighted average contribution margin per unit}}$$

Using ABC, the formula is modified as follows:

$$\text{Sales volume (to reach target profit)}$$
$$= \frac{\text{(Fixed costs + Batch-level costs + Product-level costs + Target profit)}}{\text{Contribution margin per unit}}$$

THE IMPACT OF TAXES

The payment of income taxes also needs to be considered in the target profit formula. If Happy Daze sells 38,572 games and earns the projected $100,000 in target profit, the company still won't have $100,000 cash flow to distribute to the owners as dividends because it must pay income tax on the profit. If we assume that the income tax rate for

Happy Daze is 35 percent, then the company will have to pay $35,000 in income tax ($100,000 × 35%) and will be left with after-tax profit of $65,000. The after-tax profit can be found by multiplying the before-tax profit by (1 − tax rate). Correspondingly, the before-tax profit is equal to the after-tax profit divided by (1 − tax rate):

$$\text{Before-tax profit} = \text{After-tax profit}/(1 - \text{tax rate})$$

If Happy Daze desires to earn an after-tax profit of $100,000, the company must earn a before-tax profit of $153,846 (rounded).

$$\text{Before-tax profit} = \$100,000/(1 - .35) = \$153,846$$

Modifying the before-tax target profit equation accordingly, we have

$$\text{Sales volume (to reach an after-tax target profit)} = \frac{[\text{FC} + \text{After-tax profit}/(1 - \text{tax rate})]}{\text{CM}}$$

Consequently, Happy Daze must sell 53,956 units in order to reach a before-tax profit of $153,846 and an after-tax profit of $100,000.

$$\text{Sales volume (to reach an after-tax target profit)} = \frac{(\$35,000 + \$153,846)}{\$3.50}$$
$$= 53,956 \text{ units}$$

This is confirmed in the income statement for Happy Daze shown below.

Happy Daze Game Company

Sales (53,956 units)	$674,450
Less: Variable costs	485,604
Contribution margin	$188,846
Less: Fixed costs	35,000
Net income	$153,846
Less: Income tax @ 35%	53,846
Net income after tax	$100,000

 Key Concept: *The payment of income taxes is an important variable in target profit and other CVP decisions.*

Not accounting for the impact of income taxes in profit planning and break-even decisions can be a costly error.

> **APPLICATION IN BUSINESS**   www.irs.gov
>
> The top federal income tax rate applicable to corporations is currently 35 percent. The top federal income tax rate applicable to individuals and small businesses operated as sole proprietorships is currently 39.6 percent. Most states also levy some kind of tax on the earnings of businesses. It is not unusual for a business to face total income tax rates of 40 percent or higher.

ASSUMPTIONS OF CVP ANALYSIS

LO8
Identify the assumptions inherent in CVP analysis

As in any form of analysis involving projections of the future, there are certain assumptions that must be taken into consideration. The major assumptions are as follows:

1. The selling price is constant throughout the entire relevant range. In other words, we assume that the sales price of the product will not change as volume changes.

2. Costs are linear throughout the relevant range. As discussed in Chapter 5, although costs may behave in a curvilinear fashion, they can often be approximated by a linear relationship between cost and volume within the relevant range.

3. The sales mix used to calculate the weighted average contribution margin is constant.

4. The amount of inventory is constant. In other words, the number of units produced is equal to the number of units sold.

Although some of these assumptions appear to be violated often in real business settings, the violations are usually minor and have little or no impact on management decisions. CVP analysis can still be considered valid and very useful in decision making.

COST STRUCTURE AND OPERATING LEVERAGE

LO9
Identify the differences between variable costing and absorption costing and the use of variable costing for decision making

As mentioned in Chapter 5, cost structure refers to the relative proportion of fixed and variable costs in a company. Highly automated manufacturing companies with large investments in property, plant, and equipment are likely to have cost structures dominated by fixed costs. On the other hand, labor-intensive companies like home builders are likely to have cost structures dominated by variable costs. Even companies in the same industry can have very different cost structures. A company's cost structure is important because it directly affects the sensitivity of a company's profits to changes in sales volume. Consider, for example, two companies that make the same product (furniture), with the same sales and same income. Company A is highly automated and uses state-of-the-art machinery to design, cut, and assemble its products. On the other hand, Company B is highly labor intensive and uses skilled craftspeople to cut and assemble its products. Contribution margin income statements for both companies are provided in Exhibit 6-3.

Concept Question: Which company would you prefer to be?

Concept Answer: Although you might opt for Company A with its high level of automation and correspondingly higher contribution margin ratio relative to Company B, consider the impact of changes in sales volume on the net income of each company. Although *increasing* sales will benefit Company A more than Company B, what happens when sales *decline*? If sales decline by 10 percent ($20,000), the income of Company A will decline by $16,000 ($20,000 × 80%) while the income of Company B will decline by $12,000 ($20,000 × 60%). ■

EXHIBIT 6-3   Contribution Margin Ratio and Operating Leverage

	Company A	Company B
Sales	$200,000	$200,000
Less: Variable costs	40,000	80,000
Contribution margin	$160,000	$120,000
Less: Fixed costs	80,000	40,000
Net income	$ 80,000	$ 80,000
Contribution margin ratio	80%	60%
Operating leverage	2.0	1.5

A company with a cost structure characterized by a large proportion of fixed costs relative to variable costs will see wider fluctuations in income as sales increase and decrease than a company with more variable costs in its cost structure.

OPERATING LEVERAGE

Operating leverage is a measure of the proportion of fixed costs in a company's cost structure and is used as an indicator of how sensitive profit is to changes in sales volume. A company with high fixed costs in relation to variable costs will have a high level of operating leverage. In this case net income will be very sensitive to changes in sales volume. In other words, a small percentage increase in sales dollars will result in a large percentage increase in net income. On the other hand, a company with high variable costs in relation to fixed costs will have a low level of operating leverage and income will not be as sensitive to changes in sales volume. Operating leverage is computed using the following formula:

$$\text{Operating leverage} = \frac{\text{Contribution margin}}{\text{Net income}}$$

In Exhibit 6-3, Company A has an operating leverage of 2.0 $\left(\frac{\$160,000}{\$80,000}\right)$ while Company B has an operating leverage of 1.5 $\left(\frac{\$120,000}{\$80,000}\right)$. What does this mean? When sales increase (decrease) by a given percentage, the income of Company A will increase (decrease) by 2 times that percentage increase (decrease) while the income of Company B will increase (decrease) by 1.5 times the percentage change in sales. When sales increase by 10 percent, the income of Company A will increase by 20 percent or $16,000 ($80,000 × 20%). In other words, when sales of Company A increase to $220,000, income will increase to $96,000. The income of Company B will increase by 15 percent or $12,000 ($80,000 × 15%) to a new income of $92,000. Likewise, when sales decrease by 10 percent, the income of Company A will decrease by 20 percent while the income of Company B will decrease by 15 percent.

Concept Question: *Using operating leverage and the income statements in Exhibit 6-3, calculate the net income of Company A and Company B when sales increase (decrease) by 50 percent or $100,000.*

Concept Answer: When sales increase by 50 percent, the income of Company A will increase by 100 percent (2 × 50%) to $160,000 ($80,000 + $80,000). The income of Company B will increase by 75 percent (1.5 × 50%) to $140,000 ($80,000 + $60,000). When sales decrease by 50 percent, the income of Company A will decrease by 100 percent to $0 ($80,000 − $80,000) and the income of Company B will decrease by 75 percent to $20,000 ($80,000 − $60,000). ∎

PAUSE
& Reflect

You should note that the same answers can be found using the contribution margin per unit or the contribution margin ratio.

Unlike measures of contribution margin, operating leverage changes as sales change. Consider the table below, which provides contribution margin income statements for Company B at different levels of sales.

Company B

	500 Units	1,000 Units	2,000 Units
Sales	$100,000	$200,000	$400,000
Less: Variable costs	40,000	80,000	160,000
Contribution margin	$ 60,000	$120,000	$240,000
Less: Fixed costs	40,000	40,000	40,000
Net income	$ 20,000	$ 80,000	$200,000
Operating leverage	$ 60,000 / $ 20,000 = 3.0	$120,000 / $ 80,000 = 1.5	$240,000 / $200,000 = 1.2

At a sales level of 1,000 units ($200,000), Company B's operating leverage is 1.5. A 10 percent increase in sales increases net income by 15 percent. At a sales level of 500 units, operating leverage increases to 3.0 and a 10 percent increase in sales will increase net income by 30 percent (3 × 10%). At a sales level of 2,000 units, operating leverage is reduced to 1.2 and a 10 percent increase in sales will increase income by 12 percent.

As a company gets closer and closer to the break-even point, operating leverage will continue to increase and income will be very sensitive to changes in sales. Company B's break-even point is 334 units (rounded). At this level of sales, contribution margin is equal to $40,080, income is equal to $80, and operating leverage is equal to $501 \left(\frac{$40,080}{$80} \right)$! A 10 percent increase in sales at this point will increase net income by 5,010 percent!

Company B

Sales (334 units)	$66,800
Less: Variable costs	26,720
Contribution margin	$40,080
Less: Fixed costs	40,000
Net income	$ 80

 Key Concept: *A company operating near the break-even point will have a high level of operating leverage and income will be very sensitive to changes in sales volume.*

Understanding the concepts of contribution margin and operating leverage and how they are used in CVP analysis are very important in managerial decision making. Using these tools, managers can quickly estimate the impact on net income of changes in cost, sales volume, and price.

VARIABLE COSTING FOR DECISION MAKING

In Chapter 2, a system of product costing was introduced in which all manufacturing costs, fixed and variable, were treated as product costs. Product costs included direct materials, direct labor, and all manufacturing overhead (both fixed and variable). You will recall that product costs attach to the product and are only expensed when the product is sold. On the other hand, selling and administrative costs (period costs) are expensed immediately in the period in which they are incurred. Commonly called **absorption costing or full costing,** this method is required for both external financial statements prepared under generally accepted accounting principles (GAAP) and for income tax reporting.

On the other hand, **variable costing or direct costing** treats only variable production costs (direct material, direct labor, and variable manufacturing overhead) as product costs, whereas fixed manufacturing overhead is treated as a period cost (along with selling and administrative costs). Variable costing is more consistent with CVP's focus on differentiating fixed from variable costs and provides useful information for internal decision making that is often not apparent when using absorption costing.

Exhibit 6-4 provides a summary of the two costing methods. As you can see, *the only difference between absorption and variable costing is the treatment of fixed overhead.* Under absorption costing, fixed overhead is treated as a product cost, added to the cost of the product and only expensed when the product is sold (as cost of goods sold). Under variable costing, fixed overhead is treated as a period cost and is expensed as incurred. The impact of this difference on reported income becomes evident when a company's production and sales are different (units produced are greater than units sold or units sold are greater than units produced).

Because absorption costing treats fixed overhead as a product cost, if units of production remain unsold at year-end, fixed overhead remains attached to those units and is included on the balance sheet as an asset (the cost of inventory). Using variable costing, all fixed manufacturing overhead is expensed each period regardless of the level of production or sales. Consequently, when production is greater than sales and inventories increase, absorption costing will result in higher net income than variable costing.

Let's look at a simple example in which HD Inc. produces 100,000 units each year. The cost of each unit includes direct material of $.30, direct labor of $.35, and variable overhead of $.10 per unit. In addition, fixed manufacturing overhead costs of $30,000 are incurred. Variable selling and administrative costs are $.05 per unit sold, and fixed selling and administrative costs are equal to $10,000. The selling price of one unit is

EXHIBIT 6-4 Absorption and Variable Costing

ABSORPTION COSTING		VARIABLE COSTING	
Product Costs	**Period Costs**	**Product Costs**	**Period Costs**
Direct materials		Direct materials	
Direct labor		Direct labor	
Variable overhead		Variable overhead	
Fixed overhead			**Fixed overhead**
	Selling & admin.		Selling & admin.

$2. The cost of one unit of product under absorption and variable costing is calculated as follows:.

Product Costs

Absorption Costing		Variable Costing	
Direct material	$ .30	Direct material	$.30
Direct labor	.35	Direct labor	.35
Variable overhead	.10	Variable overhead	$.10
Fixed overhead	$ .30		
Total per unit	$1.05	Total per unit	$.75

The only difference between the two methods is $.30 of fixed overhead $\left(\frac{\$30,000}{\$100,000 \text{ units}}\right)$, which is treated as a product cost under absorption costing and a period cost under variable costing. If all 100,000 units are sold in Year 1, how much income is reported under each method?

Under absorption costing, fixed manufacturing costs are expensed as part of cost of goods sold. Under variable costing, fixed manufacturing overhead costs are deducted as a fixed period cost. Regardless, when all units produced are sold, the net income reported under each method would be the same.

Year 1 Comparison of Absorption and Variable Costing

Absorption Costing		Variable Costing	
Sales	$200,000	Sales	$200,000
Less: Cost of goods sold	105,000	Less: Variable costs	80,000
Gross profit	$ 95,000	Contribution margin	$120,000
Less: Selling & admin. costs	15,000	Less: Fixed costs	40,000
Net income	$ 80,000	Net income	$ 80,000

In Year 2, assume that 100,000 units are produced but only 80,000 units are sold. In this case, the variable costing method would expense the entire $30,000 of fixed manufacturing overhead as a period cost, whereas the absorption method would only expense $24,000 (80,000 units × $.30 per unit). When production exceeds sales, absorption costing will report higher net income than variable costing. Part of the $30,000 of fixed overhead (20,000 units × $.30 per unit or $6,000) remains in inventory until those units are sold.

Year 2 (80,000 units sold)

Absorption Costing		Variable Costing	
Sales	$160,000	Sales	$160,000
Less: Cost of Goods sold[1]	84,000	Less: Variable Costs	64,000
Gross Profit	76,000	Contribution Margin	96,000
Less: Selling & Admin. Costs	14,000	Less: Fixed Costs[2]	40,000
Net Income	$ 62,000	Net Income	$ 56,000

[1]Cost of Goods Sold includes $24,000 (80,000 × $.30) of fixed manufacturing overhead.

[2]Fixed Costs include $30,000 of fixed manufacturing overhead.

In Year 3, assume that 100,000 units are produced and 120,000 units are sold. (The 20,000 remaining units from Year 2 are sold.) In this case, under variable costing, $30,000 of fixed manufacturing overhead would continue to be expensed as a period cost. Under absorption costing, the $30,000 would get expensed plus an extra $6,000 related to the 20,000 units produced last year and sold this year (20,000 units $\times$ $.30 per unit = $6,000). When units sold exceed units produced, variable costing will report higher net income than absorption costing.

Year 3 (120,000 units sold)

Absorption Costing		Variable Costing	
Sales	$240,000	Sales	$240,000
Less: Cost of Goods Sold[1]	126,000	Less: Variable Costs	96,000
Gross Profit	114,000	Contribution Margin	144,000
Less: Selling & Admin. Costs	16,000	Less: Fixed Costs[2]	40,000
Net Income	$ 98,000	Net Income	$104,000

[1]Cost of Goods Sold includes $36,000 (120,000 $\times$ $.30) of fixed manufacturing overhead.

[2]Fixed Costs include $30,000 of fixed manufacturing overhead.

To summarize the three rules:

1. When units sold equal units produced, net income is the same under both costing methods.
2. When units produced exceed units sold, absorption costing will report higher income than variable costing.
3. When units sold exceed units produced, variable costing will report higher net income than absorption costing.

The use of absorption costing for internal decision making can result in less than optimal decisions. For example, consider the case of the unemployed executive that offered his services to a manufacturing company for only $1 per year in salary and a bonus equal to 50 percent of any increase in net income generated for the year. Reviewing the absorption costing income statement for the previous year, he learned that while 10,000 units of product were produced and sold, the company had the capacity to produce 20,000 units. In addition, variable production costs were $40 per unit, variable selling and administrative costs were $10 per unit sold, fixed manufacturing overhead costs were equal to $300,000 ($30 per unit produced), and fixed selling and administrative costs were equal to $100,000. As shown below, last year's net income was $100,000.

Absorption Costing Income (10,000 units produced)

Sales (10,000 units)	$1,000,000
Less: Cost of Goods Sold[1]	700,000
Gross Profit	300,000
Less: Selling & Admin. Costs	200,000
Net Income	$ 100,000

[1]Includes $300,000 (10,000 units $\times$ $30) of fixed manufacturing overhead.

By increasing production to 20,000 units, the per-unit allocation of fixed manufacturing overhead is reduced to $15 $\left(\frac{\$300,000}{20,000 \text{ units}} = \$15 \right)$. Remember that under absorption costing, fixed overhead is a product cost and is only expensed when the product is sold. Therefore, only $150,000 of fixed overhead costs will be expensed. The remaining $150,000 of fixed manufacturing overhead costs is included in inventory and is reported as an asset on the balance sheet. The cost of goods sold is reduced to $550,000 and net income is increased by $150,000 to $250,000. The manager is entitled to a bonus of $75,000, while the company is saddled with 10,000 units of unsold inventory and the attendant costs of storing and insuring it.

Absorption Costing Income (20,000 units produced)

Sales (10,000 units)	$1,000,000
Less: Cost of Goods Sold[1]	550,000
Gross Profit	450,000
Less: Selling & Admin. Costs	200,000
Net Income	$ 250,000

[1]Includes $150,000 (10,000 units × $15) of fixed costs.

If income had been measured using a variable costing approach, net income would be the same each year and the manager would not be able to pull off this scheme.

 Key Concept: *Variable costing is consistent with CVP's focus on differentiating fixed from variable costs and provides useful information for decision making that is often not apparent when using absorption costing.*

Many other decisions such as whether to accept special orders, to make or buy component parts, and to add or drop product lines are influenced by the costing approach used by a company. These decisions are discussed in more detail in Chapter 7. In addition, you should note that problems like these are minimized in a just-in-time (JIT) environment in which inventory levels are minimized and companies strive to produce only enough product to meet demand.

SUMMARY OF KEY CONCEPTS

- The contribution margin income statement is structured to emphasize cost behavior as opposed to cost function. (p. 147)
- For every unit change in sales, contribution margin will increase or decrease by the contribution margin per unit multiplied by the increase or decrease in sales volume. (p. 148)
- The contribution margin per unit and the contribution margin ratio will remain constant as long as sales vary in direct proportion to volume. (p. 149)
- For every dollar change in sales, contribution margin will increase or decrease by the contribution margin ratio multiplied by the increase or decrease in sales dollars. (p. 149)
- The payment of income taxes is an important variable in target profit and other CVP decisions. (p. 165)
- A company operating near the break-even point will have a high level of operating leverage and income will be very sensitive to changes in sales volume. (p. 168)

• Variable costing is consistent with CVP's focus on differentiating fixed from variable costs and provides useful information for decision making that is often not apparent when using absorption costing. (p. 172)

KEY DEFINITIONS

Cost-volume-profit analysis (CVP) A tool that focuses on the relationship between a company's profits and (1) the prices of products or services, (2) the volume of products or services, (3) the per-unit variable costs, (4) the total fixed costs, and (5) the mix of products or services produced (p. 146)

Gross profit The difference between sales and cost of goods sold (p. 146)

Contribution margin per unit The sales price per unit of product less all variable costs to produce and sell the unit of product; used to calculate the change in contribution margin resulting from a change in unit sales (p. 147)

Contribution margin ratio The contribution margin divided by sales; used to calculate the change in contribution margin resulting from a dollar change in sales (p. 148)

Break-even point The level of sales where contribution margin just covers fixed costs and net income is equal to zero (p. 156)

Operating leverage The contribution margin divided by net income; used as an indicator of how sensitive net income is to the change in sales (p. 167)

Absorption (full) costing A method of costing in which product costs include direct material, direct labor, and fixed and variable overhead. Required for external financial statements and for income tax reporting (p. 169)

Variable (direct) costing A method of costing in which product costs include direct material, direct labor, and variable overhead. Fixed overhead is treated as a period cost. Consistent with CVP's focus on cost behavior (p. 169)

CONCEPT REVIEW

1. Discuss why cost-volume-profit analysis could be useful to managers.

2. The cost-volume-profit model is consistent with what type of costing?

3. Describe decisions that use the cost-volume-profit model.

4. If the total contribution margin is decreased by a given amount, what will be the effect on operating profit?

5. Define the term *contribution margin.*

6. Describe the formula for computing the break-even point.

7. Give the formula to calculate the contribution margin ratio and describe what it represents.

8. If a firm has a negative contribution margin, what options are available to management to reach the break-even point?

9. Describe different options to increase the break-even point.

10. Discuss the meaning of the term *break-even.* Why would a manager be concerned with the break-even point? Does a break-even calculation provide absolute accuracy? Why or why not? Discuss the impact of multiple products on the calculation of the break-even point.

11. How does cost-volume-profit analysis allow management to determine the relative profitability of a product?

12. Sensitivity analysis refers to what?

13. At the break-even point, fixed cost is always what amount?

14. A company's break-even point in sales dollars may be affected by equal percentage increases in both selling price and variable cost per unit (assume all other factors are equal within the relevant range). The equal percentage changes in selling price and variable cost per unit will cause the break-even point in sales dollars to behave in what manner?

15. Name an activity for which cost-volume-profit analysis would not provide useful data.

16. If fixed expenses decrease and the variable expenses (as a percentage of sales) decrease, what will be the effect on the contribution margin ratio (CMR) and the break-even point (BEP)?

17. If fixed expenses decrease while variable cost per unit remain constant, what will happen to the contribution margin?

18. In using cost-volume-profit analysis to calculate the expected sales level expressed in units, how would a predicted operating loss be included?

19. What are the major assumptions as to cost and revenue behavior underlying conventional cost-volume-profit calculations?

20. What is the basic difference between absorption costing and variable costing?

21. When using variable costing, are selling and administration considered product or period costs?

22. Describe how fixed manufacturing costs can be shifted between periods using absorption costing.

23. Discuss why variable costing might be preferred over absorption costing.

24. Discuss why absorption costing might be preferred over variable costing.

25. If units sold exceed units produced, which method, variable or absorption, would show the higher net income? Why?

26. If units produced exceed units sold, which method, variable or absorption, would show the higher net income? Why?

27. If a company is using absorption costing is it possible to increase net income without increasing sales? How?

28. Discuss how the use of JIT inventory systems could reduce the difference between net income reported between variable and absorption costing.

APPLICATION OF CONCEPTS

29. MacAulay Company produces one type of machine with the following costs and revenues for the year:

Total revenues	$4,200,000
Total fixed costs	$1,400,000
Total variable costs	$2,800,000
Total units produced and sold	700,000

Required

  A. What is the selling price per unit?

  B. What is the variable cost per unit?

  C. What is the contribution margin per unit?

  D. What is the break-even point in units?

  E. How many units must be sold to make an operating profit of $1 million for the year?

30. If Johnston Plumbing Company's sales price per house call is $100, variable costs per call are $60, and fixed costs for the year are $200,000. How many house calls must the company make to break even?

31. If Krygowski Company has variable costs of $20 per unit, fixed costs of $3,000 per month, and sells its product for $50, how many units must it sell to earn a profit of $6,000?

32. If Lannefeld Company's selling price per unit is $10, variable costs per unit are $4, and fixed costs for the year are $105,000, how many units must it sell to earn a 10 percent return on sales?

33. Lause's Family Restaurant currently breaks even at 1,000 meals. Its fixed costs are $25,000 and its variable costs are $10 per meal. What is the Lause's average selling price per meal?

34. Leake Fishing Rod Company's selling price is $12 per fishing rod, variable cost is $3 per rod, and fixed costs are $36,000. If fixed costs increased by $3,000, how many additional fishing rods must be sold to break even?

35. Lincoln Company's selling price is $18 per unit, variable cost is $6 per unit, and fixed costs are $36,000. If fixed costs increased by $3,000, how many additional units must be sold to break even?

36. Lockwood Company currently sells its deadbolt locks for $30. The variable costs are $10 and the annual fixed costs are $150,000. The company's tax rate is 40 percent. Calculate number of units needed to earn an after-tax profit of $24,000.

37. Long Company produces two products, A and B, and sells 60 percent product A and 40 percent product B. A sells for $16 and has variable costs of $8; B sells for $12 and has variable costs of $9. Fixed costs for the period are $36,000. What is the break-even point in total units?

38. Lubin Company produces two products, A and B. A sells for $16 and has variable costs of $10; B sells for $12 and has variable costs of $8. Fixed costs for the period are $35,000. An equal number of A and B units are sold. At the break-even volume, how many units of A will be sold?

39. Lutz Company produces two products, widgets and gizmos. Widgets sell for $16 and have variable costs of $6; Gizmos sell for $12 and have variable costs of $8. Fixed costs for the period are $40,000. Normally, four units of widgets are sold for every two units of gizmos. How many units of gizmos must be sold if the company expects profits of $50,000?

40. If Martinez Company has a break-even of 200 units with variable expenses of $200 and fixed expense of $100, what would the 201st unit sold contribute to net income before tax?

41. If Massey Company increased the selling price of a widget from $.50 to $.55 and fixed expenses increased from $200,000 to $240,000 while variable expense per unit remained stable, what would be the effect on the break-even point?

42. Matthews Lawn Service sells lawn mowing for $35 per yard with variable expenses of $21 per yard. If the company raises its selling price 40 percent, how much can unit sales decline before total net income declines?

43. Last year, Mayes Company had a contribution margin of 30 percent. This year, fixed expenses are expected to remain at $120,000, and sales are expected to be $550,000, which is 10 percent higher than last year. For the company to increase income by $15,000 in the coming year, the contribution margin ratio must be what level?

44. McGarity Company plans to sell 200,000 special Rose Bowl footballs with fixed costs of $400,000 and variable expenses at 60 percent of sales. To have a net income of $100,000 McGarity's management must set the sales price at what?

45. MacMaster Inc. is considering the introduction of a new custom neon signage product with the following price and costs:

Sales price	$75 each
Variable cost	$25 each
Fixed cost	$300,000 per year

It expects to sell 7,000 units for the year.

Required

A. How many signs must be sold to break even?

B. How many signs must be sold to make an operating profit of $15,000?

C. If 7,000 signs are sold, what operating profit is expected?

D. What would be the break-even point if the sales price decreased by 20 percent?

E. What would be the break-even point if variable costs per sign decreased by 40 percent?

F. What would be the break-even point if fixed costs were increased by $50,000?

46. In planning its operations for next year based on a sales forecast of $3,000,000, ZIA Motors prepared the following estimated costs and expenses:

	Variable	Fixed
Direct material	$ 800,000	
Direct labor	700,000	
Factory overhead	300,000	$450,000
Selling expense	120,000	180,000
General admin. expense	30,000	70,000
	$1,950,000	$700,000

Required

A. What would be the amount of sales dollars at the break-even point?

B. If ZIA must show a net income of $700,000, what options do they have to achieve their goal?

C. What qualitative factors should be considered for each option in B?

| Step 3 | IDENTIFY AND ANALYZE AVAILABLE OPTIONS |

47. Marshall Advertising Company is contemplating an expansion program based on the following budget data:

Projected sales	$300,000
Variable expenses	210,000
Fixed expense	60,000

Required

A. Based on this projection, what would be the budgeted break-even point in sales dollars?

B. What would sales have to be to make a net income of $100,000?

48. Martin's Rock Company has provided the following information:

Sales (25,000 units)	$500,000
Direct materials	100,000
Direct labor	50,000
Variable factory overhead	20,000
Fixed factory overhead	35,000
Selling & admin. expense:	
Variable	5,000
Fixed	30,000

Required

A. Compute the break-even point in units for Martin's Rock Company.

B. Compute the contribution margin ratio for Martin's Rock Company.

C. If Martin Rock Company were to spend $10,000 on advertising, they project that sales would increase by $20,000. Should they increase the advertising? Why?

49. HD Inc. produces CD burners. The following information concerning last year is provided:

sell price	120
Units produced	100,000
Units sold	95,000
Direct material per unit	$ 55
Direct labor per unit	$ 25
Variable manufacturing overhead per unit	$ 15
Fixed manufacturing overhead	$300,000

Required

A. Compute the cost per unit using absorption costing.

B. Compute the cost per unit using variable costing.

| Step 3 | IDENTIFY AND ANALYZE AVAILABLE OPTIONS |

C. Compute the difference in net income between the two methods. Which costing method results in a higher net income?

| Step 4 | SELECT THE BEST OPTION |

D. Assume that production was 90,000 units and sales were 100,000 units. What would be the difference in net income between the two methods? Which costing method shows the greater net income?

E. Assuming that production was 100,000 units and sales were 100,000 units. What would be the difference in net income between the two methods?

F. Which method is required by GAAP?

50. Parker Company produces watches. The following information concerning last year is provided:

Beginning inventory (units)	25,000
Units produced	90,000
Units sold	95,000
Direct material per unit	$ 15
Direct labor per unit	$ 5
Variable manufacturing overhead per unit	$ 10
Fixed manufacturing overhead	$100,000

Required

A. Gail, the owner of Parker Company, is going to the bank to negotiate a line of credit and wants to show the maximum amount of income without changing last year's results. What costing method of inventory (variable or absorption) should she choose? Why?

B. If the bank requires GAAP financial statements, what method would she choose?

C. The bank sends her off with the comment, "We need more net income for a couple of months before we can grant you the line of credit." Because Gail projects no increase in demand for her watches in the next few months, what options are available to her?

> **Step 3** IDENTIFY AND ANALYZE AVAILABLE OPTIONS

D. Which option should she choose and why? Are the options legal? Are they ethical?

> **Step 4** SELECT THE BEST OPTION

51. Oliver Inc. produces an oak rocking chair that is designed to ease back problems. The chairs sell for $200 each. The results of last year's operations are as follows:

Units in beginning inventory		0
Units produced during the year		20,000
Units sold during the year		18,000
Units left in ending inventory		2,000
Variable manufacturing costs per unit:		
Direct materials	$	70
Direct labor		20
Variable manufacturing overhead		15
Variable selling and administrative		10
Total variable cost per unit	$	115
Fixed costs:		
Fixed manufacturing overhead		$500,000
Fixed selling & admin.		530,000
Total fixed costs		$850,000

Required

A. Assume that the company uses variable costing. Compute the unit product cost to produce one rocking chair.

B. Prepare an income statement based on variable costing.

C. Assume that the company uses absorption costing. Compute the unit product cost to produce one rocking chair.

D. Prepare an income statement based on absorption costing.

E. Compare the two and analyze the difference. What causes the net incomes to differ?

F. If production was 18,000 chairs and sales were 20,000 chairs (assume 2,000 chairs in beginning inventory), what would be the impact on the two income statements?

G. If the manager of the business was paid a bonus based on net income and had a choice of methods to use to report income, what method would he choose using the original income statement? If the situation described in F was to occur, would that change his decision? Why?

52. McGuinness Company produces two beers, Light and Stout, with the following characteristics:

	Light	Stout
Selling price per case	$10	$15
Variable cost per case	$ 8	$10
Expected sales (cases)	20,000	5,000

Total fixed costs for the company are $39,000.

Required

A. What is the anticipated level of profits for the expected sales volume?

B. Assuming the product mix would be the same at the break-even point, compute the break-even point in terms of each of the products.

C. If only Stout was sold, how many units would be needed to break even?

D. If only Light was sold, how many units would be needed to break even?

E. If the product mix changed so that equal units of Light and Stout were sold, what would be the new break-even point in total units?

F. Discuss the accuracy of these calculations with regards to planning. What types of occurrences could affect the accuracy of the calculations? What assumptions must be made to use the calculations in planning and decision making?

53. Mebust Company sells three products, X, Y, and Z. The company has fixed costs in the amount of $2,600. The following information is presented to you:

	X	Y	Z
Price per unit	$11	$15	$17
Variable costs per unit	$ 6	$12	$16
Number of units sold	1,000	2,000	2,000

Required

A. Assuming the product mix will be the same at the break-even point, compute the break-even in total units.

B. What are the break-even units for each product line?

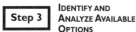

C. What options are available to change the break-even point?

54. Meng Delivery Corporation wishes to earn a 30 percent return on its $100,000 investment in bicycles and cars used to make deliveries. Based on estimated sales of 10,000 delivery jobs, the cost per job would be as follows:

Variable manufacturing costs	$5
Fixed selling and administrative costs	$2
Fixed costs	$1

Required

A. What sales price should be set for each delivery?

B. What is the break-even point?

C. What options does Meng have to increase return to 35 percent?

D. What qualitative factors must be considered in this decision?

Step 3 IDENTIFY AND ANALYZE AVAILABLE OPTIONS

55. Miller Company has the following revenue and cost budgets for the two types of eyeglasses it sells:

	Plastic Frames	Metal Frames
Sales price	$10.00	$15.00
Direct materials	(2.00)	(3.00)
Direct labor	(3.00)	(5.00)
Variable overhead	(3.00)	(4.00)
Net income per unit	$ 2.00	$ 3.00
Budgeted unit sales	100,000	300,000

The budgeted unit sales equal the current unit demand, and total fixed overhead for the year is budgeted at $975,000. Assume that the company plans to maintain the same proportional mix. In numerical calculations, Miller rounds to the nearest cent and unit.

Required

A. What is the total number of units Miller needs to produce and sell to break even?

B. What is the total number of units needed to break even if the budgeted direct labor costs were $2 for plastic frames instead of $3?

C. What is the total number of units needed to break even if sales were budgeted at 150,000 units of plastic frames and 300,000 units of metal frames with all other costs remaining constant?

56. Mistry Company produces two products, Alfa and Beta. Alfa sells for $16 and has variable costs of $10. Beta sells for $12 and has variable costs of $8. Fixed costs for the period are $35,000. Normally, two units of Alfa are sold for every one unit of Beta.

Required

A. What is the break-even point?

B. How many units of Beta must be sold if the company expects profits of $50,000?

57. Moore Inc. invented a secret process to double the growth rate of hatchery trout and manufactures a variety of products related to this process. Each product is independent of the others and is treated as a separate profit/loss division. Product managers have a great deal of freedom to manage their divisions as they think best. Failure to produce target division income is dealt with severely; however, rewards for exceeding one's profit objective are, as one division manager described them, lavish.

The Morey Division sells an additive that is added to the pond water. Morey has had a new manager in each of the three previous years because the predecessor manager failed to reach Moore's target profit. Kassy Morgan has just been promoted to manager and is studying ways to meet the current target profit for Morey.

The target profit for Morey for the coming year are $800,000 (20 percent return on the investment in the annual fixed costs of the division). Other constraints on division operations are as follows:

• Production cannot exceed sales because Moore's corporate advertising stresses completely new additives each year, even though the "newness" of the models may be only cosmetic.

• The Morey selling price may not vary above the current selling price of $200 per gallon, but it may vary as much as 10 percent below $200 ($180).

Morgan is now examining data gathered by her staff to determine if Morey can achieve its target profit of $800,000.

- Last year's sales were 30,000 units at $200 per gallon.
- The present capacity of Morey's manufacturing facility is 40,000 gallons per year, but capacity can be increased to 80,000 gallons per year with an additional investment of $1,000,000 per year in fixed costs.
- Present variable costs amount to $80 per unit, but if commitments are made for more than 60,000 gallons, Morey's vendors are willing to offer raw material discounts amounting to $20 per gallon, beginning with gallon number 60,001.

Morgan believes that these projections are reliable, and she is now trying to determine what Morey must do to meet the profit objectives assigned by Moore's board of directors.

Required

A. Calculate the dollar value of Morey's current annual fixed costs.

B. Determine the number of gallons that Morey must sell at $200 in order to achieve the profit objective. Be sure to consider any relevant constraints. What if the selling price is $180?

C. Without prejudice to your previous answers, assume Kassy Morgan decides to sell 40,000 gallons at $200 per gallon and 24,000 gallons at $180 per gallon. Prepare a pro forma income statement for Morey showing whether Kassy Morgan's decision will achieve Morey's profit objectives.

58. Happy Daze Game Company expects its sales during the next two months, July and August, to be $250,000 and $210,000, respectively. Variable costs at these levels will be $150,000 and $126,000, respectively, and fixed costs will be $100,000. July sales are expected to be 5,000 units and August sales are expected to be 4,200 units.

Required

A. What is the expected break-even point in July and August?

B. If the selling price is increased by 20 percent, what is the new variable cost ratio?

C. If the selling price is increased by 20 percent, what is the new break-even point?

D. Independent of your answer to C, if fixed costs decrease by 20 percent and variable costs increase by 20 percent per unit, what is the new break-even point?

59. Peter Nasta, cost accountant for Southeast Construction, has just finished his break-even analysis for each product line within the company. The analysis reveals a deficiency with three product lines, Townhouses, Basic houses, and Customhouses. A different division manufactures each of these houses. Based on current sales forecasts, the company as a whole will not reach the sales volume needed to break even. If two of the three product lines (Townhouses, Basic houses, and Customhouses) are dropped, the company will be able to remain profitable. Peter recommended that Townhouses and Customhouses be dropped.

When Peter started with the company he worked for the division that manufactures Basic houses. In fact, his wife, Mary, still works for that division. What are the ethical issues involved in this decision?

60. David Nurkiewicz assisted in developing break-even points for various products within his company. He was hired by another company to determine selling prices of the company's products. David feels it is unacceptable to use the information he gathered for his previous employer, but he is being pressured by his new supervisor to divulge this information. What should David do?

During the third year of operations, Big Al's estimates that 415,000 pizzas will be produced (385,000 meat pizzas and 30,000 veggie pizzas). Direct materials are purchased at the silver level for each pizza. Direct labor costs are estimated to be the same in Year 3 (per unit) as in Year 2. Selling and administrative costs are likewise estimated to be the same in Year 3 as in Year 2.

Required

A. Compute the breakeven point in Year 3 for Big Al's Pizza. Use the regression results from Chapter 5 to estimate variable and fixed overhead costs. Assume a 50 percent markup on cost to arrive at the sales price for each pizza.

B. What options does Big Al's have if they desire to reduce the breakeven point? Discuss both the quantitative and qualitative factors that must be considered with each option.

C. How many meat and veggies pizzas would Big Al's need to sell in Year 3 to earn a before-tax profit of $150,000?

D. If Big Als tax rate is 30 percent, how many pizzas does Big Al's need to sell in Year 3 to earn an after-tax profit of $150,000?

E. How will the break-even point change if the sales mix changes to 80 percent meat pizzas and 20 percent veggie pizzas?

ACCOUNTING INFORMATION, RELEVANT COSTS, AND DECISION MAKING

Study Tools

A Review of the Previous Chapter
Chapter 6 provided students with a set of tools including contribution margin, contribution margin ratio, and operating leverage that are the cornerstones of cost-volume-profit analysis and used by managers to make a number of day-to-day decisions.

A Preview of This Chapter
In this chapter, we analyze a variety of decisions affecting managers. Each of these decisions is dependent on an analysis of relevant costs and relevant qualitative factors.

Key concepts include:
- The price of a product must be sufficient to cover all the costs of the product and to provide a profit.
- The price of a special order must be higher than the additional variable costs incurred in accepting the special order plus any opportunity costs incurred.
- A product should continue to be made internally and labor incurred internally if the avoidable costs are less than the additional costs that will be incurred by buying or outsourcing.
- A product should be dropped when the fixed costs avoided are greater than the contribution margin lost.
- Resource utilization decisions hinge on an analysis of the contribution margin earned per unit of the limited resource.
- A product should be processed further if the additional revenue is greater than the additional cost.

LEARNING OBJECTIVES

After studying the material in this chapter, you should be able to:

LO1 Identify factors and issues affecting the pricing of goods and services

LO2 Analyze the pricing of a special order

LO3 Analyze a decision involving the outsourcing of labor or making or buying a component

LO4 Analyze a decision dealing with adding or dropping a product, product line, or service

LO5 Analyze a decision dealing with scarce or limited resources

LO6 Analyze a decision dealing with selling a product or processing it further

LO7 Evaluate the impact of ABC on relevant costs and decision making

A Preview of Upcoming Chapters
Chapter 8 completes our study of the nature of costs in decision making and develops a set of tools that allow managers to consider the time value of money in making long-term capital investment decisions.

In Chapter 5, we emphasized that only relevant costs and factors should be considered by managers when making decisions. Following the decision-making framework developed in Chapter 1 and building on what we know about the nature of costs from Chapter 5, in Chapter 7 we analyze a variety of decisions affecting managers. These decisions include an examination of general pricing issues and the pricing of special orders; whether to outsource labor; whether to make or buy a component used to manufacture a product; whether to add or drop a product, product line, or service; and how to utilize limited resources to maximize profit. We also consider the impact of ABC on these decisions. ■

INTRODUCTION

As we discussed in Chapter 1, operating activities include a wide range of decisions that managers make on a day-to-day basis. The manager of a local florist shop must determine the selling prices of its floral arrangements. Managers of a company that makes T-shirts must determine the price for a special one-time order. The manager of a restaurant must constantly assess the status of its menu items just as managers of a large manufacturer of stereo components must consider whether to add new products or to drop unprofitable ones. Managers of a company that makes bicycles must decide whether to buy tires from another manufacturer or to make them internally. The manager of a local video store must determine whether to hire employees to repair VCRs or to outsource that service to someone else. The manager of a hardware store must determine which products to put on the shelves and a book publisher must determine which books to publish. All of these decisions require relevant, timely accounting information to aid in the decision-making process. In this chapter we discuss the tools that managers use to make these and other business decisions.

PRICING OF PRODUCTS AND SERVICES

LO1
Identify factors and issues affecting the pricing of goods and services

In a competitive marketplace, consumers will seek out the best product at the most favorable price. Determining the selling price of products is one of the most important decisions that management will be required to make. If the price of the product is too high, market demand for that product may be less than is needed to earn a fair profit. On the other hand, if the price of the product is too low, the demand may be very high but the product may produce minimal profit or even show a negative contribution margin.

IN THE NEWS	www.omnihotels.com

Many hotel chains and airlines use sophisticated yield management computer software that constantly monitors and adjusts rates based on a variety of factors including historical trends and expected occupancy. This can result in constantly changing prices for rooms and airfares. At the Omni Park West in Dallas, Texas, rooms are priced as high as $199 on strong demand nights and as low as $59 on low-demand nights. The Omni Park West estimates that the software has increased revenues by 4 percent to 6 percent. When installed company wide, Omni expects annual revenue to increase by $15 million to $20 million (*The Wall Street Journal,* May 5, 1999, B1).

In some business situations, the cost of the product or service does not really affect the sales price. In these circumstances, the market determines the selling price and the company will produce the product as efficiently as possible and sell it for a predetermined market price. Many agricultural products fall into this category in which the market determines the selling price. However, in most instances the cost of a product or service is very important in establishing price. Consider, for example, the manufacture of furniture or automobiles. In these situations, higher cost items are typically priced higher than lower cost items. In other words, if the car costs more to produce, then the price to the consumer will be higher because the extra costs usually mean higher quality or more options.

The demand for products at different stages in their life cycles also affects pricing. For example, when Sony introduced direct stream digital CD players to the marketplace in 1999, their price was expected to exceed $4,000. However, as demand and production in-

IN THE NEWS

Even when cost is used to help establish the price of products or services, other factors may be equally or more important. Although the price of lumber has risen over the past couple of years, furniture manufacturers have been reluctant to pass on those price increases to retailers. For example, furniture manufacturers may try to help retailers maintain key "price points," knowing that consumers may be reluctant to spend above some threshold dollar amount on a new dresser or bed (*Raleigh News and Observer,* October 17, 1998, 1D).

crease, Sony expects the price of the players to come down to mass-market levels, probably within three years. This phenomenon has already been seen in products such as the VCR, which when introduced in the 1980s sold for up to $1,000 but now sells for as low as $99.

In the long run, the selling price of a product or service must be sufficient to cover the "cost" of the product plus provide a profit. The question then becomes what is the cost of the product? As we have discussed throughout the book, there are a number of ways to compute the cost of a product. In Chapter 6, we learned that absorption or full costing includes fixed manufacturing overhead as a product cost, whereas variable costing includes only direct material, direct labor, and variable manufacturing costs. Chapters 3 and 4 stated that some companies will assign overhead to products using traditional volume-based cost drivers, whereas others will use activity-based costing. In Chapter 4 we saw that the use of ABC can have a tremendous impact on the calculation of cost. Using conventional volume-based cost drivers has the general effect of overcosting simple products and undercosting complex products. The use of multiple cost drivers in ABC generally results in more accurate product costs. **Life cycle cost** refers to the costs accumulated over the entire life cycle of a product. As was discussed in Chapter 2, the product life cycle refers to the entire life span of a product from initial research and development to the time when customer support of the product is finished.

Regardless of the way companies compute the cost of their product or service, it should be obvious that in the long run the price of a product must be sufficient to cover all the costs incurred in developing, designing, manufacturing, marketing, distributing, and servicing the product. In practice, companies use a variety of approaches to determine prices.

Key Concept: *The price of a product must be sufficient to cover all the costs of the product and to provide a profit.*

TARGET PRICING

Target pricing is used when a price is preset by market conditions or when a company wishes to set a price in order to capture a predetermined market share or meet other marketing goals. In situations in which the price is preset by market conditions (as with agricultural products), the product manufacturer or service provider has little control over sales price. In these cases, the decision is really not one of establishing a price at all but rather deciding whether a product can be developed and manufactured at a cost low enough to provide an acceptable profit. In other situations, a company has control over setting prices but sets a price based on the marketing goals (to enter a new market, establish a predetermined market share, etc.) rather than the cost of the product or service. Surveys of U.S. companies indicate that almost 20 percent routinely use some sort of market-based target pricing.

Target pricing is used to determine the maximum cost that can be incurred in order to earn a desired profit (the target profit). This maximum cost is often called the target cost and is calculated by subtracting the target profit from the target selling price:

> **Target cost = Target price − Target profit**

Target pricing (and target costing) is prevalent in the computer industry where the goal may be to produce a computer that can be marketed for under $500. After determining an acceptable profit on the computer ($100 for example), the goal is to determine how to design, develop, manufacture, sell, and service the computer for a cost no higher than $400. If the target cost is within the range of acceptable estimates, then the computer can be manufactured. In reality, most production costs are determined during the early stages of the value chain (research and development and design) and very little can be done to control these costs once the product is in production. This means that estimating costs accurately and at an early stage in the value chain is crucial in deciding if a product can ultimately be sold at a profit.

CROSS FUNCTIONAL APPLICATIONS *Target pricing requires the cooperation of marketing, engineering, production, accounting, and finance managers in multidisciplinary teams.*

APPLICATION IN BUSINESS

Determining a target cost is more difficult when the target price is not known with certainty. For example, in the agricultural market, coffee bean prices are set by auction and are not known until after the beans are grown and harvested.

COST PLUS PRICING

When the market allows some flexibility in setting prices, companies often use some sort of **cost-plus pricing** to determine the selling price of products or services.

The general formula for determining a target selling price using a cost-plus approach is

> **Target selling price = Cost + (Markup % × Cost)**

In cost-plus pricing, managers determine the cost of the product or service and then add a markup percentage to that cost to arrive at the sales price. In some cases, costs are estimated and selling prices are set based on those estimates. In other cases, companies can wait until they know their actual costs before setting the selling price in a cost-plus contract. For example, a builder of custom homes would probably use cost-plus pricing. In Chapter 4, TopSail Construction used full costing and ABC to determine the total manufacturing costs of a custom house to be $237,371 (see Table 4-8). The selling price of $285,000 was determined by adding a predetermined markup of 20 percent on the total manufacturing costs (and rounding up to the nearest thousand). If TopSail uses estimated costs to determine a selling price (and enters a contract to build a house for a predetermined price), it becomes critically important for TopSail to accurately estimate those costs. If costs are estimated too high and the selling price is too high, TopSail will not be awarded the construction job; if costs are estimated too low (and the price is too low), the company may lose money or make less profit than desired.

Some companies use only variable costs to price their products; others use absorption costs or life cycle costs. There are advantages and disadvantages to each. Using variable costs is consistent with the economic model of maximizing profit by setting prices in which marginal cost is equal to marginal revenue. However, it can be misleading to managers focusing on long-run decisions. Using full costs has the benefit of motivating managers to control fixed costs. ABC has also made the practice of allocating fixed costs to products more accurate. In practice, full costs are used by almost 70 percent of U.S. companies, whereas variable costs are used by only 12 percent (Shim and Sudit, "How Manufacturers Price Products," *Management Accounting,* February 1995). Although the use of life cycle costs is appealing, as a practical matter, they are also difficult to estimate.

The **markup percentage** is a very important component of the preceding formula. The markup must be sufficient to cover any costs not included in the company's definition of product cost plus produce an acceptable profit. For a company using variable costing as the starting point in cost-plus pricing, the markup must cover fixed manufacturing costs, all selling and administrative costs, other life cycle costs incurred in the design, development and servicing of the product, and a profit. At the other extreme, the markup for a company using life cycle costing will only include a desired profit. The amount used can be a simple rule of thumb or an industry standard. Whatever method is used, the markup percentage should be reviewed often.

Some companies use a combination of target pricing and cost-plus pricing. For example, Parker Brothers (a division of Hasbro Inc.) manufactures and sells board games such as Monopoly and Scrabble. The company's approach to pricing is to first have the marketing department estimate the probable retail-selling price of a prototype game—the target price. Parker Brothers then backs into the maximum cost (the target cost) that can be incurred in manufacturing the game by applying predetermined profit margins at the retail and wholesale levels. If the target cost is too low (the company cannot manufacture the game at or below the target cost), Parker Brothers then takes a cost-plus approach to pricing and goes back to the marketing department with a higher suggested wholesale price. It is then up to the marketing department to decide whether the game can be successfully marketed at this higher price.

www.hasbro.com

TIME AND MATERIAL PRICING

In service industries where labor is the primary cost incurred, prices are often set based on time and material used. For example, CPA firms that provide audit services must provide a client with an estimate of an audit fee prior to starting the work. This fee usually will not vary unless additional work is needed that was unanticipated before the engagement began. Also, extreme problems can arise that cause the firm to spend much more time on the engagement, which could cause the fee to increase. The price is based on the estimated number of hours needed to complete the audit. Obviously more complex audit engagements will require more time and will be priced at a higher rate. As another example of **time and material pricing,** an auto shop bills customers based on mechanic labor hours plus any parts used in the repair.

MANAGEMENT ACTIONS AND DECISIONS   www.hasbro.com

GARY BERGMANN
Hasbro Games

One of the questions that comes up when we discuss pricing in the classroom is "How are prices determined in the real world?" Gary Bergmann, vice president of product acquisition and product design for Hasbro Games in Beverly, Massachusetts, gives some insight on how they view pricing. Mr. Bergmann, who has both a B.S. and an M.B.A. from Drexel University, has been with Hasbro since 1979. His job is to meet with game inventors throughout the world to review their game concepts as candidates for the Milton Bradley and Parker Brothers game lines, collectively known as Hasbro Games. Mr. Bergmann says that Hasbro is presented with about 3,000 game concepts per year. Of those, only about 15 to 20 actually reach the retail marketplace.

"When a game is considered to be marketable, we first ask the marketing team what the suggested retail price on the game might be (target pricing). We then reduce that amount by the required markups and arrive at the target cost to manufacture (target costing). If the calculated cost to manufacture is too low to allow for a properly designed game, we reverse the process by asking the manufacturing team to calculate the cost to produce the game as we would design it, then add the needed markups to arrive at the new suggested retail price. This new price is delivered to the marketing team for a sales projection using the new parameters. This procedure allows us to approach the project from two different angles and in some cases gives a candidate game a second chance at being manufactured and sold."

VALUE PRICING

In special circumstances, the price of services is based on the perceived or actual value of the service provided to a customer. A good example of **value pricing** occurs in the consulting business. Consulting firms may charge clients based on a percentage of cost savings that result from an engagement. Large CPA firms often enter into these types of arrangements. For example, a CPA firm may contract with a client to evaluate its property tax assessments and to negotiate reductions in those taxes based on faulty valuations of property. Rather than establishing a fixed price for the services (or working on a cost-plus contract), the firm may set a price equal to 30 percent of the cost savings.

LEGAL AND ETHICAL ISSUES IN PRICING

LO2
Analyze the pricing of a special order

Do you think value pricing is ethical?

A variety of laws at the local, state, and national levels prevent companies from using predatory pricing to prevent or eliminate competition. Many types of price discrimination are illegal unless the differences in price are based on cost differences in servicing and selling to different customers. Price gouging or setting the price higher for unusual situations, such as doubling the price of plywood when a hurricane is approaching, may also be illegal in some cases. In addition to the legal implications of pricing decisions, companies must also consider the ethical issues involved in pricing products and services. For example, pharmaceutical companies may choose to sell a drug below cost and doctors may treat some patients at little or no cost. However, examples also abound of companies taking advantage of customers by increasing the prices of products and services that are in high demand.

SPECIAL ORDERS

Deciding whether to accept a special order is really just a pricing decision. However, unlike the pricing decisions discussed earlier, **special-order decisions** are short-run decisions. Management must decide what sales price is appropriate when customers place orders that are different from those placed in the regular course of business (larger quantity, one-time sale to a foreign customer, etc.).[1] These decisions are affected by whether the company has excess production capacity (can produce additional units with existing machinery, labor, and facilities). Qualitative factors like the reaction of regular customers must also be considered when establishing the price of a special order. As with other decisions discussed in this chapter, managers must consider the relevant costs associated with each specific special order.

Consider the case of Sunset Airlines. The company has been asked by a major corporation to provide 150 seats to San Diego for corporate executives attending a convention. The corporation offers the airline $150 per ticket when the normal fare for this route is $275. The tickets can only be used on one day, but the executives need to be able to fly one of the five flights offered that day. The aircraft that Sunset Airlines flies on this route carries 180 passengers and Sunset has five scheduled flights each day resulting in a seat capacity of 900 seats. The normal passenger load on the day requested is between 77 percent and 78 percent of available capacity (700 passengers) so Sunset should have plenty of excess capacity (40 seats per plane or 200 seats total). However, should Sunset accept the special order at the discounted price of $150 per ticket? Referring back to the decision model presented in Chapter 1, the first step in any decision is to accurately define the problem.

In this case, the problem is clear—should Sunset Airlines sell 150 tickets at a reduced price of $150 per ticket? Step 2 in the decision process is identifying the objectives.

The objective of Sunset Airlines is to maximize income in the short run without reducing income in the long run. The third step is to identify and analyze the available options.

The options in this case include selling the tickets for $150 (accepting the special order), letting the marketplace determine the level of sales at a predetermined price of $275, or selling the tickets at some other price. The risk in this situation is that the airline will have to turn away full-fare passengers if it accepts the special order. An analysis of the options requires that the relevant costs and other factors be identified. The accounting department of Sunset Airlines has provided the following information:

Step 1 DEFINE THE PROBLEM

Step 2 IDENTIFY OBJECTIVES

Step 3 IDENTIFY AND ANALYZE AVAILABLE OPTIONS

	Per Passenger	Per Flight
Cost of meals and drinks	$ 3.25	$ 585
Cost of fuel	138.89	25,000
Cost of cabin crew (four flight attendants)	9.38	1,688
Cost of flight crew	13.89	2,500
Depreciation of aircraft	5.56	1,000
Aircraft maintenance	4.17	750
Total	$175.14	$31,523

[1]Although rush orders and orders requiring special handling, packaging, or different manufacturing specifications might be considered "special orders," these types of decisions are not discussed here.

Step 4 | SELECT THE BEST OPTION

This decision appears to be an easy one since the special-order price of $150 is less than the total cost per passenger of $175.14. Based on the full cost reported by the accounting department, Sunset Airlines would be losing $25.14 on each passenger purchasing a ticket for $150. But would it? To analyze the options in this decision problem correctly, only the relevant costs should be considered. In this decision, the only costs that are relevant are those that will differ depending on whether the special order is accepted. Another way to look at the problem is by determining which costs can be avoided by choosing one alternative over the other.

In this case, almost all of the costs are fixed with respect to the number of passengers on the plane. In fact, due to the unique nature of the airline business, most operating costs are fixed. For example, the aircraft will require the same maintenance and flight crew costs regardless of how many passengers are on board. Although the costs of the cabin crew may vary, in this situation let us assume that regulations require four flight attendants for any flight with more than 125 passengers. In this case, four flight attendants are required regardless of whether the plane carries 125 passengers or 180 passengers and acceptance of the special order will not change the cost of the cabin crew. In essence, the cost of the flight crew is fixed. Likewise, depreciation is a fixed cost. Even fuel costs would not be expected to vary much with the addition of 30 to 40 passengers. In fact, the only costs that would vary with the number of passengers on the plane is likely to be the small additional costs of meals and drinks. Because Sunset Airlines appears to have plenty of excess capacity (empty seats), any sales price above the variable costs of providing the seats will increase the income of the company. If the cost of meals and drinks is the only variable cost, Sunset should be willing to accept the special order at any price over $3.25. In situations in which excess capacity exists, the general rule is that in order to maximize income, the special-order price must simply be higher than the additional variable costs incurred in accepting the special order.

What if Sunset does not have any excess capacity? If the airline expects to sell out all its tickets at the regular price of $275, then accepting the special order involves an opportunity cost. Remember from Chapter 1 that an opportunity cost is the benefit forgone from choosing one alternative over another. If Sunset Airlines accepts the special order, it will forgo the receipt of $271.75 of contribution margin on each ticket ($275 selling price less the $3.25 variable cost of meals and drinks). Therefore, it would not be willing to accept a special order for any price below the $275 market price. The relevant costs in this case are the variable costs of $3.25 and the opportunity cost of $271.75.

Fixed costs can be relevant to a special-order decision when they change depending on the option chosen. For example, let's consider the case of flight attendants again. Instead of requiring four flight attendants for any flight with more than 125 passengers, let's assume that regulations require one flight attendant for every 35 passengers. Whereas four attendants are sufficient for a flight of 140 passengers, adding 30 additional passengers will require the addition of an extra flight attendant at a cost of $422 or $14 per additional passenger. Assuming excess capacity exists, the special-order price would need to exceed $17.25 to be acceptable to Sunset Airlines.

> **Key Concept:** The price of a special order must be higher than the additional variable costs incurred in accepting the special order plus any opportunity costs incurred.

Concept Question: Instead of 150 extra passengers flying on the five regularly scheduled flights, assume that Sunset Airlines has an additional airplane that is currently idle but can be chartered for the flight. In this case, what costs are likely to be relevant in the decision to accept the special order?

Concept Answer: In this case, fuel costs, the cost of the flight and cabin crews, and maintenance are likely to be relevant. Depreciation is still not a relevant cost, but the other costs probably are. It is important to note that determining what is relevant and what is not depends on the specific situation. ■

A number of qualitative factors must also be considered in special-order decisions. First, if it accepts the special order and its passenger-load predictions are wrong, Sunset Airlines may have to turn away passengers that would otherwise pay full fare. If that happens and these passengers turn to competing airlines, Sunset Airlines faces the potential of losing long-term customers. Second, the impact of selling seats at a discount on those customers paying regular fares must be considered.

IN THE NEWS | www.aa.com

Sometimes the most important qualitative factor in business decisions is the potential effect on customers. In February 1999, American Airline pilots decided to stage a sick-out to protest the low pay received by pilots flying for a subsidiary airline. This sick-out stranded hundreds of thousands of passengers all over the country during a key vacation period. This action could very well hurt the long-term customer loyalty to American Airlines.

Concept Question: *Historically, airlines charge much higher fares to last-minute travelers when the relevant costs associated with these additional passengers are very small. Ironically, business travelers who are the airline's most frequent flyers often pay these higher fares. Why haven't airlines been willing to offer special pricing to customers in these situations?*

Concept Answer: Many airlines are beginning to do just that. Faced with added competition from discount airlines that offer cheaper fares with no advance purchase requirements, many of the major airlines also offer last-minute flyers fares at deep discounts. However, these fares are often restricted to flights on certain days and may not be convenient for business travelers. In addition, although these fares are discounted, they are still much higher than the true relevant costs of flying the additional passengers. ■

In 1997 workers of UPS went on strike protesting a labor dispute.

www.ups.com

OUTSOURCING AND OTHER MAKE-OR-BUY DECISIONS

LO3
Analyze a decision involving the outsourcing of labor or making or buying a component

A decision to outsource labor or purchase components used in manufacturing from another company rather than to provide the services or produce the components internally is an important decision. This **outsourcing or make-or-buy decision** affects a wide range of manufacturing, merchandising, and service organizations. For example, a university can contract with an outside company to provide janitorial and repair services for on-campus dormitories or it can provide those services using university employees. A local florist can provide payroll processing internally or it can hire a CPA to provide those services. Hewlett-Packard can make carrying cases for its calculators internally or it can buy them from an outside supplier.

STRATEGIC ASPECTS OF OUTSOURCING AND MAKE-OR-BUY DECISIONS

Although these decisions might appear to be simple on the surface, they require an in-depth analysis of relevant quantitative and qualitative factors and a consideration of the costs and benefits of outsourcing and vertical integration. The decision to outsource labor requires a consideration of a variety of factors including the impact of taxes, the payment of fringe benefits to salaried employees, and the impact on the remaining workforce. Advantages to outsourcing include reduced costs. Although hourly rates paid to independent contractors may be higher than hourly wages paid to salaried employees, a company may benefit from cost reductions as a result of not being required to pay payroll taxes and fringe benefits (medical insurance, retirement plan contributions, etc.). However, outsourcing can have disadvantages such as a perceived lack of stability in the company and a resulting lack of loyalty in the workforce (plus other negative impacts outsourcing may have on the remaining workforce). For example, if a company decided to outsource maintenance and laid off all the maintenance workers, other workers in the company such as the cafeteria personnel may perceive that move as meaning that the company is going to outsource more of the service functions. Workers who feel they are just "treading water" and waiting for their area to be eliminated will be less motivated to do the best job possible and may very well leave the company if and when a better opportunity presents itself.

Universities such as the University of California–Davis can choose to outsource their food service to national restaurant chains in an effort to focus costs on institutional core competencies, such as faculty.

www.subway.com

Vertical integration is accomplished when a company is involved in multiple steps of the value chain. In an extreme example, the same company might own a gold mine, a manufacturing facility to produce gold jewelry, and a retail jewelry store. Most companies operate with some form of vertical integration (they market the products they produce or they develop the products that they manufacture), but the extent of integration varies greatly from company to company and indeed from product to product within a company. All elements of the value chain from initial research and development through design, manufacture of the product, marketing, distribution, and customer service must be considered for making or buying components needed for production of the final product.

There are advantages to making components internally instead of buying them from an outside supplier. Vertically integrated companies are not dependent on suppliers for timely delivery of services or components needed in the production process or for the quality of those services and components. However, as you can see in the following "In the News" feature, vertically integrated companies have disadvantages as well.

IN THE NEWS   www.gm.com

In the summer of 1998, General Motors (GM) found it difficult to restart production in its vehicle plants because of strikes in two of its *own* plants that supplied body stampings and other parts used in GM cars. In this case, the lack of alternative suppliers forced GM to shut down plants that were not directly affected by the strike (*The Wall Street Journal*, July 8, 1998, A3).

There are other disadvantages to making parts internally. The supplier may be able to provide a higher-quality part for less cost. For this reason, computer manufacturers do not produce their own computer chips. The producers of those chips produce in such large quantities that they can provide the chips cheaper than the company could produce them internally. Chip manufacturers also spend billions of dollars on research and development to ensure high-quality and high-performance chips.

THE MAKE-OR-BUY DECISION

Birdie Maker Golf Company produces custom sets of golf clubs that are advertised to be far superior to other golf clubs on the market. These golf clubs sell for $1,000 per set and Birdie currently sells about 1,000 sets each year. Birdie Maker currently manufactures all the golf clubs in the set but is considering acquiring the putter from Flutter Putter Inc., a manufacturer of custom putters. The purchased putter would be customized for Birdie and matched to the other clubs so customers should not be able to distinguish it from the rest of the clubs in the set. The costs incurred in the manufacture of the putter are provided in the following figure:

Birdie Maker

	Total (1,000 clubs)	Per Unit
Direct materials	$ 5,000	$ 5.00
Direct labor	9,000	9.00
Variable manufacturing overhead	3,000	3.00
Fixed manufacturing overhead	9,500	9.50
Total cost	$26,500	$26.50

CASE I

Birdie Maker

Step 1   DEFINE THE PROBLEM

Step 2   IDENTIFY OBJECTIVES

Step 3   IDENTIFY AND ANALYZE AVAILABLE OPTIONS

Step 4   SELECT THE BEST OPTION

The expected production for the year is 1,000 sets of clubs, so the full cost of each putter is $26.50 ($26,500/1,000). Flutter Putter Inc. is offering to sell the putters to Birdie Maker for $25 per putter. Although this decision seems to be a very easy one ($25 is less than $26.50), the decision is more complex than it appears. If we refer back to the decision model presented in Chapter 1 and repeated in Exhibit 7-1, we can once again structure our decision using that framework.

Step 1 in our decision-making model is to accurately define the problem. In this case, Birdie Maker must decide whether to continue making the putter or to purchase it from Flutter Putter Inc. Step 2 requires Birdie Maker to consider its objectives in making the decision.

Although Birdie Maker would like to maximize income by producing or buying the putter at the lowest possible cost, the company is also very concerned about the quality of the putter and the potential impact of the putter on sales of other clubs. Step 3 requires an identification of options and an analysis of the costs and other factors that are relevant in the decision.

Relevant costs and factors are those that differ between alternatives. As we discussed in Chapter 5, relevant costs are those that can be avoided by choosing one alternative over another. The key then is to analyze the costs of manufacturing the putter with an eye toward identifying those costs that can be *avoided* or eliminated if the putter is purchased from Flutter Putter. If Birdie Maker continues to manufacture the putter internally, it will incur costs of $26,500. If Birdie Maker decides to purchase the putters from Flutter Putter Inc., it will incur costs of $25,000 ($25 × 1,000 putters) *plus* any manufacturing costs that are not avoidable. Although the costs related to direct material, direct labor, and variable manufacturing overhead are variable (and thus avoidable), fixed manufacturing overhead is not.

So though it appears on the surface that Birdie Maker can save $1,500 ($26,500 − $25,000) by buying the putters from Flutter Putter Inc., as you can see in the following figure, in reality buying the club from Flutter Putter will cost Birdie an additional $8 per club or $8,000. What is the best solution? From a purely quantitative perspective, Birdie Maker would maximize its income by choosing to continue making putters. However, before making this decision, the company must be convinced that it can manufacture a putter of acceptable quality and that it will be able to keep up with any technological changes affecting the manufacture of the putter in the future.

	Cost to Make (per unit)	Cost to Buy (per unit)
Direct materials	$ 5.00	
Direct labor	9.00	
Variable manufacturing overhead	3.00	
Fixed manufacturing overhead	9.50	$ 9.50
Purchase price from Flutter Putter Inc.		25.00
	$26.50	$34.50

CASE II

flutter putter

Sometimes, fixed costs are relevant to the analysis. For example, assume that $5,500 of the fixed manufacturing cost is for specialized machinery that is currently being leased under a month-to-month contract. If the putters are purchased from Flutter Putter Inc., the equipment will be returned to the lessor. That means that $5.50 of the fixed manufacturing costs ($5,500/1,000 putters) is avoidable if the putter is bought from Flutter Putter and that only $4.00 of fixed overhead will be incurred if the putter is purchased from Flutter Putter. The resulting analysis is shown in the following:

EXHIBIT 7-1   The Decision-Making Model

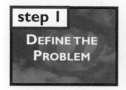 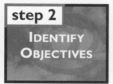  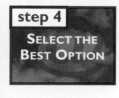

	Cost to Make	Cost to Buy
Direct materials	$ 5.00	
Direct labor	9.00	
Variable manufacturing overhead	3.00	
Fixed manufacturing overhead	9.50	$ 4.00
Purchase price from Flutter Putter Inc.		25.00
	$26.50	$29.00

Although it still remains preferable to make the putters internally, the cost difference shrinks to $2.50 per putter instead of $8.00. In this situation, Birdie Maker must carefully consider the qualitative factors relevant to the decision including the quality of the putters, the importance of keeping up with changing technology, and the dependability of the supplier.

Another way to look at this analysis is to compare the total avoidable costs to the purchase price. In this case, if the putter is purchased from Flutter Putter, the avoidable costs include direct materials ($5.00), direct labor ($9.00), variable manufacturing overhead ($3.00), and $5.50 per putter for fixed manufacturing overhead. The $22.50 of total avoidable costs should then be compared to the $25.00 purchase price. Regardless of how you choose to look at the problem, Birdie Maker is better off by $2.50 per putter if it continues making the putter.

Step 4 SELECT THE BEST OPTION

CASE III

Make-or-buy decisions can be volume dependent. Assuming the same facts as in Case II, if Birdie Maker has a decrease in production volume to 500 sets of golf clubs, the full cost to make each putter will increase to $36. The increase is due to the behavior of fixed costs.

Remember that fixed costs stay the same in total but vary on a per-unit basis as volume changes. In this example, if volume decreases to 500 putters, the unavoidable fixed costs of $4,000 increase to $8 per putter from $4 in Case II. This increase in per-unit production cost will change the decision and make it advantageous for the company to purchase the putter rather than to continue making it ($33 compared to $36).

Step 4 SELECT THE BEST OPTION

	Cost to Make	Cost to Buy
Direct materials	$ 5.00	
Direct labor	9.00	
Variable manufacturing overhead	3.00	
Fixed manufacturing overhead	19.00	$ 8.00
Purchase price from Flutter Putter Inc.		25.00
	$36.00	$33.00

CASE IV

The last case to be considered is one involving an opportunity cost. Using the same facts as in Case I, consider the impact of renting out the factory space that is now used to manufacture putters for $10,000.

By effectively reducing the cost to purchase the putters by $10,000 or $10 per putter, we find that the effective cost to purchase the putter from Flutter Putter is reduced to $24.50 and Birdie Maker would be better off by $2.00 per putter by purchasing the putters.

Step 4 | **SELECT THE BEST OPTION**

Birdie Maker

	Cost to Make	Cost to Buy
Direct materials	$ 5.00	
Direct labor	9.00	
Variable manufacturing overhead	3.00	
Fixed manufacturing overhead	9.50	$ 9.50
Purchase price from Flutter Putter Inc.		25.00
Rental of unused factory space		(10.00)
	$26.50	$24.50

Once again, as an alternative, we could treat the $10 opportunity cost as a relevant cost of making the putter internally. In that case, the total relevant costs of making the putter increase to $36.50 compared to the purchase price of $34.50. In addition to quality and reliability considerations, other factors to consider in this case include the long-term potential for renting out the unused space, potential other uses of the space, and so on.

 Key Concept: *A product should continue to be made internally and labor incurred internally if the avoidable costs are less than the additional costs that will be incurred by buying or outsourcing.*

IN THE NEWS	**www.llbean.com**

Rol Fessenden, the vice president of product acquisition for L.L. Bean, selects the factories to supply Bean with the multitude of products available in its catalogs. Rather than focusing on price, his first criterion in choosing a supplier is product quality, the second is delivery reliability, and the third is price. All of these factors are captured in Mr. Fessenden's view of cost as a concept that includes the entire spectrum of value—price, quality, reliability, and the ultimate success of the product in the marketplace (*The Wall Street Journal*, April 16, 1999, B1).

THE DECISION TO DROP A PRODUCT OR SERVICE

LO4
Analyze a decision dealing with adding or dropping a product, product line, or service

The decision to drop a product or service is among the most difficult that a manager can make. Like other decisions discussed in this chapter, deciding whether to drop an old product or product line hinges on an analysis of the relevant costs and qualitative factors affecting the decision. As you can see in the following "In the News" feature, qualitative factors are sometimes more important than focusing solely on income.

Clayton Herring Tire Co. is considering dropping one of the ten models of tires that it manufactures and sells. Sales of a special mud and snow tire have been disappointing, and based on the latest financial information (shown in the following table) the tires appear to be losing money:

Clayton Herring Tire Co.

CLAYTON HERRING TIRE CO.

	Mud and Snow	All Other Tires	Total
Sales	$25,500	$150,000	$175,500
Less: Direct material	12,000	50,600	62,600
Direct labor	5,000	30,000	35,000
Variable overhead	2,000	12,000	14,000
Contribution margin	$ 6,500	$ 57,400	$ 63,900
Less: Fixed overhead	7,000	21,000	28,000
Net income	$ (500)	$ 36,400	$ 35,900

Chris (the CEO of Clayton Herring Tire) asked Karen (the controller) why the mud and snow tires were losing money. Karen explained that the tires required more machine time than other tires. Consequently, they were allocated a greater portion of fixed overhead. Chris then asked Karen whether she would recommend that production of the mud and snow tires be discontinued. Karen explained that although it appears that net income for the company would increase to $36,400 if the mud and snow tires were dropped from the product line, further analysis revealed that a large portion of the fixed overhead allocated to the tires resulted from the rental of machines used to make the tires. On further inspection, Karen determined that these machines were used to make several models of tires and could not be disposed of if the mud and snow tires were dropped. Consequently, $5,000 of the fixed costs allocated to mud and snow tires would have to be reallocated to other product lines. These costs would remain even if the mud and snow tires were discontinued. Based on this new information, Karen prepared another report for Chris showing the effect of dropping the mud and snow tires:

CLAYTON HERRING TIRE CO.

	With Snow Tires	Without Snow Tires
Tire Sales	$175,500	$150,000
Less: Direct material	62,600	50,600
Direct labor	35,000	30,000
Variable overhead	14,000	12,000
Contribution margin	$ 63,900	$ 57,400
Less: Fixed overhead	28,000	26,000
Net income	$ 35,900	$ 31,400

Clayton
Herring
Tire Co.

Why did the net income for the company decrease by $4,500 (from $35,900 to $31,400) when the mud and snow tires were dropped even though they appeared to be losing money? The answer is that contribution margin decreased by $6,500, whereas fixed costs decreased by only $2,000 when the tires were dropped. Only $2,000 of the fixed costs were avoidable and relevant to this decision. The other $5,000 of fixed costs originally allocated to the mud and snow tires would simply be reallocated to one or more of the other models of tires. A simple way to analyze this problem is to compare the contribution margin lost when the product line is dropped to the fixed costs that are avoided. In this case, Clayton Herring Tire Company loses $6,500 of contribution margin while saving (avoiding) only $2,000 of fixed overhead.

▶ **Key Concept:** A product should be dropped when the fixed costs avoided are greater than the contribution margin lost.

Concept Question: If the machine used to produce the tires was unique and could be disposed of resulting in a savings of $5,000, how much would income increase (decrease) if the mud and snow tires were discontinued? (Assume that the other $2,000 of fixed overhead could still be avoided.)

Concept Answer: Although contribution margin would still be reduced by $6,500, the entire $7,000 of fixed costs would be avoided, resulting in an overall increase in net income of $500. But what about qualitative factors in this decision? As we discussed earlier, qualitative factors are sometimes more important than quantitative factors in these decisions. For example, what impact will discontinuing the sale of mud and snow tires have on sales of the remaining product lines? Tire retailers are likely to prefer purchasing tires from a company offering a full line of tires. They may have difficulty selling tires to individuals if they cannot offer mud and snow tires to those customers in the winter. On the other hand, like Procter & Gamble with its Prell brand, Clayton Herring Tire may choose to discontinue the tires even if they are profitable. ■

RESOURCE UTILIZATION DECISIONS

A company faces a **constraint** when the capacity to manufacture a product or provide a service is limited in some manner. A **resource utilization decision** requires an analysis of how best to use a resource that is available in limited supply. The limited resource may be a rare material or component used in manufacturing a product, but more likely is related to the time required to make a product or provide a service or the space required to store a product. For example, building custom furniture requires skilled craftspeople that may be in short supply. Deciding how best to utilize the limited labor time available is a resource utilization decision. The manufacture of golf clubs requires special machinery. If a company has only one machine that can be used to manufacture shafts for putters and other clubs, machine time may be a limited resource.

LO5
Analyze a decision dealing with scarce or limited resources

Concept Question: What is likely to be a limited resource in a grocery store?

Concept Answer: Grocery stores and other retail stores have limited shelf space. The resource utilization decision involves an analysis of how best to use this limited resource. Which products should be carried? How many? Although it may seem easy to conclude that stores should carry those products that are most profitable, decisions like this are complicated by the fact that the multitudes of products carried in large stores require different amounts of shelf space. Multipacks of paper towels take up several times the shelf space required for a box of macaroni and cheese. Although the multipack of paper towels may be more profitable per unit, this has to be balanced with the requirement of more shelf space. A decision concerning how much of each product to have on hand must also consider the impact of qualitative factors such as customer reaction if a product is not carried, the impact on sales of other products, and so on. ■

Resource utilization decisions are typically short-term decisions. In the short run, resources like machine time, labor hours, and shelf space are fixed and cannot be increased. However, in the long run, new machines can be purchased, additional skilled laborers can be hired, and stores can be expanded. When faced with short-run constraints, rather than focusing on the profitability of each product, managers must focus on the contribution margin provided by each product per unit of limited resource.[2]

Sun Devil Golf Balls produces two different golf balls, the pro model and the tour model. The balls are sold to retailers in cartons containing 360 balls (30 boxes containing 4 sleeves per box with each sleeve holding 3 balls). Both golf balls are made using the same machines. The constraint or limited resource is the number of hours that the machines can run. The pro-model golf ball takes 30 minutes of machine time to produce 360 balls, whereas the tour ball takes 45 minutes to produce the same number. The difference in

SUN
DEVIL
GOLF
BALLS

---

[2]Decisions involving limited resources or constraints often include multiple constraints, such as storage space, machine time, labor hours, and even dollars available to invest. When we have more than one constraining factor, the decision-making process becomes more complicated and is facilitated by the use of computerized linear programming models. A discussion of linear programming is beyond the scope of this text.

production time is mainly due to the different materials used in construction. Although weekend golfers purchase both models, professionals on the PGA Tour use the tour model. The relevant data concerning the two golf balls is presented in the following figure:

	Pro Model	Tour Model
Sales price (per carton)	$450	$540
Less: Direct material	200	265
Direct labor	50	50
Variable overhead	50	75
Contribution margin	$150	$150

In this case the contribution margin per carton is the same for both the pro model and the tour model. Other things being equal, each model is equally profitable. However, if we compute contribution margin per unit of the constrained or limited resource, we see that each carton of pro-model balls has a contribution margin of $300 per hour of machine time, whereas each carton of tour-model balls has a contribution margin of $200 per hour of machine time:

**SUN
DEVIL
GOLF
BALLS**

	Pro Model	Tour Model
Sales price (per carton)	$450	$540
Less: Direct material	200	265
Direct labor	50	50
Variable overhead	50	75
Contribution margin	$150	$150
Required machine time	.50 hours	.75 hours
Contribution margin per machine hour	$300 ($150/.50)	$200 ($150/.75)

If demand is not a factor and qualitative considerations are not important, Sun Devil Golf Balls will maximize profit by producing and selling only pro-model golf balls. However, if demand for either product is limited, then Sun Devil must decide on the optimal product mix. For example, if machine time is limited to 300 hours per month and the demand for the pro model is 400 cartons per month whereas demand for the tour model is 150 cartons, how much of each product should Sun Devil produce? Although Sun Devil has the capacity to produce 600 cartons (300 hours/.5 hours) of pro-model balls, it can sell only 400 cartons. Producing 400 cartons requires 200 machine hours leaving 100 additional machine hours per month for the production of tour balls. Sun Devil can maximize income by producing 400 cartons of pro balls and 133 cartons of tour balls each month.

Qualitative factors, including the impact of discontinuing the sale of the tour ball, must also be considered. Visibility of the tour ball on the professional tour may be a valuable source of advertising contributing to sales of the pro model.

Other options include adding additional machines to increase the amount of available machine hours or reducing the machine time needed to produce a carton of balls. Maximizing profits by focusing on the constraint itself in order to loosen the constraint is the focus of the theory of constraints.

 Key Concept: *Resource utilization decisions hinge on an analysis of the contribution margin earned per unit of the limited resource.*

THE THEORY OF CONSTRAINTS

The theory of constraints is a management tool for dealing with constraints. The theory of constraints identifies **bottlenecks** in the production process. Bottlenecks limit throughput, which can be thought of as the amount of finished goods that result from the production

EXHIBIT 7-2   An Example of a Production Bottleneck

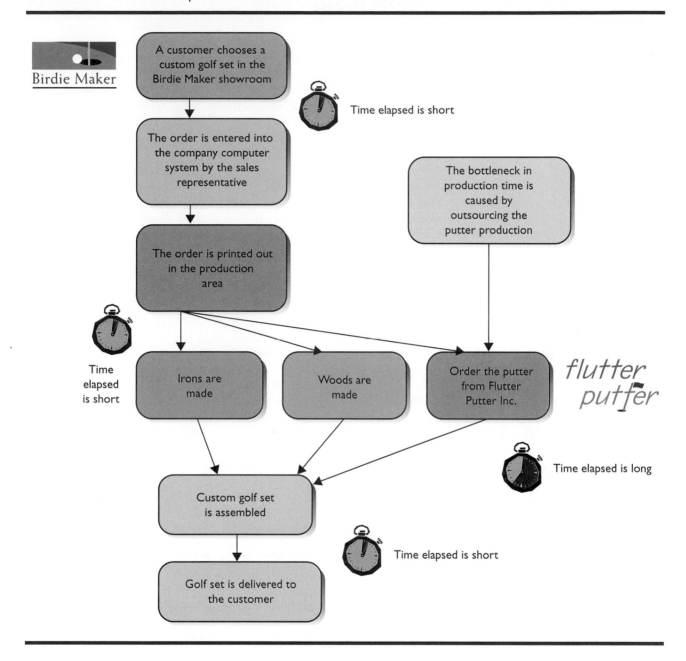

process. In the previous example, machine time is a bottleneck that limits the amount of throughput. Another example is the airline industry where certain tasks performed while the aircraft is on the ground delay departure and increase the turnaround time for the plane.

The key to the theory of constraints is identifying and managing bottlenecks. Once a bottleneck is identified, management must focus its time and resources on relieving the bottleneck. Utilizing resources to increase the efficiency of a non-bottleneck operation will rarely increase throughput. For example, increasing the efficiency of machines with excess capacity in a factory or reducing flight time for an airline will result in very limited increases in throughput (if any) until bottlenecks are relieved.

In Exhibit 7-2, Birdie Maker has discovered that delays in delivery of golf clubs to customers are a result of the extra time it takes to order and receive putters from Flutter Putter Inc. Reducing the time spent manufacturing irons or woods would not reduce overall delivery time until the bottleneck with the putters is relieved.

SELL-OR-PROCESS-FURTHER DECISIONS

LO6

Analyze a decision dealing with selling a product or processing it further

The decision to sell a product as is or to process it further to generate additional revenue is another common management decision. For example, furniture manufacturers may sell furniture unassembled and unfinished, assembled and unfinished, or assembled and finished. Pizza parlors may sell ready-to-bake pizzas or fully cooked pizzas. The key in making these and other sell-or-process-further decisions is that all costs that are incurred up to the point where the decision is made are sunk costs and therefore not relevant.

The relevant costs are the incremental or additional processing costs. Managers should compare the additional sales revenue that can be earned from processing the product further with the additional processing costs. If the additional revenue is greater than the additional costs, the product should be processed further. If the additional costs exceed the revenues, the product should be sold as is. For example, the cost to finish a piece of furniture must be less than the additional revenue that can be expected from selling finished furniture. As with limited resource problems, demand of the products must also be considered.

  Key Concept: *A product should be processed further if the additional revenue is greater than the additional cost.*

IN THE NEWS   www.wsj.com

Sometimes, further processing of an undesirable by-product can even be profitable. Since 1970, electric utilities have been scrubbing the smoke emitted from their smokestacks to remove sulfur and ash from the atmosphere. They do this by spraying a mixture of water and ground limestone into the smoke. Until recently, the utilities collected the toothpaste-like mixture that collected at the bottom of the stacks and buried it in landfills. However, adding oxygen turns the mixture into calcium sulfate, which has the same chemical composition as gypsum. The gypsum can be sold to farmers as a soil enhancer or to wallboard manufacturers as a raw material (*The Wall Street Journal,* October 5, 1998, B1).

ABC AND RELEVANT COST ANALYSIS

LO7

Evaluate the impact of ABC on relevant costs and decision making

As described in Chapter 4, activity based costing (ABC) uses multiple cost drivers to trace overhead costs directly to products. ABC's focus on activities that cause costs to be incurred sheds new light on the concept of relevant costs. Whereas traditional cost analysis focuses on changes in costs associated with volume, ABC focuses on changes in costs associated with a variety of different activities including material handling, inspection, purchasing, and machine setups. Although fixed costs may not appear to be avoidable (and therefore relevant) under traditional costing because they do not vary with changes in volume, these same costs may be avoidable when the amount of material, inspections, purchase orders, or setups is changed. ABC helps managers to identify what costs are really avoidable in a relevant cost analysis.

However, it is important to remember that not all traceable costs are relevant costs. For example, ABC may trace depreciation of a machine directly to a product. However, if the depreciation relates to an existing piece of equipment, the depreciation is a sunk cost and is still not relevant.

SUMMARY OF KEY CONCEPTS

- The price of a product must be sufficient to cover all the costs of the product and to provide a profit. (p. 186)
- The price of a special order must be higher than the additional variable costs incurred in accepting the special order plus any opportunity costs incurred. (p. 190)
- A product should continue to be made internally and labor incurred internally if the avoidable costs are less than the additional costs that will be incurred by buying or outsourcing. (p. 196)
- A product should be dropped when the fixed costs avoided are greater than the contribution margin lost. (p. 198)
- Resource utilization decisions hinge on an analysis of the contribution margin earned per unit of the limited resource. (p. 200)
- A product should be processed further if the additional revenue is greater than the additional cost. (p. 202)

KEY DEFINITIONS

Life cycle cost The costs accumulated over the entire life cycle of a product (p. 185)

Target pricing A pricing method used when a price is pre-set by market conditions or when a company wishes to set a price in order to capture a predetermined market share or meet other marketing goals (p. 186)

Cost-plus pricing A method of pricing in which managers determine the cost of the product or service and then add a markup percentage to that cost to arrive at the sales price (p. 186)

Markup percentage The amount added to cost to determine the sales price in cost-plus pricing. The markup must be sufficient to cover any costs not included in the company's definition of product cost plus produce an acceptable profit (p. 187)

Time and material pricing A pricing method often used in service industries where labor is the primary cost incurred (p. 187)

Value pricing A pricing method that bases the price of services on the perceived or actual value of the service provided to a customer (p. 188)

Special-order decisions Short-run pricing decisions in which management must decide what sales price is appropriate when customers place orders that are different from those placed in the regular course of business (larger quantity, one-time sale to a foreign customer, etc.) (p. 189)

Outsourcing and make-or-buy decisions Short-term decisions to outsource labor or purchase components used in manufacturing from another company rather than to provide services or produce components internally (p. 192)

Vertical integration Accomplished when a company is involved in multiple steps of the value chain (p. 193)

Constraints Restrictions that occur when the capacity to manufacture a product or provide a service is limited in some manner (p. 199)

Resource utilization decisions Decisions that require an analysis of how best to use a resource that is available in limited supply (p. 199)

The theory of constraints A management tool for dealing with constraints that identifies and focuses on bottlenecks in the production process (p. 200)

Bottlenecks Steps in the production process that limit throughput or the number of finished products that go through the production process (p. 200)

CONCEPT REVIEW

1. What term is used to describe the approach to pricing where a markup is added to the firm's cost?

2. What is target pricing and when would it be appropriate to use it?

3. What makes a cost relevant for decision making?

4. Why aren't fixed costs relevant for most short-term decisions?

5. Compare and contrast the terms *relevant* and *nonrelevant* costs in decision making.

6. Production of a special order will increase income when the additional revenue from the special order is greater than what?

7. In considering a special order that will enable a company to make use of presently idle capacity, list the costs that would more than likely be relevant in the decision-making process.

8. What costs are usually relevant in a make-or-buy decision?

9. Name some qualitative factors that would cause a decision maker to favor the buy choice in a make-or-buy decision.

10. In deciding whether to manufacture a part or buy it from an outside supplier, name a cost that would not be relevant to that short-run decision.

11. The decision to drop a product line should be based on what factors?

12. In the short run, which element is most critical to limited-resource decisions?

13. What steps should be taken when dealing with a production bottleneck?

14. How does ABC affect relevant cost analysis?

APPLICATION OF CONCEPTS

15. The variable production costs of a product are $15. Fixed costs are $4 per unit, based on 8,000 units produced during this period. The company has adequate capacity to accept a special order of 500 units. What is the minimum price that could be charged for this special order?

16. The Old Balance Company manufactures lacrosse sticks. The company's capacity is 4,500 sticks per month; however, it currently is selling only 3,000 sticks per month. LongMeadow Sports has asked Old Balance to sell 700 lacrosse sticks at $50 each. Normally, Old Balance sells its sticks for $65. The company records report the cost of each stick to be $40, which includes fixed costs of $20. If Old Balance was to accept LongMeadow's offer, what would be the impact on Old Balance's operating income?

17. Scott Inc. sells a product for $25 per unit. It incurs the following costs for the product: Direct materials $11, Direct labor 7, Variable overhead 2, Fixed overhead 1, Total $21. Scott Inc. received a special order for 75 units of the product. The order would require rental of a special tool. The tool rents for $300 for the period needed. What is the minimum price per unit Scott Inc. could charge for this special order if management requires a $500 minimum profit on any special order? Scott Inc. has sufficient idle capacity to produce the needed product for this order.

18. Husky Sports manufactures footballs. The forecasted income statement for the year before any special orders is as follows:

	Amount	Per Unit
Sales	$4,000,000	$10.00
Manufacturing cost of goods sold	3,200,000	8.00
Gross profit	$ 800,000	$ 2.00
Selling expenses	300,000	.75
Operating income	$ 500,000	$ 1.25

Required

A. Fixed costs included in the above forecasted income statement are $1,200,000 in manufacturing cost of goods sold and $100,000 in selling expenses. Husky Sports received a special order for 50,000 footballs at $7.50 each. There will be no additional selling expenses if the company accepts. Assume Husky Sports has sufficient capacity to manufacture 50,000 more footballs. What is the relevant unit cost?

B. By what amount would operating income of Husky Sports be increased or decreased as a result of accepting the special order?

19. Great Falls Brewery's regular selling price for a case of product is $15. Variable costs are $8 per case. Fixed costs total $2 per case based on 250,000 cases and remain unchanged within the relevant range of 50,000 cases to total capacity of 300,000 cases. After sales of 180,000 cases were projected for the year, a special order was received for an additional 30,000 cases. What is Great Falls Brewery's minimum acceptable selling price for this special order?

20. Violette Inc. uses 10,000 pounds of a certain product in the production of life preservers each year. Presently, this product is purchased from an outside supplier at $11 per pound. For some time now there has been idle capacity in the factory that could be utilized to make this product. The costs associated with manufacturing the product internally rather than buying it from the outside supplier are as follows:

Direct materials	$3 per unit
Direct labor	$3 per unit
Variable overhead	$2 per unit
Fixed overhead (based on production of 10,000 pounds per month)	$2 per unit
Annual salary of new supervisor	$32,000

Required

A. At what price per pound from the outside supplier would the company be indifferent (on economic grounds) to buying or making the product internally?

B. If Violette Inc. chooses to make the product instead of buying it from the outside vendor, what would be the change, if any, in the company's net income per year?

21. Langer Company has three products that use common facilities. The relevant data concerning these three products follow:

Product	A	B	C	Total
Sales	$10,000	$30,000	$ 40,000	$ 80,000
Variable costs	5,000	20,000	25,000	50,000
Contribution margin	$ 5,000	$10,000	$ 15,000	$ 30,000
Fixed costs	5,000	15,000	30,000	50,000
Operating loss	0	$ (5,000)	$(15,000)	$(20,000)

Required

A. If fixed costs allocated to Product Line C are not avoidable and if Product Line C is dropped, what will be the impact on operating profits?

B. If $15,000 of the fixed costs allocated to Product Line C are avoidable and Product Line C is dropped, what will be the impact on operating profits?

C. What other qualitative factors should Langer Company consider before it makes the decision to drop Product Line C?

22. Paul Allyn Productions produces music videos. They are produced in two lengths on separate videocassettes. The company can sell its entire production of either product. The relevant data for these two products follow:

	Video 1	Video 2
Machine time per unit	5 hours	2 hours
Selling price per unit	$10	$20
Variable costs per unit	$ 2	$ 4

Total fixed overhead is $240,000. The company has only 100,000 machine hours available for production. Because of the constraint on the maximum number of machine hours, Paul Allyn Productions must decide which cassette to produce to maximize its return. Which product should the company select to maximize operating profits?

23. Grace Sullivan & Company has two sales offices, one located in Portland and one in Portsmouth. The company's records report the following information:

	Portland	Portsmouth
Sales	$40,000	$50,000
Direct costs:		
Variable	$15,000	$25,000
Fixed	$10,000	$10,000

Management is considering dropping the Portland office. What will be the resulting operating income if Portland is eliminated and half of its fixed costs are avoidable?

24. Kenny Washburn Toys manufactured 500 stuffed lobsters that were defective. The manufacturing costs of the lobsters follow:

Direct materials	$30
Direct labor	$24
Variable overhead	$10
Fixed overhead	$12

The lobsters normally sell for $100. The company can rework the lobsters, which will cost $20 for direct materials, $20 for direct labor, and $2 for variable overhead. In addition, fixed overhead will be applied at the rate of 75 percent of direct labor cost. Alternatively, the company could sell the lobsters "as is" for a selling price of $70. What should management do to maximize profits?

25. Foley Corporation makes motorcycle engines. The company's records show the following costs to manufacture part #61645:

Direct materials	$12
Direct labor	$15
Variable overhead	$20
Fixed overhead	$10

Another manufacturer has offered to supply Foley Corporation with part #61645 for a cost of $50 per unit. Foley Corporation uses 1,000 units annually. If Foley Corporation accepts the offer, what will be the short-run impact on operating income?

Birdie Maker

26. If Birdie Maker Golf Company needs to mark up all costs by 30 percent to earn the desired profit, what would the selling price be if the costs of a set of golf clubs were as follows:

a. cost of clubs = $500

b. cost of clubs = $700

c. Recalculate the selling price if the markup percentage drops to 25 percent.

27. If Pryor Construction marks up the cost of construction by 24 percent, what would the selling price be on a house that cost $225,000 to build? What if the markup percentage increased to 30 percent?

Birdie Maker

28. If Birdie Maker Golf Company is limited to a selling price of $700 for a set of golf clubs because of market constraints, but still must maintain a 30 percent markup on cost, what is the target cost for a set of golf clubs? What if the market price is $800 and the markup is 35 percent?

29. Clayton Herring Tire Co. is considering adding a special tire for sports cars. The market research indicates that the maximum price for this type of tire is $75. If they must have at least a 40 percent markup on all tires, what is the maximum cost to produce the new tire? If the production department estimates the cost to be $50, what options do they have at this point?

30. Old Balance Company would like to introduce a new high-tech lacrosse stick. The new stick would sell for $75. If Old Balance marks up the cost of all products by 20 percent, what is the maximum cost they can incur to produce the new stick? What if they decide to raise the price of the stick to $80?

31. Potts Sports is considering outsourcing its maintenance work. The total labor cost for the maintenance department is $150,000 and they have an offer from Robyn Maintenance to provide the service for $125,000. The maintenance equipment currently used cannot be sold and has annual depreciation of $10,000. The overhead allocated to the maintenance department is $20,000 per year and would not be avoidable. Based on the information given, what should they do? What if the equipment could not be sold, but the overhead allocation would decrease to $10,000? What other non-quantitative factors should be considered?

32. Mandy Lifeboats produces life preservers with a cost of $10 per unit. The cost is broken down in the following manner:

Direct materials	$3
Direct labor	$3
Variable overhead	$2
Fixed overhead	$2 (based on 20,000 units)

Mandy Lifeboats can outsource the service function on the manufacturing equipment to U. R. Saved Service Co. for $12,000 per year. Currently the service function is included in variable overhead at $.50 per unit. If they do outsource the service function, the fixed overhead would also decrease by $.50 per unit. Based on these amounts, what should they do? Suppose fixed costs remain the same. Would that change the decision? What other non-quantitative factors should be considered?

33. Watson Company manufactures beach balls with a special compound. They have two models of beach balls: the bouncer and the floater. The floater uses 10 ounces of the compound and the bouncer uses 7 ounces. The maximum amount of special compound available each month is 200 pounds. Watson Company can sell up to 225 floaters and up to 300 bouncers. The compound costs $5 per pound. The floater sells for $7 and the bouncer sells for $6.50. Each ball takes ½ hour to produce and the average wage rate is $7 per hour. Overhead amounts to $.50 per ball. Which ball should they make first?

34. Porker Enterprises produces hams from locally raised pigs. The cost of getting the meat ready for market is $1 per pound. Hams weigh an average of 12 pounds and sell for $1.50 per pound. Porker can smoke the hams for an additional $.50 per pound. The smoked hams would sell for $2.25 per pound. Should they smoke the hams? What if the selling price for smoked hams was $1.75 per pound?

35. For the past 10 years, Gutmann Company has produced the small gas motors that fit into its main product line of weed-cutting machines. As material costs have steadily increased, the Controller of Gutmann Company is reviewing the decision to continue to make the small motors and has identified the following facts:

a. The equipment used to manufacture the gas motors has a book value of $350,000.

b. The space now occupied by the gas motor manufacturing department could be used to eliminate the need for storage space now being rented.

c. Comparable units can be purchased from an outside supplier for $89.95.

d. Five of the people who work in the gas motor manufacturing department would be terminated and given eight weeks' severance pay.

e. A $25,000 unsecured note is still outstanding on the equipment used in the manufacturing process.

f. Some communities where Gutmann operates have a noise-reduction law.

Required

A. Which of the items above are relevant to the decision that the controller has to make? Give a reason or reasons why each item is relevant or not.

B. Suppose the motor supplied by the outside supplier has a muffler that exceeds the noise level allowed in some communities in which you sell. Would that change your decision? Suppose the outside supplier could provide the motors with a quieter muffler for $95. What other factors should be considered?

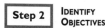

36. Jain Simmons Company needs 10,000 units of a certain part to be used in production. If Jain Simmons Company buys the part from Sullivan Company instead of making it, Jain Simmons Company could not use the present facilities for another manufacturing activity. Sixty percent of the fixed overhead applied will continue regardless of what decision is made.

The following quantitative information is available regarding the situation presented:

Cost to Jain Simmons Company to make the part:

Direct materials	$ 6
Direct labor	24
Variable overhead	12
Fixed overhead applied	15
	$57

Cost to buy the part from Sullivan Company: $53

Required

A. In deciding whether to make or buy the part, how much are Jain Simmons's total relevant costs to make the part?

B. Which alternative is more desirable for Jain Simmons and by what amount?

C. Suppose that Jain Simmons Company is in an economically depressed area of the country with a high unemployment rate and that it is unlikely that displaced direct labor employees will be able to find alternative employment. How might that impact your decision?

37. The Hemp Division of West Company produces rope. One-third of the Hemp Division's output is sold to the Hammock Products Division of West; the remainder is sold to outside customers. The Hemp Division's estimated sales and cost data for the fiscal year ending Sept. 30 are as follows:

	Hammock Products	**Outsiders**
Sales	$15,000	$40,000
Variable costs	(10,000)	(20,000)
Fixed costs	(3,000)	(6,000)
Gross margin	2,000	14,000
Unit sales	10,000	20,000

The Hemp Division has an opportunity to purchase 10,000 feet of identical-quality rope from an outside supplier at a cost of $1.25 per unit on a continuing basis. Assume that the Hemp Division cannot sell any additional product to outside customers.

Required

A. Should West allow its Hemp Division to purchase the rope from the outside supplier? Why or why not?

B. Assume the Hemp Division is now at full capacity and sufficient demand exists to sell all production to outsiders at present prices. What is the differential cost (benefit) of producing the rope internally?

C. Assume that the quality of the rope is found to be of a lesser, but still satisfactory, quality. What factors should be considered?

D. Assume that the quality of the rope is found to be of questionable quality, but the price is $1.00 per unit. What factors should be considered in the decision?

38. Patterson Manufacturing Company manufactures part #52749 for use in its production cycle. The costs per unit for 10,000 units of part #52749 are as follows:

Direct materials	$ 3
Direct labor	15
Variable overhead	6
Fixed overhead	8

Blundell Company has offered to sell Patterson 10,000 units of part #52749 for $30 per unit. If Patterson accepts Blundell's offer, the released facilities could be used to save $45,000 in relevant costs in the manufacture of part #60657. In addition, $5 per unit of the fixed overhead applied to part #52749 would be totally eliminated.

Required

A. What are the total relevant costs to manufacture part #52749?

B. What are the total relevant costs to buy part #52749?

C. What alternative is more desirable and by what amount?

D. Suppose that the purchased part is of lower quality than the part being produced internally. How would that influence your decision? What if the price of the part is reduced to $25 per unit?

39. The Schoof Manufacturing Co. manufactures part #81199 for use in producing a mountain bike. The costs per unit for 20,000 units of part #81199 are as follows:

Direct material	$ 6
Direct labor	30
Variable overhead	12
Fixed overhead	<u>16</u>
	$64

Kelley Manufacturing has offered to sell Schoof 20,000 units of part #81199 for $60 per unit. The company will decide to buy the part from Kelley if the savings total $250,000. If the part is purchased from the outside supplier, Schoof will realize savings of $9 per part for fixed overhead. Furthermore, the released facilities could be leased for additional revenue. What amount of lease payment must be charged to reach the required $250,000 savings? What qualitative factors should be considered before making a final decision? Why?

40. Foggy Mountain Company manufactures several different styles of banjos. Management estimates that during the second quarter of the current year the company will be operating at 80 percent of normal capacity. Because Foggy Mountain wants to increase utilization of the plant, the company has decided to consider special orders for its products.

Foggy Mountain has just received inquiries from a number of companies concerning the possibility of a special order and has narrowed the possibilities down to two companies. The first is from CCR Company who would like to market a banjo very similar to one of Foggy Mountain's. The CCR banjo would be marketed under CCR's own label. CCR has offered Foggy Mountain $57.50 per banjo for 20,000 banjos to be shipped by June 1. The cost data for the Foggy Mountain banjo are as follows:

Regular selling price per banjo	$90
Costs per unit:	
Raw material	$25
Direct labor (5 hours @ $6)	30
Overhead (2.5 machine hours @ $4)	10
Total costs	$65

According to the specifications provided by CCR, the banjo that the company wants would require less-expensive raw material. Consequently, the raw material would only cost $22 per banjo. Management has also estimated that the remaining costs would stay the same.

The second special order was submitted by Seager & Buffet Company for 7,500 banjos at $75 per banjo. These banjos would be marketed under the Seager & Buffet label and also should be shipped by June 1. However, the Seager & Buffet model is different from any banjo in the Foggy Mountain product line. The estimated per-unit costs are as follows:

Raw materials	$32.50
Direct labor (5 hours @ $6)	30.00
Overhead (5 machine hours @ $4)	20.00
Total costs	$82.50

In addition, Foggy Mountain will incur $15,000 in additional setup costs and will have to purchase a $25,000 special machine to manufacture these banjos; this machine will be discarded once the special order is completed.

The Foggy Mountain manufacturing capabilities are limited in the total machine hours available. The plant capacity under normal operations is 900,000 machine hours per year or 75,000 machine hours per month. The budgeted fixed overhead for the year is $2,160,000. All manufacturing overhead costs are applied to production on the basis of machine hours at $4 per hour.

Foggy Mountain will have the entire second quarter to work on the special orders. Management does not expect any repeat sales to be generated from either special order. Company practice precludes Foggy Mountain from subcontracting any portion of an order when special orders are not expected to generate repeat sales.

Required

A. What is the excess capacity of machine hours available in the second quarter?

B. What is the variable overhead rate per machine hour?

C. Based on the above information and your analysis, would you accept CCR's offer?

D. What is the unit contribution margin per banjo for the Seager & Buffet order?

E. What is the actual gain (loss) incurred by accepting Seager & Buffet's offer?

41. Cecilia Louse Inc. has the following cost structure for the upcoming year:

Sales (20,000 units @ $25)	$500,000
Manufacturing costs:	
Variable	$10 per unit
Fixed	$180,000
Marketing and administrative costs:	
Variable	$5 per unit
Fixed	$ 20,000

Required

A. What is the expected level of operating profits?

B. Should the company accept a special order for 1,000 units at a selling price of $20 if variable marketing expenses associated with this special order would be $2 per unit? Calculate the incremental profits if the order is accepted.

C. Suppose the company received a special order for 3,000 units at a selling price of $19 with no variable marketing expenses. Calculate the impact on operating profits.

D. Assume that if the special order is accepted, all the regular customers would be aware of the price paid for the special order. Would that influence your decision? Why?

42. The Belik Company has the capacity to produce 5,000 units per year. Its predicted operations for the year are as follows:

Sales (4,000 units @ $20 each)	$80,000
Manufacturing costs:	
Variable	$5 per unit
Fixed	$10,000
Marketing and administrative costs:	
Variable	$1 per unit
Fixed	$8,000

The accounting department has prepared the following projected income statement for the coming year for your use in making decisions.

Sales	$80,000	
Variable costs:		
Manufacturing ($5 × 4,000)	$20,000	
Marketing ($1 × 4,000)	4,000	24,000
Contribution margin		$56,000
Fixed costs:		
Manufacturing	$10,000	
Marketing	8,000	18,000
Operating profit		$38,000

Required

A. Should the company accept a special order for 500 units at a selling price of $8? Assuming that there are no variable marketing and administrative costs for this order and that regular sales will not be affected, what is the impact of this decision on company profits?

B. Suppose there was a one-time setup fee of $1,000 for the preceding order. Should the special order be accepted? Why?

C. What other factors should be considered and how would they impact your decision to accept the special order?

D. Suppose that regular sales would be reduced by 200 units if the special order were accepted. What impact would this have on the company's decision?

43. Avery Inc. is a wholesale distributor supplying a wide range of moderately priced sporting equipment to large chain stores. About 60 percent of Avery's products are purchased from other companies while the remainder of the products are manufactured by Avery. The company has a plastics department that is currently manufacturing molded fishing tackle boxes. Avery is able to manufacture and sell 8,000 tackle boxes annually, making full use of its direct labor capacity at available workstations.

The following table presents the selling price and costs associated with Avery's tackle boxes:

Selling price		$86.00
Costs per box:		
Molded plastic	$ 8.00	
Hinges, latches, handle	9.00	
Direct labor ($15/hour)	18.75	
Manufacturing overhead	12.50	
Selling and administrative cost	17.00	65.25
Profit per box		$20.75

Because Avery believes it could sell 12,000 tackle boxes, the company has looked into the possibility of purchasing the tackle boxes for distribution. Craig Products, a steady supplier of quality products, would be able to provide up to 9,000 tackle boxes per year at a price of $68 per box delivered to Avery's facility.

Bart Johnson, Avery's product manager, has suggested that the company could make better use of its plastics department by purchasing the tackle boxes and manufacturing skateboards. To support his position, Johnson has a market study that indicates an expanding market for skateboards and a need for additional suppliers. Johnson believes that Avery could expect to sell 17,500 skateboards annually at a price of $45.00 per skateboard. Johnson's estimate of the costs to manufacture the skateboards is presented here:

Selling price per skateboard	$45.00
Costs per skateboard:	
Molded plastic	$ 5.50
Wheels, plastic	7.00
Direct labor ($15/hour)	7.50
Manufacturing overhead	5.00
Selling and administrative cost	9.00
Total cost per skateboard	34.00
Profit per skateboard	$11.00

In the plastics department, Avery uses direct labor hours as the application base for manufacturing overhead. Included in the manufacturing overhead for the current year is $50,000 factory-wide, fixed manufacturing overhead that has been allocated to the plastic department.

Step 1	DEFINE THE PROBLEM
Step 2	IDENTIFY OBJECTIVES
Step 3	IDENTIFY AND ANALYZE AVAILABLE OPTIONS
Step 4	SELECT THE BEST OPTION

Required

A. Define the problem faced by Avery Inc. based on the facts as presented.

B. What are the relevant objectives in this problem?

C. What options are available to Avery Inc. in solving the problem?

D. Rank the options in order of preference.

E. What qualitative factors should Avery consider in the decision?

F. Should Avery consider the potential liability that comes with selling skateboards? It has been shown that skateboards are responsible for 25 deaths per year and over 500 serious accidents. Would that change your decision to make skateboards?

44. Big Ben Tours Inc. operates a large number of tours throughout the southwestern United States. A careful study has indicated that some of the tours are not profitable, and the management of Big Ben Tours is considering dropping these tours in order to improve the company's overall operating performance.

One such tour is a two-day bus trip to the world famous London Bridge on the Colorado River. An income statement from one of these tours is given in the following table:

Ticket revenue (100 seats ×			
45% occupancy × $80 ticket price)		$3,600	100%
Less: Variable expenses ($24 per person)		1,080	30%
Contribution margin		$2,520	70%
Less tour expenses:			
Tour promotion	$620		
Salary of bus driver	400		
Tour guide fee	825		
Fuel for bus	100		
Depreciation for bus	400		
Liability insurance, bus	250		
Overnight parking fee, bus	50		
Room and meals, bus driver, and tour guide	75		
Bus maintenance and preparation	325		
Total tour expenses	3,045		
Net loss	$ (525)		

The following additional information is available about the tour:

a. Bus drivers are paid fixed annual salaries; tour guides are paid for each tour conducted.

b. The "bus maintenance and preparation" cost above is an allocation of the salaries of mechanics and other service personnel who are responsible for keeping the company's fleet of buses in good operating condition.

c. This particular tour is very important to Ben, the founder and owner, who often takes the tour himself as driver or tour guide. He would like to see the tour retained.

Required

A. Prepare an analysis showing what the impact will be on company profits if this tour is discontinued.

B. Ben has criticized the company's tour director, Amy, because only about 50 percent of the seats on the London Bridge tours are being filled as compared to an average of 60 percent for the industry. The tour director has explained that the company's average seat occupancy could be improved considerably by eliminating about 10 percent of the tours, but doing so would reduce profits. Do you agree with the tour director's conclusion? Explain your response.

C. What other options are available to Big Ben Tours Inc.?

D. List qualitative factors that you think should be considered in this decision and discusss the potential impact of each factor on the decision.

> **Step 3** IDENTIFY AND ANALYZE AVAILABLE OPTIONS

45. Smoluk Mining Company currently is operating at less than 50 percent of capacity. The management of the company expects sales to drop below the present level of 10,000 tons of ore per month very soon. The sales price per ton is $3 and the variable cost per ton is $2. Fixed costs per month total $10,000.

Management is concerned that a further drop in sales volume will generate a loss and, accordingly, is considering the temporary suspension of operations until demand in the metals markets rebounds and prices once again rise. Management has implemented a cost-reduction program over the past year that has been successful in reducing costs to the point that suspending operations appears to be the only viable alternative. Management estimates that suspending operations would reduce fixed costs from $10,000 to $4,000 per month.

Required

A. Why does management estimate that the fixed costs will persist at $4,000 even though the mine is temporarily closed?

B. At what sales volume will the loss be greater or less than the shutdown cost of $4,000 per month?

C. List any qualitative factors that you think they should consider in this decision and discuss the potential impact of each factor on the decision.

46. Jagolinzer Company is currently operating at 80 percent capacity. Worried about the company's performance, Phil, the general manager, reviewed the company's operating performance.

	SEGMENT			
	North	**South**	**East**	**West**
Sales	$30	$40	$20	$10
Less variable costs	12	8	21	8
Contribution margin	$18	$32	$ (1)	$ 2
Less fixed costs	9	12	6	3
Operating profit (loss)	$ 9	$20	$ (7)	$ (1)

Required

A. What is the current operating profit for the company as a whole?

B. If Phil eliminated the unprofitable segments, what would be the new operating profit for the company as a whole?

C. What options does management have to maximize profits?

D. What qualitative factors do you think management should consider before making this decision? What impact could these qualitative factors have on the decision?

Step 3   IDENTIFY AND ANALYZE AVAILABLE OPTIONS

47. Sanders Manufacturing uses 10 hours of labor to produce one piece of radar equipment. The unit cost to manufacture this unit is presented in the following table:

Direct materials	$1,000
Materials handling (20 percent of direct material cost)	200
Direct labor	150
Manufacturing overhead (150 percent of direct labor)	225
Total manufacturing cost	$1,575

Material handling represents the direct variable costs of the receiving department that are applied to direct materials and purchased components on the basis of their cost. This is a separate charge in addition to manufacturing overhead. Sanders's annual manufacturing overhead budget is one-third variable and two-thirds fixed. John's Supply, one of Sanders's reliable vendors, has offered to provide the labor to produce the radar equipment for $175 per unit.

Required

A. If Sanders outsources the labor to John's Supply, they will avoid all direct labor costs. If Sanders decides to outsource the labor, by what amount would the unit cost increase or decrease? Be sure to consider the impact of overhead on your answer.

B. Assume that Sanders must pay six months' severance pay to all employees laid off as a result of this decision. Sanders has 10 employees who are paid $1,200 per month who would be affected by this decision. If Sanders produces 160 radar units per month, what is the time needed to recapture the severance pay?

C. What qualitative factors should they consider before making this decision? What impact would each have on the decision?

48. Voyer Company manufactures plugs used in its manufacturing cycle at a cost of $36 per unit that includes $8 of fixed overhead. Voyer needs 30,000 of these plugs annually, and John Company has offered to sell these units to Voyer at $33 per unit. If Voyer decides to purchase the plugs, $60,000 of the annual fixed overhead applied will be eliminated, and the company may be able to rent the facility previously used for manufacturing the plugs.

Required

A. If Voyer Company purchases the plugs but does not rent the unused facility, what is the per-unit impact on the company?

B. If the plugs are purchased and the facility rented, Voyer Company wishes to realize $100,000 in savings annually. To achieve this goal, what must be the minimum annual rent on the facility?

49. John Carey Company produces computer games that have a maximum market price of $50. The company is considering introducing some new games to be used with a just-released enhanced game machine manufactured by another company. The company must realize a profit of 30 percent of cost in order to remain profitable with this division of the company.

Required

A. What is the target cost for these games given the constraints presented?

B. Suppose that the production department has projected the production costs of the game to be $40. What is the problem facing the company?

C. What are the relevant costs in this problem?

D. What additional information do you need to make the optimal decision?

E. Under what circumstances might the company consider producing the games?

50. Regina Johnson Company produces children's books that must sell for $10 or less. The company is considering a proposal to introduce a series of books. The company has always tried to realize a profit of 50 percent on the cost of all new projects undertaken.

Step 1	DEFINE THE PROBLEM
Step 2	IDENTIFY OBJECTIVES
Step 3	IDENTIFY AND ANALYZE AVAILABLE OPTIONS

Required

A. What is the target cost for producing these books?

B. Part of the cost of producing the books is the royalties paid to the author. They have typically paid 10 percent royalties on the cost of the book. In other words, 10 percent of the cost to produce the book will be allocated to royalties. The author of these new books wants a 12 percent royalty on the entire series. If the market will not allow an increase in sales price, what are the options available to the company? Show calculations of the impact on company profits.

51. Vincent Martinez Company is considering taking over a hot dog vending booth at the local AA Minor League baseball stadium. Because of limitations on the retail price that may be charged for hot dogs in the stadium and a limitation on the profit percentage that may be earned, the company has very limited options. The stadium owner has set a limit on the price of a hot dog at $1.75 and limits all vendors to no more than 30 percent profit on any food sold.

Required

A. Given the limits imposed by the stadium owner, what is the maximum price that Vincent Martinez Company can pay for all ingredients needed?

B. After computing the maximum cost of the ingredients the company finds that to purchase all ingredients at the quality level expected, the cost is $1.50.

C. Accurately define the problem faced by Vincent Martinez Company.

Step 1 DEFINE THE PROBLEM

Step 2 IDENTIFY OBJECTIVES

Step 3 IDENTIFY AND ANALYZE AVAILABLE OPTIONS

Step 4 SELECT THE BEST OPTION

D. What are the key variables in this decision problem?

E. What are the available options, within the limits imposed, to solve the problem?

F. What is the best option? Why?

52. Janie Pierce-Bratcher Company wants to provide lawn maintenance services to a condo association. The company has typically priced services by adding a 60 percent markup to the costs of providing the service. The costs of providing the lawn maintenance service are as follows:

Direct labor (5 men @ 2 hours each @ $10/hour)	$100
Gas and oil for mowers @ $2.50 per hour	25
Maintenance on mowers @ $2.00 per hour	20
Total costs	$145

Required

A. What price should Janie Pierce-Bratcher Company bid for the condo association lawn maintenance service?

B. What additional costs, if any, should the company consider?

C. Based on your answer in Part A and any estimated costs you considered in Part B, how profitable will this venture be?

53. Refer to the information in Problem 52. The condo association also has asked Janie Pierce-Bratcher Company to bid on additional services needed. The association would like the company to trim all sidewalks and driveways and fertilize the lawns three times per year.

Required

A. What additional information does the company need to accurately bid on the preceding services?

B. If the costs of the additional services are $50 per mowing and $250 for each fertilization, what would the bid price be?

54. Carrillo Snow Plowing has been asked to bid on the snow-plowing needs of a large private subdivision. Assume that if the bid is successful the company will have to acquire equipment and new employees to provide the service. Carrillo has a number of these types of contracts and always marks up the estimated costs by 70 percent due to the unpredictable nature of winter storms. All labor hired has to be for the entire winter, so the snowplow operators are paid even if there is no snow to plow.

Required

A. What types of information must be gathered for the bid to be completed? Be specific but do not estimate amounts.

B. If the total cost of all labor, equipment, and supplies is $5,000 for the five-month winter period, how much should the bid price be?

C. If the bid is not accepted and Carrillo stills wants to try and get the business, what can the company do?

D. If we assume that Carrillo decides to mark up the costs by only 50 percent, what potential risks will the company face by underbidding the normal markup?

55. Cheney, Christiansen, and Clements CPAs has decided to bid on the audit of Comeau Inc., a local manufacturing firm. After learning all they can about the potential new client, the partners have estimated the following:

Staff accountant hours	1,500
Manager hours	200
Partner hours	100
Out-of-pocket costs (estimated)	$10,000

All staff, managers, and partners are paid on average 30 percent of the desired client billing rate ($75, $125, $250). Fringe benefits average 30 percent of the pay rate. Out-of-pocket costs include supplies, travel, and clerical costs and are usually fairly accurate.

Required

A. If the firm normally marks up non-labor costs by 20 percent to arrive at the client fee, what should the bid price be?

B. Using the information available to you, compute the actual out-of-pocket cost to the CPA firm to complete this audit. Out-of-pocket costs do not include any profit built into the client billing rate.

C. Using your answer in Part B, what is the lowest price the CPA firm could charge and not lose money?

D. If Comeau Inc. rejects the bid and states that it will pay no more than $200,000 for the audit, what are the options open to the CPA firm?

56. Sunset Airlines is considering a frequent flyer program. The airline would offer a free round-trip ticket for every 10,000 miles of travel. The average round-trip ticket on Sunset Airlines is 1,000 miles, so the airline would be giving a free ticket for every 10 tickets purchased. The cost structure for Sunset Airlines is given in the following table:

Sunset Airlines

	Per Passenger	Per Flight
Cost of meals and drinks	$ 3.25	$ 585
Cost of fuel	138.89	25,000
Cost of cabin crew (4 flight attendants)	9.38	1,688
Cost of flight crew	13.89	2,500
Depreciation of aircraft	5.56	1,000
Aircraft maintenance	$ 4.17	750
Total	$175.14	$31,523

The maximum capacity of the airplanes used by Sunset Airlines is 180 seats with an average load of 140 passengers per flight.

Required

A. What is the cost to Sunset Airlines to provide a free ticket to passengers under the proposed frequent flyer program?

B. What are the risks to Sunset Airlines of providing free tickets with the frequent flyer program?

C. What qualitative factors should management consider before deciding to implement the frequent flyer program, and how would they affect the decision?

D. If Sunset Airlines was already flying at 95 percent capacity, or filling up 171 seats on every flight, would the airline still be as motivated to start the frequent flyer program? Why or why not?

57. Birdie Maker Golf Company produces custom sets of golf clubs that are advertised to be far superior to other golf clubs on the market. These golf clubs sell for $1,000 per set and Birdie currently sells about 1,000 sets each year. Birdie Maker currently manufactures all the golf clubs in the set but is considering acquiring the putter from Flutter Putter Inc., a manufacturer of custom putters. The purchased putter would be customized for Birdie and matched to the other clubs so customers should not be able to distinguish it from the rest of the clubs in the set. The costs incurred in the manufacture of the putter are given in the following table:

Birdie Maker

	Total	Per Unit
Direct materials	$ 5,000	$ 5.00
Direct labor	$ 9,000	$ 9.00
Variable manufacturing overhead	$ 3,000	$ 3.00
Fixed manufacturing overhead	$ 9,500	$ 9.50
Total cost	$26,500	$26.50

The expected production for the year is 1,000 sets of clubs, so the full cost of each putter is $26.50 ($26,500/1,000). Flutter Putter Inc. is offering to sell the putters to Birdie Maker for $20 per putter.

Required

A. Compute the cost to make the putters and compare that to the cost to buy. What is the best choice for Birdie Maker?

B. What qualitative factors should Birdie Maker consider before making a final decision?

58. Refer to the facts in Problem 57. Now assume that $5,500 of the fixed manufacturing cost is for specialized machinery that is currently being leased under a month-to-month contract. If the putters are purchased from Flutter Putter Inc., the equipment will be returned to the lessor.

Required

A. Compute the cost to make the putters and compare that to the cost to buy. What is the best choice for Birdie Maker?

B. What qualitative factors should Birdie Maker consider before making a final decision?

Birdie Maker

59. Refer to the facts in Problem 57. Now assume that Birdie Maker has a decrease in production volume to 600 sets of golf clubs, and all other costs stay the same as presented in Problem 57.

Required

A. Compute the cost to make the putters and compare that to the cost to buy. What is the best choice for Birdie Maker?

B. What qualitative factors should Birdie Maker consider before making a final decision?

60. Refer to the facts in Problem 57. Birdie Maker can rent out the factory space that is now used to manufacture putters for $10,000. All other costs stay the same as presented in Problem 57.

Required

A. Compute the cost to make the putters and compare that to the cost to buy. What is the best choice for Birdie Maker?

B. What qualitative factors should Birdie Maker consider before making a final decision?

Clayton Herring Tire Co.

61. Clayton Herring Tire Co. is considering dropping one of the ten models of tires that it manufactures and sells. Sales of a special raised white-letter truck tire have been disappointing, and based on the latest financial information the tires appear to be losing money.

CLAYTON HERRING TIRE CO.

	Truck Tires	All Other Tires	Total
Sales	$15,500	$150,000	$165,500
Less: Direct material	8,000	50,600	58,600
Direct labor	2,000	30,000	32,000
Variable overhead	1,000	12,000	13,000
Contribution margin	$ 4,500	$ 57,400	$ 61,900
Less: Fixed overhead	7,000	21,000	28,000
Net Income	$ (2,500)	$ 36,400	$ 33,900

If the truck tires are dropped from the product line, $5,000 of the fixed costs allocated to truck tires would have to be reallocated to other product lines.

Required

A. What would be the effect on net income if the truck tires are dropped from the product line?

B. If the total fixed costs of $7,000 could be eliminated by discontinuing the truck tires, what would be the effect on net income?

C. If the result in Part B leads to dropping the product line, what qualitative factors should be considered before making a final decision? How would those factors impact the decision?

62. Cooney Grocery Store is a small corner grocery store in rural Montana. Because of its size, shelf space is very limited. Management must decide how to allocate shelf space for salsa. Cooney's has been given an opportunity to sell a very popular brand of salsa produced by Bob DeLucia, a popular rock star. The unique bottle is taller and thinner than the other popular brands on the market to give it visibility on the shelf. The sales and cost data for the new salsa and the three other brands presently sold are given in the following table:

	Salsa #1	Salsa #2	Salsa #3	New Salsa
Sales price per jar	$2.50	$2.75	$3.00	$4.00
Cost to purchase	$1.25	$1.35	$1.50	$2.80
Contribution margin	$1.25	$1.40	$1.50	$1.20
Bottles per foot of shelf space	10	9	7	12

Required

A. Rank the salsas based on expected revenue if each is given 10 feet of shelf space.

B. Based on the information given, which salsa should get the most shelf space? Why?

C. What qualitative factors should be considered in this decision? How would these factors impact the decision?

63. Sun Devil Golf Balls produces two different golf balls, the pro model and the tour model. The balls are sold to retailers in cartons containing 360 balls (30 boxes containing 4 sleeves per box with each sleeve holding 3 balls). Both golf balls are made using the same machines. It takes 30 minutes of machine time to produce 360 pro-model golf balls, whereas it takes 45 minutes to produce the same number of the tour balls. The difference in production time is mainly due to the different materials used in construction. The relevant data concerning the two golf balls are presented in the following table:

SUN
DEVIL
GOLF
BALLS

	Pro Model	Tour Model
Sales price (per carton)	$450	$540
Less: Direct material	200	265
Direct labor	50	50
Variable overhead	50	75
Contribution margin	$150	$150
Required machine time	.50 hours	.75 hours

Required

  A. If the amount of machine time available to Sun Devil Golf Balls is limited, which golf ball should be produced in the largest quantity?

  B. If the total machine time available is 200 hours per month and the demand for each model of golf ball is 100,000 balls per month, how many of each golf ball should be produced to maximize profit?

  C. What other factors should be considered in this decision, and how would they impact the decision?

64. DePaulis Furniture Manufacturers makes unfinished furniture for sale to customers from its own stores. Recently the company has been considering taking the production one additional step and finishing some of the furniture for sale as finished furniture. To analyze the problem, DePaulis is going to look at only one product, a very popular dining room chair. The chair can be produced now for $65 and sells for $85 unfinished. If DePaulis were to finish the chair, the cost would increase to $90 but the company could sell the finished chairs for $125.

Required

  A. Should DePaulis finish the chairs or continue to sell them unfinished? Show computations to support your decision.

  B. What other information should be considered in this decision?

  C. What if DePaulis decided it needed a new store to sell the finished furniture and the cost of the new store would add $20 to the cost of each chair. Would that change the decision? Why or why not?

65. DeVito's Fish House buys fish from local fishermen and sells the fish to the public from its booth at the public market. Lately the fish house has had a number of requests for smoked salmon and has decided to investigate whether that would be a profitable item. The salmon DeVito's buys now costs the company $2 per pound. DeVito's would have to take the fish to a smoke house to have it smoked, which would increase the total cost to $3.25 for each pound of salmon. The salmon sells now for $5.50 per pound but would sell for $6.50 per pound if it were smoked.

Required

  A. Based on the facts given, would it be profitable to smoke the salmon? Why or why not?

  B. The owner of DeVito's feels strongly that the company will lose customers if smoked salmon is not available for purchase. Based on your analysis in Requirement A and considering this information, should the company reconsider its decision?

  C. If the cost of the smoking process could be reduced by 50 cents per pound, would that change the decision?

  D. What qualitative factors should be considered before making the final decision?

Currently, Big Al's prices their products using cost-plus pricing using a markup of 50 percent on total manufacturing costs. However, competitors are offering similar meat and veggie pizzas for $6 each.

Required

A. Comment on Big Al's current pricing strategy. What recommendations would you make?

B. In year 3, Big Al's receives a special offer from an athletic arena to purchase 5,000 meat pizzas and 3,000 veggie pizzas for a special event. Assuming sufficient excess capacity, what is the minimum price that Big Al's would be willing to accept for this special order? If there is no excess capacity, what minimum price would be acceptable? What qualitative factors should Big Al's consider?

C. Big Al's is considering purchasing all ingredients separately rather than buying them prepackaged from Pizza Products, Inc. This will reduce direct material costs by 5 percent but will require the hiring of 5 new employees at a cost of $2,000 each per month to prepare dough, sauce, cheese, and meat. This will raise the cost of labor by $.16 per pizza. Should Big Al's continue to buy the prepackaged ingredients from the outside supplier or buy them separately and assemble them in-house? What qualitative factors should Big Al's consider in making this decision?

D. Big Al's is nearing their manufacturing capacity and needs to consider ways to increase their throughput. What options does Big Al's have to increase capacity? What bottlenecks do they face? What recommendations would you make?

LONG-TERM (CAPITAL INVESTMENT) DECISIONS

Study Tools

A Review of the Previous Chapter

In Chapter 7, we analyzed pricing decisions and special orders, make or buy decisions, decisions to drop a product or service, resource utilization decisions, and sell or process further decisions. Each of these decisions is dependent on an analysis of relevant costs and qualitative factors.

A Preview of This Chapter

In this chapter, we provide students with a set of tools that allow managers to consider the time value of money in making long-term capital investment decisions.

Key concepts include:
- Long-term investment decisions require a consideration of the time value of money. The time value of money is based on the concept of a dollar received today being worth more than a dollar received in the future.
- The time value of money is considered in capital investment decisions using one of two techniques: the net present value (NPV) method or the internal rate of return (IRR) method.
- If the present value of cash inflows is greater than or equal to the present value of cash outflows (the NPV is greater than or equal to zero), the investment provides a return at least equal to the discount rate (the minimum required rate of return) and the investment is acceptable.
- The internal rate of return (IRR) is the actual yield or return earned by an investment.
- Taxes are a major source of cash outflows for many companies and must be taken into consideration in time value of money calculations.
- Analyzing the cost and benefits of investments in automated and computerized design and manufacturing equipment and robotics requires careful consideration of both quantitative and qualitative factors.

LEARNING OBJECTIVES

After studying the material in this chapter, you should be able to:

LO1 Discuss the importance of focusing on cash flow in capital investment decisions

LO2 Apply the decision model to capital investment decisions

LO3 Evaluate capital investment decisions using discounted cash flow analysis (NPV and IRR)

LO4 Discuss key assumptions of the NPV and IRR methods

LO5 Evaluate the impact of taxes on capital investment decisions

LO6 Discuss the impact of the new manufacturing environment on capital investment decisions

LO7 Discuss appropriate applications of nondiscounting methods (the payback method) in capital investment decisions

- The payback method can be useful as a fast approximation of the discounted cash flow methods when the cash flows follow similar patterns.

A Preview of Upcoming Chapters

In Chapter 9, we introduce the concept of budgeting and discuss how budgets assist managers in planning and decision making. In Chapter 10, we expand the discussion of flexible budgeting, and introduce the concept of standard costs and variance analysis as tools to help managers "manage by exception" and evaluate performance in their control function.

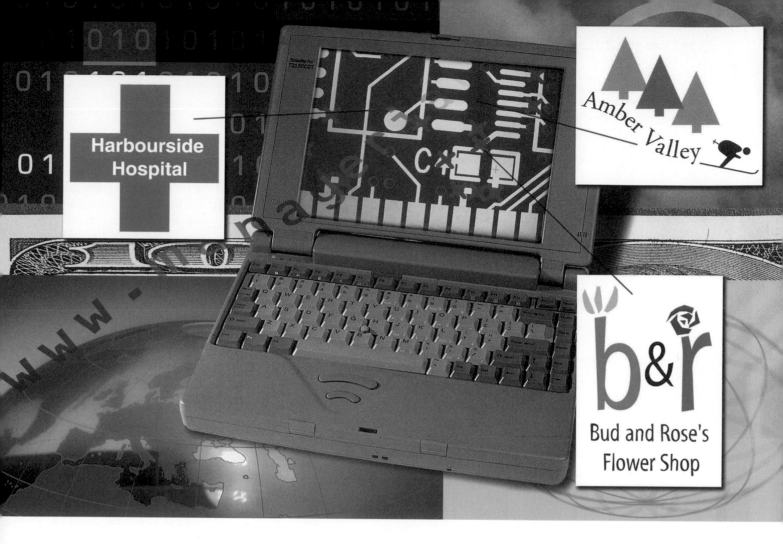

Long-term decisions require a consideration of the time value of money in addition to cost behavior and the relevance of costs. In this chapter, we develop tools that aid managers in making long-term decisions to purchase new property, plant, and equipment (capital investment decisions). These tools help managers quantify the impact of paying or receiving cash flows in different time periods.

The net present value and internal rate of return methods allow for the explicit consideration of the time value of money. The use of these tools in both screening decisions and preference decisions is discussed, as is the impact of income taxes on the analysis. The impact of new manufacturing techniques on capital investment decisions and the importance of qualitative factors in the analysis are also discussed. An approach to long-term purchasing decisions that does not take into consideration the time value of money, the payback method, is also mentioned. ∎

INTRODUCTION

Capital investment decisions are made by all types and sizes of organizations and involve the purchase (or lease) of new machinery and equipment and the acquisition or expansion of facilities used in a business. A decision by a local florist to purchase or lease a new delivery van is a capital investment decision as is the decision to upgrade the computer system at a law firm. Wal-Mart's decision to build and open a new store and Ford's decision to invest in new automated production equipment are capital investment decisions. Long-term purchasing decisions like these often involve large sums of money and considerable risk because they commit companies to a chosen course of action for many years.

One of the key factors to be considered in a long-term purchasing decision is the return of the investment and also the return on the investment—in other words, whether the benefits of the investment exceed its cost. The costs and benefits include both qualitative and quantitative factors. Qualitative costs and benefits include employee, customer, and community reaction to changes in location, the impact of automation on displaced employees, quality improvements that result from new equipment, and so forth. Quantitative costs and benefits include large initial outlays of cash and the need for future repairs and maintenance, the potential for increased sales, and reductions in production and other costs.

FOCUS ON CASH FLOW

LO1

Discuss the importance of focusing on cash flow in capital investment decisions

Because capital investments involve large sums of money and last for many years, a quantitative analysis of the costs and benefits of capital investment decisions must consider the **time value of money.** In addition, the focus of the time value of money is on cash flow, not accounting net income. Accounting net income and cash flow are often not the same. Accounting net income is calculated based on the accrual of income and expenses rather than on the receipt and payment of cash. Whereas measurements of income and cash flow are both useful to managers, investors, and creditors, time value of money calculations are based on the concept of a dollar received (paid) today being worth more (less) than a dollar received (paid) in the future and thus focus on the cash flow of an organization.

 Key Concept: *Long-term investment decisions require a consideration of the time value of money. The time value of money is based on the concept of a dollar received today being worth more than a dollar received in the future.*

IN THE NEWS

While stock analysts and investors have traditionally focused on current and expected earnings of a company in assessing its potential as an investment, analysts increasingly favor the use of cash flow. Analysts like focusing on cash flow because they say it "ignores accounting tricks and shows the true economic health of companies" (*Wall Street Journal,* "Heard on the Street," April 1, 1999).

Typical cash outflows include the original investment in the project, any additional working capital needed during the life of the investment, repairs and maintenance needed for machinery and equipment, and additional operating costs that may be incurred.

Concept Question: Working capital is the excess of current assets over current liabilities. In making a decision to open a new store, what kind of increases in working capital might be expected by a large retail store like Wal-Mart?

www.walmart.com

Concept Answer: In addition to the construction costs of the new store, Wal-Mart would incur additional costs related to stocking the store with inventory, putting cash in the cash registers, and so on. ■

Typical cash inflows include projected incremental revenues from the project, cost reductions in operating expenses, the salvage value (if any) of the investment at the end of its useful life, and the release of working capital at the end of a project's useful life.

With the exception of the initial cash outflow associated with the investment, other cash inflows and outflows are likely to be estimates. The extended time period involved in long-term purchasing decisions makes the projection of these cash inflows and outflows difficult at best. The impact of uncertainty on capital investment decisions and the use of sensitivity analysis are discussed in more detail later in the chapter.

SCREENING AND PREFERENCE DECISIONS

Capital investment decisions typically fall into one of two categories: screening decisions or preference decisions. **Screening decisions** involve deciding if an investment meets some predetermined company standard, whereas **preference decisions** involve choosing between alternatives. The decision model introduced in Chapter 1 (and presented here as Exhibit 8-1) is especially useful in analyzing preference decisions.

LO2
Apply the decision model to capital investment decisions

Typical problems addressed in capital investment decisions are as follows:

1. Should old equipment be replaced with new equipment that promises to be more cost efficient?
2. Should a new delivery vehicle be purchased or leased?
3. Should a manufacturing plant be expanded?
4. Should a new retail store be opened?

Once the problem is defined, the next step is to identify objectives. Objectives include both quantitative factors (increase production, increase sales, reduce costs) and qualitative factors (make a higher quality product, provide better customer service). Step 3 involves both a quantitative analysis of the options using tools that recognize the time value of money and a qualitative analysis. Once the potential investments are screened and analyzed in Step 3, the best option is chosen in Step 4.

| **Step 3** | **IDENTIFY AND ANALYZE AVAILABLE OPTIONS** |
| **Step 4** | **SELECT THE BEST OPTION** |

EXHIBIT 8-1 The Decision Model

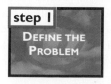 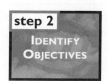  

step 1 DEFINE THE PROBLEM

step 2 IDENTIFY OBJECTIVES

step 3 IDENTIFY AND ANALYZE AVAILABLE OPTIONS

step 4 SELECT THE BEST OPTION

DISCOUNTED CASH FLOW ANALYSIS

LO3

Evaluate capital investment decisions using discounted cash flow analysis (NPV and IRR)

The time value of money is considered in capital investment decisions using one of two techniques: the **net present value (NPV)** method or the **internal rate of return (IRR)** method.[1] In both methods, two simplifying assumptions are made when discounting cash flows to their present value. The first is that all cash flows are assumed to occur at the end of each period (typically at the end of a year). Although most cost reductions and cash inflows resulting from increased sales are likely to occur uniformly throughout the year, this assumption greatly simplifies present value calculations. The second is that all cash inflows are immediately reinvested in another project or investment. This is analogous to the immediate reinvesting of dividends in a stock investment. The rate of return assumed earned on the reinvested amounts depends on whether the net present value or internal rate of return method is used. Under the NPV method, cash inflows are assumed to be reinvested at the discount rate used in the analysis. Under the IRR method, cash inflows are assumed to be reinvested at the internal rate of return of the original investment.

 Key Concept: *The time value of money is considered in capital investment decisions using one of two techniques: the net present value (NPV) method or the internal rate of return (IRR) method.*

NET PRESENT VALUE

The net present value (NPV) method requires the choice of a discount rate to be used in the analysis. Many companies choose to use the cost of capital. The **cost of capital** represents what the firm would have to pay to borrow (issue bonds) or raise funds through equity (issue stock) in the financial marketplace. In NPV analysis, the discount rate serves as a hurdle rate or a minimum required rate of return—the return that the company feels must be earned in order for any potential investment to be profitable. The **discount rate** is often adjusted to reflect the risk and uncertainty of cash flows expected to occur many years in the future. Adjusting the rate for uncertainty is discussed in more detail later in the chapter.

Computing net present value requires a comparison of the present value of all cash inflows associated with a project with the present value of all cash outflows. If the present value of the inflows is greater than or equal to the present value of the outflows (the NPV is greater than or equal to zero), the investment provides a return at least equal to the discount rate (the minimum required rate of return) and the investment is acceptable. If the present value of the outflows is greater than the present value of the inflows, the NPV will be negative and the investment will not be acceptable because it provides a return less than the discount rate.

 Key Concept: *If the present value of cash inflows is greater than or equal to the present value of cash outflows (the NPV is greater than or equal to zero), the investment provides a return at least equal to the discount rate (the minimum required rate of return) and the investment is acceptable.*

**Bud and Rose's
Flower Shop**

To illustrate NPV decisions let's discuss Bud and Rose's Flower Shop, which is considering the purchase of a new refrigerated delivery van that will cost $50,000. It will allow the company to accept large flower orders for weddings, receptions, and so on and is expected to increase cash income from sales (net of increased expenses) by $14,000 per year for six years. The van is not expected to have any salvage value at the end of the six years. Bud

---

[1] The following discussion assumes that readers are already familiar with the basic concepts of discounting and the calculation of present value for single sums and annuities. If not, you should study the appendix at the end of this chapter.

and Rose have a minimum required rate of return of 12 percent and use that as their discount rate.

The only cash outflow in this case is the initial purchase price of $50,000. The annual cash inflow of $14,000 can most easily be viewed as an ordinary annuity for purposes of calculating present value. NPV calculations using present value factors from Table 8A-3 (see the appendix) are shown below.

Cash Flow	Year	Amount	12% Factor	Present Value
Initial investment	Now	$(50,000)	1.0000	$(50,000.00)
Annual cash income	1–6	14,000	4.1114	57,559.60
Net present value				$ 7,559.60

Using the built-in function in Microsoft Excel, =PV(12%,6,–14000,0,0) returns a present value for the cash inflows equal to $57,559.70 (see Exhibit 8-2). The $.10 difference is due to rounding.

Because the NPV is positive, the delivery van should be purchased. Although the positive NPV tells us that the return on the investment is at least 12 percent, it does not tell us exactly what the return is. Is it 14 percent, 16 percent, or even some higher number? We could find the actual return by trial and error. Remember, an NPV of zero means that an investment is earning exactly the discount rate used in the analysis. Increasing the discount rate to 14 percent reduces the NPV to $4,446.[2] Going up to 16 percent reduces the NPV to $1,590 but going up to 18 percent results in a negative NPV of $1,028. The true yield of the investment must be somewhere between 16 percent and 18 percent and would be closer to 18 percent. The present value of an annuity table can also be used to find the true rate of return for the delivery van.

As discussed in the appendix, the present value of an annuity (PVA) can be found using the following formula:

$$PVA = R(DFA_{n,r})$$

In this case, we know the PVA, the annual cash inflow (R), and the number of periods (n) and can solve indirectly for the interest rate (r).

Exhibit 8-2

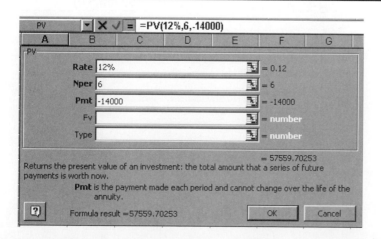

---

[2] Extended present value tables can be found on pages 254 and 255.

$$PVA_{6,??} = \$14,000(DFA_{6,??})$$
$$\$50,000 = \$14,000(DFA_{6,.??})$$
$$DFA_{6,.??} = 3.5714$$

From Table 8A-3 (appendix), looking at the row for an n of 6, we see that a DFA of 3.5714 is about halfway between an r of 16 percent and an r of 18 percent.

INTERNAL RATE OF RETURN

The internal rate of return (IRR) is the actual yield or return earned by an investment. We can find the yield of an investment in a number of ways. One way of looking at the IRR is that it is the discount rate that equates the present value of all cash inflows to the present value of all cash outflows. In other words, IRR is the discount rate that makes the NPV = 0.

 Key Concept: The internal rate of return (IRR) is the actual yield or return earned by an investment.

Although a present value table *can* be used to calculate IRR, it is inconvenient in this case because the true yield lies between the rates provided on the table. However, IRR can easily be calculated using a financial calculator or Microsoft Excel (see appendix). In Excel, = RATE (6,−14000,50000,0,0) generates an annual yield of 17.191 percent (see Exhibit 8-3).

Net present value and internal rate of return calculations get significantly more difficult when cash inflows and outflows are more numerous and when the cash flows are uneven. Consider an example in which Harbourside Hospital is considering the purchase of a new X-ray machine for cardiac catheterizations. Harbourside is a nonprofit hospital and has a slightly lower hurdle rate of 10 percent. In addition, one of the hospital's objectives is to improve the quality of care provided to cardiac patients in the area. Currently, patients have to travel as far as 100 miles to a hospital equipped with this type of X-ray machine. The machine will cost $1,200,000 plus installation costs of another $50,000 and will have a useful life of approximately six years. Due to frequent changes in technology,

Harbourside
Hospital

EXHIBIT 8-3

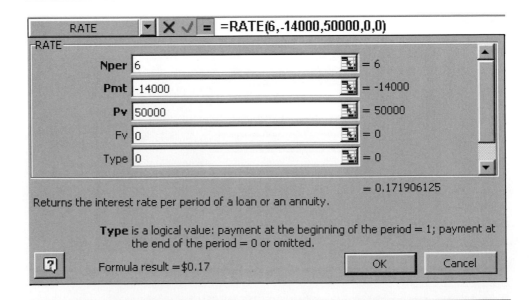

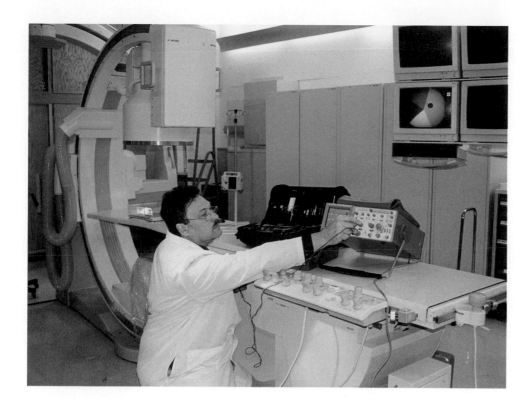

the machine would have little salvage value at the end of its useful life. Harbourside expects that it can sell the machine to a hospital in a developing country for $20,000. It is expected to increase revenues by $400,000 per year but will require the hiring of two new technicians at $40,000 per year for each technician and it will require maintenance and repairs averaging $20,000 per year, which results in a net annual cash flow of $300,000 ($400,000 − $80,000 − $20,000). In addition, it is expected to require the installation of a new X-ray tube at the end of Years 3 and 5 at a cost of $50,000 each. The table below provides a detailed NPV analysis using discount factors from Tables 8A-2 and 8A-3 in the appendix.

Cash Flow	Year	Amount	10% Factor	Present Value
Initial investment	Now	$(1,250,000)	1.0000	$(1,250,000)
Net annual cash inflow	1–6	300,000	4.3553	1,306,590
New X-ray tube	3	(50,000)	.7513	(37,565)
New X-ray tube	5	(50,000)	.6209	(31,045)
Salvage value	6	20,000	.5645	11,290
Net present value				$ (730)

In this case, the NPV is negative indicating that this investment would earn Harbourside less than its minimum required rate of return of 10 percent. Using Microsoft Excel's IRR function, the internal rate of return of the X-ray machine is 9.9796 percent (see Exhibit 8-4).

Although the quantitative analysis performed in Step 3 of our decision model would indicate that the investment is not acceptable, Harbourside should also consider qualitative factors in its decision.[3] In this case, because improving the quality of patient care is

 Step 3 **IDENTIFY AND ANALYZE AVAILABLE OPTIONS**

---

[3]Harbourside must also consider the impact of uncertainty on the decision. In this case, the only cash flow known with certainty is likely to be the initial purchase price. Changes in assumptions about future revenue and costs are likely to affect the decision. Adjusting the discounted cash flow analysis for the impact of uncertainty is discussed in more depth later in the chapter.

EXHIBIT 8-4

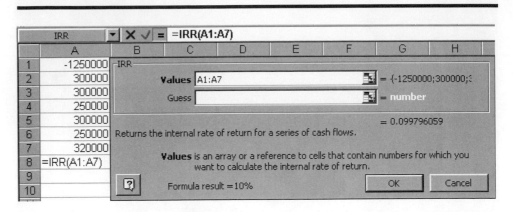

very important to Harbourside, it may very well approve the investment even though its IRR is slightly below the normal acceptable level.

SCREENING VERSUS PREFERENCE DECISIONS

LO4
Discuss key assumptions of the NPV and IRR methods

Both NPV and IRR can be used as a screening tool. They allow a manager to identify and eliminate undesirable projects. Although the methods accomplish the same objective, it is important to remember that they are used in different ways. When using net present value, the cost of capital is typically used as the discount rate to compute the net present value of each proposed investment. Any project that has a negative net present value should be rejected unless qualitative reasons exist for considering the project further.

When using the internal rate of return, the cost of capital or other measure of a company's minimum required rate of return is compared to the computed internal rate of return method. If the internal rate of return is equal to or greater than the minimum required rate of return, the investment is acceptable unless qualitative reasons exist for rejecting the project (see Exhibit 8-5).

The net present value method does have some advantages over the internal rate of return method when making screening decisions. Adjusting the discount rate to take into account the increased risk and uncertainty of cash flows expected to occur many years in the future is possible with the net present value method. When using the IRR method, users would have to adjust cash flows directly to adjust for risk.

However, NPV (without adjustment) cannot be used to compare investments (make preference decisions) unless the competing investments are of similar magnitude. Consider for example two competing investments each with a five-year useful life. The first requires an investment of $10,000 and generates cash savings with a present value of $12,000 (cash inflows of $3,165.56 per year for five years discounted at 10 percent). Its NPV is therefore $2,000. The second requires an initial investment of $20,000 and generates cash inflows with a present value of $22,000 (cash inflows of $5,803.52 per year for five years). As you can see, both investments have the same NPV of $2,000.

	Investment 1	Investment 2
Initial investment	$(10,000)	$(20,000)
PV of cash inflows	12,000	22,000
Net present value	$ 2,000	$ 2,000

EXHIBIT 8-5 Choosing the Right Investment Evaluation Method

```
                    ┌─────────────┐
                    │  Decision   │
┌──────────────┐    │   on what   │    ┌──────────────────────────┐
│ Net Present  │◄───│   method    │───►│ Internal Rate of Return  │
│ Value (NPV)  │    │   to use    │    │         (IRR)            │
└──────────────┘    └─────────────┘    └──────────────────────────┘
```

Net Present Value (NPV)

Decision on what method to use

Internal Rate of Return (IRR)

NPV is greater than or equal to 0

NO

YES

Invest in project

YES

IRR is greater than or equal to cost of capital

NO

Reject Project

Consider all qualitative (non-number) factors in the decision!

Reject Project

Which is preferred? Intuitively, the $10,000 investment should be preferred to the $20,000 investment. Think of it this way. You could invest in two $10,000 projects and generate cash inflows of $6,331.12 per year instead of the $5,803.52 generated from one $20,000 investment. The NPV analysis can be modified slightly through the calculation of a profitability index to better allow the comparison of investments of different size. The **profitability index (PI)** is calculated by dividing the present value of the cash inflows by the initial investment. A profitability index greater than 1.0 means that the NPV is positive (the PV of the inflows is greater than the initial investment) and the project is acceptable. When comparing the profitability index of competing projects, the project with the highest PI is preferred. The PI of Investments 1 and 2 is calculated below.

	Investment 1	Investment 2
PV of cash inflows	$12,000	$22,000
Initial investment	10,000	20,000
Profitability index	= 1.20	= 1.10

PAUSE & *Reflect*

What is the NPV of a project with a PI exactly equal to 1.0? Is a project with a PI of 1.0 acceptable?

The $10,000 investment has a higher PI of 1.20 and is preferred over the $20,000 investment with a PI of 1.10.

Concept Question: What is the IRR of Investments 1 and 2?

Concept Answer: Using Microsoft Excel's RATE function, the IRR of Investment 1 is 17.55 percent [=RATE (5, 3165.56, −10000,0,0) = 17.55%], whereas the IRR of Investment 2 is only 13.84 percent [=RATE (5, 5803.52, −20000,0,0) = 13.84%]. ■

In cases like this, in which the investment lives are equal and the cash flows follow similar patterns (annual cash flows for five years), IRR can be used to make preference decisions. However, when asset lives are unequal and cash flows follow different patterns, the use of IRR can result in incorrect decisions even when the initial investment is the same.

Consider the example below in which two $20,000 projects are being considered. Project A reduces cash operating costs (increases cash flow) by $12,500 per year for the next two years, whereas Project B reduces operating costs by $5,000 per year for six years. Assuming a discount rate of 10 percent, the NPV, PI, and IRR of each investment are calculated below.

	Project A	Project B
Initial investment	$(20,000.00)	$(20,000.00)
PV of cash inflows	21,693.75	21,776.50
NPV	1,693.75	1,776.50
PI	1.085	1.089
IRR	16.26%	12.98%

Although IRR would indicate that Project A is preferable to Project B, NPV and PI indicate that Project B is best. Which is right? Well, it depends. As we discussed earlier in the chapter, the IRR method assumes that cash inflows are immediately reinvested at the IRR earned on the original investment—in this case over 16 percent. In contrast, the NPV method assumes that cash inflows are reinvested at the cost of capital or other discount rate used in the analysis—10 percent in our analysis. If you can reinvest the large cash inflows received in Project A at the end of Years 1 and 2 at a high rate of return, Project A would indeed be preferred. If not, Project B offering a return of almost 13 percent for six years would be preferred. The use of IRR generally favors short-term investments with high yields, whereas NPV favors longer-term investments even if the return is lower.

THE IMPACT OF TAXES ON CAPITAL INVESTMENT DECISIONS

LO5
Evaluate the impact of taxes on capital investment decisions

Nonprofit organizations like Harbourside Hospital don't pay income taxes and don't need to consider the impact of income taxes on capital investment decisions (or other decisions for that matter).[4] However, profit-making companies must pay income taxes on any taxable income earned (just like individuals) and must therefore consider the impact of income taxes on capital investment and other management decisions. With federal income

---

[4]Hospitals, museums, churches, and a multitude of other organizations are often structured as organizations exempt from federal and state income taxes. In order to qualify, they must meet certain requirements as specified by Congress and the Internal Revenue Service. These organizations may also be exempt from local property taxes.

tax rates on corporations ranging from 15 percent to 35 percent of taxable income (and state income taxes typically adding another 5 to 10 percent), taxes are a major source of cash outflows for many companies and must be taken into consideration when considering any long-term investment decision.

As demonstrated in Chapter 5, the after-tax benefit or cost of a taxable cash inflow or tax deductible cash outflow is found by multiplying the before-tax cash inflow or before-tax cash outflow by (1 − tax rate). For a company with a combined federal and state income tax rate of 40 percent, a taxable cash inflow of $100,000 results in a $60,000 after-tax cash inflow [$100,000 × (1 −.40)]. Likewise, a $20,000 tax-deductible cash outflow for repairs results in an after-tax outflow of only $12,000.

The disposal of assets may also have tax consequences. When assets are sold or otherwise disposed of, gain or loss is calculated on the difference between their sales price and book value. Because current tax law rules do not consider salvage value in the computation of depreciation (assets are depreciated to zero even if they have a salvage value), the book value of an asset at the end of its useful life will be zero, and any salvage value realized will be taxed as gain. The after-tax cash flow associated with the sale of an asset for its salvage value is therefore found by multiplying the salvage value by (1 − tax rate).[5] For simplicity, we will assume that a gain on disposal of an asset is taxed at the same rate as operating income of a company. In practice, the tax calculation on the sale of depreciable assets can be quite complicated.

Not all tax-deductible expenses involve cash outflows. Depreciation is a tax-deductible expense that does not involve a direct payment of cash. Although depreciation does not result in a direct cash outflow, it does result in an indirect cash *inflow* due to the impact of depreciation on income taxes paid. Depreciation expense reduces a company's taxable income and thus its income tax, resulting in an increase in cash flow.

 Key Concept: *Taxes are a major source of cash outflows for many companies and must be taken into consideration in time value of money calculations.*

As an example, let's go back to Bud and Rose's Flower Shop and consider the purchase of a delivery van. The van cost $50,000 and will be depreciated using the straight-line method over six years for federal income tax purposes.[6] Depreciation expense is equal to $5,000 for Years 1 and 6 and $10,000 for Years 2 through 5. Assuming an income tax rate

Bud and Rose's
Flower Shop

The Impact of Depreciation on Cash Flow

Year	Depreciation	Tax Savings from Depreciation
1	$ 5,000	$2,000
2	10,000	4,000
3	10,000	4,000
4	10,000	4,000
5	10,000	4,000
6	5,000	2,000

---

[5]When assets are sold during their useful life, it is possible to generate tax-deductible losses as well as taxable gains. When assets are sold at a loss, their after-tax cash flow is more difficult to compute. It consists of the cash received from the sale *plus* the tax savings generated from the deductible loss.

[6]While the van would be depreciated over a useful life of 5 years, tax law generally requires the use of a half-year convention in which ½ year's depreciation is deducted in the year of acquisition (regardless of when the asset is purchased) and ½ year's depreciation is deducted in the 6th year. In addition, the tax law currently allows the use of an accelerated method of depreciation for machinery and equipment. The intricacies of tax depreciation rules are beyond the scope of this book.

of 40 percent, the depreciation deduction results in tax savings of $2,000 for Years 1 and 6 ($5,000 × 40%) and $4,000 for Years 2 through 5 ($10,000 × 40%).

Concept Question: Refer to the NPV calculation of the delivery van on page 227. What other adjustments need to be made in order to calculate the NPV after taxes?

Concept Answer: In the figure below, the annual cash inflow of $14,000 has been adjusted to the equivalent after-tax amount ($14,000 × .6 = $8,400). In addition, the discount rate has been changed to its equivalent after-tax rate (12% × .6 = 7.2%). Note that the discount factors in the table can be calculated using the mathematical formulas in the appendix. ■

Cash Flow	Year	After-Tax Amount	7.2% Factor	Present Value
Initial investment	Now	($50,000)	1.0000	($50,000.00)
Annual cash income	1–6	8,400	4.7375	39,795.00
Tax savings from depreciation				
	1	2,000	.9328	1,865.60
	2	4,000	.8702	3,480.80
	3	4,000	.8118	3,247.20
	4	4,000	.7572	3,028.80
	5	4,000	.7064	2,825.60
	6	2,000	.6589	1,317.80
Net present value				$5,560.80

PAUSE & Reflect

Why isn't the original purchase price of $50,000 adjusted for the impact of income tax?

The NPV of the new delivery van is still positive, indicating that it will provide a return greater than the company's 7.2 percent after-tax cost of capital. Using Excel's IRR function, the after-tax return of the investment is 10.715 percent (See Exhibit 8-6).

AN EXTENDED EXAMPLE

Amber Valley

Amber Valley Ski Resort is considering installing a chair lift for a new undeveloped area that would expand the amount of area available for skiing. The options are to put in a double, triple, or quadruple chair lift to carry two, three, or four skiers on each chair. The costs of the chair lifts are $3,000,000, $5,000,000, and $7,000,000, respectively. The chair lifts all have a 25-year life and will be depreciated using the straight-line method. The operating costs (in-

EXHIBIT 8-6

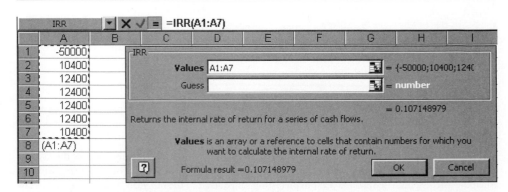

cluding routine maintenance) of the new lifts are $250,000, $300,000, and $350,000 per year. In addition, the chair lifts require major repairs every five years (at the end of years 5, 10, 15, and 20) of $100,000, $125,000, and $150,000, respectively. The lifts are difficult to resell and are assumed to have no salvage value at the end of their 25-year useful life.

Lift tickets are $49 per day, which allows the skiers to ride any of the lifts at the resort. Any increase in revenue from the new chair lift will have to come from increasing the number of skiers that visit the resort. The management of Amber Valley believes that with the addition of a new lift and the new slopes, they can attract more skiers to the resort. Right now the lift lines at the existing chair lifts are considered too long by most skiers. The overall use of the resort is down and part of the blame is attributed to the crowded conditions. Amber Valley averages 5,000 skiers per day at the present time. The projections used for the new lifts assume that the average number of skiers per day will increase by 100, 200, and 260 skiers, respectively. Assuming 120 ski days per year, this will increase revenue by $588,000, $1,176,000, and $1,528,800, respectively.

The managers of Amber Valley are confident that the new lift will increase the number of skiers sufficiently to justify its addition. However, they have asked the controller to analyze the proposed acquisition and to provide a recommendation concerning the purchase of the double, triple, or quadruple lift. Amber Valley's combined federal and state income tax rate is 40 percent and it has an after-tax cost of capital of 8 percent.

Before-tax cash inflows and outflows associated with the purchase of each chair lift are summarized below.

Before-Tax Cash Inflows and Outflows

Cash Flows	Double Chair Lift	Triple Chair Lift	Quad. Chair Lift
Purchase price	3,000,000	5,000,000	7,000,000
Additional revenue	588,000	1,176,000	1,528,800
Annual operating costs	(250,000)	(300,000)	(350,000)
Major repairs (every 5 years)	(100,000)	(125,000)	(150,000)

After-tax cash flows as adjusted are shown below.

After-Tax Cash Inflows and Outflows

Cash Flows	Double Chair Lift	Triple Chair Lift	Quad. Chair Lift
Purchase price	3,000,000	5,000,000	7,000,000
Additional revenue	352,800	705,600	917,280
Annual operating costs	(150,000)	(180,000)	(210,000)
Major repairs (every 5 years)	(60,000)	(75,000)	(90,000)
Annual tax savings from depreciation*	80,000	133,333	186,667

*Although the lifts have a useful life of 25 years, for tax purposes they would likely be depreciated over 15 years. To simplify calculations, depreciation was calculated using the straight-line method ignoring the half-year convention (a full year's depreciation was assumed for each of the 15 years). Once again, the intricacies of the tax rules for depreciation are beyond the scope of this book.

Concept Question: *Is this a screening or a preference decision? What discounted cash flow method(s) would be appropriate to analyze this decision?*

Concept Answer: The problem is a preference decision. In addition, because it involves investments of different sizes, NPV should not be used without calculating a profitability index. Because the investments have similar useful lives and patterns of cash flow, IRR can also be used to provide the quantitative analysis for the problem. ■

PAUSE & Reflect

What qualitative factors should Amber Valley consider in its decision?

As you can see in Exhibit 8-7, the NPV of the double lift is negative (and the PI is less than one) indicating that the investment is not acceptable. The IRR of 6.93 percent confirms the fact that the project provides a return below the minimum acceptable rate of return of 8 percent. Both the triple lift and quadruple lift are acceptable investments with positive NPVs, PIs greater than 1.0, and IRRs exceeding the cost of capital. Note however, that when comparing the triple lift with the quadruple lift, the quadruple lift has the highest NPV but the triple lift has the highest PI and IRR. Given the different size investments required, management should focus on the PI or IRR and choose to purchase the triple lift.

EXHIBIT 8-7

	DOUBLE-LIFT		
	Years	Cash Flow	Present Value
Cost to Purchase	now	$(3,000,000.00)	$(3,000,000.00)
After-Tax Cash Flow	1 through 25	202,800.00	2,164,844.61
Tax Savings from Depreciation	1 through 15	80,000.00	684,758.30
Major Repairs	5, 10, 15, 20	(60,000.00)	(100,414.00)
Discount rate	8%		
Net Present Value			$ (250,811.09)
Profitability Index			0.916
Internal Rate of Return			6.93%

EXHIBIT 8-7 Continued

	TRIPLE-LIFT		
	Years	**Cash Flow**	**Present Value**
Cost to Purchase	now	$(5,000,000.00)	$(5,000,000.00)
After-Tax Cash Flow	1 through 25	525,600.00	5,610,662.36
Tax Savings from Depreciation	1 through 15	133,333.00	1,141,260.97
Major Repairs	5, 10, 15, 20	(75,000.00)	(125,517.49)
Discount rate	8%		
Net Present Value			$ 1,626,405.84
Profitability Index			1.325
Internal Rate of Return			11.83%

	QUADRUPLE-LIFT		
	Years	**Cash Flow**	**Present Value**
Cost to Purchase	now	$(7,000,000.00)	$(7,000,000.00)
After-Tax Cash Flow	1 through 25	707,280.00	7,550,055.70
Tax Savings from Depreciation	1 through 15	186,667.00	1,597,772.21
Major Repairs	5, 10, 15, 20	(90,000.00)	(150,620.99)
Discount rate	8%		
Net Present Value			$ 1,997,206.92
Profitability Index			1.285
Internal Rate of Return			11.38%

THE IMPACT OF UNCERTAINTY ON CAPITAL INVESTMENT DECISIONS

As discussed previously, all long-term purchasing decisions involve some uncertainty. Any time decisions involve long periods of time, there is uncertainty. In fact, the longer the projected time frame of the project, the more the uncertainty. As has been discussed, one way to adjust for risk is to increase the cost of capital used in the NPV calculation. Raising the discount rate has the effect of reducing the present value of future cash inflows, thus reducing the NPV of an investment.

Concept Question: If Amber Valley increases the discount rate used in its NPV and PI analyses to 10 percent, is the triple lift still an acceptable investment? Exhibit 8-7 is provided as an Excel template on the disk that came with your textbook. Using the template, compute the NPV and PI for each lift if the discount rate is 10 percent instead of 8 percent.

Concept Answer: The triple lift is still acceptable and the best choice. Its NPV is positive and it has the highest PI of the three lifts. In fact, had we simply focused on the IRR of the triple and quadruple lifts in Exhibit 8-7, we could have surmised that both the triple and quadruple lifts would be acceptable at a discount rate of 10 percent because the internal rate of return of both exceeded 10 percent. ■

SENSITIVITY ANALYSIS

Amber Valley estimates an increase in skiers of 100, 200, or 260 per day for each of the lifts. What if the number of skiers increases by only 150 per day for the triple lift? Will the

acquisition of the new lift still result in a sufficient return of and on investment? **Sensitivity analysis** is used to highlight decisions that may be affected by changes in expected cash flows. We can use what-if analysis to determine how sensitive capital investment decisions are to these changes.

Concept Question: Exhibit 8-7 is provided as an Excel template on the disk that came with your textbook. Using the template, compute the NPV, PI, and IRR for the triple lift if the number of skiers increases by only 150 per day. Hint: The after-tax cash flow (additional revenues less annual operating costs) will be $349,200.

Concept Answer: With an increase of only 150 skiers, the NPV of the triple lift will be negative and the PI will be slightly less than 1.0. The IRR of 7.35 percent is a little less than the cost of capital of 8 percent. Based on a quantitative analysis, the triple lift will not be an acceptable investment with an increase of 150 skiers per day. ■

Concept Question: What increase in skiers would be required in order for the triple lift to be acceptable? Hint: Using the template, compute the number of skiers necessary in order to provide a PI of 1.0 or an IRR of 8 percent.

Concept Answer: Increasing the number of skiers to 157 per day would result in additional after-tax cash flows of $373,896. This would result in a PI of 1.001 and an IRR of 8.02 percent. ■

All decisions should be evaluated after they are implemented in order to see if they accomplished their objectives. However, in this example, as in most long-term purchasing decisions, the project is very difficult to reverse. Once a ski lift is installed, it must be used even if the projected skier volume is not reached. At that point other decisions would be made regarding how to increase the numbers of skiers. Thus, short-term decisions may become critical in making long-term capital investment decisions successful.

THE IMPACT OF THE NEW MANUFACTURING ENVIRONMENT ON CAPITAL INVESTMENT DECISIONS

LO6

Discuss the impact of the new manufacturing environment on capital investment decisions

Investments in automated and computerized design and manufacturing equipment and robotics tend to be very large, although many of the benefits may be indirect and intangible or at the very least difficult to quantify (increased quality resulting in fewer warranty expenses). These types of investments may be difficult to evaluate using purely quantitative data. For this reason, it is critically important to consider the impact of qualitative factors in these decisions.

Automating a process in a manufacturing environment is much more extensive and expensive than just purchasing a piece of equipment. The total cost of automating a process can be as much as 30 or 40 times that for installation of a single machine due to software needed, training of personnel and complementary machines, and processes needed. The benefits of automating production processes include the following:

1. Decreased labor costs
2. An increase in the quality of the finished product or a reduction in defects, resulting in fewer inspections, less waste in the production process, less rework of defective goods, and less warranty work on defective goods
3. Increased speed of the production process
4. Increased reliability of the finished product
5. An overall reduction in the amount of inventory

These improvements will not only save costs but will allow the company to maintain or increase market share. When the competition has automated production systems, companies must often follow suit or risk loss of business. Although some of the preceding benefits are difficult to measure, nevertheless they must be considered when making capital investment decisions in the new manufacturing environment.

 Key Concept: *Analyzing the cost and benefits of investments in automated and computerized design and manufacturing equipment and robotics requires careful consideration of both quantitative and qualitative factors.*

THE PAYBACK METHOD

LO7
Discuss appropriate applications of nondiscounting methods (the payback method) in capital investment decisions

Capital investment tools that recognize the time value of money and use discounted cash flow techniques are preferred by most decision makers when dealing with capital investment decisions. However, nondiscounting methods are still used by some managers in practice. Although these methods are declining in popularity, the payback method can still be useful in some cases as a fast, easy approximation of the more complicated, discounted cash flow methods.

The **payback period** is defined as the length of time needed for a long-term project to recapture or pay back the initial investment. In other words, how long does it take for a project to pay for itself? Obviously, the quicker the payback the more desirable the investment. The formula used to compute the payback period is as follows:

$$\text{Payback period} = \frac{\text{Original investment}}{\text{Net annual cash inflows}}$$

Because the payback method ignores the time value of money, it must be used with caution. Consider an example in which we are considering investing in Project A or Project B, each requiring an initial investment of $20,000. (This is the same example as used earlier, on page 232.) Project A promises cash inflows of $12,500 per year for two years, whereas Project B promises cash inflows of $5,000 per year for six years.

	Project A	Project B
Initial investment	$(20,000.00)	$(20,000.00)
Annual cash inflows	12,500.00	5,000.00
PV of cash inflows	21,693.75	21,776.50
NPV	$ 1,693.75	$ 1,776.50
PI	1.085	1.089
IRR	16.26%	12.98%
Payback	1.6 years (20,000/12,500)	4 years (20,000/5,000)

Although a manager using the payback method would prefer Project A, the method ignores the time value of money and ignores any cash flow received after the initial investment is paid for. Even when NPV and IRR give the same signal, payback can provide managers with misleading information.

Payback calculations are slightly more complicated with uneven cash flows. Using Amber Valley Ski Resort as an example, we can calculate the payback period for the three chair lifts being considered. The first column for each ski lift in Exhibit 8-8 shows the

EXHIBIT 8-8

| Year | DOUBLE-LIFT | | TRIPLE-LIFT | | QUADRUPLE-LIFT | |
	Cash Flow	Unrecovered	Cash Flow	Unrecovered	Cash Flow	Unrecovered
0	$(3,000,000.00)		$(5,000,000.00)		$(7,000,000.00)	
1	282,800.00	$(2,717,200.00)	658,933.00	$(4,341,067.00)	893,947.00	$(6,106,053.00)
2	282,800.00	(2,434,400.00)	658,933.00	(3,682,134.00)	893,947.00	(5,212,106.00)
3	282,800.00	(2,151,600.00)	658,933.00	(3,023,201.00)	893,947.00	(4,318,159.00)
4	282,800.00	(1,868,800.00)	658,933.00	(2,364,268.00)	893,947.00	(3,424,212.00)
5	222,800.00	(1,646,000.00)	583,933.00	(1,780,335.00)	803,947.00	(2,620,265.00)
6	282,800.00	(1,363,200.00)	658,933.00	(1,121,402.00)	893,947.00	(1,726,318.00)
7	282,800.00	(1,080,400.00)	658,933.00	(462,469.00)	893,947.00	(832,371.00)
8	282,800.00	(797,600.00)	658,933.00		893,947.00	
9	282,800.00	(514,800.00)	658,933.00		893,947.00	
10	222,800.00	(292,000.00)	583,933.00		803,947.00	
11	282,800.00	(9,200.00)	658,933.00		893,947.00	
12	282,800.00		658,933.00		893,947.00	
13	282,800.00		658,933.00		893,947.00	
14	282,800.00		658,933.00		893,947.00	
15	222,800.00		583,933.00		803,947.00	
16	202,800.00		525,600.00		707,280.00	
17	202,800.00		525,600.00		707,280.00	
18	202,800.00		525,600.00		707,280.00	
19	202,800.00		525,600.00		707,280.00	
20	142,800.00		450,600.00		617,280.00	
21	202,800.00		525,600.00		707,280.00	
22	202,800.00		525,600.00		707,280.00	
23	202,800.00		525,600.00		707,280.00	
24	202,800.00		525,600.00		707,280.00	
25	202,800.00		525,600.00		707,280.00	
Payback		11.033 years		7.702 years		7.931 years

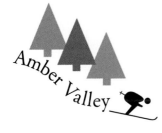

cash flow each year. The second column shows the amount of original investment that still must be recovered at the end of each year. For the double lift, the investment is almost fully recovered after the 11th year. At the end of Year 11, only $9,200 of the original $3,000,000 investment has not been paid back. In Year 12, another $282,800 of cash inflows are received. Thus it takes an additional .033 of a year $\left(\frac{9,200}{282,800}\right)$ to fully recover the investment. The calculations for the triple and quadruple lifts are similar.

If we use payback period to evaluate the desirability of these options, the triple lift is preferable. It has a payback of 7.7 years versus a payback of 7.9 years for the quadruple lift and slightly more than 11 years for the double lift. In this case, this is the same preference ordering that we got using the profitability index and IRR to evaluate the lifts. The payback method can be useful as a fast approximation of the discounted cash flow methods when the cash flows follow similar patterns. It can also be useful in screening decisions if cash flow is a serious concern and management wants to eliminate projects that would have adverse cash flow consequences. For example, smaller businesses such as Bud and Rose's Flower Shop may be very concerned about cash flow in the short run even if the long-term profitability of a project is lower than with alternative projects. In these situations the amount of time needed to recover cash outlays may be a very important criteria when evaluating capital investment decisions.

 Key Concept: *The payback method can be useful as a fast approximation of the discounted cash flow methods when the cash flows follow similar patterns.*

APPENDIX

TIME VALUE OF MONEY AND DECISION MAKING

When decisions are affected by cash flows that are paid or received in different time periods, it is necessary to adjust those cash flows for the time value of money (TVM). Because of our ability to earn interest on money invested, we would prefer to receive $1 today rather than a year from now. Likewise, we would prefer to pay $1 a year from now rather than today. A common technique used to adjust cash flows received or paid in different time periods is to discount those cash flows by finding their present value. The **present value (PV)** of cash flows is the amount of future cash flows discounted to their equivalent worth today. To fully understand the calculations involved in finding the present value of future cash flows, it is necessary to step back and examine the nature of interest and the calculation of interest received and paid. Interest is simply a payment made to use someone else's money. When you invest money in a bank account, the bank pays you interest for the use of your money for a period of time. If you invest $100 and the bank pays you $106 at the end of the year, it is clear that you earned $6 of interest on your money (and 6 percent interest for the year).

What interest rate do you earn on your checking and savings account at the local bank? How is the interest compounded?

FUTURE VALUE

Mathematically, the relationship between your initial investment (present value), the amount in the bank at the end of the year (future value), and the interest rate (r) is as follows:

$$FV_{(year\ 1)} = PV(1 + r)$$

In our example, $FV_{(year\ 1)} = 100(1 + .06) = \$106$. If you leave your money in the bank for a second year what happens? Will you earn an additional $6 of interest? It depends on whether the bank pays you simple interest or compound interest. **Simple interest** is interest on the invested amount only, whereas **compound interest** is interest on the invested amount plus interest on previous interest earned but not withdrawn. Simple interest is sometimes computed on short-term investments and debts (i.e., those that are shorter than six months to a year). Compound interest is typically computed for financial arrangements longer than one year. We will assume that interest is compounded in all examples in this book. Extending the future value formula to find the amount we have in the bank in two years gives us the following formula:

$$FV_{(year\ 2)} = PV(1 + r)(1 + r) \text{ or}$$
$$FV_{(year\ 2)} = PV(1 + r)^2$$

In our example, $FV_{(year\ 2)} = 100(1 + .06)^2$ or $112.36. We earned $6.36 of interest in Year 2—$6 on our original $100 investment and $.36 on the $6 of interest earned but not withdrawn in year 1 ($6 \times .06$).

In this example, we have assumed that compounding is on an annual basis. Compounding can also be calculated semiannually, quarterly, monthly, daily, or even continually. Go back to our original $100 investment in the bank. If the bank pays 6 percent interest compounded semiannually instead of annually, we would have $106.09 after one year. Note that the interest rate is typically expressed as a percentage rate per year. We are really earning 3 percent for each semiannual period, not 6 percent. Graphically, it is usually easier to visualize the concept of interest rate compounding with the help of time lines. Exhibit 8A-1 graphically demonstrates the impact of annual, semiannual, and monthly compounding of the 6 percent annual rate on our original $100 investment.

Exhibit 8A-1

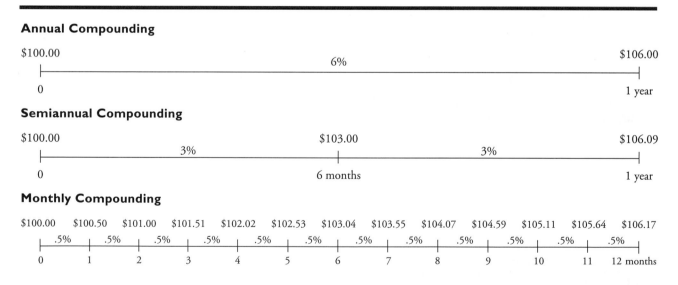

Annual Compounding

$100.00 — 6% — $106.00, 0 to 1 year

Semiannual Compounding

$100.00 — 3% — $103.00 — 3% — $106.09, 0 to 6 months to 1 year

Monthly Compounding

$100.00 $100.50 $101.00 $101.51 $102.02 $102.53 $103.04 $103.55 $104.07 $104.59 $105.11 $105.64 $106.17, .5% each month, 0 to 12 months

Mathematically, our formula for future value can once again be modified slightly to account for interest rates compounded at different intervals. $FV_{(n\ periods\ in\ the\ future)} = PV(1 + r)^n$, where n is the number of compounding periods per year multiplied by the number of years and r is the annual interest rate divided by the number of compounding periods per year. Before the advent of hand-held calculators and computers, tables were developed to simplify the calculation of FV by providing values for $(1 + r)^n$ for several combinations of n and r. These tables are still commonly used and an example is provided in Table 8A-1. The factors in Table 8A-1 are commonly referred to as cumulative factors (CF) and are simply calculations of $(1 + r)^n$ for various values of n and r.

TABLE 8A-1 Future Value of $1

n/r	0.5%	1%	2%	3%	4%	5%	6%	7%	8%	10%	12%
1	1.0050	1.0100	1.0200	1.0300	1.0400	1.0500	1.0600	1.0700	1.0800	1.1000	1.1200
2	1.0100	1.0201	1.0404	1.0609	1.0816	1.1025	1.1236	1.1449	1.1664	1.2100	1.2544
3	1.0151	1.0303	1.0612	1.0927	1.1249	1.1576	1.1910	1.2250	1.2597	1.3310	1.4049
4	1.0202	1.0406	1.0824	1.1255	1.1699	1.2155	1.2625	1.3108	1.3605	1.4641	1.5735
5	1.0253	1.0510	1.1041	1.1593	1.2167	1.2763	1.3382	1.4026	1.4693	1.6105	1.7623
6	1.0304	1.0615	1.1262	1.1941	1.2653	1.3401	1.4185	1.5007	1.5869	1.7716	1.9738
7	1.0355	1.0721	1.1487	1.2299	1.3159	1.4071	1.5036	1.6058	1.7138	1.9487	2.2107
8	1.0407	1.0829	1.1717	1.2668	1.3686	1.4775	1.5938	1.7182	1.8509	2.1436	2.4760
9	1.0459	1.0937	1.1951	1.3048	1.4233	1.5513	1.6895	1.8385	1.9990	2.3579	2.7731
10	1.0511	1.1046	1.2190	1.3439	1.4802	1.6289	1.7908	1.9672	2.1589	2.5937	3.1058
11	1.0564	1.1157	1.2434	1.3842	1.5395	1.7103	1.8983	2.1049	2.3316	2.8531	3.4785
12	1.0617	1.1268	1.2682	1.4258	1.6010	1.7959	2.0122	2.2522	2.5182	3.1384	3.8960
24	1.1272	1.2697	1.6084	2.0328	2.5633	3.2251	4.0489	5.0724	6.3412	9.8497	15.1786
36	1.1967	1.4308	2.0399	2.8983	4.1039	5.7918	8.1473	11.4239	15.9682	30.9127	59.1356
48	1.2705	1.6122	2.5871	4.1323	6.5705	10.4013	16.3939	25.7289	40.2106	97.0172	230.3908

Using this new terminology the future value formula is simply

$$FV_{(n\ periods\ in\ the\ future)} = PV(CF_{n,r})$$

With 6 percent annual compounding, our $100 investment grows to

$$\$100(CF_{1,6\%}) = \$100(1.060) = \$106.00$$

With 6 percent semiannual compounding,

$$\$100(CF_{2,3\%}) = \$100(1.0609) = \$106.09$$

With 6 percent monthly compounding,

$$\$100(CF_{12,.5\%}) = \$100(1.0617) = \$106.17$$

Most financial calculators will compute future value after the user inputs data for present value, the annual interest rate, the number of compounding periods per year, and the number of years. For example, computing the future value of $100.00 with 6 percent annual compounding using a business calculator requires the following steps:

Keys	Display	Description
1 [P/YR]	1.00	Sets compounding periods per year to 1 because interest is compounded annually
100 [±] [PV]	−100.00	Stores the present value as a negative number
6.0 [I/YR]	6.0	Stores the annual interest rate
1 [N]	1	Sets the number of years or compounding periods to 1
[FV]	106.00	Calculates the future value

Calculating the future value of $100 with 6 percent monthly compounding simply requires changing both the compounding periods per year (P/YR) and number of compounding periods (N) to 12.

Keys	Display	Description
12 [P/YR]	12	Sets the compounding periods per year to 12
12 [N]	12	Sets the number of compounding periods to 12
[FV]	106.17	Calculates the future value

Likewise, many spreadsheet programs (Microsoft Excel, Lotus 1-2-3, etc.) have built-in functions (formulas) that calculate future value. The Excel function called FV simply requires input of an interest rate (Rate), number of compounding periods (Nper), and present value (Pv) in the following format =FV(Rate, Nper, Pmt, Pv, Type).[7] Entries for Pmt and Type are not applicable to simple future value problems. To calculate the future value of $100 in one year at 6 percent interest compounded monthly, enter = FV(.5%, 12, , 100, ,). Excel returns a value of $106.17.

PRESENT VALUE

A present value formula can be derived directly from the future value formula. If

$$FV_{\text{(n periods in the future)}} = PV(1+r)^n$$

EXHIBIT 8A-2

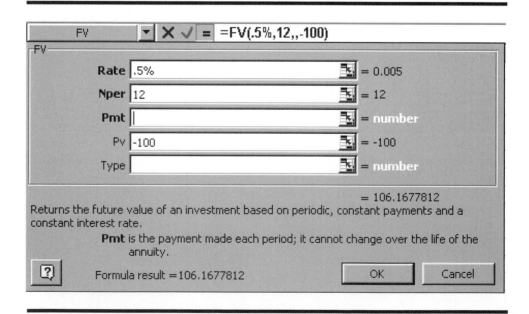

then

$$PV = FV \div (1 + r)^n \text{ or } PV = FV[1 \div (1 + r)^n]$$

Just as a cumulative factor table was developed to calculate $(1 + r)^n$, present value tables calculate $1 \div (1 + r)^n$ for various combinations of n and r. These factors are called discount factors or DFs. An example of a DF table is provided in Table 8A-2. Our PV formula can now be rewritten as follows:

$$PV = FV(DF_{n,r})$$

TABLE 8A-2 Present Value of $1

n/r	0.5%	1%	2%	3%	4%	5%	6%	7%	8%	10%	12%
1	0.9950	0.9901	0.9804	0.9709	0.9615	0.9524	0.9434	0.9346	0.9259	0.9091	0.8929
2	0.9901	0.9803	0.9612	0.9426	0.9246	0.9070	0.8900	0.8734	0.8573	0.8264	0.7972
3	0.9851	0.9706	0.9423	0.9151	0.8890	0.8638	0.8396	0.8163	0.7938	0.7513	0.7118
4	0.9802	0.9610	0.9238	0.8885	0.8548	0.8227	0.7921	0.7629	0.7350	0.6830	0.6355
5	0.9754	0.9515	0.9057	0.8626	0.8219	0.7835	0.7473	0.7130	0.6806	0.6209	0.5674
6	0.9705	0.9420	0.8880	0.8375	0.7903	0.7462	0.7050	0.6663	0.6302	0.5645	0.5066
7	0.9657	0.9327	0.8706	0.8131	0.7599	0.7107	0.6651	0.6227	0.5835	0.5132	0.4523
8	0.9609	0.9235	0.8535	0.7894	0.7307	0.6768	0.6274	0.5820	0.5403	0.4665	0.4039
9	0.9561	0.9143	0.8368	0.7664	0.7026	0.6446	0.5919	0.5439	0.5002	0.4241	0.3606
10	0.9513	0.9053	0.8203	0.7441	0.6756	0.6139	0.5584	0.5083	0.4632	0.3855	0.3220
11	0.9466	0.8963	0.8043	0.7224	0.6496	0.5847	0.5268	0.4751	0.4289	0.3505	0.2875
12	0.9419	0.8874	0.7885	0.7014	0.6246	0.5568	0.4970	0.4440	0.3971	0.3186	0.2567
24	0.8872	0.7876	0.6217	0.4919	0.3901	0.3101	0.2470	0.1971	0.1577	0.1015	0.0659
36	0.8356	0.6989	0.4902	0.3450	0.2437	0.1727	0.1227	0.0875	0.0626	0.0323	0.0169
48	0.7871	0.6203	0.3865	0.2420	0.1522	0.0961	0.0610	0.0389	0.0249	0.0103	0.0043

Now we are ready to calculate the present value of a future cash flow. For example, how much must be invested today at 8 percent compounded annually to have $1,000 in two years? Mathematically,

$$PV = \$1,000[1 \div (1 + .08)^2] = \$857.34$$

or using the DF table,

$$PV = \$1,000(DF_{2,.08}) = \$1,000(.8573) = \$857.30 \text{ (rounded)}$$

Once again, the frequency of compounding affects our calculation. Just as more frequent compounding *increases* future values, increasing the frequency of compounding decreases present values. This is demonstrated in Exhibit 8A-3 for annual, semiannual, and quarterly compounding.

EXHIBIT 8A-3

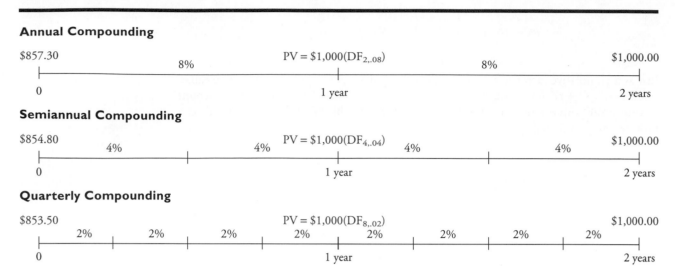

Annual Compounding

$857.30   8%   PV = $1,000(DF$_{2,.08}$)   8% $1,000.00

0   1 year   2 years

Semiannual Compounding

$854.80   4%   4%   PV = $1,000(DF$_{4,.04}$)   4%   4% $1,000.00

0   1 year   2 years

Quarterly Compounding

$853.50   2%   2%   2%   PV = $1,000(DF$_{8,.02}$)   2%   2%   2%   2% $1,000.00

0   1 year   2 years

PAUSE & Reflect

Why does more frequent compounding increase future values and decrease present values?

Computing present value using a business calculator is similar to computing future value. For example, the present value of $1,000 received or paid in two years at 8 percent compounded quarterly requires the following steps:

Keys	Display	Description
4 [P/YR]	4.00	Sets the compounding periods per year to 4
1,000 [FV]	1000.00	Stores the future value as a positive number
8.0 [I/YR]	8.0	Stores the annual interest rate
8 [N]	8.0	Sets the number of compounding periods to 8
[PV]	−853.49	Calculates the present value

In Microsoft Excel, the built-in function is called PV and requires input of the applicable interest rate (Rate), number of compounding periods (Nper), and future value (Fv) in the following format [=PV(Rate, Nper, Pmt, Fv, Type)]. In the previous example, entering =PV(2%, 8, , −1000, ,) returns a value of $853.49. Note once again that Pmt and Type are left blank in simple present value problems as they were in future value calculations (see Exhibit 8A-4).

PAUSE & Reflect

Why does a 50 percent increase in return from 8 percent to 12 percent result in almost a 100 percent increase in future value (from $20,000 to $40,000)?

Concept Question: *Eighteen years from now, the cost of one year of education at a state university is expected to cost more than $20,000 and the cost of a year at a private institution is expected to exceed $40,000. How much would parents of a newborn baby have to invest today in order to accumulate the $20,000 (or $40,000) in 18 years? Assume you can earn an 8 percent return on your money. What if you earn 12 percent?*

Concept Answer: Using the built-in functions in Microsoft Excel, the present value of $20,000 ($40,000) in 18 years at a discount rate of 8 percent is $5,004.98 and $10,009.96 respectively. At 12 percent, the present value decreases to $2,600.79 and $5,201.58, respectively. In other words, a $5,000 investment that earns 8 percent a year for 18 years will be worth almost $20,000. If you can earn 12 percent on your investment, a $5,200 investment will grow to almost $40,000. ■

EXHIBIT 8A-4

| PV | ▼ | X | ✓ | = | =PV(2%,8,,-1000) |

PV

Rate	2%		= 0.02
Nper	8		= 8
Pmt			= number
Fv	-1000		= -1000
Type			= number

= 853.4903712

Returns the present value of an investment: the total amount that a series of future payments is worth now.

    Fv is the future value, or a cash balance you want to attain after the last payment is made.

[?]   Formula result =853.4903712   [OK]   [Cancel]

IN THE NEWS

Many states now offer students and their parents prepaid tuition plans. Some of these plans allow parents to prepay a fixed amount today that is guaranteed to cover tuition when their child enters college. For example, in Ohio, a $3,600 investment for a newborn child will cover a year of tuition at any public university in the state when the child enters college 18 years later. Note, however, that admission is not guaranteed and although refunds are typically made if a child does not choose to go to college or drops out, penalties may apply.

www.texastomorrowfund.com

When FV and PV are known, either formula can be used to calculate one of the other variables in the equations (n or r). For example, if you know that your $100 bank deposit is worth $200 in six years, what rate of interest compounded annually did you earn? Using the mathematical present value formula,

$$PV = FV[1 \div (1 + r)^n]$$

or

$$\$100 = \$200[1 \div (1 + r)^6]$$

Simplifying by dividing each side by $100, $1 = 2 \div (1 + r)^6$ and multiplying each side by $(1 + r)^6$, the equation is simplified to $(1 + r)^6 = 2$. The value of r can be calculated using a financial calculator or mathematically using logarithmic functions.[8] Using a business calculator, the following steps are typical:

Keys	Display	Description
1 [P/YR]	1.00	Sets compounding periods per year to 1
200 [FV]	200	Stores the future value
100 [±] [PV]	−100	Stores the present value as a negative number
2 [N]	2.0	Sets the number of compounding periods to 2
[I/YR]	.122462	Calculates the annual interest rate

The tables can also be used to solve for n and r. Using our table formula, $PV = FV(DF_{n,r})$, if PV = 100 and FV = 200, then DF must be equal to .5. If we know that n is equal to 6, then we can simply move across the table until we find a factor close to .5. The factor at 12 percent is .5066. If we examine the factors at both 10 percent (.5645) and 14 percent (.456), we can infer that the actual interest rate will be slightly higher than 12 percent. Our logarithmic calculation is 12.2462 percent. In Microsoft Excel, the RATE function requires input of Nper, Pv, and Fv in the following format: =RATE(Nper, Pmt, Pv, Fv, Type, Guess). Since Excel uses an iterative trial-and-error method to calculate the interest rate, Guess provides a starting point. It is generally not necessary but may be required in complicated problems. Entering =RATE(6, ,−100, 200, ,) returns an interest rate of 12.2462% (see Exhibit 8A-5).

The calculation of n is done in a similar fashion. If we know that our investment earns 12 percent but do not know how long it will take for our $100 to grow to $200, mathematically, we have the following:

$$PV = FV[1 \div (1 + r)^n]$$

or

$$\$100 = \$200[1 \div (1 + .12)^n]$$

---

[8]In logarithmic form, $(1+r)^6 = 2$ can be rewritten as $\log(1+r)^6 = \log 2$ or $6\log(1+r) = \log 2$. Therefore, $\log(1+r) = \log 2 \div 6$ which simplifies to $\log(1+r) = .1155245$. Switching back to the equivalent exponential form, $e^{.1155245} = (1+r)$, $(1+r) = 1.122462$ and $r = .122462$ (12.2462%).

EXHIBIT 8A-5

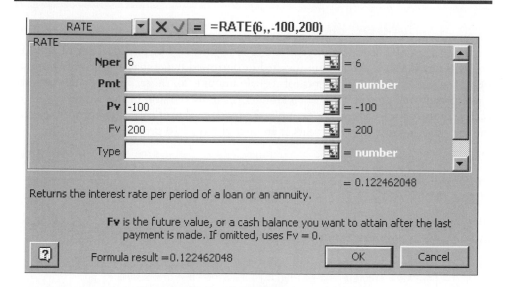

Solving the equation using logarithms or a financial calculator gives us an n of 6.116 years.[9] Using the DF formula, DF must again be equal to .5. If r is known to be 12 percent, we simply move down the 12 percent column until we find a DF close to .5. Not surprisingly, we find a factor of .5066 for an n of 6. Examining the factors for an n of 5(.5674) and 7(.4523), we can infer that the actual time will be something slightly greater than 6 years. The NPER function in Microsoft Excel requires input of Rate, Pmt, Pv, Fv, and Type in the following format: [=NPER(12%, , −100, 200,)] and returns a value of 6.116 years. Note that Pv is entered as a negative amount and that Pmt and Type are not necessary since this is essentially a present value problem (see Exhibit 8A-6).

EXHIBIT 8A-6

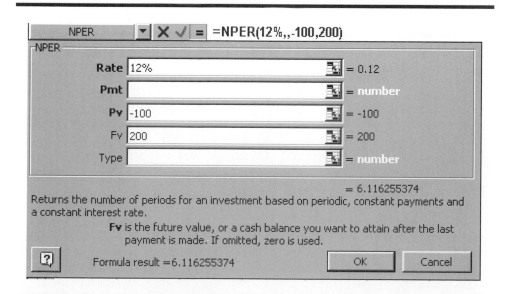

---

[9]Using a business calculator, simply input 1 P/YR, 200 FV, 100 PV, and 12 I/YR and solve for n. In logarithmic form, $(1+.12)^n = 2$ can be rewritten as $\log(1+.12)^n = \log 2$ or $n \log 1.12 = \log 2$. Therefore, n = $(\log 2)/(\log 1.12) = 6.116$.

ANNUITIES

An **annuity** is a series of cash flows of equal amount paid or received at regular intervals.[10] Common examples include mortgage and loan payments. The present value of an ordinary annuity (PVA) is the amount invested or borrowed today that will provide for a series of withdrawals or payments of equal amount for a set number of periods. Conceptually, the present value of an annuity is simply the sum of the present values of each withdrawal or payment. For example, the present value of an annuity of $100 paid at the end of each of the next four years at an interest rate of 10 percent looks like this:

Although cumbersome, the present value of an annuity can be calculated by finding the present value of each $100 payment using the present value table on page 245.

$$PVA = \$100(DF_{1,.10}) + \$100(DF_{2,.10}) + \$100(DF_{3,.10}) + \$100(DF_{4,.10})$$
$$= \$100(.9091) + \$100(.8264) + \$100(.7513) + \$100(.6830)$$
$$= \$316.98$$

The mathematical formula for PVA can be derived from the formula for PV and is equal to:

$$PVA_{n,r} = R\left(\frac{1 - \dfrac{1}{(1+r)^n}}{r}\right)$$

where R refers to the periodic payment or withdrawal (commonly called a rent). Calculated values for various combinations of n and r are provided in Table 8A-3.

TABLE 8A-3 Present Value of an Ordinary Annuity

n/r	0.50%	1%	2%	3%	4%	5%	6%	7%	8%	10%	12%
1	0.9950	0.9901	0.9804	0.9709	0.9615	0.9524	0.9434	0.9346	0.9259	0.9091	0.8929
2	1.9851	1.9704	1.9416	1.9135	1.8861	1.8594	1.8334	1.8080	1.7833	1.7355	1.6901
3	2.9702	2.9410	2.8839	2.8286	2.7751	2.7232	2.6730	2.6243	2.5771	2.4869	2.4018
4	3.9505	3.9020	3.8077	3.7171	3.6299	3.5460	3.4651	3.3872	3.3121	3.1699	3.0373
5	4.9259	4.8534	4.7135	4.5797	4.4518	4.3295	4.2124	4.1002	3.9927	3.7908	3.6048
6	5.8964	5.7955	5.6014	5.4172	5.2421	5.0757	4.9173	4.7665	4.6229	4.3553	4.1114
7	6.8621	6.7282	6.4720	6.2303	6.0021	5.7864	5.5824	5.3893	5.2064	4.8684	4.5638
8	7.8230	7.6517	7.3255	7.0197	6.7327	6.4632	6.2098	5.9713	5.7466	5.3349	4.9676
9	8.7791	8.5660	8.1622	7.7861	7.4353	7.1078	6.8017	6.5152	6.2469	5.7590	5.3282
10	9.7304	9.4713	8.9826	8.5302	8.1109	7.7217	7.3601	7.0236	6.7101	6.1446	5.6502
11	10.6770	10.3676	9.7868	9.2526	8.7605	8.3064	7.8869	7.4987	7.1390	6.4951	5.9377
12	11.6189	11.2551	10.5753	9.9540	9.3851	8.8633	8.3838	7.9427	7.5361	6.8137	6.1944
24	22.5629	21.2434	18.9139	16.9355	15.2470	13.7986	12.5504	11.4693	10.5288	8.9847	7.7843
36	32.8710	30.1075	25.4888	21.8323	18.9083	16.5469	14.6210	13.0352	11.7172	9.6765	8.1924
48	42.5803	37.9740	30.6731	25.2667	21.1951	18.0772	15.6500	13.7305	12.1891	9.8969	8.2972

---

[10]An ordinary annuity is paid or received at the end of each period while an annuity due is paid or received at the beginning of each period. In examples throughout this book, we will assume the annuity is ordinary.

The PVA formula can therefore be rewritten as follows:

$$PVA = R(DFA_{n,r})$$

As previously discussed, common examples of annuities are mortgages and loans. For example, say you are thinking about buying a new car. Your bank offers to loan you money at a special 6 percent rate compounded monthly for a 24-month term. If the maximum monthly payment you can afford is $399, how large a car loan can you get? In other words, what is the present value of a $399 annuity paid at the end of each of the next 24 months assuming an interest rate of 6 percent compounded monthly? Using a time line, the problem looks like this:

PVA $399 $399 $399 $399 $399 $399 $399 $399 $399 $399 $399 $399 $399 $399 $399 $399 $399 $399 $399 $399 $399 $399 $399 $399

.5% .5% .5% .5% .5% .5% .5% .5% .5% .5% .5% .5% .5% .5% .5% .5% .5% .5% .5% .5% .5% .5% .5% .5%

0   24 months

Mathematically,

$$PVA_{24,.005} = 399 \left(\frac{1 - \dfrac{1}{(1 + .005)^{24}}}{.005} \right)$$

Using the DFA table,

$$PVA_{24,.005} = \$399(DFA_{24,005}) = \$399(22.5629) = \$9,002.60 \text{ (rounded)}$$

Using a business calculator, the following steps are common:

Keys	Display	Description
12 [P/YR]	12.00	Sets periods per year
2 × 12 [N]	24.00	Stores numer of periods in loan
0 [FV]	0	Stores the amount left to pay after 2 years
6 [I/YR]	6	Stores interest rate
399 [±] [PMT]	−399.00	Stores desired payment as a negative number
12 [P/YR]	12.00	Sets periods per year
[PV]	9,002.58	Calculates the loan you can afford with a $399 per month payment

In Microsoft Excel, the PV function is used to calculate the present value of an annuity with additional entries for the payment amount (Pmt) and type of annuity (Type). The payment is entered as a negative number and the annuity type is 0 for ordinary and 1 for an annuity due. The format is therefore PV(Rate, Nper, Pmt, Fv, Type). Entering =PV(.5%, 24, −399, 0, 0) returns a value of $9,002.58 (see Exhibit 8A-7).

The PVA formula can also be used to calculate R, r, and n if the other variables are known. This is most easily accomplished using the DFA table or using a financial calculator. If the car you want to buy costs $20,000 and you can afford a $3,000 down payment

EXHIBIT 8A-7

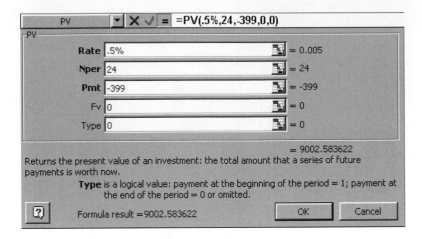

(your loan balance is $17,000), how much will your 36 monthly payments be assuming the bank charges you 6% interest compounded monthly?

Using the DFA table,

$$PVA_{36,.005} = R(DFA_{36,.005})$$
$$\$17,000 = R(32.871)$$
$$R = \$517.17$$

Using a business calculator, the following steps are common:

Keys	Display	Description
12 $\boxed{P/YR}$	12.00	Sets periods per year
3 × 12 $\boxed{N}$	36.00	Stores numer of periods in loan
0 $\boxed{FV}$	0	Stores the amount left to pay after 3 years
12 $\boxed{P/YR}$	12.00	Sets periods per year
6 $\boxed{I/YR}$	6	Stores interest rate
17,000 $\boxed{PV}$	17,000	Stores amount borrowed
$\boxed{PMT}$	−517.17	Calculates the monthly payment

In Microsoft Excel, the calculation is simply =PMT (.005, 36, −17000, 0, 0) (see Exhibit 8A-8).

In a similar fashion, assume a used-car dealer offers you a "special deal" in which you can borrow $12,000 with low monthly payments of $350 per month for 48 months. What rate of interest are you being charged in this case? Using the DFA table,

$$PVA_{48,.??} = \$350(DFA_{48,.??})$$
$$\$12,000 = 350(DFA_{48,.??})$$
$$DFA_{48,.??} = 34.2857$$

Looking at the row for an n of 48, we see that a DFA of 34.2857 is about halfway between an r of 1 percent and r of 2 percent (closer to 1 percent), which means you are being

Exhibit 8A-8

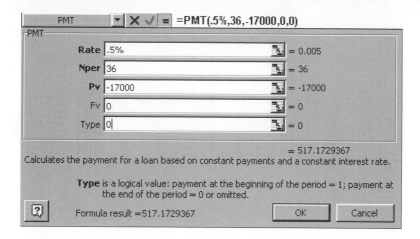

charged an annual rate of almost 18 percent (1.5% × 12)—not such a good deal after all! Using a business calculator, observe the following:

Keys	Display	Description
12 [P/YR]	12.00	Sets periods per year
4 × 12 [N]	48.00	Stores numer of periods in loan
0 [FV]	0	Stores the amount left to pay after 4 years
12,000 [PV]	12,000	Stores amount borrowed
350 [±] [PMT]	−350	Stores the monthly payment
[I/YR]	17.60	Calculates the annual interest rate

In Excel, =RATE(48, −350, 12,000, 0, 0, 0) generates a monthly rate of 1.4667 percent and an annual rate of 17.60 percent.

The use of the RATE function requires that the payments are the same each period. Excel's IRR function is more flexible allowing different payments. However, each payment has to be entered separately. For example, if the car is purchased for $17,000 with annual payments of $4,000, $5,000, $6,000, and $7,000 at the end of each of the next four years, the interest rate charged on the car loan can be calculated using the IRR function (see Exhibit 8A-9).

Exhibit 8A-9

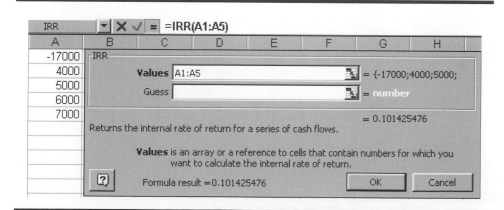

TABLE 8-1   Present Value of $1 Due in n Periods

$$\text{Factor} = \frac{1}{(1+r)^n}$$

(n) Period	1%	2%	3%	4%	5%	6%	7%	8%	9%	10%	12%	14%	15%	16%	18%	20%	24%
1	.9901	.9804	.9709	.9615	.9524	.9434	.9346	.9259	.9174	.9091	.8929	.8772	.8696	.8621	.8475	.8333	.8065
2	.9803	.9612	.9426	.9246	.9070	.8900	.8734	.8573	.8417	.8264	.7972	.7695	.7561	.7432	.7182.	.6944	.6504
3	.9706	.9423	.9151	.8890	.8638	.8396	.8163	.7938	.7722	.7513	.7118	.6750	.6575	.6407	.6086	.5787	.5245
4	.9610	.9238	.8885	.8548	.8227	.7921	.7629	.7350	.7084	.6830	.6355	.5921	.5718	.5523	.5158	.4823	.4230
5	.9515	.9057	.8626	.8219	.7835	.7473	.7130	.6806	.6499	.6209	.5674	.5194	.4972	.4761	.4371	.4019	.3411
6	.9420	.8880	.8375	.7903	.7462	.7050	.6663	.6302	.5963	.5645	.5066	.4556	.4323	.4104	.3704	.3349	.2751
7	.9327	.8706	.8131	.7599	.7107	.6651	.6227	.5835	.5470	.5132	.4523	.3996	.3759	.3538	.3139	.2791	.2218
8	.9235	.8535	.7894	.7307	.6768	.6274	.5820	.5403	.5019	.4665	.4039	.3506	.3269	.3050	.2660	.2326	.1789
9	.9143	.8368	.7664	.7026	.6446	.5919	.5439	.5002	.4604	.4241	.3606	.3075	.2843	.2630	.2255	.1938	.1443
10	.9053	.8203	.7441	.6756	.6139	.5584	.5083	.4632	.4224	.3855	.3220	.2697	.2472	.2267	.1911	.1615	.1164
11	.8963	.8043	.7224	.6496	.5847	.5268	.4751	.4289	.3875	.3505	.2875	.2366	.2149	.1954	.1619	.1346	.0938
12	.8874	.7885	.7014	.6246	.5568	.4970	.4440	.3971	.3555	.3186	.2567	.2076	.1869	.1685	.1372	.1122	.0757
13	.8787	.7730	.6810	.6006	.5303	.4688	.4150	.3677	.3262	.2897	.2292	.1821	.1625	.1452	.1163	.0935	.0610
14	.8700	.7579	.6611	.5775	.5051	.4423	.3878	.3405	.2992	.2633	.2046	.1597	.1413	.1252	.0985	.0779	.0492
15	.8613	.7430	.6419	.5553	.4810	.4173	.3624	.3152	.2745	.2394	.1827	.1401	.1229	.1079	.0835	.0649	.0397
16	.8528	.7284	.6232	.5339	.4581	.3936	.3387	.2919	.2519	.2176	.1631	.1229	.1069	.0930	.0708	.0541	.0320
17	.8444	.7142	.6050	.5134	.4363	.3714	.3166	.2703	.2311	.1978	.1456	.1078	.0929	.0802	.0600	.0451	.0258
18	.8360	.7002	.5874	.4936	.4155	.3503	.2959	.2502	.2120	.1799	.1300	.0946	.0808	.0691	.0508	.0376	.0208
19	.8277	.6864	.5703	.4746	.3957	.3305	.2765	.2317	.1945	.1635	.1161	.0829	.0703	.0596	.0431	.0313	.0168
20	.8195	.6730	.5537	.4564	.3769	.3118	.2584	.2145	.1784	.1486	.1037	.0728	.0611	.0514	.0365	.0261	.0135
21	.8114	.6598	.5375	.4388	.3589	.2942	.2415	.1987	.1637	.1351	.0926	.0638	.0531	.0443	.0309	.0217	.0109
22	.8034	.6468	.5219	.4220	.3418	.2775	.2257	.1839	.1502	.1228	.0826	.0560	.0462	.0382	.0262	.0181	.0088
23	.7954	.6342	.5067	.4057	.3256	.2618	.2109	.1703	.1378	.1117	.0738	.0491	.0402	.0329	.0222	.0151	.0071
24	.7876	.6217	.4919	.3901	.3101	.2470	.1971	.1577	.1264	.1015	.0659	.0431	.0349	.0284	.0188	.0126	.0057
25	.7798	.6095	.4776	.3751	.2953	.2330	.1842	.1460	.1160	.0923	.0588	.0378	.0304	.0245	.0160	.0105	.0046
26	.7720	.5976	.4637	.3607	.2812	.2198	.1722	.1352	.1064	.0839	.0525	.0331	.0264	.0211	.0135	.0087	.0037
27	.7644	.5859	.4502	.3468	.2678	.2074	.1609	.1252	.0976	.0763	.0469	.0291	.0230	.0182	.0115	.0073	.0030
28	.7568	.5744	.4371	.3335	.2551	.1956	.1504	.1159	.0895	.0693	.0419	.0255	.0200	.0157	.0097	.0061	.0024
29	.7493	.5631	.4243	.3207	.2429	.1846	.1406	.1073	.0822	.0630	.0374	.0224	.0174	.0135	.0082	.0051	.0020
30	.7419	.5521	.4120	.3083	.2314	.1741	.1314	.0994	.0754	.0573	.0334	.0196	.0151	.0116	.0070	.0042	.0016

TABLE 8-2 Present Value of an Annuity of $1 per Period

$$\text{Factor} = 1 - \frac{1 - \frac{1}{(1+r)^n}}{r}$$

(n) Period	1%	2%	3%	4%	5%	6%	7%	8%	9%	10%	12%	14%	15%	16%	18%	20%	24%
1	0.9901	0.9804	0.9709	0.9615	0.9524	0.9434	0.9346	0.9259	0.9174	0.9091	0.8929	0.8772	0.8696	0.8621	0.8475	0.8333	0.8065
2	1.9704	1.9416	1.9135	1.8861	1.8594	1.8334	1.8080	1.7833	1.7591	1.7355	1.6901	1.6467	1.6257	1.6052	1.5656	1.5278	1.4568
3	2.9410	2.8839	2.8286	2.7751	2.7232	2.6730	2.6243	2.5771	2.5313	2.4869	2.4018	2.3216	2.2832	2.2459	2.1743	2.1065	1.9813
4	3.9020	3.8077	3.7171	3.6299	3.5460	3.4651	3.3872	3.3121	3.2397	3.1699	3.0373	2.9137	2.8550	2.7982	2.6901	2.5887	2.4043
5	4.8534	4.7135	4.5797	4.4518	4.3295	4.2124	4.1002	3.9927	3.8897	3.7908	3.6048	3.4331	3.3522	3.2743	3.1272	2.9906	2.7454
6	5.7955	5.6014	5.4172	5.2421	5.0757	4.9173	4.7665	4.6229	4.4859	4.3553	4.114	3.8887	3.7845	3.6847	3.4976	3.3255	3.0205
7	6.7282	6.4720	6.2303	6.0021	5.7864	5.5824	5.3893	5.2064	5.0330	4.8684	4.5638	4.2883	4.1604	4.0386	3.8115	3.6046	3.2423
8	7.6517	7.3255	7.0197	6.7327	6.4632	6.2098	5.9713	5.7466	5.5348	5.3349	4.9676	4.6389	4.4873	4.3436	4.0776	3.8372	3.4212
9	8.5660	8.1622	7.7861	7.4353	7.1078	6.8017	6.5152	6.2469	5.9952	5.7590	5.3282	4.9464	4.7716	4.6065	4.3030	4.0310	3.5655
10	9.4713	8.9826	8.5302	8.1109	7.7217	7.3601	7.0236	6.7101	6.4177	6.1446	5.6502	5.2161	5.0188	4.8332	4.4941	4.1925	3.6819
11	10.3676	9.7868	9.2526	8.7605	8.3064	7.8869	7.4987	7.1390	6.8052	6.4951	5.9377	5.4527	5.2337	5.0286	4.6560	4.3271	3.7757
12	11.2551	10.5753	9.9540	9.3851	8.8633	8.3838	7.9427	7.5361	7.1607	6.8137	6.1944	5.6603	5.4206	5.1971	4.7932	4.4392	3.8514
13	12.1337	11.3484	10.6350	9.9856	9.3936	8.8527	8.3577	7.9038	7.4869	7.1034	6.4235	5.8424	5.5831	5.3423	4.9095	4.5327	3.9124
14	13.0037	12.1062	11.2961	10.5631	9.8986	9.2950	8.7455	8.244	7.7862	7.3667	6.6283	6.0021	5.7245	5.4675	5.0081	4.6106	3.9616
15	13.8651	12.8493	11.9379	11.1184	10.3797	9.7122	9.1079	8.5595	8.0607	7.6061	6.8109	6.1422	5.8474	5.5755	5.0916	4.6755	4.0013
16	14.7179	13.5777	12.5611	11.6523	10.8378	10.1059	9.4466	8.8514	8.3126	7.8237	6.9740	6.2651	5.9542	5.6685	5.1624	4.7296	4.0333
17	15.5623	14.2919	13.1661	12.1657	11.2741	10.4773	9.7632	9.1216	8.5436	8.0216	7.1196	6.3729	6.0472	5.7487	5.2223	4.7746	4.0591
18	16.3983	14.9920	13.7535	12.6593	11.6896	10.8276	10.0591	9.3719	8.7556	8.2014	7.2497	6.4674	6.1280	5.8178	5.2732	4.8122	4.0799
19	17.2260	15.6785	14.3238	13.1339	12.0853	11.1581	10.3356	9.6036	8.9501	8.3649	7.3658	6.5504	6.1982	5.8775	5.3162	4.8435	4.0967
20	18.0456	16.3514	14.8775	13.5903	12.4622	11.4699	10.5940	9.8181	9.1285	8.5136	7.4694	6.6231	6.2593	5.9288	5.3527	4.8696	4.1103
21	18.8570	17.0112	15.4150	14.0292	12.8212	11.7641	10.8355	10.0168	9.2922	8.6487	7.5620	6.6870	6.3125	5.9731	5.3837	4.8913	4.1212
22	19.6604	17.6580	15.9369	14.4511	13.1630	12.0416	11.0612	10.2007	9.4424	8.7715	7.6446	6.7429	6.3587	6.0113	5.4099	4.9094	4.1300
23	20.4558	18.2922	16.4436	14.8568	13.4886	12.3034	11.2722	10.3711	9.5802	8.8832	7.7184	6.7921	6.3988	6.0422	5.4321	4.9245	4.1371
24	21.2434	18.9139	16.9355	15.2470	13.7986	12.5504	11.4693	10.5288	9.7066	8.9847	7.7843	6.8351	6.4338	6.0726	5.4509	4.9371	4.1428
25	22.0232	19.5235	17.4131	15.6221	14.0939	12.7834	11.6536	10.6748	9.8226	9.0770	7.8431	6.8729	6.4641	6.0971	5.4669	4.9476	4.1474
26	22.7952	20.1210	17.8768	15.9828	14.3752	13.0032	11.8258	10.8100	9.9290	9.1609	7.8957	6.9061	6.4906	6.1182	5.4804	4.9563	4.1511
27	23.5596	20.7069	18.3270	16.3296	14.6430	13.2105	11.9867	10.9352	10.0266	9.2372	7.9426	6.9352	6.5135	6.1364	5.4919	4.9636	4.1542
28	24.3164	21.2813	18.7641	16.6631	14.8981	13.4062	12.1371	11.0511	10.1161	9.3066	7.9844	6.9607	6.5335	6.1520	5.5016	4.9697	4.1566
29	25.0658	21.8444	19.1885	16.9837	15.1411	13.5907	12.2777	11.1584	10.1983	9.3696	8.0218	6.9830	6.5509	6.1656	5.5098	4.9747	4.1585
30	25.8077	22.3965	19.6004	17.2920	15.3725	13.7648	12.4090	11.2578	10.2737	9.4269	8.0552	7.0027	6.5660	6.1772	5.5168	4.9789	4.1601

SUMMARY OF KEY CONCEPTS

- Long-term investment decisions require a consideration of the time value of money. The time value of money is based on the concept of a dollar received today being worth more than a dollar received in the future. (p. 224)

- The time value of money is considered in capital investment decisions using one of two techniques: the net present value (NPV) method or the internal rate of return (IRR) method. (p. 226)

- If the present value of cash inflows is greater than or equal to the present value of cash outflows (the NPV is greater than or equal to zero), the investment provides a return at least equal to the discount rate (the minimum required rate of return) and the investment is acceptable. (p. 226)

- The internal rate of return (IRR) is the actual yield or return earned by an investment. (p. 228)

- Taxes are a major source of cash outflows for many companies and must be taken into consideration in time value of money calculations. (p. 233)

- Analyzing the cost and benefits of investments in automated and computerized design and manufacturing equipment and robotics requires careful consideration of both quantitative and qualitative factors. (p. 239)

- The payback method can be useful as a fast approximation of the discounted cash flow methods when the cash flows follow similar patterns. (p. 240)

KEY DEFINITIONS

Capital investment decisions Long term decisions involving the purchase (or lease) of new machinery and equipment, and the acquisition or expansion of facilities used in a business (p. 224)

Time value of money The concept that a dollar received (paid) today is worth more (less) than a dollar received (paid) in the future (p. 224)

Screening decisions Decisions about whether an investment meets some predetermined company standard (p. 225)

Preference decisions Decisions that involve choosing between alternatives (p. 225)

Net present value (NPV) A technique for considering the time value of money in which the present value of all cash inflows associated with a project is compared with the present value of all cash outflows (p. 226)

Internal rate of return (IRR) The actual yield or return earned by an investment (p. 226)

Cost of capital What the firm would have to pay to borrow (issue bonds) or raise funds through equity (issue stock) in the financial marketplace (p. 226)

Discount rate Used as a hurdle rate or minimum rate of return in time value of money calculations; adjusted to reflect risk and uncertainty (p. 226)

Profitability index (PI) Calculated by dividing the present value of cash inflows by the initial investment (p. 231)

Sensitivity analysis Used to highlight decisions that may be affected by changes in expected cash flows (p. 238)

Payback period The length of time needed for a long-term project to recapture or pay back the initial investment (p. 239)

Present value (PV) The amount of future cash flows discounted to their equivalent worth today (p. 241)

Simple interest Interest on the invested amount only (p. 241)

Compound interest Interest on the invested amount plus interest on previous interest earned but not withdrawn (p. 241)

Annuity A series of cash flows of equal amount paid or received at regular intervals (p. 250)

CONCEPT REVIEW

1. Define capital investment decisions.

2. Define what is meant by the term *time value of money.*

3. Compare screening decisions with preference decisions.

4. Compare net present value (NPV) with internal rate of return (IRR). What are the principal differences in the two methods?

5. Define the term *cost of capital.* How would cost of capital be used in an investment decision?

6. Which method of project selection ignores the time value of money?

7. Define profitability index and discuss how it is used in capital investment decisions.

8. Define payback period.

9. Describe how internal rate of return equates to net present value.

10. Describe the process by which projects are accepted using the internal rate of return.

11. For the internal rate of return to rank projects the same way as the present value, which condition must exist?

12. The calculation of the net present value of a proposed project requires estimates of what?

13. If the net present value of a proposed project is negative, then the actual rate of return is what?

14. Competing investment projects where accepting one project eliminates the possibility of taking the remaining projects is referred to as what?

APPLICATION OF CONCEPTS

15. A planned factory expansion project has an estimated initial cost of $800,000. Using a discount rate of 20 percent, the present value of the future cost savings from the expansion is $843,000. To yield exactly a 20 percent return on investment, the actual investment expenditure should not exceed the $800,000 estimate by more than what amount?

16. If the present value of future cash flows is $17,000 and the initial investment is $10,000, what is the profitability index?

17. If the future cash flows are expected to be $4,000 for Year 1 and $3,000 for Years 2 through 5, and the initial investment is $10,000, the payback period is how many years?

18. The Orr Golf Club is considering an investment into golf carts that requires $20,000 and promises to return $28,090 in 3 years. The company's income tax rate is 40 percent. What is the internal rate of return?

19. The Nassy Day Care Center is considering an investment that will require an initial cash outlay of $300,000 to purchase nondepreciable assets that have a 10-year life. The organization requires a minimum 4-year payback. What must be the annual cash flows generated by the project in order for the company to make the investment?

20. The Pearce Club Inc. is considering investing in an exercise machine that would increase revenues by $2,000 a year for five years. The machine would be depreciated using the straight-line method over its useful life (with no half-year convention). The company's marginal tax rate is 30 percent. If the company pays $5,000 for the machine, what is the internal rate of return on the equipment?

21. Powers Inc. has a project that requires an initial investment of $43,000 and has the following expected stream of cash flows:

Year 1	$20,000
Year 2	$30,000

What is the project's internal rate of return?

22. Rechtin Company has a project that requires an initial investment of $35,000 and has the following expected stream of cash flows:

Year 1	$25,000
Year 2	$20,000
Year 3	$10,000

The company's cost of capital is 12 percent. What is the profitability index for the project?

23. Relue Inc. has a project with an expected cash flow of $1 million at the end of Year 5. Relue has a second project with an expected cash flow of $200,000 to be received at the end of each year for the next five years. What can be said of the net present value of the first project compared to the second project?

24. Rupp Inc. purchased an asset at a cost of $80,000. Annual operating cash flows are expected to be $30,000 each year for four years. At the end of the asset life, there will be no residual (salvage) value. What is the net present value if the cost of capital is 12 percent (ignore income taxes)?

25. Schaefer Organic Farms purchased a new tractor at a cost of $80,000. Annual operating cash flows are expected to be $30,000 each year for four years. At the end of life, the salvage value of the tractor is expected to be $5,000. What is the net present value if the cost of capital is 12 percent (ignore income taxes)?

26. Schaller Company purchased an asset at a cost of $40,000. Annual operating cash flows are expected to be $20,000 each year for four years. At the end of the asset life, there will be no residual (salvage) value. The income tax rate is 30 percent and the company uses straight-line depreciation with no half-year convention. What is the net present value if the cost of capital is 10 percent?

27. Schanz Quick Photo Company purchased a new photo developing machine at the cost of $80,000. Annual operating cash flows are expected to be $25,000 each year for four years. At the end of the asset life, the salvage value is expected to be $5,000. The income tax rate is 30 percent and the company uses straight-line depreciation with no half-year convention. What is the net present value if the cost of capital is 12 percent?

28. Schlue Company invested $180,000 in a new machine. The machine will generate cash flows before taxes at year-end of $90,000, $80,000, and $70,000 for the next three years. The company uses a 15 percent cost of capital. What is the net present value of purchasing the machine?

29. Seeger Company recently invested in a computerized manufacturing system. The project required an initial investment of $100,000 and is expected to provide equal cost savings over the next eight years. Based on an 8 percent discount rate, the project generated a net present value of zero. The investment is not expected to have any salvage value at the end of its life. Ignoring income taxes, what are the expected annual cost savings of the project?

30. Simmons Trucking is considering replacing its moving truck. The truck is expected to cost $60,000 and is expected to last 10 years with no salvage value. The truck is expected to generate additional net cash flows of $15,000 a year. Based on Simmons's analysis, the project has a net present value of $39,450. What cost of capital rate did the company use to compute the net present value?

31. At the end of its five-year life, Speakman Company will dispose of an asset for $6,000. If the asset is fully depreciated and Speakman's tax rate is 40 percent, what is the present value of the future cash flow? Assume that Speakman's cost of capital is 12 percent.

32. Stamenkovich Law Associates is evaluating a capital investment proposal for new computers for this current year. The initial investment would be $50,000. It would be depreciated on a straight-line basis over five years with no salvage value. The before-tax annual cash inflow due to this investment is $15,000, and the income tax rate is 40 percent paid in the same year as incurred. The desired after-tax rate of return is 15 percent. All cash flows occur at year-end. What is the net present value of the capital investment proposal? Should the proposal be accepted? Why or why not?

33. Each of two projects being considered by Stein Company require an investment of $1,000 in equipment. The firm's cost of capital is 12 percent. The cash flow patterns are as follows:

Year	Cash Flows	
	C	D
1	600	300
2	600	600
3	600	800
4	600	700

Calculate the present value of each project at each of the following costs of capital: (1) 8 percent, (2) 10 percent, (3) 12 percent. Indicate which project should be accepted at each of these costs of capital.

34. Stembridge Medical Associates is planning to acquire a $250,000 X-ray machine that will provide increased efficiencies, thereby reducing annual patient operating costs by $80,000. The machine will be depreciated by the straight-line method over five years (no half-year convention) with no salvage value at the end of five years. Assuming a 40 percent income tax rate, compute the machine's after-tax payback period.

35. Stephens Industries is contemplating four projects: Project P, Project Q, Project R, and Project S. The capital costs and estimated after-tax net cash flows of each mutually exclusive project are listed below. Stephens' desired after-tax cost of capital is 12 percent, and the company has a capital budget for the year of $450,000. Idle funds cannot be reinvested at greater than 12 percent.

	Project P	**Project Q**	**Project R**	**Project S**
Initial cost	$200,000	$235,000	$190,000	$210,000
Annual cash flows				
Year 1	$ 93,000	$ 90,000	$ 45,000	$ 40,000
Year 2	93,000	85,000	55,000	50,000
Year 3	93,000	75,000	65,000	60,000
Year 4	0	55,000	70,000	65,000
Year 5	0	50,000	75,000	75,000
Net present value	$ 23,370	$ 29,827	$ 27,233	$ (7,854)
Internal rate of return	18.7%	17.6%	17.2%	10.6%
Profitability index	1.12	1.13	1.14	0.95

Required

A. Which project will the company choose?

B. If they can only accept one project, which one should the company choose?

36. Stewart Corporation is reviewing an investment proposal. The initial cost as well as other related data for each year are presented in the following schedule. The cash flows are all assumed to take place at the end of the year. All salvage value of the investment at the end of each year is equal to its net book value, and there will be no salvage value at the end of the investment's life.

INVESTMENT PROPOSAL

Year	Initial Cost and Book Value	Annual Net After-Tax Cash Flows	Annual Net Income
0	$105,000	$ 0	$ 0
1	70,000	50,000	15,000
2	42,000	45,000	17,000
3	21,000	40,000	19,000
4	7,000	35,000	21,000
5	0	30,000	23,000

Stewart uses a 24 percent after-tax target rate of return for new investment proposals.

Required

A. What is the traditional payback period for the investment proposal?

B. What is the net present value of the investment proposal?

37. Stoehr Company manufactures three different models of paper shredders including the waste container, which serves as the base. Whereas the shredder heads are different for all three models, the waste container is the same. The number of waste containers that Stoehr will need during the next five years is estimated as follows:

Year	Number of Containers
2000	50,000
2001	50,000
2002	52,000
2003	55,000
2004	55,000

The equipment used to manufacture the waste container must be replaced because it has broken and cannot be repaired. The new equipment would have a purchase price of $945,000. The equipment is expected to have a salvage value of $12,000 at the end of its economic life in 2004. The new equipment would be more efficient than the old equipment, resulting in a 25 percent reduction in direct material and a one-time decrease in working capital requirements of $2,500 resulting from a reduction in direct material inventories. This working capital reduction would be recognized at the time of equipment acquisition.

The old equipment is fully depreciated and is not included in the fixed overhead. The old equipment from the plant can be sold for a salvage amount of $1,500. Stoehr has no alternative use for the manufacturing space at this time, so if the waste containers were purchased, the old equipment would be left in place.

Rather than replace the equipment, one of Stoehr's production managers has suggested that the waste containers be purchased. One supplier has quoted a price of $27 per container. This price is $8 less than the current manufacturing cost, which is as follows:

Direct materials	$10.00	
Direct labor	8.00	
Variable overhead	6.00	$24.00
Fixed overhead:		
Supervision	$ 2.00	
Facilities	5.00	
General	4.00	$11.00
Total manufacturing cost per unit		$35.00

Stoehr employs a plantwide fixed overhead rate in its operations. If the waste containers were purchased outside, the salary and benefits of one supervisor, included in the fixed overhead at $45,000, would be eliminated. There would be no other changes in the other cash and noncash items included in fixed overhead.

Stoehr is subject to a 40 percent income tax rate. Management assumes that all annual cash flows and tax payments occur at the end of the year and uses a 12 percent after-tax discount rate.

Required

Step I   DEFINE THE PROBLEM

A. Define the problem that Stoehr faces.

B. Calculate the net present value of the estimated after-tax cash flows at December 31, 2000, for each option you identify.

38. The Strength Corporation sells computer services to its clients. The firm is contemplating the acquisition of a computer but is undecided as to whether it should be leased or purchased. Information regarding the computer follows:

Cash purchase price	$275,000
Maintenance taxes per year	25,000
Rental price (includes maintenance and taxes)	75,000 plus 10 percent of billings
Salvage value at the end of three years	120,000
Estimated billings:	
Year 1	230,000
Year 2	250,000
Year 3	240,000
Operating expenses per year	75,000
Setup expense charge to Year 1	20,000
Income tax rate	40 percent
Depreciation method	Straight-line
Minimum desired rate of return	12 percent

Step 1	DEFINE THE PROBLEM
Step 2	IDENTIFY OBJECTIVES
Step 3	IDENTIFY AND ANALYZE AVAILABLE OPTIONS
Step 4	SELECT THE BEST OPTION

Prepare an analysis using the decision model that will indicate which alternative should be selected. Identify that alternative.

39. Stutesman Enterprises has three possible projects. Each project requires the same initial investment of $1,000,000. The cash flows are as follows:

Year	Project X	Project Y	Project Z
1	$1,250,000	$ 0	$ 500,000
2	1,250,000	0	2,000,000
3	1,250,000	0	2,000,000
4	1,250,000	5,000,000	500,000

Ignoring taxes, compute the net present value of each project at a 15 percent cost of capital. Which project should be chosen? Be sure to show supporting calculations.

40. Sullivan Company will acquire a new asset that costs $400,000 and is anticipated to have a salvage value of $30,000 at the end of four years. The new asset

(1) will replace an old asset that currently has a tax basis of $80,000 and can be sold for $60,000 now, and

(2) will continue to generate the same operating revenues as the old asset ($200,000 per year)

However, savings in operating costs will be experienced as follows: a total of $120,000 in each of the first three years and $90,000 in the fourth year. Sullivan is subject to a 40 percent tax rate.

Required

A. What is the present value of the depreciation tax shield for the new asset for Year 1?

B. What are the cash flows (net of tax) associated with the disposal of the old asset?

C. What is the investment's net present value (after tax)?

41. Sutherlin Corporation has agreed to sell some used computer equipment to Brett Sullivan, one of the company's employees.

Required

A. Assuming a 6 percent discount rate, if Sutherlin sells the computers to Sullivan for a $1,000 down payment paid immediately followed by $1,000 payments at the end of each of the next four years what value is Sutherlin placing on the computer equipment?

B. Sullivan agrees to the immediate down payment of $1,000 but would like the note for $4,000 to be payable in full at the end of the fourth year. What impact does this change have on Sutherlin?

C. How much would the payment need to be at the end of four years to make Sutherlin indifferent to receiving $1,000 at the end of each of the next four years or one payment at the end of year 4?

42. Swanson Products is considering a project that requires an initial investment of $400,000 and will generate the following cash inflows for the next four years:

Year	Cash Inflow at End of Year
1	$150,000
2	$130,000
3	$180,000
4	$150,000

Required

A. Ignoring tax effects, calculate the net present value of this project if Swanson's cost of capital is 20 percent.

B. Should the company accept the project if the cost of capital is 20 percent? Explain.

C. Ignoring tax effects, calculate the net present value of this project if Swanson's cost of capital is 12 percent.

D. Should the company accept the project if the cost of capital is 12 percent? Explain.

43. Tate Enterprises is a nonprofit organization that has a cost of capital of 10 percent. The organization is considering the replacement of their computer system. The old computer has a book value of $3,000 and a remaining estimated life of five years with no salvage value at that time. The salvage value of the old computer is currently $1,500. The new computer will cost $10,000. It has an estimated life of five years with no salvage value. Annual cash operating costs are $4,000 for the old computer and $2,000 for the new computer.

Required

A. What is the present value of the operating cash outflows for the old machine?

B. What is the present value of the operating cash outflows for the new machine?

C. What is the present value of the salvage value of the old machine if it is replaced now?

D. Would you advise the organization to replace the machine?

44. Taylor Company is considering opening a new sales territory. Management expects the initial investment to be $150,000 and subsequent investments of $100,000 and $50,000 at the end of the first and second years. Net cash flow from the sales territory is expected to yield an after-tax cash inflow for five more years: $75,000 for the first two years and $60,000 for the remaining years. The company's cost of capital is 12 percent. Calculate the net present value of this project.

45. Rob Thorton is a member of the planning and analysis staff for Thurston Inc., an established manufacturer of frozen foods. Rick Ungerman, chief financial officer of Thurston Inc., has asked him to prepare a net present value analysis for a proposed capital equipment expenditure that should improve the profitability of the Southwestern Plant. This analysis will be given to the board of directors for expenditure approval.

Several years ago, as director of planning and analysis, Ungerman was instrumental in convincing the board to open the Southwestern Plant. However, recent competitive pressures have forced all of Thurston's manufacturing divisions to consider alternatives to improve their market position. To Ungerman's dismay, the Southwestern Plant may be sold in the near future unless significant improvements in cost control and production efficiency are achieved.

Southwestern's production manager, an old friend of Ungerman's, has submitted a proposal for the acquisition of an automated materials movement system. Ungerman is anxious to have this proposal approved as it will ensure the continuance of the Southwestern Plant and preserve his friend's position. The plan calls for the replacement of a number of forklift trucks and operators with a computer-controlled conveyor belt system that feeds directly into the refrigeration units. This automation would eliminate the need for a number of materials handlers and increase the output capacity of the plant.

Ungerman has given this proposal to Thorton and instructed him to use the following information to prepare his analysis:

MATERIALS MOVEMENT SYSTEM PROJECTIONS

Projected useful life	10 years
Purchase/installation of equipment	$4,500,000
Increased working capital needed*	1,000,000
Increased annual operating costs (exclusive of depreciation)	200,000
Equipment repairs to maintain production efficiency (end of Year 5)	800,000
Increase in annual sales revenue	700,000
Reduction in annual manufacturing costs	500,000
Reduction in annual maintenance costs	300,000
Estimated salvage value of conveyor belt system	850,000

*The working capital will be released at the end of the 10-year useful life of the conveyor belt system.

The forklift trucks have a net book value of $500,000 with a remaining useful life of five years and no salvage value for depreciation purposes. If the conveyor belt system is purchased now, these trucks will be sold for $100,000. Thurston has a 40 percent effective tax rate, has chosen the straight-line depreciation method, and uses a 12 percent discount rate. For the purpose of analysis, all tax effects and cash flows from the equipment acquisition and disposal are considered to occur at the time of the transactions, whereas those from operations are considered to occur at the end of each year.

When Thorton completed his initial analysis, the proposed project appeared quite healthy. However, after investigating equipment similar to that proposed, he discovered that the estimated residual value of $850,000 was very optimistic; information previously provided by several vendors' estimates this value to be $100,000. He also discovered that industry trade publications considered eight years to be the maximum life of similar conveyor belt systems. As a result, he prepared a second analysis based on this new information. When Ungerman saw the second analysis, he told Thorton to discard this revised material, warned him not to discuss the new estimates with anyone, and ordered him not to present any of this information to the board of directors.

Required

A. Prepare a net present value analysis of the purchase and installation of the materials movement system using the revised estimates obtained by Thorton. Be sure to present supporting calculations.

B. Accurately describe the decision problem facing Thorton.

C. What alternatives does he have?

D. What is the best alternative from a quantitative analysis?

E. What other qualitative factors should be considered and why?

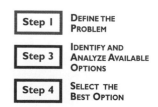

Step 1	**DEFINE THE PROBLEM**
Step 3	**IDENTIFY AND ANALYZE AVAILABLE OPTIONS**
Step 4	**SELECT THE BEST OPTION**

CONTINUING CASE | BIG AL'S PIZZA INC.

As discussed in earlier chapters, Big Al's currently leases its equipment from Pizza Products Inc. for $2,500 per month. While the lease term is 5 years (with 2 years remaining), Big Al's can terminate the lease at any time by paying a penalty of $10,000. Big Al's is considering purchasing equipment to replace the equipment being leased. Big Al's can purchase equipment at the following prices.

Equipment	Price (per unit)
Dough ball press	$5,450.00
Assembly table	$2,100.00
Cardboard cutter	$4,100.00
Plastic sealer	$2,695.00
Label Installer	$1,000.00

Note: One unit of each piece of equipment is used on each of Big Al's ten assembly lines. (Big Al's must purchase ten units of each piece of equipment.) If purchased, all equipment will be depreciated over five years using straight-line depreciation and will have no salvage value. Big Al's tax rate is 40 percent.

Required

A. Using NPV analysis, compare the present value of the lease payments with the cost of buying the equipment. Assuming a discount rate of 10 percent, which option is preferable?

B. Big Al's has the option of purchasing equipment from another supplier at a cost of $190,000. The supplier promises that the new equipment will reduce operating costs by $1,000 per month over the life of the equipment. Assuming a 10 percent discount rate, which option is preferable?

C. Calculate the after-tax NPV for each option discussed above. Is your decision still the same?

D. What factors other than cost savings should Big Al's consider in these decision problems?

Part III

PLANNING, PERFORMANCE EVALUATION, AND CONTROL

Chapter 9

THE USE OF BUDGETS IN PLANNING AND DECISION MAKING

Study Tools

A Review of the Previous Chapter
Chapter 8 completed our study of the nature of costs in decision making and provided students with a set of tools that allow managers to consider the time value of money in making long-term capital investment decisions.

A Preview of This Chapter
In this chapter we introduce the concept of budgeting and discuss how budgets assist managers in planning and decision making.

Key concepts include:
- Budgets must start with a top-down strategic plan that guides and integrates the whole company and its individual budgets.
- Budgeting is a management task, not a bookkeeping task.
- Budgets are used throughout the planning, operating, and controlling activities of managers.
- Budgets are future oriented and make extensive use of estimates and forecasts.
- Flexible budgets are based on the actual number of units produced rather than the budgeted units of production.

A Preview of Upcoming Chapters
In Chapter 10, we expand the discussion of flexible budgeting and introduce the concept of standard costs and variance analysis as tools to help managers "manage by exception" and evaluate performance in their control function. The chapter ends with a discussion of budgeting culture and the various behavioral issues involved in the budgeting process.

LEARNING OBJECTIVES

After studying the material in this chapter, you should be able to:

LO 1 Understand the concept and purpose of budgets

LO 2 Understand the use of financial budgets in operational planning and decision making

LO 3 Prepare and apply the sales budget to decision problems

LO 4 Prepare and apply production and purchases budgets to decision problems

LO 5 Prepare cash receipts and disbursements budgets

LO 6 Prepare and apply the summary cash budget to decision problems

LO 7 Prepare budgeted income statements and balance sheets and evaluate the importance of budgeted financial statements for decision making

LO 8 Understand the importance of financial budgets for merchandising and service companies

LO 9 Understand the use and importance of nonfinancial budgets

LO 10 Prepare flexible budgets and understand how they are used in activity-based costing environments

In this chapter we introduce the concept of budgeting and discuss how budgets assist managers in planning and decision making. As discussed in Chapter 1, planning involves the development of both short-term (operational) and long-term (strategic) goals and objectives. Budgeting helps managers determine the resources needed to meet their goals and objectives and thus is a key ingredient in good decision making. In this chapter, we discuss and demonstrate the preparation of operational budgets for a traditional manufacturing company with inventory, as well as for a company operating in a JIT environment. We also discuss the use of operational budgets in merchandising and service companies.

The focus of budgeting is planning—planning for production requirements, planning for purchases of raw materials, planning for the use of direct labor and other resources, and, most important, planning for cash needs. In this chapter, we pay special attention to the preparation and use of the cash budget for managerial decision making and tie it into the preparation of the statement of cash flows used extensively by external users.

In the last section of the chapter, static and flexible budgets are discussed with particular emphasis on the impact of ABC on flexible budgets. Nonfinancial budgets are also introduced. ∎

INTRODUCTION

Budgets are plans dealing with the acquisition and use of resources over a specified time period. Everyone budgets, from the college student to the large multinational corporation. Although budgets are often thought of in terms of dollars (monetary or financial budgets), budgets are used for other purposes as well. For example, a college student carrying 15 credit hours, working 20 hours a week in a part-time job, and volunteering 10 hours per week at the local hospital might need to prepare a time budget to plan his or her use of time throughout the week. A monetary budget for a college student can be as simple as jotting down expected cash inflow from loans, parents, and maybe a part-time job and expected outflows for school and living expenses.

At the other end of the budgeting spectrum, multinational companies may have very sophisticated budgets, used to plan for the acquisition and use of thousands of different materials, the manufacture of hundreds of products, and the sale of those products.

Have you ever prepared a budget? Was it a monetary or non-monetary budget? How did you use it?

Budgets for entertainment business are based on projected attendance figures. How flexible must the master budget be for the Portland Seadogs minor league franchise? How might this compare to the budget of a blockbuster movie which just opened for the summer season?
www.portlandseadogs. com

THE BUDGET DEVELOPMENT PROCESS

Traditionally, budgeting is a bottom-up process dependent on departmental managers providing a detailed plan for the upcoming month, quarter, or year. Some companies start their budget process based on last year's numbers, whereas others employ zero-based budgeting. **Zero-based budgets** require managers to build budgets from the ground up each year rather than just add a percentage increase to last year's numbers. Although we typically think of budgets as being prepared annually, as discussed in the preceding "In the News" feature, changing expectations often require that budgets be revised frequently.

LO1
Understand the concept and purpose of budgets

APPLICATION IN BUSINESS

Many state governments prepare budgets biannually (every two years). This can cause major problems when unexpected costs are incurred due to natural disasters or when tax revenue falls due to unexpected downturns in the economy.

TECHNOLOGY FOCUS

In recent years, spreadsheets have given way to enterprise resource planning (ERP) software as a key budgeting tool. ERP systems link data from across all areas of a business—a key for effective budgeting and planning. ERP systems are discussed in more depth in Chapter 13.

Regardless of the specific process used, to be successful, budgets must start with a top-down strategic plan that guides and integrates the whole company and its individual budgets. In addition, in order to motivate managers and other employees to meet the objectives and goals provided in budgets, companies must structure bonuses, merit pay, and other tangible and intangible rewards in ways that link these rewards to measurable goals outlined in the budgets.

 Key Concept: *Budgets must start with a top-down strategic plan that guides and integrates the whole company and its individual budgets.*

DILBERT BY SCOTT ADAMS

DILBERT reprinted by permission of United Features Syndicate, Inc.

One of the misconceptions about budgeting is that the budgeting process is just a mechanical number-crunching task for bookkeepers. While the preparation of budgets is often very mechanical (and can be a little tricky), the use of spreadsheets like Lotus 1-2-3 and Microsoft Excel make their preparation much simpler. In reality, budgeting is a management task not a mechanical bookkeeping task, and it requires a great deal of planning and thoughtful input from a broad range of managers in a company. This concept of budgeting as a management task will focus our discussion of the budgeting process in this chapter.

 Key Concept: *Budgeting is a management task, not a bookkeeping task.*

BUDGETS FOR PLANNING, OPERATING, AND CONTROL

LO2
Understand the use of financial budgets in operational planning and decision making

Managers use budgeting as they go about their **planning, operating,** and **control** activities (see Exhibit 9-1). Planning is the cornerstone of good management. Planning involves developing objectives and goals for the organization as well as the actual preparation of budgets. Operating involves day-to-day decision making by managers, which is facilitated by budgets. Control involves ensuring that the objectives and goals developed by the organization are being attained. Control often involves a comparison of budgets to actual performance and the use of budgets for performance evaluation purposes. The use of budgets for cost control and performance evaluation is discussed in more depth in Chapter 10.

 Key Concept: *Budgets are used throughout the planning, operating, and controlling activities of managers.*

EXHIBIT 9-1 Budgeting Is an Integral Part of the Planning, Operating, and Control Activities of Managers

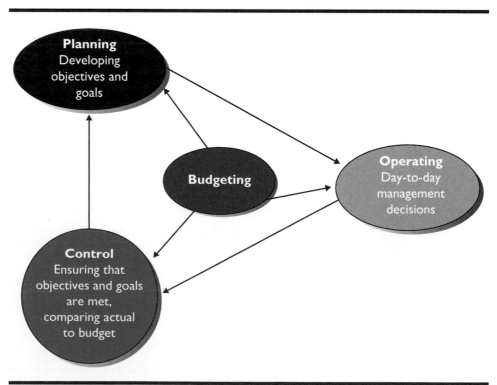

EXHIBIT 9-2 The Operating Cycle

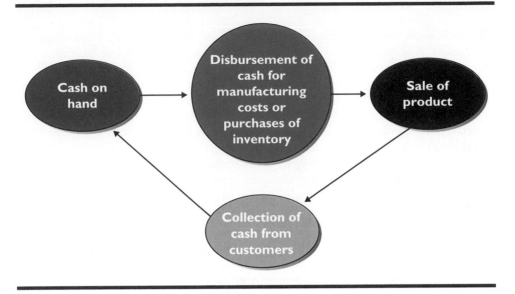

In this chapter, we emphasize the use of budgets in planning and operating activities including decisions concerning how much of a product to produce, how much material to buy, how much labor to hire, and the borrowing and investment of cash. The concept of budgeting for cash is tied back to the operating cycle discussed in your financial accounting course. The operating cycle focuses on cash flow, beginning with the investment of cash in inventory or the use of cash to manufacture products, the sale of those products to customers, and ending with the collection of cash from those customers (see Exhibit 9-2).

One of the main causes of small business failure is the lack of adequate planning for cash needs. A small business that views budgeting for cash as too time consuming or expensive is destined for failure. With the availability and affordability of computers in today's business environment, even the smallest business can very easily perform the analysis necessary to successfully plan and budget for the future.

ADVANTAGES OF BUDGETING

Although the previous introduction pointed out the clear need for budgeting as a planning, operating, and control tool requiring managers to think about organizational goals and objectives, budgeting has other advantages as well.

1. The budgeting process forces communication throughout the organization.

2. The budgeting process forces management to focus on the future and not be distracted by daily crisis in the organization.

3. The budgeting process can help management identify and deal with potential bottlenecks or constraints before they become major problems.

4. The budgeting process can increase the coordination of organizational activities and help facilitate goal congruence. Goal congruence refers to making sure that the personal goals of the managers are closely aligned with the goals of the organization.

5. The budgeting process can define specific goals and objectives that can become benchmarks, or standards of performance, for evaluating future performance.

BUDGETING FOR SALES

LO3
Prepare and apply the sales budget to decision problems

All organizations require the forecasting of future sales volume and the preparation of a sales budget. A professional baseball team needs to forecast the number of fans that attend home games each season. Airlines need to forecast the number of passengers that fly on each route and hotels need to forecast occupancy rates for different days and months. Retail stores such as Wal-Mart and J.C. Penney must forecast retail sales of many different products at many different locations. Manufacturing firms such as Ford, Chrysler, and General Motors must forecast consumer demand for each different model of car or truck that they sell.

The **sales forecast** and **sales budget** are the starting points in the preparation of production budgets for manufacturing companies, purchases budgets for merchandising companies, and labor budgets for service companies. The sales budget is also used in planning the cash needs for manufacturing, merchandising, and service companies.

CROSS FUNCTIONAL APPLICATIONS

In large companies, preparation of the sales forecast is usually accomplished by the marketing department and requires significant effort in the area of market research to arrive at an accurate forecast of expected sales. In smaller companies, the sales forecast may be made by an individual or small group of managers.

There are many different ways to forecast sales. Most forecasting will combine information from many different sources either informally or through the use of computer programs. Regardless of the size of the company or the sophistication of the forecasting methods used, the usual starting point in sales forecasting is last year's level of sales. Other factors and information sources typically used in sales forecasting are as follows:

1. Historical data such as sales trends for the company, competitors, and the industry (if available).
2. General economic trends or factors such as inflation rates, interest rates, population growth, and personal spending.
3. Regional and local factors expected to affect sales.
4. Anticipated price changes in both purchasing costs and sales prices.
5. Anticipated marketing or advertising plans.
6. The impact of new products or changes in product mix on the entire product line.
7. Other factors such as political and legal events and weather changes.

This list is not meant to be all inclusive and every organization will have unique factors that it needs to consider. Each organization will also attach a different level of importance to each factor.

IN THE NEWS

Sometimes weather can affect your business in ways that cannot be easily predicted. In the winter of 1999, New England ski areas had plenty of snow but the communities at lower elevations (from which most of their customers came) did not. Even though the ski resorts used extensive advertising to promote the good ski conditions, skiers stayed away from the slopes because of the warm weather and lack of snow at home.

The size and complexity of the organization will often determine the complexity of the sales forecasting system. Some companies will use elaborate econometric planning models

and regression analysis to forecast sales volume. Others may use very informal models and rely heavily on the intuition and opinions of managers. Regardless of the level of sophistication used in forecasting models, it is important to remember that sales forecasting is still just that—a forecast.

As you will see in the rest of this chapter, all the remaining budgets and the decisions that are made based on their forecasts are dependent on this estimate of sales. For that reason, it is important to estimate sales with as much accuracy as possible. A small error in a sales forecast can cause larger errors in other budgets that depend on the sales forecast.

 Key Concept: *Budgets are future oriented and make extensive use of estimates and forecasts.*

What unique factors might a CPA firm specializing in tax planning and the preparation of tax returns consider in forecasting sales?

OPERATING BUDGETS—AN EXAMPLE

Operating budgets are used by companies to plan for the short term—usually one year or less. As an example of the budgeting process, let's consider the case of Tina's Fine Juices, a bottler of orange juice located in the Northeast. Tina's produces bottled orange juice from fruit concentrate purchased from suppliers in Florida, Arizona, and California. The only ingredients in the juice are water and concentrate. The juice is blended, pasteurized, and bottled for sale in 12-ounce plastic bottles. The process is heavily automated and is centered on five machines that control the mixing and bottling of the juice. Each machine is run by one employee and can process 10 bottles of juice per minute or 600 bottles per hour. The amount of labor required is very small per bottle of juice. The average worker can process 10 bottles of juice per minute or 600 bottles per hour.

The juice is sold by a number of grocery stores under their store brand name and in smaller restaurants, delis, and bagel shops under the name of Tina's Fine Juices. Tina's has been in business for several years and uses a sophisticated sales forecasting model based on prior sales, expected changes in demand, and economic factors affecting the industry.

Fine Juices

What kind of costing system is Tina's likely to use?

Fine Juices

Sales of juice are highly seasonal, peaking in the first quarter of the year. Forecasted sales for the first quarter of 2000 are as follows:

Sales Forecast

January	250,000 bottles
February	325,000 bottles
March	450,000 bottles

Tina's sells the juice for $1.05 per 12-ounce bottle, in cartons of 50 bottles. A sales budget for the first quarter of the year is as follows.[1] A sales budget is the projected volume of product to be sold times the expected sales price per unit.

Sales Budget

	January	February	March	First Quarter
Projected sales (bottles)	250,000	325,000	450,000	1,025,000
Price per Bottle	$1.05	$1.05	$1.05	$1.05
Total projected sales	$262,500	$341,250	$472,500	$1,076,250

BUDGETING FOR A TRADITIONAL MANUFACTURING COMPANY WITH INVENTORY

LO4
Prepare and apply production and purchases budgets to decision problems

PRODUCTION BUDGET

For manufacturing companies, the next step in the budgeting process is to complete the **production budget.** Once the sales volume has been projected, companies must forecast how many units of product to produce in order to meet the sales projections. Although this might seem to be an easy task—just manufacture what you plan to sell—as you will recall from Chapter 2, traditional manufacturing companies often choose to hold a minimum level of finished goods inventory (as well as direct material inventory) to serve as buffers in case of unexpected demand for products or unexpected problems in production.

In this case, the sales forecast must be adjusted to account for any expected increase or decrease in finished goods inventory. A basic production budget is as follows:

Basic Production Budget

Sales forecast (in units)
+ Projected ending inventory
= Total projected production needs
− Beginning inventory
= Projected production volume

---

[1]The sales budget and the remaining operating budgets and budgeted financial statements for Tina's Fine Juices were prepared using Microsoft Excel (see the Chapter 9 template on the diskette accompanying the textbook). All dollar amounts on the spreadsheets are rounded to the nearest dollar resulting in some math "errors" in the budgets. As you will see, the use of spreadsheets greatly simplifies the mechanical budget process particularly when changes are made to the sales or production budgets.

In the basic production budget, the key term is *projected*. The overriding concept in budgeting is that *budgets are estimates.*

Tina's Fine Juices tries to maintain at least 10 percent of the next month's sales forecast in inventory at the end of each month. Since sales have been projected to increase very rapidly, the company does not want to run the risk of running out of juice to ship to customers so Tina's Fine Juices keeps a minimum amount on hand at all times. Other problems such as shipping delays or weather could also affect the amount of desired ending inventory. Based on these requirements Tina's would want to have 32,500 bottles of juice on hand at the end of January (10 percent of February's forecasted sales of 325,000). A production budget for Tina's Fine Juices is as follows:

Production Budget

	January	February	March	First Quarter
Projected sales (bottles)	250,000	325,000	450,000	1,025,000
+ Projected ending inventory	32,500	45,000	50,000	50,000
Total projected needs	282,500	370,000	500,000	1,075,000
− Beginning inventory	25,000 (given)	32,500	45,000	25,000
Projected production (bottles)	257,500	337,500	455,000	1,050,000

You should note that to complete the production budget for the first quarter we need to have some additional information. We need to know the forecasted sales for April so the projected ending inventory can be determined for the end of March. April sales are projected to be 500,000 units, so the projected ending inventory is 50,000 units.[2] The beginning inventory for January is 25,000 bottles. (This amount is also the ending inventory for December.) Closer examination of the production budget model will show that projected production needs are just the projected sales, plus or minus any projected change in inventory during the month. In January, the projected sales are 250,000 units and inventories are projected to increase by 7,500 units (from 25,000 to 32,500). If we add the projected inventory increase to the sales projection we have a projected production level of 257,500 (250,000 + 7,500). You should also note that the arrows in the exhibit point out that the projected ending inventory for any month is the projected beginning inventory for the next month.

Projected production = Projected sales + Change in finished goods inventory

One other important concept in the production budget model is that the projected ending inventory for the quarter is the ending inventory on the last day of the quarter, in this case March 31, and the projected beginning inventory is the beginning inventory on the first day of the quarter or January 1.

MATERIAL PURCHASES BUDGET

Once the production budget is completed, the next budget to be prepared is the **material purchases budget.** Once again, because many traditional companies desire to keep materials

---

[2]The Microsoft Excel template shows both December and April sales and the links between those months and the first quarter production budget.

Fine Juices

on hand at all times in order to plan for unforeseen changes in demand, the desired ending inventory for materials must be added to the projected production needs for materials to arrive at the total expected needs for materials. Then an adjustment is made for any inventory on hand at the beginning of the month.

Tina's Fine Juices needs to prepare two purchases budgets—one for the concentrate used in its orange juice and one for the bottles that are purchased from an outside supplier. Tina's has determined that it takes one gallon of orange concentrate for every 32 bottles of finished product. Each gallon of concentrate costs $4.80. Tina's also requires 20 percent of next month's direct material needs to be on hand at the end of the budget period. The material purchases budget for orange concentrate follows. Note that the starting point for this budget is the production budget. The next step in the preparation of the direct materials purchases budget is to compute the raw material needed based on the projected production. In this case we take the number of bottles to be produced and divide by 32, which is the number of bottles that can be produced with one gallon of concentrate. The ending inventory needs are then added to that figure to arrive at the projected direct materials needed to fulfill the production and ending inventory needs. Beginning inventory is then subtracted from the projected needs to arrive at the projected purchases in gallons and the last step is to convert that amount to dollars by taking the number of gallons times the price per gallon.

To calculate the projected ending inventory in March, Tina's must estimate sales for May. (April sales were already estimated to be 500,000 bottles.) If May sales are estimated at 400,000 bottles, April ending inventory will be estimated to be 40,000 (.10 × 400,000), and April production will be 490,000 bottles (April sales of 500,000 + ending inventory of 40,000 − beginning inventory of 50,000). The production of 490,000 bottles in April requires 15,313 gallons of concentrate $\left(\frac{490,000 \text{ gallons of concentrate}}{32 \text{ bottles per gallon}}\right)$. Accordingly, Tina's will plan on holding 3,063 gallons of concentrate in inventory at the end of March (20 percent of the material usage for April).

Materials Purchases Budget—Orange Concentrate

	January	February	March	First Quarter
Projected production (bottles)	257,500	337,500	455,000	1,050,000
Orange concentrate needed (gallons) for production[1]	8,047	10,547	14,219	32,813
+ Projected ending inventory	2,109	2,844	3,063[2]	3,063
Projected needs	10,156	13,391	17,281	35,875
− Projected beginning inventory	1,609[3]	2,109	2,844	1,609
Gallons to be purchased	8,547	11,281	14,438	34,266
Projected purchases[4]	$41,027	$54,150	$69,300	$164,477

[1] Projected production divided by 32 bottles per gallon.

[2] May sales are projected to be 400,000 bottles, so April ending inventory is 40,000 bottles and production for April is projected to be 490,000 bottles. The production of 490,000 bottles requires 15,313 gallons of concentrate. Twenty percent of 15,313 gallons is 3,063 gallons.

[3] This is the actual beginning inventory (given).

[4] Projected gallons times $4.80 per gallon.

Note: Table may not foot due to rounding on the accompanying Excel spreadsheet.

Tina's will prepare a similar budget for bottles. The bottles are purchased from an outside supplier for $.10 per bottle. The supplier provides labels and caps for the bottles as part of the purchase price. Tina's has the same inventory policy for bottles and orange concentrate. A material purchases budget for bottles is as follows:

Materials Purchases Budget—Bottles

	January	February	March	First Quarter
Projected production (bottles)	257,500	337,500	455,000	1,050,000
+ Projected ending inventory	67,500	91,000	98,000[1]	98,000
Projected needs	325,000	428,500	553,000	1,148,000
− Projected beginning inventory	51,500[2]	67,500	91,000	51,500
Bottles to be purchased	273,500	361,000	462,000	1,096,500
Projected purchases ($)[3]	$27,350	$36,100	$46,200	$109,650

[1] May sales are projected to be 400,000 bottles so April ending inventory is 40,000 bottles and production for April is projected to be 490,000 bottles. Twenty percent of 490,000 bottles is 98,000.

[2] This is the actual beginning inventory of bottles (given).

[3] Projected bottles times $.10 per bottle.

DIRECT LABOR BUDGET

The **direct labor budget** is one of the easiest budgets to prepare. As with the material purchases budget, the direct labor budget starts with the production budget. However, unlike the material budget, no adjustments need to be made for beginning and ending inventory.

The direct labor budget is prepared by simply multiplying the units to be produced by the number of direct labor hours required to produce each unit. As was discussed earlier, the production process utilizes a worker assigned to each of the five mixing and bottling machines. Each machine (and thus each worker) can process 600 bottles of orange juice per hour. At Tina's Fine Juices, factory workers are paid an average of $15 per hour including fringe benefits and payroll taxes. If the production schedule doesn't allow for full utilization of the workers and machines, the worker is temporarily moved to another department. Dividing the labor rate of $15 by the time required per bottle shows that the amount of direct labor cost per bottle of juice is $.025 ($\frac{\$15}{600}$ bottles). A direct labor budget for the first quarter is as follows:

PAUSE & Reflect

Why are we not concerned with inventories in the direct labor purchases budget?

Direct Labor Budget

	January	February	March	First Quarter
Projected production (bottles)	257,500	337,500	455,000	1,050,000
Direct labor time per 600 bottles	1 hour	1 hour	1 hour	1 hour
Direct labor hours needed for production	429.17 hours (257,500/600)	562.5 hours (337,500/600)	758.33 hours (455,000/600)	1,750 hours (1,050,000/600)
Direct labor rate per hour	$15/hr	$15/hr	$15/hr	$15/hr
Projected direct labor cost	$6,438	$8,438	$11,375	$26,250

MANUFACTURING OVERHEAD BUDGET

Fine Juices

Preparation of the **manufacturing overhead budget** involves estimating overhead costs. As was discussed in detail in Part 1 of this book, estimating overhead can be accomplished in a number of ways using plantwide or departmental predetermined overhead rates or activity-based costing. At Tina's Fine Juices most of the production process is automated, the juice is mixed by machine, and machines do the bottling and packaging. Overhead costs are incurred almost entirely in the mixing and bottling process. Consequently, Tina's has chosen to use a plantwide cost driver (machine hours) to apply manufacturing overhead to products.

However, as you will recall from Chapter 5, not all overhead is expected to behave in the same fashion as production increases and decreases each month. Although variable overhead costs will vary in direct proportion to the number of bottles of juice produced, fixed overhead costs will remain constant regardless of production. For budgeting purposes, Tina's separates variable overhead from fixed overhead and calculates a predetermined overhead rate for variable manufacturing overhead costs.

Tina's Fine Juices has estimated that variable overhead will total $438,000 for the year and that the machines will run approximately 8,000 hours at the projected production volume for the year (4,775,000 bottles). The estimated machine hours are 80 percent of capacity for the five machines. Therefore, Tina's predetermined overhead rate for variable overhead is $54.75 per machine hour ($\frac{\$438,000}{8,000}$ machine hours). Tina's has also estimated fixed overhead to be $1,480,000 per year ($123,333 per month) of which $1,240,000 per year ($103,333 per month) is depreciation on existing property, plant, and equipment.

The manufacturing overhead budget is presented next. Note that variable overhead is budgeted based on the predetermined overhead rate and varies with production each month while fixed manufacturing overhead is budgeted at a constant $123,333 per month.

Manufacturing Overhead Budget

	January	February	March	First Quarter
Budgeted Machine Hours*	429.17	562.5	758.33	1,750
Variable Overhead Rate	$54.75	$54.75	$54.75	$54.75
Projected Variable Overhead	$23,497	$30,797	$41,519	$95,813
Budgeted Fixed Overhead	$123,333	$123,333	$123,333	$370,000
Total Projected Manufacturing Overhead	$146,830	$154,130	$164,852	$465,813

*Budgeted machine hours are the same as budgeted labor hours. Each machine can process 600 bottles of orange juice per hour.

The material purchases budget, the direct labor budget, and the manufacturing overhead budget, are summarized in a total manufacturing cost budget. This budget provides Tina's Fine Juices with an estimate of the total manufacturing costs expected to be incurred in the first quarter of 2000:

Total Manufacturing Cost Budget

	January	February	March	First Quarter
Projected material cost—Concentrate	$41,027	$54,150	$69,300	$164,477
Projected material cost—Bottles	27,350	36,100	46,200	109,650
Projected direct labor cost	6,438	8,438	11,375	26,250
Projected manufacturing overhead cost	146,830	154,130	164,852	465,813
Total projected manufacturing costs	221,645	252,818	291,727	766,189

Note: Table may not foot due to rounding on the accompanying Excel spreadsheet.

CASH BUDGETS

WHY FOCUS ON CASH?

LO5
Prepare cash receipts and disbursements budgets

Many managers consider managing cash flow to be the single most important consideration in running a successful business. After all, cash pays the bills, *not* income. Whereas income (earnings per share) is often important to external investors, cash flow often takes center stage for managers.

IN THE NEWS

In fact, external investors sometimes focus on cash flow as well. Cash flow valuations are now in vogue in the cable, high-tech, Internet, pharmaceutical, and financial-services sectors. Stock analysts sometimes use cash flow to help value companies because it "ignores accounting tricks and thus shows the true economic health of companies" ("Analysts Increasingly Favor Using Cash Flow over Reported Earnings in Stock Valuations," by Elizabeth MacDonald, *Wall Street Journal,* April 1, 1999, C2).

The timing of cash inflows and outflows is critical to the overall planning process. When cash inflows are delayed because of the extension of credit to buyers, there may not be sufficient cash to pay suppliers, creditors, and employee wages. Timely payment is necessary to maintain good business relationships with suppliers (and to keep employees happy) and to take the maximum discounts that may be available on purchases. Cash budgeting forces managers to focus on cash flow and plan for the purchase of materials, the payment of creditors, and the payment of salaries. Sufficient cash must be available to pay dividends to stockholders and to acquire new fixed assets. As can be seen in the following example, cash budgets also point out the need for borrowing cash or when excess cash can be invested or used to repay debt.

THE CASH RECEIPTS BUDGET

The first cash budget that must be prepared is the **cash receipts budget.** The cash receipts budget shows cash receipts that are generated from operating activities—cash sales of inventory or services and customer payments on account. Other cash receipts (from the sale of property, investment income, etc.) are included in the summary cash budget.

TINA'S
Fine Juices

All of the sales of Tina's Fine Juices are on account. Based on their experience in previous years, Tina's estimates that 50 percent of the sales each month will be paid for in the month of sale. They also estimate that 35 percent of the month's sales will be collected in the month following sale and 15 percent of each month's sales will be collected in the second month following sale.[3] A cash receipts budget for cash received from operating activities is presented in the following table. As you will recall from the sales budget, sales for January, February, and March were projected to be $262,500, $341,250, and $472,500, respectively. Since collections lag sales by up to two months (some of November's sales will not be collected until January and some of December's sales will not be collected until February), completing the cash receipts budget also requires that we include sales for November and December. November's sales were $200,000 while December's sales were $250,000.

Cash Receipts Budget—Operating Activities

	CASH RECEIPTS			
	January	February	March	First Quarter
50% of January sales ($262,500)	$131,250			$131,250
35% of December sales ($250,000)	$ 87,500			$ 87,500
15% of November sales($200,000)	$ 30,000			$ 30,000
50% of February sales ($341,250)		$170,625		$170,625
35% of January sales ($262,500)		$ 91,875		$ 91,875
15% of December sales ($250,000)		$ 37,500		$ 37,500
50% of March sales ($472,500)			$236,250	$236,250
35% of February sales ($341,250)			$119,438	$119,438
15% of January sales ($262,500)			$ 39,375	$ 39,375
Totals	$248,750	$300,000	$395,063	$943,812

Note: Table may not foot due to rounding on the accompanying Excel spreadsheet.

The preparation of the cash receipts budget is straightforward once the payment scheme is set. In each month we collect 50 percent of that month's sales (50 percent of January's sales are collected in January), 35 percent of the previous month's sales (35 percent of December's sales are collected in January), and 15 percent of the second previous month's sales (15 percent of November's sales are collected in January). And then the payment scheme is repeated for the remainder of the months in the budget.

An alternative way to look at the cash receipts budget is provided below:

Cash Receipts Budget—Operating Activities

	CASH RECEIPTS			
Sales	January	February	March	First Quarter
November ($200,000)	$ 30,000 (15%)			$ 30,000
December ($250,000)	$ 87,500 (35%)	$ 37,500 (15%)		$125,000
January ($262,500)	$131,250 (50%)	$ 91,875 (35%)	$ 39,375 (15%)	$262,500
February ($341,250)		$170,625 (50%)	$119,438 (35%)	$290,063
March ($472,500)			$236,250 (50%)	$236,250
Totals	$248,750	$300,000	$395,063	$943,812

Note: Table may not foot due to rounding on the accompanying Excel spreadsheet.

---

[3]It would not be unusual for some of the sales to never be collected. If Tina's thinks that some of the accounts receivable are uncollectible, they should adjust the cash receipts budget accordingly.

A closer look at the cash receipts budget shows that budgeted cash receipts are significantly different than budgeted sales revenue. In February and March, cash receipts are expected to be less than sales revenue. When sales are increasing, and there is a lag between sales and the collection of cash, this is usually the case. It seems ironic but businesses that are growing rapidly will often be short of cash. The next component in the cash budgeting process is the **cash disbursements budget.** The cash disbursements budget includes cash outflows resulting from operating activities—payments to suppliers for materials, cash outflows for salaries and other labor costs, and cash outflows for overhead expenditures. Cash disbursements for selling and administrative costs are also included although other cash outflows (for equipment purchases, payment of dividends, etc.) are usually not included.[4] These nonoperating disbursements will be included in the summary cash budget but not in the cash disbursements budget for operating activities.

Budgeting for the cash disbursements related to materials, labor, and overhead is not as easy as just looking at the material, labor, and overhead budgets. Purchases of material are often made on account resulting in lags between the date items are purchased and the date cash actually changes hands. The manufacturing overhead budget often includes noncash items like depreciation that must be adjusted as well.

A cash disbursements budget for Tina's Fine Juices follows. Tina's has a policy of paying 50 percent of the direct materials purchases in the month of purchase and the balance in

Cash Disbursements Budget—Operating Activities

| | CASH DISBURSEMENTS | | | |
	January	February	March	First Quarter
Material purchases: Concentrate				
December	$ 18,220			$ 18,220
January	$ 20,513	$ 20,513		$ 41,025
February		$ 27,075	$ 27,075	$ 54,150
March			$ 34,650	$ 34,650
Material purchases: Bottles				
December	$ 12,146			$ 12,146
January	$ 13,675	$ 13,675		$ 27,350
February		$ 18,050	$ 18,050	$ 36,100
March			$ 23,100	$ 23,100
Total disbursements for material	$ 64,554	$ 79,313	$102,875	$246,741
Total disbursements for direct labor	$ 6,438	$ 8,438	$ 11,375	$ 26,250
Manufacturing overhead: December	$ 20,917			$ 20,917
Manufacturing overhead: January	$ 21,748	$ 21,748		$ 43,497
Manufacturing overhead: February		$ 25,398	$ 25,398	$ 50,797
Manufacturing overhead: March			$ 30,759	$ 30,759
Total disbursements for overhead	$ 42,666	$ 47,147	$ 56,158	$145,971
Total disbursements for selling and administrative costs	$100,000 (given)	$100,000 (given)	$100,000 (given)	$300,000
Total cash disbursements	$213,657	$234,897	$270,408	$718,962

---

[4]A separate budget for selling and administrative expenses (period costs) would likely be prepared by Tina's Fine Juices. It would include both variable selling and administrative expenses like commissions and shipping costs as well as fixed selling and administrative expenses related to advertising, salaries, insurance, rent, depreciation of equipment used in selling and administrative activities, etc. An example of a selling and administrative expense budget for a merchandising company is shown later in the chapter.

Fine Juices

Can you trace each of the amounts in the cash disbursements budget back to the original budget in which it appears?

LO6
Prepare and apply the summary cash budget to decision problems

the month after purchase. This policy offsets to a certain extent the lag in cash receipts from sales. Purchases of direct material are taken directly off of the material purchases budgets (adjusted for the payment lag). All direct labor costs are paid in the month incurred and come directly from the direct labor budget. Manufacturing overhead costs are paid on a lag with 50 percent paid for in the month incurred and 50 percent in the following month. However, the manufacturing overhead budget must be adjusted for depreciation of property, plant, and equipment, which does not have a direct impact on cash flow.[5] As was discussed earlier, of the total budgeted fixed overhead included in the manufacturing overhead budget ($123,333 per month), $103,333 per month pertains to depreciation and will not be included in the cash disbursements budget. Cash disbursements for selling and administrative costs are expected to be $100,000 per month.

A **summary cash budget** consists of three sections, (1) cash flows from operating activities, (2) cash flows from investing activities, and (3) cash flows from financing activities. These three sections are the same as used in the cash flow statement prepared under generally accepted accounting principles. Preparation and use of the statement of cash flows is covered in detail in Chapter 15.

Cash flows from operating activities have already been discussed. Cash flows from investing activities include purchases and sales of property, plant, equipment and other investments, and interest and dividends earned on investment assets. Cash flows from financing activities include payments for the retirement of any debt issued by the company, sales or repurchases of stock, payment of dividends, and any borrowing or repayments of other long-term liabilities.

Summary Cash Budget

	January	February	March	First Quarter
Beginning cash balance	$ 50,000	$ 50,000	$ 50,000	$ 50,000
Cash Flows from Operating Activities:				
Cash receipts	$ 248,750	$ 300,000	$ 395,063	$ 943,812
Cash disbursements	$(213,657)	$(234,898)	$(270,408)	$(718,962)
Income taxes			$ (3,190)[1]	$ (3,190)
Cash Flows from Investing Activities				
Equipment purchases		($ 75,000)		($ 75,000)
Cash Flows from Financing Activities				
Payment of dividends	($ 50,000)			($ 50,000)
Interest on long-term debt			$ (30,000)[2]	$ (30,000)
Cash balance before borrowing/Repayment	$ 35,093	$ 40,102	$ 141,464	$ 116,659
Borrowing from line of credit	$ 14,907[3]	$ 9,898[4]		$ 24,805
Repayments of line of credit			$ (24,805)[5]	$ (24,805)
Interest on line of credit			$ (538)[6]	$ (538)
Final cash balance	$ 50,000	$ 50,000	$ 116,122	$ 116,122

[1]See the Pro-forma Income Statement.
[2]Long-term liabilities (see the Pro-forma Balance Sheet) are $1,500,000. Interest is paid quarterly at an annual rate of 8%. $1,500,000 × 8% × 3/12 = $30,000.
[3]The minimum cash balance at the end of each month is $50,000. $50,000 − $35,093 = $14,907.
[4]The minimum cash balance at the end of each month is $50,000. $50,000 − $40,102 = $9,898.
[5]Since there is excess cash at the end of March, the draws on the line of credit ($14,097 and $9,898) are repaid at the end of March.
[6]The line of credit is borrowed against in January and February and repaid in March. Interest on the line of credit is calculated as $14,907 × 10% × 3/12 + $9,898 × 10% × 2/12.
Note that interest on the repaid amounts is also paid in March.

---

[5]You will recall from Chapter 8 that depreciation can have an indirect impact on cash flow through its impact on income taxes. The impact of income tax is taken into account in the summary cash budget.

Summary cash budgets can be fairly straightforward or very complex depending on the size and complexity of the company. Tina's Fine Juices has a fairly simple summary cash budget (see page 282).

Cash receipts and disbursements from operating activities have already been summarized in the cash receipts and disbursements budgets. Tina's plans to buy some new machinery in February at a cost of $75,000. The company also plans on paying a dividend of $50,000 in January. Tina's also desires to keep a cash balance of at least $50,000 on hand at the end of any month. If the projected cash balance is less than that, a line of credit at Tina's local bank will be used to make up the shortage. If they draw on the line of credit, they are charged an interest rate of 10 percent annually. If the line of credit is used, money is borrowed at the beginning of the month. Repayments are made at the end of months in which there is sufficient excess cash (over $50,000) to pay back the entire line of credit. Last, but not least, Tina's pays estimated income taxes on a quarterly basis (in March, June, September, and December) on the income earned during the respective quarter. Tina's estimates that its total tax liability (federal and state) is around 35 percent of taxable income.

BUDGETED FINANCIAL STATEMENTS

Companies may also desire to prepare budgeted financial statements. These are used both for internal planning purposes and to provide information to external users. For example, a bank might want to examine a pro-forma income statement and balance sheet before lending money to a company. The budgeted financial statements are often called **pro-forma financial statements.**

A pro-forma statement of cost of goods manufactured and cost of goods sold is as follows:

LO7
Prepare budgeted income statements and balance sheets and evaluate the importance of budgeted financial statements for decision making

Pro-forma Cost of Goods Manufactured (Absorption Costing)

	Amount	Where Information Obtained
Beginning inventory—Raw materials	$ 12,873	Material purchases budgets (pp. 276, 277) (1,609 gallons of concentrate × $4.80 per gallon + 51,500 bottles × $.10 per bottle)
Purchases of raw material	274,127	Material purchases budgets (pp. 276, 277)($164,477 + $109,650)
Raw materials available for use	287,000	
Ending inventory—Raw materials	(24,500)	Material purchases budgets (pp. 276, 277) (3,063 gallons × $4.80 per gallon + 98,000 bottles × $.10 per bottle)
Raw material used	262,500	
Direct labor cost	26,250	Direct labor budget (p. 277)
Manufacturing overhead	465,813	Manufacturing overhead budget (p. 278)
Total manufacturing costs	754,563	
Beginning inventory—WIP	—	Assumed to be $0
Ending inventory—WIP	—	Assumed to be $0
Cost of goods manufactured	$754,563	
Beginning inventory—Finished goods	$ 17,966	Production budget (p. 275) (25,000 bottles × $.71864 per bottle (given))
Cost of goods manufactured	754,563	Pro-forma cost of goods manufactured (p. 283)

(continued)

Pro-forma Cost of Goods Sold (Absorption Costing)

Description	Amount	Where Information Obtained
Beginning inventory—Finished goods	$ 17,966	Production budget (p. 275) (25,000 bottles × $.71864 per bottle (given))
Cost of goods manufactured	754,563	Pro-forma cost of goods manufactured (p. 283)
Less: Ending inventory—Finished goods	35,932	Production budget (p. 275) and the pro-forma cost of goods manufactured (50,000 bottles of juice × $754,563 cost of goods manufactured / 1,050,000 bottles produced)
Cost of goods sold	$736,597	

Note that the cost of goods manufactured and the cost of goods sold are calculated using absorption costing. Likewise, the following pro-forma income statement is prepared using the traditional format:

Pro-forma Income Statement (Traditional format)

Description	Amount	Where Information Obtained
Sales revenue	$1,076,250	Sales budget (p. 274)
Cost of goods sold	736,597	Pro-forma cost of goods sold (p. 284)
Gross margin	339,653	
Selling, general, and administrative expenses	300,000	Cash disbursements budget (p. 281)
Operating income	39,653	
Interest expense	30,538	Summary cash budget (pp. 282)
Income (before taxes)	9,116	
Income taxes	3,191	(Income × 35%)
Net Income	5,925	

Note: Table may not foot due to rounding on the accompanying Excel spreadsheet.

Variable costing statements of cost of goods manufactured and cost of goods sold and a contribution format income statement are provided as part of the Chapter 9 template on the disk accompanying the textbook.

Concept Question: The operating income on the contribution margin format income statement (on the template) is $30,844. Why is the income reported under the two methods different?

Concept Answer: As you will recall from Chapter 6, variable costing and absorption costing will result in different levels of operating income when a company's production and sales are different (units produced are greater than units sold or vice versa). In this case, Tina's Fine Juices produces 1,050,000 bottles during the quarter but only sells 1,025,000 bottles. Because production is greater than sales, absorption costing will report higher income than variable costing. Further, the difference in the amount of operating income reported under the two methods ($8,809) is solely a result of treating fixed overhead differently and can be found by multiplying the fixed overhead per unit of production ($\frac{\$370,000}{1,050,000}$ bottles = $.35238 per bottle) by the difference between units produced and units sold (25,000 bottles). 25,000 × $.35238 = $8,809. ■

The pro-forma balance sheet is as follows:

Pro-forma Balance Sheet

Description	Amount	Where Information Obtained
Current Assets		
Cash	$ 116,122	Summary cash budget (p. 282)
Accounts receivable	287,438	Sales budget (p. 274)
		($341,250 × .15 + $472,500 × .50)
Inventory: Direct materials	24,500	Pro-forma cost of goods manufactured (p. 283)
Inventory: Finished goods	35,932	Pro-forma cost of goods sold (p. 284)
Total current assets	463,991	
Fixed assets	5,075,000	$5,000,000 beginning balance (given) and
		summary cash budget (p. 282)
Total assets	5,538,991	
Current Liabilities		
Accounts payable	88,509	Material purchases budgets (pp. 276, 277)
		and manufacturing overhead budget (p. 278)
		($69,300 × .5 + $46,200 × .5 + ($164,852
		− $103,333 × .5))
Line of credit	—	Summary cash budget (p. 282)
Total current liabilities	88,509	
Long-term liabilities	1,500,000	Beginning balance (given)
Total liabilities	1,588,509	
Stockholders Equity		
Common stock	3,500,000	Beginning balance (given)
Retained earnings	450,481	Beginning balance of $494,556 (given) +
		income of $5,925 (pro-forma income
		statement) − dividends paid of $50,000
		(summary cash budget)
Total liabilities and stockholders equity	$5,538,991	

Note: Table may not foot due to rounding on the accompanying Excel spreadsheet.

As you can see, the set of operating budgets (sometimes called the master budget) form an interrelated set of planning tools for managers that are vital for decisions affecting the number of units to produce, the amount of materials to purchase, how many employees to schedule for a particular time period (and when to schedule training, for example), the timing of major acquisitions and sales of equipment, and the overall management of cash. However, what happens when key assumptions change? For example, in mid February, Tina's receives a large new order for juice increasing its budgeted sales to 350,000 bottles. Changing the sales budget changes all of the budgets following it. If prepared by hand, changing assumptions like sales or the price of materials or desired inventory levels would involve a long and tedious revision of each and every succeeding budget. However, when prepared as a template using spreadsheet software, the changes can be made in just a few seconds.

Fine Juices

Concept Question: *Using the Chapter 9 template on the disk accompanying the textbook, what is the impact on ending cash and income of changing February sales to 350,000 bottles?*

Concept Answer: Ending cash increases to $123,511 and income (after tax) is increased to $16,843. ■

Concept Question: What happens to the amounts borrowed and repaid on the summary cash budget if February sales change to 375,000 bottles?

Concept Answer: Interestingly, the amount borrowed in January increases when February sales increase. Why? Because more materials must be purchased and other costs must be incurred in January to meet the increased production schedule for February. Note that the repayment of the line of credit still occurs in March since the cash balance at the end of February is not sufficient to repay the entire loan balance (without reducing the cash balance below $50,000). ■

BUDGETS FOR A MANUFACTURING COMPANY IN A JIT ENVIRONMENT

As we discussed more fully in Chapter 2, the physical flow of goods is streamlined in companies adopting just-in-time (JIT) techniques. Raw materials are immediately placed into production, and all goods are typically finished and shipped out immediately to customers resulting in little raw material, work in process, or finished goods inventory. Just as this process simplified cost flows, budgeting is simplified as well. In JIT companies, production is typically equal to sales so the production budget and sales budget are essentially the same. Materials are purchased for current production, eliminating the need to account for beginning and ending inventories of raw materials. With no beginning or ending inventories of work in process (WIP) or finished goods, the cost of goods manufactured and cost of goods sold are the same and are simply budgeted as the sum of raw materials used in production, direct labor costs incurred, and overhead costs incurred.

BUDGETS FOR MERCHANDISING COMPANIES AND SERVICE COMPANIES

LO8
Understand the importance of financial budgets for merchandising and service companies

The budgeting process for merchandising companies is similar to that of manufacturing companies with a few important differences. Merchandising companies are not involved in manufacturing the goods they sell. A merchandising company buys finished goods from manufacturing companies and sells them to other companies for resale (wholesalers) or to final customers (retailers). Merchandising companies will still produce a sales budget but will not prepare budgets for production, direct material purchases, direct labor, or manufacturing overhead. However, merchandising companies will prepare a purchases budget (for finished goods) based on the projections in the sales budget. In addition, many merchandising companies hold some level of finished goods inventory and will need to estimate desired inventory balances and adjust sales projections accordingly.

In addition, selling and administrative expenses are often carefully budgeted in merchandising companies. A selling and administrative expense budget will include variable expenses like commissions, shipping costs, and some clerical expenses related to order taking and filling. The budget will also include fixed costs such as rent, utilities, insurance, advertising, salaries of clerical workers and administrators, depreciation of property, plant and equipment, and so on. An example of a selling and administrative expense budget for a merchandising company is as follows:

Selling and Administrative Expense Budget

	January	February	March	First Quarter
Commissions	$ 50,000	$ 55,000	$ 45,000	$150,000
Shipping Costs	10,000	12,000	8,000	30,000
Clerical Salaries	15,000	16,000	13,000	44,000
Supplies	2,000	2,100	1,900	6,000
Rent	10,000	10,000	10,000	30,000
Utilities	2,500	2,500	2,500	7,500
Insurance	3,500	3,500	3,500	10,500
Advertising	5,000	5,000	5,000	15,000
Depreciation	20,000	20,000	20,000	60,000
Total	$118,000	$126,100	$108,900	$353,000

The preparation of cash budgets and budgeted financial statements in merchandising companies is similar to that of manufacturing companies. Although the budgeting process for merchandising is a little less complex than manufacturing companies, it is just as important to effective decision making.

Service companies have the same need to budget for effective decision making but once again the budgets needed will differ slightly from those used in manufacturing companies. Service companies will prepare sales budgets and may prepare modified "production" budgets as well. For example, a CPA firm may budget not only for total revenues but the amount of revenue expected to be generated by each type of engagement (tax, audit, etc.), the number of those engagements expected (how many tax returns will be prepared), and the number of labor hours expected to be incurred in each. As a result, the main focus of budgeting for service companies will often be the labor budget. The use of time budgets by service companies is discussed in more detail in a later section on nonmonetary budgets.

Overhead is another important area of concern for service companies. A detailed budget of expected overhead expenditures (rent, utilities, insurance, etc.) is extremely useful in planning for cash outflows.

LIFE CYCLE COSTS, THE VALUE CHAIN, AND BUDGETING

As discussed earlier in the book, a company must consider all the costs incurred throughout a product's life cycle (the value chain) in making production and pricing decisions. This includes costs incurred in product planning (research and development), product design, product testing, actual production, the distribution (sale) of the product, and customer service provided both during and after the sale.

EXHIBIT 9-3 Life Cycle Costing

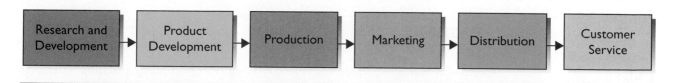

In making decisions to introduce new products, the forecasted sales over the life of the product must exceed its life cycle costs. The product life cycle can be very short (a year or less) in some industries like electronics and computers while in other industries and with other products it can exceed several years. Given that a significant percentage of total costs are incurred before a new product is actually produced and sold, early and accurate budgeting is critically important in making good decisions regarding the introduction of new products.

BUDGETING IN AN INTERNATIONAL ENVIRONMENT

What type of issues might Tina's Fine Juices face if they build a new bottling plant in Brazil?

In today's environment, many companies operate across national borders. Companies may make sales to foreign countries, purchase supplies internationally, manufacture products in other countries, or have foreign branches and subsidiaries. In budgeting, companies with international operations must consider such things as the following:

1. Translating foreign currency into U.S. dollars (and vice versa). Because of constant fluctuations in exchange rates, this can be challenging.

2. Predicting inflation rates (and prices) in countries with unstable economies. This can add a great deal of complexity and uncertainty to the budgeting process.

3. Predicting sales in countries with different consumer preferences.

4. Dealing with different labor laws, social customs, and norms affecting wage rates and the productivity of workers.

Company budgets must allow for volatile currency fluctuations around the globe.

NONMONETARY BUDGETS

LO9
Understand the use and importance of non-financial budgets

Companies may also prepare nonmonetary budgets to help in the planning, operating, and control functions of managers. These budgets are just as important and in some cases may be more important than financial budgets focusing on costs and cash flows.

Examples of nonfinancial budgets are the following:

1. *Time budgets.* In service firms such as CPA firms and law offices, time budgets are used to plan the number of hours expected to be incurred in each engagement (tax return preparation, audit, etc.). This allows firms to better plan the timing of engagements and to utilize employees as efficiently as possible. For example, if a time budget shows that professional staff will not be fully utilized in the summer, continuing education and other training courses might be planned at that time.

2. *Customer satisfaction measures.* Customer satisfaction is an important measure of success for many companies. Consequently, many companies prepare budgets and measure key indicators of customer satisfaction. Although businesses may have many different measures of customer satisfaction, common indicators include the number of returned or defective items, the number of customer complaints, time waiting to be served, and so on.

Can you think of any measures of customer satisfaction that are not mentioned here? How are you affected when you are not satisfied with a purchasing experience?

APPLICATION IN BUSINESS

As the manager of a local restaurant, you have been considering the use of a time budget to focus your staff's attention on "table turns." Table turns are the number of meals served at each table over a specified time period. Some restaurants see this as a very important measure of profitability—the higher number of table turns the higher the profit. However, you are also concerned about the impact of increasing table turns on customer satisfaction. If you rush people from their tables, they are likely to not come back again. How might you balance these conflicting concerns?

STATIC VERSUS FLEXIBLE BUDGETS

Static budgets are budgets that are set at the beginning of the period and remain constant throughout the budget period. The budgets that are presented for Tina's Fine Juices are static budgets. Although static budgets are useful for planning and operating purposes, they can be problematic when used for control. As we discussed in Chapter 1, control involves the motivation and monitoring of employees and the evaluation of people and other resources used in the operations of an organization. The purpose of control is to make sure the goals of the organization are being attained. Control requires the comparison of actual outcomes (cost of products, sales, etc.) with desired outcomes as stated in the organization's operating and strategic plans (including budgets). The idea is to compare budgeted amounts to actual results and then to analyze any differences for likely causes. However, when static budgets are used and actual sales are different from budgeted sales, such a comparison is like comparing apples to oranges. If actual sales differ from projected sales, differences in production, material purchases, labor costs, and variable overhead should be expected. If actual sales are lower than budgeted sales, actual costs of materials, labor, and variable overhead *should* be lower than budgeted costs. The fact that a company's actual costs are lower than those budgeted under static conditions does not necessarily mean that the company (or its employees) spent less or was more efficient than budgeted.

For example, assume that Tina's Fine Juices produces 250,000 bottles of juice in January instead of the budgeted amount of 257,500 bottles. The projected direct labor cost (see direct labor budget on page 277) based on a static budget of 257,500 bottles was

LO10
Prepare flexible budgets and understand how they are used in activity-based costing environments

Fine Juices

$6,438. At the end of January, Tina's had actual direct labor costs of $6,300. So Tina's spent $138 *less* than provided for in the static budget.

	Static Budget	Actual	Difference
Projected production (bottles)	257,500	250,000	
Direct labor time per 600 bottles	1 hour		
Direct labor hours needed for production	429		
Direct labor rate per hour	15		
Projected direct labor cost	$6,438	$6,300	$138

However, the comparison of actual labor costs to make 250,000 bottles with the budgeted labor costs to produce 257,500 bottles really does not make sense. Tina's ought to spend less for labor because fewer bottles were produced. The question becomes, how much less? What we would really like to know is how much the labor costs should have been had we known that production was going to be 250,000 bottles instead of 257,500.

Flexible budgets do just that. Flexible budgets take differences in cost due to volume differences out of the analysis by budgeting for labor (and other costs) based on the *actual* number of units produced.

 Key Concept: *Flexible budgets are based on the* actual *number of units produced rather than the budgeted units of production.*

A flexible direct labor budget for Tina's Fine Juices would budget labor costs based on the actual January production of 250,000 bottles. Based on the labor time needed to produce 600 bottles and the direct labor rate per hour of $15, Tina's projected labor costs would be

$6,250 ($\frac{\$250{,}000}{600}$ bottles per hour = 416.666 hours × $15 per hour) instead of $6,438. If we now compare the actual direct labor cost of $6,300 to the flexible budget amount of $6,250, we see that Tina's actually spent $50 *more* than expected instead of $138 *less* than expected.

	Flexible Budget	Actual	Difference
Projected production (bottles)	250,000	250,000	
Direct labor time per 600 bottles	1 hour		
Direct labor hours needed for production	417		
Direct labor rate per hour	15		
Projected direct labor cost	$6,250	$6,300	$(50)

Why the turnaround? By using flexible budgeting, Tina's removes any differences in cost caused by differences in volume of production and focuses only on differences arising from other factors.

What are those other factors? Perhaps Tina's paid over $15 per hour for labor. However, another explanation is that Tina's used more than 417 labor hours or even some combination of the two. Without further analysis, we simply don't know. In Chapter 10, the use of flexible budgets is expanded to allow managers to break down these differences into variances resulting from either spending too much (or too little) or using too much (or too little). This process is called variance analysis.

ABC AND FLEXIBLE BUDGETS

The use of activity-based costing (ABC) makes flexible budgets even more useful (although a bit more complicated). As we discussed in Chapter 4, companies utilizing ABC to assign costs to products and services identify activities (the procedures and processes that cause work to be accomplished) and the cost drivers associated with those activities. For example, Tina's Fine Juices might identify the movement of materials (orange juice concentrate and bottles) as an activity that consumes resources, and the number of times the material is moved as the driver of the costs incurred. In preparing a flexible budget for manufacturing overhead costs, Tina's would budget costs for moving materials based on the budgeted cost per move and the actual number of moves made during the month. Likewise, Tina's would compute the per-unit budget amounts for other batch-level and product-level costs and include those in the flexible budget along with the regular variable (unit-level) costs and fixed costs. A detailed example of a flexible budget for a company utilizing ABC is provided in Chapter 10 as well.

SUMMARY OF KEY CONCEPTS

- Budgets must start with a top-down strategic plan that guides and integrates the whole company and its individual budgets. (p. 269)
- Budgeting is a management task, not a bookkeeping task. (p. 270)
- Budgets are used throughout the planning, operating, and controlling activities of managers. (p. 271)
- Budgets are future oriented and make extensive use of estimates and forecasts. (p. 273)
- Flexible budgets are based on the *actual* number of units produced rather than the budgeted units of production. (p. 290)

KEY DEFINITIONS

Budgets Plans dealing with the acquisition and use of resources over a specified time period (p. 268)

Zero-based budgeting Requires managers to build budgets from the ground up each year (p. 269)

Planning The cornerstone of good management. Planning involves developing objectives and goals for the organization as well as the actual preparation of budgets. (p. 270)

Operating Involves day-to-day decision making by managers, which is often facilitated by budgeting (p. 270)

Control Involves ensuring that the objectives and goals developed by the organization are being attained; control often involves a comparison of budgets to actual performance and the use of budgets for performance evaluation purposes (p. 270)

Sales forecast Combines with the **sales budget** to form the starting points in the preparation of production budgets for manufacturing companies, purchases budgets for merchandising companies, and labor budgets for service companies (p. 272)

Sales budget Used in planning the cash needs for manufacturing, merchandising, and service companies (p. 272)

Operating budget Used to plan for the short term (typically one year or less) (p. 273)

Production budget Used to forecast how many units of product to produce in order to meet the sales projections (p. 274)

Material purchases budget Used to project the dollar amount raw material purchased for production (p. 275)

Direct labor budget Used to project the dollar amount of direct labor cost needed for production (p. 277)

Manufacturing overhead budget Used to project the dollar amount of manufacturing overhead needed for production (p. 278)

Cash receipts budget Used to project the amount of cash expected to be received from sales and cash collections from customers (p. 279)

Cash disbursements budget Used to project the amount of cash to be disbursed during the budget period (p. 280)

Summary cash budget Consists of three sections: (1) cash flow from operating activities, (2) cash flows from investing activities, and (3) cash flows from financing activities; these three sections are the same as used in the cash flow statement prepared under generally accepted accounting principles (GAAP) (p. 282)

Pro-forma financial statements Budgeted financial statements that are sometimes used for internal planning purposes but more often are used by external users (p. 283)

Static budgets Budgets that are set at the beginning of the period and remain constant throughout the budget period (p. 289)

Flexible budgets Take differences in spending due to volume differences out of the analysis by budgeting for labor (and other costs) based on the *actual* number of units produced (p. 290)

CONCEPT REVIEW

1. Discuss why budgeting is a management task as opposed to a bookkeeping task.

2. Define the term *budgets* and discuss how budgets are used in decision making.

3. Discuss how budgets relate to the operating cycle.

4. Outline, using no amounts, a budget that you might use in budgeting your personal finances.

5. What is the main cause of business failure today? What is one potential safeguard against business failure?

6. Define planning as used in management decision making.

7. Define control as used in management decision making.

8. Compare and contrast planning and control in decision making.

9. What are some advantages of budgeting?

10. What are some of the characteristics of a typical budget?

11. Why is the sales budget the most important piece of the budgeting process?

12. List and describe some of the major factors and information sources typically used in sales forecasting.

13. If you were forecasting revenue for a ski area, what factors might you consider in your decision?

14. If you were forecasting revenues for a CPA firm, what factors might you consider in your decision?

15. If you were forecasting revenues for an airline, what factors might you consider in your decision?

16. Discuss ways that regression analysis might be used to aid the revenue-forecasting task.

17. What type of decisions could management address using the cash receipts budget?

18. What type of decisions could management address using the cash disbursements budget?

19. Why are budgets focused on cash flow?

20. Discuss why financial budgets for merchandising companies are different from those for manufacturing companies.

21. Discuss why financial budgets for service companies are different from those for manufacturing and merchandising companies.

22. Discuss the difference between static and flexible budgets.

23. Discuss how activity-based costing (ABC) impacts the preparation and use of flexible budgets.

24. Give some examples of nonfinancial budgets and how management uses them.

25. Discuss life cycle budgeting. What are the five distinct phases in the life of a product and how does budgeting change over those phases?

26. What types of problems must be considered when budgeting in an international environment?

APPLICATION OF CONCEPTS

27. Ringle Brothers sells pretzels for $1.50 per bag. The marketing department prepared the following first quarter sales forecast:

January	25,000 bags
February	22,000
March	26,000
Total	73,000 bags

Required

   a. What is the sales budget for January?

   b. What is the sales budget for the first quarter?

   c. If the brothers try to maintain 10 percent of the next month's forecasted sales in inventory, what is the projected production for February?

28. Pat's Pacifiers sells pacifiers for $1.25 each. The marketing department prepared the following first quarter sales forecast:

January	125,000
February	135,000
March	170,000
Total	430,000

   Pat tries to maintain 10 percent of the next month's forecasted sales in inventory. January's beginning inventory was 14,000. April sales are expected to be 195,000.

Required

Prepare a sales budget and a production budget for each month of the quarter.

29. Babs' Bicycles produces and sells bicycles. The production manager prepared the following second quarter production forecast:

April	60,000
May	35,000
June	80,000
Total	175,000

   Each bicycle requires two identical tires. Babs tries to maintain 10 percent of the next month's forecasted production needs in inventory. April's beginning inventory was 6,000. July production is expected to be 75,000.

Required

Prepare a purchases budget for each month of the quarter.

30. Greybar Inc. sells plastic baby bottles for $1.25 each. The marketing department prepared the following semiannual sales forecast:

January	150,000
February	125,000
March	180,000
April	165,000
May	165,000
June	155,000
Total	940,000

   Historically, the cash collection of sales has been as follows: 55 percent of sales collected in month of sale, 35 percent of sales collected in month following sale, and 9 percent of sales collected in second month following sale.

Required

Prepare a sales budget for each month and a cash receipts budget for each month of the second quarter (April, May, and June).

31. Granny sells homemade cookies locally for $2.50 per box. Grandpop prepared the following first quarter sales forecast:

January	1,500 boxes
February	1,200
March	1,600
Total	4,300 boxes

For scheduling purposes, Granny and Grandpop try to maintain 10 percent of the next month's forecasted sales in inventory.

Granny and Grandpop expects cash collection of sales to be as follows:

55 percent of sales collected in month of sale,

35 percent of sales collected in month following sale, and

8 percent of sales collected in second month following sale.

Required

A. Prepare a sales budget for the first quarter.

B. Prepare a schedule of cash collections, beginning with January sales.

C. Prepare a production budget for the first quarter. Beginning inventory in January is 150 boxes; April sales are expected to equal 1,100.

32. Clapton Company's sales budget shows the following projections for the year ending December 31, 2000:

Quarter	Guitars
First, 2000	30,000
Second, 2000	40,000
Third, 2000	22,500
Fourth, 2000	27,500
Total	120,000
First, 2001	34,500

Inventory at December 31 of the prior year was budgeted at 6,000 guitars. The quantity of finished goods inventory at the end of each quarter is to equal 20 percent of the next quarter's budgeted unit sales. How much should the production budget show for units to be produced for each quarter in 2000?

33. Abraham Company's sales budget shows the following projections for the year ending December 31, 2000:

Month	Units
January	25,000
February	27,000
March	32,000
April	28,500
May	31,400
June	34,500
July	36,700

Inventory at December 31 of the prior year was budgeted at 6,250 units. The desired quantity of finished goods inventory at the end of each month in 2000 is to be equal to 25 percent of the next month's budgeted unit sales. Prepare a production budget for January through June of 2000.

34. Allen Company's sales budget shows the following projections for the year ending December 31, 2000:

Month	Units
January	10,000
February	17,000
March	13,000
April	18,500
May	22,100
June	24,300
July	26,200

Inventory at December 31 of the prior year was budgeted at 1,500 units. The desired quantity of finished goods inventory at the end of each month in 2000 is to be equal to 15 percent of the next month's budgeted unit sales. Prepare a production budget for January through June of 2000.

Prepare a purchases budget for January.

35. Alvarez Company's sales budget shows the following projections for the year ending December 31, 2000:

Month	Units
January	25,000
February	27,000
March	32,000
April	28,500
May	31,400
June	34,500
July	36,700
August	35,000

Inventory at December 31 of the prior year was budgeted at 6,250 units. The desired quantity of finished goods inventory at the end of each month in 2000 is to be equal to 25 percent of the next month's budgeted unit sales. Each unit of finished product requires three pounds of raw material. The company wants to have 30 percent of next month's required raw material on hand at the end of each month. Prepare production and purchases budgets for January through June of 2000, assuming that each pound of raw material costs $22.

36. Anderson Company's sales budget shows the following projections for the year ending December 31, 2000:

Month	Units
January	10,000
February	17,000
March	13,000
April	18,500
May	22,100
June	24,300
July	26,200
August	27,000

Inventory at December 31 of the prior year was budgeted at 1,500 units. The desired quantity of finished goods inventory at the end of each month in 2000 is to be equal to 15 percent of the next month's budgeted unit sales. Each completed unit of finished product requires 1.5 gallons of raw material. The company has determined that it needs 20 percent of next month's raw material needs on hand at the end of each month. Prepare production and purchases budgets for January through June of 2000, assuming that raw material costs are $10 per gallon.

37. Ash Company's production budget shows the following projections for the period ending June 30:

Month	Units
January	25,000
February	27,000
March	32,000
April	28,500
May	31,400
June	34,500

Each unit of finished product requires 2.5 hours of direct labor. The company applies overhead at the rate of $7 per direct labor hour. Prepare direct labor and overhead budgets for January through June of 2000 assuming that the direct labor rate is $15 per hour.

38. Babcock Builder's production budget shows the following projections for the year ending December 31, 2000:

Month	Units
January	10,000
February	17,000
March	13,000
April	18,500
May	22,100
June	24,300
July	26,200

Each completed unit of finished product requires 3.5 hours of direct labor. Each hour of direct labor is $25. The company applies overhead at the rate of $3 per direct labor hour. Prepare direct labor and overhead budgets for January through June of 2000.

39. Barrera's Outdoor Outfitters' sales budget shows the following projections for the period ending July 31, 2000:

Month	Scarfs
January	25,000
February	27,000
March	32,000
April	28,500
May	31,400
June	34,500
July	36,700

The sales price per scarf is $12. The company estimates that it collects 70 percent of each month's sales in the month of sale and 20 percent the following month. The remaining outstanding sales are collected in the next month. The balance of accounts receivable at December 31, 1999, was $141,600. Of the accounts receivable balance, $33,600 represents uncollected November sales. Prepare a cash receipts budget for January through June of 2000.

40. Baum Company's sales budget shows the following projections for the period ending July 31, 2000:

Month	Units
January	10,000
February	17,000
March	13,000
April	18,500
May	22,100
June	24,300
July	26,200

The average sales price of each unit is $15. The company estimates that it collects 50 percent of each month's sales in the month of sale, with 30 percent being collected in the second month and 15 percent being collected in the third month after sale. The remaining 5 percent is estimated to be bad debt expense. The balance in accounts receivable at December 31,1999, is $180,000 with $135,000 of that balance being from December. Prepare a cash receipts budget for January through June of 2000.

41. Donny's Donuts has requested that you prepare a cash budget for the month of June. The following information has been provided:

a. The beginning cash balance is $10,000

b. The actual sales for April and May and the budgeted sales for June are as follows:

	April	May	June
Cash sales	$16,500	$15,500	$17,500
Sales on account	30,000	40,000	50,000
Total sales	$46,500	$55,500	$67,500

Sales on account are collected over a two-month period with 70 percent being collected in the first month and the remainder being collected in the second month.

c. Inventory purchases will be $35,000 in the month of June. The company pays for inventory purchases in the month following purchase. The balance of May's purchases is $22,000.

d. Selling and administrative expenses are budgeted to be $14,000 for June. Of that amount, 50 percent is depreciation.

e. Equipment costing $14,000 will be purchased in June for cash, and dividends will be paid in the amount of $2,500.

f. The company wants to maintain a minimum cash balance of $10,000 and has set up a line of credit to cover any shortage. If the company must borrow, the loan will be made at the beginning of the month and any repayment will be made at the end of the month of repayment.

Required

A. Prepare a cash receipts budget for June.

B. Prepare a cash disbursements budget for June.

C. Using the preceding budgets, prepare a schedule of any financing needed.

42. Baxter Bagels has requested that you prepare a cash budget for the month of June. The following information has been provided:

The beginning cash balance is $10,000. The budgeted sales for March, April, May, and June are as follows:

	March	April	May	June
Cash sales	$14,000	$16,500	$15,500	$17,500
Sales on account	29,000	30,000	40,000	50,000
Total sales	$43,000	$46,500	$55,500	$67,500

Sales on account are collected over a two-month period with 70 percent being collected in the first month and the remainder being collected in the second month.

Inventory purchases are budgeted to be 60 percent of budgeted sales each month. The company pays for inventory purchases in the month following purchase.

Selling and administrative expenses are budgeted to be 30 percent of each month's sales. Of that amount, 50 percent is depreciation.

Equipment costing $24,000 will be purchased in April for cash, and dividends will be paid in the amount of $12,500 in the same month.

The company wants to maintain a minimum cash balance of $10,000 and has set up a line of credit to cover any shortage. If the company must borrow, the loan will be made at the beginning of the month and any repayment will be made at the end of the month of repayment.

Required

A. Prepare a cash receipts budget for April, May, and June.

B. Prepare a cash disbursements budget for April, May, and June.

C. Using the preceding budgets, prepare a schedule of any financing needed for the months of April, May, and June.

43. The following records from Benson Inc. are provided. Benson Inc. requires a minimum cash balance of $7,000 to start each quarter.

	QUARTER			
	1	**2**	**3**	**4**
Beginning cash balance	$10	$?	$?	$?
Cash collections	?	?	126	80
Total cash available	86	?	?	?
Inventory purchases	41	59	?	33
Operating expenses	?	43	55	?
Equipment purchases	11	9	8	5
Dividends	3	3	3	3
Total disbursements	?	111	?	?
Excess (deficiency) of cash	(4)	?	30	?
Financing:				
Borrowings	?	21	—	—
Repayments*	—	—	(?)	(8)
Total	?	?	?	?
Ending cash balance	$?	$?	$?	$?

* Includes interest.

Fill in the missing amounts.

44. Benzinger Motors is preparing a sales budget for the service department based on last year's actual amounts. Last year's sales amounts are as follows:

	Mechanic Hours	**Total Revenues**
January	1,174	$11,681
February	1,057	10,538
March	1,125	11,261
April	1,516	15,008
May	1,724	16,981
June	2,515	25,014
July	2,746	27,185
August	3,107	30,604
September	2,421	23,823
October	2,211	22,154
November	1,709	17,090
December	1,524	15,164
January 2000	1,495	15,050

Required

A. Compute the average revenue per mechanic hour for 1999.

B. Assuming that sales volume will grow by an average of 10 percent in 2000, prepare a monthly sales budget for 2000.

C. Assuming the average sales price increased by 5 percent, prepare a monthly sales budget for 2000.

D. For the year in total, is it more advantageous to increase sales price or sales volume by 10 percent? Remember the impact of variable and fixed cost on these projections.

45. Dip Em Donuts Inc. had 20,000 pounds of flour on hand at the beginning of the year. The company plans to produce 200,000 boxes of 12 donuts each during the year. Each box of donuts takes half a pound of flour. The company would like to have 10,000 pounds of flour on hand at the end of each year. How many pounds of flour must be purchased during the year to have enough for production needs and the desired ending inventory?

46. Clayton's FunLand Inc. had 14,000 games on hand at the end of the previous year. The company has a policy of maintaining 10 percent of the current year's requirements in ending inventory of any year. During the current year, the company sold 150,000 games. How many games did Clayton's FunLand purchase during the current year?

47. Berger Inc. sold 100,000 video games at $10 each last year. The company anticipates that volume will increase by 25 percent. In addition, the new price for a video game will increase by 20 percent. What are the expected sales revenues for the coming year?

48. Bernys Modems Inc. forecasts sales of 420,000 modems during the coming year. Each modem requires three internal memory chips. The inventory of memory chips at the beginning of the year was 20,000 units. Management desires to maintain an inventory of all parts equal to 10 percent of the current year's usage. How many memory chips must Bernys Modems purchase during the year?

49. Martinez's Ointments is a chemical company that manufactures a very popular ointment used in a variety of cosmetic products. Forecasted sales for the next year are 100,000 pounds of ointment. The beginning finished goods inventory consists of 20,000 pounds. The desired amount for each year's ending inventory is 15,000 units. How many units should be scheduled for production this year?

50. Blanchard Company budgets on an annual basis for its fiscal year. The following beginning and ending inventory levels (in units) are planned for the fiscal year of July 1, 1999, through June 30, 2000:

	July 1, 1999	June 30, 2000
Raw material*	40,000	50,000
Work-in-process	10,000	10,000
Finished goods	80,000	50,000

*Two (2) units of raw material are needed to produce each unit of finished product.

Required

A. If Blanchard Company plans to sell 480,000 units during the 1999–2000 fiscal year, how many units would it have to manufacture during the year?

B. If Blanchard Company were to manufacture 500,000 finished units during the 1999–2000 fiscal year, how many units of raw material would it need to purchase?

51. Bochet Company expects to begin the coming year with 12,000 units of Product X in the inventory of finished goods. It expects to sell 130,000 units of the product and end the year with 15,800 units in finished goods inventory. Five pounds of Material A go into each unit of Product X. The company expects to have 2,000 pounds of Material A on hand at the beginning of the coming year and wishes to end the year with 3,400 pounds in inventory.

Required

A. Calculate the number of units of Product X that the company must manufacture in carrying out these plans.

B. Calculate the number of pounds of Material A the company must purchase during the year.

52. Tina's Fine Juices is a bottler of orange juice located in the Northeast. Tina's produces bottled orange juice from fruit concentrate purchased from suppliers in Florida, Arizona, and California. The only ingredients in the juice are water and concentrate. The juice is blended, pasteurized, and bottled for sale in 12-ounce plastic bottles. The process is heavily automated and is centered on five machines that control the mixing and bottling of the juice. Each machine is run by one employee and can process 10 bottles of juice per minute or 600 bottles per hour. The amount of labor required is very small per bottle of juice. The average worker can process 10 bottles of juice per minute or 600 bottles per hour. The juice is sold by a number of grocery stores under their store brand name and in smaller restaurants, delis, and bagel shops under the name of Tina's Fine Juices. Tina's has been in business for several years and uses a sophisticated sales forecasting model based on prior sales, expected changes in demand, and economic factors affecting the industry. Sales of juice are highly seasonal, peaking in the first quarter of the year.

Forecasted sales for 2001 are as follows:

Sales Forecast

November, 2000	375,000 bottles
December, 2000	370,000
January	350,000
February	425,000
March	400,000
April	395,000
May	375,000
June	350,000
July	375,000
August	385,000
September	395,000
October	405,000
November	400,000
December	365,000

Other information:

1. Tina's sells the juice for $1.05 per 12-ounce bottle, in cartons of 50 bottles.

2. Tina's Fine Juices tries to maintain at least 10 percent of the next month's sales forecast in inventory at the end of each month.

3. Tina's Fine Juices needs to prepare two purchases budgets—one for the concentrate used in its orange juice and one for the bottles that are purchased from an outside supplier. Tina's has determined that it takes one gallon of orange concentrate for every 32 bottles of finished product. Each gallon of concentrate costs $4.80. Tina's also requires 20 percent of next month's direct material needs to be on hand at the end of the budget period. Bottles can be purchased from an outside supplier for $.10 each.

4. At Tina's Fine Juices, factory workers are paid an average of $15 per hour including fringe benefits and payroll taxes. If the production schedule doesn't allow for full utilization of the workers and machines, the worker is temporarily moved to another department.

5. At Tina's Fine Juices most of the production process is automated, the juice is mixed by machine, and machines do the bottling and packaging. Overhead

costs are incurred almost entirely in the mixing and bottling process. Consequently, Tina's has chosen to use a plantwide cost driver (machine hours) to apply manufacturing overhead to products.

6. Although variable overhead costs will vary in direct proportion to the number of bottles of juice produced, fixed overhead costs will remain constant regardless of production. For budgeting purposes, Tina's separates variable overhead from fixed overhead and calculates a predetermined overhead rate for variable manufacturing overhead costs.

7. Tina's Fine Juices has estimated that variable overhead will total $438,000 for the year and that the machines will run approximately 8,000 hours at the projected production volume for the year (4,775,000 bottles). The estimated machine hours are 80 percent of capacity for the five machines. Therefore, Tina's predetermined overhead rate for variable overhead is $54.75 per machine hour ($\frac{\$438,000}{8,000}$ machine hours). Tina's has also estimated fixed overhead to be $1,480,000 per year ($123,333 per month) of which $1,240,000 per year ($103,333 per month) is depreciation on existing property, plant, and equipment.

8. All of the sales of Tina's Fine Juices are on account. Based on the company's experience in previous years, Tina's estimates that 50 percent of the sales each month will be paid for in the month of sale. The company also estimates that 35 percent of the month's sales will be collected in the month following sale and 15 percent of each month's sales will be collected in the second month following sale.

9. Tina's has a policy of paying 50 percent of the direct materials purchases in the month of purchase and the balance in the month after purchase.

10. Tina's plans to buy some new machinery in February at a cost of $75,000. The equipment will have a useful life of 10 years and uses straight-line depreciation. The company also plans on paying a dividend of $50,000 in January. Tina's also desires to keep a cash balance of at least $50,000 on hand at the end of any month. If the projected cash balance is less than that, a line of credit at First National Bank will be used to make up the shortage. If the company draws on the line of credit, Tina's is charged an interest rate of 10 percent annually. If the line of credit is used, money is borrowed at the beginning of the month. Repayments are made at the end of months in which there is sufficient excess cash (over $50,000) to pay back the entire line of credit. Last, but not least, Tina's pays estimated income taxes on a quarterly basis (in March, June, September, and December) on the income earned during the respective quarter. Tina's estimates that its total tax liability (federal and state) is around 35 percent of taxable income.

Required

A. Prepare a sales budget for 2001.

B. Prepare a production budget for 2001.

C. Prepare a purchases budget for 2001.

D. Prepare a direct labor budget for 2001.

E. Prepare an overhead budget for 2001.

F. Prepare cash receipts and disbursements budgets for 2001.

G. Prepare a summary cash budget for 2001.

H. Prepare a pro-forma income statement for 2001.

Big Al's Pizza Inc. needs a cash budget for Year 3 and has provided you with the following information. Sales are all on account and are estimated to be collected over a three month period with 70 percent collected in the month of sale, 25 percent collected the next month and 4 percent collected the third month. The remaining 1 percent is estimated to not be collectible. December and November sales from the previous year were $201,638 and $185,000, respectively.

Because of the lag in collecting cash from sales on account, Big Al's delays payment on some of their purchases of materials. They estimate that 60 percent of each month's material purchases are paid in the month of purchase and 40 percent in the following month. The accounts payable balance for materials at the end of the previous year was $20,000.

Big Al's also requires a minimum balance of $50,000 in cash at the end of each month. They will use their line of credit when needed to bring the balance up to that minimum level. If they are required to borrow money, the interest rate is 10 percent compounded annually. For simplicity, you can assume that cash is borrowed on the first day of the month and that loan repayments are made at the end of the month.

Big Al's plans to exercise the option on the leased production equipment in March (as described in Chapter 2).

The purchase price on the equipment will be $153,450 with payments of $3,260.36 per month. Big Al's also plans on expanding the existing production space in May at a cost of $500,000. They want to finance the expansion out of current earnings so will use the line of credit if they are short of cash in May. The expansion will cause fixed manufacturing overhead to increase by $10,000 per month starting in May.

Required

A. Prepare a cash receipts budget for Year 3 assuming estimated sales of 385,000 meat pizzas and 30,000 veggie pizzas and the following monthly distribution of sales. Assume sales prices as calculated in Chapter 6.

January	8.3%	July	8.5%
February	9.2	August	9.8
March	10.3	September	7.5
April	7.6	October	9.1
May	8.0	November	7.2
June	6.9	December	7.6

B. Prepare a cash disbursements budget for the year.

C. Prepare a summary cash budget for the year showing any borrowing and repayment of debt with interest.

Chapter 10

THE USE OF BUDGETS FOR COST CONTROL AND PERFORMANCE EVALUATION

Study Tools

A Review of the Previous Chapter
In Chapter 9, we introduced the concept of budgeting and discussed how budgets assist managers in planning and decision making.

A Preview of This Chapter
In this chapter we expand the discussion of flexible budgeting and introduce the concept of standard costs and variance analysis as tools to help managers "manage by exception" and evaluate performance in their control function.

Key concepts include:
- The purpose of the control function in management is to make sure that the goals of the organization are being attained.
- Management by exception is the key to effective variance analysis and involves taking action only when actual results deviate significantly from planned.
- The flexible budgeting process removes any differences or variances due only to variations in volume.
- "Favorable" and "unfavorable" designations for variances do not always refer to "good" or "bad."
- The variable overhead efficiency variance does not measure the efficient use of overhead but rather the efficient use of the cost driver or overhead allocation base used in the flexible budget.
- Total over- or underapplied overhead is the sum of the four overhead variances.
- The fixed overhead volume variance should not be interpreted as favorable or unfavorable or as a measure of the efficient utilization of facilities.
- The advantages of variance analysis for overhead costs are enhanced in companies using activity-based costing.

A Preview of Upcoming Chapters
In Chapter 11, we discuss financial measures of per-

LEARNING OBJECTIVES

After studying the material in this chapter, you should be able to:

LO 1 Apply and use standard costing in variance analysis

LO 2 Understand how managers use flexible budgets to help control operations and evaluate performance

LO 3 Compute and analyze the flexible budget variance

LO 4 Analyze the flexible budget variance using the sales volume variance, cost variances related to direct material, direct labor, variable and fixed overhead, and selling and administrative variances

LO 5 Compute and interpret price and usage variances for material and labor

LO 6 Compute and interpret variable and fixed manufacturing overhead variances

LO 7 Evaluate the impact of activity-based costing systems on flexible budgets

LO 8 Analyze important considerations in using and interpreting variances including the concept of management by exception

LO 9 Evaluate behavioral considerations in using standard costing and variance analysis

formance and other tools for cost control and performance evaluation in a decentralized environment. Nonfinancial performance measures are discussed in more detail in Chapter 12.

In Chapter 9, the use of budgets for planning and decision making was discussed. We focused on the preparation of operating budgets beginning with the sales budget and ending with budgeted financial statements. Special emphasis was placed on the use of budgeting in cash planning and the use of operating budgets to plan production, material purchases and use, and labor requirements. We also introduced the concept of flexible budgets and their use as a control and evaluation mechanism. In this chapter, we expand the discussion of flexible budgeting and introduce the concept of standard costs and variance analysis as tools to help managers "manage by exception" and evaluate performance in their control function. We also demonstrate the calculation of variances for direct material, direct labor, variable overhead, and fixed overhead and discuss the use of variance analysis for selling and administrative costs. The chapter ends with a discussion of variance analysis in an ABC environment, the limitations of standard costing and variance analysis, and behavioral considerations. ■

INTRODUCTION

As discussed in the previous chapter, budgeting is a tool that managers use to plan and make decisions. In this chapter, we expand our discussion of budgeting to include its use as a control tool. **Control** involves the motivation and monitoring of employees and the evaluation of people and other resources used in the operations of the organization. The purpose of control is to make sure the goals of the organization are being attained. It includes the use of incentives and other rewards to motivate employees to accomplish an organization's goals and mechanisms to detect and correct deviations from those goals.

 Key Concept: *The purpose of the control function in management is to make sure that the goals of the organization are being attained.*

A control mechanism is a little like a thermostat in your house. If you desire to keep your house at 70 degrees (the budgeted temperature), the thermostat constantly measures the actual temperature in the room and compares the actual temperature to the budgeted temperature. If the actual temperature deviates from 70 degrees, the thermostat will signal the heating system to come on (if the actual temperature is less than 70 degrees) or will turn on the air conditioning (if the temperature is above 70 degrees). Managers need a similar type of control system to control budgetary differences.

In business, control often involves the comparison of actual outcomes (cost of products, units sold, sales prices, etc.) with desired outcomes as stated in the organizations' operating and strategic plans. Control decisions include questions of how to evaluate performance, what measures to use, and what type of incentives to use. At the end of an accounting period (month, quarter, year, etc.), managers can use the budget as a control tool by comparing budgeted sales, budgeted production, and budgeted manufacturing costs with actual sales, production, and manufacturing costs. These comparisons are typically made through a process called **variance analysis.** Variance analysis allows managers to see whether sales, production, and manufacturing costs are higher or lower than planned and, more important, *why* actual sales, production, and costs differ from those budgeted.

The key to effective variance analysis is **management by exception.** Management by exception is the process of taking action only when actual results deviate significantly from planned. The key term in this definition is *significant.* Managers typically don't have the time to investigate every deviation from budget (nor would such investigations likely add value to the organization) so they tend to focus on material or significant differences. This allows managers to focus their energy where they are needed and where they are likely to make a difference. The concept of materiality and its use in variance analysis is discussed in more depth later in the chapter.

 Key Concept: *Management by exception is the key to effective variance analysis and involves taking action only when actual results deviate significantly from planned.*

STANDARD COSTING

LOI
Apply and use standard costing in variance analysis

To facilitate the use of flexible budgeting for control purposes, it is useful to examine the budget at a micro level rather than a macro level—that is, to develop a budget for a single unit of a product or service rather than for the company as a whole. A budget for a single unit of a product or service is known as its **standard cost.** Just as the cost of a product consists of three components—direct materials, direct labor, and manufacturing overhead—a standard cost will be developed for each component. In addition, each component consists of two separate standards—a standard quantity and a standard price. The **standard quantity** tells us the budgeted *amount* of material, labor, and overhead in a product, whereas the **standard price** tells us the budgeted *price* of the material, labor, or overhead for each unit (gallon, hour, etc.).

Standards can be determined in a couple of different ways. Management can analyze historical cost and production data to determine how much material and labor was used in each unit of product and how much the material and labor cost. Likewise, management can look at historical data to determine the amount of overhead costs incurred in the past in producing a certain number of units. For companies with a long history of producing the same product, historical data can be very useful in forecasting future prices and quantities. However, historical data must be used with caution and adjusted when necessary. For example, changes in product design or manufacturing processes can dramatically change both the amounts and prices of materials, labor, and overhead.

Another method of setting standards is called **task analysis.** Task analysis examines the production process in detail with an emphasis on determining what it *should* cost to produce a product, not what it cost last year. Task analysis typically involves the use of engineers who perform time and motion studies to determine how much material should be used in a product, how long it takes to perform certain labor tasks in manufacturing the product, how much electricity is consumed, and so on. Typically some combination of task analysis and historical cost analysis will be used in determining standard costs.

IN THE NEWS	www.ups.com

Fifteen years ago, United Parcel Service (UPS) went so far as to develop standards for how fast drivers should walk to a customer's door (three feet per second) and how long it should take to handle a customer's package ("Up to Speed: United Parcel Service Gets Deliveries Done by Driving Its Workers," *Wall Street Journal,* April 22, 1986).

IDEAL VERSUS PRACTICAL STANDARDS

Because standard costs are used to evaluate performance, human behavior can influence how the standards are determined. Should standards be set so they are easy to attain or set so they can rarely be attained? An **ideal standard** is one that is attained only when near-perfect conditions are present. An ideal standard assumes that every aspect of the production process, from purchasing through shipment, is at peak efficiency. Some managers like ideal standards because they believe that employees will be motivated to achieve more when the goals are set very high. Others would argue that employees are discouraged by standards that are not attainable. Employees may be motivated to cut corners, use less than optimum material, or skimp on labor to achieve the standards. This type of behavior can lead to poor quality and an increase in defective units produced, which may cost the company more in the long run.

Practical standards should be attainable under normal, efficient operating conditions. Practical standards take into consideration that machines break down occasionally, that employees are not always perfect, that waste in materials does occur. Most managers would agree that practical standards would encourage employees to be more positive and productive.

How do you think you would react to being evaluated using ideal standards? Practical standards?

USE OF STANDARDS BY NONMANUFACTURING ORGANIZATIONS

The use of standard costing applies to merchandising and service organizations as well. Just as Panasonic needs to determine how much it should cost to make a telephone, an automobile dealership needs to know how much it should cost to sell a car, the city of Atlanta needs to know how much it should cost to provide garbage pickup to a residence,

The estimated cost of providing an education to a student at a typical state university has been estimated to exceed $30,000 per year. However, in-state tuition at most public universities rarely exceeds $3,000 to $5,000 per year. Who is paying the rest of the cost?

and North Carolina State University needs to determine how much it should cost to provide an education to an incoming student. CPA firms have standards for the amount of time needed to prepare certain types of tax forms or returns, auto repair shops have standards for the time needed to make each repair, and airlines have standards for on-time departures. The use of standards is very common in all types of businesses.[1]

APPLICATION IN BUSINESS

Some managed health care companies have gone so far as to develop a standard amount of time for doctors seeing patients for particular ailments. For example, an initial office visit might have a standard time of 20 minutes, whereas a full physical for a patient might have a standard time of 45 minutes.

FLEXIBLE BUDGETING WITH STANDARD COSTS

LO2

Understand how managers use flexible budgets to help control operations and evaluate performance

Corinne's

Country Rockers

In Chapter 9, we introduced the concept of flexible budgeting based on the actual volume of production rather than the planned level of production. Flexible budgets based on standard costs are the centerpiece of effective variance analysis.

To illustrate the concept of flexible budgets, consider the case of Corinne's Country Rockers. Corinne's builds a high-quality rocking chair with a reputation for lasting a lifetime. They also use a unique (and patented) rocking mechanism not found on other rockers. The chairs are sold directly by Corinne's through mail order and the Internet and have a retail price of $250 each. Corinne's produces each chair to order and has the capacity to produce 600 chairs per month. The standard quantity, standard price, and standard cost of direct material, direct labor, and variable overhead in each chair is summarized as follows. Estimated variable selling and administrative costs (per unit) and total fixed overhead and fixed selling and administrative costs are also provided.

Standard Costs for Corinne's Country Rockers

	Standard Quantity	Standard Price	Standard Cost
Direct material	20 linear feet of oak	$2 per foot	$ 40
Direct labor	5 labor hours	12 per hour	60
Variable overhead	5 labor hours	3 per hour	15
Total variable production costs			$ 115
Variable selling and administrative costs			25
Total variable costs			$ 140
Fixed overhead ($5,000 per month or $15,000 per quarter)			$15,000
Fixed selling and administrative costs			
($6,000 per month or $18,000 per quarter)			18,000
Total fixed costs			$33,000

---

[1]Companies also use standard costs to price products and services. For example, a CPA firm may use its budget for the time normally needed to prepare a variety of schedules on a tax return to compute the price of the tax return. Likewise, auto repair shops may use the amount of time budgeted for each type of repair to determine a price for the repair service.

A static budget based on estimated production and sales of 1,500 chairs is provided in the following table. In addition, a flexible budget based on the actual production and sale of 1,600 rockers is provided.

Corinne's Country Rockers
Comparison of Budget to Actual (Quarter 1, 2000)

	Static Budget	Flexible Budget	Actual Results
Units sold	1,500	1,600	1,600
Units produced	1,500	1,600	1,600
Sales revenue	$375,000	$400,000	$396,800
− Variable manufacturing costs	172,500	184,000	189,200
− Variable selling and administrative	37,500	40,000	40,800
= Contribution margin	165,000	176,000	166,800
− Fixed manufacturing costs	15,000	15,000	16,000
− Fixed selling and administrative costs	18,000	18,000	16,000
= Operating income	$132,000	$143,000	$134,800

As you can see, the actual operating income for Corinne's is somewhere in the middle of that predicted by the static budget and the flexible budget. What does that mean? Unfortunately, not much! It means that Corinne's earned more than budgeted at the beginning of the year. But remember the static budget was based on expected production and sales of 1,500 units. Corinne's ended up producing and selling 1,600 units. Comparing the static budget to the actual results is like comparing apples with oranges. It just does not make sense!

It can be useful to compare the static budget to the flexible budget. Differences in the static budget and the flexible budget are solely a result of differences in budgeted production and sales and actual production and sales. The sales volume variance is the difference between the operating income of $132,000 (based on the static budget) and the operating income of $143,000 (based on the flexible budget). Note that this $11,000 difference in operating income is the same as the $11,000 difference in contribution margin.

Concept Question: *Why is the difference between the static budget and flexible budget contribution margin the same as the difference between the static budget and flexible budget operating income?*

Concept Answer: *Because budgeted fixed costs are the same in a static and flexible budget, differences in contribution margin are directly reflected as differences in income.* ■

SALES VOLUME VARIANCE

The **sales volume variance** is computed by taking the difference between the actual sales volume used in the flexible budget and the budgeted sales volume and multiplying that difference by the budgeted contribution margin per unit.

LO3
Compute and analyze the flexible budget variance

$$\text{Sales Volume Variance} =$$
$$(\text{Actual} - \text{Budgeted sales volume}) \times (\text{Budgeted contribution margin per unit})$$

Corinne's Country Rockers

The sales volume variance for Corinne's is as follows:

(Actual − Budgeted sales volume) × (Budgeted contribution margin per unit)
(1,600 − 1,500) × $110 = $11,000

This variance is obviously a result of actual sales used for the flexible budget exceeding the budgeted sales used for the static budget. However, beyond that it is not particularly informative. We don't know *why* actual sales were greater than budgeted. A reduction in sales price, a change in advertising strategy, or simply a downturn in demand may have caused it.

Corinne's Country Rockers
The Sales Volume (Activity) Variance (Quarter 1, 2000)

	Static Budget	Sales Volume (Activity) Variance	Flexible Budget
Units sold	1,500		1,600
Units produced	1,500		1,600
Sales revenue	$375,000	$25,000	$400,000
− Variable manufacturing costs	172,500	11,500	184,000
− Variable selling and administrative	37,500	2,500	40,000
= Contribution margin	165,000	11,000	176,000
− Fixed manufacturing costs	15,000		15,000
− Fixed selling and administrative costs	18,000		18,000
= Operating income	$132,000	$11,000	$143,000

Comparing the flexible budget amounts with the actual results is more meaningful. Remember that the flexible budget was calculated based on the actual production and sales

Corinne's Country Rockers
The Flexible Budget Variance (Quarter 1, 2000)

	Flexible Budget	Flexible Budget Variance	Actual Results
Units sold	1,600		1,600
Average sales price per unit	$ 250		$ 248
Units produced	1,600		1,600
Sales revenue	$400,000	$3,200 under	$396,800
− Variable manufacturing costs	184,000	5,200 over	189,200
− Variable selling and administrative	40,000	800 over	40,800
= Contribution margin	176,000	9,200 under	166,800
− Fixed manufacturing costs	15,000	1,000 over	16,000
− Fixed selling and administrative costs	18,000	2,000 under	16,000
= Operating income	$143,000	**$8,200 under**	$134,800

of 1,600 units. It represents the amount of revenue and cost that Corinne's expected to incur during the first quarter for the actual number of units produced and sold. The difference between the flexible budget operating income and actual operating income is called the **flexible budget variance.** As shown in the preceding table, the flexible budget variance for Corinne's is $8,200.

As we mentioned in Chapter 9, the flexible budget removes any differences due to volume. However, we still don't have much information concerning exactly *why* operating income is $8,200 below budget. It appears to be caused by a combination of factors—sales are $3,200 below budget and variable manufacturing and selling and administrative costs are $6,000 over budget (resulting in contribution margin that is $9,200 below budget). Fixed manufacturing costs are $1,000 over budget and fixed selling and administrative costs are $2,000 under budget.

 Key Concept: *The flexible budgeting process removes any differences or variances due only to variations in volume.*

Now the question becomes, why didn't Corinne's reach the sales dollar budget? Once we have eliminated the volume component of the variance, the only explanation is that the average sales price of $248 $\left(\frac{\$396,800}{1,600 \text{ units}}\right)$ was lower than budgeted sales price of $250 $\left(\frac{\$400,000}{1,600 \text{ units}}\right)$.

SALES PRICE VARIANCE

The **sales price variance** is computed by comparing the actual sales price to the flexible budget sales price and multiplying that amount by the actual sales volume.

> Sales price variance = (Actual − Expected sales price) × Actual volume

Plugging in the numbers for Corinne's, the sales price variance is as follows:

> ($248 − $250) × 1,600 = −$3,200

LO4
Analyze the flexible budget variance using the sales volume variance, cost variances related to direct material, direct labor, variable and fixed overhead, and selling and administrative variances

The sales price variance can direct management's attention to a potential problem area. However, at this point, it is difficult to tell if the unfavorable variance is the result of reducing the sales price of all rockers by $2 or perhaps the result of accepting a special order of 100 rockers at a price of $218 per chair. The variance simply points out that the actual sales price is different from the budgeted sales price. Management should investigate it further to determine its cause.

VARIABLE MANUFACTURING COST VARIANCES

While the flexible budget variance shows us that actual variable manufacturing costs were $5,200 higher than budgeted, determining the true cause of that variance is a little more difficult. Did Corinne's spend too much on material or use too much? Did the company incur more labor costs than usual due to paying a higher wage or did it spend more time making each chair than budgeted? Did Corinne's spend more than budgeted on electricity, supplies, and other variable overhead or use more than budgeted? We simply don't know. In fact, the real reason may be a combination of any or all of the above.

To analyze the variable cost variances based on a flexible budget, we must step back and examine the flexible budget in more detail. Based on the standard cost information provided on page 308, the flexible budget for variable manufacturing costs is shown in the following table. More detail concerning the actual variable overhead costs of $189,200 is also provided.

Corinne's Country Rockers
Variable Manufacturing Cost Budget

	Flexible Budget	Actual Costs	Flexible Budget Variance
Direct material	64,000[1]	63,840[4]	160 F
Direct labor	96,000[2]	101,640[5]	5,640 U
Variable overhead	24,000[3]	23,720[6]	280 F
Total variable manufacturing costs	184,000	189,200	5,200 U

[1]Flexible budget for direct materials = (20 feet per unit × 1,600 units) × $2 per unit = $64,000
[2]Flexible budget for direct labor = (5 hours per unit × 1,600 units) × $12 per hour = $96,000
[3]Flexible budget for variable overhead = (5 hours per unit × 1,600 units) × $3 per unit = $24,000
[4]33,600 feet × $1.90 per foot = $63,840
[5]8,400 hours × $12.10 per hour = $101,640
[6]Actual variable overhead costs consist of the variable portion of utilities ($16,390), shop supplies and indirect materials ($4,140), and repairs and maintenance ($3,190).

The total variance for variable manufacturing costs is $5,200. Note that this is the same as the flexible budget variance for variable manufacturing costs shown on page 310. Because actual costs are greater than budgeted, this variance is treated as "unfavorable" (indicated by a "U" following the amount in the last column of the table). Even though Corinne's actual expenditures for total variable production costs were greater than budgeted, Corinne's spent slightly less than the amount budgeted for direct materials and variable overhead but much more for direct labor.

Because actual costs for direct materials are less than the flexible budget amount, the $160 difference is "favorable." As you will see later in the chapter, "favorable" should not necessarily be confused with "good." Although it is useful to know that we spent less than budgeted for direct material, this type of analysis still does not tell us *why* Corinne's spent less. Did the company use less lumber than budgeted or pay less for each foot? To fully utilize the available information, we need to break down the total direct material variance presented earlier into its components and calculate both price and usage (quantity) variances.

 Key Concept: *"Favorable" and "unfavorable" designations for variances do not always refer to "good" or "bad."*

We can examine the direct labor variance in the same way. Because actual labor costs are greater than the flexible budget amount, the variance is unfavorable. However, once again we don't really know *why* Corinne's spent more than budgeted. It could be because the company used more labor hours than budgeted or paid more for each hour of labor or some combination of the two. In addition, as with favorable variances, unfavorable variances are not necessarily "bad." Further analysis is necessary to break down the total labor variance into its price and usage components and to fully understand the cause of the variances.

Analyzing variable overhead is much like analyzing direct material and direct labor. Of course, direct material and direct labor are also variable costs. Although we know that Corinne's spent less on variable overhead than budgeted (the variance is favorable), we do not know whether the price paid for electricity, supplies, and other variable overhead was less than budgeted or whether Corinne's used less.

As you will recall, rather than budget each individual item, we prepared the flexible budget in Chapter 9 by combining all variable overhead costs and budgeting these separately from fixed overhead costs. The flexible budget for variable overhead for Corinne's was prepared by multiplying the predetermined overhead rate of $3 per direct labor hour by the number of direct labor hours expected to be incurred in producing 1,600 units (8,000 hours).

Unfortunately, although traditional variance analysis of variable overhead can help provide answers to questions about whether a company spent more or less or used more or less in total, it does not provide us with information concerning the components of overhead. In other words, traditional analysis does not tell us if we spent more than budgeted on electricity or supplies, just that the overall amount of spending was higher than budgeted. Companies adopting activity-based costing to allocate overhead to products can extend variance analysis to look at the overhead costs associated with each activity and its associated cost driver. This provides much more detailed information than provided by traditional variance analysis. The analysis of overhead variances for companies using ABC is discussed in more detail later in the chapter.

A MODEL FOR VARIANCE ANALYSIS

The next step in variance analysis is to break down the direct material, direct labor, and variable overhead variances into their components (a price variance and a usage or quantity variance) using the basic variance model shown here:

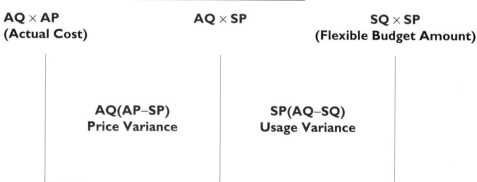

Basic Variance Analysis Model

AQ × AP
(Actual Cost)

AQ × SP

SQ × SP
(Flexible Budget Amount)

AQ(AP–SP)
Price Variance

SP(AQ–SQ)
Usage Variance

AQ = Actual Quantity, or Actual Hours; AP = Actual Price or Actual Rate
SP = Standard Price or Standard Rate; SQ = Standard Quantity or Standard Hours

Usage variance = Standard price(SP) × [Actual quantity(AQ) − Standard quantity (SQ)]
Price variance = Actual quantity(AQ) × [Actual price (AP) − Standard price(SP)]

Whereas AQ, AP, and SP are self-explanatory, the calculation of SQ needs to be elaborated a little. In Chapter 9, the flexible budget was prepared based on the cost that should have been incurred to manufacture the actual number of units produced. SQ is a similar concept. It is the standard (budgeted) quantity of material or number of hours that should be incurred for the actual level of production. As you can see, the **material price variance** is the difference between the actual quantity multiplied by the actual price (AQ × AP) and the actual quantity multiplied by the standard price (AQ × SP). Simplifying, (AQ × AP) − (AQ × SP) = AQ(AP − SP). The price variance is simply the difference in price multiplied by the actual quantity. Likewise, the **usage variance** is the difference between the actual quantity multiplied by the standard price (AQ × SP) and the standard quantity multiplied by the standard price (SQ × SP). Simplifying, (AQ × SP) − (SQ × SP) = SP(AQ − SQ). The usage variance is simply the difference in quantity multiplied by the standard price. The variance model separates the overall flexible budget variance (AQ × AP) − (SQ × SP) into two components—one the result of paying more or less than budgeted and the other the result of using more or less than budgeted.

DIRECT MATERIAL VARIANCES

LO5
Compute and interpret price and usage variances for material and labor

Using the standard cost data for Corinne's Country Rockers provided on page 308 and the breakdown of actual direct material costs shown on page 312, direct material variances are calculated as shown here:

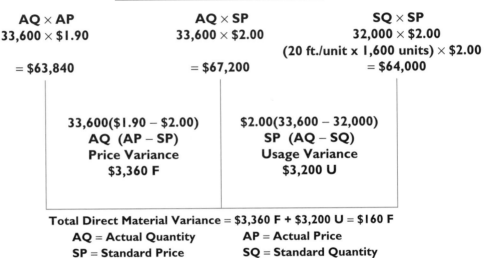

Analysis of Direct Material Variances

AQ × AP	AQ × SP	SQ × SP
33,600 × $1.90	33,600 × $2.00	32,000 × $2.00
		(20 ft./unit x 1,600 units) × $2.00
= $63,840	= $67,200	= $64,000

33,600($1.90 − $2.00)	$2.00(33,600 − 32,000)
AQ (AP − SP)	SP (AQ − SQ)
Price Variance	Usage Variance
$3,360 F	$3,200 U

Total Direct Material Variance = $3,360 F + $3,200 U = $160 F

AQ = Actual Quantity   AP = Actual Price
SP = Standard Price   SQ = Standard Quantity

The price variance is calculated by multiplying the actual amount of material purchased (33,600 feet) by the difference in the actual price paid per foot ($1.90) and the standard or budgeted price per foot ($2.00). This variance of $3,360 is considered favorable because the actual price was less than the budgeted price.

The usage variance for direct materials is found by multiplying the standard price by the difference in the actual quantity used and standard quantity allowed. Remember that the standard quantity allowed is the amount of direct material that *should* have been used to produce the actual output (the flexible budget amount). In this case, the budget for materials is 20 feet of lumber per chair. Corinne's actually produced 1,600 chairs during the quarter and should have used 32,000 feet of lumber (1,600 chairs × 20 feet per chair = 32,000 feet). The variance of $3,200 is considered unfavorable because the actual quantity of material used (33,600 feet) was greater than the flexible budget amount (32,000 feet).

The total favorable variance of $160 for direct materials can now be examined in more detail. It is the sum of a favorable price variance of $3,360 and an unfavorable usage variance of $3,200. Although the overall direct material variance was quite small, you can see that both the price variance and usage variance are quite large and just happen to offset each other. Possible reasons for a favorable price variance include taking advantage of unexpected quantity discounts or negotiating reduced prices with suppliers. However, favorable direct material price variances can also result from the purchase of low-quality materials. Unfavorable material usage variances can likewise be caused by a number of reasons—poorly trained workers, machine breakdowns, or perhaps even the use of low-quality materials if they result in more defective units, machine downtime, rework, and so on.

Concept Question: *What are some possible reasons for an unfavorable direct material price variance and a favorable material usage variance?*

Concept Answer: Unfavorable material price variances might result from rush orders (requiring faster delivery and higher prices), purchasing in small lot sizes (and not taking advantage of quantity discounts), and purchasing higher-quality materials than budgeted. Favorable material usage variances are likely a result of highly efficient workers and well-maintained machinery and equipment. However, a favorable variance should not *necessarily* be considered "good." For example, the highly trained, efficient worker might require a higher salary than budgeted. ■

The investigation of variances and their causes using the decision model framework is discussed in more detail later in the chapter.

If the amount of material purchased is not the same as the amount of material used in production, the variance model for materials must be slightly modified. To isolate the variances as soon as possible, the price variance should be calculated using the total amount of material purchased while the usage variance should be calculated based on the amount of material actually used in production. For example, if Corinne's purchases 35,000 feet of lumber but only uses 33,600 feet, the price variance would be calculated as follows:

$$AQ_{purchased} \ (AP - SP)$$

or

$$35,000 \ (\$1.90 - \$2.00) = \$3,500 \ F$$

The usage variance is calculated as before, that is

$$SP \ (AQ_{used} - SQ)$$

or

$$\$2.00 \ (33,600 - 32,000) = \$3,200 \ U$$

Analysis of Direct Material Variances When Quantity Purchased Is Different from Quantity Used

AQ × AP	AQ × SP	AQ × SP	SQ × SP
35,000 × \$1.90	35,000 × \$2.00	33,600 × \$2.00	32,000 × \$2.00
= \$66,500	= \$70,000	= \$67,200	= \$64,000

35,000(\$1.90 − \$2.00)	\$2.00(33,600 − 32,000)
AQ (AP − SP)	SP (AQ − SQ)
Price Variance	Usage Variance
\$3,500 F	\$3,200 U

AQ = Actual Quantity	AP = Actual Price
SP = Standard Price	SQ = Standard Quantity

You should note that when the amount of material purchased is not equal to the amount of material used, the price and usage variances cannot be added together to calculate the total direct material variance.

DIRECT LABOR VARIANCES

Direct labor variances are calculated using the same basic variance model used to calculate direct material variances. Because we are talking about labor instead of material, we substitute rates for price (AR and SR instead of AP and SP) and hours for quantity (AH and SH instead of AQ and SQ). In addition, the direct labor usage variance is often referred to as an efficiency variance. Using the standard cost data for Corinne's Country Rockers provided on page 308 and the breakdown of actual direct labor costs on page 312, direct labor variances are calculated below:

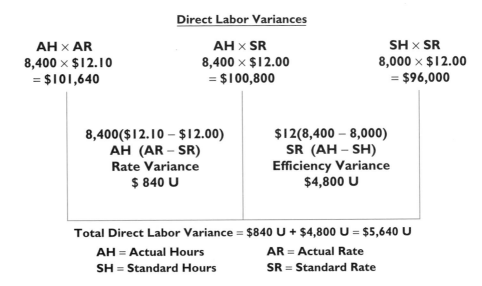

Direct Labor Variances

AH × AR	AH × SR	SH × SR
8,400 × $12.10	8,400 × $12.00	8,000 × $12.00
= $101,640	= $100,800	= $96,000

8,400($12.10 – $12.00)	$12(8,400 – 8,000)
AH (AR – SR)	SR (AH – SH)
Rate Variance	Efficiency Variance
$ 840 U	$4,800 U

Total Direct Labor Variance = $840 U + $4,800 U = $5,640 U

AH = Actual Hours	AR = Actual Rate
SH = Standard Hours	SR = Standard Rate

If the two components of the direct labor variance are evaluated, we see that most of the variance is due to inefficiencies in the use of labor. Potential causes of an unfavorable direct labor efficiency variance include poorly trained workers, machine breakdowns, the use of poor-quality raw materials (resulting in more time spent in production), or just general employee inefficiencies resulting from poor supervision. In this case, the unfavorable direct labor rate variance is small but still may be important. Potential causes of unfavorable direct labor rate variances include the use of higher-paid workers than budgeted, unexpected increases in wages due to union negotiations, and so on.

Concept Question: *What are some possible reasons for* favorable *direct labor rate and efficiency variances?*

Concept Answer: Hiring workers at a lower wage rate is one obvious reason for a favorable direct labor rate variance. However, that may be problematic if the workers are less skilled than required. On the other hand, favorable labor efficiency variances most often result from using highly skilled workers. Obviously, there are tradeoffs here. Paying higher wage rates can result in unfavorable labor rate variances and favorable labor efficiency variances whereas paying lower wage rates can result in favorable labor rate variances and unfavorable labor efficiency variances. ■

VARIABLE OVERHEAD VARIANCES

With slight modifications, variable overhead variances are calculated using the same variance model as direct material and direct labor variances. As with direct material and direct labor, (AQ × AP) is simply the actual cost incurred—in this case the actual variable over-head costs. SR is the variable predetermined overhead rate (sometimes called SVR). Be-cause variable overhead was estimated using direct labor as the cost driver, AH is simply the actual number of labor hours incurred. Likewise, SH is the standard number of labor hours allowed for actual production. Consequently, SH × SVR is the amount of applied variable overhead.[2] The price variance is often called a variable overhead spending vari-ance and like the labor usage variance, the usage variance for variable overhead is called an efficiency variance.

The variable overhead spending and efficiency variances are calculated as follows:

Variable Overhead Variances

Actual Variable Overhead Expense	AH × SVR 8,400 × $3.00	SH × SVR 8,000 × $3.00
= $23,720	= $25,200	= $24,000

Actual − (AH × SVR) $23,720 − (8,400 × $3.00) **Spending Variance** $1,480 F	SVR (AH − SH) $3.00(8,400 − 8,000) **Efficiency Variance** $1,200 U

Total Variable Overhead Variance = $1,480 F + 1,200 U = $280 F

AH = Actual Hours	SH = Standard Hours
SVR = Standard Variable Rate	SR = Standard Rate

What do these variances tell us? Whereas the price variance for materials and the rate variance for labor tell us if the price of materials and the rate for labor are more or less than budgeted, the interpretation of the variable overhead spending variance is a little dif-ferent. Whereas a spending variance for variable overhead indicates that the actual price of variable overhead items like supplies, utilities, repairs, and maintenance was more or less than the flexible budget amount, it is also affected by excessive *usage* of overhead caused by inefficient operations or waste. For example, although the rates for electricity usage (charged by the utility) might be exactly as budgeted, excessive usage might result from poorly maintained equipment. Likewise, even if the price of supplies was lower than bud-geted, excessive use of the supplies due to waste could still result in an unfavorable vari-able overhead spending variance.

The variable overhead efficiency variance is also interpreted differently than the direct material and direct labor usage variances. It does not measure the efficient use of overhead at all but rather the efficient use of the cost driver or overhead allocation base used in the flexible budget. The efficiency variance has nothing to do with the efficient use of utilities, maintenance, and supplies. The efficiency variance only shows how efficiently the organi-zation used the base chosen to apply overhead to the cost of product produced.

 Key Concept: *The variable overhead efficiency variance does not measure the efficient use of overhead but rather the efficient use of the cost driver or overhead allocation base used in the flexible budget.*

In the case of Corinne's Country Rockers, the favorable variable overhead spending vari-ance tells us that Corinne's spent less than budgeted on the items included in the variable

---

[2]Of course, overhead can be applied using cost drivers other than direct labor. If overhead is applied based on machine hours, AH is simply the actual number of machine hours used and SH is the budgeted number of machine hours allowed for actual production.

LO6
Compute and interpret variable and fixed man-ufacturing overhead variances

overhead portion of its flexible budget. Although this might have resulted from paying less per kilowatt-hour for electricity, it might also have resulted from using less electricity than expected. A detailed analysis of each line item would provide more information. The unfavorable variable overhead efficiency variance tells us simply that more *direct labor hours* were used than budgeted. It does not tell us anything about the efficient use of electricity, supplies, or repairs and maintenance.

The interpretation of variable overhead spending and efficiency variances is made difficult by the use of a single cost driver to apply variable overhead to products and services. The use of multiple cost drivers and ABC makes the interpretation of these variances much more useful. This is illustrated in more detail later in the chapter.

FIXED OVERHEAD VARIANCES

Corinne's Country Rockers

Corinne's fixed manufacturing overhead variance (see page 310) is $1,000 over budget ($16,000 actual costs compared to the flexible budget amount of $15,000). Unlike variable overhead, fixed overhead (and other fixed costs) should not be affected when production increases or decreases. Consequently, the variance model used in analyzing variable costs (direct material, direct labor, and variable overhead) is not appropriate for analyzing the fixed overhead variance.

Fixed overhead variances consist of a budget variance and a volume variance. The **budget variance** (or spending variance) is simply the difference between the amount of fixed overhead actually incurred and the flexible budget amount. Because fixed overhead is not dependent on production volume, no activity levels are used in its calculation.

> Fixed overhead budget (spending) variance
> = Actual fixed overhead − Budgeted fixed overhead

The **volume variance** is the difference between the flexible budget amount and the amount of fixed overhead *applied* to products. Overhead is applied by multiplying the predetermined overhead rate (for fixed overhead) by the standard hours (or budgeted hours) allowed to complete the actual units produced.

> Fixed overhead volume variance = Budgeted fixed overhead − Applied fixed overhead

APPLICATION IN BUSINESS

A company using variable (direct) costing rather than absorption (full) costing treats fixed overhead as a period cost and expenses it immediately (see Chapter 6). In these companies, there won't be a fixed overhead volume variance because fixed overhead is not "applied" to products. It is simply expensed in the period incurred.

Fixed overhead variances for Corinne's Country Rockers are calculated in the following table. The predetermined fixed overhead rate is $2 per labor hour ($15,000 budgeted fixed overhead divided by 7,500 budgeted labor hours (1,500 budgeted units × 5 hours per unit)). Applied fixed overhead is $16,000 ($2 predetermined overhead rate × 8,000 hours (1,600 actual units × 5 hours per unit)).

Fixed Overhead Variances

Actual Fixed Overhead Expense	Budgeted Fixed Overhead (7,500 labor hours × $2.00/hour) (1,500 chairs × 5 hours)	Applied Fixed Overhead (8,000 labor hours x $2.00) (1,600 chairs × 5 hours)
= $16,000	= $15,000	= $16,000

Actual – Budget Spending Variance $1,000 U	Budget – Applied Volume Variance $1,000 F

The spending variance is unfavorable because Corinne's spent more on fixed overhead items than the company had budgeted. As you can see, the volume variance is simply a result of Corinne's manufacturing more chairs than budgeted (1,600 instead of 1,500). Everything else in the comparison of budgeted and applied overhead is the same. The fixed overhead volume variance is calculated primarily as a method of reconciling the amount of overhead applied to products under an absorption costing system with the amount of overhead actually incurred—and consequently the over- or underapplied overhead. The total amount of the variable overhead spending variance, variable overhead efficiency variance, fixed overhead spending variance, and fixed overhead volume variance will equal the company's over- or underapplied overhead for a period.

 Key Concept: *Total over- or underapplied overhead is the sum of the four overhead variances.*

For Corinne's, manufacturing overhead was overapplied by $280 for the quarter. This is the sum of Corinne's $1,480 favorable variable overhead spending variance, $1,200 unfavorable variable overhead efficiency variance, $1,000 unfavorable fixed overhead spending variance, and $1,000 favorable fixed overhead volume variance.[3]

Concept Question: *What was Corinne's actual overhead for variable and fixed costs? What was Corinne's applied overhead for variable and fixed costs?*

Concept Answer: Actual variable overhead cost was $23,720 and the actual fixed overhead cost was $16,000 resulting in actual total overhead of $39,720. The applied variable overhead was $24,000 (8,000 labor hours × the variable predetermined overhead rate of $3 per hour) and the applied fixed overhead was $16,000 (8,000 labor hours × the fixed predetermined overhead rate of $2 per hour) resulting in total applied overhead of $40,000. The difference between actual and applied overhead? $280! ▪

The fixed overhead volume variance generally should not be interpreted as favorable or unfavorable and should not be interpreted as a measure of over- or underutilization of facilities. This can be particularly problematic when the applied overhead is smaller than the budgeted amount (when a company produces fewer products than budgeted). Companies may reduce production for a number of reasons including reduced demand for products, temporary material or labor shortages, and so on.

---

[3]The fixed overhead volume variance is considered favorable for this purpose because actual production was greater than budgeted production.

Key Concept: *The fixed overhead volume variance should not be interpreted as favorable or unfavorable or as a measure of the efficient utilization of facilities.*

ACTIVITY-BASED COSTING AND VARIANCE ANALYSIS

LO7

Evaluate the impact of activity-based costing systems on flexible budgets

The advantages of variance analysis for overhead costs are enhanced in companies using activity-based costing. Because ABC systems break down overhead into multiple cost pools associated with activities (with a cost driver for each), companies that employ ABC can analyze price and usage variances for each activity making up the total overhead variance. Just as the use of ABC systems enhances the quality of information available for decision making, analyzing variances by activity has a similar effect.

 Key Concept: *The advantages of variance analysis for overhead costs are enhanced in companies using activity-based costing.*

Corinne's flexible budget for variable overhead was $24,000, whereas the flexible budget for fixed overhead was $15,000. When Corinne's analyzes this overhead using ABC, the $39,000 of budgeted overhead is traced to six activities—material handling, setting up machinery, assembly, finishing, maintenance, and inspections. The costs associated with each activity and their respective cost drivers are as follows:

Corinne's Country Rockers
Activity-Based Costing Flexible Budget

Activity	Flexible Budget Amount	Cost Driver	Budgeted Volume	Cost Formula
Material handling	$ 6,000	Number of moves	200	$30 per move
Setting up machinery	4,000	Number of setups	80	50 per setup
Assembly	14,000	Number of assembly (labor) hours	6,000	2.33 per assembly hour
Finishing	4,800	Number of finishing (labor) hours	2,000	2.40 per finishing hour
Maintenance	4,800	Number of maintenance hours	160	30 per maintenance hour
Inspections	5,400	Number of inspections	2,400	2.25 per inspection
Total	**$39,000**			

The cost formula is simply the predetermined overhead rate for each activity. It is found by dividing the estimated overhead for each activity by the estimated activity level of the cost driver. Once the actual cost associated with each activity and the actual volume of cost driver associated with each activity are known, a spending variance and efficiency variance can be computed. The detailed calculations of variances for each of the six activities identified at Corinne's Country Rockers are at the top of the following page.

Although the preceding example is very simple, the ABC flexible overhead budget with variance analysis provides a wealth of information for managerial decision making. Although the total overhead variance is only $720, the detailed analysis shows us that the efficiency variances are almost all unfavorable. In all cases (except maintenance), Corinne's used more of the relevant cost driver than budgeted. On the other hand, the spending variances include an even number of favorable and unfavorable variances. Spending on machine setups, assembly, and finishing was favorable, whereas spending related to material handling, maintenance, and inspections was unfavorable. As always, Corinne's should pay special attention to any possible interactions between the variances.

Spending Variances and Efficiency Variances by Activity

Activity	Actual Cost	Spending Variance	Actual Base × Std Rate	Efficiency Variance	Standard Base × Std Rate	Total Variance
Material handling	$ 6,200	$ 50 U	205 × $30 = $6,150	$150 U	200 × $30 = $6,000	$200 U
Setting up machinery	4,150	350 F	90 × $50 = $4,500	500 U	80 × $50 = $4,000	150 U
Assembly	13,925	754 F	6,300 × $2.33 = $14,679	679 U	6,000 × $2.33 = $14,000	75 F
Finishing	4,775	265 F	2,100 × $2.40 = $5,040	240 U	2,000 × $2.40 = $4,800	25 F
Maintenance	5,120	620 U	150 × $30 = $4,500	300 F	160 × $30 = $4,800	320 U
Inspections	5,550	60 U	2,440 × $2.25 = $5,490	90 U	2,400 × $2.25 = $5,400	150 U
Totals	**$39,720**	**$639 F**	**$40,359**	**$1,359 U**	**$39,000**	**$720 U**

SELLING AND ADMINISTRATIVE EXPENSE VARIANCE

As shown in the flexible budget variance calculation on page 310, Corinne's had an $800 unfavorable variance for variable selling and administrative costs and a $2,000 favorable variance for fixed selling and administrative costs. Variable selling and administrative costs include things like commissions on sales, advertising brochures that are sent out with each chair purchased, administrative time to process each sale, and so on. Fixed selling and administrative costs include the salaries of the sales manager and personnel manager, and facility costs like rent and insurance. Like overhead variances, selling and administrative

Selling and administrative expense variances are vitally important to home shopping companies and others that sell products via mail order.

variances are difficult to analyze and interpret. However, companies utilizing ABC systems may have sufficient detail to analyze portions of this variance in more detail. For example, Corinne's is interested in reducing the costs associated with processing mail-order sales made by telephone and has established a quantity standard for the time spent to process each call (6 minutes). Likewise, they have established a price standard for this activity consisting of the salary costs incurred by sales representatives handling the call ($1 per call based on a salary of $10 per hour) plus the direct costs of the toll-free line ($.60 at $.10 per minute). The actual costs incurred in handling sales calls can then be compared to the flexible budget amount, and price and usage variances can be calculated.

INTERPRETING AND USING VARIANCE ANALYSIS

LO8
Analyze important considerations in using and interpreting variances including the concept of management by exception

Although standard costs and variance analysis can be useful to managers attempting to diagnose organizational performance, they are most effective in stable companies with mature production environments characterized by a heavy reliance on direct labor. On the other hand, they may not be much help in rapidly changing companies, companies with flexible manufacturing systems (in which more than one product is manufactured on an assembly line), companies with heavily automated manufacturing processes, or companies that emphasize continuous improvement and reducing non-value-added activities in the production process. Although variance analysis may still be of value as a summary report for top management, it has a number of drawbacks when used in many modern manufacturing environments:

1. The information from variance analysis is likely to be too aggregated for operating managers to use. To be useful, material variances may need to be broken down into detail by specific product lines and even batches of product, whereas labor variances may need to be calculated for specific manufacturing cells.

2. The information from variance analysis is not timely enough to be useful to managers. As product life cycles are reduced, timely reporting is even more critical than in the past.

3. Traditional variance analysis of variable and fixed overhead provides little useful information for managers. As the relative proportion and importance of overhead grows in comparison to direct material and direct labor, the usefulness of traditional overhead variances has declined.

4. Traditional variance analysis focuses on cost control instead of product quality, customer service, delivery time, and other nonfinancial measures of performance. These measures are discussed in more detail in Chapter 12.

 Key Concept: *Variance analysis is most effective in stable companies with mature production environments and has a number of drawbacks when used in many modern manufacturing environments.*

Even in traditional and stable manufacturing environments, the effective use of variance analysis for control and performance purposes requires the proper application of "management by exception" and careful interpretation of variances (including understanding their causes).

The proper application of "management by exception" requires an understanding that it is neither necessary nor desirable to investigate all variances. If you think about it, it is likely that actual costs will always deviate from budgeted costs to some extent. Utility prices are affected by the weather and prices of raw materials can change suddenly due to shortages, surpluses, and new sources of competing products. Unexpected machine breakdowns affect the amount of time workers spend manufacturing products. Even fixed costs can differ from budgeted costs when rent is unexpectedly increased, new equipment is purchased, or insurance rates go up. Because of these random fluctuations, managers should generally only investigate those variances that are material in amount and outside some normal acceptable range. Traditionally, materiality thresholds were often based on absolute size (investigate everything over $1,000) or relative size (investigate everything over 10 percent of the budgeted amount) or some combination of the two. Today, companies are more likely to use statistical techniques and to investigate variances that fall outside of some "normal" range of fluctuations. For example, companies may investigate variances that are more than two standard deviations from the mean. Regardless of materiality, trends in variances might also warrant investigation. For example, constantly occurring and increasing material price variances might be vitally important to a restaurant regardless of their absolute size.

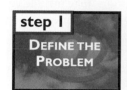   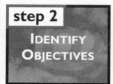

The decision model introduced in Chapter 1 (and shown above) aids the proper use and interpretation of variances and their causes. Step 1 of the decision model requires an accurate definition of the problem. This requires input from managers across all functional areas of a company. For example, consider a company investigating an unfavorable direct labor efficiency variance. Although on the surface, the unfavorable variance would seem to indicate a "problem" in worker efficiency, the real problem may be the combination of a workforce that is "fixed" in the short run and a lack of sufficient orders to keep workers busy.[4]

Likewise, an unfavorable direct material usage variance generally points to a problem in production. However, further analysis might reveal that usage was high because of an unusual number of defective parts and the large number of defective parts was a result of the purchasing manager buying materials of inferior quality. The problem becomes one of the purchasing manager buying inferior materials, not the production manager using excessive amounts of material.

Identifying management's objectives (Step 2) is vitally important in deciding how to use and interpret variances. If the problem is one of insufficient orders and management is truly concerned about controlling costs, management must be careful *not* to use the direct labor efficiency variance for purposes of motivating and controlling the production supervisor. Although this may seem counterintuitive, put yourself in the shoes of the production manager. The production supervisor really has two options—either continue producing products to keep workers busy or have an unfavorable labor efficiency variance. But keeping workers busy has definite drawbacks. Building inventory levels is costly. Holding high levels of inventory results in additional costs of storage and insurance and can result in increased waste due to theft and obsolescence.

In other situations, understanding whether the primary objective of management is cost control or producing a high-quality product is important. If cost control is paramount, an unfavorable direct material price variance might well be considered "bad"; however, if management's objective is to provide a high-quality product, an unfavorable material price variance might be acceptable if the higher price is necessary to obtain high-quality materials.

Even though the purchasing manager caused the "problem," the material price variance would be favorable. As we discussed earlier, favorable variances are not necessarily "good."

---

[4]Companies may be reluctant to lay off workers for short periods of time when demand is unexpectedly reduced or other problems make it difficult to keep them fully employed. It may be costly to rehire workers or they may find other jobs. As discussed elsewhere, this often makes direct labor a fixed cost in the short run.

Step 3	IDENTIFY AND ANALYZE AVAILABLE OPTIONS

Step 3 in the decision model involves the identification and analysis of available options. With respect to variance analysis, options can be considered at two points in the process. The first involves deciding how the variances should be used and interpreted and who should be held responsible (if anyone). As we have already discussed, assigning responsibility for variances can be problematic when managers use the information without understanding the root causes of problems. Options may include controlling costs and evaluating performance using other measures along with variance analysis. Some of these other measures are discussed in more detail in Chapters 11 and 12.

Step 4	SELECT THE BEST OPTION

Once managers are sure of the root cause(s) of a variance, they can intelligently consider options available to deal with the problem. This step in the decision process includes a careful consideration of the relevant factors affecting the problem. For example, if management finds that an unfavorable direct labor efficiency variance is caused by a lack of customer orders and a workforce that is "fixed" in the short run, options may include accepting special orders, utilizing the workers in other areas, utilizing the time to train workers or to repair machinery, and so on.

The last step in the decision model involves choosing the best option. This involves paying special attention to management's objectives as discussed in Step 2. If the primary objective is cost control, managers are likely to choose a different option than if their primary objectives are qualitative.

BEHAVIORAL CONSIDERATIONS

LO9
Evaluate behavioral considerations in using standard costing and variance analysis

As you have seen throughout this chapter, although useful for control and performance evaluation, the use of standard costs and variance analysis can also cause dysfunctional behavior among employees and management. The use of ideal standards can cause resentment among managers when constantly faced with "unfavorable" variances. Some companies tie compensation to performance that is at least partly measured by variances. Even though this is likely to make managers aware of costs, it may have undesirable side effects. Too much emphasis on the direct material usage variance can cause production managers to increase production so as to appear efficient, causing inventories to rise above acceptable levels. By focusing on variances, a purchasing manager may be encouraged to purchase inferior products to make his or her performance appear better even though the manager knows that the poor-quality material will cause problems in the production area. It is important to understand the root causes of variances and to assign responsibility accordingly. It is also important to remember that variance analysis provides just one measure of performance. The uses of other financial and nonfinancial measures of performance are discussed in Chapters 11 and 12.

Book store managers may face "unfavorable variances" when too many books are ordered from publishers. However, too much emphasis on controlling purchases and inventory may result in students not being able to obtain the books they need for class.

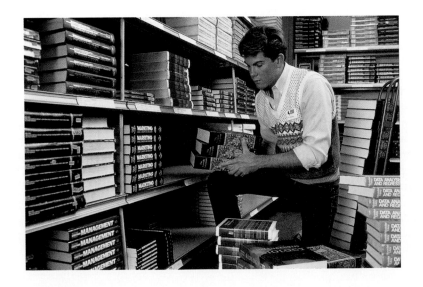

SUMMARY OF KEY CONCEPTS

- The purpose of the control function in management is to make sure that the goals of the organization are being attained. (p. 306)
- Management by exception is the key to effective variance analysis and involves taking action only when actual results deviate significantly from planned. (p. 306)
- The flexible budgeting process removes any differences or variances due only to variations in volume. (p. 311)
- "Favorable" and "unfavorable" designations for variances do not always refer to "good" or "bad." (p. 312)
- The variable overhead efficiency variance does not measure the efficient use of overhead but rather the efficient use of the cost driver or overhead allocation base used in the flexible budget. (p. 317)
- Total over- or underapplied overhead is the sum of the four overhead variances. (p. 319)
- The fixed overhead volume variance should not be interpreted as favorable or unfavorable or as a measure of the efficient utilization of facilities. (p. 320)
- The advantages of variance analysis for overhead costs are enhanced in companies using activity-based costing. (p. 320)
- Variance analysis is most effective in stable companies with mature production environments and has a number of drawbacks when used in many modern manufacturing environments. (p. 322)

KEY DEFINITIONS

Control Involves the motivation and monitoring of employees and the evaluation of people and other resources used in the operations of the organization (p. 306)

Variance analysis Allows managers to see whether sales, production, and manufacturing costs are higher or lower than planned and, more important, *why* actual sales, production, and costs differ from budget (p. 306)

Management by exception The process of taking action only when actual results deviate significantly from planned (p. 306)

Standard cost A budget for a single unit of product or service (p. 306)

Standard quantity The budgeted amount of material, labor, or overhead for each product (p. 306)

Standard price The budgeted price of the material, labor, or overhead for each unit (p. 307)

Task analysis A method of setting standards that also examines the production process in detail to determine what it should cost to produce a product (p. 307)

Ideal standard A standard that is attained only when near-perfect conditions are present (p. 307)

Practical standard A standard that should be attained under normal, efficient operating conditions (p. 307)

Sales volume variance The difference between the actual sales volume and the budgeted sales volume times the budgeted contribution margin (p. 309)

Flexible budget variance The difference between the flexible budget operating income and actual operating income (p. 311)

Sales price variance Computed by comparing the actual sales price to the flexible budget sales price times the actual sales volume (p. 311)

Material price variance The difference between the actual price and the standard quantity price times the actual volume purchased (p. 313)

Usage variance The difference between the actual quantity and the standard quantity times the standard price (p. 313)

Budget variance Also known as the spending variance, the difference between the amount of fixed overhead actually incurred and the flexible budget amount (p. 318)

Volume variance The difference between the flexible budget and the fixed overhead applied to a product (p. 318)

CONCEPT REVIEW

1. Discuss the purpose of the planning and control process.

2. Discuss ideal versus practical standards and how they might affect employee behavior.

3. Discuss the pros and cons of management by exception.

4. Discuss the value of a flexible budget to management decision making.

5. What is the primary difference between a static budget and a flexible budget?

6. Which area of management would normally be responsible for sales price variances? Why?

7. What factors are considered when measuring the sales volume variance?

8. Give the formula for computing the generic price variance and explain each term.

9. Give the formula for computing the generic usage variance and explain each term.

10. Discuss the impact on fixed and variable cost per unit when production volume decreases when using a flexible budget.

11. Usage variances focus on what?

12. The predetermined fixed overhead application rate is a function of a predetermined "normal" activity level. If standard hours allowed for good output equal this predetermined activity level for a given period, what will the volume variance be?

13. Husky Manufacturing relies on unfavorable material variances to signal quality problems that require excessive rework and materials use. Discuss the pros and cons of this practice.

14. Incentive compatible compensation schemes often create many opportunities as well as problems. Identify two negative outcomes of incentive compensation systems, and suggest how companies can overcome them.

15. Discuss the meaning of the terms *favorable* and *unfavorable* with regards to variances. How does each type of variance affect operating profits? Do the terms refer to good or bad variances? Give an example of each with the effect on profits and the interpretation of the meaning of the term.

APPLICATION OF CONCEPTS

16. Total production costs for Sun Devil Advertising Agency are budgeted at $330,000 for 60,000 hours of budgeted output and $380,000 for 70,000 hours of budgeted output. How much is Sun Devil's budgeted variable costs per hour of output?

17. Grizzly Manufacturing uses the following flexible budget formula for annual maintenance cost:

> Total cost = $9,200 + .80 per machine hour

The current month's budget is based upon 30,000 hours of planned machine time. What is the maintenance cost included in this flexible budget?

18. The budget formula for manufacturing costs is $13,500 + $5.00 per unit produced. The budget formula for marketing and administrative costs is $10,000 + $7.50 per unit sold. If 10,000 units are expected to be produced, but only 8,000 units are expected to be sold, what are the total budgeted operating expenses for the period?

19. A direct marketing company expects to incur fixed expenses of $50,000 per month and variable costs of $4 per sales call and $2 per telephone call in generating sales of $75,000. During the month the sales force made 100 sales calls and 500 telephone calls and generated sales of $70,000. Actual costs incurred included $52,000 for fixed costs and $1,200 for variable costs. Compute the flexible budget variance.

20. The Brisick Quick Copy Shop had an unfavorable sales price variance of $150. The budgeted selling price was $10 per unit, and the number of units sold was 50. What was the actual selling price?

21. Burke Long Distance Company expects to sell 100 phone card units at a selling price of $15 each. Variable costs are expected to be $10 each. What is the sales volume variance if the company actually sells 110 phone card units at $16 and its variable costs are $12?

22. Simpson Company's budget shows straight-line depreciation on factory equipment of $258,000. The budget was prepared at an annual production volume of 103,200 units of product. This production volume is expected to occur uniformly throughout the year. During September, Simpson produced 8,170 units of product, and the accounts reflected actual depreciation on factory machinery of $20,500. Simpson controls manufacturing costs with a flexible budget. What would the flexible budget amount for depreciation on factory machinery for September be?

23. Morgan Corporation's budget calls for the production of 5,000 units of product monthly. The budget includes indirect labor of $144,000 annually; Morgan considers indirect labor to be a variable cost. During the month of April, 4,500 units of product were produced, and indirect labor costs of $10,100 were incurred. What would be the budget variance for indirect labor utilizing flexible budgeting?

24. Fort Worth Company prepared a budget last period that called for sales of 10,000 units at a price of $10 each. The costs per unit were estimated to amount to $5 variable and $2 fixed. During the period, production was exactly equal to actual sales of 12,000 units. The selling price was $9.50 per unit. Variable costs were $6 per unit. Fixed costs actually incurred were $21,000. Prepare a report to show the difference between the actual contribution margin and the budgeted contribution margin per the static budget. Now compare the actual contribution margin with the budgeted contribution margin per the flexible budget.

25. As a hobby, Janie makes knitted caps for sale at ski resorts. Her budget for the production and sale of 150 caps is as follows:

Sales revenue	$1,500.00
Variable costs:	
Direct material (yarn)	375.00
Direct labor	750.00
Commission to resort	112.50
Fixed costs	75.00
Net income	$ 187.50

Janie came down with a bad case of the flu and was only able to make and sell 125 caps.

Required

Prepare a flexible budget for the production and sale of 125 caps.

26. As a hobby, Jim makes souvenir wood sculptures for sale at ski resorts. His budgeted revenue and expenses are as follows:

Sales revenue	$100 per sculpture
Variable costs:	
Direct material	25 per sculpture
Direct labor	15 per sculpture
Commission to resort	10 per sculpture
Fixed costs	$ 50 for the production of up to 75 sculptures

Required

Prepare a flexible budget for the production and sale of 50 sculptures.

27. Last year, Wheeler Corporation budgeted for production and sales of 1,200 items. They actually produced and sold 1,100 items. Each item has a standard requiring 1

foot of material at a budgeted cost of $1.50 per foot and 2 hours of assembly time at a cost of $12 per hour. The items sell for $30. Actual costs for the production of 1,100 items were $1435.50 for materials (990 feet at $1.45 per foot) and $29,161.10 for labor (2,420 hours at $12.05 per hour).

Required

A. Calculate the budgeted contribution margin per unit

B. Calculate the actual contribution margin per unit

C. Calculate the sales volume variance

D. Calculate the flexible budget variance

E. Calculate the direct materials price variance

F. Calculate the direct materials usage variance

G. Calculate the labor rate variance

H. Calculate the labor efficiency variance

28. Last year, Boring Corporation budgeted for production and sales of 1,000 items. They actually produced and sold 1,100 items. Each item has a standard requiring 1 pound of material at a budgeted cost of $5.00 per pound and 2 hours of assembly time at a cost of $12 per hour. The items sell for $40. Actual costs for the production of 1,100 items included 1,150 pounds of material at $4.75 per pound and 2,220 labor hours at $12.05 per hour.

Required

A. Calculate the direct materials price variance

B. Calculate the direct materials usage variance

C. Calculate the labor rate variance

D. Calculate the labor efficiency variance

29. Simon Enterprises had actual variable overhead expenses totaling $33,750 and actual fixed overhead expenses totaling $21,500 last year for production of 6,000 units. Variable overhead is applied at a rate of $1.50 per direct labor hour, while fixed overhead is applied at a rate of $1.75 per direct labor hour. Two direct labor hours are budgeted for each unit. 11,990 direct labor hours were incurred.

Compute the variable overhead efficiency variance, the variable overhead spending variance, and the fixed overhead volume variance.

30. Garfunkel Company, which uses standard costing, shows the following overhead information for the current period:

Actual overhead incurred:	
Fixed	$10,500
Variable	$66,810
Budgeted fixed overhead	$11,000
Variable overhead rate per direct labor hour	$ 5
Standard hours allowed for actual production	13,100
Actual labor hours used	13,000

Required

A. What is the variable overhead spending variance?

B. What is the variable overhead efficiency variance?

31. Last year, Bachman Corporation budgeted for production and sales of 5,000 units of their product. They actually produced and sold 6,000 units. Each unit has a standard requiring 1.5 pounds of material at a budgeted cost of $1.52 per pound and 2 hours of assembly time at a cost of $12.50 per hour. The product sells for $32. Actual costs for the production of 6,000 units were $12,900 for materials

(8,600 pounds at $1.50 per pound) and $161,700 (13,200 at $12.25 per hour) for labor.

Required

    A. What was the budgeted contribution margin per unit?

    B. What was the actual contribution margin per unit?

    C. What was Banana's sales volume variance?

    D. What was Banana's flexible budget variance?

    E. What was Banana's direct materials price variance?

    F. What was Banana's direct materials usage variance?

    G. What was Banana's labor rate variance?

    H. What was Banana's labor efficiency variance?

    I. If each Bachman product actually sold for $33, the sales price variance would be:

32. Last year, Turner Corporation budgeted for production and sales of 12,000 overdrive transmission parts. They actually produced 11,000 and sold 10,500 parts. Each part has a standard requiring 1 pound of material at a budgeted cost of $1.50 per pound and 20 minutes of assembly time at a cost of $.25 per minute. The parts sell for $8. Actual costs for the production of 11,000 parts were $16,940 for materials (11,000 pounds at $1.54 per pound) and $58,080 (242,000 minutes at $.24 per minute) for labor.

Required

    A. What was the budgeted contribution margin per unit?

    B. What was the actual contribution margin per unit?

    C. What was Turner's sales volume variance?

    D. What was Turner's flexible budget variance?

    E. What was Turner's direct materials price variance?

    F. What was Turner's direct materials usage variance?

    G. What was Turner's labor rate variance?

    H. What was Turner's labor efficiency variance?

33. Pooh Enterprises had the following standard costs for the production of one bear:

Direct materials	1.5 lbs of stuffing @ $2 per lb.
Direct labor	2 hrs of assembly @ $15 per hr.

    Actual production costs for the production of 1,000 bears included 1,750 pounds of stuffing @ $1.95 per pound and 1,950 labor hours at $15.25 per hour.

Required

    A. What is the direct materials price variance?

    B. What is the direct materials usage variance?

    C. What is the labor rate variance?

    D. What is the labor efficiency variance?

34. Byrd Company's actual results with a sales volume of 400,000 units are as follows:

Sales Revenues		$2,440,000
Variable Costs		
Manufacturing	$1,060,000	
Marketing and administrative	748,000	1,808,000
Contribution margin		$ 632,000
Fixed Costs		
Manufacturing	$ 400,000	
Marketing and administrative	200,000	600,000
Operating profit		$ 32,000

The company planned to produce and sell 375,000 at $6 each. At that volume variable manufacturing costs were budgeted at $2.50, and variable marketing and administrative costs were budgeted at $2.00 each. In addition, the company expected an operating profit of $62,500.

Required

   A. Re-create the static budget.

   B. Prepare the flexible budget.

   C. Calculate the sales price variance.

   D. Calculate the sales volume variance.

   E. Calculate the variable manufacturing variances.

   F. Calculate the fixed cost variances.

   G. Reconcile the budgeted operating profits of $62,500 to the actual operating profits of $32,000 by fully explaining all variances.

35. Each year, the Patterson Company begins its budgeting process in September. Managers are asked to provide sales forecasts by product line. The president, Jim Sr., wishing to provide an incentive to improve performance, always increases the forecast by 25 percent. Discuss the impact of the president's actions on the sales force as well as the production personnel.

36. The Short Sheets Company established standard costs as follows:

Materials: 5 pieces of fabric @ $1 per piece
Labor: 2 hours @ $7 per hour

In October, 1,000 units were completed. During the month, 5,400 pieces of fabric were purchased at $1.08 per piece. Labor costs were $13,650 for 2,100 hours.

Required

   A. What is the material price variance?

   B. What is the material efficiency variance?

   C. What is the labor price variance?

   D. What is the labor efficiency variance?

37. The following information pertains to the Assembly Department of MacPage Manufacturing for the month of February:

Units produced	5,500 units
Materials purchased	$26,400 ($2.20/pound)
Materials used	13,000 pounds
Labor costs incurred	$9,187.50
Labor hours worked	2,450 hours
Standard price/pound for materials	$2.10/pound

Standard labor time/finished unit	30 minutes
Material usage variance	$1,575 F
Total labor variance	$712.50 F

Required

A. What is the standard usage of material per finished unit?

B. What is the labor efficiency variance?

C. If the given information remains unchanged except for the number of units produced and if the standard wage rate per hour were $3.30, then how many units would have been produced during February?

D. If the given information remains unchanged except for the number of units produced and the standard time per finished unit, and the number of units produced were 825 units while the standard wage rate per hour was $4, then the standard time per finished unit would have been how much?

38. The planned activity level for the assembly department of Guice Manufacturing during the month of December was 10,000 direct labor hours. The actual number of direct labor hours worked during December was 9,000. Overhead is allocated on the basis of actual direct labor hours. What kind of variance occurred?

39. The Comet Company's budget contains these standards for materials and direct labor for a unit:

Material	5 pounds @ $1 per pound	$ 5
Labor	2 hours @ $5 per hour	$10

Although 2,500 units were budgeted, 3,000 were actually produced. Materials weighing 16,000 pounds were purchased for $18,400. Materials weighing 15,500 were issued to production. Direct labor costs were $33,075 for 6,750 hours.

Required

A. Compute the materials purchase price variance.

B. Compute the materials efficiency variance.

C. Compute the labor price variance.

D. Compute the labor efficiency variance.

40. Surfs Up Company, which uses standard costing, shows the following overhead information for the current period:

Actual Overhead Incurred	
Fixed	$10,500
Variable	$66,810
Budgeted fixed overhead	$11,000
Variable overhead rate per direct labor hour	$ 5
Standard hours allowed for actual production	13,100
Actual labor hours used	13,000

Required

A. What is the variable overhead spending variance?

B. What is the variable overhead efficiency variance?

C. What is the fixed overhead budget variance?

41. The Small Tykes World Company mass produces wooden chairs. The standard costs follow:

Plastic	10 pounds at $4.50 per pound
Molding	3 feet at $3.00 per foot
Direct labor	4 hours at $6.00 per hour
Variable overhead	$3 per direct labor hour
Fixed overhead	$55,000 per period

Transactions during June follow:

a. Small Tykes purchased plastic at $4.45 per pound and issued 185,000 pounds to production.

b. Small Tykes purchased at $3.10 per foot and issued 50,000 feet of molding to production.

c. The direct labor payroll was 72,500 hours at $6.00.

d. Overhead costs were $275,000 of which $221,125 was variable.

e. Small Tykes produced 18,000 chairs during the month.

Required

A. Calculate all variances to the extent permitted by the data.

B. Interpret the variances (in other words, tell the story of the variances). What do they tell us about the performance of the company?

C. Suggest what areas need to be investigated as a result of your analysis of the variances.

D. What options are available?

E. In your opinion, what are the best options? Why?

42. Seats R Us manufactures office chairs. Recently it established standard costs as follows:

> Material: 4 pieces per unit at $2 per piece
> Labor : 1½ hours per unit at $8 per hour

In April, 6,000 pieces of material were purchased for $2.25 per piece. Of that number, 5,500 pieces of material were used to produce 1,325 units. Labor costs were $16,300 for 2,000 hours.

Required

A. Compute the materials price variance.

B. Compute the material usage variance.

C. Compute the labor price variance.

D. Compute the labor efficiency variance.

43. The following overhead data of the Simon Travel Company are presented for analysis of the variances from standard:

Forecast Data (expected capacity)

Direct labor hours	40,000
Estimated overhead	
Fixed	$16,000
Variable	$30,000

Actual Results

Direct labor hours	37,200
Overhead	
Fixed	$16,120
Variable	$28,060

Allowed or standard hours for actual production was 37,000 hours.

Required

A. Calculate the variable overhead spending variance.

B. Calculate the variable overhead efficiency variance.

C. Calculate the fixed overhead budget variance.

44. Oil Inc. uses from one to three chemicals to manufacture oil products. Variance data for the month follow (F indicates a favorable variance, U indicates unfavorable variance):

	Chemical X	**Chemical Y**	**Chemical Z**
Materials price variance	$ 84,000 F	$ 50,000 F	$ 42,000 U
Material usage variance	$ 80,000 U	$ 60,000 U	$ 96,000 U
Total materials variance	$ 4,000 F	$ 10,000 U	$138,000 U
Oil products requiring this chemical	200,000	220,000	250,000

The budget allowed one pound for each kind of chemical for each oil product requiring that kind of chemical. For Chemical X the average price paid was $.40 per pound less than standard; for Chemical Y it was $.20 less; for Chemical Z it was $.14 greater. The company purchased and used all chemicals in a given period.

Required

A. For Chemical X, calculate the following:

(1) The number of pounds of material purchased

(2) The standard cost per pound of material

(3) The total standard material cost

B. For Chemical Y, calculate the following:

(1) The number of pounds of material purchased

(2) The standard cost per pound of material

(3) The total standard material cost

C. For Chemical Z, calculate the following:

(1) The number of pounds of material purchased

(2) The standard cost per pound of material

(3) The total standard material cost

45. Sparky Electric produces a single product: outlets. The standard costs per unit for direct materials and direct labor are as follows:

Cost Standards

Material A	2 pounds at $6.00/pound	$12.00
Material B	3 gallons at $3.00/gallon	$ 9.00
Labor	4 hours at $3.20/hour	$12.80
Total standard unit cost		$33.80

The performance report for the month of February appears as follows (F denotes favorable, U denotes unfavorable):

COMPARISON OF ACTUAL AND STANDARD

	Actual	**Standard**	**Total Variance**
Material A	$37,515	$38,400	$ 885 F
Material B	30,195	28,800	1,395 U
Direct labor	39,525	40,960	1,435 F

Analysis of Total Variance

	Total	**Price**	**Usage**
Material A	$ 885 F	$ 615 U	$1,500 F
Material B	1,395 U	495 U	900 U
Direct labor	1,435 F	1,275 F	160 F

There were no beginning or ending inventories of Material A or Material B.

Required

A. What was the number of units produced during February?

B. What was the actual price paid per pound for Material A during February?

C. What was the actual number of pounds of Material A used during February?

D. What was the actual price paid per gallon for Material B during February?

E. What was the actual number of gallons of Material B purchased during February?

F. What was the actual wage rate per hour during February?

G. What were the actual labor hours used during February?

46. Ben Inc. manufactures video games. Market saturation and technological innovations have caused pricing pressures, which have resulted in declining profits. To stem the slide in profits until new products can be introduced, top management has turned its attention to both manufacturing economics and increased production. To realize these objectives, an incentive program has been developed to reward production managers who contribute to an increase in the number of units produced and effect cost reductions.

    The production managers have responded to the pressure of improving manufacturing in several ways that have resulted in increased completed units over normal production levels. The video game machines are put together by the programming group (PG) and the graphics group (GG). To attain increased production levels, PG and GG groups commenced rejecting games that previously would have been tested and modified to meet manufacturing standards. Preventive maintenance on machines used in the production of these games has been postponed with only emergency repair work being performed to keep production lines moving. The maintenance department is concerned that there will be serious breakdowns and unsafe operating conditions.

    The more aggressive assembly group production supervisors have pressured maintenance personnel to attend to their machines at the expense of other groups. This has resulted in machine downtime in the PG and GG groups, which, when coupled with demands for accelerated delivery by the assembly group, has led to more frequent rejections and increased friction among departments.

    Ben Inc. operates under a standard cost system. The standard costs for video games are as follows:

Cost Item	Quantity	Cost	Total
Direct Materials			
CD	1	$20	$20
Package	1	15	15
Labels	2	1	2
Direct Labor			
Assembly group	2 hours	8	16
PG group	1 hour	9	9
GG group	1.5 hours	10	15
Variable overhead	4.5 hours	2	9
Total standard cost per unit			$ 86

Ben's prepares monthly performance reports based on standard costs. Presented in the following table is the contribution report for May 1999, when production and sales both reached 2,200 units:

Ben's Inc. Contribution Report
For the Month of May 1999

	Budget	Actual	Variance
Units	2,000	2,200	200 F
Revenue	$200,000	$220,000	$20,000 F
Variable Costs			
Direct material	74,000	85,600	11,600 U
Direct labor	80,000	93,460	13,460 U
Variable overhead	18,000	18,800	800 U
Total variable costs	172,000	197,860	25,860 U
Contribution margin	$ 28,000	$ 22,140	$ 5,860 U

Ben's top management was surprised by the unfavorable contribution to overall corporate profits in spite of the increased sales in May. Al Miller, the cost accountant, was assigned to identify and report on the reasons for the unfavorable contribution results as well as the individuals or groups responsible. After review, Miller prepared the following usage report:

Ben Inc. Usage Report
For the Month of May 1999

Direct Materials	Quantity	Actual Cost
CDs	2,200 units	$ 44,000
Package	2,200 units	35,000
Labels	4,400 units	6,600
Direct Labor		
Assembly	3,900 hours	31,200
CDs	2,400 hours	23,760
Packages/labels	3,500 hours	38,500
Variable overhead	9,900 hours	18,800
Total variable cost		$197,860

Miller reported that the PG and GG groups supported the increased production levels but experienced abnormal machine downtime causing idle labor, which required the use of overtime to keep up with the accelerated demand for parts. The idle time was charged to direct labor. Miller also reported that the production managers of these two groups resorted to parts rejection as opposed to testing and modification procedures formerly applied. Miller determined that the assembly group met management's objectives by increasing production while using lower than standard hours.

Required

A. For May 1999, Ben Inc.'s labor rate variance was $5,660 unfavorable, and the labor efficiency variance was $200 favorable. By using these two variances and calculating the following five variances, prepare an explanation of the $5,860 unfavorable variance between budgeted and actual contribution margin during May 1999.

   (1) Materials price variance

   (2) Materials quantity variance

   (3) Variable overhead efficiency variance

   (4) Variable overhead spending variance

   (5) Sales volume variance

Step 2 IDENTIFY
OBJECTIVES

Step 3 IDENTIFY AND
ANALYZE AVAILABLE
OPTIONS

B. Tell the story of the variances.

C. Identify and briefly explain the behavioral factors that may promote friction among the production managers and between the production managers and the maintenance manager.

D. Evaluate Al Miller's analysis of the unfavorable contribution results in terms of its completeness and its effect on the behavior of the production groups. What decisions need to be made with regards to increasing the contribution margin?

47. Franklin Glass Works' production budget for the year ended November 30, 1999, was based on 200,000 units. Each unit requires two standard hours of labor for completion. Total overhead was budgeted at $900,000 for the year, and the fixed overhead rate was estimated to be $3 per unit. Both fixed and variable overhead are assigned to the product on the basis of direct labor hours. The actual data for the year ended November 30, 1999, are as follows:

Actual production in units	198,000
Actual direct labor hours	440,000
Actual variable overhead	$352,000
Actual fixed overhead	$575,000

Required

A. What are the standard hours allowed for actual production for the year ended November 30,1999?

B. What is Franklin's variable overhead efficiency variance for the year?

C. What is Franklin's variable overhead spending variance for the year?

D. What is Franklin's fixed overhead spending variance for the year?

E. What is the fixed overhead applied to Franklin's production for the year?

48. JanDan Inc. (JDI) is a specialty frozen food processor located in the southeastern states. Since its founding in 1992, JDI has enjoyed a loyal local clientele that is willing to pay premium prices for the high-quality frozen foods it prepares from specialized recipes. In the past two years, the company has experienced rapid sales growth in its operating region and has had many inquiries about supplying its products on a national basis. To meet this growth, JDI expanded its processing capabilities, which resulted in increased production and distribution costs. Furthermore, JDI has been encountering pricing pressure from competitors outside its normal marketing region.

As JDI desires to continue its expansion, Nick Guice, CEO, has engaged a consulting firm to assist JDI in determining its best course of action. The consulting firm concluded that, while premium pricing is sustainable in some areas, if sales growth is to be achieved, JDI must make some price concessions. Also, in order to maintain profit margins, costs must be reduced and controlled. The consulting firm recommended the institution of a standard cost system that would also facilitate a flexible budgeting system to better accommodate the changes in demand that can be expected when serving an expanding market area.

Guice met with his management team and explained the recommendations of the consulting firm. Guice then assigned the task of establishing standard costs to his management team. After discussing the situation with their respective staffs, the management team met to review the matter.

Janie Morgan, purchasing manager, advised that meeting expanded production would necessitate obtaining basic food supplies from other than JDI's traditional sources. This would entail increased raw material and shipping costs and might result in lower-quality supplies. Consequently, these increased costs would need to be made up by the processing department if current cost levels are to be maintained or reduced.

Dan Walters, processing manager, countered that the need to accelerate processing cycles to increase production, coupled with the possibility of receiving lower-grade supplies, can be expected to result in a slip in quality and a greater product rejection rate. Under these circumstances, per-unit labor utilization cannot be maintained or reduced, and forecasting future unit labor content becomes very difficult.

Corinne Kelly, production engineer, advised that if the equipment is not properly maintained and thoroughly cleaned at prescribed daily intervals, it can be anticipated that the quality and unique taste of the frozen food product will be affected. Kent Jackson, vice president of sales, stated that if quality cannot be maintained, JDI cannot expect to increase sales to the levels projected.

When Guice was apprised of the problems encountered by his management team, he advised them that if agreement could not be reached on appropriate standards he would arrange to have them set by the consulting firm, and everyone would have to live with the results.

Required

A. List the major advantages of using a standard cost system.

B. List disadvantages that can result from using a standard cost system.

C. Identify those who should participate in setting standards, and describe the benefits of their participation in the standard setting process.

D. Explain the general features and characteristics associated with the introduction and operation of a standard cost system that make it an effective tool for cost control.

E. What could be the consequences if Nick Guice, CEO of JanDan Inc., has the standards set by an outside consulting firm?

F. Explain what is meant by variance and variance analysis.

G. Discuss the materials variances and why they would occur.

H. Explain the overhead variances. Include a discussion of variable and fixed overhead variances.

In December (month 24) of the second year of operations, Big Al's produced and sold 32,675 pizzas, consisting of 30,570 meat pizzas and 2,105 veggie pizzas. The budgeted sales price for meat pizzas was $6.15 and the budgeted sales price for veggie pizzas was $5.85. The estimated production and sales during December was 31,678 meat pizzas and 2,595 veggie pizzas.

Required

A. Compute the price and volume variances for sales assuming that Big Al's sold all pizzas produced for $189,534 (meat) and $12,104 (veggie). What might explain these variances?

B. Compute the price and quantity variances for direct materials for each type of pizza assuming that Big Al's paid $58,185 for 32,325 units of raw material for meat pizzas and $3,265.36 for 2,401 units of raw material for veggie pizzas. (A unit consists of dough shells, sauce, cheese, meat or veggies and assembly materials). In addition they used 30,955 units in production of meat pizzas and 2,149 units in production of veggie pizzas. The budgeted (standard) costs of materials were based on the purchase of silver-quality level ingredients. How would these variances be interpreted? What might explain these variances? Would you consider them to be material.

C. Compute the labor rate and efficiency variances assuming that Big Al's paid $47,444 in labor costs for 7,150 hours of labor for meat pizzas and $4,193 in labor costs for 650 hours of labor for veggie pizzas. How would these variances be interpreted? What might explain these variances? Would you consider them to be material?

D. Compute the variable overhead rate and efficiency variances assuming that Big Al's paid $20,852 in total overhead costs consisting of $17,002 of variable overhead and $3,850 of fixed overhead. Use the predetermined overhead rate using direct labor hours as a base from Chapter 3. How would these variances be interpreted? What might explain these variances? Would you consider them to be material?

E. How might Big Al's extend their variance analysis to be compatible with their use of activity based costing as discussed in Chapter 4?

Chapter 11

OTHER TOOLS FOR COST CONTROL AND PERFORMANCE EVALUATION

Study Tools

A Review of the Previous Chapter

In Chapter 10 we discussed flexible budgeting and introduced the concept of standard costs and variance analysis as tools to help managers "manage by exception" and evaluate performance in their control function. The chapter also included a discussion of the use of variance analysis in an ABC environment, the limitations of standard costing, and variance analysis and behavioral considerations.

A Preview of This Chapter

In this chapter we discuss cost control and performance evaluation in a decentralized environment and the impact of responsibility accounting and segment reporting on decision making in decentralized organizations. We discuss performance evaluation in cost, profit, and investment centers utilizing variance analysis and other financial measures of performance including the segmented income statement, return on investment (ROI), residual income, and economic value added (EVA).

Key concepts include:
- There are advantages and disadvantages to decentralized companies.
- Decentralized organizations require very well-developed and well-integrated information systems.
- The key to effective decision making in a decentralized organization is responsibility accounting—holding managers responsible for only those things under their control.
- Evaluating investment centers requires focusing on the level of investment required in generating a segment's profit.

LEARNING OBJECTIVES

After studying the material in this chapter, you should be able to:

LO 1 Understand the structure and organization of decentralized operations

LO 2 Evaluate how responsibility accounting is used to help manage in decentralized operations

LO 3 Understand the concept of cost, profit, and investment centers and how managers of each must be evaluated differently

LO 4 Compute segment margin to evaluate the performance of managers and the segments under their control

LO 5 Compute and interpret return on investment (ROI), residual income, and economic value added (EVA) as measures of financial performance for investment centers

LO 6 Evaluate the impact of transfer pricing on segment performance and decision making

- The transfer price that provides the most benefit to the company as a whole is the one that should be chosen.

A Preview of Upcoming Chapters

In Chapter 12 we discuss a variety of nonfinancial and qualitative measures used in a "balanced scorecard" approach to measuring performance.

In this chapter we discuss organizations with an emphasis on cost control and performance evaluation in a decentralized environment. We also discuss the impact of responsibility accounting and segment reporting on decision making in decentralized organizations. We discuss performance evaluation in cost, profit, and investment centers utilizing variance analysis and other financial measures of performance including the segmented income statement, return on investment (ROI), residual income, and economic value added (EVA). Nonfinancial performance measures are discussed in more detail in Chapter 12. We conclude the chapter with a discussion of transfer pricing issues with respect to cost control and performance evaluation. ■

INTRODUCTION

As the owner and CEO of a chain of local retail shoe stores, you would be responsible for all aspects of your company's performance—from purchasing shoes to setting prices to investing in new fixtures or even expanding operations by opening new stores. Consequently, your performance should be evaluated based on all of these factors—the costs incurred, the revenue generated, and the investment made in the company. Contrast the responsibilities of the CEO of the company to the responsibilities of a manager of a specific store. As the store manager, you are likely to have some authority over setting prices of shoes, but purchasing decisions are made for the entire chain. Likewise, although you are likely to have some responsibility over making improvements to your store, major renovations and expansions can only be made with the approval of the CEO. Obviously it would not be fair to the store manager to evaluate his or her performance based on the profit earned by the entire chain. In addition, it would probably not be appropriate to evaluate the store manager's performance based on the profit of his or her store since a major component of the costs (the costs of shoes sold) is out of the store manager's control. In general, managers should be held responsible for only those things over which they have control. The dilemma for companies is to find tools that allow the evaluation of managers at all levels in the organization—from a plant manager in a factory, to the manager of a retail store, to the regional sales manager, to the CEO.

MANAGEMENT OF DECENTRALIZED ORGANIZATIONS

LO1
Understand the structure and organization of decentralized operations

A **decentralized organization** is one in which decision-making authority is spread throughout the organization as opposed to being confined to top-level management. When a few individuals at the top of an organization retain decision-making authority, the organization is referred to as centralized. In a decentralized environment managers at various levels throughout the organization make key decisions about operations relating to their specific area of responsibility. These areas are called segments. Segments can be branches and divisions or individual products. Any activity or part of the business for which a manager needs cost, revenue, or profit data can be considered a segment. Reporting financial and other information by segments is called segment reporting. This chapter discusses segment reporting and cost control and performance evaluation issues in segments of decentralized organizations.

Decentralization varies from organization to organization. Most organizations are decentralized to some degree. At one end of the spectrum, managers are given complete authority to make decisions at their level of operations. At the other extreme, managers have little, if any, authority to make decisions. Most firms will fall somewhere in the middle. However, the tendency is to move toward more, rather than less, decentralization.

IN THE NEWS   **www.ford.com**

Ford Motor Company recently reorganized its senior management by shifting authority to its regional operations in an effort to react faster to changing market conditions and boost sales. Under the new structure, Ford's regional and brand executives will have more authority in deciding what kinds of cars and trucks to make and how to market them ("Ford's Wallace Gets Top Financial Post, and Some Management Is Decentralized," *Wall Street Journal,* October 18, 1999, B4).

There are many benefits to decentralization. Generally those closest to a problem are most familiar with the problem and its root causes. In the past, decentralization has been key in improving customer service. By pushing decision-making authority down to lower levels, managers most familiar with a problem have the opportunity to solve it. At the same time, top management is left with more time to devote to long-range strategic planning since decentralization removes the responsibility for much of the day-to-day decision making. Third, studies have shown that managers allowed to make decisions in a decentralized environment have higher job satisfaction than managers in centralized organizations. Finally, managers who are given increased responsibility for decision making early in their careers generally become better managers because of the on-the-job training they receive. In other words, experience is the best teacher. Ford's recent decentralization was designed in part to help develop new talent by giving more executives responsibilities for entire businesses (see the previous "In the News").

However, there can be drawbacks. When decision-making authority is spread among too many managers, a lack of company focus can occur. Managers may become so concerned with their own area of responsibility that they lose sight of the big picture. Because of this lack of focus on the company as a whole, managers may tend to make decisions benefiting their own segment, which may not always be in the best interest of the company. In addition, managers may not be adequately trained in decision making at the early stages of their careers. The costs of training managers can be high and the potential costs of bad decisions while new managers are being trained should be considered.

 Key Concept: *There are advantages and disadvantages to decentralized companies.*

ACCOUNTING INFORMATION SYSTEMS AND DECENTRALIZED ORGANIZATIONS

Decentralized organizations require very well-developed and well-integrated information systems. The flow of information and open communication between divisions and upper and lower management is critical. This can be a problem for companies whose systems simply don't provide the kind of quantitative and qualitative information needed at the segment level. For this reason, the use of enterprise resource planning (ERP) systems has been particularly helpful in decentralized organizations. ERP systems (which are discussed in more detail in Chapter 13) integrate and provide information to managers throughout an organization. Information on individual segments and business lines is more readily available than ever before.

 Key Concept: *Decentralized organizations require very well-developed and well-integrated information systems.*

RESPONSIBILITY ACCOUNTING AND SEGMENT REPORTING

The key to effective decision making in a decentralized organization is **responsibility accounting**—holding managers responsible for only those things under their control. In reality, the amount of control a manager has can vary greatly from situation to situation. For example, 75 percent of the shoes offered for sale at the shoe department of your local Penney's may be purchased regionally or nationally to obtain quantity purchase discounts from suppliers, whereas 25 percent are purchased at the discretion of the individual store manager. Should the manager of the shoe department of the local Penney's be held responsible for the cost of shoes purchased and the profit earned on shoe sales?

LO2
Evaluate how responsibility accounting is used to help manage in decentralized operations

In the previous chapter, variance analysis was used to help evaluate the performance of managers by focusing on who had responsibility for a variance. Usage variances were typically the responsibility of production managers and price variances were typically the responsibility of purchasing managers. However, as you will recall, general rules like this must be used with caution. For example, the purchasing manager might be responsible for a usage variance if low-quality materials contributed to excessive waste.

In decentralized organizations, detailed information is needed to evaluate the effectiveness of managerial decision making. Company-wide budgets, cost standards, income statements, and so on are not sufficient to evaluate the performance of each of a company's segments. For example, in evaluating the performance of the myriad of managers at General Motors, overall financial statements generated for external reporting purposes would be of limited use. The manager of the Chevy truck division would be evaluated just on the results of the Chevy truck division, whereas the manager of the GM car division would be evaluated just on the results of that division. Going down a step further, a production manager dealing only with the manufacture of the Chevy S-10 pickup would be evaluated using different information than a production manager that only works with the C/K Silverado series of full-size trucks. Even within a product line, managers should only be held responsible for those things under their control. A manager on an engine assembly line should not be evaluated and held responsible for a production problem dealing with the vehicle body. Plant managers would be evaluated based on activities in their plant, regional sales managers would be held responsible for sales in their region, and so on.

www.gm.com

▶ **Key Concept:** *The key to effective decision making in a decentralized organization is responsibility accounting—holding managers responsible for only those things under their control.*

COST, PROFIT, AND INVESTMENT CENTERS

To enhance the use of responsibility accounting for decision making, organizations typically identify the different segments or levels of responsibility as cost, revenue, profit, or investment centers and attach different levels of responsibility to each segment. A **cost center** manager has control over costs but not over revenue or capital investment (purchasing) decisions. The purchasing manager of a store, the production manager for a particular type of CD player, the maintenance manager in a hotel, and the human resources manager of a CPA firm would likely be considered managers of cost centers. The manager of a cost center should be evaluated on how well he or she controls costs in the respective segment. Consequently, performance reports typically focus on differences between budgeted and actual costs using variance analysis. A **performance report** provides key financial and nonfinancial measures of performance appropriate for a particular segment.

A **revenue center** manager has control over the generation of revenue but not costs. Examples include the sales manager of a retail store, the sales department of a production facility, and the reservation department of an airline. Performance reports of a revenue center often focus on sales volume and sales price variances (discussed in Chapter 10).

A **profit center** manager has control over both cost and revenue but not capital investment decisions. Whereas the purchasing manager of a retail store was a manager of a cost center, the overall manager of the store would probably be a profit center manager. Likewise, the manager of an entire product line in a factory, the manager of a particular hotel location, and the partner in charge of the tax department at a CPA firm would be considered profit center managers. It is important to understand that profit center managers still don't have control over making investment decisions. For example, the profit center managers described here could not make decisions to remodel a store, buy new manufacturing equipment, add a swimming pool to a hotel, or open a new office.

The manager of a profit center should be evaluated on both revenue generation and cost control. Consequently, performance reports typically focus on income measures like

the overall flexible budget variance (discussed in Chapter 10). The flexible budget variance is the difference between the actual and budgeted operating income. However, this can be a problem when uncontrollable fixed costs are included in the analysis. Segment managers should only be held responsible for those costs under their control. Consequently, other measures of profit center performance like segment margin are also commonly used.

In addition to being responsible for a segment's revenue and expenses, an **investment center** manager is responsible for the amount of capital invested in generating its income. Investment centers (also called **strategic business units or SBUs**) are in essence separate businesses with their own value chains. An investment center manager is involved in decisions ranging from research and development to production to marketing and sales and customer service.

Although the manager of an investment center can be evaluated using some of the same tools as profit centers, the amount of assets or investment under the manager's control must also be considered. Measures of performance for investment centers are discussed later in the chapter.

PAUSE
& *Reflect*

The JCPenney store in your local shopping mall is likely treated as a profit center. What about a small independently owned and operated store like the one pictured?

www.jcpenney.com

PROFIT CENTER PERFORMANCE AND SEGMENTED INCOME STATEMENTS

Segmented income statements calculate income for each major segment of an organization in addition to the company as a whole. Although it is usually easy to keep records of sales by segment, tracing costs to a particular segment and deciding how to treat costs that are incurred for more than one segment can be very difficult.

Variable costs (unit-level costs) are generally traced directly to a segment. Remember, variable costs vary in direct proportion to sales volume. Therefore, they can be allocated to a segment based on sales volume.

Deciding which fixed costs to assign or allocate to a segment requires an analysis of the overall company and the individual areas of responsibility (segments) within an organization. **Segment costs** should include *all* costs attributable to that segment, but *only* those costs that are actually caused by the segment. Fixed costs that can be easily and conveniently traced to a segment should obviously be assigned to that segment. The problem is that many fixed costs are indirect in nature. Should indirect fixed costs be allocated to segments? A good test for deciding whether to allocate indirect fixed costs is to determine if the cost would be reduced or eliminated if the segment were eliminated. If the cost cannot

LO3
Understand the concept of cost, profit, and investment centers and how managers of each must be evaluated differently

CAMELBACK MOUNTAIN COMMUNITY BANK

be reduced or eliminated, it is referred to as a common cost. **Common costs** are indirect costs that are incurred to benefit more than one segment and cannot be directly traced to a particular segment or allocated in a reasonable manner based on what causes the cost to be incurred. In general, common costs should not be allocated to segments.

For example, Camelback Mountain Community Bank (headquartered in Phoenix, Arizona) has six branches located in and around the Phoenix metropolitan area. One of those branches is located in Tempe. The Tempe branch incurs fixed lease expense to rent the building in which the bank is located. Obviously, this lease expense is directly traceable to the individual branch (a segment) and should be allocated to that segment. However, if the lease expense is for the corporate headquarters building in Phoenix, the cost is an indirect one and probably should not be allocated to the Tempe branch. In this case, it is doubtful that the lease expense for the headquarters building would be reduced or eliminated if the Tempe branch were eliminated. Therefore, it is probably best treated as a common cost and not allocated to the segment.[1]

Other indirect costs can be allocated to segments if there is a sufficient causal relationship between the cost and the segment. For example, all loan processing for Camelback Mountain Community Bank is done in the headquarters building in Phoenix. Although these costs (credit checks, loan processing costs, staff salaries, etc.) may be difficult to directly trace to the Tempe branch, they can be allocated in a manner that reflects the cause of the costs (the number of loans processed, the dollar amount of loans processed, etc.). In addition, it is reasonable to assume that at least some of the loan processing costs would be reduced or eliminated if the branch were closed.

To allocate indirect costs, there should be a causal relationship between the allocation base and a segment's use of the common cost. Allocating costs using an arbitrary allocation base is inappropriate. Although Camelback Mountain Community Bank could allocate the lease cost of the headquarters building to its branches based on an allocation base such as square footage or total deposits, such a base would be completely arbitrary. There is no causal relationship between the square footage or total deposits in a branch and the lease expense in the headquarters building. Arbitrary allocations like this may result in a profitable segment appearing unprofitable and may lead to less than optimal decisions concerning that segment.

IN THE NEWS   www.jcpenney.com

J.C. Penney Co. allocates the corporate costs of auditing, legal, and personnel services to its subsidiaries based on the time spent providing the services to each subsidiary. In the past, the allocation was made based on the revenue earned by each subsidiary ("Teamwork Pays Off at Penney's," *Business Week,* no. 2734, pp. 107–108).

GARCIA&BUFFET CPAS

THE SEGMENTED INCOME STATEMENT

Garcia and Buffett is a full-service local CPA firm offering services in three departments: tax, audit, and consulting. The tax department is further broken down into individual and business divisions. Garcia and Buffett have annual client billings of $1,000,000 with 50 percent generated from the tax department, 40 percent from the audit department, and the remaining 10 percent from the consulting department. The following table shows

---

[1]In practice, companies sometimes allocate common costs from headquarters to segments without using them for evaluation purposes. This practice has the advantage of making the segment manager aware that the cost is being incurred and that the cost must ultimately be paid for by revenue generated by the segment.

a segmented income statement broken down into three segments based on the three practice departments:

LO4
Compute segment margin to evaluate the performance of managers and the segments under their control

Segmented Income Statement Using Contribution Format
Segments Defined as Departments

	Total Firm	Tax Department	Audit Department	Consulting Department
Client billings	$1,000,000	$500,000	$400,000	$100,000
Less: Variable expenses	400,000	200,000	160,000	40,000
Contribution margin	$ 600,000	$300,000	$240,000	$ 60,000
Less: Traceable fixed	200,000	100,000	75,000	25,000
Segment margin	$ 400,000	$200,000	$165,000	$ 35,000
Less: Common fixed	200,000			
Net income	$ 200,000			

The $100,000 of fixed costs traceable to the tax department include advertising specifically geared to the tax department, the salary of the tax manager, the costs of research material used in the tax library, and computer software used for tax preparation. Common fixed costs (for the firm as a whole) include salaries of the managing partner of the firm, the human resources manager, and the receptionist, and depreciation of the office building.

In the following table, Garcia and Buffett go a step further and provide a segmented income statement for the two divisions within the tax department. Note that the statements are based on the contribution margin format introduced in Chapter 6. The primary difference is the separation of fixed costs into traceable fixed costs and common fixed costs and the interim calculation of segment margin.

Segmented Income Statement Using Contribution Format
Segments Defined as Divisions

	Tax Department	Individual Tax Division	Business Tax Division
Client billings	$500,000	$100,000	$400,000
Less: Variable expenses	200,000	80,000	120,000
Contribution Margin	$300,000	$ 20,000	$280,000
Less: Traceable fixed	80,000	30,000	50,000
Divisional segment margin	$220,000	$ (10,000)	$230,000
Less: Common fixed	20,000		
Departmental segment margin	$200,000		

Note that although $100,000 of fixed costs were traced to the tax department in the first figure (when segments were defined as departments), only $80,000 are subsequently traced to the individual and business divisions; $20,000 of traceable costs have become common costs. In this case, the advertising costs for the tax division and the cost of research materials in the tax library cannot be traced directly to either the individual or business division.

As discussed in Chapter 6, contribution margin is primarily a measure of short-run profitability, as it ignores fixed costs. It is used extensively in short-run decisions such as CVP analysis and evaluation of special orders. On the other hand, **segment margin** is a measure of long-term profitability and is more appropriate in addressing long-term decisions such as whether to drop product lines.

In the case of Garcia and Buffett, the segment margin of the tax department is positive but the segment margin of the individual tax division is negative. In the long run, the

Garcia and Buffett have considered allocating the advertising costs to each division based on the revenue generated in each division. Comment on whether this is appropriate allocation base.

EXHIBIT 11-1 The Value Chain

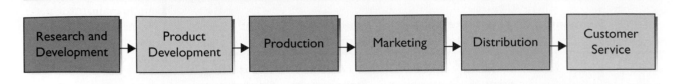

GARCIA&BUFFET CPAS

individual tax division is not profitable. However, before the firm decides to eliminate the individual tax division, it should consider other factors (both quantitative and qualitative), including the impact on its highly profitable business tax division.

For example, it may be important for the firm to be perceived as a full-service firm where owners of small businesses can come for help with all of their tax and business problems. In addition, planning for a small business must often be integrated with planning for the individual owner of the business. For these reasons, the firm may decide to retain the division even if it has not been profitable. Instead of eliminating the division, Garcia and Buffett may decide to focus on ways to make the division profitable through expanding the array of services offered to clients. For example, they may begin offering personal financial planning services to their clients to help them meet their overall financial goals.

SEGMENT PERFORMANCE AND THE VALUE CHAIN

When segment margin is used to evaluate performance and to make decisions like whether a segment should be discontinued, it is important to remember that costs are incurred throughout the value chain, not just in the manufacturing process. The value chain includes costs associated with research and development, product design, manufacturing, marketing, distribution, and customer service (see Exhibit 11-1). When making long-run decisions regarding the profitability of a segment (for example, whether to stop manufacturing a product or providing a service), it is imperative that managers consider all costs incurred in the value chain.

SEGMENT PERFORMANCE AND ACTIVITY-BASED COSTING

The use of activity-based costing (ABC) can affect the classification of costs as traceable or common. As you will recall from the discussion in Chapter 4, when ABC is used, many costs that were previously considered "fixed" are found to vary with respect to batch- or product-level cost drivers. In manufacturing firms, batch-level and product-level activities and costs are often driven by factors such as the number of setups, the number of parts, the number of customer orders, the number of supervision hours, and so on. In service-oriented companies, these costs may vary with the number of customers serviced, the size of the client, or the number of hours spent reviewing files. For example, the "fixed" costs of a research aid in the tax research library at Garcia and Buffett might be driven by the number of research hours provided to each division.

APPLICATION IN BUSINESS

CPA firms incur a variety of costs related to auditing and providing other services to large clients that are publicly held (have stock owned by the general public). These costs (additional training for employees, peer reviews and other quality reviews mandated by regulators, etc.) might traditionally be considered fixed because they don't vary with revenue or other measures of volume. However, they are in fact driven by the size of clients serviced. If a firm has only a few large publicly held clients, it may choose to stop servicing those clients in order to eliminate a variety of these product-level costs.

INVESTMENT CENTERS AND MEASURES OF PERFORMANCE

In addition to being responsible for a segment's revenue and expenses, an investment center manager is responsible for the amount of capital invested in generating its income. Investment center managers can make capital purchasing decisions including decisions to remodel facilities, purchase new equipment, expand facilities, or add new locations. Investment centers are typically major divisions or branch operations of a company involved in all aspects of the value chain. In addition to being evaluated using the approaches discussed earlier for cost and profit centers, evaluating investment centers requires focusing on the level of investment required in generating a segment's profit. For this reason, performance reports focus on measures specifically developed for this purpose—return on investment, residual income, and economic value added.

LO5
Compute and interpret return on investment (ROI), residual income, and economic value added (EVA) as measures of financial performance for investment centers

 Key Concept: *Evaluating investment centers requires focusing on the level of investment required in generating a segment's profit.*

Concept Question: *Does the manager of a local branch of a national bank likely manage a profit or investment center? What about the manager of the local Pizza Hut? What about the manager of an independent pizza restaurant or clothing store who is also the owner of that store?*

Concept Answer: Although the answer depends on exactly what the manager of each segment controls, the managers of the local branch of the bank and the Pizza Hut franchise are likely to be evaluated as the managers of profit centers whereas the owners of the independent stores would likely be treated as managers of investment centers. ■

Managers of investment centers are given complete control over all activities in their respective segments. In fact, an investment center is often treated like a separate business—hence the name *strategic business units.* Managers want to be associated with well-run, profitable divisions. Competition between investment center managers within an organization is sometimes intense. Because of compensation issues such as year-end bonuses based on performance, managers of investment centers must also be evaluated. Although all of the financial measures of performance used in evaluating the managers of cost, revenue, and profit centers apply to investment center managers, they are not sufficient. To some extent, controlling costs and generating revenue (and income) is a function of the investment assets under a manager's control. For example, if a manager had unlimited resources, production costs could be reduced by buying the most efficient equipment available regardless of the cost. Likewise, sales might be maximized by additional spending on advertising. Income is often larger in big companies than small companies. However, an investment center manager with low costs, high revenues, and high income cannot really be evaluated without reference to the size of the investment center being managed and the assets under the manager's control.

RETURN ON INVESTMENT (ROI)

DuPont was the first major company in the United States to recognize that the performance of an investment center must consider the level of investment along with the income generated from that investment. **Return on investment (ROI)** measures the rate of return generated by an investment center's assets.

www.dupont.com

ROI can be a very simple concept. For example, if you invest $1,000 in a bank certificate of deposit for one year and receive $50 at the end of the year, your return on that investment is 5 percent ($50/$1,000). However, the calculation of return gets a little more complicated when the income is reinvested in another certificate, the amount of assets change, and costs are incurred to manage the money.

In business, the calculation of ROI is generally broken down into two components—a measure of operating performance (called margin) and a measure of how effectively assets are used during a period (called asset turnover). **Margin** is found by dividing an investment center's net operating income by its sales. As such, it can be viewed as the profit that is earned on each dollar of sales. A margin of 10 percent indicates that 10 cents of every sales dollar is profit. **Asset turnover** is calculated by dividing an investment center's sales by its average operating assets during a period. It measures the sales that are generated for a given level of assets.

The formula for return on investment (ROI) is as follows:

$$ROI = Margin \times Turnover$$
$$Margin = Net\ operating\ income/Sales$$
$$Turnover = Sales/Average\ operating\ assets$$
$$So\ ROI = \frac{Net\ operating\ income}{Sales} \times \frac{Sales}{Average\ operating\ assets}$$

or

$$ROI = \frac{Net\ operating\ income}{Average\ operating\ assets}$$

In graphical form, the elements comprising ROI are shown in Exhibit 11-2.

Although different investment centers (including companies) may have similar ROIs, their margin and turnover may be very different. For example, a grocery store and furniture store both have an ROI of 20 percent. However, the grocery store's ROI may be made up of a profit margin of $.02 per dollar of product sold and a turnover of 10 while the furniture store may have a margin of $.10 per dollar of product sold and a turnover of 2. In this case, the grocery store does not make much from each dollar of sales but generates a lot of sales for the amount of its assets. On the other hand, the furniture store makes more from each sale but does not generate as many sales for the amount of assets under its control.

Net operating income is most frequently used as the measure of income in the ROI formula. Net operating income is defined as income before interest and taxes.

Likewise, the most common measure of investment is average operating assets. **Operating assets** typically include cash, accounts receivable, inventory, and property, plant, and equipment needed to operate a business. Land and other assets held for resale or assets that are idle (a plant that is not being used) are typically not included in operating assets. Since

Inventory turnover in a grocery store is likely to be much higher than turnover in a furniture store.

EXHIBIT 11-2   Elements of Return on Investment (ROI)

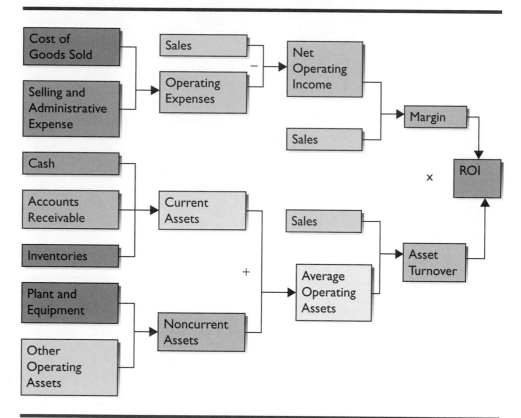

income is measured over time, assets are also generally measured as an average of beginning and end of period numbers. By focusing on operating income and average operating assets, ROI attempts to isolate the financial performance of a company's core operations.

Whereas cash, accounts receivable, and inventory are generally easy to measure, the measurement of depreciable property, plant, and equipment for purposes of determining ROI poses some interesting questions. The use of net book value (the cost of the assets less accumulated depreciation) is consistent with the calculation of operating income (which includes depreciation expense) but can have some undesirable consequences. For example, as an asset ages, the net book value of the asset decreases. Using the net book value method can cause ROI to increase over time simply because of the reduction in book value of assets used in the calculation. Choice of depreciation method can also affect ROI calculations. By choosing an accelerated method over straight-line, the book value of the asset decreases more rapidly, increasing ROI. Both of these factors may discourage managers from replacing old assets like manufacturing equipment. If managers are evaluated based on ROI, they may be very reluctant to replace aging machinery with a very low book value with an expensive but more efficient piece of equipment.

The use of gross book value to measure operating assets eliminates age of an asset as a factor in the ROI calculation and any distortions that can be caused by the depreciation method chosen. To illustrate the use of ROI, consider the financial results of Big Al's Pizza Emporium. During 1999, Big Al's had average operating assets of $100,000 consisting of cash, accounts receivable, inventory, and furniture and equipment at book value. All are considered operating assets. Big Al's sales for the year were $350,000 (consisting of $275,000 for 23,000 pizzas and $75,000 for drinks and other side orders). Operating income was $17,500. The ROI for Big Al's using the net book value method would be 17.5 percent consisting of margin of .05 $\left(\frac{\$17,500}{\$350,000}\right)$ and asset turnover of 3.5 $\left(\frac{\$350,000}{\$100,000}\right)$.

PAUSE & Reflect

Why might investing in new assets decrease ROI? Will ROI always go down when new equipment is purchased?

A contribution format income statement for Big Al's is provided in the following table:

Big Al's Pizza Emporium
Contribution Format Income Statement

Sales Revenue		$350,000	100%
Variable Costs			
Production	$175,000		
S G & A	75,000	250,000	
Contribution margin		100,000	28.57
Fixed Costs			
Production	50,000		
S G & A	32,500	82,500	
Net operating income		$ 17,500	

If Big Al would like to increase ROI, what are his options? In general, sales can be increased, operating expenses can be reduced, or the investment in operating assets can be reduced. The first two alternatives increase operating income and the last option decreases net operating assets.

INCREASE SALES VOLUME OR SALES PRICE

Sales revenue can be raised by either increasing sales volume without changing the sales price or by increasing the sales price without affecting volume. Remember that when sales volume increases, variable costs increase by the same proportional amount because variable costs stay the same per unit but increase in total as more units are sold. In addition, fixed costs remain the same. Thus if sales volume increases by 5 percent (resulting in sales revenue of $367,500), income will increase by $5,000 to $22,500. ROI will correspondingly increase to 22.5 percent $\left(\frac{\$22,500}{\$100,000}\right)$.

Big Al's Pizza Emporium
Contribution Format Income Statement

Sales Revenue		$367,500	100%
Variable Costs			
Production	$183,750		
S G & A	78,750	262,500	
Contribution margin		105,000	28.57
Fixed Costs			
Production	50,000		
S G & A	32,500	82,500	
Net operating income		$ 22,500	

Remember that the contribution margin ratio can be used to quickly calculate the impact on income of a change in sales. If sales increase by $17,500, income will increase by 28.57 percent × $17,500 or $5,000.

Concept Question: *How much would sales volume have to increase to increase Big Al's ROI to 20 percent?*

Concept Answer: Net operating income of $20,000 would generate a ROI of 20 percent ($20,000/$100,000). Using the contribution margin ratio of 28.57 percent, increasing income by $2,500 would require a $8,750 increase in sales revenue to $358,750. ■

If Big Al just changes the price of his products, the analysis is a little different. Increasing sales prices (without a corresponding change in volume) does *not* affect variable costs or fixed costs. Thus if revenue were increased by $17,500 because of a 5 percent increase in sales price, income would increase by the same $17,500. ROI would increase to 35 percent $\left(\frac{\$35,000}{\$100,000}\right)$.

Concept Question: *How might Big Al increase sales volume without decreasing sales prices or increasing other costs like advertising, or increase sales prices without affecting volume?*

Concept Answer: Neither is likely. As a practical matter, changing sales volume or sales price is likely to impact other variables as well. For this reason, Big Al might try to increase ROI using other options discussed below. ■

DECREASE OPERATING COSTS

ROI can also be increased by decreasing operating costs. The decrease in costs can be concentrated in variable or fixed costs or both. The key is that any decrease in operating costs will increase operating income and have a positive impact on ROI. In the following income statement, variable production costs are reduced by 5 percent by using a different supplier for direct materials. Income increases by $8,750 resulting in ROI of 26.25 percent $\left(\frac{\$26,250}{\$100,000}\right)$.

Big Al's Pizza Emporium
Contribution Format Income Statement

Sales Revenue		$350,000	100%
Variable Costs			
Production	$166,250		
S G & A	75,000	241,250	
Contribution margin		108,750	31.07
Fixed Costs			
Production	50,000		
S G & A	32,500	82,500	
Net operating income		$ 26,250	

Concept Question: *Why did the contribution margin percentage increase when the variable costs were lowered? Would it change if fixed costs were lowered?*

Concept Answer: Remember the structure of the contribution format income statement. Contribution margin is equal to sales minus all the variable costs, so when the variable costs are lowered the contribution margin will increase as will the percentage. Because fixed costs are deducted from contribution margin, a change in fixed cost would not affect contribution margin. ■

Decrease the Amount of Operating Assets

The third way to increase ROI is to decrease the amount invested in operating assets. Although this may be difficult to do in the short run with property, plant, and equipment, the amount of average operating assets can be decreased through better management of accounts receivable, a reduction in inventory levels, and so on. For example, let's assume that Big Al's reduces operating assets by 10 percent by lowering the amount of materials kept in inventory and more prudently collecting accounts receivable. Reducing average operating assets to $90,000 will increase ROI to 19.44 percent.

In some cases, evaluating the performance of an investment center and its manager using ROI can cause problems. For example, Big Al is thinking about opening a second location and bringing in a new manager to run the business at the existing location. (Since the new location will be substantially larger than the existing location, he wants to devote his full attention to the successful startup of the new location.) Before leaving, Big Al worked diligently to reduce operating costs and increased the location's net operating income to $22,500. He also reduced the location's average operating assets to $90,000 through actively managing his inventory. ROI was therefore 25 percent. His goal and minimum acceptable return for both locations is to maintain a ROI of 20 percent. However, the new manager may reject potential projects or investments that are profitable (and earn a return greater than 20 percent) but would lower the location's overall ROI. For example, the new manager is considering purchasing a new automated pizza oven that will reduce the time it takes to make a pizza and the electricity consumed. The equipment costs $15,000 and is expected to result in increased income of $3,200. Although the return on investment for this particular piece of equipment is over 21 percent, the manager is likely to reject the purchase because it will reduce his overall ROI.

Using ROI to compare segments within a company can also be a problem. For example, a consulting division of a company operated as an investment center is likely to have few tangible assets compared to an asset-intensive manufacturing division operated as an investment center. If both generate an ROI of 15 percent, which appears to be doing better? Rather than comparing the ROI of divisions with different assets, costs, and revenue streams, it is often preferable to compare the ROI of a segment to a budget or goal for that segment.

RESIDUAL INCOME

As an alternative to ROI, the manager of an investment center can be evaluated based on the residual income generated by the strategic business unit (SBU). **Residual income** is the amount of income earned in excess of some predetermined minimum level of return on assets. All other things being equal, the higher the residual income of an investment center, the better.

$$\text{Residual income} =$$
$$\text{Net operating income} - (\text{Average operating assets} \times \text{Minimum required rate of return})$$

In the case of Big Al's (discussed earlier) at the time the new location is opened, the residual income at the existing location would be as follows:

$$\$22,500 - (\$90,000 \times 20\%) = \$4,500$$

If the new manager has the opportunity to purchase a new pizza oven at a cost of $15,000 and expects that profits will increase by $3,200, evaluating the new manager using residual income will result in the manager purchasing the new oven. The residual income of the existing location will increase from $4,500 to $4,700 as follows:

$$\$25,700 - (\$105,000 \times 20\%) = \$4,700$$

Concept Question: *If Big Al's has a minimum required rate of return equal to 20 percent and generates a residual income of zero on sales of $350,000 and average operating assets of $90,000, what is its ROI?*

Concept Answer: Big Al's income must be equal to $18,000 resulting in a ROI of 20 percent $\left(\dfrac{\$18,000}{\$90,000}\right)$.

Residual income has its problems as well. It should not be used to compare the performance of investment centers of different size. For example, Big Al's new location will be considerably larger than the existing location. As shown here, average operating assets in the new location total $300,000 compared to $105,000 in the existing location.

Return on Investment and Residual Income

	Existing Location	New Location
Average operating assets	$105,000	$300,000
Minimum required return	20%	20%
Net operating income	$ 25,700	$ 70,000
Residual income	$ 4,700	$ 10,000
ROI	24.5%	23.3%

In this case, the residual income of the new location (run by Big Al) is higher than the residual income of the existing location (run by the new manager). However, Big Al did not necessarily manage the new location better, it's just bigger. As you can see, the ROI of the new division is actually lower than the ROI of the existing location. Which measure is best? Both are useful but often for different purposes. Residual income is most useful as a performance measure for a single investment center while ROI is better suited as a comparative measure. However, as mentioned earlier, ROI must be used cautiously when comparing investment centers with different core businesses or those with markedly different revenue and cost structures.

TECHNOLOGY FOCUS

E-business and Internet companies often have very few tangible assets. On the other hand, they may have large investments in employee resources and intellectual capital. How might traditional measures like ROI and residual income be adjusted to reflect these new types of businesses?

APPLICATION IN BUSINESS   **www.daimlerchrysler.com**

Large international companies may have several core businesses. For example, Daimler Chrysler has over a half dozen major business components operating as strategic business units. During the first half of 1999, the revenue generated from the SBUs ranged from $34 billion in the passenger car and truck division (generating more than $3 billion of operating profit) to $400 million in revenues in their diesel engine division. They also have a financial services and information technology division with revenues of more than $6 billion and operating profit of more than $700 million.

ECONOMIC VALUE ADDED (EVA)

The most contemporary measure of investment center performance is **economic value added (EVA).**[2] In a nutshell, EVA tells management whether shareholder wealth is being created by focusing on whether after-tax profits are greater than the cost of capital. Although it is primarily a measure of shareholder wealth, companies may use it internally as part of incentive compensation plans or to encourage managers to undertake desired behavior.

> Economic value added = After-tax operating profit − [(Total assets −
> Current liabilities) × Weighted average cost of capital]

As you can see, the calculation of EVA is very similar to that for residual income. However, EVA does have several important differences. First, EVA is based on after-tax operating profit, not before-tax operating profit. Second, assets are often shown net of current liabilities. In addition, companies may modify income and asset measurements based on generally accepted accounting principles (GAAP) to better reflect the changing nature of business today. For example, to encourage investments in research and development, employee training, and customer development, expenditures in these areas may be capitalized as an asset for EVA purposes rather than expensed against income. Inventories may be restated to their replacement cost and the value of assets may be restated to reflect their true economic value.

Finally, EVA considers the actual cost of capital, both debt and equity, as compared to a minimum required rate of return. The calculation of the cost of debt is straightforward and is equal to the interest paid on that debt. However, the cost of equity is more complex and is basically assumed to be the amount that an investor could earn on an investment with similar risk.

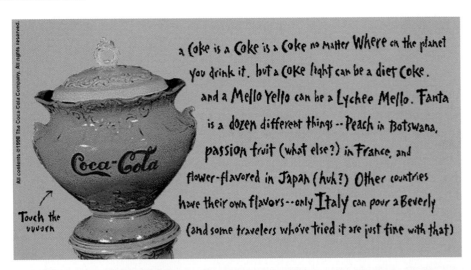

a Coke is a Coke is a Coke no matter Where on the planet you drink it. but a Coke light can be a diet Coke. and a Mello Yello can be a Lychee Mello. Fanta is a dozen different things -- Peach in Botswana, passion fruit (what else?) in France, and flower-flavored in Japan (huh?) Other countries have their own flavors -- only Italy can pour a Beverly (and some travelers who've tried it are just fine with that)

Touch the vuvurn

IN THE NEWS | www.cocacola.com

Roberto Goizueeta, the past CEO of Coca-Cola, explains EVA this way: "We raise capital to make concentrate, and sell it and make operating profit. Then we pay the cost of capital. Shareholders pocket the difference" ("The Real Key to Creating Wealth," by Shawn Tully, *Fortune,* September, 20, 1993).

---

[2]EVA is a registered trademark of Stern Stewart & Company.

MANAGEMENT ACTIONS AND DECISIONS

www.sprint.com

At Sprint, managers are given recommendations on how to incorporate EVA into their everyday decisions.

BUILD

Commit new capital to value-creating projects. For example:

- What equipment should we buy to provide new and better products and services to our customers?
- What new marketing efforts will improve customer satisfaction and result in increased sales and profits?
- What new business opportunities should we pursue?

Increase profits without using additional capital. For example:

- How can we reduce customer churn or sell more products without spending more?
- What costs can be reduced through Business Process Improvement efforts?
- How can we change government regulation to make our business operate more efficiently?

STREAMLINE

EXIT

Withdraw capital from activities that produce inadequate returns compared to other uses for that capital. For example:

- What products and customers are not as profitable as we expect?
- How can accounts receivable or inventories be reduced to free up cash?
- What assets should be sold or redeployed?

EVA is used in a variety of business management processes to align our actions with creating value.

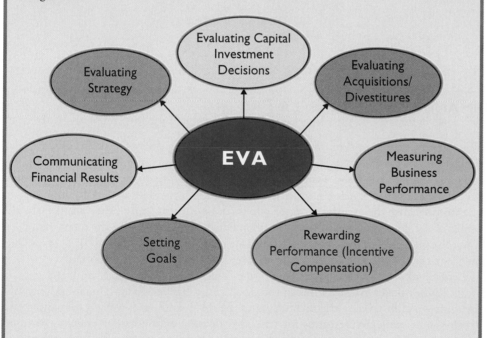

As an example, assume that a division operating as an SBU has the following results:

Operating income per GAAP financial statements (before tax)	$1,000,000
Total assets per GAAP financial statements	4,000,000
Expenditures related to employee training, research and development, and customer development[1]	1,000,000
Fair market value of property, plant, and equipment[2]	2,500,000
Current liabilities	500,000
Tax rate	40%
Weighted average cost of capital	10%

[1] These expenditures were expensed on the GAAP financial statements. Management chooses to capitalize them for purposes of calculating EVA.

[2] Included on the balance sheet at cost of $2,000,000. Management chooses to use the fair market value of assets in calculating EVA.

After adjusting for the impact of capitalizing expenditures related to employee training, research and development, and customer development, operating income is equal to $2,000,000 and after-tax operating income is $1,200,000 [($2,000,000 × (1 − .40)]. Total assets of $4,000,000 (per GAAP) are increased by $1,500,000 to reflect the impact of the capitalized expenses of $1,000,000 and to increase property, plant, and equipment to fair market value. After adjusting for current liabilities, assets used in the EVA calculation are equal to $5,000,000.

$$EVA = \$1,200,000 - [\$5,000,000 \times 10\%)]$$
$$= \$1,200,000 - \$500,000$$
$$= \$700,000$$

SEGMENT PERFORMANCE AND TRANSFER PRICING

LO6

Evaluate the impact of transfer pricing on segment performance and decision making

When segments within the same company sell products or services to one another, special problems arise when evaluating performance of the segments. For example, when an automobile manufacturer also manufactures car batteries, what price does the battery division charge the auto division for the battery? This may seem like an easy or unimportant question because the transfer is made within the same company. After all, if I am the owner of the company, what comes out of one pocket simply goes in the other. However, when the managers of the separate divisions are evaluated based on profit or other performance measures like ROI or EVA, the **transfer price** becomes very important.

Let's refer back to Chapter 7 and use Birdie-Maker Golf Inc. as an example. As you will recall, Birdie-Maker manufactures and sells golf clubs. Birdie-Maker is organized into two divisions—a club division that manufactures the shafts and heads for its clubs and a grip division that manufactures grips for its clubs. Because Birdie-Maker evaluates division managers based on the profit generated in their respective profit centers, the manager of the grip division will want to charge the highest possible price for its product and the manager of the club division will want to buy grips at the lowest possible price. Therein lies the problem in transfer pricing. The amount to set for the transfer price is a complex problem with no easy solution.

There are basically three approaches to establishing transfer prices. The first is to use a market price if available. The second is to base the transfer price on the cost of the product transferred. The third is to let the buyer and seller negotiate the price.

TRANSFER PRICE AT MARKET

If there is an outside market for the product being transferred between divisions, the transfer price should be based on the market price of the product. However, in order to be effective, the manager of the buying division must have the authority to purchase from an outside supplier if the selling division does not want to meet the market price, and the manager of the selling division must have the authority to sell to outside buyers if he can earn a higher profit. The use of a market price thus provides an incentive for both the selling division and the buying division to maximize their profits. In reality, few transfers take place at exactly the market price. For example, the grip division of Birdie-Maker can sell grips to another club manufacturer for $10 per grip. However, if the grip division sells internally to the Birdie-Maker club division, it will realize some cost savings due to reduced storage and shipping costs. This may lead to negotiations between the manager of the grip division and the manger of the club division and a transfer at a price somewhat under $10.

Birdie Maker

If the selling division is not at full capacity, the transfer price will often be adjusted as well. For example, if the grip division has the capacity to make 20,000 grips but can only sell 10,000 to outside buyers, it is likely that the two divisions will set transfer prices based on cost or negotiate a transfer price below the full market price of the grips.

TRANSFER PRICE AT COST

When no outside market exists, or when the selling division has excess capacity, transfer prices are often established based on the cost of the product being transferred.

No Outside Market Let's assume that Birdie-Maker's grip is unique and therefore cannot be sold to other club manufacturers. Birdie-Maker's grip division manufactures grips for $6, which consists of $4 of direct material, direct labor, and variable overhead and $40,000 of fixed manufacturing costs (based on a capacity of 20,000 grips). Administrative costs include $1 of variable costs and $20,000 of fixed costs.

If Birdie-Maker chooses to set the transfer price using product cost as the basis, the question becomes, at what cost? Variable manufacturing costs are $4 per grip, and total variable costs are $5 per grip while the full absorption cost of making a grip is $6. Total costs including the fixed administrative costs are $7. In order for the grip division to truly operate as a profit center (and to be evaluated as such), it must be able to earn a profit. However, the club division may be reluctant to "buy" at whatever price is established by the grip division. What price is fair?

When we use our decision model to address this problem (see Exhibit 11-3), we first define the decision to be made. The decision to be made is to establish a transfer price for grips that are to be sold to the club division. The objectives of the decision are to set a price that does not adversely affect either manager or the firm and to maximize Birdie-Maker's overall profit. The options in this situation are to establish the transfer price at the variable manufacturing costs of making the grips, the full cost of making the grips, or even to set the price so that the grip division earns an acceptable profit.

EXHIBIT 11-3 The Decision-Making Model

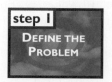
step 1 DEFINE THE PROBLEM

step 2 IDENTIFY OBJECTIVES

step 3 IDENTIFY AND ANALYZE AVAILABLE OPTIONS

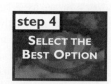
step 4 SELECT THE BEST OPTION

If the transfer is made at cost (either variable or full), the grip division cannot be evaluated as a profit center. Rather it should be evaluated as a cost center and held responsible only for the costs incurred in manufacturing grips. Transfers based on costs also can result in some problems from the buying division's perspective. If the selling division is simply allowed to pass along all costs to the buying division, inefficiencies in cost control in the selling division will be passed along to the buying division in the form of a higher "price."

Birdie Maker

Outside Market and Excess Capacity When an outside market exists for the product and Birdie-Maker can sell grips to other club manufacturers, the transfer price hinges on whether the manufacturing facility has excess capacity. As we already discussed, if the grip division has no excess capacity and can sell all its grips to an outside buyer, the transfer price should be based on the market price (potentially adjusted for cost savings). If the grip division has excess capacity, the problem gets more difficult. As in the case of accepting special orders, in the short run, the grip division will benefit as long as the transfer price exceeds all the variable costs associated with the product. Thus, the grip division should be willing to sell grips to the club division at any price over $5. The actual price is likely to be negotiated between the grip division and the club division.

NEGOTIATED TRANSFER PRICES

In many cases, transfer prices are negotiated between buyer and seller and end up somewhere between cost and the market price. Negotiated prices work best where there is no reliable market price or in situations where the general transfer pricing formula (discussed in the next section) provides different minimum and maximum transfer prices.

A GENERAL MODEL FOR COMPUTING TRANSFER PRICES

Regardless of the method chosen, a general formula for computing transfer prices can be developed in which the minimum transfer price is the variable cost of making and selling the product plus any contribution margin that may be lost to the selling division as a result of giving up sales to outside customers.

> Minimum transfer price = Variable costs of producing and selling
> + Contribution margin lost on outside sales

The contribution margin lost on outside sales is an opportunity cost—the benefit the selling division would forgo by not selling to an outside buyer. The maximum price of the transfer should be the market price (if available).

Continuing our example, if the grip division has no outside market for grips, the minimum transfer price will be $5 + 0 = $5. Because there is no outside market, there is no lost contribution margin. It is likely that the actual transfer price would be negotiated up from this $5 minimum. If the grip division is at full capacity and can sell all its grips to an outside buyer for $10, the minimum transfer price will be $5 + $5 = $10. For every grip that is sold internally, the grip division will lose $5 of contribution margin on outside sales. Note that the maximum price will also be $10 (the market price). If the grip division is not at full capacity but still has an outside market for its product, the pricing gets more interesting. For example, let's assume that the grip division has a capacity of 12,000 clubs and can only sell 8,000 to outside buyers. If the club division needs all 12,000 clubs, the transfer price on the first 8,000 should be set at the market price of $10. The other 4,000 can be sold at any price greater than the $5 of variable costs. If all 12,000 grips are sold internally, the general pricing formula in this case gives us a minimum price of $8.33. The variable costs of making the grips equal $5 while the contribution margin lost on outside sales equals $3.33 per club (8,000 clubs sold at market price of $10 − variable costs of $5 = a lost contribution margin of $40,000; spread over the entire 12,000 clubs, the lost contribution margin per club is $3.33).

Note that if all 12,000 clubs are sold at an internal price of $8.33, the total revenue to the grip division is equal to $100,000. This is the same as the revenue earned if the grip division sells 8,000 clubs at $10 each to outside buyers while selling 4,000 clubs internally at the minimum transfer price of $5.

A key concept in transfer pricing is that no matter what the desires of the division managers, the transfer price that provides the most benefit to the company as a whole is the one that should be chosen. Forcing a transfer when the best course of action for the company is to buy outside or preventing a transfer when the best choice is to transfer the product internally results in inefficient use of a company's resources.

 Key Concept: *The transfer price that provides the most benefit to the company as a whole is the one that should be chosen.*

INTERNATIONAL ASPECTS OF TRANSFER PRICING

When an organization has international divisions the same type of problems arise, but the focus of transfer pricing changes.[3] The focus of transfer pricing when international divisions are involved centers on minimizing taxes, duties, and foreign exchange risks. By artificially setting high transfer prices, selling divisions in low-tax countries can show high levels of income while correspondingly reducing the income of a buying division located in a high-tax country. If the selling division is in a high-tax country, the transfer price can likewise be set at an artificially low price to reduce income in the high-tax country and increase income in the low-tax country.

Selling and shipping goods internationally introduces many opportunities for manipulating transfer prices.

---

[3]This discussion also applies to divisions located in different states if income tax rates differ between the states.

IN THE NEWS

A recent study estimates that multinational companies avoided paying $35.6 billion in income taxes in 1998 by artificially manipulating transfer prices. Examples of under-priced exported items include ice cream exported to the Cayman Islands for 20 cents per kilogram, laser printers exported to Mexico at $50 per printer, and missile and rocket launchers exported to Turkey at $12.44 each. By lowering the price, the U.S. operations show no profit and pay no or little taxes. U.S. companies also buy products from related companies at artificially high prices including razor blades from Panama for $24.98, toothbrushes from India for $171.80, and molasses from Lebanon for $103.70 per liter (Simon Pak and John Zdanowicz, "An Estimate of 1998 Lost U.S. Federal Income Tax Revenues Due to Over-Invoiced Imports and Under-Invoiced Exports").

Issues of international competition and foreign government relations are also important components of any transfer pricing decision. Managers must be aware and sensitive to geographic, political, and economic circumstances in the environment in which they operate. The goal of transfer pricing in any environment is to optimize the performance of the total company, not just the individual divisions.

SUMMARY OF KEY CONCEPTS

- There are advantages and disadvantages to decentralized companies. (p. 343)
- Decentralized organizations require very well-developed and well-integrated information systems. (p. 343)
- The key to effective decision making in a decentralized organization is responsibility accounting—holding managers responsible for only those things under their control. (p. 344)
- Evaluating investment centers requires focusing on the level of investment required in generating a segment's profit. (p. 349)
- The transfer price that provides the most benefit to the company as a whole is the one that should be chosen. (p. 361)

KEY DEFINITIONS

Decentralized organization An organization in which decision-making authority is spread throughout the organization (p. 342)

Responsibility accounting An accounting system that assigns responsibility to a manager for those areas that are under that manager's control (p. 343)

Cost center A segment or division of an organization where the manager has control over costs, but not over revenue or investment decisions. (p. 344)

Performance report Provides key financial and nonfinancial measures of performance for a particular segment (p. 344)

Revenue center A segment or division of an organization where the manager has control over revenue, but not costs or investment decisions (p. 344)

Profit center A segment or division of an organization where the manager has control over both costs and revenue, but not investment decisions (p. 344)

Investment center A segment or division of an organization where the manager has control over cost, revenue, and investment decisions (p. 345)

Strategic business unit (SBU) Another term for investment center (p. 345)

Segmented income statements Calculate income for each major segment of an organization in addition to the company as a whole (p. 345)

Segment costs All costs attributable to a particular segment of an organization but only those costs that are actually caused by the segment (p. 345)

Common costs Indirect costs that are incurred to benefit more than one segment and cannot be directly traced to a particular segment or allocated in a reasonable manner (p. 346)

Segment margin The profit margin of a particular segment of an organization, typically the best measure of long-run profitability (p. 347)

Return on investment (ROI) Measures the rate of return generated by an investment center's assets (p. 349)

Margin The percentage of each sales dollar that is recognized as net profit (p. 350)

Asset turnover The measure of activity used in the ROI calculation; it measures the sales that are generated for a given level of assets (p. 350)

Net operating income Net income from operations before interest and taxes (p. 350)

Operating assets Typically include cash, accounts receivable, inventory, and property, plant, and equipment (p. 350)

Residual income The amount of income earned in excess of some predetermined minimum level of return on assets (p. 354)

Economic value added (EVA) A contemporary measure of performance focusing on shareholder wealth (p. 356)

Transfer price The price charged by one segment or division to another segment or division within the same organization for the transfer of goods or services (p. 358)

CONCEPT REVIEW

1. What is a decentralized organization?
2. Why might firms choose to decentralize?
3. Identify the benefits and disadvantages of decentralization.
4. Discuss the impact of accounting information systems (AIS) on decentralization.
5. What is responsibility accounting and what is its impact on decision making?
6. How is the philosophy of "management by exception" employed in a decentralized organization to control operations?
7. What type of information should the accounting information system provide for effective decision making in decentralized organizations?
8. Define a cost center.
9. Define a profit center.
10. Define an investment center.
11. Describe the function of segmented income statements in performance evaluation.
12. Describe segment costs and compare them to common costs.
13. Discuss the impact of the value chain on segment margin reporting.
14. Discuss the impact of ABC costing on segment margin reporting.
15. How does the number of turns impact margin in the ROI calculation?
16. Define residual income and discuss how it compares to ROI.
17. Define EVA and discuss how it compares to ROI and residual income.
18. Other factors remaining the same, how could the rate of return on investment be improved?
19. Define transfer pricing, what it is, and why it is necessary.
20. Discuss some of the disadvantages of transfer prices when using actual cost.
21. What is the general rule in establishing transfer prices consistent with economic decision making?
22. What would be the appropriate transfer price for a firm operating at full capacity?
23. When is it appropriate to negotiate transfer prices?
24. Explain how transfer pricing relates to decentralization.
25. Explain return on investment (ROI).
26. Describe alternative ways transfer prices are established.
27. What benefits can arise from using transfer prices for service organizations?
28. Discuss the following statement: "The complexity of the transfer-pricing problem is a function of the size and growth rate of a company."
29. Discuss transfer pricing rules, issues, and methods.
30. Each divisional manager at Lakewood Inc. is evaluated based on ROI. A downturn in sales leaves cost as the only factor managers can control to maintain an adequate ROI. Cost can be cut in each division if they fail to implement pollution control devices recommended by local authorities. Discuss the ethical considerations.

APPLICATION OF CONCEPTS

31. Bachman Inc. produces and sells two main products. Revenue and cost information relating to the products are as follows:

	PRODUCT	
	Turner	**Overdrive**
Selling price per unit	$ 10.00	$ 27.00
Variable expenses per unit	4.30	19.00
Traceable fixed expenses per year	$142,000	$54,000

Common fixed expenses in the company total $125,000 per year. Last year, Bachman Inc. produced and sold 42,500 units of Turner and 19,000 units of Overdrive.

Required

Prepare a report showing the profit for each product.

32. Simon Company operates two divisions, Garfunkel and Robinson. A segmented income statement for the company's most recent year is as follows:

	Total Company	**Garfunkel Division**	**Robinson Division**
Sales	$850,000	$250,000	$600,000
Less variable expenses	505,000	145,000	360,000
Contribution margin	345,000	105,000	240,000
Less traceable fixed costs	145,000	45,000	100,000
Division segment margin	200,000	$ 60,000	$140,000
Less common fixed costs	130,000		
Net income	$ 70,000		

Required

A. If Garfunkel Division increased its sales by $85,000 per year, how much would the company's net income change? Assume that all cost behavior patterns remained constant.

B. If Robinson Division increased sales by $100,000 and Garfunkel Division sales remained the same and there was no change in fixed costs,
(1) compute the net income amounts for each division and the total company;
(2) compute the segment margin ratios before and after these changes and comment on the results. Explain the changes.

33. Paradise Company makes two products in separate divisions, Cheese and Burger. Segmented income statements for the most recent year follow:

	Total Company	**Cheese Division**	**Burger Division**
Sales	$850,000	$250,000	$600,000
Less variable expenses	505,000	185,000	360,000
Contribution margin	345,000	65,000	240,000
Less traceable fixed costs	145,000	45,000	100,000
Division segment margin	200,000	$ 20,000	$140,000
Less common fixed costs	130,000		
Net income	$ 70,000		

Paradise Company would like to initiate a special advertising campaign on the Super Bowl television show. The company can only feature one product because of the expense and needs to decide which product to feature. The campaign will cost $28,000. Marketing studies have indicated that such a campaign could increase sales of the Cheese Division by $100,000 or increase sales of the Burger Division by $75,000.

Required

Which product should be featured in the campaign? Why? Show computations.

34. The ABC Division reported 1995 sales of $150,000, an asset turnover ratio of 3.0, and a rate of return on average assets of 18 percent. The percentage of net income to sales is how much?

35. The VCR division of Allied Electronics has sales of $400,000, operating profit of $40,000, and investment of $1,000,000. What is the ROI for the division?

36. The Tea Division of A Cup of Joe's Coffee has sales of $600,000, operating profit of $15,000, and investment of $1,200,000. What is the asset turnover for the Tea Division?

37. Watson Investments generates sales of $2,500,000 and operating profits of $75,000 on $1,500,000 of assets under its control. What is the profit margin?

38. A division has $3,000,000 in sales, operating profit of $250,000, and investment of $1,250,000. Assuming a 10 percent cost of capital, what is the division's residual income?

39. An advertising company purchased computer equipment costing $400,000 which will be depreciated over four years with no salvage value. The company started the year with nondepreciable assets of $100,000. Annual cash profits are expected to be $150,000. The company uses end-of-year asset values in determining ROI.

Required

A. What is the ROI for Year 1 using net book value?

B. What is the ROI for Year 1 using gross book value?

C. If sales for Year 1 totaled $700,000, what was the profit margin?

40. The Upstart Shoe Company has two divisions, Stitching and Soles. The Soles division has a total cost of $15 per unit for its product, rubber soles, of which $10 is fixed. The Soles division also has idle capacity for up to 25,000 units per month. The Stitching division would like to purchase 20,000 units from the Soles division but feels the $15 price is too high. What is the lowest price the Soles division can sell at in order to suffer no additional losses?

41. The Newton Company has two divisions, X and Y. Division X has a total cost of $30 per unit for its product of which $20 is fixed. Division X is at full capacity. Division Y would like to purchase 20,000 units from Division X, but thinks the $35 price Division X normally charges on the outside is too high. At what price should Division X sell to Division Y in order to suffer no additional losses?

42. A division can sell externally for $60 per unit. Its variable manufacturing costs are $26 per unit, and its fixed manufacturing cost per unit is $10. What is the opportunity cost of transferring internally if the division is operating at capacity?

43. Miller company has two divisions, B and S, each operated as a profit center. Division B charges Division S $35 per unit for each unit transferred to Division S. Other data are as follows:

B's variable cost per unit	$ 30
B's fixed costs	$10,000
B's annual sales to S	5,000 units
B's sales to outsiders	50,000 units

Division B is planning to raise its transfer price to $50 per unit. Division S can purchase units at $40 each from outside vendors, but doing so would idle Division B's facilities now committed to producing units for Division S. Division B cannot increase its sales to outsiders. From the perspective of the company as a whole, from whom should Division S acquire the units, assuming Division S's market is unaffected?

44. Eat More Food Company began business in January 1999. It produces various food products that pass through two divisions. Division A processes the food, and Division B packages it. During 1999, Division A processed 100,000 pounds of food at a cost of $250,000. Its administration and other expenses amounted to $50,000. Division B incurred $100,000 of additional manufacturing costs in completing the 100,000 pounds. Division B sold the 100,000 pounds of completed units for $450,000. Division B's selling and administrative expenses for the year were $30,000.

Required

A. Prepare divisional income statements for 1999 for each of these two divisions assuming the transfer price is equal to Division A's total cost.

B. Prepare divisional income statements for 1999 for each of these two divisions assuming the transfer price is based on the external market price of $3.50 per pound.

C. Which statement presents a better measure of each division's performance? Why?

45. The following information summarizes the operations of one division of Goods Enterprises for 1999:

Sales	$2,500,000
Variable expenses	(1,000,000)
Fixed expenses	(1,000,000)
Income before taxes	$ 500,000
Average total assets	4,000,000
Company cost of capital	10 percent

Required

A. Compute the return on investment (ROI).

B. Compute the residual income (RI).

46. You are the manager of a franchise operating division of a "Kwik-Copies" Company. Your division has $9,000,000 in assets, and your budgeted income statement for the fiscal year is as follows:

Revenue	$16,500,000
Variable Costs and Fixed Costs	
Variable	3,000,000
Fixed	7,750,000
Depreciation	2,375,000
Division profit	$ 3,375,500

Your company evaluates your division using ROI, computed with end-of-year gross asset balances. Your bonus is based on the percentage increase in ROI over the prior year.

During the year, you consider buying a new copy machine for $4,000,000, which will enable you to expand the output of your division and save costs. The copy machine would have no salvage value and would be depreciated over five years using straight-line depreciation. It will increase output by 10 percent while reducing fixed costs by $4,000,000. If you accept the copy machine, it will be installed in late December but will not be placed in use until the following year. As a result, no depreciation will be taken on it this year.

If you do buy the copy machine, you will have to dispose of the copy machine you are not using, which you just purchased during the current year. The old copy machine cost you $4,000,000 but has no salvage value. Of the depreciation in the income statement, $1,000,000 is for this machine.

In the ROI calculations, the company includes any gains or losses from copy equipment disposal as part of the numerator.

Required

A. What is your division's ROI this year if you do not acquire the new machine?

B. What is your division's ROI this year if you do acquire the new copy machine?

C. What is your division's expected ROI for next year if the copy machine is acquired and meets expectations? Assume that unit costs and prices do not change.

D. As the manager, what action will you take and why?

47. Top management is trying to determine a consistent but fair valuation system to use to evaluate each of its four divisions. This year's performance data is summarized as follows:

	DIVISION			
	1	**2**	**3**	**4**
Income	$1,000	$1,200	$ 1,600	$1,600
Operating assets	4,000	6,000	15,000	8,000
Current liabilities	400	2,000	2,400	200

Required

A. Which division would earn a bonus if top management used return on investment based on operating assets?

B. Which division would earn a bonus if top management used return on investment based on operating assets minus current liabilities?

C. Which division would earn a bonus if top management used return on investment based on operating assets assuming a minimum desired ROI of 12 percent?

D. Which division would earn a bonus if top management used return on investment based on operating assets minus current liabilities assuming a minimum desired ROI of 12 percent?

48. A manufacturing company is presented with the following report on its two divisions:

	Division A	**Division B**
Sales	$100,000	$200,000
Cost of goods sold	(50,000)	(160,000)
Gross profit	50,000	40,000
Marketing and administrative	(20,000)	(10,000)
Operating profit	$ 30,000	$30,000

Top management plans to award equal bonuses to the divisions based on their identical operating profits.

Required

A. What problems do you see in the bonus plan suggested by top management?

B. What questions should be addressed by top management before concluding that the operating performance of Division A and Division B are identical?

C. What alternatives would you suggest to top management?

49. Adler Industries is a vertically integrated firm with several divisions that operate as decentralized profit centers. Adler's Systems Division manufactures scientific instruments and uses the products of two of Adler's other divisions. The Board Division manufactures printed circuit boards (PCBs). One PCB model is made exclusively for the Systems Division using proprietary designs, whereas less complex models are sold in outside markets. The products of the Transistor Division are sold in a well-developed competitive market; however, one transistor model is also used by the Systems Division.

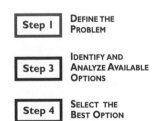

The costs per unit of the products used by the Systems Division are as follows:

	PCB	**Transistor**
Direct materials	$2.50	$ .80
Direct labor	4.50	1.00
Variable overhead	2.00	.50
Fixed overhead	.80	.75
Total cost	$9.80	$3.05

The Board Division sells its commercial products at full cost plus a 25 percent markup and believes the proprietary board made for the Systems Division would sell for $12.25 per unit on the open market. The market price of the transistor used by the Systems Division is $3.70 per unit.

Required

A. What would be the impact on the Transistor Division if the per-unit transfer price from the Transistor Division to the Systems Division was the full cost of $3.05?

B. Assume the Systems Division is able to purchase a large quantity of transistors from an outside source at $2.90 per unit. The Transistor Division, having excess capacity, agrees to lower its transfer price to $2.90 per unit. What would be the result of this action for the company as a whole?

C. The Board and Systems Divisions have negotiated a transfer price of $11.00 per printed circuit board. What is the likely response from each division if this negotiated price is used?

50. Raddington Industries produces tool and die machinery for manufacturers. The company expanded vertically in 1999 by acquiring one of its suppliers of alloy steel plates, Regis Steel Company. In order to manage the two separate businesses, the operations of Regis Steel are reported separately as an investment center.

Raddington monitors its divisions on the basis of both unit contribution and return on average investment (ROI) with investment defined as average operating assets employed. Management bonuses are determined on ROI. All investments in operating assets are expected to earn a minimum return of 11 percent before income taxes.

Regis's cost of goods sold is considered to be entirely variable, whereas the division's administrative expenses are not dependent on volume. Selling expenses are a mixed cost with 40 percent attributed to sales volume. Regis's ROI has ranged from 11.8 percent to 14.7 percent since 1999. During the fiscal year ended November 30, 1999, Regis contemplated a capital acquisition with an estimated ROI of 11.5 percent; however, division management decided against the investment because it believed that the investment would decrease Regis's overall ROI.

The 1999 operating statement for Regis is presented here. The division's operating assets employed were $15,750,000 at November 30, 1999, a 5 percent increase over the 1998 year-end balance.

Regis Steel Division Operating Statement
For the Year Ended November 30, 1999
($000 omitted)

Sales revenue		$25,000
Less: Cost of goods sold	$16,500	
Administrative expenses	3,955	
Selling expenses	2,700	23,155
Income from operations before income taxes		$ 1,845

Required

   A. Calculate the unit contribution for Regis Steel Division if 1,484,000 units were produced and sold during the year ended November 30, 1999.

   B. Calculate the pretax return on average investment in operating assets employed (ROI) for 1999 Regis Steel Division.

   C. Calculate the residual income using the average operating assets employed for 1999 for the Regis Steel Division.

   D. Explain why the management of Regis Steel Division would have been more likely to accept the contemplated acquisition if residual income rather than ROI were used as a performance measure.

> **Step 2** | IDENTIFY OBJECTIVES

> **Step 3** | IDENTIFY AND ANALYZE AVAILABLE OPTIONS

   E. The Regis Steel Division is a separate investment center within Raddington Industries. Identify several items that Regis Steel should control if it is to be evaluated fairly by either the ROI or residual income performance measure.

CONTINUING CASE | BIG AL'S PIZZA INC.

Big Al's Pizza Emporium, a subsidiary of Big Al's Pizza Inc., has decided to sell frozen pizzas in their restaurants. These pizzas will be taken home and cooked by restaurant customers. The restaurants will sell frozen meat pizzas for $10 and frozen veggie pizzas for $11.50.

While the restaurants would like to purchase the pizzas from Big Al's Pizza Inc., Big Al's Pizza Emporium has found an unrelated supplier who will provide the meat pizzas for $4.55 and veggie pizzas for $5.75. Assume that Big Al's Pizza Inc. has excess capacity and can supply the frozen pizzas to Big Al's Pizza Emporium without affecting their sales.

Required

A. Using estimated cost data for Year 3, at what minimum price should Big Al's Pizza Inc. agree to transfer meat and veggie pizzas to Big Al's Pizza Emporium?

B. What is the maximum price that Big Al's Pizza Emporium should pay Big Al's Pizza, Inc. for the pizzas?

C. If Big Al's Pizza Emporium purchases pizzas from Big Al's Pizza Inc., what is the ideal transfer price? Why?

D. Should Big Al's Pizza Emporium buy pizzas from Big Al's Pizza Inc.? What qualitative factors should be considered in making this decision?

E. What should the transfer price be if Big Al's Pizza Inc. is at full capacity?

Chapter 12

NONFINANCIAL MEASURES OF PERFORMANCE

Study Tools

A Review of the Previous Chapter

In Chapter 11 we discussed the impact of responsibility accounting and segment reporting on decision making in decentralized organizations. We also discussed performance evaluation in cost, revenue profit, and investment centers utilizing variance analysis and other financial measures of performance including the segmented income statement, return on investment (ROI), residual income, and economic value added (EVA).

A Preview of This Chapter

In this chapter we expand the discussion of performance evaluation to include a variety of nonfinancial and qualitative measures used in a "balanced scorecard" approach.

Key concepts include:

- The balanced scorecard approach integrates financial and nonfinancial performance measures.
- The balanced scorecard approach requires looking at performance from four different but related perspectives: financial, customer, internal business, and learning and growth.
- The four perspectives of the balanced scorecard revolve around measures of quality, productivity, efficiency and timeliness, and marketing success.

A Preview of Upcoming Chapters

Part IV of the textbook introduces two contemporary topics in management decision making dealing with information and knowledge management in Chapter 13 and management fraud and internal control in Chapter 14.

LEARNING OBJECTIVES

After studying the material in this chapter, you should be able to:

LO 1 Apply the concept of the balanced scorecard approach to performance measurement

LO 2 Understand key dimensions of the financial, customer, internal business, and learning and growth perspectives of the balanced scorecard

LO 3 Apply key measures of performance based on quality

LO 4 Interpret the costs of quality and the tradeoffs between prevention costs, appraisal costs, internal failure, and external failure costs

LO 5 Apply key measures of performance based on productivity

LO 6 Apply key measures of performance based on efficiency and timeliness

LO 7 Apply key measures of performance based on marketing effectiveness

LO 8 Understand the use of quality, productivity, efficiency and timeliness, and marketing effectiveness measures within the four perspectives of the balanced scorecard

In the previous two chapters, we discussed cost control and performance evaluation in cost, revenue, profit, and investment centers using financial measures like variance analysis, segmented income statements, return on investment, residual income, and economic value added. In this chapter we expand that analysis to include a variety of nonfinancial and qualitative measures used in a "balanced scorecard" approach to measuring performance. Because of changing technology, global competition, and an increased awareness of the need to focus on customer needs, these nonfinancial and qualitative performance measures have become an integral component of effective managerial decision making.

The balanced scorecard looks at performance from four unique but related perspectives—financial, customer, internal business, and learning and growth perspectives of the balanced scorecard. The chapter concludes with a discussion of key measures of quality, productivity, efficiency and timeliness, and marketing effectiveness within the four perspectives of the balanced scorecard. ■

INTRODUCTION

When customers choose a restaurant for a meal, they are probably *not* concerned with how well the restaurant meets its cost goals, whether its segment margin is positive or the level of its return on investment (ROI). Customers probably *are* concerned with the price of the meal, how long they have to wait to be seated and waited on, and the quality of the food that is served.

Customers who have a bad experience may choose to not return to the restaurant. Those customers also have a tendency to inform friends or relatives about the bad experience. These factors are difficult to measure but are critically important to the success of the restaurant. The manager of the restaurant can be very competent at controlling costs but if customers go elsewhere, the restaurant will not be financially successful and will eventually fail.[1]

In today's competitive business environment characterized by rapidly changing technology, global competition, and a focus on meeting and exceeding customer's expectations, in order to be successful, managers must focus on factors other than financial performance. Traditional measures of financial performance are simply not adequate to fully assess the performance of companies and their segments in this environment. Quality may be more important than cost, timeliness more important than meeting budget, and customer service more important than ROI.[2]

THE BALANCED SCORECARD

LO1
Apply the concept of the balanced scorecard approach to performance measurement

Nonfinancial measures must be used with caution. For example, table turns may be an important nonfinancial measure of performance for restaurants. However, if too much emphasis is placed on the quick turnover of tables, customers may feel that they are being rushed and, once again, choose to go elsewhere. Can you identify restaurants that emphasize table turns? How about restaurants that do not emphasize table turns? What was your overall opinion of each type?

Traditional accounting measures of performance dealing with historical financial data are of little use in making decisions concerning customer satisfaction, quality issues, productivity, efficiency, and employee satisfaction. Managers also need information concerning the success or failure of new products or marketing campaigns and the success of programs designed to enhance customer value. The **balanced scorecard** approach to performance measurement uses a set of financial and nonfinancial measures that relate to the critical success factors of the organization. By integrating financial and nonfinancial performance measures, the balanced scorecard approach helps to keep management focused on all of a company's critical success factors, not just its financial ones. The balanced scorecard also helps to keep short-term operating performance in line with long-term strategy.

 Key Concept: *The balanced scorecard approach integrates financial and nonfinancial performance measures.*

As shown in Exhibit 12-1, utilizing a balanced scorecard approach requires looking at performance from four different but related perspectives: financial, customer, internal business, and learning and growth.

---

[1]It should be noted that financial measures of performance would eventually capture customer service problems when they impact income. A decrease in customer satisfaction will eventually lead to reduced sales, which will reduce income and have a negative impact on ROI. However, these measures are not timely enough nor detailed enough to help management correct any customer service problems.

[2]While quality, timeliness, customer service, and other nonfinancial measures may be more important than their financial counterparts, it should be noted that traditional transaction-based accounting information systems may not even capture this type of information.

EXHIBIT 12-1   The Balanced Scorecard Strategy

LO2
Understand key dimensions of the financial, customer, internal business, and learning and growth perspectives of the balanced scorecard

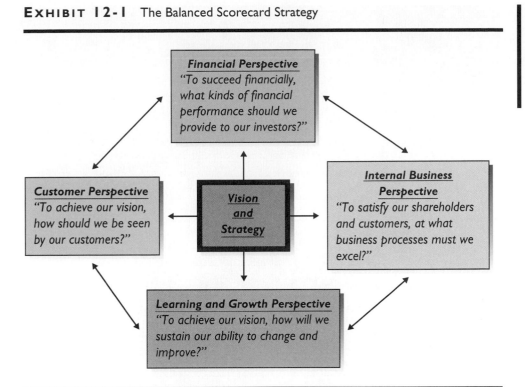

FINANCIAL PERSPECTIVE

The primary goal of every profit-making enterprise is to show a profit. Profit allows the enterprise to provide a return on investment to investors, to repay creditors, and to adequately compensate management and employees. Financial measures of success (costs, variances, earnings, segment margin, ROI, EVA) have been discussed in the earlier chapters in this book. Increasing sales, reducing costs, and increasing profits are critical success factors in many companies. However, under the balanced scorecard approach, financial performance is seen in the larger context of the company's overall goals and objectives relating to its customers and suppliers, internal processes, and employees.

CUSTOMER PERSPECTIVE

Many successful businesses have found that focusing on customers and meeting or exceeding their needs is more important in the long run than simply focusing on financial measures of performance. After all, it is the customer who ultimately incurs the costs of producing products and contributes to a company's profits. Considering the customer perspective is therefore critical in attaining the financial goals of a company. Critical success factors under this perspective are likely to include increasing the quality of products and services, reducing delivery time, and increasing customer satisfaction. Measures of performance appropriate under this perspective include the number of warranty claims and returned products (for quality), customer response time and the percentage of on-time deliveries (for reducing delivery time), and customer complaints and repeat business (for customer satisfaction). A second dimension of the customer perspective deals with increasing market share and penetrating new markets. Measures of performance appropriate for this dimension include market share, market saturation, and new products introduced into the marketplace.

SATURN SURVEY

Your name _Mike Sheridan_ Age _30_

Occupation _TRAFFIC REPORTER_

Where is your Saturn retailer located? _Saturn of Warwick_

If you had to share one story or experience about your Saturn, what would it be?

I see hundreds of cars every day. If not thousands. But for some reason, the Saturns seemed to stand out. Anyway, I took a test-drive, and ended up getting an SL2. And I've been really happy with it. It handles well. And it's very quick. Unless you happen to be driving in the morning, between 7 and 9. Or in the afternoon, between 5 and 7.

Which Saturn do you drive? _Saturn SL2_ Color _Silver_

124-horsepower, dual-overhead-cam engine. The new, redesigned Saturn S-Series.
A Different Kind of Company. A Different Kind of Car.

The 2000 Saturn SL2, M.S.R.P. of $13,335 including AC, retailer prep and transportation. Options, tax and license are extra. 1-800-522-5000 or www.saturn.com. ©1999 Saturn Corporation.

www.saturn.com

Saturn relies on customer surveys and other measures in evaluating the customer perspective of the balanced scorecard.

INTERNAL BUSINESS PERSPECTIVE

The internal business process perspective deals with objectives across the company's entire value chain from research and development to postsale customer service. It is linked to the financial perspective through its emphasis on improving the efficiency of manufacturing processes and with the customer perspective through its focus on improving processes and products to better meet customer needs. Every company will approach this perspective differently as these products and processes will all be unique in what adds value to products and services which are sold to the customer. However, critical success factors are likely to include improving quality throughout the production process, increasing productivity, and increasing efficiency and timeliness.

LEARNING AND GROWTH PERSPECTIVE

The learning and growth perspective links the critical success factors in the other perspectives and ensures an environment that supports and allows the objectives of the other three perspectives to be achieved. Critical success factors center around three areas. The first is the efficient and effective use of employees (employee empowerment). Measures include improving employee morale, increasing skill development, increasing employee satisfaction, reducing employee turnover, and increasing the participation of employees in the decision process. The second critical success factor is increasing information systems capabilities through improving the availability and timeliness of information. The third critical success factor involves measures of product innovation like increasing the number of new products, new patents, and so on.

 Key Concept: *The balanced scorecard approach requires looking at performance from four different but related perspectives: financial, customer, internal business, and learning and growth.*

IN THE NEWS	www.llbean.com

Rol Fessenden, the head of global procurement for L.L. Bean, says that "good working conditions go hand in hand with high quality, high reliability, and, in the broad view, lower costs." When L.L. Bean recently replaced a supplier for keeping poor wage records, the new supplier not only had better administrative practices but better products as well ("A Humanist Executive Leads by Thinking in Broader Terms," *Wall Street Journal,* April 16, 1999, B1).

A FOCUS ON QUALITY

Over the past 20 years or so, the demand by customers for quality products and services at an affordable price has drastically changed the way companies do business. Quality is no longer just a buzzword but a way of life. Managers have come to realize that improving quality increases sales through higher customer satisfaction and demand, reduces costs, and increases the long-term profitability of companies. However, before we go any further, just what is meant by quality? Although you may "know it when you see it," most businesses describe **quality** as "meeting or exceeding customers' expectations." Of course, this requires that a product performs as it is intended but also requires that a product be reliable and durable, and that these features are provided at a competitive price.

LO3
Apply key measures of performance based on quality

Companies have focused on improving the quality of the products or services they sell through a variety of initiatives such as total quality management (TQM), market-driven quality, and strategic quality management. Although the details of these methods may differ, all focus on meeting or exceeding customer expectations, continuous improvement, and employee empowerment. Continuous improvement is an idea pioneered by Japan's Toyota Motor Corp. Called **kaizen** in Japan, it refers to a system of improvement based on a series of gradual and often small improvements rather than major changes requiring very large investments.[3] Effective kaizen requires active participation by all of a company's employees—from the CEO to the worker on the assembly line. Kaizen takes the view that everyone is responsible for continuous improvement. Employee empowerment refers to companies providing appropriate opportunities for training, skill development, and advancement so those employees can become active participants and active decision makers in an organization. As discussed earlier, empowering employees is a key dimension of the innovation and growth perspective of the balanced scorecard.

www.toyota.com

Along with their quality improvement initiatives, many companies seek ISO 9000 certification. **ISO 9000** is a set of guidelines for quality management focusing on the design,

---

[3]In addition to quality improvements, kaizen techniques are used to continually reduce the cost of products and services.

production, inspection, testing, installing, and servicing of products, processes, and services. Though originally developed by the International Standards Organization (ISO) to control the quality of products sold in Europe, it has been widely adopted in the United States and in other countries worldwide. U.S. companies may also compete for the Malcolm Baldridge National Quality Award. This award was created in 1987 to recognize quality excellence in manufacturing, small business, service, education, and health care.

IN THE NEWS **www.fedex.com**

Total quality management (TQM) pays off handsomely. The results of a study published in *Business Week* found that quality award winners did two to three times as well in growth of operating income, sales, assets, and employment and 50 percent better in stock appreciation, compared with a corporate control group ("Rewards of Quality Rewards," *Business Week,* September 21, 1998).

Officials from Federal Express Corp. receiving the Malcolm Baldridge Award from President Bush.

Improving the quality of products and services is an important component in both the customer perspective and the internal business perspective of the balanced scorecard. From a customer perspective, one of the most important measures of quality is customer satisfaction and the number of customer complaints. If the number of meals returned to the kitchen is increasing, management should probably infer that customers are unhappy with the quality of the meal. The number of warranty claims can also serve as a measure of quality. The increase in warranty work performed on a certain model of automobile indicates a potential problem with the production process and the quality of the car produced. If customer complaints and warranty claims are increasing, they provide a signal to management that quality may be a problem. However, poor quality is not the only explanation for increasing customer complaints. In addition, these measures are not perfect in that customers do not always complain or return products when quality problems are evident. For example, restaurant patrons may not complain about sub-par meals and customers may simply discard defective merchandise instead of returning it. Therefore, management must be careful to provide a mechanism to make it easy for customers to complain, easy to return defective products, and so on.

From the internal business perspective, quality measures center around improving output yields, reducing defects in raw materials and finished products, and reducing downtime due to quality problems. Defects are hopefully detected before they leave the factory, and the manufacturing process adapted accordingly. The amount of scrap can also indicate potential quality problems in the production process. Although a certain amount of scrap is acceptable and even necessary in most manufacturing environments, an excessive amount should raise a red flag indicating possible problems in the process that are causing an increase in the number of defective units.

THE COSTS OF QUALITY

LO4
Interpret the costs of quality and the tradeoffs between prevention costs, appraisal costs, internal failure, and external failure costs

Improving quality can be costly. On average, U.S. companies spend 20 to 30 percent of every sales dollar on quality costs.[4] However, improving quality can also prove very prof-

---

[4]Michael R. Ostrega, "Return on Investment Through the Costs of Quality," *Journal of Cost Management* (Summer 1991): p. 37.

itable. Xerox estimates that it saved more than $200 million over a four-year period by improving quality.[5]

In evaluating managers based on quality concerns, it is useful to have a framework for comparing the benefits of providing a high-quality product or service with the costs that result from poor quality. To facilitate this comparison, quality costs are typically classified into four general categories: (1) prevention costs, (2) appraisal costs, (3) internal failure costs, and (4) external failure costs.

Prevention costs are costs incurred to prevent product failure from occurring. These costs are typically incurred early in the value chain and include design and engineering costs as well as training, supervision, and the costs of quality improvement projects. If parts are purchased from an outside supplier, these costs may include providing training and technical support to the supplier in order to increase the quality of purchased materials. Prevention costs are incurred to eliminate quality problems before they occur. Most companies find that incurring prevention costs up front is less expensive in the long run than product failure costs.

Appraisal (detection) costs are incurred in inspecting, identifying, and isolating defective products and services before they reach the customer. These include the costs of inspecting raw materials, testing of goods throughout the manufacturing process, and final product testing and inspection. In practice, it is very difficult to ensure quality through inspection. It is time consuming and costly to inspect every unit of product. Therefore, sampling is usually used to identify the problems with the production process. However, sampling is certainly not foolproof and is not likely to catch all quality problems. In general, it is more effective to design quality into a product through prevention activities rather than inspect quality into a product using appraisal activities.

If a product or service is defective in any way or does not meet customer expectations, failure costs are incurred. **Internal failure costs** are costs incurred once the product is produced and then determined to be defective (through the appraisal process) but before it is sold to customers. Internal failure costs include the material, labor, and other manufacturing costs incurred in reworking defective products and the costs of scrap and spoilage. Internal failure costs also include downtime caused by quality problems, design changes, and the costs of reinspections and retesting. If no defects exist, internal failure costs will be zero. On the other hand, a high level of internal failure costs should be an indication to management that more attention needs to be spent in preventing quality problems to eliminate or reduce the number of defective products during the production process.

External failure costs are incurred after a defective product is delivered to a customer. External failure costs include the cost of repairs made under warranty or the replacement of defective parts, product recalls (such as in the automobile industry), liability costs arising from legal actions against the seller, and eventually lost sales. Although the cost of potential lawsuits and lost sales may be difficult to measure, the cost of external failures is likely to exceed other quality costs. Failure costs, both internal and external, are like bandages—they only address symptoms rather than fix the underlying problem. When unhappy customers decide not to purchase products from a company because of quality problems, the domino effect can be devastating—particularly when safety is a concern.

Although quality costs in many U.S. companies may reach 20 to 30 percent of sales, experts suggest that the total costs of quality should not exceed 2 to 4 percent of sales. The problem faced by management is to reduce the costs of quality while maintaining a high-quality product or service. The goal, of course, is to minimize all of the quality costs. However, it may be prudent to increase expenditures in one or more areas in order to decrease other costs. For example, as you have seen, external failure costs are serious and potentially devastating to companies. Both external and internal failure costs can be reduced (theoretically to zero) by paying more attention to quality issues early in the value chain. Products can be designed to emphasize quality and durability, suppliers can be certified,

[5]Lawrence P. Carr, "How Xerox Sustains the Costs of Quality," *Management Accounting* (August 1995): pp. 26-32.

In the summer of 1999, Coke faced one of the most serious crises in its 113-year history. The problem? A Coke bottling plant in Antwerp, Belgium, failed to follow crucial quality control procedures including receiving quality assurances from its suppliers and simply making sure the carbon dioxide used to give Coke its fizz tasted and smelled fresh. As a result, contaminated carbon dioxide was pumped into the holding tanks at the bottling plant resulting in bad-smelling Coca-Cola and hundreds of sick consumers. In the aftermath, Coke products were recalled all over Europe. Coca-Cola Enterprises Inc. (the bottling company owned 40 percent by Coca-Cola.) estimates that the problems resulted in a charge against earnings of more than $100 million (*Wall Street Journal,* June 29, 1999, A1, and July 13, 1999, A4).

employees can be trained, and the manufacturing process can be improved to increase quality throughout the value chain. Increasing expenditures related to prevention and appraisal can result in significant overall cost savings in the long run. As you can see in Exhibit 12-2, the traditional view of managing total quality costs suggests that increasing prevention and appraisal costs will reduce defective units (and failure costs) but that there are tradeoffs in doing so. The traditional view suggests that total quality costs are minimized at a level of product quality below 100 percent.

Exhibit 12-2 implies that total quality costs are minimized at a point less than that associated with zero defects. However, additional prevention and appraisal activities are likely to reduce defects even further. Should companies continue to incur prevention and appraisal costs beyond this point?

A more contemporary view of quality costs recognizes that a number of failure costs are difficult to measure. For example, poor quality can lead to lost sales. This tends to increase the costs of external failures as the percentage of defective units increases. In addition, rather than continually increasing as quality improves (as in Exhibit 12-2), prevention and appraisal costs may actually decrease as a company nears a level of zero defects. As you can see in Exhibit 12-3, this implies that total quality costs are minimized at a level of zero defects.

PRODUCTIVITY MEASURES

LO5
Apply key measures of performance based on productivity

In a company's effort to continually improve products and processes, improvements in productivity are often emphasized. **Productivity** is simply a measure of the relationship between outputs and inputs. How many cars are produced per labor hour, how many loaves of bread are baked per bag of flour, how many calculators are produced per machine hour, how many customers are serviced per shift, and how many sales dollars are generated per full-time sales clerk are all measures of productivity. Measures of output per unit of input such as labor or machine hours can be very important when evaluating the efficiency of a production process. These measures are similar to the traditional financial measures used in variance analysis (direct material and direct labor efficiency variances). However, the focus when using productivity measures is on continually improving productivity rather than simply using less material or incurring fewer labor hours than budgeted.

EXHIBIT 12-2 Traditional View of the Costs of Quality

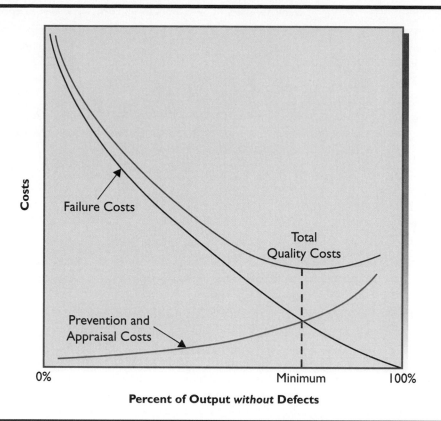

Percent of Output *without* Defects

EXHIBIT 12-3 Contemporary View of the Costs of Quality

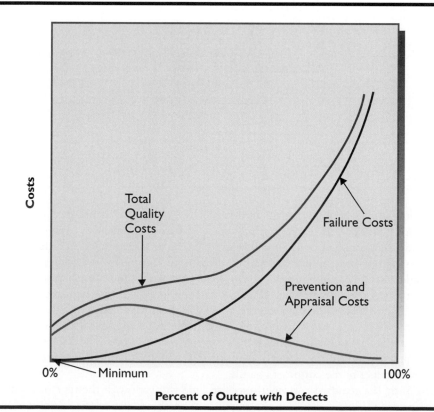

Percent of Output *with* Defects

PAUSE & Reflect

What type of productivity measures might be appropriate for a nonprofit organization like Motheread Inc., whose mission is to educate mothers and fathers of the benefits of reading and to provide hands-on literacy training for parents and their children?

In service organizations, productivity measures are important when evaluating the efficiency of personnel. In HMOs the number of patients seen per physician in a given time period can be an important measure of profitability. Likewise, advertising agencies and CPA and law firms are very concerned with the revenue generated per partner.

To be useful, productivity measures must be used in conjunction with quality measures. A company that uses fewer workers, machines, materials, and other resources to generate the same amount of goods and services as its competitors will only realize a competitive advantage if the quality of products and services is not compromised in the process.

EFFICIENCY AND TIMELINESS MEASURES

LO6
Apply key measures of performance based on efficiency and timeliness

Although quality is certainly a primary focus of the customer perspective, products and services must also be provided on a timely basis. **Customer response time** is the time it takes to deliver a product or service after an order is placed. As shown in Exhibit 12-4, it includes such non-value-added time as order receipt time (time between when the order is placed and when the order is ready for setup) and order wait time (time between when the order is ready for setup and when the setup is complete). Order receipt time can occur when orders are mailed or when there is a delay between the placing of an order and its production. This can occur when products are made in batches or when an order is too small to initiate a production run. Total customer response time also includes the time that the order spends in the actual manufacturing process and any delivery time required to get the product in the customer's hands.

Obviously the standard customer response time will vary with the type of product or service provided. In a restaurant the response time should be relatively short. On the

EXHIBIT 12-4 Elements of Customer Response Time

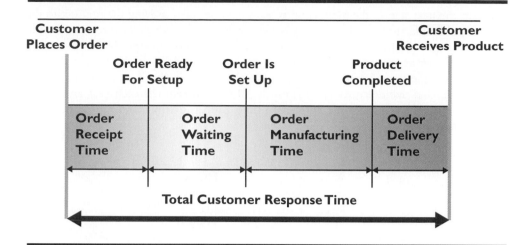

other hand, when ordering an automobile with special options or a custom piece of furniture, the customer response time can be considerably longer. Another measure of timeliness applicable to the customer service perspective is the number of on-time deliveries.

From an internal business perspective, efficiency and timeliness are often measured using manufacturing cycle time, velocity, throughput, and manufacturing cycle efficiency. **Manufacturing cycle time** is the amount of time it takes to produce a good unit of product from the time raw material is received until the product is ready to deliver to customers. As such it is one element in the customer response time (see Exhibit 12-4). In addition to actual processing time, cycle time includes time spent moving materials and products from one place to the next, time spent waiting for machine availability, and time spent inspecting materials and finished goods. The concept of manufacturing cycle time is directly related to velocity or **throughput.** Whereas manufacturing cycle time is the time required to produce a unit of product, throughput refers to the number of good units that can be made in a given period of time. The shorter the manufacturing cycle time, the greater the throughput. Because manufacturing cycle time and throughput focus on the production of good units, they are directly influenced by quality. As such you can view throughput and manufacturing cycle time as directly related to quality and productivity measures:

Are any of the activities in the order manufacturing time likely to be non-value-added activities? What about the delivery time?

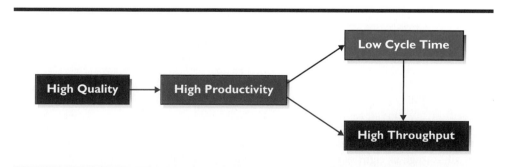

Manufacturing cycle efficiency (MCE) is the value-added time in the production process divided by the total manufacturing cycle time:

$$MCE = \frac{\text{Value-added time}}{\text{Manufacturing cycle time}}$$

Value-added time includes time spent in the actual manufacturing of a product (machining, assembly, painting, etc.). Non-value-added time includes the time a product is waiting to move to the next step in the production process or time spent moving the product to the next step. Manufacturing cycle efficiency is a key measure of performance directly related to the customer service perspective as well as the internal operations perspective. By increasing MCE, customer response time is reduced and non-value-added activities are reduced.

As an example, consider Northern Lights Custom Cabinets (introduced in Chapter 2). Northern Lights manufactures approximately 30 custom cabinets each year and maintains records related to wait time, inspection time, processing time, and move time of its cabinets as follows:

Wait time	12 hours
Inspection time	2 hours
Processing time	48 hours
Move time	2 hours

The cabinets are shipped to the job site as soon as they are complete. Northern Lights used these amounts to compute the following values:

Manufacturing Cycle Time
= Wait time + Processing time + Inspection time + Move time
= 12 + 48 + 2 + 2 = 64 hours
= 8 days

Throughput
$$= \frac{250 \text{ work days}}{8 \text{ days}} = 31.25 \text{ units}$$

Value-Added Time
= Processing time
= 48 hours or 6 days

Non-Value-Added Time
= Wait time + Inspection time + Move time
= 12 hours + 2 hours + 2 hours
= 2 days

Manufacturing Cycle Efficiency (MCE)
= Value added time/ Manufacturing cycle time
= 6 days/8 days
= 75 percent

So what do these values mean? Once raw materials are received by Northern Lights, it takes an average of eight days to manufacture a set of custom cabinets. Seventy-five percent of the manufacturing cycle time is value added (related to actual processing of the cabinets), whereas only 25 percent is non-value-added resulting in a MCE of 75 percent.

Although an MCE of 75 percent would likely be considered very good, these numbers can really only be analyzed by comparison to previous months or to industry standards for this type of business. Regardless, the MCE of 75 percent highlights the non-value-added waiting time, which Northern Lights may be able to reduce.

Can you think of other examples in which wait time would be considered value-added?

Concept Question: In a brewery, beer must sit in storage vats for a period of time while waiting to be bottled or packaged for delivery. Is this "wait time" value-added or non-value-added?

Concept Answer: Although wait and storage times are normally considered non-value-added activities, the real question is whether the wait time adds value to the finished product. In the case of the brewery, the wait time is necessary, as the beer must age to be a better quality, so the wait time is value-added. ■

MARKETING MEASURES

Marketing measures are linked to the financial, customer, and learning and growth perspectives of the balanced scorecard. Market share is directly associated with financial performance and is indirectly linked to customer satisfaction. As an example, a large supermarket chain in the northeast recently started giving customers double credit for manufacturer coupons in order to increase market share by enticing customers away from competing stores. They stated that each 1 percent increase in market share in New England was worth $50 million dollars in annual sales.

Other measures of marketing effectiveness include the success of new products. The number of new products introduced by a toy company, the number of new patents applied for by a drug company, and the number of new services offered and used by customers of a bank are market measures linked to both the customer service and innovation and growth perspectives of a business.

To illustrate how nonfinancial measures of performance might be used in a variety of companies, let's go back and look at some of the companies featured throughout the book. As previously discussed, Northern Lights Custom Cabinets manufactures custom kitchen and bathroom cabinets. The following table shows a variety of performance measures Northern Lights might use to assess the customer, internal business, and learning and growth perspectives of the balanced scorecard using measures of quality, productivity, efficiency and timeliness, and marketing success.

LO7
Apply key measures of performance based on marketing effectiveness

Northern Lights Custom Cabinets
Nonfinancial Measures of Performance

Quality Measures	Method of Measuring
Customer satisfaction	Customer complaints/Warranty claims
Defects per unit	Hours of time to rework defective cabinets
Percentage of external failures	Warranty claims/Returns
Percentage of scrap	Pounds of scrap lumber compared to raw material put into production

Efficiency and Timeliness Measures	
Customer response time	Time between customer order and delivery
Service time	Time spent servicing cabinets already installed
Delivery performance	Time from completion to installation of cabinets
Manufacturing cycle time	Total production time
Manufacturing cycle efficiency	Value-added time divided by cycle time

Marketing Measures	
Growth in market share	Percentage of remodeling jobs and new homes installing Northern Lights cabinets
Product innovation	The number of new features and designs offered
New market saturation	Percentage of new homes installing Northern Lights cabinets

Productivity Measures	
Output per unit of input	Output per hour of labor, machine time, and board foot of lumber

Likewise, the following table provides similar measures for Big Al's Pizza Emporium. Although Big Al's is also in the business of providing a product to customers, the specific measures used by Big Al's are likely to differ substantially from those used by Northern Lights.

Big Al's Pizza Emporium
Nonfinancial Measures of Performance

Quality Measures	Method of Measuring
Customer satisfaction	Customer complaints/Returned meals/Amount of leftover food
Inspections of raw material	Amount of food not meeting quality criteria
Percentage of scrap	Food discarded in kitchen

Efficiency and Timeliness Measures	
Customer response time	Time from customer order to delivery of meal
Manufacturing cycle time	Meals served per hour

Marketing Measures	
Growth in market share	Percentage change in sales compared to industry standards
Product innovation	Sales of new menu items

Productivity Measures	
Output per unit of input	Finished meals per measure of key ingredients, meals per table per hour (table turns), sales dollars per table, etc.
Machine availability and utilization	Output per hour of pizza oven use

LO8
Understand the use of quality, productivity, efficiency and timeliness, and marketing effectiveness measures within the four perspectives of the balanced scorecard

The next table illustrates potential nonfinancial measures of performance for Garcia and Buffett CPAs, a service firm discussed in Chapter 11. Once again we see differences in the specific measures of performance due to differences in the business itself. For example, the number of billable hours per professional employee is very important to a professional services firm.

GARCIA&BUFFET CPAS

Garcia and Buffett CPAs
Nonfinancial Measures of Performance

Quality Measures	Method of Measuring
Customer satisfaction	Client complaints/Number of lost clients/Number of new clients referred by current clients
Percentage of external failures	IRS audits/Mistakes on client financial statements

Efficiency and Timeliness Measures	
Customer response time	Total time between client delivering tax information and completion of tax return
Delivery performance	Number of extended tax returns

Marketing Measures	
Growth in market share	Percentage change in sales compared to industry standards
Product innovation	Sales of new services to existing clients
New market saturation	Percentage of new businesses that become clients

Productivity Measures	
Output per unit of input	Revenue per dollar of payroll, revenue per partner, billable hours per professional staff member

Although specific measures used in companies will differ, virtually every organization has a need to measure performance using nonfinancial measures of quality, productivity, efficiency and timeliness, and marketing success. Combined with traditional financial measures of performance like cost variances, segment margin, ROI, and EVA, these measures allow companies to integrate the financial, customer, internal business, and learning and growth perspectives of the balanced scorecard.

Consider some of the other companies introduced in the book (TopSail Construction, Tina's Fine Juices, and Happy Daze Game Company). Can you think of nonfinancial measures of performance that might be appropriate for these companies?

 Key Concept: *The four perspectives of the balanced scorecard revolve around measures of quality, productivity, efficiency and timeliness, and marketing success.*

SUMMARY OF KEY CONCEPTS

- The balanced scorecard approach integrates financial and nonfinancial performance measures. (p. 372)
- The balanced scorecard approach requires looking at performance from four different but related perspectives: financial, customer, internal business process, and learning and growth. (p. 375)
- The four perspectives of the balanced scorecard revolve around measures of quality, productivity, efficiency and timeliness, and marketing success. (p. 385)

KEY DEFINITIONS

Balanced scorecard Uses a set of financial and nonfinancial measures that relate to the critical success factors of any organization (p. 372)

Quality Usually defined as meeting or exceeding customers' expectations (p. 375)

Kaizen A system of improvement based on a series of gradual and often small improvements (p. 375)

ISO 9000 A set of guidelines for quality management focusing on the design, production, inspection, testing, installing, and servicing of products, processes, and services (p. 375)

Prevention costs Costs incurred to prevent product failures from occurring, typically related to design and engineering (p. 377)

Appraisal costs Costs incurred to inspect finished products or products in the process of production (p. 377)

Internal failure costs Costs incurred once the product is produced and then determined to be defective (p. 377)

External failure costs Costs incurred when a defective product is delivered to a customer (p. 377)

Productivity A measure of the relationship between outputs and inputs (p. 378)

Customer response time The time it takes to deliver the product of service after the order is received (p. 380)

Manufacturing cycle time The total time a product is in production which includes process time, inspection time, wait time, and move time; cycle time will include both value- and non-value-added time (p. 381)

Throughput The amount of product produced in a given amount of time such as a day, week, or month (p. 381)

Manufacturing cycle efficiency (MCE) The value-added time in the production process divided by the throughput or cycle time (p. 381)

CONCEPT REVIEW

1. Based on the material covered in this chapter, why do you think a firm should be aware of its customers' needs?

2. Describe a balanced scorecard and explain how it helps an organization meet its goals.

3. Discuss the financial perspective of the balanced scorecard. How does this perspective differ from financial measures of performance discussed earlier in this textbook? How does this perspective relate to the other balanced scorecard perspectives?

4. Discuss the customer perspective of the balanced scorecard. How does this perspective relate to the other balanced scorecard perspectives?

5. Discuss the internal operations perspective of the balanced scorecard. How does this perspective relate to the value chain? How does it relate to the other balanced scorecard perspectives?

6. Discuss the innovation and learning perspective of the balanced scorecard. How does this perspective relate to the other three perspectives of the balanced scorecard?

7. Discuss the need for both financial and nonfinancial measures of performance and how they relate to the balanced scorecard.

8. Comment on the phrase "Managers will devote most of their time to activities that can be measured."

9. Discuss the use of performance measurement and the impact on improvement of performance.

10. Discuss why managers could be tempted to manipulate performance measures and how the design of performance measures should take that possibility into consideration.

11. Discuss the use of throughput. What does it measure?

12. Discuss what is meant by quality in today's manufacturing environment.

13. Describe continuous improvement and how it might impact decision-making in today's business environment.

14. Discuss "kaizen" costing and relate it to continuous improvement.

15. How does "employee empowerment" relate to continuous improvement?

16. Describe in detail the three critical success factors that relate to meeting customer quality requirements.

17. Describe the two costs of *controlling quality* and the two costs of *failing to control quality*.

18. Although the "cost of quality" concept is prevalent among companies throughout the world, a current theme in business today is that "quality is free." Discuss what that statement means.

19. Operational measures of time indicate the speed and reliability with which organizations supply products and services to customers. Companies generally use which two measures of time? Describe each of these measures.

20. What are the four quality costing categories? Include in your answer at least three examples for each category.

21. Describe ISO 9000 and comment on its importance. Research and compare other quality certification programs.

22. Describe value-added time. Give examples.

23. Describe non-value-added time. Give examples.

24. Describe how each element of manufacturing cycle efficiency impacts the overall measurement.

25. Discuss marketing measures of performance and the impact of these measures on the balanced scorecard.

APPLICATION OF CONCEPTS

26. The following information has been gathered from Three Dog Nite Company:

Warranty claims	$ 120,000
Product liability lawsuits	200,000
Rework costs	600,000
Quality training	305,000
Inspection of incoming materials	900,000
Statistical process control	650,000
Waste	300,000
Product quality audits	475,000
Total yearly sales	$50,000,000

Required

    A. What are total prevention costs?

    B. What are total appraisal costs?

    C. What are total internal failure costs?

    D. What are total external failure costs?

E. Compare prevention and appraisal costs to internal and external failure costs.

27. The following information was received from Two Black Cats Restaurant Chain:

Warranty claims	$ 120,000
Food poisoning liability lawsuits	200,000
Remaking entree costs	600,000
Quality training	305,000
Inspection of incoming ingredients	900,000
Statistical process control	650,000
Spoilage and waste	300,000
Product quality audits	475,000
Total sales	$50,000,000

Required

A. Compute the total prevention costs.

B. Compute the total appraisal costs.

C. Compute the total internal failure costs.

D. Compute the total external failure costs.

E. Compare prevention and appraisal costs to internal and external failure costs.

F. Two Black Cats Restaurant Chain is considering spending more on inspections, what is the likely impact on other failure costs? What do you recommend?

28. The following information was received from Down East Coffee Company:

Warranty claims	$ 60,000
Product liability lawsuits	100,000
Rework costs	300,000
Quality training	152,500
Inspection of incoming material	450,000
Statistical process control	325,000
Waste	150,000
Product quality audits	237,500
Total sales	$25,000,000

Required

Prepare a report for Down East Coffee Company showing total prevention, appraisal, internal failure, and external failure costs as a percentage of sales. Based on the report, what recommendations would you make?

29. Rebecca's Pottery Loft makes a variety of handmade pottery items. She has asked for your advice on one of the items manufactured—a clay pelican. The following information is provided:

Defective pelicans	$1,100
Number of pelicans returned	150
Pelicans reworked	200
Profit per good pelican	10
Profit per defective pelican	5
Cost to rework defective pelican	4
Processing cost of a returned pelican	20
Appraisal costs	3,400
Prevention costs	6,000

Required

A. Calculate the total profits lost, because Rebecca sold some defective pelicans.

B. Calculate the rework cost.

C. Calculate the cost of processing customer returns.

D. Calculate total failure cost.

E. Calculate total quality cost.

30. Cheryl's Country Creations is a chain of craft stores. The company evaluates its managers on the basis of both financial and nonfinancial performance measures. One of the nonfinancial measures used is throughput to measure performance in the manufacturing divisions. The following data pertain to the company's branch in Biloxi, Mississippi. The unit of measurement is units.

Units started into production	180,000
Total good units completed	135,000
Total hours of value-added production time	90,000
Total production hours	120,000

Required

A. Compute the manufacturing cycle efficiency.

B. What was the total throughput per hour?

31. Dan Foley's Pubs is a chain of brewpubs in the Pacific Northwest. The company evaluates its managers on the basis of both financial and nonfinancial performance measures. One of the nonfinancial measures used is throughput to measure performance in the brewing divisions. The following data pertain to the company's brewpub in Federal Way, Washington. The unit of measurement is gallons:

Units started into production	280,000
Total good units completed	235,000
Total hours of value-added production time	190,000
Total production hours	220,000

Required

A. Compute the manufacturing cycle efficiency.

B. What was the total throughput per hour?

32. Mandy Lifeboats Yacht Company has always measured divisional performance using only financial measures. Top management has started to question this approach to evaluating performance and is evaluating alternative measures. The managers are specifically interested in focusing on activities that generate value for their customers so are considering using throughput. They have gathered the following data and have asked for your opinion.

Units started into production	3,000
Total good units completed	2,900
Total hours of value added production time	180,000
Total hours of division production time	210,000

Required

A. What is the manufacturing cycle efficiency?

B. What is the total throughput per hour?

C. Is there evidence of potentially poor quality in the production process as measured by the number of defective units? (Remember the type of business.)

Part IV

THE IMPACT OF MANAGEMENT DECISIONS

Chapter 13

THE MANAGEMENT OF INFORMATION AND KNOWLEDGE FOR BETTER DECISIONS

Study Tools

A Review of the Previous Chapter
In Chapter 12 we discussed a variety of nonfinancial and qualitative measures used in a "balanced scorecard" approach to measuring performance.

A Preview of This Chapter
In this chapter, we introduce the concept of knowledge management—the process of formally managing information and knowledge resources in order to facilitate access and reuse of that information and knowledge. Knowledge management tools facilitate human resource management, supply-chain management, and customer relationship management ultimately leading to better and faster decision making.

Key concepts include:
- Data becomes information when organized, processed, and summarized, and information becomes knowledge when it is shared and exploited to add value to an organization.
- E-business can be used to support an organization's entire value chain. One of the key benefits of e-business is the ability to quickly access and share knowledge inside and outside an organization.
- The combination of enterprise resource planning (ERP), electronic data interchange (EDI), and e-business via the Internet has vastly changed the traditional supply chain allowing organizations to link employees, suppliers, and customers into a communications network whose benefits extend well beyond simple exchanges of data.
- The use of the Internet facilitates customer relationship (CRM) by allowing data to be gathered, stored, accessed, and shared more easily and by providing a feedback loop from customers to companies.

LEARNING OBJECTIVES

After studying the material in this chapter, you should be able to:

LO1 Understand changes in the business environment that require more effective information and knowledge management

LO2 Evaluate the impact of technological innovations like the Internet and electronic business on information and knowledge management

LO3 Identify key tools for effective knowledge management

LO4 Explain the use and benefits of knowledge warehouses and enterprise resource planning (ERP) systems as knowledge management tools

LO5 Analyze the impact of ERP, EDI, and e-business on supply-chain management and customer-relationship management

A Preview of Upcoming Chapters
In Chapter 14, we discuss management fraud and the importance of good internal control systems on the reliability of accounting information in decision making. The chapter describes common types of management and employee fraud and looks at the role of the internal auditor and external auditor in assuring that financial information is fairly presented and reliable.

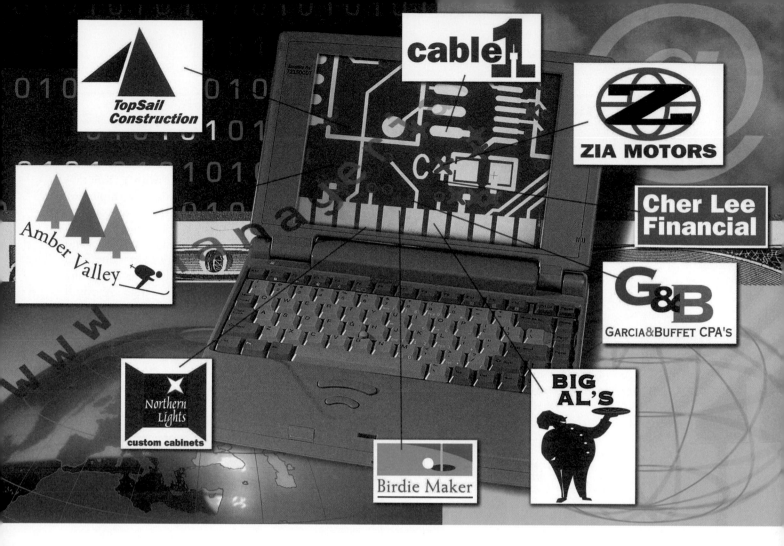

In this chapter, we introduce the reader to the concept of knowledge management—the process of formally managing information and knowledge resources in order to facilitate access and reuse of that information and knowledge. Information and knowledge resources may vary for each company but include traditional sources of data provided by the accounting information system as well as such things as internal memos, training manuals, and information supplied by customers and suppliers.

Just as information and knowledge resources vary among companies, knowledge management tools may vary as well. Typical knowledge management tools include knowledge warehouses and enterprise resource planning (ERP) systems. Knowledge management tools facilitate human resource management, supply-chain management, and customer relationship management ultimately leading to better and faster decision making. ■

INTRODUCTION

LO1

Understand changes in the business environment that require more effective information and knowledge management

Business environments have changed dramatically in the past few decades. Companies of all sizes can now compete in a dynamic global marketplace through electronic commerce (e-business) and other emerging technologies. Downsizing, combined with a more mobile workforce, has placed a premium on retaining talented, knowledgeable employees. Customers demand specialized products and services and real-time information concerning product availability, order status, and delivery times. Suppliers need information on their buyers' sales and inventory levels in order to tailor their production schedules and delivery times to meet the buyers' demands. Shareholders demand greater value from their investments. Although these changes have provided opportunities for companies able to adapt and take advantage of them, they have also resulted in challenges. Above all else, these changes require more effective management of knowledge within an organization. In today's business environment, knowledge is power and must be managed for companies to remain competitive.

Although sometimes used interchangeably, knowledge should not be confused with data or information. Companies generate literally tons of **data**—financial statements, customer lists, inventory records, and the number and type of products and services sold. However, getting that data into an accessible and usable form is another matter. When data are organized, processed, and summarized, they become **information.** When that information is shared and exploited so that it adds value to an organization, it becomes **knowledge.**

 Key Concept: *Data becomes information when organized, processed, and summarized and information becomes knowledge when it is shared and exploited to add value to an organization.*

THE EVOLUTION OF DATA, INFORMATION, AND KNOWLEDGE MANAGEMENT

Many of us take for granted that a computer will be available to assist us in the completion of our everyday business and personal tasks (letter writing, note taking, basic word processing, accounting/bookkeeping, presentations, etc.). But those of us who are old enough remember when the entire process of running an organization, from human resources (hiring, firing, and employee benefits) to accounting (source documents, cost sheets, financial statements, etc.) to production (machine specifications, product output, and inventory records) was manually accounted for and documented without the benefit of computers. Business data were recorded on reams of paper, information was stored in file cabinets, and knowledge resided in people's minds.

Data and information management evolved with the introduction and availability of mainframe computers in the 1960s and 1970s and personal computers in the 1980s. Accounting information systems were often computerized, and training manuals, internal memos, and customer records could all be stored electronically. However, the problems of knowledge management did not go away. The stored data were not easily organized, accessed, or searched. Although information was arguably available, just how did one find it and use it? Until the widespread adoption of relational databases in the 1980s, it was still difficult to access and retrieve data. Sales staff still did not always know what was going on in production, and customer service representatives had no way of knowing that a customer's problem had already been addressed by another representative dealing with a different customer in a different city. In addition, key employees still left for other jobs, taking with them all their knowledge that was not written down or otherwise shared. Although the widespread use of Intranets (networks of linked computers inside a company) made access to information faster and easier, exploiting that information as usable knowledge was and still is difficult.

THE INTERNET AND ELECTRONIC COMMERCE

LO2
Evaluate the impact of technological innovations like the Internet and electronic business on information and knowledge management

Yet another transformation in data and information management was made possible with the wide-scale use of the Internet and electronic commerce in the 1990s. Electronic business or **e-business** includes a vast array of business activities conducted electronically. The first widespread application of e-business involved direct sales of products to customers over the Internet. Today, more than 17 million U.S. households shop on-line with retail sales expected to exceed $20 billion (The Internet Economy Indicators Web site, www.internetindicators.com, November 8, 1999). A wide variety of products and services are sold on-line via electronic catalogs. Examples of companies that offer customers the opportunity to shop on-line include computer manufacturers such as Dell (www.dell.com) and Gateway (www.gateway.com), resellers such as Amazon books (www.amazon.com) and wine sellers (www.wine.com), and PeaPod, an online grocery (www.peapod.com).

From a purely operational perspective, on-line business has the ability to increase sales, reduce customer response time, increase efficiency, and quicken new products' time to market while decreasing transaction costs. Sales via the Internet allow a raw material producer to sell directly to the end consumer, eliminating costs of the intermediary without reducing value to the consumer. From the consumer's perspective, 24-hour access to products as well as the company's ability to help develop and tailor products should increase customer satisfaction and thus increase customer retention rates. In summary, on-line sales allow companies to reach new markets, remain open for business 24 hours a day, 7 days a week, and potentially enhance customer service.

IN THE NEWS   www.seafoodnow.com

In the four months after launching its Web site, Internet sales accounted for 25 to 30 percent of total sales of Hanson Bros. Fresh Seafood in Portland, Maine. According to the owner, Brian Hanson, being on the Web broadened Hanson's customer base and generated sales in slower months to keep money flowing into the business (Associated Press Newswires, Darlene Superville, May 27, 1999).

In addition to the benefits of on-line sales, e-business can be used to support an organization's entire value chain. As introduced in Chapter 2, the value chain describes the linked set of value-creating activities required by today's competitive business environment (Exhibit 13-1).

Although we often think of e-business as consumer-related purchases of goods and services, e-business covers the entire spectrum of business activities. In fact, business-to-business (B2B) sales are expected to hit $2.4 trillion by 2004. (Forrester Research, Inc. (www.forrester.com), Press Release, February 7, 2000).

IN THE NEWS   **www.intel.com**

Intel averages $1 billion in on-line orders each month from customers (other companies) in 46 countries. These companies can use the Internet to check product specifications, pricing, availability, order status, and delivery dates in real time. Data are personalized for every company and for every type of user (*Wall Street Journal* advertisement, September 20, 1999, B11).

**www.gm.com &
www.ford.com**

In addition to the direct links to the value chain, one of the major benefits of e-business is the ability to quickly access and share knowledge inside and outside an organization. As an example, General Motors (GM) and Ford recently announced plans to set up "on-line bazaars for all of the goods and services they buy—everything from paper clips to stamping presses and contract manufacturing." Suppliers are expected to be active participants in the on-line activities, not only by selling to GM and Ford, but also by doing business with each other. For example, a company that provides parts to GM might use the on-line bazaar to get a more favorable price on steel by piggybacking with other suppliers. Likewise, a supplier with excess steel might sell to another supplier. Other initiatives include directly linking dealerships to a manufacturer so that warranty problems can be reported on-line. This would allow manufacturers to immediately correct assembly line problems, reducing the huge postsale costs caused by recalls and repairs made under warranty ("How GM, Ford Think Web Can Make Splash on the Factory Floor," *Wall Street Journal,* December 3, 1999, A1).

 Key Concept: *E-business can be used to support an organization's entire value chain. One of the key benefits of e-business is the ability to quickly access and share knowledge inside and outside an organization.*

www.ey.com

Even with these technological innovations in data and information management occurring in the past 30 to 40 years, Ernst & Young estimates that up to 80 percent of a company's accumulated knowledge is not utilized in business decisions ("Knowledge Based

EXHIBIT 13-1 The Value Chain

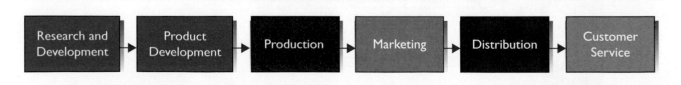

Businesses, Overview: Knowledge is Power," Ernst and Young (www.ey.com), 1999). The reasons are varied. One possible explanation is that accounting information systems still may not provide timely information that is easily accessible and easily shared.

As discussed in Chapter 1, traditionally the accounting information system (AIS) was simply a transaction processing system that captured financial data resulting from accounting transactions. Other nonmonetary information was likely collected and processed outside the traditional AIS if collected at all. Useful information concerning transactions such as the quality of the material purchased and the timeliness of its delivery or customer satisfaction with an order might not be captured at all and therefore not evaluated by management. Although the contemporary view of accounting information has been broadened to include both nonmonetary quantitative data and qualitative data (see Exhibit 13-2), this information was not readily accessible and readily shared until the advent of enterprise resource planning (ERP) systems in the past few years.

Other potential reasons that knowledge is not effectively used and managed in businesses may include geographic and cultural barriers resulting from international expansion and the continued mobility of key employees and managers leaving for other jobs and taking critical knowledge with them.

EXHIBIT 13-2   A Contemporary View of Accounting Information

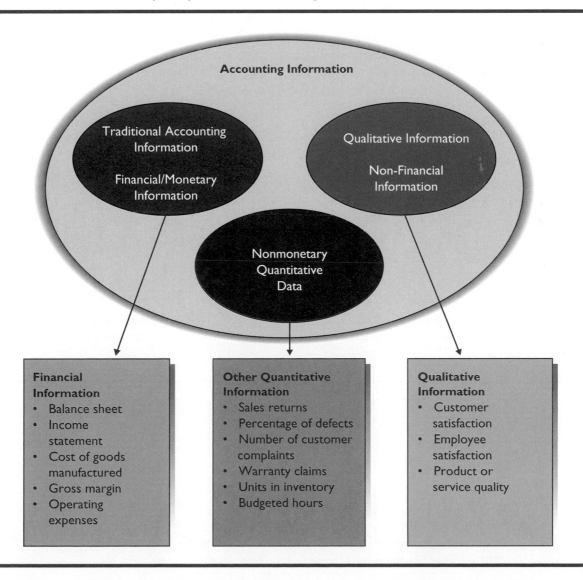

KNOWLEDGE MANAGEMENT TOOLS

LO3
Identify key tools for effective knowledge management

Effective knowledge management can result in faster and better business decisions leading ultimately to increased profitability through better strategic planning, more timely development of products and completion of projects, improved customer service, and cost savings. A variety of knowledge management tools including data and knowledge warehouses and ERP systems facilitate effective knowledge management.

DATA AND KNOWLEDGE WAREHOUSES

Data warehouses are simply central depositories for electronic data. Data warehouses often contain many years of transactions, which can be accessed and browsed electronically. Although data warehouses contain the ingredients for good business decisions, turning that data into information and knowledge requires other tools. A variety of technological tools are available to help managers dig out the information they need to make business decisions. The term **data mining** was coined as a way to express, in modern day technical terms, how a manager can search for and extract information from the corporate computer system much like a coal miner searches for and extracts coal from a mine. Data mining software like SAS Institute's Enterprise Miner is used to help find business opportunities in large amounts of data. For example, every time you make a purchase using a value card at a grocery store, the grocery store collects data on what you purchase, how much you purchase, whether you use coupons, and whether you pay with cash, check, or credit card. Data mining software looks for patterns in the data that can be used to help managers make decisions concerning product placement, product pricing, inventory management, and advertising campaigns.

Knowledge warehouses are organized to provide access to a wide variety of qualitative data. Memos, news articles, client and customer notes, product specifications, documentation of problem resolution, employee information (education, skills, and specialty areas), and competitor intelligence may all be a part of a searchable knowledge warehouse. Data-mining techniques can be used to determine the available skill set of employees, identify untapped expertise and opportunities for growth, and identify needs for additional skills and training. Technological tools like Lotus Notes were traditionally used to store this type of data and to facilitate its access and use. Today, Web-based tools such as Internet newsgroups are often used to collect and share knowledge. As discussed in the next section, ERP systems are another tool allowing organizations the ability to gather information and disseminate knowledge to their employees.

ENTERPRISE RESOURCE PLANNING SYSTEMS

Companies use **enterprise resource planning (ERP) systems** to collect, organize, report, and distribute data throughout an organization and to transform that data into usable

Think of other ways that data can be collected on your buying habits to help marketing efforts.

DILBERT BY SCOTT ADAMS

DILBERT reprinted by permission of United Features Syndicate, Inc.

knowledge necessary for managers to make proper business decisions. These systems typically integrate payroll, purchasing, sales, manufacturing, inventory, product costing, and billing, providing a more comprehensive view of the organization.

An ERP system digitally records every business transaction a company makes regardless of whether it is inputted through accounting, purchasing, sales, or manufacturing and automatically updates all connected systems to reflect each transaction. This approach provides real-time information to decision makers throughout a company. When a sales associate on the road places an order for a product, the information is automatically conveyed to purchasing, accounts receivable, and production so that materials can be ordered, invoices can be processed, and production can be scheduled.

ERP systems help businesses evolve from data generators to information gatherers to knowledge creators and sharers. The ultimate goal of the ERP system is to get the right information to the right people at the right time. With better knowledge management, an organization can better identify its strengths, pinpoint its weaknesses, uncover new opportunities, capitalize on trends, and make better business decisions.

When used effectively, ERP systems can allow an organization to achieve higher levels of profitability. They can provide more accurate and complete information resulting in reduced purchasing and manufacturing costs, reduced customer response time, increased quality of products and services, increased customer satisfaction, and better business decisions. After the installation of an ERP system at Belvedere Co. (a $30 million manufacturer and distributor of beauty salon furnishings), customer response time was reduced from 5 days to 2 days, inventory was reduced by 30 percent, order-processing capacity was increased by 15 percent, and customer complaints dropped (Piturro, Marlene, "How Midsize Companies are Buying ERP," *Journal of Accountancy,* September 1999, 41).

The benefits of ERP are not limited to manufacturing companies. Service organizations have also come to realize the increased benefits of ERP systems. Organizational efficiencies such as improved customer service and better communication provide benefits to all types of companies.

IN THE NEWS

According to Computer Economics Inc. as of June 1999, the leading industries in implementing ERP systems are manufacturing (40.5%), professional services (26.2%), distribution (18.4%), utilities (15.4%), banking and finance (12.9%), state and local governments (12.5%), trade services (12.3%), transportation (9.5%), health care (9.7%), insurance (7.7%), and the federal government (4.0%).

Although ERP systems have provided benefits to many companies, they are not without their costs. ERP systems tend to involve large-scale financial, human resource, time, and information technology costs. As the following "In the News" demonstrates, when there are glitches in the systems, the results can be disastrous.

IN THE NEWS   **www.hersheys.com**

In July of 1999, Hershey Foods Corp. (the nations largest candy producer) went on-line with its $112 million ERP system designed to do everything: track raw ingredients, schedule production, set prices, measure the effectiveness of promotional campaigns, schedule delivery, and decide how to stack products inside trucks. However, glitches in the system left many distributors and retailers with empty candy shelves in the season leading to Halloween. At one point, Hershey could not even tell what had been shipped or who it had been shipped to ("Hershey's Biggest Dud Has Turned Out to Be New Computer System," *Wall Street Journal,* October 29, 1999, A1).

Great Plains Software, head-quartered in Fargo, North Dakota, is a rapidly growing firm, which designs ERP software for mid-sized companies.

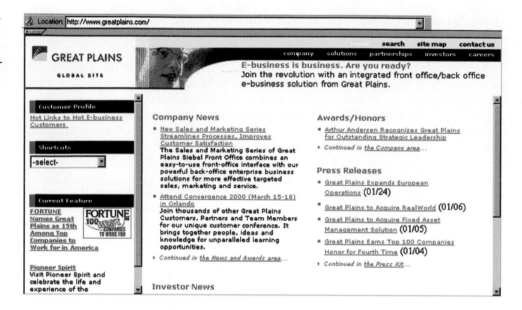

ERP systems are generally not meant to *solve* business inefficiencies. Rather, they can point to where inefficiencies exist within an organization and allow corporate decision makers to take appropriate corrective measures. A number of companies have reengineered their business processes through involvement with ERP systems resulting in substantial returns from their ERP investments.

The success of an ERP system usually depends on how quickly it can provide useful information for managerial decision making. This need favors rapid implementation, which shortens the time needed to recapture the investment. However, the average implementation time of a system is 23 months. In addition, it can take up to two years after implementation for a company to achieve a quantifiable return on investment.

Many small corporations have been reluctant to invest in ERP systems due to the high cost and the implementation time involved. However, several of the larger ERP system vendors have begun to market scaled-down versions of their ERP packages in order to tap the small to medium-sized company market. Companies who either could not afford ERP systems in the past or were merely too small to integrate the applications can now compete with their larger counterparts.

ERP, EDI, AND E-BUSINESS

LO5

Analyze the impact of ERP, EDI, and e-business on supply-chain management and customer-relationship management

www.nabisco.com

Electronic data interchange (EDI) and e-business via the Internet allow suppliers and customers to be brought into the ERP network so that on-line orders from customers initiate a series of highly integrated transactions that ultimately fulfill the request—from materials acquisition, to manufacturing, to shipping. EDI is simply the electronic transmission of data such as purchase orders and invoices. Though originally limited to large companies with a direct data connection or companies on the same network, the Internet has made EDI technology available to a wide range of medium and small businesses. EDI has several benefits. It increases the speed and quality of information exchange, reduces lead times, and reduces processing costs. Nabisco estimates that the cost of processing a paper-based purchase order is $70 while the same transaction performed through EDI costs less than $1 (Millman, H., "A Brief History of EDI," *Infoworld*, April 6, 1998, 83). Government agencies and a variety of service organizations also use EDI. Wisconsin's Worker's Compensation Division uses EDI to allow electronic reporting of injury claims. Reporting electronically saves time and money for both the division and for insurance carriers, employers, and injured workers. It also increases the accuracy of claims and enhances data flexibility by providing a rich database for future use (Greenstein and Feinman, *Electronic Commerce: Security Risk Management and Control*, McGraw-Hill Higher Ed., 2000).

SUPPLY-CHAIN MANAGEMENT

Supply-chain management includes a variety of activities centered around making the purchase of materials and inventory more efficient and less costly. When coupled with ERP systems, EDI allows a company to place a great deal of the burden of inventory management and raw materials ordering in the hands of its suppliers, resulting in an evolution of supply-chain management from "loosely coupled relationships into virtual organizations" (O'Leary, Daniel E., "Supply Chain Processes and Relationships for Electronic Commerce," *Handbook of Electronic Commerce,* Springer Verlag, 2000, 431–444). In these organizations, suppliers monitor sales in real time and determine order quantities and order times for buyers. Wal-Mart shares data on sales, profit margin, and inventory levels with more than 7,000 suppliers who access Wal-Mart's database 120,000 times per week. This allows suppliers to more closely match their production schedules to Wal-Mart's peak selling seasons and to deliver products when Wal-Mart needs them ("Wal-Mart Expands Access to Product Sales History," *Wall Street Journal,* August 18, 1999, B8).

In other companies, e-business, ERP, and EDI are changing the supply chain in other ways. When Coca-Cola rolled out its ERP system, it included 11 of its major worldwide bottling partners including Coca-Cola Enterprises. This allowed Coca-Cola and the bottlers to pool requisitions for raw materials like corn syrup and aluminum and to coordinate shipping resulting in volume discounts and other cost savings ("ERP: Extending the Enterprise," *Discount Store News,* May 24, 1999, 7).

 Key Concept: *The combination of ERP, EDI, and e-business via the Internet has vastly changed the traditional supply chain allowing organizations to link employees, suppliers, and customers into a communications network whose benefits extend well beyond simple exchanges of data.*

CUSTOMER RELATIONSHIP MANAGEMENT

The goal of **customer relationship management (CRM)** is to bring a company closer to its customers in order to serve them better. Whether customers are served by in-store representatives, outside sales associates, or call-center operators, the use of ERP and the Internet facilitates CRM by allowing information to be gathered, stored, and most important, easily accessed and shared. CRM utilizing the ERP and the Internet allows organizations to focus sales efforts on what the customer values and to anticipate and react to customer needs.

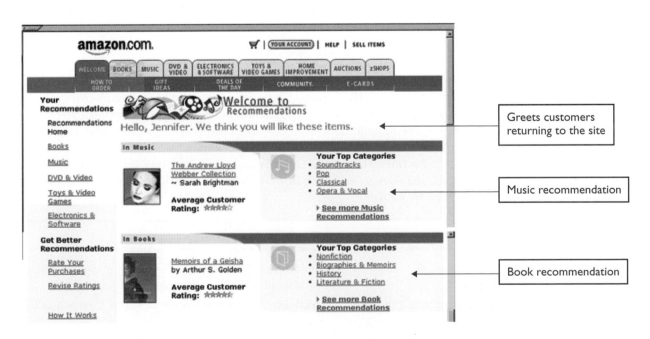

Greets customers returning to the site

Music recommendation

Book recommendation

IN THE NEWS   www.amazon.com

Amazon.com collects data on each customer and anticipates the customer's preferences and buying habits. This allows Amazon to e-mail the customer with the latest products that fit the particular customer and to greet each customer accessing their Web site with personalized suggestions based on previous purchases.

Who owns customer information? Is collecting customer information without the customer's knowledge and sharing that information with other parties ethical?

The use of the Internet creates an interactive feedback "loop" from customers to companies, making it possible to more accurately and consistently forecast, manage, and meet customer expectations. Through the Internet, an organization can manage the entire life cycle of its customer relationships, including marketing analysis and planning, customer acquisition and retention, order management, and customer service and support. A variety of car manufacturers including Toyota and GM are using the Web to enhance their CRM efforts. Up to now, car manufacturers tried to forecast consumer demand for different models and delivered vehicles to dealers based on those forecasts. However, if consumer tastes changed, dealers (and the manufacturer) were often left with a large inventory of cars that were difficult to sell. Both Toyota and GM have recently announced goals of manufacturing and delivering a custom vehicle within 10 to 12 days of receiving an on-line order from a customer. This benefits all stakeholders by reducing inventory carrying costs for the manufacturer and dealer, allowing manufacturers to quickly identify and react to changes in customer demand, and providing built-to-order products in a timely fashion to consumers ("General Motors Looks to the Future with Internet Unit," *Wall Street Journal,* August 11, 1999, B4; see also www.gm.com and www.toyota.com).

 Key Concept: *The use of the Internet facilitates CRM by allowing data to be gathered, stored, accessed, and shared more easily and by providing a feedback loop from customers to companies.*

SUMMARY OF KEY CONCEPTS

- Data becomes information when organized, processed, and summarized, and information becomes knowledge when it is shared and exploited to add value to an organization. (p. 392)
- E-business can be used to support an organization's entire value chain. One of the key benefits of e-business is the ability to quickly access and share knowledge inside and outside an organization. (p. 394)
- The combination of ERP, EDI, and e-business via the Internet has vastly changed the traditional supply chain allowing organizations to link employees, suppliers, and customers into a communications network whose benefits extend well beyond simple exchanges of data. (p. 399)
- The use of the Internet facilitates CRM by allowing data to be gathered, stored, accessed, and shared more easily and by providing a feedback loop from customers to companies. (p. 400)

KEY DEFINITIONS

Data Reports such as financial statements, customer lists, inventory records, and so on (p. 392)

Information Data that have been organized, processed, and summarized (p. 392)

Knowledge Information that is shared and exploited so that its adds value to an organization (p. 392)

E-business Business activities conducted electronically (p. 393)

Data warehouses Central depositories for electronic data (p. 396)

Data mining A process of searching and extracting information from data (p. 396)

Knowledge warehouses Used to store and provide access to a wide variety of qualitative data (p. 396)

Enterprise resource planning (ERP) systems Used to collect, organize, report, and distribute data from all aspects of a company's business and to transform that data into useful knowledge (p. 396)

Electronic data interchange (EDI) The electronic transmission of data such as purchase orders and invoices (p. 398)

Supply-chain management Includes a variety of activities centered around making the purchase of materials and inventory more efficient and less costly (p. 399)

Customer relationship management (CRM) Designed to bring a company closer to its customers in order to serve them better (p. 399)

CONCEPT REVIEW

1. Explain how e-business has impacted the business environment today. How has e-business changed your life specifically?

2. Discuss the relationship between data, information, and knowledge.

3. Visit www.internetindicators.com and go to the case studies section. Choose any company and write a short (1–2 page) report on the success or failure of the case study chosen. Print out the case study as a reference for your paper.

4. Go to www.dell.com and visit the higher education, faculty, staff, and student area. Price the latest special computer offered for purchase. Print out the material.

5. Go to www.gateway.com and price a remanufactured computer of your choice. Print out the material.

6. Go to www.llbean.com and research and write a short report on discovery schools. Print out the material to support your paper.

7. Go to www.landsend.com and research what luggage is offered. Print out the material.

8. Go to www.intel.com and research employment opportunities. Print out the material.

9. Go to www.gmc.com and research any current special offers for automobiles. Print out the material.

10. Go to www.sap.com and write a short paper about what the company provides in the way of ERP systems. What is the company's competitive advantage?

11. Go to www.oracle.com and write a short paper about what the company provides in the way of ERP systems. What is the company's competitive advantage?

12. Go to www.peoplesoft.com and write a short paper about what the company provides in the way of ERP systems. What is the company's competitive advantage?

13. Go to www.baan.com and write a short paper about what the company provides in the way of ERP systems. What is the company's competitive advantage?

14. Go to www.jdedwards.com and write a short paper about what the company provide in the way of ERP systems. What is the company's competitive advantage?

15. Visit all the sites of software vendors offering ERP systems that were mentioned in the chapter and contrast and compare them. What company would you choose to provide an ERP system to your business? Why?

16. Discuss on-line sales and the impact they can have on business today.

17. Do you think on-line sales can actually reduce the price to the consumer? Why or why not?

18. Discuss why traditional accounting information systems may not provide all the information needed for effective decision making.

19. Discuss what is meant by "effective knowledge management."

20. Discuss how ERP systems can enhance effective knowledge management.

21. Discuss the impact of data and knowledge warehouses on decision making.

22. Discuss the benefits and limitations of ERP systems.

23. Discuss the impact of electronic data interchange (EDI) technology on decision making in business.

24. Discuss the impact of the Internet on customer relationship management (CRM).

25. Using the *Wall Street Journal* and other business resources, research how companies are using online supply networks to facilitate their business operations. What problems are companies facing?

Chapter 14

INTERNAL CONTROL AND THE PREVENTION OF FRAUD

Study Tools

A Review of the Previous Chapter
In Chapter 13, we introduced the concept of knowledge management—the process of formally managing information and knowledge resources in order to facilitate access and reuse of that information and knowledge. Typical knowledge management tools include knowledge warehouses and enterprise resource planning (ERP) systems. Knowledge management tools facilitate supply-chain management and customer relationship management, ultimately leading to better and faster decision making.

A Preview of This Chapter
In this chapter, we discuss the importance of internal control systems in detecting fraud. We also discuss key characteristics of an internal control system, common internal control procedures and the impact of e-business on fraud and internal control.

Key concepts include:
- Fraud is more narrowly defined in a business context than in common law.
- Management fraud can be very difficult to detect.
- Good internal control systems can usually detect and prevent most types of employee fraud.
- Individuals engage in fraudulent activity as a result of situational pressures, opportunity, and personal characteristics.
- The internal control system's impact on promoting effective and efficient operations is perhaps even more important than detecting fraudulent activity.
- Upper-level management sets the tone of ethical behavior and the overall atmosphere of the organization.
- To be effective, internal control systems must be communicated throughout an organization and modified as new risks are identified.

LEARNING OBJECTIVES

After studying the material in this chapter, you should be able to:

LO1 Distinguish management fraud from employee fraud

LO2 Understand ethical issues surrounding earnings management

LO3 Explain the typical causes of fraudulent activities

LO4 Understand the role of the internal audit department and the external auditor

LO5 Explain the objectives, design, and characteristics of good internal control systems

LO6 Understand common internal control procedures

LO7 Understand the behavioral implications of internal control systems

LO8 Understand the impact of e-business on internal control

- E-business activities entail new risks and require new internal control procedures.

A Preview of Upcoming Chapters
In Chapter 15 and Chapter 16, we discuss the preparation and use of the statement of cash flows and the analysis of financial statement information.

This chapter examines the importance of internal control systems in detecting and controlling management and employee fraud. The chapter explores common types of fraud and the role of internal managers and external auditors in detecting and preventing fraud. The chapter also introduces characteristics of an internal control system (including the key internal control procedures that are used to prevent and detect fraudulent activities). The chapter concludes with a discussion of the impact of e-business on internal control systems and risk. ∎

INTRODUCTION

www.kpmg.com

A 1998 survey of executives at more than 5,000 corporations, universities, and federal, state, and local governments and agencies found that 59 percent of respondents believed that fraud will become more of a problem in the future (1998 Fraud Survey, KPMG LLP). Although fraud has been a problem as long as businesses have been in existence, organizations may face increased risks in today's business environment for a number of reasons. The sheer size of many corporations makes it difficult to monitor thousands of employees. In some cases, globalization has increased opportunities for fraud as companies expand internationally without a firm understanding of the culture of the country. Reduced stability in the workforce and a resulting reduction in corporate loyalty may increase fraud, as may increasing pressure to meet earnings expectations of shareholders or the expectations of other stakeholders. Most recently, the increased computerization of accounting systems and growing reliance on the Internet as a sales tool and as a way to share information and knowledge with customers and suppliers has led to new concerns about the security of data and the manipulation of data by hackers and disgruntled employees.

FRAUD

LO1
Distinguish management fraud from employee fraud

What exactly is **fraud**? Common law requirements for fraud include a false representation of a material fact made by one party to another party with the intent to deceive and induce the other party to justifiably rely on the fact to his or her detriment.

In a business context, the meaning of fraud is narrower than the common law definition. Fraud may include internal deceptions by management, a manipulation of financial data, or a misappropriation of the organization's assets. Misappropriation of assets can include embezzling funds, stealing assets, or causing the organization to pay for goods or services it did not receive. Fraudulent acts may involve falsifying documents or accounting records and can involve one or more individuals at any level in the organization.

 Key Concept: *Fraud is more narrowly defined in a business context than in common law.*

MANAGEMENT FRAUD

Management fraud typically involves misstating financial statements in order to mislead readers of those statements or to take advantage of incentives or other benefits tied to earnings. The most common types of management fraud involve improper revenue recognition, overstating assets, or understating liabilities. These types of frauds typically are the result of pressure on management to report good operating results. This pressure may come from stockholders to meet earnings expectations but may also be a result of unrealistic sales goals or other budgets set internally or compensation plans that are tied directly to the financial results of the organization. For example, sales managers may record sales in the wrong period to meet sales quotas. If a large order is received on January 2, 2000, the paperwork might be altered to record the sale in 1999. This type of fraud increases sales and earnings for 1999 but will correct itself by the end of 2000. In other words, the combined sales for 1999 and 2000 will be correct although one year will be overstated and the other year understated.

Revenues can also be inflated by recording false sales or not recording returned merchandise. This has the impact of falsely inflating revenues and overstating accounts receivable. Other examples of financial statement manipulation include inflating inventory values by leaving obsolete inventory on the books or creating fake documents to show purchases of inventory.

IN THE NEWS

One of the most famous examples of fraudulent manipulation of revenue involved ZZZZ Best Company Inc. Founded by Barry Minkow in 1982 as a carpet cleaning business run out of his parents' garage, the company's reported net income grew from $200,000 in 1984 to $5 million in 1987 on revenues of $50 million. In 1987, the stock market valued the company at over $200 million. However, by 1989 Barry Minkow was serving a 25-year sentence for 57 counts of securities fraud. ZZZZ Best recorded revenues from restoration of damaged buildings, when in fact it did no actual restoration work at all. When the company was liquidated in July 1987, the assets brought in only $62,000 (Domanick, *Faking It in America: Barry Minkow and the Great ZZZZ Best Scam*).

Management fraud can be difficult to detect and can cause irreparable damage to the financial position of a company. This type of fraud is often called **performance fraud** because the manipulation of the financial information is often designed to inflate earnings or to cover up a decline in financial position.

How might companies reduce the risk of management fraud?

 Key Concept: *Management fraud can be very difficult to detect.*

Although the examples of financial statement manipulation discussed here are clearly fraudulent, earnings "management" is another story entirely.

EARNINGS MANAGEMENT

Generally accepted accounting principles (GAAP) are the principles that guide the preparation of financial statements for external users. However, the very same financial statements may be used by internal decision makers for a number of different purposes including promotion decisions, compensation levels, and year-end bonuses to management. In addition, GAAP leaves considerable leeway to managers to make choices that can impact earnings. For example, management has control over depreciation methods and determining the useful lives of assets. Management also has control over when to write off obsolete inventory, when to write off bad debts, and increases or decreases in the allowance for bad debts account. These and other choices provide management with ample opportunities to manage earnings. **Earnings management** may be used to "smooth" earnings from quarter to quarter or to otherwise manipulate financial results for a variety of reasons. Is earnings management fraudulent behavior? Probably not. However, the press and others are increasingly questioning it as inappropriate.

LO2
Understand ethical issues surrounding earnings management

IN THE NEWS   www.microsoft.com

Microsoft came under fire in 1999 for earnings management related to a memo from Microsoft's CFO to Bill Gates urging that the company "do all we can do" to smooth its profits and keep a "steady state earnings model." Microsoft was accused of setting aside revenue not needed to make current sales and profit targets as a "reserve" that could be used to increase revenue and earnings in the future. The Security and Exchange Commission (SEC) strongly objects to this practice and considers it a manipulation of financial statements.

How do you feel about "earnings management"? Which stakeholders should management consider in making decisions to smooth earnings? Is earnings management ethical?

EMPLOYEE FRAUD

In contrast to the financial statement manipulation common in management fraud, **employee fraud** typically involves the theft of cash or other assets of the organization. Employee fraud is almost always carried out for the personal benefit of the employee or employees involved in the scheme. However, thefts must be concealed in order to avoid detection. As discussed later, good internal control systems can usually detect and prevent most types of employee fraud.

 Key Concept: *Good internal control systems can usually detect and prevent most types of employee fraud.*

CAUSES OF FRAUD

LO3
Explain the typical causes of fraudulent activities

EXHIBIT 14-1
The Balance of High Situational Pressures and Fraud to a Business

People engage in fraudulent activity as a result of an interaction of forces both within an individual's personality and the external environment. These forces include situational pressures, opportunity, and personal characteristics ("Auditors and the Detection of Fraud," *Journal of Accountancy,* May 1980, 63). Situational pressures include things like real or imagined grievances against the company or management and management pressure to meet budgets. They may also include societal factors like the inadequate punishment of convicted criminals and the overall weakening of society's values. Opportunity can arise as a result of ongoing transactions with related parties or as a result of insufficient internal controls. Personal characteristics include things like high levels of stress and economic pressure resulting from large amounts of personal financial debt, an extravagant lifestyle, or drug, alcohol, and gambling addictions. Ethical standards are also very important personal characteristics.

Combinations of high situational pressures, high opportunity, and low ethical standards are more likely to lead to fraud than situations characterized by low situational pressure, low opportunity, and high ethical standards. Ethical standards and behavior typically have more impact on the scale than the other factors. Even when situational pressures and opportunity are high, high ethical values will sometimes tip the scale back toward nonfraudulent behavior (see Exhibit 14-1).

 Key Concept: *Individuals engage in fraudulent activity as a result of situational pressures, opportunity, and personal characteristics.*

Concept Question: *Just as fraudulent activities have increased in business, fraudulent activities like cheating and plagiarism are rampant in many colleges and universities. What are some possible causes of fraudulent activities in an academic setting?*

Concept Answer: Even though specific causes vary, the same forces impacting the behavior of managers in business are likely to influence students and professors at a college or university—situational pressures, opportunity, and personal characteristics. ∎

Although personal characteristics of employees and managers are difficult to control, situational pressures and opportunities for fraudulent behavior can be controlled. One role of the internal audit department of a company is to develop internal control systems that reduce situational pressures and opportunities for fraudulent behavior.

ROLE OF THE INTERNAL AUDIT DEPARTMENT

An **internal auditor** is responsible for improving the ability of an organization to meet its operational and strategic goals. Internal auditing also deals with the quality and reliability of the accounting information supplied to management for decision making. As such, the internal audit department is responsible for the design and maintenance of an internal control system. Internal auditors also conduct periodic audit procedures to ensure that errors and irregularities in financial information are detected. However, an internal audit department is not only responsible for the integrity of the financial information but for evaluating the effectiveness and efficiency of operations of the various departments and divisions of the company. These evaluations are often called *operational audits.* Although internal auditors must become very familiar with the operations of the divisions or departments being audited, they must also be independent of all department and divisions and should report directly to the board of directors.

ROLE OF THE EXTERNAL AUDITOR

The main objective of the financial statement audit conducted by the independent **external auditor** is to attest to the fairness of a company's financial statements and to report any discovered fraud or irregularities to shareholders. Although external auditors are required to design their audit tests to minimize the risk of financial statement misstatements, their role is not to prevent fraud but rather to plan and perform an audit to obtain reasonable assurance that material misstatements due to fraud will be detected. Fraud prevention is left to the internal auditor and the internal control system.

LO4
Understand the role of the internal audit department and the external auditor

---

INTERNAL CONTROL SYSTEMS AND THE PREVENTION OF FRAUD

Internal control is defined as follows:

> A process, effected by an entity's board of directors, management, and other personnel, designed to provide reasonable assurance regarding the achievement of objectives in the following categories: 1) reliability of financial reporting, 2) compliance with applicable laws and regulations, and 3) effectiveness and efficiency of operations (Rittenberg and Schwieger, *Auditing: Concepts for a Changing Environment,* 2d ed., Dryden Press, 1998).

LO5
Explain the objectives, design, and characteristics of good internal control systems

Internal control involves the methods used by an organization to make sure that financial reporting is accurate and reliable, that applicable laws and regulations are followed, and that assets are protected and used to promote effective and efficient use in the operation of the business. Internal control is the key ingredient in preventing losses due to management and employee fraud. However, internal control is more than just a fraud prevention measure. Good internal controls promote quality decision making by providing reliable information to internal managers. Good internal control can also help ensure that policies and strategic plans are being followed and can help prevent costly legal action by preventing violation of applicable laws and regulations. Although an effective system of internal controls is a must for preventing fraudulent activities, the internal control systems impact on promoting effective and efficient operations is perhaps even more important.

 Key Concept: *The internal control system's impact on promoting effective and efficient operations is perhaps even more important than detecting fraudulent activity.*

DESIGN OF INTERNAL CONTROL SYSTEMS

The need for internal control systems is predicated on the assumption that managers and employees of a company will not always exhibit behavior that is in the best interest of the owners or shareholders of the company. If we consider a very small business in which the owners/shareholders and managers/employees are one and the same, internal control concerns are negligible. On the other hand, the internal control system of Amber Valley Ski Resort, which has dozens of managers and hundreds of employees, is likely to be quite complex. Fraud by managers and employees is a real concern and the internal control

What types of fraudulent activities might the employees of Amber Valley undertake?

system must be designed to minimize opportunities for fraudulent activity and to detect it if it occurs.

CHARACTERISTICS OF AN INTERNAL CONTROL SYSTEM

Although internal control systems will vary from company to company, a good internal control system must consider the following:[1]

- The organizational environment in which the system exists
- The risks that affect the ability of a company to meet its objectives and the activities a company uses to control its risks (risk assessment and risk control)
- The methods and procedures a company uses to communicate and to monitor its internal control system to make sure it is functioning properly (communication and monitoring procedures)

TopSail Construction

Organizational Environment Upper-level management sets the tone for ethical behavior in an organization. If upper management has high ethical standards and shares those standards with the rest of the organization, other managers and employees are likely to exhibit similar high standards. As an example, if upper management of Top-Sail Construction behaves ethically in its dealings with customers, employees who are actually constructing the homes will have a tendency to act in a similar manner. On the other hand, if management makes a practice of inflating costs or using low-quality materials in construction, employees will receive a signal that this type of behavior is acceptable and the risk of employee theft or other types of less than desirable behavior increases.

 Key Concept: *Upper-level management sets the tone of ethical behavior and the overall atmosphere of the organization.*

GARCIA&BUFFET CPAS

The organizational environment can also be influenced through the adoption and use of a formal code of ethical conduct. For example, partners and employees of Garcia and Buffett CPAs are governed by a code of ethical conduct that spells out ethical responsibilities to their clients. Among other things, Garcia and Buffett does not allow partners or other employees to own stock or have any financial interest in an audit client of the firm. Owning stock in a company, which is audited by the firm, raises questions of independence on the part of the CPA firm.

Why would owning stock in an audit client raise concerns about independence?

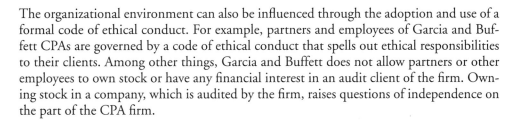

IN THE NEWS   www.pwcglobal.com

As reported in the *Wall Street Journal* on June 29, 1999, partners and employees of PriceWaterhouseCoopers (the largest CPA firm in the world) were ordered to dump their investments in companies the firm audits. The charges centered on the firm's Tampa office where 11 employees owned stock in 70 publicly held companies that the firm audited and the company-wide retirement plan that owned stock in 45 audit clients. Five PriceWaterhouseCoopers partners and an undisclosed number of associates were fired for not selling their stocks in a timely manner.

Risk Assessment and Risk Control Risk assessment and control involves identifying potential risks to the organization and ways to minimize or manage those

---

[1]The content of this section was adapted from: The Committee of Sponsoring Organizations of the Treadway Commission, "Internal Control—Integrated Framework," 1992.

risks. All companies face risks. These risks can come from internal or external sources. Internal risks can be minimized with the cooperation of upper management and affected employees. Minimizing external risks requires understanding competitive pressures facing a company and its managers, and the impact of new products, technology changes, and changes in laws and regulations on a company. When a company introduces new products, places new equipment on-line, makes management changes, or enters new markets, the corresponding level of risk must be assessed.

The manner in which an organization manages and controls risk is very important. After specific risks are identified, the likelihood of occurrence must be established. An identified risk with a low probability of occurrence should be given low priority. If a risk has a high probability of occurrence, then the potential loss from that occurrence should be determined. If the risk has a high likelihood of occurring, and the amount of potential loss is material, an organization must design internal controls to manage and control the risk. For example, Zia Motors has determined that it faces risks due to the theft of automobile parts held in inventory. If the likelihood of theft is high and the potential losses are material, ZIA must develop specific controls to manage and control the risk. Potential controls might involve installing more lighting, hiring security guards, and so forth.

Communication and Monitoring Procedures Internal control procedures are also impacted by the methods, records, and reports a company uses to communicate with employees and external decision makers and the procedures a company uses to monitor its internal control system to make sure it is functioning properly. As discussed in more detail later in the chapter, internal control systems must be constantly monitored and modified as new risks are identified.

INTERNAL CONTROL PROCEDURES

Companies use **internal control procedures** to address areas of risk identified during the risk assessment process. Most internal control procedures are designed to prevent specific events (such as the theft of assets) from occurring. Typical types of internal control procedures are shown in Exhibit 14-2.

LO6
Understand common internal control procedures

Internal control procedures are designed to focus on activities that are determined to increase the risk of management or employee fraud. These activities typically involve transactions affecting cash, accounts receivable, inventory, and payroll.

REVIEWING FINANCIAL REPORTS THAT COMPARE ACTUAL RESULTS TO BUDGETED AMOUNTS

This internal control procedure is very easy to implement and is effective in detecting large errors or irregularities. Every month when financial statements are prepared they

EXHIBIT 14-2 Internal Control Procedures

1. Reviewing financial reports that compare actual results to budgeted amounts
2. Checking the accuracy of recorded transactions
3. Segregation of duties between employees so that people who authorize transactions do not also record them and have access to related assets
4. Securing assets such as cash, inventory, and property, plant, and equipment
5. Comparing financial data with other supporting data such as sales and shipping documents

should be compared to budgeted amounts for the same month. For example, if Big Al's projects selling 2,000 pizzas per week but actually sells 3,000 pizzas per week, internal auditors should expect variable costs to be 50 percent higher than budgeted in the static budget at the beginning of the year. Comparing actual amounts to flexible budget estimates using variance analysis can provide information about the possible theft of materials and products and the efficient (or inefficient) use of corporate resources.

CHECKING THE ACCURACY OF RECORDED TRANSACTIONS

Checking the accuracy of recorded transactions is especially important in businesses that have a high volume of cash transactions. For example, Big Al's Pizza Emporium and Amber Valley Ski Resort have a high volume of small cash transactions. On the other hand, Northern Lights Custom Cabinets and TopSail Construction have a smaller volume of mostly larger dollar transactions. Most large transactions will involve checks that are deposited directly into the bank. Not only are smaller amounts easier to steal, they are more likely to go unnoticed. If Big Al's sells $10,000 of pizzas a night, a few missing $10 receipts may be explained by errors, whereas large checks would be difficult to hide.

Internal control procedures at Big Al's might include the use of sequentially numbered sales tickets and detailed deposit information. In most retail businesses, bar coding and automatic scanners are used to control inventory and to check the accuracy of sales transactions. Timely bank reconciliations are a common control technique used to check the accuracy of sales and purchase transactions.

SEGREGATION OF DUTIES

Segregation of duties is a crucial internal control procedure. Separation of duties in the cash area is of particular importance. Employees who collect cash should not be responsible for recording its collection. Likewise, employees who prepare deposits should not have duties related to cash collection or recording. In a clothing store, the clerk that handles customer returns of merchandise should not be responsible for recording the returned merchandise in inventory. Segregation of duties can be difficult in small companies with only a few employees. In these cases, other internal control procedures become even more important.

SECURING ASSETS

Securing assets is a common internal control procedure. Cash can be physically isolated in vaults and safes and access to it can be limited. Inventory is often susceptible to theft by customers and employees. Although a number of tools (clothing tags for example) can be used to reduce theft by customers, controlling theft by employees can be more difficult. Good internal control procedures can include restricting access to merchandise or requiring employees to "check out" each night with a security guard. Periodic inventory counts can also be used to combat this problem.

COMPARING FINANCIAL DATA WITH OTHER SUPPORTING DATA

Another useful internal control procedure—comparing financial data with supporting physical documents—can take many shapes and forms. At Amber Valley, using two-part lift tickets is likely to be an effective internal control tool. The part of the lift ticket retained can be compared to the cash collected to ensure that all sales are recorded and that cash is collected. At Big Al's, matching invoices for food purchases to receiving reports is a useful tool for ensuring that inventory is properly recorded in the company's financial records.

COMMON FRAUDS AND EFFECTIVE INTERNAL CONTROLS

Companies with large amounts of sales on account are especially susceptible to theft through a scheme called lapping. CableOne, a cable TV company, bills all customers monthly. The customer then mails a check to CableOne or pays the bill at the office with a check or cash. The employee collecting the cash can steal payments and cover the theft by using a technique called lapping. Lapping involves using a subsequent payment to cover the payment that was taken. When payments are typically of the same amount, lapping can be difficult to detect. For example, assume that the cashier at CableOne collects all payments made at the office. The employee takes a cash payment for the normal monthly fee of $25 and keeps it rather than crediting it to a customer's account. The customer, Susan Schumaker, gets a receipt and then leaves. The next customer, Sheri Armstrong, pays her bill for $25 and the cashier uses Sheri's payment to record the missing payment on Susan's account. Then the next payment for $25 can be used to cover Sheri's missing payment and so on.

CableOne can minimize the likelihood of lapping through segregation of duties and by simply requiring that employees take two weeks of vacation at least once per year. The lapping scheme just described would likely be discovered very quickly when the cashier couldn't continue applying the collected amounts to the accounts previously shorted. External auditors use confirmations sent directly to customers and returned to the auditors to verify the accuracy of amounts that are owed. These confirmations can detect a lapping scheme when the time lag between collection and posting increases. In other words, if the cashier continues lapping for an extended period of time, it may be days or weeks before payments can be applied to amounts owed by customers.

Requiring vacations can be a useful internal control tool in other types of fraud as well. CherLee Financial is a loan company that approves personal loans up to $2,500 over the phone. Because of a unique state law, CherLee can make these loans without a customer's signature. Loan papers are simply signed by a loan officer and mailed to the customer

along with a check for the loan proceeds. This procedure led to an interesting fraud case when an employee, whose duties included keeping track of delinquent loans, processed loan applications for herself. Loan officers signed and disbursed funds without paying attention to the payee on the checks and the employee simply never reported the delinquent loans to her supervisors. However, during a required two-week vacation, the scheme was uncovered by another employee.

Payroll is another area that is susceptible to theft by mangers and other employees. Schemes include simple plans involving the fraudulent reporting of overtime and requesting reimbursement of fictitious travel expenses to complex schemes involving fictitious employees. Computer systems may also be susceptible to manipulation. For example, a computer programmer may change a payroll program to round down all payroll checks to an even dollar amount while adding the difference to his or her check. However, internal control procedures such as segregation of duties and timely bank reconciliations should be effective in detecting these frauds.

Employee theft can also occur by employees setting up fictitious companies to sell merchandise to the employee's company. For example, an employee at Northern Lights Custom Cabinets working in the accounts payable area could set up a fake company and sell Northern Lights material for cabinet construction. When invoices are submitted by the fake company, the employee simply authorizes payment, even though the materials are never received. These types of schemes can also be controlled through periodic inventory counts and adequate segregation of duties.

BEHAVIORAL IMPLICATIONS OF INTERNAL CONTROL SYSTEMS

LO7
Understand the behavioral implications of internal control systems

Well-designed internal control systems can detect many types of fraudulent activity. However, the real goal of an internal control system is to prevent the fraudulent activity in the first place. To prevent fraudulent activity from occurring, internal controls must be communicated throughout an organization. If adequate internal controls are in place and employees and managers are aware of the controls, fraudulent activity is much less likely to take place. However, in order for an internal control system to continue to be effective, the procedures must be monitored and modified as the environment changes and new risks are identified.

 Key Concept: *To be effective, internal control systems must be communicated throughout an organization and modified as new risks are identified.*

INTERNAL CONTROL IN AN E-BUSINESS ENVIRONMENT

www.irs.gov

LO8
Understand the impact of e-business on internal control

As discussed in Chapter 13, e-business involves direct sales to customers (b2c) as well as business-to-business applications (b2b). The government is also using the Internet to conduct business with citizens. The Internal Revenue Service now accepts electronic tax returns and some state and local governments are allowing vehicle registration to be done on-line.

Although e-business has provided new opportunities to companies, it also entails new risks. Because it is conducted on a public network (the World Wide Web), the information is susceptible to being viewed, copied, or altered by nonusers who gain access to the data. Although much work is being done to raise the level of comfort with the security and reliability of information being transmitted over the Internet, risks remain that data can be stolen, corrupted, misused, altered, or falsely generated when transmitted over a public network. As shown in Exhibit 14-3, threats can come from a variety of directions and sources.

EXHIBIT 14-3 Threats in an E-Business Environment

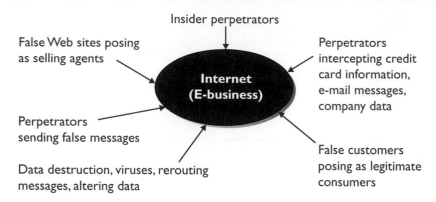

SOURCE: Adapted from Greenstein and Geinman, *Electronic Commerce: Security, Risk Management, and Control,* McGraw-Hill Higher Education, 2000, 132.

IN THE NEWS

In a recent survey, more than one-third of information technology professionals said their company's information systems had been compromised in the past year. Financial losses from these break-ins exceeded more than $120 million (J. B. Earp, L. R. Ingraham, and J. G. Jenkins, "The Newest Technology Tools: (Un)Limited Access?" *CPA Journal,* January 2000, 58–59).

Specific risks to e-business providers include the following:

- *Customer impersonation.* False customers can enter a seller's computer system and corrupt data or place false orders using the assumed customer's identification.
- *Denial of service attacks.* These are used to destroy, shut down, or degrade a system. The goal of this type of attack is to flood the site with information so that legitimate messages or orders cannot be received.
- *Unauthorized access to data.* Data is particularly vulnerable at intermediate network junctions that handle the transfer of information from one site to another.
- *Sabotage by former employers.* Former employees who are laid off, fired, or leave under unpleasant circumstances are a threat because of their knowledge of the systems and the organization.
- *Threats by current employees.* These types of threats include stealing trade secrets to sell to competitors and embezzling assets from the company.

How does an organization reduce the risks associated with e-business activities? Overall, the same types of internal controls that we have discussed previously will serve to reduce the risks. However, specific internal controls associated with e-business activities are also useful. These include the following:

- Passwords to limit access to computer systems
- Firewalls to limit access to computer networks by screening all network traffic and controlling access to critical information
- Encryption of sensitive data so it is readable only by persons holding the decryption key
- Moving critical data to a separate server that is not connected to the outside world
- Shutting off computers during nonbusiness hours
- Staying up to date with technology

► **Key Concept:** *E-business activities entail new risks and require new internal control procedures.*

External auditors also need to consider the impact of e-business activities on the reliability of financial reports. Data that are created and stored electronically may be more vulnerable to manipulation. As a result, auditors should pay particular attention to a company's policies and procedures regarding computer security (Earp, Ingraham, and Jenkins, "The Newest Technology Tools: (Un)Limited Access?" *CPA Journal,* January 2000, 58–59).

SUMMARY OF KEY CONCEPTS

- Fraud is more narrowly defined in a business context than in common law. (p. 404)
- Management fraud can be very difficult to detect. (p. 405)
- Good internal control systems can usually detect and prevent most types of employee fraud. (p. 406)
- Individuals engage in fraudulent activity as a result of situational pressures, opportunity, and personal characteristics. (p. 406)
- The internal control system's impact on promoting effective and efficient operations is perhaps even more important than detecting fraudulent activity. (p. 407)
- Upper-level management sets the tone of ethical behavior and the overall atmosphere of the organization. (p. 408)
- To be effective, internal control systems must be communicated throughout an organization and modified as new risks are identified. (p. 412)
- E-business activities entail new risks and require new internal control procedures. (p. 414)

KEY DEFINITIONS

Fraud A false representation of a material fact made by one party to another party with the intent to deceive and induce the other party to justifiably rely on the fact to his or her detriment (p. 404)

Management fraud Typically involves misstating the financial statements in order to mislead readers of the financial statements such as stockholders and creditors (p. 404)

Performance fraud Another term for management fraud, used because the manipulation of the financial information is often designed to inflate earnings or to cover up a decline in financial position (p. 405)

Earnings management A method of recording used to "smooth" earnings from quarter to quarter or to otherwise manipulate financial results for a steady income stream (p. 405)

Employee fraud The main focus of employee fraud is taking possession of assets or cash of the organization (p. 406)

Internal auditors Auditors that are employed by the organization that they audit (p. 407)

External auditors Usually CPAs that are independent of the organization that they are auditing (p. 407)

Internal control A process, effected by an entity's board of directors, management, and other personnel, designed to provide reasonable assurance regarding the achievement of objectives in the following categories: (1) reliability of financial reporting, (2) compliance with applicable laws and regulations, and (3) effectiveness and efficiency of operations (p. 407)

Risk assessment and control Involves identifying potential risks of the organization and also ways to minimize or manage those risks (p. 408)

Internal control procedures Used to address areas of risk that were identified during the risk assessment process (p. 409)

CONCEPT REVIEW

1. What is the formal definition of fraud?

2. Discuss the common law requirements for a fraudulent act.

3. Discuss the meaning of fraud in a business context. How does that differ from the common law definition?

4. What is the formal definition of management fraud?

5. What are the most common types of management fraud?

6. What is performance fraud?

7. Discuss different ways to "manage earnings."

8. Discuss different ways to misstate revenue.

9. Discuss employee fraud. How does it differ from management fraud?

10. What are the three forces that increase the chances an individual will commit a fraudulent act?

11. What factors are reported in the 1998 KPMG fraud survey as leading to an increase in fraudulent acts?

12. Discuss how the red flags link to fraudulent behavior.

13. Why do organizations employ internal auditors? What is the function of an internal audit department?

14. What are the main objectives of an internal audit department?

15. What is meant by an operational audit?

16. What is the role of the external auditor in detecting fraud?

17. Discuss the main difference between the internal and external audit function.

18. What is the formal definition of internal control?

19. What are the goals of an internal control system?

20. What are the characteristics of a good internal control system?

21. What is meant by risk assessment?

22. Discuss different ways of reducing risk.

23. Discuss the tradeoff between cost and benefit of controls for theft.

24. Discuss typical internal control procedures.

25. Discuss control procedures that are based on human behavior patterns.

26. Discuss why e-business has increased the risk of error or fraudulent behavior.

27. What are the specific added risks to e-business providers?

28. What additional security measures are needed for good internal control with e-business?

29. Explain why risk assessment is important to the overall design of internal control systems.

APPLICATION OF CONCEPTS

30. Warren Abraham is the controller of Northern Lights Custom Cabinets. Warren stated, "Northern Lights has a very strong internal control system. The ledger must always balance, and this ensures that all transactions are properly transferred to our general ledger." What do you think of Warren's comment? Do the balanced books ensure good internal controls?

31. Upper management at TopSail Construction has been advised that the present system of internal control needs to be improved. It has recently come to management's attention that the controller who has almost complete control over cash and the accounting records is experiencing financial difficulties as the result of a personal tragedy in the family. Is this a potential "red flag" for management to be concerned with? If so, what steps should upper management take with respect to this problem?

32. Cindy is the vice president of research and development for Big Al's Pizza Inc. Cindy submits a request for expense reimbursement each month and Lori, the controller, has noticed that Cindy's requests are always higher than those of anyone else in the company. What should the controller do? Is this a potential internal control problem?

33. Terry is an accountant at Happy Daze Game Company. Her main function is to prepare production cost reports for distribution to upper management. Her good friend Tracy is the production supervisor on one of the production lines. While preparing

this month's cost report, Terry noticed a substantial increase in production costs on Tracy's production line. To make her friend look better, Terry shifted some of the costs to other lines thinking that there must be an accounting error somewhere. The shift in costs was never noticed. Did Terry act appropriately? Discuss the alternative courses of action that Terry could have taken. Would this be considered a fraudulent act?

34. Mark is a sales clerk at a clothing store in the local mall. Mark has been short of cash in the past and has prepared fake sales return forms and taken money from the cash register equal to those forms. The scheme has not been caught and now Mark is preparing to take even more money as the managers seem unaware of the scheme. What internal controls would you suggest to assist management in eliminating this opportunity?

35. LaRue's Machine Shop takes custom orders for metal parts. In order to machine some of the parts, the shop uses various solvents that must be disposed of in compliance with local hazardous waste rules. For years before the new laws went into effect, LaRue's routinely dumped the solvents in a pit behind the shop. The new law has been in effect for three years and LaRue's has yet to comply with it. What risks do you think the company faces by not properly disposing of the solvents?

36. The local credit union has a written policy that states in part: "All employees are strictly prohibited from accepting any gratuities, gifts, donations, or any other remuneration from credit union members for which the fair market value of such gift, gratuity, or donation exceeds $5." How does such a policy strengthen the credit union's system of internal control?

37. Heather Hogan, the vice president of the local credit union mentioned in the problem above, has always accepted invitations to join credit union members who own skyboxes at the local ball park. She has never paid for the tickets and, in fact, accepts free food and drink provided in the skybox. What effect will her actions have on the internal control environment at the credit union?

38. Irene's Greeting Cards sells custom greeting cards to drugstores across the country. All sales are on credit, and payment is expected within 30 days of the order. The company provides an invoice with each delivery but does not send subsequent statements. The salespeople who call on the customers are allowed to collect any outstanding invoices. If the company started sending invoices, would that have an effect on the internal control over accounts receivable?

39. Bonnie's Beautiful Lights is a wholesale lighting contractor selling to residential building contractors. The company has very few staff members, so the bookkeeper collects all payments on account, makes the bank deposits, writes checks to pay all accounts payable, and reconciles the bank statement at the end of the month. The company also does not count inventory on a regular basis. Discuss any internal control weaknesses you see and suggest possible solutions.

40. At the drive-through window of your local fast food outlet, you notice a sign that reads "If the amount you pay is not the same as your sales receipt, your meal is free." What is the restaurant trying to accomplish with the receipts?

41. Chip's Crazy Pies, the local pizza parlor, has a cash register that randomly prints a red star on the sales receipts. If you get a red star, you get a free meal on your next visit. Your friend says that the red stars are for marketing and promotion, nothing else. You have just completed studying this chapter on internal control and think there may be more to this than just promotion. Give reasons for the red stars other than promotion. Can this be a method of increasing control? How?

42. Ben's Cinema, a new 10-plex movie house, is so busy that management has decided to forgo collecting ticket stubs at the entrance to each movie and tear the stub at the register. Do you see any control problems with this practice? If so, what controls could be put in place to correct any weaknesses? If Ben's hires only high school and college students to work the theater, does that introduce any other potential weaknesses? What if they are paid only minimum wage? What solution to these problems

do you suggest? Ben's is hiring a new manager and a background check shows that the new manager has a lot of credit card debt, drives a new car, and is known to like to bet on local sporting events. Does this manager present any internal control risk? If so, what should Ben's do to reduce or eliminate this risk? What other red flags should the company look for?

43. Dolly's Antiques has decided to add a Web page and go on-line to sell merchandise, and the company has come to you for advice. What potential control problems might Dolly's face with this type of business? What controls can reduce or eliminate the risks faced by e-business providers?

44. Discuss why middle mangers are more prone to fraudulent activity. What specific internal controls could reduce this risk?

OTHER TOPICS

Chapter 15

THE STATEMENT OF CASH FLOWS: REPORTING AND ANALYZING

Study Tools

A Review of the Previous Chapter

In Chapter 14, we discussed fraud and the importance of internal control systems in detecting and controlling management and employee fraud. We discussed the primary forces impacting fraudulent behavior and the role of the internal auditor and the external auditor in preventing fraud. We also discussed characteristics of an internal control system and key internal control procedures that are used to prevent and detect fraudulent activities and the impact of e-business on fraud and internal control.

A Preview of This Chapter

In Chapter 15, we discuss the preparation and use of the statement of cash flows and its use in decision making.

Key concepts include:

- The only difference between the direct and indirect methods is in the presentation of the cash flows from operating activities. Cash flows from investing activities and cash flows from financing activities are calculated in exactly the same way.
- When using the indirect method, increases (decreases) in asset (liability) accounts during the year require deductions from net income. When asset (liability) accounts decrease (increase) during the year, the amount of decrease or increase must be added to net income in arriving at net cash provided by operating activities.

A Preview of Upcoming Chapters

In Chapter 16, we discuss the analysis of financial statement information by investors, creditors, and managers using ratio analysis and other techniques.

LEARNING OBJECTIVES

After studying the material in this chapter, you should be able to:

LO1 Understand the purpose of a statement of cash flows and why accrual accounting creates a need for the statement of cash flows

LO2 Discuss the types of transactions that result from operating, investing, and financing activities and how they are presented on the statement of cash flows

LO3 Discuss the difference between the direct and the indirect methods of computing cash flow from operating activities

LO4 Prepare a statement of cash flows

LO5 Analyze the statement of cash flows and use the information in decision making

In the previous 14 chapters of this textbook we have concentrated on using internally gen-erated accounting information for managerial decision making. In this chapter we present an in-depth discussion of the preparation and use of the statement of cash flows. Although this statement is used primarily by those external to the organization, the statement of cash flows and the related cash budget (discussed in Chapter 9) are also useful tools for manage-rial decision making. ■

INTRODUCTION

www.bostonmarket.com
www.upi.com
www.wards.com
www.filenesbasement.
com

During the 1990s there were numerous business failures of companies that appeared financially healthy and profitable in the years immediately preceding the failures. Among those businesses are some very well known companies such as Boston Market, United Press International, Montgomery Ward, and Filene's Basement. However, each of these companies filed for bankruptcy protection due to the company's inability to generate sufficient cash flow to cover operating costs, capital expansion, and debt repayment. Investors and others sometimes learn too late that to be successful, companies must generate sufficient cash to pay their bills!

This chapter discusses the statement of cash flows. The statement of cash flows reports the impact of a firm's operating, investing, and financing activities on cash flows during the accounting period. Along with the balance sheet, income statement, and the statement of changes in stockholders' equity, this statement is a required component of a company's external financial statements.

Users of financial statements have made the statement of cash flows one of the most important of the four required financial statements. In today's highly competitive global environment, users of financial accounting information have learned that cash flows may be a better indicator of financial performance than net income or earnings per share.

IN THE NEWS

Although stock analysts typically have focused on earnings in valuing companies, a recent *Wall Street Journal* article reports that stock analysts are increasingly using cash flow rather than earnings to value companies. Among other things, "it ignores accounting tricks and shows the true health of companies" ("Analysts Increasingly Favor Using Cash Flow over Reported Earnings in Stock Valuations," *Wall Street Journal,* April 1, 1999, C2).

PURPOSE OF THE STATEMENT OF CASH FLOWS

LO1
Understand the purpose of a statement of cash flows and why accrual accounting creates a need for the statement of cash flows

The main purpose of the statement of cash flows is to provide information to decision makers about a company's cash inflows and outflows during the period. The statement of cash flows provides information relating to the change in cash balances between two balance sheet dates. Balance sheets provide a "snapshot" of the financial position of a company at a particular point in time whereas the statement of cash flows reports changes over time. The statement of cash flows should be viewed as an explanation of the changes to the cash balance reported on the balance sheet. The statement of cash flows also discloses items that affect how the balance sheet changed, but that don't show up in the income statement such as issuance of stock or acquisitions of property, plant, and equipment.

THE COMPOSITION OF THE STATEMENT OF CASH FLOWS

The statement of cash flows summarizes and explains all major cash receipts (inflows) and cash payments (outflows) during the period and categorizes the changes as resulting from operating, investing, or financing activities.

OPERATING ACTIVITIES

Operating activities include acquiring and selling products in the normal course of business. Different types of businesses will have different transactions that are included in cash flows from operating activities. Typical types of items reported in this section of the statement of cash flows as inflows are cash from sales to customers, collection of cash from past sales that were made on credit, and interest and dividends received. Typical outflows of cash from operating activities are purchases of merchandise for sale or materials to manufacture products, payments for operating expenses, interest on debt, payments for services, and payments of taxes.

INVESTING ACTIVITIES

Cash flows from **investing activities** include cash inflows from the sale of property, plant, and equipment, the sale of securities (stocks and bonds) of other companies, and the receipt of loan payments. Cash outflows include the purchase of property, plant, and equipment, the purchase of securities, and making loans as investments. Loans directly related to the sale of products or services are likely classified as operating activities. The interest on loans included as an investing activity is also classified as a cash flow from operating activities.

FINANCING ACTIVITIES

Cash flows from **financing activities** include cash inflows from selling stock or from issuing bonds (see Exhibit 15-1). Cash inflows from financing activities also include contributions from owners and borrowing from banks on a long-term basis. Cash outflows from financing activities include repayment of notes and bonds, cash payments to repurchase stock (Treasury stock), and the payment of dividends. Once again all interest payments are included in cash flows from operating activities.

As an example, consider Hasbro, Inc. whose Consolidated Statements of Cash Flows are presented in Exhibit 15-2. Note than even though Hasbro's 1998 earnings increased by $71,379,000 compared to 1997, cash and cash equivalents actually decreased by $184,037,000.

www.hasbro.com

Concept Question: Review the Hasbro Consolidated Statements of Cash Flows and identify reasons why cash and cash equivalents actually decreased when net earnings increased in 1998.

Concept Answer: The reduction in cash appears to have resulted from a combination of things. Net cash provided by operating activities was much lower in 1998 ($126,587,000) than in 1997 ($543,841,000), while at the same time net cash utilized by investing activities was much higher ($792,700,000 in 1998 compared to $269,277,000 in 1997). Even with substantially more net cash provided by financing activities, the cash balance went down. ■

EXHIBIT 15-1 A Summary of Activities Making Up a Cash Flow Statement

LO2
Discuss the types of transactions that result from operating, investing, and financing activities and how they are presented on the statement of cash flows

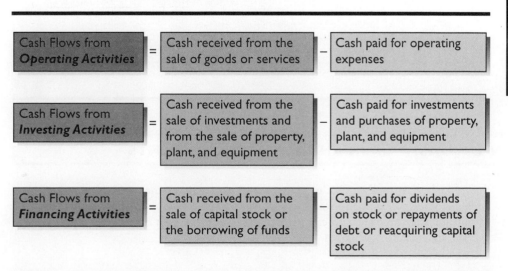

EXHIBIT 15-2 Consolidated Statements of Cash Flows

Hasbro, Inc.
CONSOLIDATED STATEMENTS OF CASH FLOWS

Fiscal Years Ended in December (Thousands of Dollars)	1998	1997	1996
Cash flows from operating activities			
Net earnings	$206,365	134,986	199,912
Adjustments to reconcile net earnings to net cash provided by operating activities:			
Depreciation and amortization of plant and equipment	96,991	112,817	98,201
Other amortization	72,208	53,767	40,064
Deferred income taxes	1,679	(40,555)	(8,120)
Acquired in-process research and development	20,000	—	—
Change in operating assets and liabilities (other than cash and cash equivalents):			
(Increase) decrease in accounts receivable	(126,842)	11,920	(22,418)
(Increase) decrease in inventories	(44,606)	40,739	42,959
(Increase) decrease in prepaid expenses and other current assets	(113,451)	20,326	(37,036)
Increase (decrease) in trade payables and other current liabilities	17,668	200,359	(35,852)
Other	(3,425)	9,482	2,283
Net cash provided by operating activities	126,587	543,841	279,993
Cash flows from investing activities			
Additions to property, plant and equipment	(141,950)	(99,356)	(101,946)
Investments and acquisitions, net of cash acquired	(667,736)	(172,116)	(33,027)
Other	16,986	2,195	7,687
Net cash utilized by investing activities	(792,700)	(269,277)	(127,286)
Cash flows from financing activities			
Proceeds from borrowings with original maturities of more than three months	407,377	295,132	265,017
Repayments of borrowings with original maturities of more than three months	(24,925)	(304,927)	(255,636)
Net proceeds (payments) of other short-term borrowings	271,895	21,599	(6,116)
Purchase of common stock	(178,917)	(134,880)	(83,657)
Stock option and warrant transactions	58,493	37,258	17,745
Dividends paid	(42,277)	(39,694)	(32,959)
Net cash provided (utilized) by financing activities	491,646	(125,512)	(95,606)
Effect of exchange rate changes on cash	(9,570)	(6,238)	840
(Decrease) increase in cash and cash equivalents	(184,037)	142,814	57,941
Cash and cash equivalents at beginning of year	361,785	218,971	161,030
Cash and cash equivalents at end of year	$177,748	361,785	218,971
Supplemental information			
Cash paid during the year for			
Interest	$ 25,135	23,480	29,430
Income taxes	$128,436	135,446	92,670
Non-cash financing activities			
6% Convertible Subordinated Notes Due 1998, converted into common stock	$ —	149,354	609

See accompanying notes to consolidated financial statements.

THE DEFINITION OF CASH: CASH AND CASH EQUIVALENTS

Before we begin our discussion of the preparation of the statement of cash flows, it is important to be specific about exactly what is meant by cash. Accounting standards define certain items as equivalent to cash, which are combined with cash on the balance sheet and the statement of cash flows.

Commercial paper (short-term notes issued by corporations), money market funds, and Treasury bills are examples of cash equivalents. A **cash equivalent** is an item that can be readily converted to a known amount of cash and has an original maturity to the investor of three months or less. For example, a three-year Treasury bill purchased three years before maturity is not a cash equivalent, but if that same Treasury bill is purchased three months prior to maturity, then it would be a cash equivalent.

NONCASH TRANSACTIONS

It is not uncommon for organizations to have exchange transactions that do not directly involve cash inflows or outflows but still warrant disclosure on a statement of cash flows. These transactions are primarily in the financing and investing areas. For example, if an exchange were made of stock for an asset, the transaction would require an accounting entry to record the issuance of the stock and the addition of the asset. This transaction would not directly affect cash flows. However, if the company sold the stock on the open market and then used that cash to purchase the asset, the transaction would directly impact cash and be shown on the statement of cash flows. The sale of stock would show up as an inflow in the financing activities section and the purchase of the asset would show up as an offsetting outflow in the investing activities section of the statement of cash flows. The key point is that the form of the transaction differs between the two transactions (exchange versus sale and purchase), whereas the substance (or result) of the two transactions is the same. Both transactions result in the same impact on the financial statements. Because we are more concerned with the substance of accounting transactions and full disclosure to users of the information, generally accepted accounting principles require that any significant noncash transaction be reported either in a separate schedule or in a footnote to the financial statements. For example, on the Hasbro statement of cash flows in Exhibit 15-2, supplemental information concerning noncash financing activities (converting preferred stock to common stock) is disclosed at the bottom of the statement.

CASH FLOWS FROM OPERATING ACTIVITIES

Organizations use two methods (direct and indirect) to report cash flows from operating activities. The **direct method** reports major classes of gross cash receipts and payments. For example, the direct method would report cash collected from customers, cash paid for inventory, cash paid for salaries and wages, and so on. The **indirect method,** in comparison, starts with net income and then removes the effect of all noncash items resulting from accruals or noncash expenses like depreciation. In other words, the indirect method essentially converts the accrual-basis income statement to a cash-basis income statement by taking out noncash items such as depreciation and nonoperating items such as accruals.

LO3
Discuss the difference between the direct and the indirect methods of computing cash flow from operating activities

Concept Question: Take a look at the Hasbro statement of cash flows and identify what method Hasbro uses to report cash from operating activities.

Concept Answer: As do most companies, Hasbro uses the indirect method. ■

In order to compare the two methods, consider the income statement and balance sheet on the next page. The company began operations on January 1, 2000, with the owners investing $100,000 in cash. The financial statements for the year ending December 31, 2000, are as follows:

Income Statement
For the Year Ended December 31, 2000

Sales revenues	$800,000
Operating expenses	640,000
Income before tax	160,000
Income tax expense	40,000
Net income	$120,000

Balance Sheet
As of December 31, 2000

Assets		Liabilities and Stockholders' Equity	
Cash	$150,000	Accounts Payable	$ 60,000
Accounts receivable	130,000	Capital Stock	100,000
		Retained earnings	120,000
Total	$280,000	Total	$280,000

DIRECT METHOD

When using the direct method, each item on the income statement must be looked at to determine how much cash each of these activities either generated or used during the year. As an example, if all sales were for cash, cash collections from customers would be equal to sales revenue. However, if sales are made on account, sales revenue must be adjusted for changes in accounts receivable:

Sales revenue + Beginning accounts receivable − Ending accounts receivable
= Cash collections from customers

or

Cash collections from customers = Sales +/− Decrease (Increase) in accounts receivable

In this case, the company had a beginning accounts receivable balance of $0. The ending accounts receivable balance is $130,000, so cash collections from customers equal $670,000 ($800,000 + $0 − $130,000).

Concept Question: *If accounts receivable decrease next year, would cash collections from customers be higher or lower than sales revenue? Why?*

Concept Answer: If the amount owed decreases, the company must have collected all of the sales from the period plus cash owed from previous periods so cash collections will be higher than sales. ■

Applying the same concept, if all operating expenses are paid in cash, cash outflows for operating expenses will equal $640,000. However, if some of the expenses are incurred on account, expenses must be adjusted for any changes in related accounts payable balances:

> Cash outflows for operating expenses = Operating expenses
> + Beginning accounts payable − Ending accounts payable

Therefore, the cash outflow from operating expenses is $580,000 ($640,000 + $0 − $60,000). Assuming that the company's tax payments are made in cash (note that there is no liability for taxes payable), cash flows from operating activities are as follows:

Cash Flows from Operating Activities (Direct Method)

Cash collected from customers	$670,000
Cash payments for operating activities	(580,000)
Cash payments for taxes	(40,000)
Net cash inflow from operating activities	$ 50,000

INDIRECT METHOD

The indirect method of preparing the cash flows from operating activities starts with the net income for the period, which is $120,000. This amount is then adjusted to arrive at the amount of cash provided by operating activities. The first adjustment to net income will be the change in accounts receivable. In this case, the increase of $130,000 will be subtracted from revenue. The next adjustment will be for the decrease in accounts payable ($60,000). The increase in accounts receivable means that some of the sales were not collected so did not result in cash flows. The decrease in accounts payable means that cash in excess of current period expenses (shown on the income statement) was used to pay expenses from prior periods. Using the indirect method, cash flows from operations are presented as follows:

Cash Flows from Operating Activities (Indirect Method)

Net income	$120,000
Adjustments to Reconcile Net Income to Net Cash	
Increase in accounts receivable	(130,000)
Increase in accounts payable	60,000
Net cash inflow from operating activities	$ 50,000

 Key Concept: *The only difference between the direct and indirect methods is in the presentation of the cash flows from operating activities. Cash flows from investing activities and cash flows from financing activities are calculated in exactly the same way.*

Proponents of the direct method point to the straightforward presentation of the cash flows from operating activities and point out that anyone, even someone with no training in accounting, can very easily use this information in decision making. Proponents of the direct method also argue that this method provides more useful information for evaluating operating efficiency.

Supporters of the indirect method argue that it focuses attention on differences between the cash and accrual basis of accounting, which is very important for decision making. They also point out that if the direct method is used, the indirect schedule must still be prepared. Consequently, more companies choose to report using the indirect method.

THE STATEMENT OF CASH FLOWS AND THE ACCOUNTING EQUATION

The basic accounting equation as presented in your financial accounting course is

$$Assets = Liabilities + Owners' \ equity$$

In more detail,

$$Cash + NCCA + LTA = CL + LTL + CS + RE$$

where

$$
\begin{aligned}
NCCA &= noncash \ current \ assets \\
LTA &= long\text{-}term \ assets \\
CL &= current \ liabilities \\
LTL &= long\text{-}term \ liabilities \\
CS &= capital \ stock \\
RE &= retained \ earnings
\end{aligned}
$$

We can rearrange the equation so that cash is on the left side and all other items are on the right side:

$$Cash = CL + LTL + CS + RE - NCCA - LTA$$

Using this equation it is apparent that any changes in cash (the left side of the equation) must be accompanied by a corresponding change on the right side of the equation. For example:

Transaction	Activity	Left Side	Right Side
Collect accounts receivable	Operating	+ Cash	− NCCA
Prepay insurance	Operating	− Cash	+ NCCA
Collect customer's deposit	Operating	+ Cash	+ CL
Pay suppliers	Operating	− Cash	− CL
Make a cash sale	Operating	+ Cash	+ RE
Sell equipment	Investing	+ Cash	− LTA
Buy equipment	Investing	− Cash	+ LTA
Issue bonds	Financing	+ Cash	+ LTL
Retire bonds	Financing	− Cash	− LTL
Issue capital stock	Financing	+ Cash	+ CS
Buy treasury stock	Financing	− Cash	− CS
Pay dividends	Financing	− Cash	− RE

PREPARING THE STATEMENT OF CASH FLOWS

LO4
Prepare a statement of cash flows

To prepare the statement of cash flows we must gather appropriate information, which includes comparative balance sheets (last year's and this year's), the current income statement, and additional information needed to analyze noncash transactions. After gathering the preceding information, we must complete six steps in preparing the statement of cash flows.

1. Compute the net change in cash (increase or decrease)

2. Compute net cash provided or used by operating activities

3. Compute net cash provided or used by investing activities

4. Compute net cash provided or used by financing activities

5. Compute net cash flow by combining the results from operating, investing, and financing activities

6. Report any significant noncash investing and/or financing activities in a separate schedule or a footnote

As an example, consider the financial statements for Robyn's Boutique, a retail store specializing in children's clothes.

Robyn's Boutique
Income Statement
For the Year Ended December 31, 2000

Revenues and Gains	
Sales revenue	$700,000
Interest income	75,000
Gain on sale of vehicle	25,000
Total revenues and gains	$800,000

ROBYN'S
BOUTIQUE

Expenses and Losses	
Cost of goods sold	500,000
Payroll expense	50,000
Insurance expense	30,000
Interest expense	7,000
Rent expense	18,000
Depreciation	35,000
Loss on sale of long-term investments	25,000
Income tax expense	40,000
Total expenses and losses	705,000
Net income	$ 95,000

Robyn's Boutique
Comparative Balance Sheets

	12/31/2000	12/31/1999
Cash	$130,000	$110,000
Accounts receivable	130,000	120,000
Inventory	225,000	215,000
Prepaid insurance	25,000	30,000
Total current assets	510,000	475,000
Long-term investments	110,000	75,000
Land	200,000	175,000
Property and equipment	215,000	95,000
Accumulated depreciation	(105,000)	(80,000)
Total long-term assets	420,000	265,000
Total assets	930,000	740,000
Accounts payable	60,000	50,000
Payroll payable	10,000	8,000
Income tax payable	10,000	9,000
Total current liabilities	80,000	67,000
Notes payable	400,000	380,000
Total long-term liabilities	400,000	380,000
Capital stock	200,000	100,000
Retained earnings	250,000	193,000
Total	$930,000	$740,000

Additional Information

1. Long-term investments were purchased for $ 85,000.

2. Long-term investments were sold for $25,000, with a book value of $50,000, resulting in a loss of $25,000.

3. Land was purchased for $25,000 by issuing a $20,000 note and a cash payment of $5,000.

4. Equipment was purchased for $180,000.

5. A vehicle with an original cost of $60,000 and a book value of $50,000 was sold for $75,000, resulting in a gain of $25,000.

6. Capital stock was issued for cash of $100,000.

7. Dividends of $38,000 were paid.

Step 1: Compute the Net Change in Cash The net change in cash as shown on the balance sheet is $20,000.

Step 2: Compute Net Cash Provided or Used by Operating Activities

DIRECT METHOD

Operating activities generating cash inflows for Robyn's Boutique include selling goods and services and collecting interest income. Sales revenue was reported as $700,000. However, we must consider the change in accounts receivable to determine how much cash was actually collected from sales. Using the formula on page 426, cash collections are equal to $690,000 ($700,000 sales + $120,000 beginning accounts receivable − $130,000 ending accounts receivable). Interest income reported on the income statement is $75,000. How can we tell if the entire $75,000 was collected in cash? In this case, because there is no "interest receivable" account on the balance sheet, the entire amount must have been collected in cash.

Operating activities generating cash outflows include buying merchandise for resale to customers, making payments to employees, and making payments for other operating expenses like insurance, interest, rent, and taxes. Cost of goods sold is reported at $500,000. However, cash outflows for purchases of inventory may be different. To determine the amount of cash expended to purchase inventory, we must analyze changes in the inventory account as well as changes in accounts payable because inventory purchases are normally made on credit. Using the cost of goods sold model for a merchandising company developed in Chapter 2 (see page 39):

Beginning inventory + Cost of goods purchased − Ending inventory = Cost of goods sold

Consequently, the cost of goods purchased equals the following:

Cost of goods purchased = Cost of goods sold − Beginning inventory + Ending inventory

Therefore, the cost of goods purchased by Robyn's is $510,000 ($500,000 − $215,000 + $225,000). However, we still don't know if all of these purchases were for cash. Using the formula developed earlier for analyzing cash expenditures for operating expenses:

Cash outflows for purchases = Cost of goods purchased + Beginning accounts payable − Ending accounts payable

Robyn's cash outflows for purchases equals $500,000 ($510,000 + $50,000 − $60,000).

Next consider payroll expense of $50,000. Once again, if any payroll expense is accrued at the end of the year for employees that are owed wages but not paid by year-end, the payroll expense must be adjusted by changes in payroll liabilities to determine the cash outflows for payroll. The formula is as follows:

Cash outflows for payroll = Payroll expense + Beginning payroll payable − Ending payroll payable

Cash outflows for payroll are therefore $48,000 ($50,000 + $8,000 − $10,000).

Another way to look at the cash outflow for payroll is to assume that Robyn's paid the amount owed from last year ($8,000) plus all of this year's expense ($50,000) except the amount owed at the end of the current year ($10,000)—in other words, $8,000 + $50,000 − $10,000 = $48,000.

ROBYN'S BOUTIQUE

The next item on the income statement is insurance expense. While there are no liabilities for insurance at the end of 1999 or 2000, you will note that the balance sheet does include an asset called prepaid insurance with a beginning of the year balance of $30,000 and an end of year balance of $25,000. The $30,000 beginning balance represents prepayments that were made in 1999 for insurance coverage provided in 2000. This $30,000 was expensed on the income statement in 2000 as insurance coverage was provided for Robyn's Boutique. Likewise, the $25,000 prepaid balance at the end of 2000 represents cash outflows for insurance that occurred in 2000. This amount will be expensed on the income statement for the year ended December 31, 2001.

Cash outflows for interest expense and rent expense are equal to $7,000 and $18,000, respectively. Note that Robyn's must have paid for these items in cash because no related liabilities or assets appear on the balance sheet. Although Robyn's also reports depreciation expense of $35,000, depreciation does not result in a cash outflow. The cash outflow occurs at the time the depreciable property is purchased and is shown in the investing activities section of the cash flow statement. Finally, income tax expense is equal to $40,000. Adjusting for related increases in income tax liabilities on the balance sheet, cash outflows for income taxes during the year must have been $39,000 ($40,000 income tax expense + Beginning income tax payable balance of $9,000 − Ending income tax payable balance of $10,000).

Net Cash Flows from Operating Activities (Direct Method)
Cash Receipts From

Sales on account	$690,000
Interest	75,000
Cash Payments For	
Inventory purchases	(500,000)
Payroll	(48,000)
Insurance	(25,000)
Interest	(7,000)
Rent expense	(18,000)
Taxes	(39,000)
Net cash provided (used) by operating activities	$128,000

INDIRECT METHOD

The indirect method reconciles net income to net cash flow from operating activities by taking the income statement amounts of revenues and expenses and adjusting for changes in related noncash assets and liabilities:

Income statement amount
+ Increases in related liabilities
+ Decreases in related noncash assets
− Increases in related noncash assets
− Decreases in related liabilities
= Cash flow amount

Additions to Net Income	**Deductions from Net Income**
Decrease in accounts receivable	Increase in accounts receivable
Decrease in inventory	Increase in inventory
Decrease in prepaid assets	Increase in prepaid assets
Increase in accounts payable	Decrease in accounts payable
Increase in accrued liabilities	Decrease in accrued liabilities

Key Concept: *When using the indirect method, increases (decreases) in asset (liability) accounts during the year require deductions from net income. When asset (liability) accounts decrease (increase) during the year, the amount of decrease or increase must be added to net income in arriving at net cash provided by operating activities.*

In addition, gains (losses) on sales of assets and securities must be deducted (added) to net income because these amounts are not operating cash flows. Although the cash received from the sale will affect cash flow, it will be reported in the investing activities section of the cash flow statement rather than the operating activities section. Likewise, because depreciation expense does not affect cash flow, it must be added back to net income using the indirect method.

Using the indirect method, the net cash provided by operating activities section of the cash flow statement for Robyn's Boutique would appear as follows:

Robyn's Boutique
Net Cash Flows from Operating Activities (Indirect Method)

Net income	$ 95,000
Adjustments to Reconcile Net Income to Net Cash Provided (Used) by Operating Activities	
Increase in accounts receivable	(10,000)
Increase in inventory	(10,000)
Decrease in prepaid insurance	5,000
Increase in accounts payable	10,000
Increase in payroll payable	2,000
Increase in income taxes payable	1,000
Gain on sale of vehicle	(25,000)
Loss on the sale of securities	25,000
Depreciation expense	35,000
Net cash provided (used) by operating activities	$128,000

Step 3: Compute Net Cash Provided or Used by Investing Activities

Investing activities for Robyn's Boutique include cash inflows from the sale of a vehicle and the sale of long-term investments and cash outflows for purchases of land, equipment, and long-term investments. As shown on the income statement, the sale of the car (shown on the balance sheet as property and equipment) generated a gain of $25,000. However, the actual cash generated from the sale was the sales price of $75,000.

The vehicle that was sold had a book value of $50,000 and originally cost $60,000, which means that accumulated depreciation was $10,000 ($60,000 − $50,000).

Concept Question: *Can you calculate the ending accumulated depreciation amount shown on the balance sheet of $105,000?*

Concept Answer: The beginning balance in accumulated depreciation ($80,000) is increased by the current year's depreciation expense of $35,000 and decreased by $10,000 of accumulated depreciation written off at the time the vehicle is sold leaving an ending balance of $105,000. ■

Likewise, the sale of securities generates cash inflows equal to the amount of cash that was received ($25,000), not the loss on securities sold.

Long-term investments increased by $35,000 during the year (from $75,000 to $110,000). However, just looking at the net change in the accounts does not really tell the

**ROBYN'S
BOUTIQUE**

complete story of what happened during the year. During the year, long-term investments were purchased for $85,000 cash (increasing the asset account by $85,000) and investments with a book value of $50,000 were sold.

Equipment was purchased for $180,000. Land was also purchased for $25,000. However, paying only $5,000 in cash made the purchase.

Concept Question: *Reconcile the beginning and ending balance of the property and equipment asset account.*

Concept Answer: The beginning balance of $95,000 was increased by $180,000 for purchases of equipment and decreased by $60,000 (the original cost of the car sold). ■

Net Cash Flows from Investing Activities	
Cash Inflows From	
Sale of note	$ 25,000
Sale of vehicle	75,000
Cash Outflows For	
Purchase of long-term investments	(85,000)
Purchase of equipment	(180,000)
Purchase of land	(5,000)
Net cash provided (used) by investing activities	$(170,000)

Because the acquisition of land also included the issuance of a note payable for $20,000, rather than the payment of cash currently, this information is disclosed on a supplemental schedule of noncash investing and financing activities as follows:

Supplemental Schedule of Noncash Investing and Financing Activities	
Acquisition of land in exchange for note payable	$20,000

Step 4: Compute Net Cash Provided or Used by Financing Activities
Activities reported in this section include a $100,000 increase in capital stock and payment of dividends of $38,000.

Net Cash Flows from Financing Activities	
Cash Inflows From	
Issuance of stock	$100,000
Cash Outflows From	
Payment of cash dividends	(38,000)
Net cash provided (used) by financing activities	$ 62,000

Step 5: Compute Net Cash Flow by Combining the Results from Operating, Investing, and Financing Activities
Combining all the information contained in the three schedules of operating, investing, and financing activities and adding the supplemental schedule we can easily prepare the completed statement of cash flows for Robyn's Boutique for the year ended December 31, 2000.

Robyn's Boutique
Statement of Cash Flows (Direct Method)
For the Year Ended December 31, 2000

Cash Flows from Operating Activities
Cash Receipts From

Sales	$690,000
Interest	75,000
Total cash receipts	765,000

Cash Payments For

Inventory purchases	500,000
Payroll	48,000
Insurance	25,000
Interest	7,000
Rent expense	18,000
Taxes	39,000
Total cash payments	(637,000)
Net cash provided (used) by operating activities	128,000

Cash Flows from Investing Activities

Sale of securities	25,000
Sale of vehicle	75,000
Purchase of equipment	(180,000)
Purchase of long-term investments	(85,000)
Purchase of land	(5,000)
Net cash provided (used) by investing activities	(170,000)

Cash Flows from Financing Activities

Issuance of stock	100,000
Payment of cash dividends	(38,000)
Net cash provided (used) by financing activities	62,000
Net increase in cash	20,000
Cash balance 12/31/99	110,000
Cash balance 12/31/00	$130,000

Step 6: Report Any Significant Noncash Investing or Financing Activities in a Separate Schedule or a Footnote

Supplemental Schedule of Noncash Investing and Financing Activities
Acquisition of land in exchange for note payable $20,000

USING THE CASH FLOW STATEMENT IN DECISION MAKING

The statement of cash flows is a major source of information to investors and creditors. Many users view the statement of cash flows as the most important of the three main financial statements. Many investors and bankers focus on cash flows as opposed to net income because they are concerned with the ability of the company to meet its short-term obligations. Accrual accounting is felt to mask cash flow problems. Sophisticated users of financial statements may determine the cash flows of a business by using only the income

LO5
Analyze the statement of cash flows and use the information in decision making

statement and balance sheet through details such as purchases of property, plant, and equipment, and details of financing and investing activities may not be evident without the separate statement of cash flows.

CASH FLOW ADEQUACY

Creditors are concerned with the ability of the organization to repay its debts and meet its interest payments. **Cash flow adequacy** is a measure designed to help users of the financial statements make better lending decisions. Cash flow adequacy measures the cash available to meet future debt obligations after payment of interest and taxes and any long-term expenditures. Analysts are concerned with the amount of cash available to repay debt after the company has replaced or updated its existing property, plant, and equipment. Cash flow adequacy is computed as follows:

$$\text{Cash flow adequacy} = \frac{\text{Cash flow from operating activities} - \text{Interest} - \text{Taxes} - \text{Capital expenditure}}{\text{Average amount of debt maturing over the next five years}}$$

How is this measure used in decision making? Looking at annual reports for Wal-Mart, Carnival Cruise Lines, and Hasbro and gathering cash flow statement data and information from the required footnote on long-term debt, cash flow adequacy ratios are calculated as follows:

Wal-Mart: (all amounts in millions)

$$\text{Cash flow adequacy (1999)} = \frac{\$7,580 - 3,734}{\$3,828} \text{ or } 1.0047$$

Carnival Cruise Lines: (all amounts in thousands)

$$\text{Cash flow adequacy (1998)} = \frac{\$1,091,840 - 1,150,413}{\$169,212} \text{ or } -.3462$$

Hasbro: (all amounts in thousands)

$$\text{Cash flow adequacy (1998)} = \frac{\$126,587 - \$141,950}{305,800} \text{ or } -.0502$$

What do these ratios mean? In general, if the ratio is less than 1, it indicates that cash flow is insufficient to repay average annual long-term debt over the next five years. Any ratio above 1 would indicate sufficient cash flow to repay long-term debt. However, as with any ratio, the results should not be used without looking at the previous year's ratios to determine trends and also to compare with industry standards. Short-term fluctuations from positive to negative are common.

Some investment analysts prefer using cash flow per share as a measure of financial health as opposed to earnings per share. The accounting profession has expressly forbidden the reporting of cash flow per share information in external financial statements. The profession believes that this type of information is not an acceptable alternative to earnings per share as an indicator of company performance. As is the case in a lot of areas of accounting disclosure, there is disagreement on what is the most useful information to disclose. Individuals will use the information that best serves their needs for each specific decision situation.

P A U S E
& *Reflect*

Visit Web sites for Wal-Mart
(www.walmart.com),
Carnival Cruise Lines,
(www.carnivalcorp.com), and
Hasbro (www.hasbro.com)
and examine their cash flow
statements. How do these
three companies compare?

SUMMARY OF KEY CONCEPTS

- The only difference between the direct and indirect methods is in the presentation of the cash flows from operating activities. Cash flows from investing activities and cash flows from financing activities are calculated in exactly the same way. (p. 427)
- When using the indirect method, increases (decreases) in asset (liability) accounts during the year require deductions from net income. When asset (liability) accounts decrease (increase) during the year, the amount of decrease or increase must be added to net income in arriving at net cash provided by operating activities. (p. 433)

KEY DEFINITIONS

Operating activities Include acquiring and selling products in the normal course of business (p. 422)

Investing activities Include the purchase and sale of property, plant, and equipment, the purchases and sales of securities, and making loans as investments (p. 423)

Financing activities Include cash flows from selling or repurchasing capital stock, long-term borrowing, and contributions from owners (p. 423)

Cash equivalent An item that can be readily converted to a known amount of cash and has an original maturity to the investor of three months or less (p. 425)

Direct method Reports cash collected from customers and cash paid for inventory, salaries, wages, and so on (p. 425)

Indirect method Starts with net income and removes the impact of noncash items and accruals (p. 425)

Cash flow adequacy A measure of cash available to meet future debt obligations (p. 436)

CONCEPT REVIEW

1. What is the purpose of the statement of cash flows?
2. Discuss how the statement of cash flows differs from an income statement.
3. What is a cash equivalent? How is it used in preparation of the statement of cash flows?
4. "The statement of cash flows is the easiest of the basic financial statements to prepare because you know the answer before you start." Do you agree with this statement? Why or why not?
5. "To prepare a statement of cash flows, all you have to do is compare the beginning and ending balances in cash on the balance sheet and compute the net inflow or outflow of cash." Do you agree with this statement? Why or why not?
6. How is depreciation expense handled on the statement of cash flows?
7. Which method for preparing the operating activities section of the statement of cash flows, the direct or indirect method, provides the most information to users of the statement? Explain your answer.
8. Explain why, when a company uses the indirect method to prepare the operating activities section of the statement of cash flows, a decrease in a current asset is added back to net income.
9. Can a company show a decrease in cash even if reporting net income? Why?
10. Can a company show an increase in cash even if reporting a net loss? Why?
11. Why do you think accounting standards require a company to separately disclose income taxes paid and interest paid if it uses the indirect method?

APPLICATION OF CONCEPTS

12. Van Buren Inc. acquires a piece of land by signing a $100,000 promissory note and making a $30,000 down payment. How should this transaction be reported on the statement of cash flows?

13. Van Patten Inc. made two purchases during September. One was a $25,000 certificate of deposit that matures in 90 days. The other was a $50,000 investment in Microsoft common stock that will be held indefinitely. How should each of these transactions be treated on the statement of cash flows?

14. Vardy Toys Inc. prepays insurance in January of each year on various policies. The beginning balance in Prepaid Insurance was $12,500, and the ending balance was $10,000. The income statement reports insurance expense of $65,000. Under the direct method, what amount would appear for cash paid for insurance in the operating section of the statement of cash flows?

15. Walden Book Buyers Inc. buys 5,000 shares of its own common stock at $25 per share. The company purchases the shares as treasury stock. How is this transaction reported on the statement of cash flows?

16. Washburn Delivery Company sold a company car for $12,000. Its original cost was $35,000 and the accumulated depreciation at the time of sale was $20,000. How does the transaction to record the sale appear on a statement of cash flows prepared using the indirect method?

17. Whitney R.V.'s Inc. declared and distributed a 10 percent stock dividend during the year. Explain how, if at all, you would report this transaction on the statement of cash flows.

18. Whitney R.V.'s Inc. has invested its excess cash in the following instruments during December 2000:

Certificate of deposit, due Jan. 31, 2001	$100,000
Certificate of deposit, due May 31, 2001	$150,000
Investment in City of Portland bonds, due June 30, 2001	$110,000
Investment in Sheetz Inc. stock	$125,000
A money market fund	$225,000
90-day Treasury bills	$125,000
Treasury note, due December 2001	$200,000

Required

A. What should be included in cash equivalents at year-end 2000?

B. Where should the amount of cash equivalents be disclosed?

19. For each of the following transactions reported on a statement of cash flows, fill in the blank to indicate if it would appear in the Operating Activities section (O), in the Investing Activities section (I), or in the Financing Activities section (F). Put an (S) in the blank if the transaction does not affect cash but is reported in a supplemental schedule of noncash activities. Assume the company uses the direct method in the Operating Activities section.

a. _____ A company purchases its own common stock in the open market and immediately retires it.

b. _____ A company issues common stock in exchange for land.

c. _____ A six-month bank loan is obtained.

d. _____ 30-year bonds are issued.

e. _____ A customer pays the balance in an open account.

f. _____ Income taxes are paid.

g. _____ Cash sales are recorded.

h. _____ Cash dividends are declared and paid.

i. _____ A creditor is given common stock in exchange for a long-term note.

j. _____ A new piece of machinery is acquired for cash.

k. _____ Stock of another company is acquired as an investment.

    l. _____ Interest is paid on a bank loan.

    m. _____ Workers are paid for one week's wages.

20. Williams Media Inc.'s comparative balance sheets included accounts receivable of $100,000 at December 31, 1999, and $125,000 at December 31, 2000. Sales of consulting services reported by Williams Media Inc. on its 2000 income statement amounted to $2,000,000. What is the amount of cash collections that Williams Media Inc. should report in the Operating section of its 2000 statement of cash flows assuming that the direct method is used?

21. Workman-Smith Co.'s comparative balance sheets included inventory of $120,000 at December 31,1999, and $110,000 at December 31, 2000. Workman-Smith's comparative balance sheets also included accounts payable of $60,000 at December 31, 1999, and $55,000 at December 31, 2000. Workman-Smith's accounts payable balances are composed solely of amounts due to suppliers for purchases on inventory. Cost of goods sold, as reported by Workman-Smith on its 2000 income statement, amounted to $850,000. What is the amount of cash payments for inventory that Workman-Smith should report in the Operating Activities section of its 2000 statement of cash flows assuming that the direct method is used?

22. The following account balances are for the noncash current assets and current liabilities of Wynn Bicycle Company for 1999 and 2000:

	DECEMBER 31	
	1999	**2000**
Accounts receivable	$ 4,000	$ 6,000
Inventory	30,000	20,000
Office supplies	5,000	8,000
Accounts payable	10,000	7,000
Salaries and wages payable	2,500	4,000
Interest payable	1,500	2,500
Income taxes payable	5,500	2,500

In addition, the income statement for 2000 is as follows:

	2000
Sales revenue	$110,000
Cost of goods sold	85,000
Gross profit	25,000
General and administrative expense	9,000
Depreciation expense	2,000
Total operating expenses	11,000
Income before interest and taxes	14,000
Interest expense	2,000
Income before tax	12,000
Income tax expense	4,800
Net income	$ 7,200

Required

    A. Prepare the Operating Activities section of the statement of cash flows using the indirect method.

    B. What does the use of the direct method reveal about a company that the indirect method does not?

23. Determine the missing amounts in the following cases:

Case 1

Accounts receivable, beginning balance	$250,000
Accounts receivable, ending balance	200,000
Credit sales for the year	275,000
Cash sales for the year	160,000
Uncollectible accounts written off	135,000
Total cash collections for the year	?

Case 2

Inventory, beginning balance	$180,000
Inventory, ending balance	155,000
Accounts payable, beginning balance	125,000
Accounts payable, ending balance	115,000
Cost of goods sold	275,000
Cash payments for inventory (assume all purchases are on account)	?

Case 3

Prepaid insurance, beginning balance	$ 27,000
Prepaid insurance, ending balance	30,000
Insurance expense	25,000
Cash paid for new insurance	?

Case 4

Interest payable, beginning balance	$105,000
Interest payable, ending balance	125,000
Interest expense	300,000
Cash payments for interest	?

Case 5

Income taxes payable, beginning balance	$ 55,000
Income taxes payable, ending balance	75,000
Income tax expense	100,000
Cash payments for income taxes	?

24. The following selected account balances are available from the records of Yuen Seafood Specialty Company:

	DECEMBER 31	
	1999	**2000**
Dividends payable	$130,000	$120,000
Retained earnings	475,000	350,000

Other information is as follows:

a. Yuen reported $385,000 in net income for 2000.

b. The company declared and distributed a stock dividend of $150,000 during the year.

c. It declared cash dividends at the end of each quarter and paid them within the next 30 days of the following quarter.

Required

A. Determine the amount of cash dividends paid during the year for presentation in the Financing Activities section of the statement of cash flows.

B. Should the stock dividend described in Part b appear on the statement of cash flows? Explain your answer.

25. Assume that a company uses the indirect method to prepare the Operating Activities section of the statement of cash flows.

Required

For each of the following items, fill in the blank to indicate whether it would be added to net income (A), deducted from net income (D), or not reported in this section of the statement under the indirect method (NR).

A. Depreciation expense _____

B. Gain on the sale of used delivery truck _____

C. Bad debt expense _____

D. Increase in accounts payable _____

E. Purchase of a new delivery truck _____

F. Loss on retirement of bonds _____

G. Increase in prepaid rent _____

H. Decrease in inventory _____

I. Increase in short-term investments (classified as available-for-sale securities) _____

J. Amortization of patents _____

26. The account balances for the noncash current assets and current liabilities of Abraham Music Company are as follows:

	DECEMBER 31	
	1999	**2000**
Dividends payable	$ 50,000	$ 40,000
Retained earnings	545,000	375,000

Other information for 2000:

a. Abraham reported $375,000 in net income for 2000.

b. The company declared and distributed a stock dividend of $85,000 during the year.

c. The company declared cash dividends at the end of each quarter and paid them within the first 30 days of the next quarter.

Required

A. Determine the amount of cash dividends paid during the year for presentation in the Financing Activities section of the statement of cash flows.

B. Should the stock dividend described in Part b appear on a statement of cash flows? Explain your answer.

27. The account balances for the noncash current assets of Allen Company are as follows:

DECEMBER 31

	1999	2000
Accounts receivable	$ 45,000	$ 38,000
Inventory	40,000	50,000
Prepaid insurance	21,000	17,000
Total current assets	$106,000	$105,000

Net income for 2000 is $35,000. Depreciation expense is $22,000. Assume that all sales and all purchases are on account.

Required

A. Prepare the Operating Activities section of the statement of cash flows using the indirect method. Explain why cash flow from operating activities is more or less than the net income for the period.

B. What additional information do you need to prepare the operating activities section of the statement of cash flow using the direct method.

C. Explain the usefulness of each method for managerial decision making.

28. For each of the following transactions, indicate how they would be reported on the statement of cash flows. Use the following legend and assume that the stocks and bonds of other companies are classified as available-for-sale securities.

II = inflow from investing activities

OI = outflow from investing activities

IF = inflow from financing activities

OF = outflow from financing activities

CE = classified as a cash equivalent and included with cash for purposes of preparing the statement of cash flows.

A. Purchased a six-month certificate of deposit

B. Purchased a 90-day Treasury bill

C. Issued 10,000 shares of common stock

D. Purchased 5,000 shares of stock of another company

E. Purchased 10,000 shares of its own stock to be held in the treasury

F. Invested $10,000 in a money market fund

G. Sold 1,500 shares of stock of another company

H. Purchased 10-year bonds of another company

I. Issued 20-year bonds

J. Repaid a nine-month bank note

29. The following account balances are taken from the records of Roadhouse Corp. for the past two years:

| | DECEMBER 31 | |
	2000	**1999**
Plant and equipment	$750,000	$500,000
Accumulated depreciation	160,000	200,000
Patents	92,000	80,000
Retained earnings	825,000	675,000

Other information available for 2000 follows:

a. Net income for the year was $200,000.

b. Depreciation expense on plant and equipment was $50,000.

c. Plant and equipment with an original cost of $150,000 were sold for $64,000 (you will need to determine the book value of the assets sold).

d. Amortization expense on patents was $8,000.

e. Both new plant and equipment and patents were purchased for cash during the year.

Required

Indicate, with amounts, how all items related to these long-term assets would be reported in the 2000 statement of cash flows, including any adjustments in the Operating Activities section of the statement. Assume that Roadhouse Corp. uses the indirect method.

Chapter 16

FINANCIAL STATEMENT ANALYSIS

Study Tools

A Review of the Previous Chapter
In the first 14 chapters of this textbook we discussed uses of accounting information in decision making by managers. In Chapter 15 we discussed the preparation and use of the statement of cash flows and its use in decision making.

A Preview of This Chapter
In this chapter we discuss ratio analysis and other techniques used by investors, creditors, analysts, and managers in decision making.

Key concepts include:
- Ratio analysis provides additional information necessary to enhance the decision-making ability of the users of the information.
- Rather than focus on a single ratio, decision makers need to evaluate a company by comparing ratios to those of previous years, budgeted amounts, and industry standards.
- Horizontal analysis is used to analyze changes in accounts occurring between years.
- Vertical analysis uses common size financial statements to remove size as a relevant variable in ratio analysis.
- Ratio analysis is useful in assessing the impact of transactions on ROI, residual income, EVA, and other key measures of performance.

LEARNING OBJECTIVES

After studying the material in this chapter, you should be able to:

LO1 Understand why decision makers analyze financial statements

LO2 Understand the limitations of financial statement analysis

LO3 Use comparative financial statements to analyze the performance of a company over time (horizontal analysis)

LO4 Prepare and use common size financial statements to compare various financial statement items (vertical analysis)

LO5 Prepare and use liquidity ratios to analyze a company

LO6 Prepare and use solvency ratios to analyze a company

LO7 Prepare and use profitability ratios to analyze a company

Financial statement analysis involves the application of analytical tools to financial statements and supplemental data included with the financial statements to enhance the ability of decision makers to make optimal decisions. Investors and creditors need to make decisions to provide a company with loans or other capital. The primary source of information provided to external users is financial statements. The management team also makes decisions using financial statement information. For both groups, the use of financial statement analysis techniques enhances the usefulness of the information contained in the financial statements. ■

INTRODUCTION

Decision makers need a variety of information in the decision-making process. Bankers and other lenders are interested in the ability of an organization to repay loans. Stockholders or potential stockholders are interested in earning a fair return on their investment. The management team of a company is concerned with these issues and more—the adequacy of cash flow to pay operating expenses, the efficient use of company resources, and how to improve the overall performance of the company. Financial statement analysis is a useful tool for both external and internal users as they make decisions about a company or for a company.

WHY ANALYZE FINANCIAL STATEMENTS?

LO1

Understand why decision makers analyze financial statements

The most compelling reason to analyze financial statements is simply that it provides useful information to supplement information directly provided in financial statements. Ratio analysis provides additional information necessary to enhance the decision-making ability of the users of the information. Although we will spend some time on the computation of the ratios, the most important aspect of the discussion is what the ratios mean and how to improve performance of the organization by analyzing trends and changes in these ratios. Financial ratios can not only show how the company has done in the past but are very useful in predicting the future direction and financial position of organizations.

 Key Concept: *Ratio analysis provides additional information necessary to enhance the decision-making ability of the users of the information.*

LIMITATIONS OF FINANCIAL STATEMENT ANALYSIS

LO2

Understand the limitations of financial statement analysis

Financial statements are prepared using generally accepted accounting principles (GAAP). However, GAAP allows financial statement preparers to use a variety of methods, estimates, and assumptions in their preparation. To properly prepare and interpret financial statement ratios, these methods, estimates, and assumptions must be taken into consideration. For example, inventory valuation methods include FIFO, LIFO, and other accepted cost flow assumptions. These methods impact the cost of inventory shown on the balance sheet. For example, a company using the LIFO method of inventory costing in a period of rising prices is always selling the most costly inventory purchased (the last inventory purchased is the first to be sold), whereas the inventory shown on the balance sheet is the oldest and least costly. As a result, inventory balances on the balance sheet may be very low and "undercosted" based on today's prices. When comparing companies, differences in accounting methods and cost flow assumptions need to be taken into consideration. If accounting methods or assumptions are changed from year to year, comparisons between years can be difficult.

Decision makers using financial statements and the resulting ratios should not place too much emphasis on any single ratio. Ratios must be looked at as a story that cannot be told without all the pieces. Ratios should be compared with prior years' results, with the budget for the current year, and with industry standards. These industry standards can be found in publications by *Dun & Bradstreet, Moody's, Standard & Poor's,* and *Dow Jones Retrieval.* These services provide up-to-date information on most industries and regions. Regional differences are very important factors in evaluating performance. In addition, due to the size and complexity of many companies, industry standards are sometimes only useful in evaluating divisions of a business. For example, hotels that are affiliated with a casino are operated differently than hotels that are only in the hotel business. Rates for

www.dnb.com
www.moodys.com
www.standardpoor.com
www.dowjones.com

rooms are different, expectations are different, and the analysis of the financial ratios must be interpreted in light of these differences.

 Key Concept: *Rather than focus on a single ratio, decision makers need to evaluate a company by comparing ratios to those of previous years, budgeted amounts, and industry standards.*

THE IMPACT OF INFLATION ON FINANCIAL STATEMENT ANALYSIS

Financial statements are prepared using historical costs and are not adjusted for the effects of increasing prices. For example, though sales may have increased by 5 percent each year for the past five years, the impact of inflation on changing prices needs to be considered. If inflation averaged 3 percent annually over that same period of time, the real increase in sales dollars is only 2 percent. The impact of changing prices on long-term assets can be even more dramatic. Consider a building purchased 30 years ago for $100,000. If inflation averages 3 percent per year over the life of the building, the market value of the building today will be more than double the historical cost used to record the building when purchased. To compound the problem, the building is likely to be almost fully depreciated so the book value of the building may be very small.

HORIZONTAL ANALYSIS

Analyzing financial statements over time is called **horizontal analysis.** To demonstrate the concept of horizontal analysis, the financial statements for Robyn's Boutique are presented here. The idea behind horizontal analysis is to analyze changes in accounts occurring between years. To facilitate this analysis, dollar changes and percentage changes in each item on the balance sheet are often provided. The percentage changes are the amount of change from the previous year. In the following example, cash increased by $20,000, which is 18.2 percent of the 1999 balance $\left(\frac{\$20,000}{\$110,000}\right)$.

LO3
Use comparative financial statements to analyze the performance of a company over time (horizontal analysis)

ROBYN'S BOUTIQUE

 Key Concept: *Horizontal analysis is used to analyze changes in accounts occurring between years.*

Robyn's Boutique
Comparative Balance Sheets
Increase (Decrease)

	2000	1999	$ Change	% Change
Cash	$130,000	$110,000	$ 20,000	18.2%
Accounts receivable	130,000	120,000	10,000	8.3
Inventory	225,000	215,000	10,000	4.7
Prepaid insurance	25,000	30,000	(5,000)	(16.7)
Total current assets	510,000	475,000	35,000	7.4
Long-term investments	110,000	75,000	35,000	46.7
Land	200,000	175,000	25,000	14.3
Property and equipment	215,000	95,000	120,000	126.3
Accum. depr.	(105,000)	(80,000)	(25,000)	(31.3)
Total assets	$930,000	$740,000	$190,000	25.7
Accounts payable	60,000	50,000	10,000	20.0
Payroll payable	10,000	8,000	2,000	25.0
Taxes payable	10,000	9,000	1,000	11.1
Total current liabilities	80,000	67,000	13,000	19.4
Notes payable	100,000	80,000	20,000	25.0
Capital stock	500,000	400,000	100,000	25.0
Retained earnings	250,000	193,000	57,000	29.5
Total liabilities and stockholders' equity	$930,000	$740,000	$190,000	25.7

Looking closely at the balance sheet for Robyn's Boutique we see two accounts with large percentage changes between 1999 and 2000. Long-term investments have increased by 46.7 percent $\left(\frac{\$35,000}{\$75,000}\right)$ and property and equipment has increased by 126.3 percent $\left(\frac{\$120,000}{\$95,000}\right)$. Although increases like these are common in growing companies, analysts and others will likely be interested in how Robyn's paid for the acquisitions.

Concept Question: *Where can analysts find information on the source of funds used to acquire the additional long-term investments and property and equipment?*

Concept Answer: As you will recall from Chapter 15, the statement of cash flows provides that information. ■

Changes in the income statement for Robyn's Boutique can be analyzed in a similar fashion:

Robyn's Boutique
Comparative Statements of Income and Retained Earnings
Increase (Decrease)

	2000	1999	$ Change	% Change
Sales revenue	$700,000	$650,000	$50,000	7.7%
Cost of goods sold	500,000	455,000	45,000	9.9
Gross profit	200,000	195,000	5,000	2.6
Payroll expense	50,000	42,250	7,750	18.3
Insurance expense	30,000	29,000	1,000	3.4

Rent expense	18,000	18,000	—	—
Depreciation	35,000	15,000	20,000	133.3
Total expenses	133,000	104,250	28,750	27.6
Operating Income	67,000	90,750	(23,750)	(26.2)
Interest expense	(7,000)	(5,000)	(2,000)	40.0
Gain on vehicle sale	25,000	—	25,000	—
Loss on sale of securities	(25,000)	—	(25,000)	—
Interest revenue	75,000	50,000	25,000	50.0
Net income before interest and taxes	135,000	135,750	(750)	(.06)
Tax	(40,000)	(40,250)	250	(.06)
Net income	95,000	95,500	(500)	(.05)
Dividends	(38,000)	(38,000)		
To retained earnings	57,000	57,500		
Retained earnings 1/1	193,000	136,000		
Retained earnings 12/31	$250,000	$193,500		

Sales increased by $50,000 (7.7 percent) from 1999 to 2000. On the surface this would appear to be a positive sign. However, further analysis shows that the cost of goods sold increased by $45,000 or 9.9 percent, whereas total operating expenses increased by $28,750 or 27.6 percent. Although sales increased, expenses appear to be rising much faster than sales! This information is likely to be important for both external users and internal managers. A large decrease in operating income can indicate serious problems with cost management.

Horizontal analysis of financial statements can and should include more than just two years of data. Many annual reports include, as supplemental information, up to 10 years of financial data. Using these supplemental reports, readers of financial statements can perform **trend analysis.** Decision makers can use trend analysis to build prediction models to forecast financial performance in the future. Trend analysis can also be used to identify problem areas by looking for sudden or abnormal changes in accounts.

Horizontal analysis can also include the statement of cash flows:

Note that focusing on net income without looking at other changes in income statement items would definitely be a mistake in this case. Although net income was virtually unchanged from 1999 to 2000, operating income decreased over 26 percent.

Comparative Statements of Cash Flow
For the Years Ended December 31, 2000 and 1999

	2000	1999	$Change	% Change
Cash Flows from Operating Activities				
Cash Receipts From				
Sales on account	$690,000	$640,000	$50,000	7.8%
Interest	75,000	50,000	25,000	50.0
Total cash receipts	$765,000	$690,000	$75,000	
Cash Payments For				
Inventory purchases	$500,000	$470,000	$30,000	6.4
Payroll	48,000	42,250	5,750	13.6
Insurance	25,000	29,000	(4,000)	(13.8)
Interest	7,000	5,000	2,000	40.0
Rent expense	18,000	18,000	—	—
Taxes	39,000	40,250	(1,250)	(3.1)
Total cash payments	(637,000)	(604,500)	32,500	5.4
Net cash provided (used) by operating activities	$128,000	$ 85,500	$42,500	49.7

Cash Flows From Investing Activities

Sale of note	$ 25,000	—	$ 25,000	—
Sale of vehicle	75,000	—	75,000	—
Purchase of equipment	(180,000)	$(20,000)	(160,000)	800
Purchase of long-term investments	(85,000)	—	(85,000)	—
Purchase of land	(5,000)	—	(5,000)	—
Net cash provided (used) by investing activities	$(170,000)	$(20,000)	$(150,000)	750

Cash Flows from Financing Activities

Issuance of stock	$ 100,000	—	$ 100,000	—
Payment of cash dividends	(38,000)	$(38,000)	—	—
Net cash provided (used) by financing activities	62,000	(38,000)	100,000	263.2
Net increase in cash	20,000	27,500	$ (7,500)	(27.3)
Cash balance 1/1	110,000	82,500		
Cash balance 12/31	$ 130,000	$110,000		

Supplemental Schedule of Noncash Investing and Financing Activities

Acquisition of land in exchange for note payable	$ 20,000	(2,000)

Robyn's Boutique shows consistent and increasing cash flows from operations, $765,000 in 2000 and $690,000 in 1999. The boutique also shows an increase in net cash provided by operating activities of $42,500 or 49.7 percent. These two changes indicate a good trend in cash flows from operating activities. Although the net increase in cash for 2000 was less than the increase in 1999, the decrease can be easily explained by the additional cash used for investing activities in 2000.

VERTICAL ANALYSIS

LO4
Prepare and use common size financial statements to compare various financial statement items (vertical analysis)

www.boeing.com,
www.cessna.com

Vertical analysis compares financial statements of different companies and financial statements of the same company across time after controlling for differences in size. When comparing companies of different sizes, it is useful to standardize the statements. **Common size financial statements** are statements in which all items have been restated as a percentage of a selected item on the statements. Common size financial statements remove size as a relevant variable in ratio analysis and can be used to compare companies that make similar products that are different in size (like Boeing and Cessna, both aircraft manufacturers). They also can be used to compare the same company across years.

 Key Concept: *Vertical analysis uses common size financial statements to remove size as a relevant variable in ratio analysis.*

Common size comparative balance sheets for Robyn's Boutique follow. Note that all asset accounts are stated as a percentage of total assets. Similarly, all liability and stockholders' equity accounts are stated as a percentage of total liabilities and stockholders' equity.

Robyn's Boutique
Comparative Balance Sheets
Increase (Decrease)

	2000	Percent	1999	% Change
Cash	$130,000	14%	$110,000	14.9%
Accounts receivable	130,000	14	120,000	16.2
Inventory	225,000	24.2	215,000	29.1

Prepaid insurance	25,000	2.7	30,000	4.1
Total current assets	510,000	54.8	475,000	64.2
Long-term investments	110,000	11.8	75,000	10.1
Land	200,000	21.5	175,000	23.6
Property and equipment	215,000	23.1	95,000	12.8
Accum. Depr.	(105,000)	(11.3)	(80,000)	(10.8)
Total assets	$930,000	100%	$740,000	100%
Accounts payable	60,000	6.5	50,000	6.8
Payroll payable	10,000	1.1	8,000	1.1
Taxes payable	10,000	1.1	9,000	1.2
Total current liabilities	80,000	8.7	67,000	9.1
Notes payable	100,000	10.8	80,000	10.8
Capital stock	500,000	53.8	400,000	54.1
Retained earnings	250,000	26.9	193,000	26.1
Total liabilities and stockholders' equity	$930,000	100%	$740,000	100%

As mentioned earlier, there are two ways to use common size financial statements. The first is a comparison between years or over a number of years. The second is a comparison of similar companies of different sizes.

When comparing across years, analysts and other decision makers look for critical changes in the composition of accounts. One important measure from the balance sheet is working capital. **Working capital** is defined as the excess of current assets over current liabilities and is a measure of an entity's **liquidity** or its ability to meet its immediate financial obligations. Robyn's Boutique had current assets and current liabilities in 2000 and 1999 as follows:

	2000	**1999**
Current assets	$510,000	$475,000
Current liabilities	(80,000)	(67,000)
Working capital	$430,000	$408,000

The amount of working capital has increased by $22,000 from 1999 to 2000, indicating that Robyn's has increased the amount of current assets available to pay current liabilities. However, without information concerning the makeup of working capital, the information is of limited use. If current assets consist primarily of inventory, the company's liquidity could still be in jeopardy. In such a case a slower conversion to cash would result than it would in a situation where current assets consisted primarily of accounts receivable.

Common size comparative income statements for Robyn's Boutique are presented here. The base on which all income statement accounts are compared is net sales, presented simply as sales revenues in our demonstration.

Robyn's Boutique
Common Size Comparative Income Statements

	2000	Percent	1999	Percent
Sales revenue	$700,000	100.0%	$650,000	100.0%
Cost of goods sold	500,000	71.4	455,000	70.0
Gross profit	200,000	28.6	195,000	30.0
Payroll expense	50,000	7.1	42,250	6.0
Insurance expense	30,000	4.3	29,000	4.5

Rent expense	18,000	—	18,000	—
Depreciation	35,000	5.0	15,000	2.3
Total expenses	133,000	19.0	104,250	16.0
Operating Income	67,000	9.6	90,750	14.0
Interest expense	(7,000)	(1.0)	(5,000)	(0.8)
Gain on vehicle sale	25,000	3.6	0	—
Loss on sale of securities	(25,000)	(3.6)	0	—
Interest revenue	75,000	10.7	50,000	7.7
Net Income before interest and taxes	135,000	19.3	135,750	20.9
Tax	(40,000)	(5.7)	(40,250)	(6.2)
Net income	$ 95,000	13.6 %	$ 95,500	14.7 %

LO5
Prepare and use liquidity ratios to analyze a company

The common size income statement points out some interesting but small changes between the two years presented. The gross profit percentage decreased from 30 percent to 28.6 percent. This is a closely watched ratio in many companies and industries.

COMPARISON OF ROBYN'S TO THE GAP

www.gap.com

An important use of common size financial statements is to compare companies that are in similar lines of business but are of different sizes. For example, the GAP had working capital of $839,399,000 at January 31, 1998, representing 25.15 percent of total assets. Robyn's working capital is 46.24 percent of total assets. Other financial statement amounts from Robyn's and the GAP are as follows:

Comparison of Robyn's Boutique and the GAP

ACCOUNT	ROBYN'S (2000)	GAP (1998)
	Percentage of Total Assets	**Percentage of Total Assets**
Cash	14	27
Inventory	24	22
Prepaids	2.7	5.5
Property and equipment (net)	33.3	40.9
Long-term investments	11.8	0

	Percentage of Liabilities and Equity	**Percentage of Liabilities and Equity**
Accounts payable	6.5	12.5
Income tax	1.1	2.5
Long-term debt	10.8	14.8
Cost of goods sold	71.4	61.8
Operating expense	19	25.1
Net income after tax	13.6	8.2

PAUSE & Reflect

Spend some time looking at the preceding comparison and speculate on what would cause the differences between the two companies.

RATIO ANALYSIS

Financial statement ratios simply refer to a relationship between two financial statement amounts stated as a percentage.

RATIO ANALYSIS AND RETURN ON INVESTMENT

As discussed in Chapter 11, managers and the investment centers under their control are often evaluated using a measure of return on invested assets. These measures include return on investment (ROI), residual income, and economic value added (EVA). The measures are similar in that they look at performance in relation to the amount of assets or investment under a manager's control. As you will recall from Chapter 11,

$$ROI = \text{Profit Margin} \times \text{Asset Turnover}$$

where

$$\text{Profit Margin} = \frac{\text{Net operating income}}{\text{Sales}}$$

$$\text{Asset Turnover} = \frac{\text{Sales}}{\text{Average operating assets}}$$

$$ROI = \frac{\text{Net operating income}}{\text{Sales}} \times \frac{\text{Sales}}{\text{Average operating assets}}$$

The elements of ROI are shown in more detail in Exhibit 16-1.

 Key Concept: *Ratio analysis is useful in assessing the impact of transactions on ROI, residual income, EVA, and other key measures of performance.*

CURRENT RATIO

The **current ratio** or working capital ratio is a measure of an entity's liquidity. The formula for the current ratio is as follows:

$$\text{Current ratio} = \frac{\text{Current assets}}{\text{Current liabilities}}$$

EXHIBIT 16-1 Elements of Return on Investment

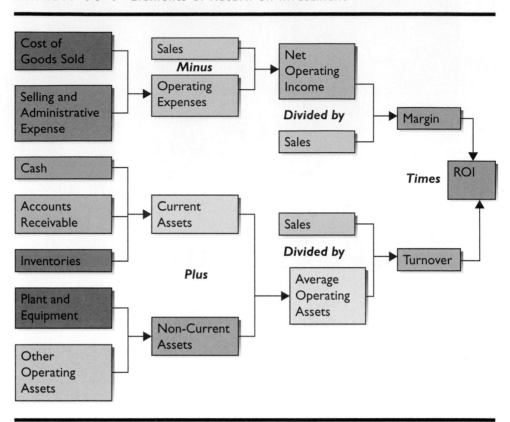

The current ratios for Robyn's Boutique for the past two years are as follows:

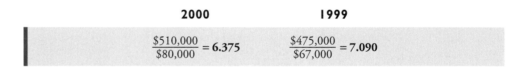

2000	1999
$\dfrac{\$510,000}{\$80,000} = \mathbf{6.375}$	$\dfrac{\$475,000}{\$67,000} = \mathbf{7.090}$

What does this ratio tell us? In 2000, Robyn's Boutique has $6.38 of current assets for every dollar of current liabilities, and in 1999 the boutique had $7.09 for every dollar of current liabilities. Although high current ratios would appear to be good (if you are a creditor of a company, a high current ratio indicates that you are more likely to be paid), a ratio that is very high may indicate that a company holds too much cash, accounts receivable, or inventory. Historically, a current ratio of 2.0 was considered good. However, many companies strive to maintain current ratios that are closer to 1.0. Internal managers look closely at the current ratio and its composition so that they can better control levels of current assets. As we have discussed elsewhere, holding inventory can be very costly for companies. High levels of accounts receivable may indicate problems collecting cash from customers and cash held in noninterest-bearing accounts might be more productively used elsewhere.

What is the impact of the current ratio on ROI, residual income, and EVA? The only way to increase the current ratio is to increase current assets or decrease current liabilities. Although decreasing liabilities has no direct impact on measures of return on investment, increasing current assets with no change in current liabilities will decrease ROI, residual income, and EVA.

ACID-TEST RATIO

One way to reduce the concern of the composition of the current accounts when computing the current ratio is to use the quick ratio or acid-test ratio. The **quick ratio** is a stricter test of a company's ability to pay its current debts with highly liquid current assets. The quick ratio removes inventories and prepaid assets from the current asset amount used in the calculation of the current ratio. These current assets are considered the least liquid. The quick ratio formula is as follows:

$$\text{Quick ratio} = \frac{\text{Quick assets}}{\text{Current liabilities}}$$

Using the amounts from Robyn's Boutique, the quick ratio becomes

2000	**1999**
$\frac{\$260,000}{\$80,000} = 3.25$	$\frac{\$230,000}{\$67,000} = 3.433$

A quick ratio less than 1.0 should be of concern to both creditors and internal managers as it indicates that liquid current assets are not sufficient to meet current obligations. On the other hand, Robyn's has unusually high quick ratios. High quick ratios may indicate other problems to management. Unless there are good reasons for holding excess cash (large purchases of property, plant, and equipment, future expansion, etc.), Robyn's should probably try to convert its excess cash into assets generating higher returns.

CASH FLOW FROM OPERATIONS TO CURRENT LIABILITIES RATIO

The current ratio and the quick ratio have two major weaknesses. The first is that all debt payments are made with cash, whereas current assets include noncash assets. The second is that both ratios focus on liquid and current assets at one point in time (the balance sheet date). However, cash, inventories, accounts receivable, and other current assets change over the course of the year. For these reasons, the amount of cash flow from operations (from the statement of cash flows) is sometimes used as the numerator in a ratio with an average balance of current liabilities in the denominator:

$$\text{Cash flow from operations to current liabilities ratio} = \frac{\text{Net cash provided by operating activities}}{\text{Average current liabilities}}$$

The computation of the 1999 ratio requires the 1998 end-of-year current liability balance. The December 31, 1998, balance sheet for Robyn's Boutique is as follows:

ROBYN'S
BOUTIQUE

Robyn's Boutique
Balance Sheet
December 31, 1998

Cash	$ 95,000
Accounts receivable	105,000
Inventory	175,000
Prepaid insurance	25,000
Total current assets	400,000
Long-term investments	45,000
Land	175,000
Property and equipment	85,000
Accumulated depreciation	(60,000)
Total long-term assets	245,000
Total assets	$645,000
Accounts payable	35,000
Payroll payable	6,500
Income tax payable	7,000
Total current liabilities	48,500
Notes payable	70,000
Total long-term liabilities	70,000
Capital stock	400,000
Retained earnings	126,500
Total liabilities and stockholders' equity	$645,000

The ratios for Robyn's Boutique are as follows:

2000	**1999**
$\dfrac{\$128,000}{\left[\dfrac{(\$80,000 + \$67,000)}{2}\right]} = 1.74$	$\dfrac{\$85,500}{\left[\dfrac{(\$67,000 + \$48,500)}{2}\right]} = 1.48$

Robyn's is generating sufficient cash from operations to pay current obligations.

ACCOUNTS RECEIVABLE ANALYSIS

The **accounts receivable turnover ratio** is one of the best measures of the efficiency of the collection process. Management's analysis of accounts receivable is very important in monitoring collection and credit-granting policies. The accounts receivable turnover ratio is

$$\text{Accounts receivable turnover ratio} = \frac{\text{Net credit sales}}{\text{Average accounts receivable}}$$

This ratio is known as an activity ratio, which means that it consists of an activity (sales) divided by a related base (accounts receivable). Using the accounts receivable balances in the 1998, 1999, and 2000 balance sheets, the ratios for Robyn's Boutique are as follows:

2000   **1999**

$$\frac{\$700,000}{\left[\frac{(\$120,000 + \$130,000)}{2}\right]} = \mathbf{5.60} \qquad \frac{\$650,000}{\left[\frac{(\$105,000 + \$120,000)}{2}\right]} = \mathbf{5.78}$$

These ratios tell us that on average, Robyn's Boutique sold on account and subsequently collected accounts receivable almost six times during the year. To convert this to a more understandable measure, consider this question: If you can do something almost six times in a year, how many days did it take you to do it once? The average number of days to collect a credit sale, computed as follows, measures this concept:

$$\text{Number of days sales are in receivables} = \frac{\text{Number of days in the period}}{\text{Accounts receivable turnover}}$$

The calculations for Robyn's for 1999 and 2000 are as follows:

2000   **1999**

$$\frac{360}{5.6} = \mathbf{64.29 \; days} \qquad \frac{360}{5.78} = \mathbf{62.28 \; days}$$

This ratio tells us that the average time to collect sales on account was 62.28 days in 1999 and 64.29 days in 2000. Is this amount of time to collect sales acceptable? That depends on the credit policy of the particular business and on industry standards. If the accounts are due in 30 days, then a collection period in excess of 60 is not good. If the credit policy allows for 60 days, then the collection period is in line with existing policy.

The accounts receivable turnover ratio will have an impact on ROI and other measures of return on invested assets. One of the key components of ROI is turnover of assets. When turnover is increased, ROI and related measures will also increase.

INVENTORY ANALYSIS

Analysis of inventory is very similar to the analysis of accounts receivable. The first ratio is the inventory turnover ratio:

$$\text{Inventory turnover ratio} = \frac{\text{Cost of goods sold}}{\text{Average inventory}}$$

The ratios for Robyn's for 1999 and 2000 are as follows:

2000   **1999**

$$\frac{\$500,000}{\left[\frac{(\$215,000 + \$225,000)}{2}\right]} = \mathbf{2.27} \qquad \frac{\$455,000}{\left[\frac{(\$175,000 + \$215,000)}{2}\right]} = \mathbf{2.33}$$

ROBYN'S
BOUTIQUE

These ratios tell us that on average, Robyn's Boutique bought inventory and then subsequently sold it 2.33 and 2.27 times per year in 1999 and 2000. This ratio does not mean that every item in inventory is sold 2.33 times but that the value of inventory was sold 2.33 times. Determining if inventory turns are good is totally dependent on industry and company standards. Some businesses expect higher inventory turns than others. For example, a grocery store would expect inventory turns of 50 or even 100 times per year. A bakery may expect inventory turns as high as 200 because it would expect to sell all fresh baked goods the same day they are produced. At the other extreme, furniture stores may only expect inventory turns of 1 or 2 per year. Retail stores should expect to turn over inventory much more frequently than 2 times per year. This is a serious concern for management. Another way to look at inventory turnover is to calculate the number of days inventory is held before it is sold:

$$\text{Number of days inventory is held before sale} = \frac{\text{Number of days in the period}}{\text{Inventory turnover}}$$

On average, Robyn's is holding inventory for more than 150 days in both 1999 and 2000, calculated as follows:

2000	**1999**
$\frac{360}{2.27} = \mathbf{158.59\ days}$	$\frac{360}{2.33} = \mathbf{154.51\ days}$

Low turnover ratios and a correspondingly high number of days in which inventory is held for sale can direct management's attention toward a variety of problems. A large amount of obsolete inventory that is not being written off can adversely impact these ratios. These ratios can also indicate problems in the sales department or problems with the product, both of which can cause decreases in sales. As with accounts receivable turnover, if inventory turnover increases, ROI and other measures of return on invested assets will also increase.

CASH-TO-CASH OPERATING CYCLE RATIO

This ratio measures the length of time between the purchase of inventory and the eventual collection of cash from sales. To calculate this ratio, we combine two measures:

$$\text{Cash-to-cash operating cycle ratio} = \text{Number of days in inventory} \\ + \text{Number of days in receivables}$$

The cash-to-cash operating cycle ratios for Robyn's Boutique are as follows:

2000	**1999**
$158.59 + 64.29 = \mathbf{222.88\ days}$	$154.51 + 62.28 = \mathbf{216.79\ days}$

On average, it took Robyn's 216.79 days in 1999 and 222.88 days in 2000 to turn purchased inventory into cash.

Solvency refers to a company's ability to remain in business over the long term. Solvency is related to liquidity but differs with respect to time frame. Liquidity measures the ability to pay short-term debt, whereas solvency measures the ability to stay financially healthy over the long run.

LO6
Prepare and use solvency ratios to analyze a company

DEBT-TO-EQUITY RATIO

The main focus of solvency analysis is capital structure. Capital structure refers to the relationship between debt and stockholders' equity. The debt-to-equity ratio is as follows:

$$\text{Debt-to-equity ratio} = \frac{\text{Total liabilities}}{\text{Total stockholders' equity}}$$

Robyn's debt-to-equity ratio at 1999 and 2000 is as follows:

2000	1999
$\frac{\$180,000}{\$750,000} = .24 \text{ to } 1$	$\frac{\$147,000}{\$593,000} = .25 \text{ to } 1$

These ratios tell us that for every $1 of capital (capital stock and retained earnings), creditors provided 25 cents in 1999 and 24 cents in 2000. Low debt-to-equity ratios indicate a preference to raise funds through equity financing and a tendency to avoid the higher risk of debt financing. What is considered a good debt-to-equity ratio? As with all other ratios this is dependent on the business, the industry, and other factors. Although a high debt-to-equity ratio may be of concern to creditors, it may be desirable and necessary for a new business to borrow money. The decision to capitalize a company with debt or equity involves many variables including the income tax impact of debt versus equity to both a corporation and its shareholders. If management borrows funds at 8 percent and earns a return on investment of 10 percent, the use of debt (leverage) is desirable. But it adds some risk due to the obligation to repay the debt and the interest on the debt. This level of risk can be measured by the next ratio, times interest earned.

TIMES INTEREST EARNED

Times interest earned measures a company's ability to meet current interest payments to creditors by specifically measuring its ability to meet current-year interest payments out of current-year earnings:

$$\text{Times interest earned} = \frac{\text{Net income} + \text{Interest expense} + \text{Income tax}}{\text{Interest expense}}$$

Both interest expense and income tax expense are added back to net income because interest is deducted from net income to arrive at taxable income. This adjustment gives us a "purer" measure of income available to pay interest. This ratio is especially important to bankers and other lenders. The times interest earned ratios for Robyn's are as follows:

2000	1999
$\frac{\$135,000 + \$7,000 + \$40,000}{\$7,000} = 26.0 \text{ to } 1$	$\frac{\$135,750 + \$5,000 + \$40,250}{\$5,000} = 36.2 \text{ to } 1$

The ratios for Robyn's Boutique are very good. Robyn's could pay (from current earnings) the interest on debt 36 times in 1999 and 26 times in 2000.

DEBT SERVICE COVERAGE RATIO

Two major weaknesses are associated with the use of the times interest earned ratio as a measure of the ability to pay creditors. First, the ratio only considers interest expense. Management and other decision makers must also be concerned with the amount of principal that must be repaid on the currently maturing debt. Second, the ratio does not take into account any noncash adjustments to net income that arise because of accrual accounting. The debt service coverage ratio is used to measure the amount of cash generated from operating activities that is available to repay principal and interest in the upcoming year. That ratio is as follows:

$$\text{Debt service coverage ratio} = \frac{\text{Cash flow from operations before interest and taxes}}{\text{Interest and principal payments}}$$

Referring back to the comparative statement of cash flows, we can compute the ratios for Robyn's:

2000	1999
$\frac{(\$128{,}000 - \$7{,}000 - \$39{,}000)}{\$25{,}000} = 3.28$	$\frac{(\$85{,}500 - \$5{,}000 - \$40{,}250)}{\$25{,}000} = 1.61$

These ratios indicate that Robyn's generated $1.61 in cash for every $1 of interest and principal paid in 1999 and $3.28 for every $1 of interest and principal paid in 2000. The 1999 ratio is weak but the improvement is dramatic.

CASH FLOW FROM OPERATIONS TO CAPITAL EXPENDITURES RATIO

This ratio measures a company's ability to use cash flow from operations to finance its acquisitions of property, plant, and equipment. The ability to use cash from operations diminishes the need to acquire outside financing such as debt. The ratio is computed as follows:

$$\text{Cash flow from operations to capital expenditures ratio} = \frac{\text{Cash flow from operations} - \text{Total dividends paid}}{\text{Cash paid for acquisitions}}$$

The calculation of these ratios for Robyn's is as follows:

2000	1999
$\frac{\$128{,}000 - \$38{,}000}{\$105{,}000} = 86\%$	$\frac{\$85{,}500 - \$38{,}000}{\$20{,}000} = 238\%$

These ratios tell us that in 1999 Robyn's generated cash from operations approximately 2.4 times greater than what was needed for acquisition of capital assets. In 2000 the ratio shows that Robyn's generated cash from operations to cover only 86 percent of the capital asset needs. Note that the amount used in 2000 to compute the ratio was net assets acquired. Robyn's had acquired $180,000 of new assets but sold a vehicle for $75,000.

Another group of ratios of importance to decision makers are those concerned with profitability analysis. Creditors are concerned with profitability because it indicates an ability to make required principal and interest payments. Stockholders are very interested in profitability because of related increases in stock prices or dividends paid to shareholders. Managers are also concerned with profitability as it is often related to performance evaluations and tangible rewards from bonus payments and other incentive compensation plans.

LO7
Prepare and use profitability ratios to analyze a company

RETURN ON ASSETS

Return ratios measure the relationship between a return and some specific investment made in the company by various groups of investors, creditors, and owners. Return on assets (ROA) considers the return to investors on all assets invested in the company. Because we are measuring a return to investors, net income is often adjusted by interest expense paid to creditors. The formula for computation of return on assets is as follows:

$$ROA = \frac{\text{Net income} + \text{Interest expense (net of tax)}}{\text{Average total assets}}$$

Assuming a 30 percent tax rate, the calculation of ROA is as follows:

	2000		**1999**	
Net income		$95,000		$95,500
Add back				
Interest expense	7,000		5,000	
× (1 − Tax rate)	× .70	4,900	× .70	3,500
Numerator:		99,900		99,000
Assets, beginning of year		$740,000		$645,000
Assets, end of year		930,000		740,000
Total		$1,670,000		$1,385,000
Denominator:				
Average total assets		$\left(\frac{1,670,000}{2}\right) = \$835,000$		$\left(\frac{1,385,000}{2}\right) = \$692,500$
ROA		$\frac{\$99,900}{\$835,000} = \textbf{11.96\%}$		$\frac{\$99,000}{\$692,500} = \textbf{14.30\%}$

Interpretation of this ratio is based on the company's required return on assets, industry standards, and trends. In this case, the decline in ROA is likely to be of concern to the owners of Robyn's Boutique.

Like return on investment, ROA can be broken down into margin and turnover components; return on sales and asset turnover. The two ratios are computed as follows:

$$\text{Return on sales} = \frac{\text{Net income} + \text{Interest expense (net of tax)}}{\text{Net sales}}$$

$$\text{Asset turnover ratio} = \frac{\text{Net sales}}{\text{Average total assets}}$$

The ratios for Robyn's are as follows:

2000	1999
$\text{Return on sales} = \dfrac{\$99,900}{\$700,000} = 14.27\%$	$\dfrac{\$99,000}{\$650,000} = 15.23$
$\text{Asset turnover ratio} = \dfrac{\$700,000}{\$835,000} = .84 \text{ times}$	$\dfrac{\$650,000}{\$692,500} = .94 \text{ times}$

Both the return on sales (income generated as a percentage of sales) and the asset turnover ratio (sales generated as a percentage of assets) declined from 1999 to 2000. Of particular concern to management is the low asset turnover ratio.

RETURN ON COMMON STOCKHOLDERS' EQUITY

Return on common stockholders' equity (ROCSE) measures the return to common stockholders (net income reduced by preferred dividends) as a percentage of stockholders' equity:

$$\text{ROCSE} = \frac{\text{Net income} - \text{Preferred dividends}}{\text{Average common stockholders' equity}}$$

The ROCSE ratios for Robyn's are as follows:

2000	1999
$\dfrac{\$95,000}{\left[\dfrac{(\$593,000 + \$750,000)}{2}\right]} = 14.15\%$	$\dfrac{\$95,500}{\left[\dfrac{(\$526,500 + \$593,000)}{2}\right]} = 17.06\%$

The ratios indicate that the common stockholders are earning a 17 percent return in 1999 and a 14 percent return in 2000. Adequacy of return on stockholders' equity is dependent on a number of factors including the risk of the investment.

EARNINGS PER SHARE

Current stockholders and potential investors use earnings per share (EPS) as a key measure of performance. In contrast to measures of net income, EPS can be used to compare the performance of companies of different sizes. However, it should be used with caution in comparing companies across different industries. EPS is calculated as follows:

$$\text{EPS} = \frac{\text{Net income} - \text{Preferred dividends}}{\text{Average number of common shares outstanding}}$$

The EPS for Robyn's is as follows:

	2000	**1999**
	EPS = $\dfrac{\$95,000}{45,000}$ = **$2.11**	EPS = $\dfrac{\$95,500}{40,000}$ = **$2.39**

Robyn's Boutique has a $10 per share par value resulting in 40,000 shares outstanding in 1999. In 2000, the boutique sold another 10,000 shares for $100,000, so 50,000 shares were outstanding at the end of 2000. The average number of shares outstanding in 2000 was 45,000 $\left(\dfrac{40,000 + 50,000}{2}\right)$.

PRICE EARNINGS RATIO

Earnings per share is a very important ratio for investors because of the relationship of earnings to dividends and the market price of a company's stock. Investors are also interested in the current price of a company's stock in comparison to its earnings. The price/earnings (P/E) ratio is computed as follows:

$$\text{Price earnings ratio} = \frac{\text{Current market price}}{\text{EPS}}$$

Assuming that the current market price for Robyn's Boutique stock is $13 per share, the P/E ratio is computed as follows:

	2000	**1999**
	$\dfrac{\$13}{\$2.11}$ = **6.16 to 1**	$\dfrac{\$13}{\$2.39}$ = **5.44 to 1**

P/E ratios are highly dependent on industry. A high P/E ratio can indicate that a stock is overpriced and a low P/E ratio can indicate that a stock is underpriced.

IN THE NEWS

The common stock of publicly held companies has generally been considered to be priced at a market value tied to historical earnings. However, many growth stocks appear to be priced based on *projected earnings,* not historical earnings.

In the past few years, Internet companies have often reflected high share prices with no historical earnings and minimal projected earnings. What do you think the prices of Internet stocks are based on? Reference values of companies such as Amazon.com, eBay.com, and priceline.com.

www.amazon.com
www.ebay.com
www.priceline.com

Summary of Key Concepts

- Ratio analysis provides additional information necessary to enhance the decision-making ability of the users of the information. (p. 448)

- Rather than focus on a single ratio, decision makers need to evaluate a company by comparing ratios to those of previous years, budgeted amounts, and industry standards. (p. 449)

- Horizontal analysis is used to analyze changes in accounts occurring between years. (p. 450)

- Vertical analysis uses common size financial statements to remove size as a relevant variable in ratio analysis. (p. 452)

- Ratio analysis is useful in assessing the impact of transactions on ROI, residual income, EVA, and other key measures of performance. (p. 455)

Key Definitions

Horizontal analysis When financial statements are analyzed over time (p. 449)

Trend analysis Horizontal analysis of multiple years of data (p. 451)

Common size financial statements Statements in which all items have been restated as a percentage of a selected item on the statements (p. 452)

Working capital The excess of current assets over current liabilities, which is a measure of an entity's liquidity (p. 453)

Liquidity A measure of the ability of a company to meet its immediate financial obligations (p. 453)

Current ratio Another measure of an entity's liquidity (p. 455)

Quick ratio A stricter test of a company's ability to pay its current debts with highly liquid current assets (p. 457)

Accounts receivable turnover ratio One of the best measures of the efficiency of the collection process (p. 458)

Concept Review

1. The rate of return on assets can be separated into what two components?

2. Discuss ways to increase the rate of return on assets.

3. Give the formula to compute accounts receivable turnover.

4. Give the formula to compute inventory turnover.

5. Give the formula to compute asset turnover.

6. If sales are $475, beginning assets are $420, and ending assets are $480, what is the asset turnover ratio?

7. If the cost of goods sold was $500, beginning inventory was $50, and ending inventory was $80, what is the inventory turnover ratio?

8. If a company's sales (all on account) equal $600, beginning accounts receivable were $68, and ending accounts receivable were $54, what is the accounts receivable turnover?

9. A company has a current ratio of 3 to 1 but would like to decrease the ratio. What types of options does it have to accomplish this?

10. At the beginning of 1999, the Golden Eagle Company had a current ratio of 2 to 1. What could Golden Eagle do to increase this ratio?

11. If current assets exceed current liabilities, what will a payment to short-term creditors do to the ratio?

12. Spendthrift Inc. has ordered goods on credit from Prudence Co. Before Prudence ships the goods, however, it would like to be sure that Spendthrift is likely to be able to pay the bill when due. Assuming Prudence has access to Spendthrift's financial statements, which ratios will Prudence find most useful? Why?

13. Explain the purpose of financial statement analysis.

14. Explain the limitations of ratio analysis.

APPLICATION OF CONCEPTS

15. Using the following financial statements for Eagle Company, compute the required ratios:

Eagle Company
Statement of Financial Position as of December 31 (in millions)

	1999	2000	2001
Assets			
Cash	$ 2.6	$ 1.8	$ 1.6
Government securities	0.4	0.2	0.0
Accounts and notes receivable	8.0	8.5	8.5
Inventories	2.8	3.2	2.8
Prepaid assets	0.7	0.6	0.6
Total current assets	14.5	14.3	13.5
Property, plant, and equipment (net)	4.3	5.4	5.9
Total assets	$18.8	$19.7	$19.4
Liabilities and Equity			
Notes payable	$ 3.2	$ 3.7	$ 4.2
Accounts payable	2.8	3.7	4.1
Accrued expenses	0.9	1.1	1.0
Total current liabilities	6.9	8.5	9.3
Long-term debt, 6 % interest	3.0	2.0	1.0
Total liabilities	9.9	10.5	10.3
Shareholders' equity	8.9	9.2	9.1
Total liabilities and equity	$18.8	$19.7	$19.4

Income Statement
For the Year Ended December 31 (in millions)

	1999	2000	2001
Net sales	$24.2	$24.5	$24.9
Cost of goods sold	(16.9)	(17.2)	(18.0)
Gross margin	7.3	7.3	6.9
Selling and administrative	(6.6)	(6.8)	(7.3)
Earnings (Loss) before taxes	0.7	0.5	(.4)
Income taxes	(0.3)	(0.2)	.2
Net income	$ 0.4	$ 0.3	$ (.2)

Required

    A. What is the rate of return on total assets for the year 2001?

    B. What is the current ratio for the year 2001?

    C. What is the quick (acid test) ratio for the year 2001?

    D. What is the profit margin for the year 2000?

    E. What is the profit margin for the year 2001?

    F. What is the inventory turnover for the year 2000?

    G. What is the inventory turnover for the year 2001?

H. What is the rate of return on stockholders' equity for the year 2000?

I. What is the rate of return on stockholders' equity for the year 2001?

J. What is the debt-equity ratio for the year 2001?

16. Recent annual reports of The Coca-Cola Company and PepsiCo Inc. reveal the following for Year 3 (in millions):

www.coca-cola.com
www.pepsico.com

	Coca-Cola	**PepsiCo**
Revenues	$8,338	$13,007
Interest expense	199	345
Net income	1,045	762
Average total assets	8,028	10,079

The income tax rate for Year 3 is 34 percent.

Required

A. Calculate the rate of return on assets for each company.

B. Break the rate of return on assets into return on sales and total asset turnover.

C. Comment on the relative profitability of the two companies for Year 3.

17. Information taken from recent annual reports of two retailers follows (amounts in millions). Dan's Duds and Handsome Hal's both sell men's clothing. The income tax rate is 34 percent. Indicate which of these companies is the discount store and which is the specialty retailer. Explain your answer.

	Dan's Duds	**Handsome Hal's**
Sales	$4,071	$20,649
Interest expense	64	136
Net income	245	837
Average total assets	2,061	5,746

18. Annual reports of Kellogg's and Quaker Oats reveal the following for the current year (amounts in millions):

www.kellogg.com
www.quakeroats.com

	Kellogg's	**Quaker Oats**
Sales	$3,793	$3,671
Accounts receivable, January 1	219	505
Accounts receivable, December 31	275	537

Required

A. Compute the accounts receivable for each company.

B. Compute the average number of days that accounts receivable are outstanding for each company.

C. Which of these two companies is managing its accounts receivable more efficiently?

19. The following relates to the activities of Eli Lilly, a pharmaceutical company (amounts in millions):

www.elililly.com

	Year 5	**Year 6**	**Year 7**	**Year 8**
Sales	$3,271	$3,720	$3,644	$4,070
Cost of goods sold	1,175	1,346	1,303	1,337
Average inventory	662	694	655	645

Required

A. Compute the inventory turnover for each year.

B. Compute the average number of days that inventories are held each year.

C. Compute the cost of goods sold to sales percentage for each year.

D. How well has the company managed its inventories over the four years?

20. The following information relates to a manufacturer of CD players (amounts in millions):

	Year 2	Year 3	Year 4
Sales	$210	$538	$1,051
Average total assets	70	145	256
Net income	36	87	137

Required

A. Compute the asset turnover ratio for each year.

B. How well has the company managed its investment in plant assets over the three years?

21. Information taken from the annual reports of National Medical Enterprises for three recent years is as follows (amounts in millions):

	Year 4	Year 5	Year 6
Revenues	$2,962	$2,881	$3,202
Net income	118	140	170
Average total assets	3,069	3,365	3,471
Average common stockholders' equity	974	968	944

Required

A. Compute the rate of return on common stockholders' equity for each year.

B. Break the rate of return on assets into the return on sales and the asset turnover ratio.

C. How has the profitability of the company changed over the three years?

22. The following data show five items from the financial statements of three companies for a recent year (amounts in millions):

	Company A	Company B	Company C
For the Year			
Revenues	$8,824	$9,000	$11,742
Income before interest and related taxes[a]	615	1,043	611
Net income to common shareholders[b]	477	974	503
Average during the Year			
Total assets	9,073	6,833	7,163
Common shareholders' equity	2,915	3,494	2,888

[a]Net income + Interest expense × (1 − tax rate)
[b]Net income − Preferred stock dividends

Required

A. Compute the rate of return on assets for each company. Separate the rate of return on assets into the return on sales and the asset turnover ratio.

B. The three companies are American Airlines, Johnson & Johnson, and May Department Stores. Which of the companies corresponds to A, B, and C? What clues did you use in reaching your conclusions?

www.aa.com
www.johnsonandjohnson.com
www.mayco.com

23. The 1999 financial statements for the Griffin Company are as follows:

Griffin Company
Statement of Financial Position

Assets	12/31/99	12/31/98
Cash	$ 40,000	$ 10,000
Accounts receivable	30,000	55,000
Inventory	110,000	70,000
Property, plant, and equipment	250,000	257,000
Total assets	$430,000	$392,000

Liabilities and Stockholders' Equity

	12/31/99	12/31/98
Current liabilities	$ 60,000	$ 50,000
5 percent mortgage payable	120,000	162,000
Common stock (30,000 shares)	150,000	150,000
Retained earnings	100,000	30,000
Total liabilities and equity	$430,000	$392,000

Griffin Company
Income Statement
For the Year Ended December 31, 1999

Sales on Account	$420,000
Less Expenses	
Cost of goods sold	$214,000
Salary expense	50,000
Depreciation expense	7,000
Interest expense	9,000
Total expenses	280,000
Income before taxes	140,000
Income tax expense (50 percent)	70,000
Net income	$ 70,000

Required

Compute the following ratios for the Griffin Company for the year ending December 31, 1999:

A. Profit margin ratio (before interest and taxes)

B. Total asset turnover

C. Rate of return on total assets

D. Rate of return on common stockholders' equity

E. Earnings per share of stock

F. Inventory turnover

G. Current ratio

H. Quick ratio

I. Accounts receivable turnover

J. Debt-to-equity ratio

K. Interest coverage ratio

24. Avantronics is a manufacturer of electronic components and accessories with total assets of $20,000,000. Selected financial ratios for Avantronics and the industry averages for firms of similar size are as follows:

	AVANTRONICS			**INDUSTRY AVERAGE**
	1997	1998	1999	
Current ratio	2.09	2.27	2.51	2.24
Quick ratio	1.15	1.12	1.19	1.22
Inventory turnover	2.40	2.18	2.02	3.50
Profit margin	0.14	0.15	0.17	0.11
Debt to equity ratio	0.24	0.37	0.44	0.35

Avantronics is being reviewed by several entities whose interests vary, and the company's financial ratios are a part of the data being considered. Each of the following parties must recommend an action based on its evaluation of Avantronics' financial position.

MidCoastal Bank. The bank is processing Avantronics' application for a new five-year term note. MidCoastal has been the banker for Avantronics for several years but must reevaluate the company's financial position for each major transaction.

Ozawa Company. Ozawa is a new supplier to Avantronics and must decide on the appropriate credit terms to extend to the company.

Drucker & Denon. A brokerage firm specializing in the stock of electronics firms that are sold over the counter, Drucker & Denon must decide if it will include Avantronics in a new fund being established for sale to Drucker & Denon's clients.

Working Capital Management Committee. This is a committee of Avantronics' management personnel chaired by the chief operating officer. The committee is responsible for periodically reviewing the company's working capital position, comparing actual data against budgets, and recommending changes in strategy as needed.

Required

A. Describe the analytical use of each of the five ratios just presented.

B. For each of the four entities described, identify the financial ratios, from those ratios presented, that would be most valuable as a basis for its decision regarding Avantronics.

C. Discuss what the financial ratios presented in the question reveal about Avantronics. Support your answer by citing specific ratio levels and trends as well as the interrelationships between these ratios.

Abnormal spoilage Spoilage resulting from unusual circumstances including improper handling, poorly trained employees, faulty equipment, and so on (p. 65)

Absorption (full) costing A method of costing in which product costs include direct material, direct labor, and fixed and variable overhead. Required for external financial statements and for income tax reporting (p. 169)

Accounting information system (AIS) A transaction processing system that captures financial data resulting from accounting transactions within a company (p. 4)

Accounts receivable turnover ratio One of the best measures of the efficiency of the collection process (p. 458)

Activities Procedures or processes that cause work to be accomplished (p. 87)

Activity-based costing (ABC) A system of allocating overhead costs that assumes that activities, not volume of production, cause overhead costs to be incurred (p. 87)

Activity-based management (ABM) A system that focuses on managing activities to reduce costs and make better decisions (p. 98)

Allocation The process of finding a logical method of assigning overhead costs to the products or services produced by a company (p. 67)

Annuity A series of cash flows of equal amount paid or received at regular intervals (p. 250)

Appraisal costs Costs incurred to inspect finished product or product in process of production (p. 377)

Asset turnover The measure of activity used in the ROI calculation; it measures the sales that are generated for a given level of assets (p. 350)

Backflush costing A costing system in which manufacturing costs are directly flushed into cost of goods sold instead of flowing through inventory (p. 75)

Balanced scorecard Uses a set of financial and nonfinancial measures that relate to the critical success factors of any organization (p. 372)

Bottlenecks Steps in the production process that limit throughput or the number of finished products that go through the production process (p. 200)

Break-even point The level of sales where contribution margin just covers fixed costs and net income is equal to zero (p. 156)

Budget variance Also known as the spending variance, the difference between the amount of fixed overhead actually incurred and the flexible budget amount (p. 318)

Budgets Plans dealing with the acquisition and use of resources over a specified time period (p. 268)

Capital investment decisions Long term decisions involving the purchase (or lease) of new machinery and equipment, and the acquisition or expansion of facilities used in a business (p. 224)

Cash disbursements budget Used to project the amount of cash to be disbursed during the budget period (p. 280)

Cash equivalent An item that can be readily converted to a known amount of cash and have an original maturity to the investor of three months or less (p. 425)

Cash flow adequacy A measure of cash available to meet future debt obligations (p. 436)

Cash receipts budget Used to project the amount of cash expected to be received from sales and cash collections from customers (p. 279)

Common costs Indirect costs that are incurred to benefit more than one segment and cannot be directly traced to a particular segment or allocated in a reasonable manner (p. 346)

Common size financial statements Statements in which all items have been restated as a percentage of a selected item on the statements (p. 452)

Compound interest Interest on the invested amount plus interest on previous interest earned but not withdrawn (p. 241)

Constraints Restrictions that occur when the capacity to manufacture a product or provide a service is limited in some manner (p. 199)

Contribution margin per unit The sales price per unit of product less all variable costs to produce and sell the unit of product; used to calculate the change in contribution margin resulting from a change in unit sales (p. 147)

Contribution margin ratio The contribution margin divided by sales; used to calculate the change in contribution margin resulting from a dollar change in sales (p. 148)

Control Involves ensuring that the objectives and goals developed by the organization are being attained. Control often involves a comparison of budgets to actual performance and the use of budgets for performance evaluation purposes. (p. 270, 306)

Controlling activities The motivation and monitoring of employees and the evaluation of people and other resources used in the operations of the organization (p. 8)

Cost behavior How costs react to changes in production volume or other levels of activity (p. 116)

Cost center A segment or division of an organization that is primarily responsible for control of costs (p. 344)

Cost drivers Factors that cause or drive the incurrence of costs (p. 67)

Cost of capital What the firm would have to pay to borrow (issue bonds) or raise funds through equity (issue stock) in the financial marketplace (p. 226)

Cost pools Groups of overhead costs that are similar; used to simplify the task of assigning costs to products using ABC costing (p. 68)

Cost-plus pricing A method of pricing in which managers determine the cost of the product or service and then add a markup percentage to that cost to arrive at the sales price (p. 186)

Cost-volume-profit analysis (CVP) A tool that focuses on the relationship between a company's profits and (1) the prices of products or services, (2) the volume of products or services, (3) the per-unit variable costs, (4) the total fixed costs, and (5) the mix of products or services produced (p. 146)

Current ratio Another measure of an entity's liquidity (p. 455)

Customer relationship management (CRM) Designed to bring a company closer to its customers in order to serve them better (p. 399)

Customer response time The time it takes to deliver the product of service after the order is received (p. 380)

Data Reports such as financial statements, customer lists, inventory records, and so on (p. 392)

Data mining A process of searching and extracting information from data (p. 396)

Data warehouses Central depositories for electronic data (p. 396)

Decentralized organization An organization in which decision-making authority is spread throughout the organization (p. 342)

Decision making The process of identifying alternative courses of action and selecting an appropriate alternative in a given decision-making situation (p. 12)

Dependent variable The variable in regression analysis that is dependent on changes in the independent variable (p. 124)

Direct labor Labor that can easily and conveniently be traced to particular products (p. 33)

Direct labor budget Used to project the dollar amount of direct labor cost needed for production (p. 277)

Direct materials Materials that can easily and conveniently be traced to the final product (p. 33)

Direct method Reports cash collected from customers and cash paid for inventory, salaries, wages and so on (p. 425)

Discount rate Used as a hurdle rate or minimum rate of return in time value of money calculations, it is adjusted to reflect risk and uncertainty (p. 226)

Diverse Products Products that consume resources in different proportions (p. 97)

E-business Business activities conducted electronically (p. 393)

Earnings management A method of recording used to "smooth" earnings from quarter to quarter or to otherwise manipulate financial results for a steady income stream (p. 405)

Economic value added (EVA) A contemporary measure of performance focusing on shareholder wealth (p. 356)

Electronic data interchange (EDI) The electronic transmission of data such as purchase orders and invoices (p. 399)

Employee fraud The main focus of employee fraud is taking possession of assets or cash of the organization (p. 406)

Enterprise resource planning (ERP) systems Systems used to collect, organize, report, and distribute organizational data and transform that data into critical information and knowledge (p. 4, 396)

Equivalent units The number of finished units that can be made from the materials, labor, and overhead included in partially completed units (p. 73)

External auditors Usually CPAs that are independent of the organization that they are auditing (p. 407)

External failure costs Costs incurred when a defective product is delivered to a customer (p. 377)

Financing activities Include cash flows from selling or repurchasing capital stock, long-term borrowing, and contributions from owners (p. 423)

Finished goods inventory Inventory of finished product waiting for sale and shipment to customers (p. 29)

Fixed costs Costs that remain the same in total when production volume increases or decreases but vary per unit (p. 116)

Flexible budget variance The difference between the flexible budget operating income and actual operating income (p. 311)

Flexible budgets Take differences in spending due to volume differences out of the analysis by budgeting for labor (and other costs) based on the *actual* number of units produced (p. 290)

Fraud A false representation of a material fact made by one party to another party with the intent to deceive and induce the other party to justifiably rely on the fact to his or her detriment (p. 404)

Fringe benefits Payroll costs in addition to the basic hourly wage (p. 66)

Gross profit The difference between sales and cost of goods sold (p. 146)

Horizontal analysis When financial statements are analyzed over time (p. 449)

Ideal standard A standard that is attained only when near-perfect conditions are present (p. 307)

Idle time Worker time that is not used in the production of the finished product (p. 66)

Independent variable The variable in regression analysis that drives changes in the dependent variable (p. 124)

Indirect labor Labor used in the production of products but not directly traceable to the specific product (p. 33)

Indirect material Material used in the production of products but not directly traceable to the specific product (p. 33)

Indirect method Starts with net income and removes the impact of noncash items and accruals (p. 425)

Information Data that have been organized, processed, and summarized (p. 392)

Internal auditors Auditors that are employed by the organization that they audit (p. 407)

Internal control A process, effected by an entity's board of directors, management, and other personnel, designed to provide reasonable assurance regarding the achievement of objectives in the following categories: (1) reliability of financial reporting, (2) compliance with applicable laws and regulations, and (3) effectiveness and efficiency of operations (p. 407)

Internal control procedures Used to address areas of risk that were identified during the risk assessment process (p. 409)

Internal failure costs Costs incurred once the product is produced and then determined to be defective (p. 377)

Internal rate of return (IRR) The actual yield or return earned by an investment (p. 226)

Investing activities Include the purchase and sale of property, plant, and equipment, the purchases and sales of securities, and making loans as investments (p. 423)

Investment center A segment or division of an organization that is primarily responsible for sales revenue, costs, and investments in operating assets (p. 345)

ISO 9000 A set of guidelines for quality management focusing on the design, production, inspection, testing, installing, and servicing of products, processes, and services (p. 375)

JIT (just-in-time) production systems The philosophy of having raw materials arrive just in time to be used in production and for finished goods inventory to be completed just in time to be shipped to customers (p. 29)

Job Costing A costing system that accumulates, tracks, and assigns costs for each job produced by a company (p. 62)

Kaizen A system of improvement based on a series of gradual and often small improvements (p. 375)

Knowledge Information that is shared and exploited so that its adds value to an organization (p. 392)

Knowledge warehouses Used to store and provide access to a wide variety of qualitative data (p. 396)

Life cycle cost The costs accumulated over the entire life cycle of a product (p. 185)

Life-cycle costing Includes all of the costs incurred throughout a product's life, not just in the manufacturing and selling of the product (p. 34)

Liquidity A measure of the ability of a company to meet its immediate financial obligations (p. 453)

Management by exception The process of taking action only when actual results deviate significantly from planned (p. 306)

Management fraud Typically involves misstating the financial statements in order to mislead readers of the financial statements such as stockholders and creditors (p. 404)

Manufacturing companies Companies that purchase raw materials from other companies and transform those raw materials into a finished product (p. 28)

Manufacturing costs Costs incurred in the factory or plant to produce a product. Typically consists of three different elements: direct materials, direct labor, and manufacturing overhead (p. 32)

Manufacturing cycle efficiency (MCE) The value-added time in the production process divided by the throughput or cycle time (p. 38)

Manufacturing cycle time The total time a product is in production which includes process time, inspection time, wait time, and move time; cycle time will include both value- and non-value-added time (p. 381)

Manufacturing overhead Indirect material and labor and any other expenses related to the production of product but not directly traceable to the specific product (p. 33)

Manufacturing overhead budget Used to project the dollar amount of manufacturing overhead needed for production (p. 278)

Margin The percentage of each sales dollar that is recognized as net profit (p. 350)

Markup percentage The amount added to cost to determine the sales price in cost-plus pricing. The markup must be sufficient to cover any costs not included in the company's definition of product cost plus produce an acceptable profit (p. 187)

Material price variance The difference between the actual price and the budgeted price times the actual volume purchased (p. 313)

Material purchases budget Used to project the dollar amount raw material purchased for production (p. 275)

Mixed costs These costs include both a fixed and a variable component. Consequently, it is difficult to predict the behavior of a mixed cost as production changes unless the cost is first separated into its fixed and variable components (p. 120)

Net operating income Net income from operations before interest and taxes (p. 350)

Net present value (NPV) A technique for considering the time value of money in which the present value of all cash inflows associated with a project is compared with the present value of all cash outflows (p. 226)

Non-value-added activities Activities that can be eliminated without affecting the quality or performance of a product (p. 99)

Nonmanufacturing costs Costs that include selling and administrative costs (p. 33)

Normal spoilage Spoilage resulting from the regular operations of the production process (p. 65)

Operating Involves day-to-day decision making by managers, which is often facilitated by budgeting (p. 270)

Operating activities The day-to-day operations of a business (p. 8, 422)

Operating assets Typically include cash, accounts receivable, inventory and property, plant, and equipment (p. 350)

Operating budget Used to plan for the short term (typically one year or less) (p. 273)

Operating leverage The contribution margin divided by net income; used as an indicator of how sensitive net income is to the change in sales (p. 167)

Operations costing A hybrid of job and process costing; used by companies that make products in batches (p. 63)

Opportunity costs The benefits forgone by choosing one alternative over another (p. 15)

Outsourcing and make-or-buy decisions Short-term decisions to outsource labor or purchase components used in manufacturing from another company rather than to provide services or produce components internally (p. 192)

Overapplied Overhead The amount of applied overhead in excess of actual overhead (p. 72)

Overtime premium The additional amount added to the basic hourly wage due to overtime worked by the workers (p. 66)

Payback period The length of time needed for a long-term project to recapture or pay back the initial investment (p. 239)

Performance fraud Another term for management fraud, used because the manipulation of the financial information is often designed to inflate earnings or to cover up a decline in financial position (p. 405)

Performance report Provides key financial and nonfinancial measures of performance for a particular segment (p. 344)

Period cost Costs that are expensed in the period incurred. Attached to the period as opposed to the product. (p. 40)

Planning The development of both the short-term (operational) and the long-term (strategic) objectives and goals of an organization and an identification of the resources needed to achieve them (p. 7, 270)

Practical standard A standard that should be attained under normal, efficient operating conditions (p. 307)

Predetermined overhead rates Used to apply overhead to products; calculated by dividing the estimated overhead for a cost pool by the estimated units of the cost driver (p. 71)

Preference decisions Decisions that involve choosing between alternatives (p. 225)

Present value (PV) The amount of future cash flows discounted to their equivalent worth today (p. 241)

Prevention costs Costs incurred to prevent product failures from occurring, typically related to design and engineering (p. 377)

Pro-forma financial statements Budgeted financial statements that are sometimes used for internal planning purposes but more often are used by external users (p. 283)

Process costing A costing system that accumulates and tracks costs for each process performed and then assigns those costs equally to each unit produced (p. 62)

Product cost Also called inventoriable costs because they attach to the products as they go through the manufacturing process (p. 40)

Production budget Used to forecast how many units of product to produce in order to meet the sales projections (p. 274)

Productivity A measure of the relationship between outputs and inputs (p. 378)

Profit center A segment or division of an organization that is primarily responsible for control of sales revenue and costs (p. 344)

Profitability index (PI) Calculated by dividing the present value of cash inflows by the initial investment (p. 231)

Qualitative Deals with nonnumerical attributes or characteristics (p. 13)

Quality Usually defined as meeting or exceeding customer's expectations (p. 375)

Quantitative Can be expressed in terms of dollars or other quantities (units, pounds, etc.) (p. 13)

Quick ratio A stricter test of a company's ability to pay its current debts with highly liquid current assets (p. 457)

R square (R^2) A measure of goodness of fit (how well the regression line "fits" the data) (p. 127)

Raw material inventory Inventory of materials needed in the production process but not yet moved to the production area (p. 29)

Regression analysis The procedure that uses statistical methods (least squares regression) to fit a cost line (called a regression line) through a number of data points (p. 123)

Relevant costs Those costs that differ between alternatives (p. 15)

Relevant range The normal range of production that can be expected for a particular product and company (p. 117)

Residual income The amount of income earned in excess of some predetermined minimum level of return on assets (p. 354)

Resource utilization decisions Decisions that require an analysis of how best to use a resource that is available in limited supply (p. 199)

Responsibility accounting An accounting system that assigns responsibility to managers for those areas that are under that managers control (p. 343)

Return on investment (ROI) Measures the rate of return generated by an investment center's assets (p. 349)

Revenue center A segment or division of an organization that is primarily responsible for generation of revenue but not costs (p. 344)

Risk assessment and control Involves identifying potential risks of the organization and also ways to minimize or manage those risks (p. 408)

Risk The likelihood that an option chosen in a decision situation will yield unsatisfactory results (p. 16)

Sales budget Used in planning the cash needs for manufacturing, merchandising, and service companies (p. 272)

Sales forecast Combines with the **sales budget** to form the starting points in the preparation of production budgets for manufacturing companies, purchases budgets for merchandising companies, and labor budgets for service companies (p. 272)

Sales price variance Computed by comparing the actual sales price to the flexible budget sales price times the actual sales volume (p. 311)

Sales volume variance The difference between the actual sales volume and the budgeted sales volume times the budgeted contribution margin (p. 309)

Screening decisions Decisions about whether an investment meets some predetermined company standard (p. 225)

Segment costs All costs attributable to a particular segment of an organization but only those costs that are actually caused by the segment (p. 345)

Segment margin The profit margin of a particular segment of an organization, typically the best measure of long-run profitability (p. 347)

Segmented income statements Calculate income for each major segment of an organization in addition to the company as a whole (p. 345)

Sensitivity analysis The process of changing the values of key variables to determine how sensitive decisions are to those changes (p. 16, 238)

Simple interest Interest on the invested amount only (p. 241)

Special-order decisions Short-run pricing decisions in which management must decide what sales price is appropriate when customers place orders that are different from those placed in the regular course of business (larger quantity, one-time sale to a foreign customer, etc.) (p. 189)

Standard cost A budget for a single unit of product or service (p. 306)

Standard price The budgeted price of the material, labor, or overhead for each unit (p. 307)

Standard quantity The budgeted amount of material, labor, or overhead for each product (p. 306)

Static budgets Budgets that are set at the beginning of the period and remain constant throughout the budget period (p. 289)

Step costs Costs that vary with activity in steps. They may look like and be treated as either variable costs or fixed costs. While step costs are technically not fixed costs, they may be treated as such if they remain constant within a relevant range of production (p. 120)

Strategic budgets Used to help managers plan many years in the future (p. 289)

Strategic business unit (SBU) Another term for investment center (p. 345)

Summary cash budget Consists of three sections: (1) cash flow from operating activities, (2) cash flow from investing activities, and (3) cash flows from financing activities. These three sections are the same as used in the cash flow statement prepared under generally accepted accounting principles (GAAP) (p. 282)

Sunk costs Costs that have already been incurred (p. 15)

Supply chain management Includes a variety of activities centered around making the purchase of materials and inventory more efficient and less costly (p. 399)

Target pricing A pricing method used when a price is preset by market conditions or when a company wishes to set a price in order to capture a predetermined market share or meet other marketing goals (p. 186)

Task analysis A method of setting standards that also examines the production process in detail to determine what it should cost to produce a product (p. 307)

Theory of constraints A management tool for dealing with constraints that identifies and focuses on bottlenecks in the production process (p. 200)

Throughput The amount of product produced in a given amount of time such as a day, week, and month (p. 381)

Time and material pricing A pricing method often used in service industries where labor is the primary cost incurred (p. 187)

Time value of money The concept that a dollar received (paid) today is worth more (less) than a dollar received (paid) in the future (p. 224)

Transfer price The price charged by one segment or division to another segment or division within the same organization for the transfer of goods or services (p. 358)

Trend analysis Horizontal analysis of multiple years of data (p. 451)

Underapplied Overhead The amount of actual overhead in excess of applied overhead (p. 72)

Usage variance The difference between the actual quantity and the standard quantity times the standard price (p. 313)

Value chain The set of activities that increase the value of an organization's products and services. The value chain typically includes research and development, design, production, marketing, distribution, and customer service activities (p. 34)

Value pricing A pricing method that bases the price of services on the perceived or actual value of the service provided to a customer (p. 188)

Variable (direct) costing A method of costing in which product costs include direct material, direct labor, and variable overhead. Fixed overhead is treated as a period cost. Consistent with CVP's focus on cost behavior (p. 169)

Variable costs Costs that stay the same per unit but change in total as production volume increases or decreases (p. 116)

Variance analysis Allows managers to see whether sales, production, and manufacturing costs are higher lower than planned and, more important, *why* actual sales, production, and costs differ from budget (p. 306)

Vertical integration Accomplished when a company is involved in multiple steps of the value chain (p. 193)

Volume variance The difference between the flexible budget and the fixed overhead applied to a product (p. 318)

Work-in-process inventory Inventory of unfinished product (in other words, what is left in the factory at the end of the period) (p. 29)

Working capital The excess of current assets over current liabilities, which is a measure of an entity's liquidity (p. 453)

Zero-based budgeting Requires managers to build budgets from the ground up each year (p. 269)

CREDITS

COMPANY INDEX

SUBJECT INDEX